CAREER OPPORTUNITIES IN CONSERVATION AND THE ENVIRONMENT

CAREER OPPORTUNITIES IN CONSERVATION AND THE ENVIRONMENT

PAUL R. GREENLAND AND ANNAMARIE L. SHELDON

Ferguson
An imprint of Infobase Publishing

Career Opportunities in Conservation and the Environment

Ferguson
An imprint of Infobase Publishing
132 West 31st Street
New York NY 10001

Library of Congress Cataloging-in-Publication Data

Greenland, Paul.
  Career opportunities in conservation and the environment / Paul Greenland and AnnaMarie Sheldon
      p. cm.
  Includes bibliographical references and index.
  ISBN-13: 978-0-8160-6742-8 (hc : alk paper)
  ISBN-10: 0-8160-6742-2 (hc : alk. paper) 1. Conservation of natural resources—Vocational guidance. 2. Ecology—Vocational guidance. I. Sheldon, AnnaMarie L. II. Title.
  S945.G74 2007
  333.72023—dc22
                        2006102569

Ferguson books are available at special discounts when purchased in bulk quantities for businesses, associations, institutions, or sales promotions. Please call our Special Sales Department in New York at (212) 967-8800 or (800) 322-8755.

You can find Ferguson on the World Wide Web at http://www.fergpubco.com

Cover design by Takeshi Takahashi

Printed in the United States of America

VB Hermitage 10 9 8 7 6 5 4 3 2 1

This book is printed on acid-free paper.

To my children:
Taylor, Nicholas, and Addison
—Paul Greenland

To my partner,
Michael, for teaching me more than you will probably
ever realize about pursuing what you want
— AnnaMarie Sheldon

CONTENTS

How to Use This Book ix
Acknowledgments xi
Industry Outlook xiii

ECOTOURISM

Camp Cook 2
Camp Counselor 5
Camp Director 8
Resort Operator 11
Resort Planner 14
River Guide 17
Tour Guide 20
Travel Agent 23
Wilderness Guide 26

ENGINEERING

Biological and Agricultural Engineers 30
Community Planner 34
Environmental Engineer 37
Geospatial Engineer 40
Mining and Geological Engineers 43
Surveying and Mapping Technician 46
Surveyor 49

FARMING AND FISHING

Agricultural Consultant 54
Commercial Beekeeper 57
Crop Farmer 60
Crop Scientist 63
Dairy Farmer 66
Farm Manager 69
Fisher 72
Fish Farmer 74
Livestock Farmer 76
Rural Appraiser 79

FORESTRY

Forester 84
Forestry Technician 87

Logger 90
Urban Forester 93

LEGAL AND REGULATORY

Environmental Attorney 98
Enivornmental Campaign Staff Worker 102
Environmental Compliance Specialist 105
Environmental Economist 108
Enivronmental Health Officer 111
Fish and Wildlife Officer 114
Irrigation Auditor 117
Occupational Safety and Health Office 120
Park Manager 123

OTHER

Grounds Maintenance Worker 128
Landscape Architect 131
Nature Photographer 134

OUTDOOR/ENVIRONMENTAL EDUCATION

Ecological Restoration Instructor 138
Environmental Education Program Director 141
Environmental Science Professor 144
Environmental Science Teacher, High School 147
Field Education Coordinator 150
Field Teacher/Naturalist 153
Forestry and Conservation Science Professors 156
Marine Science Instructor 159
Outdoor Education Instructor 162
Recreation and Fitness Studies Professor 165
Recreation Planner 168
Recreation Worker 171

SCIENTIFIC

Atmospheric Scientist 176
Chemical Laboratory Technician 179

Environmental Chemist   182
Environmental Technician   185
Geoscientist   189
Marine Biologist   192
Marine Science Technician   195
Oceanographer   198
Plant Scientist   201
Range Manager   205
Soil Scientist   208
Veterinarian   211
Wetland Scientist   214
Wildlife Rehabilitator   217
Wildlife Scientist   220

APPENDIXES

I. Education and Training Resources   224
II. Professional Associations   284
III. Professional Certifications   290
IV. Government Agencies   293
V. Internet Resources   294
VI. National Forests   296
VII. National Parks   299
VIII. State Environmental Resources   301

Glossary   304
Bibliography   306
Index   313

HOW TO USE THIS BOOK

Career Opportunities in Conservation and the Environment is intended for anyone interested in learning more about various career options related to conservation and the environment. Environmentally minded high school and college students, as well as current professionals interested in switching careers, can consult this book for ideas about what types of jobs are available in this field. The counselors advising these students can use this book to provide their students with more detailed information—including the educational requirements, typical salaries, anticipated demand, day-to-day responsibilities, and advancement opportunities—for particular careers. Parents of students interested in conservation and environmental careers can use *Career Opportunities in Conservation and the Environment* as a starting point for researching the various postsecondary programs and internship opportunities available to their children. Other potential readers include teachers, professors, academic program directors, vocational training program developers, and all other career development professionals.

Organization

The 69 job profiles in *Career Opportunities in Conservation and the Environment* are organized into eight sections: Ecotourism, Engineering, Farming and Fishing, Forestry, Legal and Regulatory, Other, and Outdoor/Environmental Education, Scientific. Each section contains between three and 15 profiles. Anywhere from two to three pages in length, each profile is formatted identically so that readers can familiarize themselves as quickly as possible with where to find the specific information contained in each profile. Readers can skip from profile to profile or section to section as they choose.

Resources

Deciding which jobs to cover in *Career Opportunities in Conservation and the Environment* and gathering information to include in each of the job profiles was no small task. The authors interviewed industry professionals at leading environmental associations, consulted Web sites from the top environmental careers organizations, reviewed data from the Bureau of Labor Statistics, reviewed environment and conservation program descriptions from colleges and universities across the United States, and perused professional journals, textbooks, handbooks, manuals, and various other print sources. They also secured the expertise of David W. Sheldon, a biological and environmental sciences professor at St. Clair County Community College with 12 years of experience not only in teaching the courses required of students pursuing careers in conservation and the environment, but also in advising those students throughout their degree programs and mentoring those students early in their careers.

Job Profiles

Truly the meat of this book, each job profile includes detailed information about one of the careers covered in *Career Opportunities in Conservation and the Environment*. Job profiles are organized into the following 11 subsections:

Career Profile is an introductory section listing key professional responsibilities, salary range, employment outlook, advancement potential, and general job prerequisites.

Career Ladder offers a visual depiction of a career path, demonstrating which positions lead to a particular job and what positions an individual might advance into beyond that job.

Position Description provides a detailed explanation of the overall responsibilities, as well as the day-to-day tasks, required for a particular job. This section also describes typical working conditions.

Salaries covers the range of earnings workers can expect given their level of education and experience.

Employment Prospects details the current and projected outlook for a particular job.

Advancement Prospects explains how individuals can gain experience to secure a specific job and describes what positions might eventually be available for advancement.

Education and Training describes the typical educational requirements of a particular job. This section also covers what type of previous on-the-job training is normally expected.

Special Requirements covers any predetermined selection processes a candidate might need to undergo, as well as any specialized certifications or credentials required for a job.

Experience, Special Skills, and Personality Traits gives an overview of the specific skills, talents, and character traits possessed by successful candidates.

Unions and Associations lists the professional organizations serving students and individuals on a particular career path.

Tips for Entry lists concrete steps individuals can take to begin preparing themselves for the career of their choice.

Appendixes

Following the job profiles are eight appendixes designed to provide more detailed information about the educational/training programs, professional associations, professional certifications, government agencies, and Internet resources mentioned throughout this book.

Education and Training Resources contains helpful listings of educational and training programs for some of the specific jobs and job categories profiled in this book. A section of general education and training resources is followed by education and training resources organized alphabetically within each job category.

Professional Associations contains full contact information for the professional associations listed throughout this book. The importance of these organizations cannot be overemphasized, as most offer career resources, including job listings, certification information, and links to education and training resources. Associations are organized alphabetically within each job category.

Professional Certifications includes mandatory and optional certifications related to some of the careers profiled in this book. Certification programs are organized alphabetically within each job category.

Government Agencies includes an alphabetical listing of federal government agencies that play a role in or offer resources related to environmental issues.

Internet Resources provides a listing of Web sites that offer useful information regarding careers and job postings in the conservation and environment field. A section of general Internet resources is followed by Internet resources organized alphabetically within each job category.

National Forests lists contact information for the national Forest Service office and each regional office, along with links to corresponding online directories with extensive department phone numbers. In addition, national forests are listed by state, along with individual Web sites when available.

National Parks provides contact information for the National Park Service headquarters and regional offices, Web pages for each individual state, and instructions for accessing a complete online index of national parks.

State Environmental Resources contains a geographic listing of state government agencies that can provide career information, as well as details about specific laws and regulations.

Glossary

Following the appendixes is a glossary that provides brief definitions of terms that may not be familiar to the reader.

Bibliography

After the glossary is a bibliography divided into two sections: Periodicals and Books. The periodicals section lists professional trade magazines and journals related to many of the careers profiled in this book, while the books section lists relevant books. In both sections, a grouping of general titles is followed by more specific titles organized alphabetically within each job category.

ACKNOWLEDGMENTS

The authors would like to extend their sincere thanks and gratitude to the many people who devoted their time and expertise to contribute to this book. Without the help of the following individuals and organizations, this project would not have been possible:

American Society of Agronomy; Andy Bacon; Caroline Bathje; George H. Bathje III; Dr. Larry Case, National FFA Adviser, National FFA Organization; Terrance W. Clark, CF, Associate Director, Science and Education, Society of American Foresters; Crop Science Society of America; Ernie Gill, Team Leader, LPS, National FFA Organization; Lauren Goschke, Henry Clepper Forest Policy Intern, Society of American Foresters; Tracey Greenland; Charles Helsten, Hinshaw & Culbertson LLP; Dolores Landeck, American Society of Agricultural and Biological Engineers; Bob Lane; Joan Lane; Michael H. Lewis Jr.; Louise Murgia, CF, Director, Field Services, Society of American Foresters; Eric Mussen, Cooperative Extension Apiculturist, University of California, Davis; Ashley Owens, Manager, Public Relations, American Society of Landscape Architects; Armour Peterson; Brian Pyles, Coordinator of Career and Technical Education, Shiawasee Intermediate School District; Eric Schilling, Team Leader, National FFA Organization; Tony Small, Executive Director, Education Division, National FFA Organization; Janet M. Smith, Chair, Division of Chemical Technicians, American Chemical Society; Soil Science Society of America; David W. Sheldon, Professor of Biology, St. Clair County Community College; Hope Steward Evans, Membership Coordinator, American Society of Farm Managers and Rural Appraisers, American Society of Agricultural Consultants; Elaine M. Thrune, Board Member, National Wildlife Rehabilitators Association; Kimberly A. Tilley, Associate Executive Director/Communications Director, ASPRS: The Imaging and Geospatial Information Society; Jodi L. Wesemann, American Chemical Society.

In addition, we would like to thank James Chambers, our editor, for his patience and guidance. Paul would like to thank his wife, Tracey, for her never-ending support and understanding. AnnaMarie would like to thank her partner, Michael, for listening, for understanding, and for being willing to work so hard, especially early on Saturday mornings.

INDUSTRY OUTLOOK

The conservation and environmental field is remarkably broad in scope. It includes organizations involved in monitoring various aspects of the environment, including air and water quality; global warming; plant, water, and energy resource conservation and development; and wildlife preservation and protection. While these organizations, many of which are activist in nature, provide a key source of jobs within the industry, other entities—some of which are not necessarily based on principals of environmental activism—also employ a sizable number of individuals who choose to work with or focus on the natural environment in some way. Examples include educators, tour guides, photographers, landscape architects, and even groundskeepers.

Constituting a significant portion of the U.S. job market, conservation and environmental jobs account for between 1 percent and 3 percent of total U.S. employment. While it is difficult to obtain an exact count of the total number of workers employed in all conservation and environmental fields, most estimates hover between 120,000 and 150,000. Since the mid-1990s, the number of conservation and environmental jobs has increased roughly 4 percent annually, outpacing general job growth rates.

U.S. job growth in this sector has slowed considerably since the 1970s, when it ranged from 9 percent to 11 percent annually, and the late 1980s, when it peaked at 12 percent to 15 percent annually. However, international job growth is expected to surge well into the first decade of the 21st century. For example, areas in Asia (outside of Japan), Latin America, and Africa are expected to experience double-digit growth in conservation and environmental jobs.

U.S. News and World Report lists 515 different undergraduate colleges and universities offering degrees in natural resources and conservation fields. A total of 266 institutions offer degree programs in environmental sciences alone, a sector that employs roughly 55,000 workers. Other popular degree programs for this sector include environmental studies, offered by 241 institutions; wildlife and wildlands science and management, offered by 53 institutions; and forestry, offered by 57 institutions.

Unlimited Opportunities

As reflected in the scope of jobs profiled in this book, students should recognize the wide range of opportunities that exist within the conservation and environmental field. If one has a general interest in working with the environment, the range of potential employment situations is virtually endless.

Within broad industry areas such as agriculture, ecotourism, education, engineering, forestry, law, and science, there are many different types of employers from which to choose. These include for-profit and nonprofit companies; consulting firms; local, state, and federal government agencies; educational institutions; research laboratories; hospitals; utilities; and other public and private organizations.

While some students might assume that conservation and environmental jobs mainly involve outdoor work, that is far from the case. While some jobs do call for extensive fieldwork in forests, wetlands, mountains, oceans, and other outdoor settings, others are limited to a lab or office setting. Many offer a blend of both indoor and outdoor work, providing variety that workers in many other fields might envy.

Trends and Predictions

There are a number of key trends that cut across many of the jobs profiled in this book and will support above-average growth for many conservation and environmental careers. One is the widespread use of geospatial technology to understand, monitor, and make important decisions about the environment. Tools such as aerial and satellite remote sensing imagery, the Global Positioning System (GPS), and computerized geographic information systems (GIS) are revolutionizing the conduct of business, science, and government alike. Professionals in virtually every field increasingly rely on geospatial information to make important decisions and carry out their work.

Geospatial technology is employed in a wide range of fields, including aerial photography, agriculture, archeology, architecture, biology, cartography, civil engineering, community and urban planning, computer science, ecology, economics, engineering, environmental science, forestry, geodesy, geography, geology, geometry, graphic arts, hydrology, industrial engineering, manufacturing, medicine, meteorology, military planning, natural resource management, photography, physics, satellite imagery, sociology, and transportation. For this reason, any form of education or training in this area will be extremely beneficial, and may increase one's employment prospects.

Another important trend is the increasing number of environmental rules and regulations with which individuals and organizations must comply. These pertain to the broad areas of air, water, and land pollution, and include many specific subcategories. Examples of laws at the federal level alone include the Clean Air Act, Clean Water Act,

Emergency Planning and Community Right to Know Act (EPCRA), Hazardous Materials Transportation Authorization Act; Resource Conservation and Recovery Act (RCRA) (hazardous waste), Safe Drinking Water Act, the Comprehensive Environmental Response, Compensation, and Liability Act (CERCLA), also known as Superfund, and the Toxic Substances Control Act (TSCA).

According to the American Academy of Environmental Engineers, major areas of focus within the environmental compliance area include air pollution control, hazardous waste management, industrial hygiene, land management, public health, radiation protection, solid waste disposal, storm water management, toxic materials control, wastewater management, and water supply. In addition to an increase in environmental compliance, there is a continued and often related need for environmental remediation initiatives that involve removing waste from contaminated sites. Opportunities to become familiar with environmental rules and regulations, or introductory courses in environmental law, will be of great help to those who wish to work in this field.

Important Developments

The Industrial Revolution led to growing concern about humankind's impact on the environment on many fronts, especially in regard to pollution. This concern eventually led to the establishment of the U.S. Environmental Protection Agency (EPA) on December 2, 1970. In recognition of its 35th anniversary in 2005, the EPA stated: "From regulating auto emissions to banning the use of DDT; from cleaning up toxic waste to protecting the ozone layer; from increasing recycling to revitalizing inner-city brownfields, EPA's achievements have resulted in cleaner air, purer water, and better protected land."

Every day, local, state, and national news sources profile new developments that illustrate the importance of conservation and environmental issues. During the early 21st century, perhaps the most significant development was global warming, a phenomenon that scientists attribute to the burning of fossil fuels. In the February 17, 2006, *Houston Chronicle*, writer Eric Berger indicated that carbon dioxide levels have increased more than 40 percent since the mid-1900s alone. This has been linked to glacial melting and rising ocean levels, which threaten the planet's coastal areas. As the world's largest emitter of carbon dioxide, the United States is closely connected to this pressing global issue.

Heading into 2007, there was a growing awareness of the need for immediate action in regard to global warming. In the April 3, 2006, issue of *Time*, a Time/ABC News/Stanford University poll was referenced, in which 85 percent of respondents acknowledged the existence of global warming. In addition, 87 percent of respondents called for government action to reduce power-plant emissions, and 85 percent supported the use of less gasoline in automobiles.

This sense of urgency transcends both political and religious affiliations. Examples include the establishment of the Evangelical Climate Initiative by 86 religious leaders, and criticism from six former EPA administrators—one democrat and five republicans—of the Bush administration's efforts to reduce greenhouse gas emissions. Another bipartisan example is the U.S. Mayors Climate Protection Agreement, in which the leaders of some 200 U.S. cities committed to reduce the emission of greenhouse gas to 1990 levels by the year 2012.

In September 2006, entrepreneur and international business magnate Richard Branson pledged to invest $3 billion from his Virgin train and airline businesses to combat global warming. According to the September 22, 2006, issue of *The Atlanta Journal-Constitution*, his pledge was "one of the biggest contributions ever to a specific social cause, and may be the largest for research into avoiding climate change from a private source."

Global warming and environmental pollution are international problems, and those who wish to pursue careers in this field may find promising jobs that deal with issues at the global level, working in fields such as international business and economic policy development. In particular, China—the world's second-leading emitter of carbon dioxide—was attracting significant attention on the environmental front in the early 21st century. Behind its burgeoning economy was evidence of rampant environmental pollution.

As Brian Bremner explained in the June 19, 2006, issue of *BusinessWeek Online*, "Yes, China is a remarkable growth story. But it is also fast becoming an ecological wasteland, home to world-class smog, acid rain, polluted rivers and lakes, and deforestation. Environmental problems play a role in the death of some 300,000 Chinese people each year, according to World Bank estimates." China's State Environmental Protection Administration indicated that pollution results in annual costs of $200 billion, due to government outlays, productivity losses, and health problems.

Beyond immediate needs, such as the reduction of annual greenhouse gas levels, a broader goal of conservation and environmental workers in the early 21st century was to make a general, positive impact on the Earth, thus ensuring its survival for future generations. *Career Opportunities in Conservation and the Environment* provides examples of many jobs that will allow you to make a difference or simply gain a greater appreciation of our planet and all that it has to offer.

ECOTOURISM

CAMP COOK

CAREER PROFILE

Duties: Prepare meals for camp attendees; order food, beverages, and related supplies; create menus in keeping with nutritional guidelines and special dietary needs of clients; determine numbers and size of portions; oversee kitchen staff and assistants; maintain cleanliness standards; monitor expenses

Alternate Title(s): Camp Chef; Culinary Director

Salary Range: $15,000 to $40,000

Employment Prospects: Good

Advancement Prospects: Good

Prerequisites:

> **Education or Training**—None required for entry-level positions
>
> **Experience**—Familiarity with pots and pans; utensils and cutlery; kitchen implements like slicers, grinders, and blenders; and appliances such as ovens, broilers, and grills; knowledge of food sanitation and safety regulations
>
> **Special Skills and Personality Traits**—Sense of taste and smell; ability to follow recipes and engage in repetitive actions; leadership skills; creativity; attention to detail and accuracy
>
> **Special Requirements**—Vary by employer

CAREER LADDER

```
┌─────────────────────────────┐
│         Camp Chef           │
└─────────────────────────────┘

┌─────────────────────────────┐
│       Head Camp Cook        │
└─────────────────────────────┘

┌─────────────────────────────┐
│         Camp Cook           │
└─────────────────────────────┘

┌─────────────────────────────┐
│     Assistant Camp Cook     │
└─────────────────────────────┘
```

Position Description

The main job of Camp Cooks is to prepare all meals served at a camp facility. As a result, they are responsible for cooking not only main meals such as spaghetti dinners and bacon and egg breakfasts, but also for baking pastries and desserts, grilling all sorts of meats, sautéing and steaming vegetables, preparing picnic lunches, creating, tossing, and dressing salads, etc. No matter their previous experience or expertise, Camp Cooks are expected to prepare a wide variety of meals.

However, the job of a Camp Cook involves much more than the cleaning, chopping, cooking, and others tasks involved in meal preparation. It also entails helping to create daily menus consistent with any special dietary needs of camp participants. Menus at camps tend to reflect both nutritional guidelines for participants and the theme of the camp or various activities undertaken there. For example, a cook at a weight-loss camp might prepare meals that are lower in fat and include more fruits and vegetables than a cook at a football camp, where pasta and other complex carbohydrates form the basis for most meals. Oftentimes, Camp Cooks are instructed to create specified portion sizes, a decision that might be based on financial considerations as well as on the desire of diners. In many cases, cooks will also actually serve food to patrons.

Cooks also work to insure that cleanliness and safety standards are upheld in the kitchen. To this end, they inspect all meat, fish, and poultry prior to use. They also regularly sanitize their work area, including all appliances, utensils, and other devices used in food preparation.

Food preparation assistants are often used for tasks like peeling and chopping fruits and vegetables; washing and trimming fat from meat and poultry; cleaning countertops, utensils, and dishes; maintaining consistent heat for ovens, stovetops, and fryers; and garnishing finished dishes. However, most cooks complete higher-level tasks—like seasoning dishes, preparing marinades, measuring and mixing ingredients, and actually cooking the food—themselves. Camp Cooks also complete a variety of administrative and supervisory duties, such as overseeing the work of assistants, ordering necessary food, beverages, and supplies, recording goods received, managing inventory, and calculating meal prices based on ingredient costs.

Larger camp facilities might require more extensive kitchen staffs that include chefs, cooks, assistant cooks, and food preparation workers. In these cases, the job of a Camp Cook can vary based on the position he or she holds. Some cooks might be in charge of a single task, such as operating a griller or fryer to prepare all the meats, or baking all the pastries and desserts. Due to the large number of patrons being served, these cooks typically prepare large amounts of a limited range of dishes, particularly if daily meals are preset. If the camp permits clients to order selections from a menu, cooks tend to prepare a much wider variety of entrees, side dishes, and desserts.

Working conditions for Camp Cooks vary considerably. While newer facilities tend to have newer equipment and ergonomically correct work spaces, along with amenities like advanced ventilation systems and air conditioning, older sites typically have smaller kitchens that may not be as well designed or well equipped. No matter the type of kitchen, cooks are required to work with hot stoves, ovens, and other potentially dangerous appliances. They also tend to stand for long periods of time and lift heavy pots, pans, and bulk containers of food. However, although burns, cuts, and other accidents do occur from time to time, they normally result in only minor injuries. Expected to work as efficiently as possible, cooks must also move quickly without compromising safety and sanitation requirements. As a result, this job might involve considerable stress during peak work periods.

Hours for Camp Cooks vary considerably, depending on the needs of the facility. Seasonal cooks may work 40 hours a week or more during the summertime and other peak seasons. During particularly busy seasons, cooks might work up to 12 hours a day, spending the morning engaged in tasks like cooking breakfast, receiving food and supplies, planning a menu for the day, and beginning meal preparations, and the afternoon and evening actually cooking the meals. Other cooks may work part time year round. In fact, nearly half of all cooks work part time.

Salaries

The median annual salary for a Camp Cook in 2004 was $19,330. However, the range of incomes in this profession is broad. Beginning part-time cooks might earn only minimum wage, while those with a few years of training might garner more than $10 an hour. More experienced cooks who specialize in certain types of meals tend to make $25,000 to $35,000 annually. Chefs, individuals who typically possess culinary arts degrees and years of experience working for expensive restaurants or resorts, can earn upwards of $45,000 a year. More upscale facilities tend to pay the most. Additional perks may include free meals and lodging, although employers are allowed to deduct these expenses from employee salaries if they choose. Full-time workers often receive standard benefit packages.

Employment Prospects

Although job growth for food service workers of all kinds, including Camp Cooks, is expected to remain high over the next several years, nearly half will be either part-time or seasonal. According to the Department of Labor's Bureau of Labor Statistics, one reason for the high number of job openings is a significant turnover rate among cooks; causes for this phenomenon include promotions within the industry, transfers to higher paying industries, and burnout from stress related to the pace of work. Job growth will also be fueled by increases in both household income and leisure time, the combination of which permits people to pay for these camps.

Advancement Prospects

Gaining entry into this field is fairly easy given that the fast food industry offers a multitude of entry-level positions. While these positions are often stressful due to the pressure to work quickly, they do afford individuals a chance to gain experience as cooks. Individuals can also gain experience with camp facilities as food preparation workers or assistant cooks. On-the-job training is common for these entry-level positions, and a year or two of experience is typically sufficient for promotion to Camp Cook.

Camp Cooks who wish to advance their careers further can seek employment with a large camp facility that employs multiple cooks, as managerial and administrative positions may be available. They may also pursue a culinary arts degree and seek employment as a chef, a job that typically allows for more control over food selection, menu creation, and experimentation.

Education and Training

While entry-level positions require no formal training or education, many Camp Cooks are expected to possess a high school diploma. Certain high schools offer training programs for students interested in pursuing this career path. Individuals can also gain experience as members of the United States Armed Forces.

Higher-level jobs typically require an apprenticeship, a degree, or certification from some sort of culinary arts school or professional association. Programs can last anywhere from six months to two years, and they typically culminate in a formal examination. The American Culinary Federation, which has accredited more than 100 culinary arts training programs throughout the U.S., offers information about apprenticeships, credentials such as the Master Chef certification, and other culinary arts training opportunities. Culinary arts programs typically offer training in the following areas:

- Cutting and chopping techniques
- Basic cooking methods
- Food handling, food storage, sanitation, and public health
- Ordering, purchasing, and controlling inventory
- Kitchen equipment care and maintenance
- Nutrition and apportionment
- Menu planning
- Food service management

Experience, Special Skills, and Personality Traits
All cooks should possess a highly developed ability to gauge food taste and smell, as well as an understanding of how seasonings work independently and in combination. Creativity is important, as those with the freedom to develop their own menus are expected to experiment with meal selections. Cooks overseeing food preparation workers or assistant cooks also need leadership skills. Some facilities require certification of some type.

Camp Cooks tend to follow recipes exactly and repeat them over and over again, if necessary. As a result, cooks must possess agile fingers, hands, and wrists and must be able to organize tasks in an order that produces efficiency. They must also be able to tolerate standing for a long period of time in rooms that are often quite warm. The ability to work in a fast-paced environment is also important, as are verbal communication skills.

Unions and Associations
The American Culinary Federation offers training and certification programs for cooks and chefs at any level. The International Association of Culinary Professionals serves cooks and chefs throughout the world. Other associations include the National Restaurant Association and the International Council on Hotel, Restaurant, and Institutional Education.

Tips for Entry
1. Visit the American Culinary Federation's Web site, http://www.acfchefs.org, for information about apprenticeship and certification programs.
2. Gain experience while in high school by working as a cook for a fast food or chain restaurant.
3. Learn more about career opportunities for cooks from the National Restaurant Association, which also publishes a directory of community colleges and universities with food service programs. For more information, go to http://www.restaurant.org.
4. Search for schools at the Culinary Institution's Web site, http://www.culinary-institutions.com.

CAMP COUNSELOR

CAREER PROFILE

Duties: Organize and lead activities for camp attendees; provide group and individual counseling; develop relationships with every member of case load; attend staff meetings

Alternate Title(s): Camp Therapist; Life Skills Coach

Salary Range: $20,000 to $30,000

Employment Prospects: Good

Advancement Prospects: Fair

Prerequisites:

Education or Training—A minimum of a high school diploma, although many positions require a college degree in social work, education, psychology, or similar field

Experience—Depends on focus of camp; experience working with children or individuals with special needs may be desired

Special Skills and Personality Traits—Energetic; responsible; creative; self-motivated; teaching, public speaking, and interpersonal communication skills

Special Requirements—Vary by employer; may need a license to practice psychotherapy

CAREER LADDER

```
┌─────────────────────────────┐
│ Camp Counseling Supervisor  │
└─────────────────────────────┘

┌─────────────────────────────┐
│      Camp Counselor         │
└─────────────────────────────┘

┌─────────────────────────────┐
│   Camp Activities Leader    │
└─────────────────────────────┘
```

Position Description

Camp Counselors work in a wide variety of settings and with highly diverse types of populations. They also provide a broad range of services. For example, those who work with physically challenged individuals provide any necessary support with tasks like eating, walking, and using the bathroom; they might also oversee appropriate adventure-based activities designed to boost self-esteem and foster a sense of accomplishment or run support groups that address emotional issues, depending on the focus of the camp. Other counselors may actually be licensed mental health professionals who provide psychotherapeutic treatment to youth with mental illnesses or who work at a recreational facility for adolescents with repeat criminal offenses. And still others simply lead various outdoor activities at standard camp sites serving mainstream individuals. Oftentimes, counselors live on-site with camp residents, who may be in attendance for days, weeks, months, or even longer. No matter the setting, counselors are responsible for the safety, health, personal needs, and general welfare of all participants assigned to them.

Camp Counselors at certain sites might work with individuals diagnosed with adjustment, attention deficit, bipolar, conduct, or obsessive-compulsive disorders, as well as post-traumatic stress syndrome and mild and major depressive episodes. To treat these diagnoses, counselors can use a specific modality, such as cognitive-behavioral therapy, to teach life skills including problem solving, self-help, coping, and socialization. In a setting such as this, the counselor will lead vocational group projects, oversee recreational activities including sports, and teach self-management, team work, and daily living skills. When conflicts arise, counselors are expected to help residents figure out how to come to amicable resolutions, rather than to actually resolve conflicts for them. Counselors may also teach alcohol and drug abuse awareness education.

Counselors working with at-risk youth—such as those with histories of truancy, running away, shoplifting, poor academic performance, drug or alcohol abuse, fighting, poor family relationships, negative peer pressure, suicide attempts, low self-esteem, or physical or sexual abuse—might conduct group therapy sessions in which they foster discussions about why residents are there, past behaviors, issues, feelings, and current goals. Individual therapy sessions often require the ability to confront irrational and self-defeating thoughts, beliefs, and behaviors. Counselors must then teach strategies for identifying problems and for substituting problematic patterns with new thoughts, beliefs, and behaviors. Counselors also encourage camp attendees to devise goals for themselves and to create steps that will allow them to reach these goals.

The daily activities of a Camp Counselor can vary considerably. Some days they might be engaged in teaching attendees specific physical skills, such as fly fishing or rock climbing. Other days they might work with modes of creative expression, such as art, dance, or therapeutic drumming. And at other times they might lead a series of trust-building exercises to teach residents to cooperate with one another. No matter what specific activities are on the agenda, counselors are always devising and implementing strategies to develop positive relationships with the attendees. Counselors are expected not only to participate in activities themselves, but also to motivate residents to make positive contributions.

Camp Counselors typically work as part of a team that plans daily activities, discusses the progress of attendees, brainstorms solutions to any problems that arise, and ensures that the needs of each of the campers is being met. They also do things like keep progress notes, which they review prior to each session and add to after each session. Sometimes, they are expected to help maintain and clean cabin and camp areas as well.

Camp Counselors tend to spend time with each of their assigned attendees outside of planned activities and sessions. As a result, their work schedule is quite demanding. They might work 10 to 12 hours a day for six days a week, and leave the campsite on their one day off to get time away from residents. This type of schedule is quite common with seasonal positions that last the duration of the summer.

Salaries

Camp Counselors can get paid per year, per season, or per camp session. Average annual wages for full-time positions range from $20,000 to $30,000, although those that require degrees and licensure tend to offer a higher salary. Seasonal positions pay $250 to $300 per week. Additional perks often include free room and board. Some positions also offer medical and dental insurance.

Employment Prospects

Full-time professional positions for camp counselors are limited compared to part-time seasonal positions, which are expected to grow at an average rate through 2014, according to the Bureau of Labor Statistics. However, employment growth for Camp Counselor positions with government-funded organizations might be reduced by anticipated budget cuts for special needs programs.

Advancement Prospects

Most Camp Counselors gain experience by volunteering for organizations that serve the populations with whom they are most interested in working. Others secure part-time or seasonal jobs, as the likelihood of securing full-time work increases with this kind of experience. Once hired, counselors also receive some form of training on topics such as group dynamics; group counseling; individual counseling; first aid and CPR; strategies for preventing and handling aggressive behavior; detecting evidence of physical and sexual abuse; and adolescent development. An orientation might also provide an overview of basic program philosophies. Oftentimes, new counselors spend a few weeks or months shadowing more experienced counselors, observing what happens in different groups and in one-on-one interactions.

Counselors who want to broaden their skill base are often able to do so while on the job. For example, counselors might work toward certification in adventure-based therapy, or gain expertise as a lifeguard, raft guide, or ropes course instructor. Individuals with entry-level Camp Counseling experience may eventually pursue careers in education, psychology, or social work, or they might decide to establish their own programs.

Education and Training

While a high school diploma is the minimum requirement for an entry-level position, most programs prefer individuals with at least one year of college course work under their belt. The most common degree requirement is a four-year degree in education, counseling, social work, behavioral science, or recreation.

Special Requirements

Licensure to provide psychotherapy or certifications in various outdoor activities, such as river rafting, might be required. Candidates are often expected to pass drug and background checks as well.

Experience, Special Skills, and Personality Traits

Knowledge of physical, cognitive, or mental disorders, as well as various treatment modalities, is helpful in securing a job of this sort. Most programs seek individuals with experience working with their target population, or at the very least an interest in working with this population. Because counselors are expected to work well with others, highly developed interpersonal communication skills are essential. Positions might also require experience leading outdoor activities or adventure-based programs.

Camp Counselors must possess the ability to manage stressful situations. As counselors are expected to arise daily with campers, eat meals with them, and supervise them during rest hours and after bedtime, a certain degree of stamina is required as well. Some positions require the ability to lift and move attendees to and from wheelchairs and beds, as well as in and out of tubs. Counselors are also expected to be cheerful, enthusiastic, energetic, patient, flexible, and compassionate.

Unions and Associations

The American Camp Association represents camp professionals of all types, including counselors. The National Recreation and Parks Association is another professional organization that Camp Counselors can join.

Tips for Entry

1. Gain experience with whatever population interests you most by volunteering with an organization that serves this population.
2. In high school, take courses in psychology, communication, child development, and physical fitness.
3. Visit the counseling section of the American Camp Association's Web site, http://www.acacamps.org/staff/counselors.php, for more information about a career as a Camp Counselor.
4. Search for jobs at the Career Center of the National Recreation and Parks Association's Web site, http://nrpa.jobcontrolcenter.com/search/.

CAMP DIRECTOR

CAREER PROFILE

Duties: Managing all operations of a camp facility; overseeing all departments, such as counseling, food and beverage, marketing, and program development; creating budgets and monitoring camp finances; hiring and supervising employees

Alternate Title(s): Camp Manager; Camp Operator

Salary Range: $30,000 to $80,000

Employment Prospects: Good

Advancement Prospects: Limited

Prerequisites:

Education or Training—A minimum of an associate's degree in parks and recreation or similar field; a bachelor's degree is desirable

Experience—Familiarity with camp settings; understanding of specific administrative and managerial issues related to various type of camps, including both day camps and longer-term residential facilities; knowledge of safety rules and regulations camp facilities are required to follow

Special Skills and Personality Traits—Strong leadership and mentoring skills; ability to delegate responsibilities; customer service, problem solving, and interpersonal communication skills; energetic, health-conscious, and team-oriented

Special Requirements—Vary by position; some require certification by the National Recreational and Parks Association or other credentials related to residential camping management; background checks; first aid and CPR certification; government positions often require U.S. citizenship, a valid driver's license, and passage of background checks and drug tests

CAREER LADDER

```
┌─────────────────────────────────┐
│         Camp Owner              │
└─────────────────────────────────┘

┌─────────────────────────────────┐
│         Camp Director           │
└─────────────────────────────────┘

┌─────────────────────────────────┐
│     Camp Assistant Director     │
└─────────────────────────────────┘

┌─────────────────────────────────┐
│     Camp Activities Leader      │
└─────────────────────────────────┘
```

Position Description

Camp Directors manage all operations of a camp facility. As a result, a single day's work might involve a broad range of tasks, such as mentoring employees, overseeing facility and grounds maintenance, tending to finance and budgeting concerns, developing various marketing strategies, and deciding which programs to offer camp attendees. While directors need the skills necessary to handle most administrative duties themselves, they might also delegate a fair number of these tasks to assistants and other employees. Ultimately, however, they bear responsibility for everything that happens at their camp.

A wide variety of seasonal and year-round camps serves all sorts of populations. Typical summer camps offer a wide variety of programs including environmental education, adventure and outdoor recreation, arts and crafts, sports, wilderness training, and more. Camps might be run by private businesses, individuals, parks and recreation departments of various jurisdictions, or nonprofit organizations like the Girl Scouts or Boy Scouts of America. More specialized camps cater to specific populations, such as physically challenged individuals, youth with mental illnesses, or adolescents with repeat criminal offenses. Camp residents may be in attendance for a single day, for a few weeks or months, or even longer. No matter what the setting, camps are run by directors who are hired to ensure that the safety, health, and personal and recreational needs of all participants are met.

Specific duties of Camp Directors include the following:

- Develop rules and regulations designed to ensure discipline and safety of all employees and attendees; monitor compliance and enforce consequences, if necessary
- Create standard procedures for handling emergency situations; conduct routine drills to prepare staff members to respond appropriately
- Oversee provision of first aid and other medical services. To this end, hire qualified staff members; order correct supplies; obtain medical information from camp attendees regarding allergies, special needs, and medications; secure any required medical releases, if appropriate
- Develop and implement activities appropriate to focus of camp; devise strategies to promote interest in activities
- Create employee schedules, as well as timetables for all events, programs, and activities
- Monitor effectiveness of camp programming, facilities, and services, modifying them when possible to meet participant needs
- Tour grounds and evaluate camp equipment and facilities on a regular basis to ensure functionality and safety
- Oversee all daily operations, including food service, ground maintenance, etc.
- Host camp orientations at which employees greet new camp participants and attendees meet one another and learn about facility rules, daily schedules, expectations, etc.
- Oversee meetings with camp counselors and other employees to plan daily activities, discuss the progress of attendees, brainstorm solutions to any problems that arise, and insure that the needs of each of the campers are being met.
- Provide supervision and mentoring directly to employees or indirectly by appointing other supervisors and mentors.
- Oversee grounds and building maintenance, including the construction of new facilities or remodeling of existing structures.

Camp Directors may live on-site or off-site, depending on the location of the camp. When camp is in session, they typically work 10-hour days and are quite often on call on their days off. For camps that operate seasonally, full-time directors may work reduced hours during the off-season, handling tasks such as program development, public relations, and recruitment of both attendees and employees.

Salaries

Camp Directors earn anywhere from $30,000 to $80,000, depending on the size and location of the camp, the duration of programming, and the type of services offered at the camp. For example, a camp that offers its residents specialized services, such as psychotherapy, oftentimes pays more for a director than a more mainstream summer camp might. At the same time, however, qualifications will be more stringent. Both year-round and seasonal positions tend to be full time for the duration of the program. Additional perks often include free room and board and standard benefits packages.

Employment Prospects

Full-time, year-round positions for camp directors are more limited than seasonal positions, which are expected to grow from 10 percent to 20 percent through 2014. According to the Bureau of Labor Statistics, this rate of growth is average.

Advancement Prospects

Many Camp Directors gain their first exposure to working in a camp environment by finding part-time employment at a summer camp while they are still in high school. After gaining entry-level experience, they may be allowed to lead certain activities or be promoted to positions like cabin leader or camp counselor. Others might volunteer for recreational programs or for organizations serving kids and other specific populations with whom they are interested in working. Many camps offer their volunteer and part-time employees training in group dynamics, first aid and CPR, strategies for working with youth and dealing with difficult behavior, and how to handle suspected physical and sexual abuse. Oftentimes, these individuals are able to maximize their experience by working toward certification as lifeguards, wilderness guides, ropes course instructors, etc.

Before securing positions as full-fledged directors, many individuals work as program managers or assistant directors for a few years, during which time they gradually increase their managerial and administrative duties. As Camp Director positions are quite high-level in the industry, advancement opportunities beyond this level are limited. Some individuals might be promoted to administrative or managerial roles in various parks and recreation departments, overseeing a variety of camps and programs. Others might eventually open their own camps.

Education and Training

While the minimum requirement for a Camp Director position is an associate's degree in parks and recreation or similar field, a bachelor's degree in parks and recreation, management, business administration, kinesiology, or physical education is desirable. Three to four years' experience managing educational, enrichment, or recreational programs is often required for a position at this level.

Special Requirements

Some positions require certification by the National Recreational and Parks Association or other credentials related to residential camping management. The National Recreation and Parks Association offers three levels of certification for industry professionals: Associate Park and Recreational Professional, Provisional Park and Recreational Professional, and Certified Park and Recreational Professional. The American Camp Association offers a class entitled Basic Camp Director Course, which is designed for site managers, experienced program directors or camp directors, with fewer than six years of experience.

Other potential requirements include criminal background checks, including the National Child Registry; U.S. citizenship; a valid driver's license; background checks; and random drug and alcohol tests. Individuals must also possess knowledge of local, state, and federal rules and regulations related to operating a camp facility and housing youth and individuals with special needs. First aid and CPR certification is also typically required of candidates.

Experience, Special Skills, and Personality Traits

Camp Directors need highly developed interpersonal communication, organizational, and leadership skills that allow them both to mentor employees and to delegate responsibilities as appropriate. Successful directors also tend to be energetic, creative, and people-oriented. Additional skills include problem solving, sales, customer service, and team building.

Unions and Associations

The American Camp Association represents camp professionals such as program managers, directors, and other types of administrators. Other organizations include the National Recreation and Parks Association, the Active Network, and the American Alliance for Health, Physical Education, Recreation, and Dance.

Tips for Entry

1. Gain experience by securing part-time work at a summer camp while in high school.
2. In high school, take courses in psychology, business, communication, and physical fitness.
3. Visit the American Camp Association's Web site, http://www.acacamps.org, for more information about a career as a Camp Director.
4. Search for jobs at the Career Center of the National Recreation and Parks Association's Web site, http://nrpa.jobcontrolcenter.com/search/.

RESORT OPERATOR

Duties: Managing all operations of one or more resorts; overseeing all departments, such as housekeeping, grounds, maintenance, public relations, and reservations; planning, developing, implementing, and evaluating resort marketing programs; managing resort finances; hiring and supervising resort employees.

Alternate Title(s): Hotel Manager; Lodging Manager

Salary Range: $40,000 to $80,000

Employment Prospects: Average

Advancement Prospects: Good

Prerequisites:

Education or Training—Minimum of an associate's degree in hotel and restaurant management, hospitality, travel and tourism, or similar field; a four-year degree is desirable

Experience—Previous customer service experience in a hotel or resort; understanding of specific issues related to resort operation, including guest relations, food and beverage services, and grounds maintenance

Special Skills and Personality Traits—Strong leadership and mentoring skills; ability to multitask and delegate responsibilities in a fast-paced environment; customer service, problem-solving, and interpersonal communication skills

Special Requirements—Ability to work with computerized reservation and billing systems; understanding of online hotel booking systems

```
┌─────────────────────────────┐
│      Resort Operator        │
└─────────────────────────────┘

┌─────────────────────────────┐
│   Resort Assistant Manager  │
└─────────────────────────────┘

┌─────────────────────────────┐
│    Resort Manager Trainee   │
└─────────────────────────────┘

┌─────────────────────────────┐
│      Resort Desk Clerk      │
└─────────────────────────────┘
```

Position Description

Resort Operators are responsible for managing an entire resort or group of resorts. Consequently, they must possess a very broad range of skills that include the oversight of personnel development, facility and grounds maintenance, finance and budgeting, marketing and brand development, and customer service. Resort Operators must know when to handle specific administrative jobs themselves and when it makes more sense to delegate them to an assistant of some sort; however, they are ultimately responsible for all happenings at their resort.

From staff recruitment and professional development to front desk coverage and housekeeping schedules, Resort Operators oversee all aspects of personnel. If the resort in question is small, operators may handle interviewing, hiring, training, and supervising staff themselves; larger operations may have a human resources manager who reports to the operator. Similarly, Resort Operators will either conduct all employee evaluations themselves, or they will delegate this task to a human resources professional. Resort Operators must also ensure compliance with all human resource laws and regulations of the jurisdiction in which the resort is located.

Resort Operators are also accountable for grounds and building maintenance, as well as the construction of new facilities and the refurbishment of existing structures. This can entail anything from contracting building engineers and construction firms to overseeing the work of housekeepers, landscape architects, and maintenance professionals. Disposal of waste and recycling of materials—two activities of particular importance to ecotourism-based resorts—are also the responsibility of Resort Operators, as is ensuring that any and all work taking place at their resort meets governmental safety standards, such as those drafted by the U.S. Occupational Safety and Health Administration (OSHA).

Resort Operators are also expected to ensure the profitability of their property. To this end, they draft and revise budgets; approve expenditures, such as the design and construction of new buildings and restaurants, as well as the refurbishment of existing accommodations; contract all necessary services, such as accounting and tax preparation; prepare for audits; and ensure compliance with all rules and regulations to avoid citations and fines. In the case of ecotourism-based resorts, concerns about environmental sustainability and minimal impact on natural environment and indigenous people are factored in to budgetary decisions.

Marketing and brand development activities include strategic planning, such as drafting a mission, vision, and goals, as well as a brand identity, which can include anything from building, room, and landscape design to specific services, such as offering free wireless Internet access to guests or placing complementary biodegradable, environmentally friendly bathing products in each room. Resort Operators often lead groups of employees in developing specific resort philosophies, including how resort conservation practices will be communicated to guests and how employees can contribute to the ideals of sustainable tourism while completing their work.

Perhaps the most important component of running a resort, customer service is a key responsibility of Resort Operators, who decide everything from how customer complaints will be handled to what housekeeping services, dining options, and banquet and meeting facilities will be offered to guests. As most ecotourism resorts make use of innovative water, waste, and energy systems to reduce impact on natural resources and residents of an area, the customer services offered to guests—such as daily laundering of each room's linens and towels—may differ considerably from more traditional resorts.

Many ecotourism resorts offer outdoor activities and other educational and recreational programs typically popular with their environmentally conscious clientele. Resort Operators decide whether to offer these programs independently or in conjunction with another organization, such as a wilderness tour outfitter. For the former option, a Resort Operator must hire qualified individuals and purchase the equipment and insurance necessary for such an endeavor. If they choose to pursue the latter option, Resort Operators can contract other companies to provide various activities and excursions to their guests.

Resort Operators work long hours. Along with logging 10 or even 12 hours a day, sometimes on weekends and during evenings, Resort Operators are typically on call 24 hours a day, seven days a week. These jobs are fast-paced and stressful, particularly during peak travel times or when guests make use of banquet facilities for events such as wedding receptions.

Salaries

According to the Bureau of Labor Statistics, Resort Operators earn between $40,000 and $80,000 a year. Compensation tends to vary considerably, depending on the size and location of the resort, the size of the company that owns the resort, and the type of clients typically served. For example, high-end resorts serving business clients in large cities tend to pay more than smaller resorts catering to tourists. Some Resort Operators earn an annual bonus based on the profitability of the resort.

Employment Prospects

Resort operation positions are expected to grow at an average rate through 2014. Personal travel, both domestic and international, is expected to increase, as is business travel. Consequently, the need for Resort Operators will grow as well. Specialty resorts, such as ecolodges, are also expected to continue gaining in popularity.

Advancement Prospects

Resort Operators can gain entry-level experience by working as a front-desk clerk and developing the customer service skills so important in the travel and tourism industry. Many large resort chains hire recent college graduates for their management training programs. After completing such a program, individuals are promoted to assistant manager positions and begin developing the managerial skills necessary to ultimately secure a position as a Resort Operator. Eventually, many Resort Operators open their own resorts; in fact, they account for nearly half of all Resort Operators.

Education and Training

Although the minimum educational requirement for Resort Operators is a two-year degree in hotel and restaurant management, hospitality, travel and tourism, or similar field, a four-year degree is becoming increasingly desirable. As a result, more than 800 postsecondary institutions offer some form of hotel and restaurant management training.

Specialized training in ecotourism management and ecolodge development is available from the Ecotourism Society, which offers distance learning certification in sustainable tourism. Also, the International Ecotourism Club Web site includes a searchable database of colleges and universities throughout the world that offer specific degrees in ecotourism. This Web site also contains information about internship opportunities for students.

Special Requirements

In nearly 500 U.S. high schools, the American Hotel and Lodging Association operates a two-year Lodging Management Program, whereby junior and senior students interested in this career can earn a Certified Rooms Division Specialist credential. Many community colleges and universities award college credits to students who complete this program.

Because nearly all reservation and billing systems are now online, Resort Operators need considerable computer skills. Computers are also used to coordinate meetings and other special events; to order supplies such as food, beverages, and linens; and to schedule housekeeping activities.

Experience, Special Skills, and Personality Traits

Resort Operators must possess a wide variety of managerial skills, including the ability to foster teamwork, mentor employees, delegate responsibilities, solve problems, and communicate effectively and efficiently with both employees and clients. Along with the stamina to work long and varied hours, Resort Operators also need to thrive in a fast-paced and often times stressful work environment.

Unions and Associations

The American Hotel and Lodging Association represents hotel owners and offers specialized management training programs. The International Council on Hotel, Restaurant, and Institutional Education is an organization comprised of postsecondary schools that offers hospitality industry training. The Hospitality Sales and Marketing Association represents individuals responsible for sales and marketing at their resorts. Resort Operators specializing in ecotourism can also join the International Ecotourism Society and the International Ecotourism Club.

Tips for Entry

1. Search for scholarships in the *Just for Students* section of the International Council on Hotel, Restaurant, and Institutional Education Web site, http://www.chrie.org.
2. Gain experience by securing a part-time job as a desk clerk at a local hotel or resort.
3. Research internships like those offered by the International Ecotourism Society, http://www.ecotourism.org, or the Student Conservation Association, http://www.sca-inc.org.
4. Search for job openings at Web sites like Hospitality Online, http://www.hotel-online.com, and ECOCLUB's Ecotourism Job Center, http://www.ecoclub.com/job.

RESORT PLANNER

CAREER PROFILE

Duties: Working with architects, landscape architects, engineers, zoning agencies, and other local officials to draft detailed plans for the development of properties and the construction of resorts; gather information about the social, economic, and environmental impact such development will have on a community; make public presentations regarding development plans; create reports that demonstrate how plans can be implemented and what they will cost

Alternate Title(s): Resort Developer

Salary Range: $30,000 to $80,000+

Employment Prospects: Good

Advancement Prospects: Good

Prerequisites:

Education or Training—Bachelor's degree in planning with a master's degree in architecture or landscape architecture, or a bachelor's degree in sociology, environmental engineering, or similar field with a master's degree in planning

Experience—Knowledge of building and landscape design issues

Special Skills and Personality Traits—Ability to work with community groups, governmental bodies, and other organizations to gather information and input from diverse perspectives; mediation skills; attention to detail; public speaking; report writing

Special Requirements—Ability to work with statistics and various computer modeling programs; interest in social, economic, and environmental issues

CAREER LADDER

```
┌─────────────────────────────┐
│       Senior Planner        │
└─────────────────────────────┘

┌─────────────────────────────┐
│          Planner            │
└─────────────────────────────┘

┌─────────────────────────────┐
│       Junior Planner        │
└─────────────────────────────┘
```

Position Description

Resort Planners develop plans for the construction of new resorts, as well as for the expansion and/or refurbishment of existing resorts. However, plans are not limited to the buildings themselves, but include considerations such as landscape design, how a site is currently used, and how development will affect this site. As a result, planners must do considerable preparatory work in assessing things like access to adequate supplies of electricity, water, and other utilities; if the possibility exists to make use of alternative forms of energy; proximity to existing structures, roads, and airports; and the anticipated impact of development on the surrounding ecology and any residents.

When drafting plans, Resort Planners do not work in isolation. Rather, while gathering all the information and input they need, Resort Planners rely on the expertise of civil and environmental engineers, building inspectors, construction contractors, landscape architects, and other industry professionals. They also do things like setting up meetings with local community groups to discuss any issues that are of concern to residents and consulting with zoning boards, building inspectors, and other regulatory bodies to be sure their plans will result in properties that comply with building codes and other rules and regulations of the jurisdictions in which their resorts will operate. When conflicts arise between two parties—a community group concerned about the proximity of a resort to a nature preserve and a developer hoping that this proximity might draw more customers to the resort, for example—planners may also act as mediators.

While gathering information and drafting ideas, Resort Planners must consider the goals of the development. Clearly, profitability is a common goal in resort development. However, if something like environmental sustainability is an objective, concerns about minimizing the resort's impact on the natural environment and indigenous people are factored into budgetary decisions. As a result, operational issues such how the resort will handle the disposal of waste, the maintenance of amenities such as pools and spas, the recycling of materials, and the laundering of items such as dishes, towels, and linens are also of concern to the planner. As a result, Resort Planners working in the ecotourism sector might also consult with environmental engineers and other specialists to devise plans for innovative water, waste, and energy systems to reduce impact on natural resources and residents of an area. Ultimately, what a Resort Planner produces is a detailed report that covers not only what exactly is planned and how it can be completed, but also outlines any and all associated costs.

Along with a standard schedule of between 40 and 50 hours per week, Resort Planners may also need to schedule evening and weekend meetings. In addition, they can work considerably longer hours when deadlines draw near or when high-profile development projects draw attention and warrant public hearings and/or meetings with various interest and citizen groups. Usually, Resort Planners will travel to potential sites to see for themselves where the property is situated, how the natural environment currently looks, and what types of structures, if any, have already been erected. They may also make site visits to view progress, to discuss any alterations to the original plan and what consequences those changes might cause, and to view projects after completion.

Salaries

Resort Planners, according to the Bureau of Labor Statistics, earned an average of $53,450 in 2004. Depending on experience and education, annual salaries total $30,000 to $80,000. Beginners tend to make between $30,000 and $40,000; those with master's degrees start at the higher end of this range. After about five years of experience, salaries increase to between $40,000 and $50,000. Senior planners, those with more than 10 years of experience, can make upwards of $80,000. Positions with the federal government and large development companies tend to pay the most.

Employment Prospects

The Bureau of Labor Statistics expects the job outlook for Resort Planners through 2014 to be equal to most other occupations. Specific areas of growth include redevelopment of existing areas and preservation of historic and natural sites.

Advancement Prospects

As all planners need at least a bachelor's degree to qualify for an entry-level position, securing an internship can be invaluable in giving a new graduate concrete experience, as well as industry contacts and a foot in the door somewhere. Most entry-level planners are hired for junior planner positions. Responsibilities include helping more experienced planners write reports, review policy, and prepare presentations. A promotion to the next level typically requires a master's degree. Responsibilities and independence increase accordingly. A senior planner typically has at least five years of experience. In larger firms, senior planners may also have managerial responsibilities and be expected to mentor less experienced planners.

Education and Training

Although the minimum educational requirement for a Resort Planner is a bachelor's degree, master's degrees make it much easier to secure a job. Nearly 70 postsecondary institutions offer master's degrees in planning; a total of 15 of these universities offer undergraduate planning degrees. Some students secure bachelor's degrees in planning and then pursue master's degrees in things like architecture or landscape architecture. Others get undergraduate degrees in sociology, geography, environmental engineering, or similar fields and then pursue a graduate degree in planning.

Special Requirements

The American Planning Association's American Institute of Certified Planners offers a certification credential for individuals who pass their examination. To be eligible to sit for the examination, planners need between two and four years of experience, depending on their level of education. Specialized training in ecotourism management and ecolodge development is available from the Ecotourism Society, which offers distance learning certification programs in a wide range of ecotourism fields.

Resort Planners must be able to grasp spacial relationships, to visualize the outcome of plans, and to understand building and landscape design issues. Technical requirements include the ability to work with statistics and computer drafting and modeling programs.

Experience, Special Skills, and Personality Traits

Resort Planners must be patient and detail-oriented enough to gather extensive information from a variety of sources with varying perspectives. A willingness to consider a broad range of factors—social, cultural, historical, economic, and environmental—is also necessary. Verbal and written communication, interpersonal communication, and mediation skills are essential for work with community groups, governmental bodies, and other organizations.

Unions and Associations

The American Planning Association represents planners throughout the United States. The Association of Collegiate Schools of Planning promotes educational options for planners and offers information on degree programs, scholarships, and awards. Resort Developers specializing in ecotourism can also join the International Ecotourism Society and the International Ecotourism Club.

Tips for Entry

1. Visit the Association of Collegiate Schools of Planning's Web site, http://www.acsp.org, to research schools that offer degrees in planning.
2. Search for jobs at the American Planning Association's Web site, http://www.planning.org/jobsonline/ads.htm.
3. Research internships like those offered by the Student Conservation Association, http://www.sca-inc.org, or the International Ecotourism Society, http://www.ecotourism.org.
4. Review industry Web sites such as Planners Web, http://www.plannersweb.com, and Planners Network, http://www.plannersnetwork.org, to learn more about the industry.

RIVER GUIDE

CAREER PROFILE

Duties: Planning, organizing, and leading river trips and tours through natural areas, such as national parks, forests, and mountains, canoeing, kayaking, white-water rafting, camping, fishing, and similar outdoor activities; instructing group members in the proper use of flotation devices, such as life jackets; explaining marine biology, wildlife, and other points of interest along riverbanks; fielding questions; teaching participants to observe rules and regulations; keeping track of all group members; and providing basic first aid, if necessary.

Alternate Title(s): River Tour Leader; White-water Rafting Guide; Adventure Guide; Tour Escort

Salary Range: $15,000 to $50,000+

Employment Prospects: Average

Advancement Prospects: Limited

Prerequisites:

Education or Training—High school diploma with certification as a river guide

Experience—Knowledge of local waterways and natural history; expertise in canoeing, kayaking, rafting, and similar activities; experience using life jackets and other floatation devices; understanding of local, state, and federal rules and regulations related to waterways used

Special Skills and Personality Traits—Ability to plan and organize events and lead groups in specific tasks; attention to detail; public speaking; problem solving

Special Requirements—Certification as river guide; basic first aid skills; CPR; ability to swim

CAREER LADDER

```
┌─────────────────────────────────────┐
│  River Guide Company Manager/Owner   │
└─────────────────────────────────────┘

┌─────────────────────────────────────┐
│        Full-Time River Guide         │
└─────────────────────────────────────┘

┌─────────────────────────────────────┐
│        Part-Time River Guide         │
└─────────────────────────────────────┘

┌─────────────────────────────────────┐
│        Volunteer River Guide         │
└─────────────────────────────────────┘
```

Position Description

River Guides lead a variety of water-based tours ranging from a fast-paced white-water rafting trip through mountain rapids to a leisurely downstream river float via inner tubes. In some cases, these tours take place in a few hours. Other tours can span several days and involve activities like portaging canoes over dry river beds and setting up and tearing down camp. As river tours attract both novices and experts, as well as those with skill levels somewhere in the middle of these two extremes, it is the job of the River Guide to ascertain which trips are open to everyone, which require experience, and how much experience is adequate. While some River Guides specialize in a single type of excursion, such as white-water rafting, others choose not to limit the types of trips they offer.

Oftentimes, River Guides are responsible for organizing their own trips. As a result, before the trip actually begins, they are busy greeting and registering participants, gathering watercraft and safety devices and checking both for defects, and reviewing trip details. More involved excursions might require a River Guide to also map out routes, plan and purchase meals and water, rent or purchase overnight camping equipment, and arrange for participants to be transported to and from starting and ending points.

River Guides also monitor weather conditions, marine forecasts, and other ecological conditions affecting areas through which they will travel. Along with remaining particularly alert to the potential for flash floods, River Guides also keep tabs on which rivers are overflowing at their banks and which riverbeds have run dry. In some cases, additional safety equipment or a change in plans might be in order. Although some river trips can take place during rainy weather, guides are vigilant about the likelihood of more perilous weather developments, such as funnel clouds or lightning storms.

Because physical fitness can be a factor in decisions about the suitability of individuals for river tours, River Guides may also need to interview candidates about their agility, stamina, and ability to swim prior to granting them access to certain trips. This information can also prove helpful when making recommendations about which trip might be appropriate. During a tour, River Guides also observe participants in an effort to match pace with ability levels and continuously monitor the progress of each participant for the duration of the trip.

Before actually getting on the water, River Guides are responsible for teaching group members things like how to board and deboard watercraft, techniques for steering and navigation, what to do if the watercraft tips over, how to fasten life jackets, and what other safety precautions members are expected to observe throughout the trip. Guides also help individuals who are struggling or lagging behind the group. In the event of a lost or seriously hurt group member, River Guides are required to organize a search party and request other necessary emergency assistance.

Resort operators, national and state parks, and adventure travel and outdoor recreation outfitters often hire part-time and seasonal River Guides. Full-time positions are more limited. Peak travel and recreation times, such as weekends and holidays, are typically the busiest time of year for River Guides. Hours tend to vary, as River Guides must work for the entire duration of a trip. In between trips, they have time off, or they might work to market an upcoming trip or to develop a new one.

Salaries

Oftentimes, River Guides are paid hourly, daily, or even per trip. Beginning part-time guides usually earn about $8 an hour. More seasoned part-time guides make more than $12 an hour. The Bureau of Labor Statistics lists the median annual salary for guides in 2004 as $19,280. Full-time guides who take on either managerial or marketing duties can garner $25,000 to $30,000 per year. Guides with specialized training and expertise typically earn a higher wage than those with more general skills. Summer resorts and other seasonal lodges may offer their River Guides an end-of-season bonus. Also, River Guides can solicit tips in an effort to increase their wages. Owners and operators of River Guide businesses can earn an annual salary of more than $50,000.

Employment Prospects

Employment for River Guides is expected to grow roughly 12 percent annually until 2012, according to the Bureau of Labor Statistics. Currently, this is considered an average rate of job growth in the United States.

Advancement Prospects

To gain experience, individuals can look for part-time work assisting a full-fledged River Guide. Part-time or volunteer positions with the Coast Guard might also provide entry into the field, as any experience on local waterways would prove helpful. Many companies that hire River Guides offer on-the-job training and certification programs that meet state requirements for guides.

Internships are also an excellent method of gaining not only experience but also a foot in the door with an organization that hires River Guides. America Outdoors: An Association of Outfitters and Guides compiles a listing of open jobs and internships. Another organization, Outdoor Ed: The Professional's Resource, offers information about outdoor, environmental, and adventure education at its online Training Center. In addition to offering three of its own scholarships, Outdoor Ed also operates a searchable database of training opportunities and internships throughout the United States.

Experienced River Guides working for large organizations that employ multiple guides may be able to advance into managerial or training positions. Many River Guides eventually open their own businesses; however, most gain their initial experience working for another employer.

Education and Training

A high school diploma is the minimum education requirement for a River Guide; however, before an individual is considered qualified to lead a river tour, some form of specialized training is typically necessary. A variety of organizations and associations offer certification programs for River Guides.

Certain vocational schools, community colleges, and universities also offer outdoor education and recreation programs for individuals interested in becoming River Guides. Those wishing to secure a college degree can also search the International Ecotourism Club Web site's global database of colleges and universities that offer degrees in various forms of ecotourism. This Web site also contains information about internship opportunities for students.

Students pursuing careers as River Guides can benefit from marine biology, natural history, and aquatic botany courses, as well as second language and public speaking classes. Those planning to operate their own companies would also benefit from business, marketing, hospitality, and tourism courses.

Special Requirements

In states that require certification, a variety of organizations and associations offer certification programs for River Guides. Individuals can also pursue general certification programs, such as the online Sustainable Tourism certification program offered by International Ecotourism Society, which includes courses such as Tourist Guide Techniques.

Certification requirements for River Guides vary depending on municipal and state waterway regulations. Many organizations that hire River Guides require some sort of safety or medical training, such as the first aid training offered by Wilderness Medical Associates. Boating safety, swimming, and lifeguard courses are also helpful.

Experience, Special Skills, and Personality Traits

Excellent public speaking skills are a requirement for every River Guide. As nearly all river trips involve some form of training or instruction, guides should be able to comfortably and clearly explain and model what it is participants need to do. Guides must also be able to speak the local language, as well as the language of group members.

Because the activities included on many river trips can be risky and physically demanding, some level of physical fitness is typically necessary for these jobs. Stamina is also a prerequisite for River Guides. Not only must they spend entire days outdoors, sometimes in intense heat and sun, but guides on more extended trips do not necessarily get a chance to rest after the group reaches its stopping point for the day. Oftentimes, while the group members rest, guides are busy setting up camp or cooking meals. Guides may also find themselves performing first aid for cuts, scrapes, sprains, and other minor injuries; although serious accidents and emergencies are rare, guides must also be able to perform CPR if necessary.

Unions and Associations

America Outdoors serves outdoor educators, as well as travel outfitters and tour companies. The National Tour Association represents tour operators, tour suppliers, and destination marketing organizations. Options for guides specializing in some form of ecotourism include the International Ecotourism Club and the Ecotourism Society.

Tips for Entry

1. Gain boating experience by working part time or volunteering in some capacity for activities related to local waterways.
2. Research internships like those offered by the Student Conservation Association, http://www.sca-inc.org, or the International Ecotourism Society, http://www.ecotourism.org.
3. Apply for outdoor education scholarships like those offered by Outdoor Ed, http://www.outdoored.com.
4. Look for jobs at ECOCLUB's Ecotourism Job Center, http://www.ecoclub.com/jobs, or at Web sites like America Outdoors, http://www.americaoutdoors.org/job-results.asp, and the Travel Industry Association of America, http://www.tia.org/express/job_intro.html.

TOUR GUIDE

CAREER PROFILE

Duties: Planning, organizing, and leading individual and group tours of art galleries, historical buildings, monuments, national parks, zoos, and other sites, as well as cruises, expeditions, and other types of travel; detailing points of interest, answering questions, explaining tour rules and regulations, and monitoring group progress to ensure the safety of all tour participants; distributing name tags, headsets, safety devices, and other materials or equipment relevant to the tour

Alternate Title(s): Travel Planner; Tour Manager; Tour Director; Tour Escort

Salary Range: $15,000 to $50,000+

Employment Prospects: Fair

Advancement Prospects: Limited

Prerequisites:

    Education or Training—High school diploma with specialized vocational training in travel and tourism

    Experience—Understanding of local culture, art, history, and ecology; familiarity with various tourist attractions and travel destinations; knowledge of local, state, and federal rules and regulations related to areas or sites visited

    Special Skills and Personality Traits—Ability to plan and organize events; time management; attention to detail; public speaking; problem solving

    Special Requirements—Basic first aid skills

CAREER LADDER

```
┌─────────────────────────────────────┐
│   Tour Company Manager/Owner         │
└─────────────────────────────────────┘

┌─────────────────────────────────────┐
│   Full-Time Tour Guide               │
└─────────────────────────────────────┘

┌─────────────────────────────────────┐
│   Part-Time Tour Guide               │
└─────────────────────────────────────┘

┌─────────────────────────────────────┐
│   Volunteer Tour Guide               │
└─────────────────────────────────────┘
```

Position Description

Tour Guides conduct individual and group tours of all sorts of tourist attractions, monuments, and other destinations, both indoors and outside. While some tours are as simple as a three-hour walk through the Sistine Chapel in Rome, others involve excursion or cruise packages that span several days or even several weeks and include several destinations and modes of transportation. For example, a Caribbean cruise tour package with several port calls might include guided walking tours of various cities in Mexico, bus travel to nearby ancient ruins, mountain or rainforest hikes, snorkeling excursions, and folkloric ballet shows. With these more complex itineraries, Tour Guides not only lead tours at various destinations, but they may also organize the entire tour, from planning daily activities and making reservations at various restaurants or entertainment venues to purchasing tickets and even driving tour buses or boats. Many guides often engage in activities, such as snorkeling, with group members.

Tour Guides also monitor weather conditions at planned destinations, provide information about the physical fitness level needed to complete a tour, and monitor the progress of members throughout a tour. Prior to beginning a tour, guides might also collect information from clients and lead them through a registration process, hand out identification cards or name tags, show a video, teach clients how to use necessary equipment, and explain safety and regulatory requirements for the tour. In addition, guides help clients resolve any problems, such as lost or stolen tickets, that might arise during a tour.

Tour Guides employed at a specific site, such as a museum, zoo, or art gallery, oftentimes offer only a single type of tour, which they repeat regularly. Many of these positions are volunteer or part-time. Other Tour Guides—often employed by larger travel agencies, tour companies, resort operators, national parks, or other governmental bodies—plan, organize, and lead a wide variety of tours to all sorts of destinations. These positions can be either part-time or full-time. Both part-time and full-time Tour Guides typically work sporadic hours, depending on the types of tours they are offering. Weekends, holidays, and other peak travel times are often the busiest for Tour Guides. As a result, work is often seasonal.

Salaries

Salaries for Tour Guides vary significantly, depending on their experience, the types of tours they offer, and the size and location of their employers. According to the Bureau of Labor Statistics, the median annual salary for a Tour Guide in 2004 was $19,280. Guides able to offer a wide variety of tours and travel extensively typically earn more than those situated at a single site. A part-time Tour Guide earns anywhere from minimum wage to $10 per hour, while a beginning full-time Tour Guide typically starts at $20,000 per year; more experienced guides earns up to $30,000 annually. Guides also typically earn tips. Tour company owners can make more than $50,000 per year.

Employment Prospects

Employment for Tour Guides is expected to grow at an average rate of 10 to 15 percent annually until 2012. This is considered an average rate of growth compared to other types of careers.

Advancement Prospects

Many tour operators begin their careers by volunteering at a local museum, art gallery, or tour company. Along with learning how to organize and lead tours, volunteer guides are also able to increase their knowledge about local culture and ecology. Finding part-time work also allows a beginning guide entry into the field, as well as the chance to increase skills and knowledge. College students interested in developing Tour Guide skills can seek part-time employment as campus guides for prospective students and parents or as orientation leaders for new students. Larger organizations that employ multiple part-time and full-time Tour Guides may offer on-the-job training and opportuni-

ties to advance into management positions. Entrepreneurs who establish their own tour companies typically first gain experience as salaried guides working for an organization of some sort.

Education and Training

The minimum education requirement for a Tour Guide is a high school diploma. However, postsecondary education is becoming increasingly common in the field. As with many careers, more education typically translates into higher wages. Many vocational schools, adult education programs, community colleges, and universities offer travel-related classes and training programs. A limited number of colleges offer bachelor's and master's degrees in travel and tourism. The International Ecotourism Club Web site includes a searchable database of colleges and universities throughout the world that offer specific degrees in ecotourism. This Web site also contains information about internship opportunities for students.

Whether in high school or college, students interested in becoming Tour Guides can benefit from taking classes in geography, history, art, culture, and literature. Language and public speaking courses are also extremely valuable. Business courses are helpful for individuals who plan to open their own tour companies.

Special Requirements

According to the National Federation of Tourist Guide Associations, only a handful of municipalities in the United States require a license to work as a Tour Guide in the United States:

- Charleston, South Carolina
- Gettysburg Battlefield, Pennsylvania
- New Orleans, Louisiana
- New York City, New York
- Savannah, Georgia
- Vicksburg Battlefield, Mississippi
- Washington, D.C.

The National Tour Association offers a Certified Tour Professional distance-learning program. The International Ecotourism Society offers an online Sustainable Tourism certification program for Tour Guides who wish to specialize in ecotourism.

Experience, Special Skills, and Personality Traits

All Tour Guides need excellent public speaking skills. Because a significant portion of most tours involves answering questions, guides must possess significant knowledge about local culture, ecology, etc. Guides must also be able to speak the local language, as well as the language of tour participants. Many tour jobs require significant amounts of walking; as a result, a basic level of physical fitness is usually necessary. For tours involving mountain or rock climbing, white-water rafting, or similar outdoor activities, specialized training is required. As minor injuries are not uncommon on these types of tours, guides must be able to perform basic first aid and also possess the knowledge and ability to get appropriate help should a more serious accident occur.

Unions and Associations

The World Federation of Tourist Guides Association represents Tour Guides across the globe. Its U.S. branch is called the National Federation of Tourist Guide Associations. The National Tour Association represents tour operators, tour suppliers, and destination marketing organizations. Tour Guides specializing in ecotourism can also join the International Ecotourism Society and the International Ecotourism Club.

Tips for Entry

1. Gain experience as a volunteer Tour Guide at a local museum, art gallery, zoo, park, or tour company.
2. Research internships like those offered by the International Ecotourism Society, http://www.ecotourism.org.
3. Search for job openings at Web sites like the Travel Industry Association of America, http://www.tia.org/express/job_intro.html; ECOCLUB's Ecotourism Job Center, http://www.ecoclub.com/jobs; America Outdoors, http://www.americaoutdoors.org/job-results.asp; and Outdoor Ed: The Professional's Resource, http://www.outdoored.com.

TRAVEL AGENT

CAREER PROFILE

Duties: Researching travel dates, location, prices, and modes of transportation for clients; booking travel arrangements, such as airplane, train, and cruise tickets, hotel accommodations, car rentals, and other forms of entertainment, such as tickets to various events; offering advice about travel destinations, dining options, area attractions and activities, climate, and related considerations

Alternate Title(s): Travel Planner; Reservation and Transportation Ticket Agent

Salary Range: $17,000 to $45,000

Employment Prospects: Fair

Advancement Prospects: Limited

Prerequisites:

    Education or Training—High school diploma with specialized vocational training in travel and tourism

    Experience—Understanding of world geography, familiarity with various travel destinations; knowledge of rules and regulations related to international travel

    Special Skills and Personality Traits—Ability to gather and organize detailed information clearly and accurately; problem solving; communication, including writing and speaking; sales

    Special Requirements—Familiarity with computers and Internet travel planning resources

CAREER LADDER

```
┌─────────────────────────────┐
│     Agency Owner/Manager     │
└─────────────────────────────┘

┌─────────────────────────────┐
│      Senior Travel Agent     │
└─────────────────────────────┘

┌─────────────────────────────┐
│         Travel Agent         │
└─────────────────────────────┘

┌─────────────────────────────┐
│       Reservation Clerk      │
└─────────────────────────────┘
```

Position Description

Travel Agents help clients identify their travel needs and desires and then book the arrangements most suited to them. Travel reservations can range from something as straightforward as a single airline ticket for a short business trip to a complex and comprehensive excursion package that might include not only flight reservations, but also car rentals, train and bus tickets, travel insurance, hotel accommodations, guided tours, and meal packages for a family interested in visiting multiple destinations.

Along with researching a multitude of destinations and booking a wide range of travel arrangements, Travel Agents stay abreast of weather conditions in various destinations; offer information about necessary documentation, such as passports and visas, for international travel; and monitor things like exchange rates and health risks in certain areas. In addition, Travel Agents help clients resolve problems, such as a stolen passport, that arise during their trips.

To build their client base, Travel Agents use media such as direct mail and the Internet to market their expertise. Oftentimes, large resort operators, cruise lines, and tour guide businesses hire Travel Agents to market special deals and specific services to clients. In some cases, Travel Agents may be required to engage in specific promotional activities, such as presenting slide shows to groups of people or manning trade show booths. Other Travel Agents narrow their services to a single specialty, such as ecotourism, and target a specific clientele, such as environmentally conscious travelers seeking unspoiled destinations, opportunities for outdoor activities, and accommodations designed to have a minimal impact on natural surroundings and inhabitants.

Travel Agents make use of a wide range of sources when building travel packages for clients. Along with consulting traditional travel publications, Travel Agents in recent years have also taken advantage of the growing number of online resources for travel information. Quite often, they also survey clients who have returned from a trip for their impressions of the destination, accommodations, and modes of transportation.

In addition to using outside sources for information about the quality of various travel-related accommodations, Travel Agents may also visit various places themselves to assess things like comfort, affordability, reliability, service, and cleanliness. In some cases, resort operators or tourism boards of certain countries might pay for a Travel Agent's visit there.

After completing their research and compiling prices, available dates and times, and customer service ratings, Travel Agents present various options to clients, handle all booking arrangements, and ultimately, provide clients with itineraries, tickets, publications, maps, and any other necessary paperwork. Whether working from an office or from home, an increasingly popular option thanks to recent technological advances, Travel Agents spend the majority of their time at a desk, either on the phone or at the computer, engaged in customer service and sales activities.

Travel agencies, tour and resort operators, and insurance companies all employ Travel Agents, some full time and some part time. Many Travel Agents are also self-employed. Full-time Travel Agents typically work eight hours a day, five days a week. However, when holidays and other peak travel times approach, many Travel Agents find themselves working longer hours to keep pace with demand. These peak times are typically the most lucrative and also the most stressful periods for Travel Agents.

Salaries

According to the Bureau of Labor Statistics, salaries for Travel Agents vary depending on the size and location of their employer. In May of 2004, the median yearly salary for a Travel Agent was $27,640. Employees working for large companies in urban areas typically earn more than those employed by smaller firms in less populated locales. Also, the pay is typically higher for agents focused on corporate sales than those serving mainly leisure travelers. A beginning Travel Agent typically earns an annual salary of $17,000 to $22,000. As an agent gains experience and a proven track record in sales, this typically increases to between $25,000 and $30,000 per year. A seasoned Travel Agent, with several years of experience, may earn more than $35,000 per year, while an agency owner typically garners a yearly income of $35,000 to $45,000.

Compensation for many salaried Travel Agents typically includes perks such as reduced airline fares and accommodation fees and even free trips. Most full-time agents also have compensation packages that include traditional benefits, including medical insurance, retirement plans, and paid vacations.

Income for self-employed Travel Agents, who account for roughly 14 percent of all Travel Agents, can be more sporadic, as it depends solely on sales and any commissions earned from international airlines (domestic airlines no longer pay commissions to Travel Agents), tour and resort operators, and other travel-related companies willing to pay commissions. To boost earnings, some agents charge clients a fee for their services. Self-employed Travel Agents are particularly susceptible to economic downturns, as both individuals and companies tend to trim their travel budgets at these times, a trend which directly impacts the earnings of a self-employed agent.

Employment Prospects

While pay for Travel Agents may be on the modest side, the fringe benefit of discounted and free trips remains a significant draw to this field of work. At the same time, the increasing popularity of easy-to-use discount Internet travel sites has significantly reduced demand for Travel Agent services, particularly for simple tasks such as booking airline tickets. As a result, competition for jobs is expected to be high. In fact, according to the Bureau of Labor Statistics, the number of Travel Agent jobs will decline through 2014. Positions will most often come available when more experienced agents retire or change occupations. As a result, the most successful agents will likely be those who specialize in niche markets, such as ecotourism, and those who are able to use Internet resources to remain as competitive as possible, finding the least expensive options for clients, particularly those with complex travel plans.

Advancement Prospects

One way to gain experience, as well as a foot in the door, is to work as a reservation clerk or receptionist at an agency. Oftentimes, experienced Travel Agents will train such individuals to take on additional responsibilities until they are capable of functioning as full-fledged Travel Agents on their own. Travel Agents can also advance their careers by gaining certifications in various specialties. And in larger agencies with multiple employees, oftentimes there exist managerial opportunities for experienced Travel Agents. Individuals who open their own agencies typically first gain experience as salaried Travel Agents working for an established agency.

Education and Training

While a high school diploma is considered the minimum education requirement for a Travel Agent, additional specialized training, in either a specific destination or a type of travel, makes it significantly easier to secure a job. Postsecondary education is particularly important for individuals with limited experience.

A variety of short-term educational options exist. For example, numerous vocational schools offer 12-week Travel Agent training programs. Adult education programs, community colleges, and universities also tend to offer travel-related classes. Finally, a limited number of colleges offer bachelor's and master's degrees in travel and tourism. The International Ecotourism Club compiles an online database of colleges and universities throughout the world that offer specific degrees in ecotourism.

Two of the industry's leading associations, the American Society of Travel Agents (ASTA) and the Institute of Certified Travel Agents (ICTA), offer online and print self-study courses for individuals wanting to advance their skills, specialize in a certain sector of the industry, learn more about a certain destination, or gain credentials such as the Certified Travel Counselor designation. The International Ecotourism Society offers an online program, which results in a Sustainable Tourism certification, for Travel Agents who wish to specialize in ecotourism.

A more general postsecondary education can also be helpful to Travel Agents looking for their first job. Many employers like to see coursework in areas such as geography, world history, computer technology, communications, languages, finance, marketing, sales, and management. Many of these courses are also invaluable for entrepreneurs hoping to establish their own travel agencies someday.

Special Requirements

While the federal government does not require a license to practice as a Travel Agent in the United States, numerous states do require specific licensure or certification for travel retailers. The Department of Commerce or the Attorney General's Office in each state can provide additional information. Individuals who launch their own agencies are eligible for commission from airlines, cruise line operators or other travel suppliers only after securing formal approval from governing bodies such as the International Airlines Travel Agency Network. Approval is granted only to financially healthy agencies staffed by a minimum of one experienced Travel Agent.

Experience, Special Skills, and Personality Traits

Whether novice, veteran, or somewhere in between, all Travel Agents need excellent communication, customer service, and sales skills to build and maintain a network of clients. As computers have become indispensable to the industry and as e-mail and Web sites have become common media for providing services to clients, Travel Agents must be familiar with both computer and Internet technology. Attention to detail is also essential, as Travel Agents frequently gather and compare information from various sites while they arrange itineraries, sometime quite complex ones, for their clients. Those agents focused on corporate sales also need the ability to work quickly as business travel often takes place with little preplanning. Personal travel experience is helpful, as firsthand knowledge of a particular destination, accommodation, airline, tour guide, etc. allows an agent to provide specific and personal recommendations to clients. For similar reasons, knowledge of world geography is valuable as well.

Unions and Associations

The American Society of Travel Agents is the world's largest association for Travel Agents and suppliers. Representing Travel Agents throughout the world, it offers a variety of online and print correspondence educational programs for beginning and experienced Travel Agents. An international, nonprofit entity, the Institute of Certified Travel Agents offers certification programs for travel industry professionals throughout the world. The National Association of Commissioned Travel Agents is the association for self-employed Travel Agents, while the Cruise Lines International Association serves cruise industry professionals. The Society for Accessible Travel and Hospitality, which advocates for travelers with disabilities, provides extensive resources for Travel Agents serving this population. Other organizations include the Travel Industry Association of America and the International Ecotourism Club.

Tips for Entry

1. Order the 25-page booklet, *Becoming a Travel Agent*, from the American Society of Travel Agents Web site, http://www.astanet.com/education/edu_becoming.asp.

2. Gain experience by working either as a receptionist or a reservation clerk at a travel agency, by securing a part-time or seasonal position during peak travel times, or by completing an internship like those offered by the International Ecotourism Society, http://www.ecotourism.org.

3. Search for job openings at the American Society of Travel Agents Web site, http://www.astanet.com; at the Travel Industry Association of America Web site, http://www.tia.org/express/job_intro.html; and at ECO-CLUB's Ecotourism Job Center, http://www.ecoclub.com/jobs.

4. Subscribe to a free monthly travel industry publication such as *RECOMMEND* Magazine (available online at http://www.recommend.com) to learn more about travel destinations from the perspective of experienced Travel Agents.

WILDERNESS GUIDE

CAREER PROFILE

Duties: Leading wilderness trips and tours through natural areas, such as national parks, forests, rivers, and mountains; engaging in mountain climbing, rock climbing, snowshoeing, cross-country skiing, kayaking, whitewater rafting, camping, hiking, and similar outdoor activities; teaching group members how to use safety equipment and related devices; explaining ecology, natural history, and other points of interest; answering questions; explaining rules and regulations; monitoring progress of all group participants to ensure safety; and providing basic first aid.

Alternate Title(s): Adventure Guide; Nature Guide; Tour Leader; Tour Escort

Salary Range: $15,000 to $50,000+

Employment Prospects: Fair

Advancement Prospects: Limited

Prerequisites:
  Education or Training—High school diploma with certifications in areas of specialization
  Experience—Knowledge of local ecology and natural history; expertise in mountain climbing, rock climbing, hiking, white-water rafting, and similar activities; experience using safety devices and equipment; understanding of local, state, and federal rules and regulations related to areas visited
  Special Skills and Personality Traits—Ability to plan and organize events and lead groups in specific tasks; attention to detail; public speaking; problem solving
  Special Requirements—Basic first aid skills; CPR; physical fitness

CAREER LADDER

```
┌─────────────────────────────┐
│  Wilderness Guide Company   │
│      Manager/Owner          │
└─────────────────────────────┘

┌─────────────────────────────┐
│  Full-Time Wilderness Guide │
└─────────────────────────────┘

┌─────────────────────────────┐
│  Part-Time Wilderness Guide │
└─────────────────────────────┘

┌─────────────────────────────┐
│  Volunteer Wilderness Guide │
└─────────────────────────────┘
```

Position Description

Wilderness Guides conduct individual and group activities at all sorts of outdoor destinations. While some tours focus on a specific type of activity, such as rock climbing, others make use of several different outdoor options, such as hiking, camping, and mountain climbing. Because wilderness tours can range in duration from a day or weekend to several weeks or even months, and because the experience level of participants can range from novice to expert, the job of the Wilderness Guide can vary considerably. Some guides specialize in a specific activity for experts only, others offer a specific activity for beginners and experts alike, and still others serve not only participants of any level, but also provide a wide variety of activities. Wilderness Guides tend to organize an entire tour, doing everything from mapping out routes, planning meals, bringing food and water, gathering camping equipment and other necessary devices, and arranging vans or other modes of transportation to where the tour is scheduled to begin.

These guides also check weather forecasts and other ecological conditions at planned destinations. For example, mountain guides must be particularly alert to the sudden snowstorms that frequently happen atop mountains, as well as mud and rock slides that can wash out roads and cause trail closures. In some cases, additional gear or the use of alternate routes might be required. And while many outdoor excursions do take place during inclement weather, guides must be aware of the potential for dangerous weather conditions such as tornadoes, severe thunderstorms, blizzards, and hurricanes. Wilderness Guides also provide information about the physical fitness level needed to complete a tour, interview and observe tour members in an effort to match ability levels with activities, and monitor the progress of members throughout a tour.

Prior to beginning a tour, guides frequently teach clients how to use necessary equipment, lead team-building exercises, and explain the safety precautions members are expected to observe throughout the trip. Guides also help individuals who are struggling or lagging behind the group. If a member gets lost or seriously hurt, the guide is responsible for organizing a search party and enlisting emergency services.

Wilderness Guides are most often employed by resort operators, national parks, and adventure travel and outdoor recreation businesses. Many positions are seasonal or part-time. Guides typically work sporadic hours; during tours, they are quite often considered on-duty for the entire duration of the trip, and between tours they may not work at all, although some spend time recruiting individuals for the next tour or researching and planning new tours. Weekends, holidays, and other peak travel times are often the busiest for Wilderness Guides.

Salaries

Many Wilderness Guides get paid per hour, per day, or per trip. Beginning part-time guides tend to make roughly $8 an hour, while experienced guides can garner more than $12 an hour. Full-time guides with management and marketing responsibilities usually earn $25,000 to $30,000 per year. According to the Bureau of Labor Statistics, the median annual salary for a guide in 2004 was $19,280. Guides with specialized training and expertise typically earn a higher wage than those with more general skills. Seasonal resorts, such as ski lodges, sometimes pay their Wilderness Guides a bonus at the end of the season, and guides can also boost their income significantly with tips. Managers and owners of Wilderness Guide companies can make upwards of $50,000 annually.

Employment Prospects

According to the Bureau of Labor Statistics, employment for Wilderness Guides is expected to grow roughly 12 percent annually until 2012. Compared to other types of careers, this is considered an average rate of growth.

Advancement Prospects

Many Wilderness Guides gain experience at lodges or resorts by taking jobs as cooks or groundskeepers or at summer camps by working as counselors or instructors. Most employers of Wilderness Guides offer on-the-job training, which allows new employees to learn how to organize and lead a wilderness tour, as well as to increase their skills in specific activities and knowledge of certain locales. Internships also provide entry into the field. An organization called Outdoor Ed compiles information about outdoor, environmental, and adventure education on its online Training Center. Along with offering three scholarships itself, Outdoor Ed also operates a searchable database of training opportunities and internships throughout the United States. America Outdoors: An Association of Outfitters and Guides also posts jobs and internships available.

Experienced guides working for organizations that employ multiple Wilderness Guides may have opportunities to advance into leadership positions with administrative and managerial duties. While some Wilderness Guides eventually launch their own businesses, most first gain experience working for an organization of some sort.

Education and Training

The minimum education requirement for a Wilderness Guide is a high school diploma. However, specialized training is typically necessary before an individual is qualified to lead wilderness-based activities, particularly high-risk ones like rock climbing. A variety of vocational schools, community colleges, and universities offer outdoor education and recreation programs for individuals interested in becoming Wilderness Guides. Those wishing to secure a college degree can also search the International Ecotourism Club's online database of colleges and universities throughout the world that offer degrees in various forms of ecotourism. This Web site also contains information about internship opportunities for students.

Whether in high school or college, students interested in becoming Wilderness Guides can benefit from taking language and public speaking classes, as well as courses in geography, topography, natural history, and botany. Business, marketing, and hospitality and tourism courses are also helpful to those planning to run their own guide businesses some day.

Special Requirements

Licensing requirements for Wilderness Guides vary by specialty, as well as by municipality and state. Industry associations typically offer certification programs to the individuals they represent. For example, the American Mountain Guide

Association offers a top rope course, a ski mountaineering program, an alpine guide program, and a rock guide program, as well as various scholarships. More general certification programs exist as well. For example, the International Ecotourism Society offers an online Sustainable Tourism certification program, which includes courses such as Tourist Guide Techniques, for guides who wish to specialize in ecotourism. Many organizations require some sort of wilderness-based safety or medical training, such as the first aid training offered by Wilderness Medical Associates.

Experience, Special Skills, and Personality Traits

All guides need excellent public speaking skills. Because nearly every wilderness trip requires some form of instruction or training, guides must be able to explain and demonstrate processes and procedures clearly and answer any questions, not only about a specific activity, but also about the environment in which it is taking place. Oftentimes, guides field questions about local history and culture. In addition, guides must be able to speak the local language, as well as the language of tour participants.

Because the activities included on many wilderness tours are physically grueling, physical fitness is usually a prerequisite. The ability to work long days is also necessary; oftentimes, when a tour reaches its destination for the day, the guide sets up camp, plans the next day's activities, or cooks a meal, while the group members rest. Guides also must be able to perform basic first aid for minor injuries, as well as CPR in the event of a more serious accident or illness.

Unions and Associations

Outdoor educators of any discipline can join America Outdoors, which also serves travel outfitters and tour companies. The National Federation of Tourist Guide Associations, the U.S. branch of the World Federation of Tourist Guides Association, represents guide organizations throughout the United States, while the National Tour Association represents tour operators, tour suppliers, and destination marketing organizations. The International Ecotourism Club and the Ecotourism Society are two options for guides specializing in some form of ecotourism. Finally, the American Mountain Guide Association represents U.S.-based mountain guides.

Tips for Entry

1. Gain experience as a counselor or instructor at a summer camp or as a cook or groundskeeper at a lodge or resort.
2. Research internships like those offered by the International Ecotourism Society, http://www.ecotourism. org, or the Student Conservation Association, http://www.sca-inc.org.
3. Apply for scholarships like those offered by the American Mountain Guide Association, http://www.amga. com, and Outdoor Ed, http://www.outdoored.com.
4. Search for job openings at Web sites like America Outdoors, http://www.americaoutdoors.org/job-results. asp; the Travel Industry Association of America, http://www.tia.org/express/job_intro.html; and ECOCLUB's Ecotourism Job Center, http://www.ecoclub.com/jobs.

ENGINEERING

BIOLOGICAL AND AGRICULTURAL ENGINEERS

CAREER PROFILE

Duties: Devise practical, efficient solutions for producing, storing, transporting, processing, and packaging agricultural products; solve problems related to systems, processes, and machines that interact with humans, plants, animals, microorganisms, and biological materials; develop solutions for responsible, alternative uses of agricultural products, byproducts and wastes, and natural resources.

Alternate Title(s): Agricultural Engineer; Agricultural Safety and Health Program Director; Agricultural Systems Specialist; Conservation Engineer; Plan Service Engineer; Product Technology Engineer; Project Engineer; Biosystems Engineer; Bioresources Engineer; Agricultural Extension Services Engineer; Consulting Engineer

Salary Range: $37,680 to $90,410

Employment Prospects: Good

Advancement Prospects: Good

Prerequisites:

   Education or Training—A bachelor's degree is a minimum requirement, but a master's degree is required for some positions

   Experience—Experience using specialized technical software may be helpful or required, as well as experience operating scientific instruments and equipment

   Special Skills and Personality Traits—Analytical thinking, problem-solving, communication, computer, technical, and mechanical skills; detail-oriented, careful, thorough, patient, logical, adaptable, and flexible

   Special Requirements—State licensure is usually required; specialized certifications may be required

CAREER LADDER

```
┌─────────────────────────────────────┐
│   Vice President of Research or      │
│      Development Director            │
│   of Technology or Research          │
└─────────────────────────────────────┘

┌─────────────────────────────────────┐
│   Engineering Manager or Consultant  │
└─────────────────────────────────────┘

┌─────────────────────────────────────┐
│            Staff Engineer            │
└─────────────────────────────────────┘

┌─────────────────────────────────────┐
│               Intern                 │
└─────────────────────────────────────┘
```

Position Description

Biological and agricultural engineering is the application of engineering principles to any process associated with producing agriculturally based goods and the management of natural resources. Biological and Agricultural Engineers ensure that humankind has safe and plentiful food to eat, pure water to drink, clean fuel and energy sources, and a safe, healthy environment in which to live.

Biological and Agricultural Engineers (BAEs) devise practical, efficient solutions for producing, storing, transporting, processing, and packaging agricultural products. They solve problems related to systems, processes, and machines that interact with humans, plants, animals, microorganisms, and biological materials. In addition, BAEs develop solutions for responsible, alternative uses of agricultural products, byproducts, and wastes, as well as natural resources such as soil, water, air, and energy. They do all of these things with a constant eye toward improved protection of people, animals, and the environment.

Regardless of the specialty, BAE students enjoy a distinct advantage when it comes time to enter the workforce. Their well-rounded engineering experiences enable them to function exceptionally well on the multidisciplinary teams in today's workforce. Because of their training and experience, BAEs are well prepared to understand the interrelationships between technology and living systems—talents needed to succeed in engineering positions today and in the future.

BAE embraces a variety of specialty areas. As new technology and information emerge, specialty areas are created, and many overlap with one or more other areas. Following are descriptions of some of the exciting specialties BAE students can choose to focus on.

Biological Engineering

One of the most rapidly growing of the BAE specialties, biological engineering applies engineering practice to problems and opportunities presented by living things and the natural environment. Engineers in this field are involved in everything from environmental protection and remediation to food and feed production to medicine and plant-based pharmaceuticals and packaging materials. Some develop strategies for natural pest control and the treatment of hazardous wastes, for composting, and for enzyme processing of biomass, food, feed, and wastes.

Natural Resources

BAEs with environmental expertise work to better understand the complex mechanics of these resources, so that they can be used efficiently and without degradation. These engineers determine crop water requirements and design irrigation systems. They are experts in agricultural hydrology principles, such as controlling drainage, and they implement ways to control soil erosion and study the environmental effects of sediment on stream quality. Natural resources engineers design, build, operate, and maintain water control structures for reservoirs, floodways, and channels. They also work on water treatment systems, wetlands protection, and other water issues.

Power Systems and Machinery Design

BAEs in this specialty focus on designing advanced equipment, making it more efficient and less demanding on natural resources. They develop equipment for food processing, highly precise crop spraying, agricultural commodity and waste transport, and turf and landscape maintenance, as well as equipment for such specialized tasks as removing seaweed from beaches.

Structures and Environment

BAEs with expertise in this area design animal housing, storage structures, and greenhouses with ventilation systems, temperature and humidity controls, and structural strength appropriate for their climate and purpose. They

also devise better practices and systems for storing, recovering, reusing, and transporting waste products.

Food and Bioprocess Engineering

Engineers in this specialty understand microbiological processes and use this expertise to develop useful products; to treat municipal, industrial, and agricultural wastes; and to improve food safety. They are experts in pasteurization, sterilization, and irradiation and in the packaging, transportation, and storage of perishable products. Food process engineers combine design expertise with manufacturing methods to develop economical and responsible processing solutions for industry. Food and bioprocess engineers also look for ways to reduce waste by devising alternatives for treatment, disposal, and utilization.

Information and Electrical Technologies

One of the most versatile of the BAE specialties, this concentration involves everything from machinery design to soil testing to food quality and safety control. Geographic information systems, global positioning systems, machine instrumentation and controls, biorobotics, and machine vision are some of the exciting information and electrical technologies being used today or developed for the future.

Forest Engineering

In this specialty, BAEs apply engineering to solve natural resource and environment problems in forest production systems and related manufacturing industries. Such problems are related to equipment design and manufacturing; forest access systems design and construction; machine-soil interaction and erosion control; forest operations analysis and improvement; decision modeling; and wood product design and manufacturing.

Energy

This specialty involves efforts to identify and develop viable energy sources—including biomass, methane, and vegetable oil—and to make these and other systems cleaner and more efficient. BAEs in this area develop energy conservation strategies to reduce costs and protect the environment. In addition, they design traditional and alternative energy systems to meet the needs of agricultural operations.

Aquacultural Engineering

In this niche, BAEs help to design farm systems for raising fish and shellfish, as well as ornamental and bait fish. They specialize in water quality, biotechnology, machinery, natural resources, feeding and ventilation systems, and sanitation. These BAEs seek ways to reduce pollution from aquacultural discharges, to reduce excess water use, and to improve farm systems. They also work with aquatic animal harvesting, sorting, and processing.

Nursery and Greenhouse Engineering

In addition to applying their expertise to matters such as irrigation, mechanization, disease and pest control, and nutrient application, in this specialty BAEs also focus on equipment for transplantation; control systems for temperature, humidity, and ventilation; and plant biology issues, such as hydroponics, tissue culture, and seedling propagation methods.

Ergonomics, Safety, and Health
BAEs in this area analyze health and injury data, the use and possible misuse of machines, and equipment compliance with standards and regulation. They constantly look for ways to improve the safety of equipment, materials, and agricultural practices, and to communicate safety and health issues to the public.

Due to their broad understanding of the interrelationships between technology and living systems, BAEs have a wide variety of employment options from which to choose. Career opportunities are found in the corporate sector with leading companies of all kinds. In addition, opportunities also existing with the likes of NASA, as well as government agencies such as the U.S. Department of Agriculture, U.S. Department of Energy, and the U.S. Environmental Protection Agency.

Salaries
According to the 2006–07 edition of the U.S. Department of Labor's *Occupational Outlook Handbook*, in mid-2004 median annual salaries for agricultural engineers ranged from $37,680 to $90,410. Data from a survey conducted by the National Association of Colleges and Employers in 2005 put average annual starting salaries for those with bachelor's degrees at $46,172.

Employment Prospects
The U.S. Department of Labor projects average employment growth for agricultural engineers through 2014. Growth will be supported by a number of factors, including an emphasis on resource conservation, the need to feed a larger population, agricultural equipment standardization, and the improvement of agricultural production efficiency.

Advancement Prospects
The U.S. Department of Labor reports that entry-level engineers normally work under the supervision of an experienced engineer. After acquiring knowledge and expertise through work experience, they are given additional responsibility and more complex assignments. Eventually, they are able to advance to positions as technical specialists or supervisors. Some engineers pursue management careers, or go on to work as consultants or sales representatives.

Education and Training
While a bachelor's degree is the minimum requirement to work in this profession, some jobs call for a master's degree. University BAE programs have many names, such as biological systems engineering, bioresource engineering, environmental engineering, forest engineering, or food process engineering. While other engineering students may study a single discipline, BAE programs traditionally include coursework in a variety of engineering disciplines, complemented by classes in biological and agricultural sciences. When they reach their advanced-level courses, BAE students then tend to choose a specialty area according to their individual interests, such as environmental systems, food production, biological resources/ecological systems, or power and machinery systems.

Special Requirements
State licensure is usually required for engineers whose work impacts public health and safety. Depending on an engineer's specialty, certifications may be required for working with hazardous materials.

Experience, Special Skills, and Personality Traits
BAEs must be detail-oriented, with the ability to perform tasks in a careful and thorough manner. They also must be logical and analytical thinkers, with excellent problem-solving abilities. Due to the many variables involved in engineering, scientific, and technical work, the ability to be patient, adaptable, and flexible also is critical for professionals in this field. BAEs must be able to closely follow established procedures and protocols.

BAEs must be self-reliant and capable of working independently at remote sites, and also on teams that involve communication with other engineers, technicians, scientists, executives, government officials, and the public. Because documentation is an important aspect of this profession, strong written communication skills also are required, along with proficiency in statistics.

Biological and Agricultural Engineers must be proficient in using computer software. Beyond word processing and spreadsheet applications, engineers in this field frequently use specialized programs related to their particular niche. Biological and Agricultural Engineers also must be mechanically inclined and skilled in the use of technology, including specialized sensors, as well as geographic information systems (GIS) and global positioning systems (GPS).

Unions and Associations
With more than 9,000 members in 100 countries, the American Society of Agricultural and Biological Engineers (ASABE) is an educational and scientific organization dedicated to the advancement of engineering applicable to agricultural, food, and biological systems. ASABE membership is open to engineers and non-engineers who are interested in the knowledge and application of engineering in agricultural, food, and biological systems.

Tips for Entry

1. In high school, take as many math and science courses as possible, including selections in the life sciences, as well as writing and speech courses that teach effective communication.

2. For a list of universities that offer BAE degrees, visit the American Society of Agricultural and Biological Engineers' (ASABE) Career Resources page at http://www.asabe.org/membership/career.html.

3. Visit the Pre-professionals/Students area of the ASABE's Web site at http://www.asabe.org/membership/students/index.html, where you can download a student membership application, learn about career resources, and apply for scholarship competitions and awards.

4. In college, pursue internships to gain valuable hands-on experience.

A portion of the information contained in this career profile was provided by the American Society of Agricultural and Biological Engineers.

COMMUNITY PLANNER

CAREER PROFILE

Duties: Conduct research; give presentations; help others with goal setting; develop short- and long-term plans related to urban, suburban, and rural areas; minimize the environmental impact of land use; improve community health and welfare; help draft legislation; manage grants; manage projects; ensure legal and regulatory compliance

Alternate Title(s): City Planner; Community Development Planner; Director of Building, Planning, and Zoning; Housing Development Specialist; Housing Grant Analyst; Neighborhood Planner; Planner; Transportation Planner; Urban Planner

Salary Range: $33,840 to $82,610+

Employment Prospects: Good

Advancement Prospects: Good

Prerequisites:

Education or Training—A master's degree is required for most positions.

Experience—Entry-level experience is usually acquired in college through internships and summer employment.

Special Skills and Personality Traits—Detail-oriented; flexible; creative; pragmatic; solid understanding of how cities, communities, and government agencies function; excellent conflict resolution, decision-making, data analysis, spatial, visualization, and written/oral communication skills

Special Requirements—Licensure is required in some states. Some positions may require optional certification from the American Planning Association.

CAREER LADDER

```
┌─────────────────────────────────────┐
│   Planning Director or City Manager  │
└─────────────────────────────────────┘

┌─────────────────────────────────────┐
│          Community Planner           │
└─────────────────────────────────────┘

┌─────────────────────────────────────┐
│      Intern or Student Employee      │
└─────────────────────────────────────┘
```

Position Description

Community Planners, also known as urban planners, city planners, or regional planners, are professionals who use their training and expertise in a wide range of areas to help communities determine the best way to use land and resources for commercial, institutional, recreational, or residential endeavors.

According to Arizona State University, Community Planners draw from a variety of different disciplines to carry out their work. These areas include everything from computer and research methods, environmental impact assessments, housing, and landscape architecture to planning and zoning, law, public policy formulation and administration, transportation, economics, and urban design. In addition, Community Planners must be adept at considering economic, physical, political, and social factors when working on a given project.

The most fundamental aspect of a Community Planner's job is developing plans. However, the planning field is very broad and there are many different types of short- and long-term plans that relate to urban and suburban areas, as well as rural communities. According to the American Planning Association, common types of plans include community action plans, comprehensive plans, economic development strategic plans, historic preservation plans, neighborhood plans, policy recommendations, redevelopment plans, regulatory and incentive strategies, and smart growth strategies.

Planning is beneficial in many ways. From a conservation standpoint, planning can help to minimize the impact that a given land use project will have on the natural environment, including a forest or wetland area. Planners also may work on projects that determine the best location for a landfill, seek to control different forms of pollution, minimize traffic congestion, and even create new areas of natural beauty. Finally, professionals in this field work on numerous initiatives to improve community health and welfare. This may involve helping officials to develop plans or draft legislation related to new schools, parks, correctional facilities, public housing complexes, transportation systems, and homeless shelters.

Planning is a highly collaborative field, and Community Planners work with a wide range of people during the planning process to help them identify their goals and cast a vision of what they would like to accomplish. These include individual citizens; citizen groups; neighborhood associations; historic preservation review boards; city councils; appointed and elected officials, including planning commissioners, city managers, and mayors; civic leaders; members of the business community; health care providers; attorneys; engineers; architects; developers; and contractors.

As the American Planning Association explains, "The planner's role is to provide the big picture and to relate the project to various goals and guidelines, such as ordinances or design review, in order to achieve a final project that meets the needs of the community. This might include appropriate design, environmental considerations, support for the local economy, or equitable access for all members of the community." While working with the many public groups during a project, Community Planners often serve as mediators between groups with opposing interests, working with them to identify mutually agreeable solutions.

After meeting with one or more of the aforementioned public groups to identify specific objectives, planners must assess and provide information about how a particular land area is currently being used. This involves conducting research and developing reports and presentations that summarize numerous characteristics about a certain area or region, from the concentration and makeup of industry to employment rates and the demographic and social characteristics of residents. This aspect of the planning process also involves assessing the location and capacity of airports, cultural and recreational sites, highways, libraries, schools, streets, utilities, water and sewer lines, and more.

Community Planners use the information obtained during the above stages to create a strategic plan that can turn a desired vision into reality. A proposed layout is created that shows how an area of land could be used, along with reports detailing the work and costs that would be involved. This information, which may include text documents, spreadsheets, and computer-generated maps, is usually presented to government officials and other decision-makers.

A Community Planner's job does not end after the plan development phase. Planners often manage the projects they design and conduct presentations to business, government, and public audiences as the project progresses through different stages. As part of a project, planners may oversee grant programs. In addition, they must stay knowledgeable about building codes, zoning codes, environmental regulations, and other laws related to their work and ensure compliance from builders, developers, and other parties involved in the project.

Community Planners use a variety of technical tools during the course of their work, namely computer software. Examples range from different computer databases and productivity applications (especially spreadsheets for forecasting) to geographic information systems (GIS) that allow them to create visual representations of data. Other high-tech tools include applications for scenario building visualization, as well as electronic polling systems.

The community planning field is highly specialized. While the majority of planners either work for or serve as consultants to governments, others specialize in a certain niche. The American Planning Association explains that "Some planners select a career in advocating, often focusing on planning concerns such as the environment, transportation, or community development. They may work for a nonprofit organization or become involved in politics. Some planners work as staff assistants to elected officials; others run for public office and serve in local, state, and national office. Many of these planners focus on policy."

In large firms, planners often specialize in a single area, while in smaller firms they may engage in many different types of planning. Examples of different areas of specialization include community activism, community development, economic development, environmental or natural resources planning; historic preservation, housing, land use and comprehensive planning, parks and recreation, planning management and finance, social planning, transportation, and urban design.

Community Planners have a variety of employment scenarios from which to choose, ranging from nonprofit and for-profit private planning firms to agencies at all levels of government. Planners work in all geographic areas, from rural communities to suburban and urban settings. According to the U.S. Department of Labor, there were 32,000 urban and regional planners employed in 2004, and approximately 70 percent of them worked for local governments; the federal government employed only a very small number of planners. In the private sector, common employers included firms specializing in engineering and architecture, as well as scientific, management, and technical consulting services.

Community planners are often required to travel to the areas where their projects are located. In some cases, this may involve extended stays away from home. While planners usually divide their time between office and field settings, those specializing in site development may spend the majority of their time performing fieldwork. Even though the majority of planners are scheduled to work regular 40-hour weeks, meetings with various groups usually require them to work during the evening or on weekends. The greatest occupational stressors associated with this job are political pressures and project deadlines.

Salaries

According to the 2006–07 edition of the U.S. Department of Labor's *Occupational Outlook Handbook*, in mid-2004 median annual salaries for urban and regional planners ranged from less than $33,840 to more than $82,610, with a median of $53,450. In the local government sector, planners earned median annual salaries of $52,520.

Employment Prospects

The U.S. Department of Labor projects average employment growth for urban and regional planners through 2014. Historic preservation and redevelopment projects are expected to drive growth in the private sector, while regulation of environmental issues, land use, commercial development, and the demand for typical public services like transportation and housing will drive growth at the local and state government levels. Opportunities will be the best for those with graduate degrees.

Advancement Prospects

Community Planners often begin their careers as interns or part-time employees during college. After working in entry-level positions for several years, planners commonly are given assignments of increased responsibility and complexity. Beyond senior-level or management planning positions, a variety of advancement opportunities exist. In the public sector, planners may advance to the position of community planning director, director of community or economic development, or city manager. In the academic world, planners may become professors, as well as deans or university presidents.

Education and Training

While a few entry-level positions in the planning field can be obtained with an undergraduate degree, a master's degree from an accredited planning program is usually required to become a planning practitioner. Before pursuing a graduate planning degree, planners may earn an undergraduate degree in planning, as well as one of several other disciplines, including architecture, geography, sociology, or urban studies.

Special Requirements

A handful of states require planners to hold a license. The American Planning Association's American Institute of Certified Planners offers optional certification to planning professionals who meet established education and experience requirements and pass a required examination.

Experience, Special Skills, and Personality Traits

While pursuing a graduate degree, students preparing for a career in planning gain considerable hands-on experience through internships and summer jobs, especially in the areas of analysis and problem solving. This experience prepares them for eventual entry-level employment. Community planners must be detail-oriented, flexible, creative, and pragmatic. In addition to a solid understanding of how cities, communities, and government agencies function, they must possess excellent conflict resolution, decision-making, data analysis, spatial, visualization, and written/oral communication skills. Finally, Community Planners must be skilled in the use of advanced computer software applications, including geographic information systems.

Unions and Associations

Approximately 36,000 planners are members of the nonprofit American Planning Association, a public interest and research organization with offices in Chicago and Washington, D.C., that is committed to urban, suburban, regional, and rural planning.

Tips for Entry

1. In high school, take classes in the natural and computer sciences, as well as advanced mathematics.
2. Learn more about colleges and universities with programs in planning by visiting the Association of Collegiate Schools of Planning at http://www.acsp.org/org/links_to_planning_schools.htm.
3. Review scholarship opportunities available from the American Planning Association (APA) by visiting http://www.planning.org/institutions/scholarship.htm.
4. In college, become a student member of the APA. More information is available at http://www.planning.org/students.
5. In college, secure internships and summer jobs that provide valuable field experience and increase your qualifications for entry-level employment.

ENVIRONMENTAL ENGINEER

CAREER PROFILE

Duties: Design, construct, inspect, and maintain waste control systems; carry out pollution prevention and environmental remediation initiatives; ensure compliance with environmental laws and regulations; solve problems; uncover pollution sources; perform administrative tasks; provide legal testimony

Alternate Title(s): Air Pollution Control Engineer; Environmental Analyst; Environmental Remediation Specialist; Hazardous Substances Engineer

Salary Range: $40,620 to $100,050+

Employment Prospects: Excellent

Advancement Prospects: Good

Prerequisites:

Education or Training—A bachelor's degree in environmental engineering is a minimum requirement, but a master's degree is required for many positions.

Experience—Experience using technical software related to environmental modeling and emergency response may be helpful or required, as well as experience operating scientific instruments and equipment.

Special Skills and Personality Traits—Analytical thinking, problem-solving, communication, computer, technical, and mechanical skills; detail-oriented; careful; thorough; patient; logical; adaptable; flexible

Special Requirements—State licensure is often required, as well as certifications for working with hazardous materials.

CAREER LADDER

```
Engineering Manager or Consultant
```

```
Environmental Engineer
```

```
Intern
```

Position Description

Environmental engineering is a major specialty within the larger engineering field. Environmental Engineers are responsible for designing, constructing, and the overall maintenance and inspection of waste control systems. These systems may pertain to the broad areas of air, water, or land pollution, along with many specific sub-categories.

According to the American Academy of Environmental Engineers, major areas of focus within this field include air pollution control, hazardous waste management, industrial hygiene, land management, public health, radiation protection, solid waste disposal, storm water management, toxic materials control, wastewater management, and water supply. In addition to their work with systems that control or treat waste, Environmental Engineers are involved in efforts to prevent pollution and in environmental remediation initiatives that involve removing waste from a contaminated site.

Environmental Engineers play a key role in ensuring compliance with numerous environmental laws at the local, state, and federal levels. These pertain to everything from the maintenance and remediation of underground storage tanks to wetlands and surface mining. Examples of laws at the federal level include:

- Clean Air Act
- Clean Water Act
- Emergency Planning and Community Right to Know Act (EPCRA)
- Hazardous Materials Transportation Authorization Act
- Resource Conservation and Recovery Act (RCRA) (hazardous waste)
- Safe Drinking Water Act
- Superfund (CERCLA)
- Toxic Substances Control Act (TSCA)

From a technical standpoint, Environmental Engineers ensure that remediation, treatment, and disposal systems are designed properly and meet regulatory specifications. They often perform regular inspections to ensure the effectiveness of operations. When environmental contamination occurs, Environmental Engineers get involved to determine what happened and why. They then advise companies or government agencies about the steps required to rectify the problem as quickly and safely as possible.

Environmental Engineers perform a number of administrative tasks. These range from data collection and documentation to preparing reports, giving presentations, and training others. While these administrative tasks may pertain to routine operations, they also may be related specifically to environmental investigations. Engineers in this field also help to develop policies, procedures, and standards, and provide related advice to their employers or government agencies. Finally, Environmental Engineers frequently appear in court to testify in environmental cases.

Environmental Engineers have many different employment situations from which to choose. Potential employers include local, state, and federal government agencies; businesses and corporations of all sizes; private consulting and research firms; testing laboratories; and universities. When they work for government agencies, Environmental Engineers function like detectives by performing investigative work, while those working for companies or consulting firms usually focus on ensuring compliance with environmental rules and regulations.

According to the U.S. Department of Labor, in 2004 nearly 1.5 million engineers of all types were employed in the United States. Of these, Environmental Engineers constituted a small portion (49,000). Within this specialty, the largest concentrations were employed in the areas of architecture, engineering, and related services (28.9 percent), while state and local governments employed 19.6 percent.

Paralleling the wide variety of potential employers, engineers in this field may work in a number of different environments, ranging from office and laboratory settings to industrial locations, water and waste treatment plants, construction sites, wetlands, and forests. While some technicians may work exclusively in one type of environment, many divide their time among different settings. Environmental Engineers usually work normal 40-hour schedules, although this can vary due to project deadlines. Travel may be required in order to visit industrial facilities or contaminated sites.

Environmental technicians may be subject to a range of occupational hazards, including chemicals, toxic waste, and potentially dangerous equipment. In the field, technicians may be exposed to extreme weather conditions. Fieldwork also can be physically demanding at times, requiring technicians to stand frequently, bend, and walk long distances. Therefore, good physical condition may be a job requirement.

In additional to occupational hazards, Environmental Engineers must contend with a number of challenging situations, no matter whom they work for. As the book *Careers in Focus: Environment* explains: "If they work on company staffs, they may face frustration over not knowing what is going on in their own plants. If they work for the government, they might struggle with bureaucracy. If they work for a consultant, they may have to juggle the needs of the client (including the need to keep costs down) with the demands of the government."

Environmental Engineers use a variety of advanced tools to perform their job. These include spectrophotometers, photometers, core drills, mass spectrometers, and devices for monitoring air velocity and temperature. In addition, they use advanced analytical and scientific software, including applications related to regulatory compliance, continuous emission management, hazardous materials management, material safety data sheets, computer programming, computer-aided design, and photo imaging.

Salaries

According to the 2006–07 edition of the U.S. Department of Labor's *Occupational Outlook Handbook*, in mid-2004 median annual salaries for Environmental Engineers ranged from $40,620 to $100,050. A survey conducted by the National Association of Colleges and Employers in 2005 indicated that the average starting salary for engineers in the environmental/environmental health field was $47,384.

Employment Prospects

While the U.S. Department of Labor projects that overall employment rates for engineers will increase about as fast as the average for all occupations through 2014, the environmental engineering specialty is expected to experience above average growth as industry is forced to comply with a growing number of environmental rules and regulations. In addition, a continued need for remediation methods, along with a focus on preventing pollution and addressing public health concerns, will support growth in the environmental engineering sector.

Advancement Prospects

After obtaining entry-level positions in the private or public sectors, Environmental Engineers can advance to supervisory or management roles. Many engineers who begin their careers at a government agency move on to positions with companies or consulting firms in the private sector. In consulting firms, Environmental Engineers may become experts in a certain niche, or become partners in their firm.

Education and Training

An undergraduate degree is required to work as an Environmental Engineer. Beyond programs specifically in environmental engineering, examples of appropriate undergraduate disciplines include civil, chemical, and mechanical engineering. A growing number of jobs require master's degrees, due to the complex nature of environmental engineering work. A doctorate degree is required for teaching at the college or university level and can be advantageous for obtaining high-level positions in the private and public sectors.

Special Requirements

State licensure is often required for engineers whose work impacts public health and safety. Depending on an engineer's specialty, certifications may be required for working with hazardous materials, such as lead, wastewater, or radiation.

Experience, Special Skills, and Personality Traits

Environmental Engineers must be detail-oriented, with the ability to perform tasks in a careful and thorough manner. They also must be logical and analytical thinkers, with excellent problem-solving abilities. Due to the many variables involved in engineering, scientific, and technical work, the ability to be patient, adaptable, and flexible also is critical for professionals in this field. Additionally, Environmental Engineers must be able to closely follow established procedures and protocols.

Environmental Engineers must be self-reliant and capable of working independently at remote sites, and also on teams that involve communication with other engineers, technicians, scientists, executives, government officials, and the public. Because documentation is an important aspect of this profession, strong written communication skills are required, along with a proficiency in statistics.

Environmental Engineers must be proficient in using computer software. Beyond common productivity applications such as word processing and spreadsheet programs, engineers in this field frequently use technical programs related to environmental modeling and emergency response. Because operating, maintaining, and repairing sophisticated instruments and equipment is often a primary job responsibility, Environmental Engineers must be mechanically inclined and skilled in the use of technology, including sensors, geographic information systems (GIS), and Global Positioning System (GPS).

Unions and Associations

Many Environmental Engineers are members of the American Academy of Environmental Engineers (AAEE). Based in Annapolis, Maryland, the AAEE is "dedicated to improving the practice, elevating the standards and advancing the cause of environmental engineering." In addition, the academy is committed to ensuring "the public health, safety, and welfare to enable humankind to co-exist in harmony with nature."

Tips for Entry

1. In high school, take courses that provide broad exposure to science, including biology, chemistry, earth science, geology, and zoology, as well as courses in mathematics, physics, and English.
2. Learn more about the many different areas of specialization within environmental engineering by subscribing to *Environmental Engineer Magazine* from the American Academy of Environmental Engineers. Subscription information is available at http://www.aaee.net/Website/Magazine.htm.
3. Identify colleges and universities that offer environmental engineering programs and request information. A list of accredited programs is available by visiting ABET Inc.'s Web site at http://www.abet.org/schoolareaeac.asp.
4. Obtain any special certifications before applying for a position, which will give you an edge over other applicants and possibly result in a higher starting salary.

GEOSPATIAL ENGINEER

CAREER PROFILE

Duties: Apply geospatial information and advanced technology to a broad range of problems; plan and supervise ground and aerial surveys; interpret and make measurements from remote sensing imagery; design maps and cartographic presentations; reproduce and distribute maps; manage projects

Alternate Title(s): Cartographer; Database Administrator; Digital Cartographer; Geographer; GIS Analyst; GIS Manager; Image Analyst; Photogrammetrist; Production Manager; Remote Sensing Specialist; Surveyor

Salary Range: $28,210 to $74,440+

Employment Prospects: Good

Advancement Prospects: Good

Prerequisites:

Education or Training—Most entry-level positions require a bachelor's degree.

Experience—Entry-level positions require little or no experience, but advanced positions usually require several years of experience or experience in a specific application area.

Special Skills and Personality Traits—Good eyesight and spatial ability; systems perspective; detail-oriented; careful; thorough; self-reliant; team player; logical and analytical thinking, problem-solving, writing, and reading comprehension skills.

Special Requirements—A state license and continuing education may be required.

CAREER LADDER

```
┌─────────────────────────────────────┐
│  GIS Manager or Research Scientist   │
└─────────────────────────────────────┘

┌─────────────────────────────────────┐
│  GIS Analyst, Photogrammetrist, or   │
│     Remote Sensing Specialist        │
└─────────────────────────────────────┘

┌─────────────────────────────────────┐
│        GIS Technician or             │
│    Photogrammetric Technician        │
└─────────────────────────────────────┘
```

Position Description

In the information-based global economy of the early 21st century, tools such as aerial and satellite remote sensing imagery, the global positioning system (GPS), and computerized geographic information systems (GIS) were revolutionizing the conduct of business, science, and government alike. Professionals in virtually every field increasingly rely on geospatial information to make important decisions and carry out their work.

In the *Journal of Geospatial Engineering*, Zhilin Li explained that the term "geospatial" encompasses spatial phenomena at geographic scales, including shapes, sizes, orientations, positions, and relations. Li further explained that the term "geospatial engineering" refers to "the science and technology used to acquire, store, manage, analyze, present and apply geospatial data in two or three dimensions, referenced to the earth by some type of real-world coordinate systems (e.g., national geodetic systems)."

Geospatial Engineers are employed in a wide range of fields, including aerial photography, agriculture, archeology, architecture, biology, cartography, civil engineering, community and urban planning, computer science, ecology, economics, engineering, environmental science, forestry, geodesy, geography, geology, geometry, graphic arts, hydrology, industrial engineering, manufacturing, medicine, meteorology, military planning, natural resource management, photography, physics, satellite imagery, sociology, and transportation.

Geospatial information is increasingly becoming the driving force for decision making across the local-to-global continuum. A staggering number of tasks can be greatly enhanced by the use of some form of geospatial technology. Examples include planning urban growth, managing a forest, implementing "precision farming," assessing groundwater contamination, improving wildlife habitats, monitoring air quality, assessing environmental impact, designing a road, studying human health statistics, minimizing water pollution, preserving wetlands, mapping natural hazards and disasters, providing famine relief, and studying the causes and consequences of global climate change.

The field of geospatial engineering is broad and includes a number of specialties including surveying, cartography (mapmaking), geodesy (studying the Earth's size and shape), and working with GPS. Three main areas in which Geospatial Engineers work are photogrammetry, remote sensing, and GIS.

Photogrammetry is the science and technology of obtaining reliable measurements, maps, digital elevation models, and other GIS data, primarily from aerial and space photography. Professional photogrammetrists are responsible for all phases of mapping projects and provide spatially accurate base maps that form a foundation for many applications of GIS. Functions can include planning and supervising ground and aerial surveys, interpreting and making measurements from remote sensing imagery, designing maps and cartographic presentations, the reproduction and distribution of map products, and managing general business and organizational aspects of photogrammetric projects.

Remote sensing is a broad geospatial specialty used in fields that range from agriculture to wildlife management. In a nutshell, remote sensing refers to any technique whereby information about objects and the environment is obtained from a distance. In the context of obtaining geospatial information, remote sensing is based on measuring variations in how electromagnetic waves interact with objects. The wavelengths typically involved include not only visible light, but also near-infrared, mid-infrared, thermal, and microwave energy. Hence, remote sensing systems often permit us to greatly expand our spectral view of the Earth and "see" the world much more clearly than we can with the unaided eye or any sensor restricted to visible wavelengths.

Today, an extremely broad range of remote sensing systems is used to collect data from both aerial and spaceborne platforms. These systems include everything from aerial cameras to Earth orbiting multispectral sensors and imaging radar systems. By 2006 the launch of commercial high-resolution Earth-orbiting systems was having a major influence on the field of remote sensing. These high-resolution sys-

tems allow objects of approximately one meter in length to be identified on the Earth's surface using a satellite in outer space. They are expected to provide a quantum jump in the commercial applications of remote sensing, and hence the demand for professionals in the field.

GIS represents another broad area of specialization for Geospatial Engineers. GIS allow the user to work with, interrelate, and analyze virtually all forms of spatial data. A GIS typically consists of three major components: a database of geospatial and thematic data and information, a capability to spatially model or analyze the data sets, and a graphical display capability.

GIS integrates remotely sensed and ground-based information into powerful decision-making analytical tools. Geographic information systems are used to provide information and knowledge data in various forms to help resolve and understand a range of complex resource issues, from ozone depletion and global warming to soil erosion and natural resource utilization.

Geospatial Engineers work with a variety of tools during the course of their jobs, including digital cameras, scanners, global positioning system receivers, radar-based surveillance systems, and plotter printers. They frequently work with advanced computer software, including programs for computer-aided design (CAD), information retrieval, map creation, photo imaging, and Web site development.

Geospatial careers are available in nearly all segments of the commercial, public, government, and academic communities. An increasing number of graduates are utilizing GIS in private firms, in environmental management, planning, and other businesses that require spatial analysis. The rise of many more commercial remote sensing firms also is a good opportunity for people with training in geospatial fields.

State government activity in these disciplines is generally carried out in agencies related to planning, environment, resources, transportation, and geology and is usually coordinated through state geographic information councils. Employment opportunities in city and county government agencies often parallel state job titles.

Federal employment opportunities exist with many agencies, including the U.S. Geological Survey (USGS), National Oceanic and Atmospheric Administration (NOAA), U.S. Forest Service (USFS), Environmental Protection Agency (EPA), National Aeronautics and Space Administration (NASA), National Imagery and Mapping Agency (NIMA), and the U.S. Bureau of Land Management (BLM).

With the increased use of computers in imaging and geospatial technology careers, most jobs involve working in an office environment. However, certain careers may require extensive fieldwork to verify results or to acquire data in the outdoors. In addition, imaging and geospatial technology disciplines are finding their way into many other applications and careers that are not traditionally associated with photogrammetry, remote sensing, and GIS.

Salaries

Starting salaries for Geospatial Engineers vary depending on background and experience. While the U.S. Department of Labor does not list salary information specifically for Geospatial Engineers, it does provide data for cartographers and photogrammetrists. According to the 2006–07 edition of the department's *Occupational Outlook Handbook*, in mid-2004 annual salaries for these professionals ranged from $28,210 to more than $74,440, with a median of $46,080.

Employment Prospects

Overall, the U.S. Department of Labor expects average job growth for cartographers and photogrammetrists through 2014. Increased productivity due to technological advancements will limit job growth somewhat. However, a large number of retiring workers will create new job opportunities.

Advancement Prospects

Many Geospatial Engineers begin their careers as technicians and move into more advanced roles after obtaining additional education and work experience. After working at the entry level, they assume more complex responsibilities and begin to manage larger projects. Some move into management roles. Geospatial Engineers with doctorate degrees often work for universities as professors or research scientists. In addition, they may do advanced work for consulting firms and scientific laboratories, where they contribute to scientific research, theory, and discoveries.

Education and Training

While some Geospatial Engineers begin their careers as technicians after completing a two-year associate's degree or certificate program, most professional-level jobs in the geospatial field require an undergraduate or graduate degree. These may be obtained in a number of fields, including geography, geomatics engineering, civil engineering, forestry, planning, surveying and mapping, or physical science. Educational preparation can be targeted toward becoming either a specialist in the field of geospatial information science and technology or a specialist in a traditional discipline with a complementary background in photogrammetry, remote sensing, and GIS.

Special Requirements

Geospatial Engineers may be required to hold a state license and meet continuing education requirements.

Experience, Special Skills, and Personality Traits

Entry-level geospatial engineering jobs can be obtained with limited or no experience, while higher-level positions require experience, depending on the level of responsibility involved. Some positions require knowledge and experience in one or several application areas such as biology/ecology or resource management.

Geospatial Engineers must possess good eyesight and spatial ability. They must be detail-oriented, with the ability to perform tasks in a careful and thorough manner. In addition, professionals in this field are logical and analytical thinkers, with excellent problem-solving skills, as well as the ability to take a systems perspective and determine how the outcome of a process can be affected by changing different variables. They must be self-reliant and capable of working independently at remote sites, and also on teams that involve verbal and written communication with others.

Geospatial Engineers usually work with advanced technology related to computer modeling, digital mapping, or data integration activities. Therefore, experience with GIS and GPS is often required.

Unions and Associations

Geospatial Engineers may join the American Society for Photogrammetry & Remote Sensing (ASPRS), a membership society that seeks to advance knowledge and improve understanding of geospatial information science and technology and to promote the responsible application of photogrammetry, remote sensing, geographic information systems, and supporting technologies.

Tips for Entry

1. Learn more about geospatial careers by reading the ASPRS career brochure at http://www.asprs.org/career/brochure.pdf.
2. For a listing of colleges and universities offering programs in GIS, remote sensing, or photogrammetry, visit the University Consortium for Geographic Information Science's Web site at http://www.ucgis.org.
3. Become a student member of ASPRS. Membership information is available from https://www.asprs.org/application.
4. Learn about travel grants, cash awards, internship stipends, and scholarships offered by the ASPRS. For complete details and application deadlines, visit http://www.asprs.org/membership/scholar.html.
5. In college, pursue internships to increase your prospects of entry-level employment.

Information contained in this career profile was derived partially from the ASPRS "Shape the Future: Careers in Imaging and Geospatial Information Science and Technology" brochure with permission from the American Society for Photogrammetry & Remote Sensing.

MINING AND GEOLOGICAL ENGINEERS

CAREER PROFILE

Duties: Identify ideal mining locations; determine appropriate mining methods; design mines; oversee mine construction; supervise mining personnel and operations; monitor production; produce schedules and reports; design and monitor mining equipment, systems, and processes; develop, implement, and manage safety programs; ensure environmental compliance

Alternate Title(s): Engineer; Mine Engineering Manager; Mine Environmental Engineer; Mine Manager; Mine Safety Manager; Planning Engineer; Safety Representative

Salary Range: $39,700 to $103,790+

Employment Prospects: Excellent

Advancement Prospects: Good

Prerequisites:

Education or Training—Undergraduate degree in mineralogy or related field

Experience—None required for entry-level positions

Special Skills and Personality Traits—Systems perspective; detail-oriented; careful; thorough; self-reliant; team player; logical and analytical thinking; problem-solving, writing, and reading comprehension skills

Special Requirements—State licensure may be required.

CAREER LADDER

```
┌─────────────────────────────────────┐
│     Mining Engineering Manager       │
└─────────────────────────────────────┘

┌─────────────────────────────────────┐
│   Mining or Geological Engineer      │
└─────────────────────────────────────┘

┌─────────────────────────────────────┐
│        Mining Technician             │
└─────────────────────────────────────┘
```

Position Description

Mining is the process of extracting valuable minerals from the earth. These are then used by a range of manufacturers to produce goods and by utilities to produce energy. The types of mines are as varied as the types of mineral resources being mined. Operations include open-pit and underground mines that contain copper, coal, salt, iron, lead, silver, gold, diamonds, and more. The mining field also includes the extraction of building materials, including stone, sand, and gravel. Humankind has relied on mining for centuries. In fact, a 45,000-year-old iron mine in Africa is recognized as the world's oldest.

As evidence of mining's economic importance, the Society for Mining, Metallurgy, and Exploration reveals that the average U.S. resident uses approximately 40,000 pounds of newly mined minerals each year. While this may seem like an astronomical figure, it includes everything from the aluminum used to make beverage containers to table salt and the coal that is used for generating electricity. Minerals are even contained in the consumer electronic devices that have become a critical aspect of modern life. For example, telephones alone contain more than 40 different minerals.

Mining and Geological Engineers work to maximize the extraction of a desired mineral while minimizing the removal of surrounding material that is not needed. Before actual mining operations can begin, Mining and Geological Engineers engage in planning and preliminary work. Some of the professionals in this field work with geologists and metallurgical engineers to locate mineral deposits, determine if they can be mined profitably, and identify ideal mining locations. This aspect of the job often includes examining undeveloped mines and mineral deposits, conducting topographical and geological surveys, reviewing maps, and visiting drilling locations.

After identifying the most appropriate mining method, Mining and Geological Engineers may design the mine, including mine shafts and tunnel systems, and then oversee its construction. When the mine has been constructed, engineers then supervise the actual mining operations. This aspect of their job can involve managing a variety of mining personnel, including other engineers, geologists, technicians, and surveyors. During the course of mining operations, engineers monitor production to ensure efficiency and productivity, and produce related schedules and reports. Mining and Geological Engineers also may design and monitor equipment, systems, and processes used during a mining operation.

Mining and Geological Engineers also work to ensure the safety of mining operations through the development, implementation, and management of mining safety programs. In addition, engineers design and maintain safety devices and equipment used to protect and rescue workers. They often conduct inspections of mining areas to identify equipment, structures, and working conditions that may be unsafe. Finally, Mining and Geological Engineers work to ensure compliance with federal and state safety regulations.

Engineers in the mining field also deal with environmental matters, including land reclamation, as well as air and water pollution. By minimizing the extraction of undesirable material during operations, they maximize efficiency and lessen environmental impact. In addition to working with other professionals, including environmental engineers and reclamation specialists, to minimize the impact that operations have on the environment, Mining and Geological Engineers ensure that environmental rules and regulations are followed.

The mining and geological engineering profession is highly specialized. For example, engineers often concentrate on one type of mineral or metal, such as gold or coal. From there, they may focus on a certain aspect of the mining process. For example, some engineers develop new equipment, while others design mines. Others may deal with mineral processing, whereby dirt, rock, and other matter are separated from a desired mineral.

According to the Society for Mining, Metallurgy, and Exploration, some other specialties in this field include mine valuation, rock excavation, ventilation, and rock mechanics. Mine valuation involves determining what a particular mineral deposit is worth in order to assure a decent return-on-investment. Rock excavation entails determining the best way to extract minerals from rock. Methods range from scraping or gouging the rock to the use of drilling and explosives. Ventilation is a critical aspect of underground mining. To ensure proper air quality, engineers in this niche must deal with the combustion gases that result from blasting, as well as equipment emissions, tempera-

ture, and humidity. Finally, engineers specializing in rock mechanics evaluate the physical properties of minerals and surrounding materials in order to determine the best way to construct a new mine.

During the course of their work, Mining and Geological Engineers use a variety of tools and technology, including satellite photography, instruments that measure variations in the earth's magnetic field, and a wide range of specialized mining machinery.

Because of the many subspecialties that exist within the field of mining and geological engineering, Mining and Geological Engineers have many different types of work environments from which to choose. These range from office settings to outdoor environments and classrooms. Many engineers divide their time between fieldwork and an office setting. Fieldwork may occur near an urban area, but often involves long travel times to remote or foreign locations, sometimes via all-terrain vehicles or helicopters. While engineers usually work normal schedules when they are in the office, in the field they may be required to work unusual hours.

Compared to engineering specialties such as electrical or mechanical engineering, the field of mining and geological engineering is highly specialized. According to the U.S. Department of Labor, of the 1.4 million engineers employed in 2004, only 5,200 (0.4 percent) were in the mining and geological field, including mining safety. Mining and Geological Engineers work in the government and private sectors and are employed in virtually every industry. However, about half are employed specifically in the mining industry.

Salaries

According to the 2006–07 edition of the U.S. Department of Labor's *Occupational Outlook Handbook*, in mid-2004 median annual salaries for Mining and Geological Engineers, including those working in mining safety, ranged from $39,700 to $103,790. Data from a survey conducted by the National Association of Colleges and Employers in 2005 put average annual starting salaries for those with bachelor's degrees at $48,643.

Employment Prospects

Although the U.S. Department of Labor projects an overall decline in the employment of Mining and Geological Engineers through 2014, a large number of retiring workers, coupled with a workforce shortage, will create many employment opportunities. In its May–June 2005 issue, the *Mineralogical Record* indicated that a decline in mineralogy programs at American colleges and universities was one factor leading to a significant workforce shortage in this profession. Some 300 graduates are needed each year just to replace retiring workers, with 500 needed to accommodate industry growth. However, only 86 mining engineers graduated in the United States in 2004.

Advancement Prospects

Entry-level Mining and Geological Engineers normally work under the supervision of an experienced engineer. After acquiring knowledge and expertise through work experience, they are given additional responsibility and more complex assignments. Eventually, Mining and Geological Engineers are able to advance to positions as technical specialists or supervisors. Some advance to positions as mine engineering managers or mine safety managers, while others pursue sales positions.

Education and Training

Entry-level Mining and Geological Engineer positions require an undergraduate degree in mineralogy or a related field. A number of programs are accredited by the Accreditation Board for Engineering and Technology, Inc. (ABET). In addition to courses specific to mining and geology, course work is provided in the areas of science and mathematics. While some schools offer students a two-year degree that is more focused on production work, a four-year degree is required for those who wish to become certified as a Professional Engineer. A graduate degree is required for those who wish to teach at the college or university level.

Special Requirements

In the United States, Mining and Geological Engineers who provide services to the public must be licensed as Professional Engineers. To receive this credential one must pass a state exam, meet certain experience requirements, and earn a degree from an engineering program that is accredited by the Accreditation Board for Engineering and Technology.

Experience, Special Skills, and Personality Traits

Entry-level positions in the field of mining and geological engineering can be obtained with no prior work experience. Mining and Geological Engineers must be detail-oriented, with the ability to perform tasks in a careful and thorough manner. In addition, they are logical and analytical think-ers, with excellent problem-solving skills, as well as the ability to take a systems perspective and determine how the outcome of a process can be affected by changing different variables. Mining and Geological Engineers must be self-reliant and capable of working independently at remote sites, and also on teams that involve communication with others. Because report writing and research are important aspects of this profession, strong writing and reading comprehension skills are required.

Unions and Associations

Many Mining and Geological Engineers are members of the Littleton, Colorado-based Society for Mining, Metallurgy, and Exploration (SME). In 2006 this international society had more than 11,500 members in almost 100 countries. The SME consists of five divisions: mining and exploration; mineral and metallurgical processing; industrial minerals; environmental; and coal and energy.

Tips for Entry

1. In high school, take classes in physics, chemistry, earth science, and computer science, as well as advanced mathematics including calculus and trigonometry.
2. Join an engineering club or participate in the Junior Engineering Technical Society (JETS).
3. Learn more about scholarship programs, student chapters, and colleges and universities with accredited minerals programs by visiting the student section of the Society for Mining, Metallurgy, and Exploration's Web site at http://www.smenet.org/education/Students/index.cfm.
4. In college, become a student member of SME. A membership application is available for download at http://www.smenet.org/education/students/reasons_to_belong.pdf.
5. In college, secure internships that provide valuable field experience and increase your qualifications for entry-level employment.

SURVEYING AND MAPPING TECHNICIAN

CAREER PROFILE

Duties: Determine and mark property boundaries; gather measurements and descriptions; record data; plot charts and maps; produce drawings; prepare land plats; perform calculations; conduct research; evaluate existing surveys and maps; download, analyze, and upload data; maintain computer systems; prepare maps; write property descriptions; engage in quality assurance activities

Alternate Title(s): Cartographic Drafter and Tracer; Chainman; Engineering Assistant; Engineering Technician; Field Crew Chief; Instrument Man (I-Man); Instrument Operator; Rodman; Survey Crew Chief; Survey Party Chief; Surveying Associate

Salary Range: $19,140 to $51,070+

Employment Prospects: Fair

Advancement Prospects: Good

Prerequisites:

Education or Training—An associate's or bachelor's degree may be required for advanced positions.

Experience—Entry-level positions require little or no experience, but advanced positions usually require one to three years of experience.

Special Skills and Personality Traits—Good eyesight and spatial ability; systems perspective; detail-oriented; careful; thorough; self-reliant; team player; logical and analytical thinking; problem-solving, writing, and reading comprehension skills.

Special Requirements—A commercial driver's license or Certified Survey Technician credentials may be required.

CAREER LADDER

```
┌─────────────────────────────────────────┐
│              Surveyor                     │
└─────────────────────────────────────────┘

┌─────────────────────────────────────────┐
│  Lead Technician or Survey Party Chief    │
└─────────────────────────────────────────┘

┌─────────────────────────────────────────┐
│         Surveying Technician              │
└─────────────────────────────────────────┘
```

Position Description

By assisting surveyors, Surveying and Mapping Technicians play a key role in humankind's relationship with the surrounding environment. Before land use activities such as property development, road construction, or mining activities can begin, surveys are conducted to measure the land; mark property, water body, and airspace boundaries; and provide data regarding a range of geographic characteristics, from location and elevation to contour and shape. The information gathered during a survey is used to create maps that a variety of end users—including engineers, attorneys, developers, and government officials at various levels—rely on to make important decisions.

As key members of the surveying team, Surveying and Mapping Technicians help surveyors to conduct a range of surveying activities, such as topographic mapping surveys, boundary surveys, control surveys, and construction staking. In the field, they search for survey points and property irons that are used to determine boundaries, and may cut down brush in order to mark lines. Technicians also gather measurements (including angles, elevations, and distances) and descriptions, and record the data in different formats.

In addition to plotting charts and maps that indicate things such as the relation of topographical elevations and contours to structures such as buildings, tunnels, retaining walls, overhead power lines, and the like, Surveying and Mapping Technicians produce a variety of drawings. Examples of the things they draw range from roads and sewage disposal systems to breakwaters, culverts, dikes, and wharfs. Technicians in this field use their math and geometry skills to prepare land plats and perform a wide range of different calculations. These are used to determine excavation volumes, azimuths, Earth curvature corrections, marker placements, and level runs.

Fieldwork is an important aspect of a Surveying and Mapping Technician's job. However, like surveyors, many technicians also spend a portion of their work time in an office setting. This portion of the job may involve conducting research, evaluating existing surveys or maps, downloading and analyzing data or photographs that were gathered in the field, uploading data for field staff, maintaining computer systems, preparing maps, writing legal property descriptions, engaging in quality assurance activities, or coordinating various aspects of a project with engineers and surveyors.

Equipment and technology are central to a Surveying and Mapping Technician's job. Technicians are often responsible for maintaining, adjusting, and operating a range of surveying instruments. Examples of tools used during the surveying process include lasers, 3D scanning systems, global positioning system (GPS) equipment, electronic levels, measuring rods, tape measures, total stations (which record and measure distances and angles at the same time), and satellite signal receivers that are used to indicate geographic position with remarkable accuracy. By the early 21st century, surveyors also rely on a range of computer applications, including geographic information systems (GIS) and software for modeling, computer-aided design (CAD), mapmaking, route navigation, and project management.

In addition to working under the direction of a licensed surveyor, Surveying and Mapping Technicians normally work on teams that may include cartographers, who specialize in producing maps, and photogrammetrists who perform analysis, make measurements, and produce drawings and maps using aerial photographs. Teams also include senior technicians, called party chiefs, who serve in a lead capacity. This role involves the training, guidance, and supervision of lower-level technicians. In addition, senior technicians perform higher-level or complex surveying tasks.

Surveying and Mapping Technicians have a variety of career options to choose from within their profession. For instance, they may work for firms that concentrate on rivers, harbors, lakes, and other water bodies. In addition to mapping the topography of a lake bed, they might measure the depth of the water and also mark the lake's shorelines. Geophysical prospecting work involves surveying areas below the surface, namely for the purpose of petroleum exploration. Finally, geodetic surveying involves the use of satellite technology to survey broad areas of the planet's surface.

According to the 2006–07 edition of the Department of Labor's *Occupational Outlook Handbook*, in 2004 most Surveying and Mapping Technicians worked for firms within the engineering, mining, energy, or architectural sectors. Opportunities also existed with federal, state, and local governments. The Army Corps of Engineers, U.S. Geological Survey, Bureau of Land Management, and National Geodetic Survey are leading federal employers.

While performing fieldwork, Surveying and Mapping Technicians are exposed to all kinds of weather—including rain, extreme heat, humidity, and bitter cold. This profession can be physically demanding, requiring frequent walking and standing. Although some outdoor work is carried out in easily accessible areas, technicians may be required to travel to proposed land development sites and construction zones to perform surveys. Such areas may consist of rough terrain. Therefore, being in good or excellent physical condition may be a requirement for this profession.

While there may be seasonal fluctuations, due to the demand for surveys in warm weather conditions, most Surveying and Mapping Technicians work normal 40-hour workweeks. However, they may be required to travel long distances. In some cases, survey projects may require overnight stays or temporary relocation.

Salaries

According to the 2006–07 edition of the Department of Labor's *Occupational Outlook Handbook*, in mid-2004 annual salaries for Surveying and Mapping Technicians ranged from less than $19,140 to more than $51,070, with a median of $30,380. Median annual salaries for technicians working in the local government sector were $34,810 in mid-2004, while those working for private sector firms were slightly lower, at $28,610.

Employment Prospects

The U.S. Department of Labor anticipates average job growth for Surveying and Mapping Technicians through 2014. Technology has reduced the size of surveying parties. While positions focused on GIS data entry were expected to be plentiful, competition is expected to be high for such jobs, given that many candidates meet the minimum requirements.

Advancement Prospects

In some cases, high school graduates are able to secure apprenticeships in the surveying field and, with some formal training, become assistants or surveying technicians. From there it is possible to advance to a senior-level technician position and, in some states, to eventually become a licensed surveyor. However, by 2006 most entry-level surveyors were required to earn an undergraduate degree.

Education and Training

Historically, Surveying and Mapping Technicians have learned what they need to know through on-the-job training and postsecondary classes in surveying. While a college degree is not required to work in this occupation, many senior or lead technician positions require an associate's degree in civil technology or surveying technology, and some jobs require a bachelor's degree. Educational programs in surveying technology take one to three years to complete, and are offered at junior and community colleges, technical schools, vocational schools, and colleges and universities.

Special Requirements

Some positions may require candidates to hold a commercial driver's license. Senior or lead technician positions may require a candidate to hold the Certified Survey Technician (CST) credential from the National Society of Professional Surveyors.

Experience, Special Skills, and Personality Traits

Entry-level surveying and mapping positions can be obtained with little or no experience, while higher-level positions may require one to three years of experience, as well as education, depending on the level of responsibility involved.

Surveying and Mapping Technicians must possess good eyesight and spatial ability, because they are regularly required to gauge distances and visualize forms and objects. They must be detail-oriented, with the ability to perform tasks in a careful and thorough manner. In addition, technicians in this field are logical and analytical thinkers, with excellent problem-solving skills, as well as the ability to take a systems perspective and determine how the outcome of a process can be affected by changing different variables.

They must be self-reliant and capable of working independently at remote sites, and also on teams that involve communication with others.

Because report writing and research are important aspects of this profession, strong writing and reading comprehension skills are required. In addition, technicians may be required to perform work with advanced technology related to computer modeling, digital mapping, or data integration. Therefore, experience with GIS and GPS may be required.

Unions and Associations

Many Surveying and Mapping Technicians are members of the American Congress on Surveying and Mapping (ACSM), which was established in 1941. ACSM members must belong to at least one of four ACSM member organizations: the American Association for Geodetic Surveying; the Cartography and Geographic Information Society; the Geographic and Land Information Society; or the National Society of Professional Surveyors, Inc.

Tips for Entry

1. In high school, take classes in computer science, drafting, mechanical drawing, algebra, geometry, and trigonometry.
2. Learn more about scholarship programs, student chapters, state affiliates, and colleges and universities with accredited surveying technology programs by visiting the student section of the American Congress on Surveying and Mapping's (ACSM) Web site at http://www.acsm.net/student.html.
3. In college, become a student member of the ACSM. A membership application is available for download at http://www.acsm.net/studentapp.pdf.
4. Earn the Certified Survey Technician credential and increase your employment prospects. Learn more by visiting the National Society of Professional Surveyors's Web site at http://www.nspsmo.org/cst/get_certified.shtml.

SURVEYOR

CAREER PROFILE

Duties: Review property records and prior surveys; mark property, water body, and airspace boundaries; measure and provide data regarding a range of geographic characteristics; create or oversee the production of sketches, property descriptions, charts, maps, and plots; provide professional testimony in legal proceedings

Alternate Title(s): County Surveyor; Engineer; Engineering Technician; Geodesist; Land Surveyor; Mine Surveyor; Survey Party Chief

Salary Range: $24,640 to $71,640+

Employment Prospects: Fair

Advancement Prospects: Good

Prerequisites:

  Education or Training—A four-year college degree is required for most Surveyor jobs.

  Experience—At least four years of experience is required to become a certified Surveyor. Experience with geographic information systems (GIS) and global positioning system (GPS) equipment is usually required.

  Special Skills and Personality Traits—Good eyesight and spatial ability; systems perspective; detail-oriented; careful; thorough; self-reliant; team player; logical and analytical thinking, problem-solving, writing, and reading comprehension skills.

  Special Requirements—Surveyors are required to be certified in all 50 states.

CAREER LADDER

```
┌─────────────────────────────┐
│         Surveyor            │
└─────────────────────────────┘

┌─────────────────────────────┐
│     Survey Party Chief      │
└─────────────────────────────┘

┌─────────────────────────────┐
│    Surveying Technician     │
└─────────────────────────────┘
```

Position Description

Surveyors play a key role in humankind's relationship with the surrounding environment. Before land use activities such as construction projects and mining activities can begin, Surveyors are responsible for measuring land; marking property, water body, and airspace boundaries; and providing data regarding a range of geographic characteristics, from location and elevation to contour and shape. The information they gather is used to create maps that a variety of end users—including engineers, attorneys, developers, and government officials at various levels—rely on to make important decisions.

The contributions of Surveyors date back to the early days of American history. Unknown to many, George Washington and Abraham Lincoln both worked as surveyors before becoming president. In the December 2002 issue of *Point of Beginning*, Emily E. Vass explained that Washington surveyed more than 200 tracts of land between 1747 and 1799, spanning some 65,000 acres.

While fieldwork is an important aspect of a Surveyor's job, there are many others. In some respects, Surveyors work like detectives to uncover details about land. This involves spending time in courthouse archives to review printed and/or computerized records of property titles, deeds, and previous surveys, which is helpful in making boundary determinations. In addition, Surveyors plan the work that must be done by assessing different factors and variables in order to determine the best method to survey a particular area of land.

In the field, Surveyors use established reference points to make accurate determinations about the location of other elements within a particular survey zone. This involves the measurement of angles, distances, elevations, contours, and directions above, on, or below the ground and documenting the various characteristics of terrain. Surveyors record what they find in written form or, more commonly, in a laptop computer.

Surveyors rely on a number of advanced tools to carry out their work, including a variety of different lasers, 3D scanning systems, GPS equipment, electronic levels, measuring rods, tape measures, total stations (which record and measure distances and angles at the same time), and satellite signal receivers that are used to indicate geographic position with remarkable accuracy. Gone are the surveying tools of yesteryear, which included plumb bobs, chains, compasses, and transits. By the early 21st century, Surveyors also relied on a range of computer applications, including GIS and software for modeling, computer-aided design (CAD), map-making, route navigation, and project management.

Back in the office, Surveyors process, analyze, and verify the accuracy of their data. This includes double checking measurements and calculations made in the field. While some Surveyors perform both fieldwork and analysis, some rely on office-based Surveyors to perform the analysis component. They then oversee the creation of various records and documents related to the survey. These may range from sketches and property descriptions to charts, maps, and plots.

Surveyors frequently work with cartographers, who create maps with computers, sometimes in a day or two. The resulting maps may become official legal documents that architects, attorneys, businesspeople, and engineers rely on for various purposes, including environmental studies, marketing, and planning. Surveyors must certify and be liable for the work they do. From time to time, they are required to appear in court and provide professional opinions as testimony in legal proceedings.

In addition to working with cartographers, Surveyors also work on teams that include photogrammetrists, who perform analysis, make measurements, and produce drawings and maps using aerial photographs. In some states, photogrammetrists may be licensed Surveyors. Surveying and mapping technicians are other members of the surveying team; they help Surveyors by collecting data in the field, performing calculations, making sketches, and performing other required tasks. Senior technicians may hold lead positions on a survey team, and are sometimes known as party chiefs.

Surveyors have a variety of career options to choose from within their profession. For instance, hydrographic or marine Surveyors concentrate on rivers, harbors, lakes, and other water bodies. In addition to mapping the topography of a lake bed, they might measure the depth of the water and also mark the lake's shorelines. Geophysical prospecting surveyors focus on surveys below the surface, and often work for companies involved in petroleum exploration. Finally, geodetic surveyors use satellite technology to survey broad areas of the planet's surface.

Even within a particular niche, some surveyors specialize in different stages or aspects of the surveying process. By the early 21st century, the U.S. Department of Labor indicated that the skills of cartographers, photogrammetrists, and Surveyors were blending together to form a new breed of "mapping scientist" known as a geographic information specialist. This new professional category uses advanced technology to collect and analyze geographic information.

According to the 2006–07 edition of the Department of Labor's *Occupational Outlook Handbook*, in 2004, Surveyors held 56,000 jobs in the United States. Many of these individuals worked for firms within the engineering, mining, energy, or architectural sectors. Opportunities also existed with federal, state, and local governments. The Army Corps of Engineers, U.S. Geological Survey, Bureau of Land Management, and National Geodetic Survey are leading federal employers.

While some Surveyors work exclusively in an office setting, most divide their time between the office and the field. Fieldwork involves working outdoors in all kinds of weather—including rain, extreme heat, humidity, and bitter cold. This profession can be physically demanding, requiring frequent walking and standing. Although some outdoor work is carried out in easily accessible areas, Surveyors often travel to proposed land development sites and construction zones to perform surveys. Such areas may consist of rough terrain. Therefore, being in good or excellent physical condition may be a requirement for this profession.

While there may be seasonal fluctuations, due to the demand for surveys in warm weather conditions, most Surveyors work normal 40-hour workweeks. However, they may be required to travel long distances to perform a survey. In some cases, survey projects may require overnight stays or temporary relocation.

Salaries

According to the 2006–07 edition of the Department of Labor's *Occupational Outlook Handbook*, in mid-2004 annual salaries for Surveyors ranged from less than $24,640 to more than $71,640, with a median of $42,980.

Employment Prospects

The U.S. Department of Labor anticipates average job growth for Surveyors through 2014. Many opportunities will result from a large number of anticipated retirements. However, advanced technology, which has increased the efficiency of

Surveyors, will limit job growth somewhat. Opportunities will be the best for those with bachelor's degrees.

Advancement Prospects

In some cases, high school graduates are able to secure apprenticeships in the surveying field and, with some formal training, become assistants or surveying technicians. From there it is possible to advance to a senior-level technician position and, in some states, to eventually become a licensed Surveyor. However, by 2006 most entry-level Surveyors were required to earn an undergraduate degree and work under the supervision of a licensed Surveyor before becoming licensed themselves.

Education and Training

Historically, Surveyors have learned what they need to know through extensive on-the-job training and postsecondary classes in surveying. While a college degree is not required to work as a Surveyor, by the mid-2000s it was becoming increasingly difficult to obtain a position without a college degree due to the training needed to work with advanced technology. In addition to vocational programs at junior and technical schools that could be completed in one to three years, universities now offer undergraduate surveying degrees. In addition to meeting continuing education requirements, some states require Surveyors to hold a bachelor's degree, sometimes from a school accredited by the Accreditation Board for Engineering and Technology.

Special Requirements

Surveyors are required to obtain a license in all 50 states. Most states require candidates to pass the National Council of Examiners for Engineering and Surveying's written exam in addition to passing a written exam offered by a state's licensing board. Licensure also is subject to minimum experience and education requirements, which differ from state to state.

Experience, Special Skills, and Personality Traits

Experience is required to become a licensed Surveyor. After passing the Fundamentals of Surveying Exam, entry-level Surveyors usually work under a licensed Surveyor for a period of about four years before obtaining their own licenses.

Surveyors must possess good eyesight and spatial ability, because they are regularly required to gauge distances and visualize forms and objects. They must be detail-oriented, with the ability to perform tasks in a careful and thorough manner. In addition, Surveyors are logical and analytical thinkers, with excellent problem-solving skills. They must be able to take a systems perspective and determine how the outcome of a process can be affected by changing different variables. Surveyors must be self-reliant and capable of working independently at remote sites, and also on teams that involve communication with others.

Because report writing and research are important aspects of this profession, strong writing and reading comprehension skills are required. In addition, Surveyors may be required to perform computer modeling, digital mapping, and data integration activities. Therefore, experience with GIS and the GPS equipment is usually required.

Unions and Associations

Many surveying professionals are members of the American Congress on Surveying and Mapping (ACSM), which was established in 1941. ACSM members must belong to at least one of four ACSM member organizations: the American Association for Geodetic Surveying; the Cartography and Geographic Information Society; the Geographic and Land Information Society; or the National Society of Professional Surveyors, Inc.

Tips for Entry

1. In high school, take classes in computer science, drafting, mechanical drawing, algebra, geometry, and trigonometry.
2. Learn more about scholarship programs, student chapters, state affiliates, and colleges and universities with accredited surveying programs by visiting the student section of the American Congress on Surveying and Mapping's (ACSM) Web site at http://www.acsm.net/student.html.
3. In college, become a student member of the ACSM. A membership application is available for download at http://www.acsm.net/studentapp.pdf.
4. In college, secure internships that provide valuable field experience and increase your qualifications for entry-level employment.

FARMING AND FISHING

AGRICULTURAL CONSULTANT

CAREER PROFILE

Duties: Provide farmers, ranchers, and agribusinesses with expertise in financial matters, business structure, human relations, personnel management, business succession planning, production, evolving technologies, current practices, operations issues, and marketing

Alternate Title(s): Research Associate; Consultant; Senior Consultant; Junior or Senior Partner

Salary Range: $52,000 to $319,000

Employment Prospects: Poor

Advancement Prospects: Good

Prerequisites:

   Education or Training—Bachelor's degree in agribusiness, business administration, or related field.

   Experience—Internships and an agricultural background are extremely helpful for new graduates.

   Special Skills and Personality Traits—Creative, self-motivated, patient, enthusiastic, tactful, independent, cooperative, dependable, confident, determined, and detail-oriented; strong oral communications; mathematical, analytical, computer, communication, customer service, organizational, technical, business, and leadership skills.

   Special Requirements—The American Society of Farm Managers and Rural Appraisers offers the designation of Accredited Agricultural Consultant (AAC).

CAREER LADDER

```
┌─────────────────────────────┐
│     Senior Partner or       │
│   Independent Contractor    │
└─────────────────────────────┘

┌─────────────────────────────┐
│   Agricultural Consultant   │
└─────────────────────────────┘

┌─────────────────────────────┐
│     Research Associate      │
└─────────────────────────────┘
```

Position Description

Consulting is the fastest growing field in agriculture. The role of Agricultural Consultants is becoming more and more critical as agriculture enters the fast-paced era of consolidation, technology, specialization, mergers, and reformation. Agricultural Consultants provide farmers, ranchers, and agribusiness operators with independent, objective advice that can help them to lower costs and maximize yield while at the same time minimizing environmental impact. They value honesty and fair dealing in a manner that promotes the interests of clients, employees, and shareholders.

With technology changing so rapidly, Agricultural Consultants provide specialized knowledge to business operators, enabling them to keep up with changes and developments needed to adapt and remain profitable. They have expertise in a wide range of areas, including financial matters, business structure, human relations, personnel management, business succession planning, production, evolving technologies, current practices, operations issues, and marketing.

Agricultural Consultants must have extensive knowledge of both the agricultural industry and the world of business. During the course of their job, consultants in this field manage, analyze, and control financial accounts and examine business operations to find ways to improve efficiency and profits for farmers, ranchers, and agribusinesses. They look at procedures to uncover causes of problems. They then find ways to eliminate problems and increase productivity by devising more efficient and less costly ways to accomplish the goals of the farmer, rancher, or agribusiness.

More specifically, Agricultural Consultants analyze financial records and make suggestions on how financial stability and profitability could be increased. They analyze, manage, check, and prepare business and financial records such as income statements, balance sheets, cost studies, and tax returns. Agricultural Consultants also offer advisory services on a variety of business transactions, such as purchasing, selling, leasing, or contracting, or ways to increase profits and productivity. They study company procedures, establish budgets, assist in the purchase or sale of a business, and establish financial plans.

Providing advice regarding money and taxes is another important function of the Agricultural Consultant. They are experts in tax planning strategies and are able to prepare estate, gift, inheritance, and income tax statements. Agricultural Consultants work with lawyers and insurance and trust experts to set up or carry out estate plans and resolve other money matters.

Other services provided by Agricultural Consultants include weed and pest control evaluations, livestock waste management, soil sampling, and fertilizer recommendations. Consultants in this field also engage in research activities, such as conducting surveys, collecting and analyzing data, and writing reports. In addition to participating in industry research studies, their research may be used to help a client determine the feasibility of engaging in a new agricultural practice or expanding a business activity.

Most Agricultural Consultants work in rural or suburban settings near agricultural areas. Generally speaking, large firms dominate the field of management, scientific, and technical consulting as a whole. According to the U.S. Department of Labor, of those consulting firms with more than 20 employees, 4 percent represented more than half of all consulting jobs in 2004. However, most consulting businesses are small firms with less than five employees. In addition, many consultants are self-employed. Beyond the 779,000 management, scientific, and technical consultants employed on a wage and salary basis, the U.S. Department of Labor reported an additional 256,000 self-employed or unpaid family workers in the field during 2004.

Agricultural Consultants mainly work indoors in an office setting, although their profession also involves traveling to farms, ranches, and locations owned or operated by their clients. According to the U.S. Department of Labor, management, scientific, and technical consultants worked an average of 35 hours per week in 2004. However, this varies depending on the consulting service being performed, the nature of specific projects, and the size of the consulting business. Consultants may be required to work long hours, including weekends, in order to meet deadlines.

Salaries

Agricultural Consultants' salaries vary, depending on their level of experience, the nature of their job, and their specific credentials. According to the 2006–07 edition of the U.S. Department of Labor's *Occupational Outlook Handbook*, 2004 data from the Association of Management Consulting Firms indicated that research associates received total compensation of $52,482, followed by $65,066 for entry-level consultants; $89,116 for management consultants; and $123,305 for senior consultants. Junior partners earned $191,664, while total compensation for senior partners totaled $319,339. Self-employed consultants are often well paid.

Employment Prospects

According to the U.S. Department of Labor, the larger field of management, scientific, and technical consulting is expected to be the economy's fifth-fastest growing industry through 2014, with strong growth projected in all areas. However, increasing competition is expected from law firms, accounting firms, and investment banks. Professionals concentrating in agriculture and food science work within the subcategory of scientific and technical consulting, which in mid-2004 included 66,215 workers (about 8.5 percent of the industry total). The highly specialized field of agricultural consulting is an even smaller subclassification. For this reason, job availability will be more limited than in other areas of the larger consulting profession.

Advancement Prospects

In larger firms, entry-level consultants often begin as research associates and, with additional education and experience, progress up the ladder to consultant, management consultant, and senior consultant. Eventually, one may attain the level of junior or senior partner. Rather than work for an existing firm, many consultants choose to go into business as independent contractors or start their own consulting firms with several partners. Some consultants provide services on a part-time basis while continuing to work for another employer.

Education and Training

A bachelor's degree in agribusiness, business administration, or a related field is the minimum education required to work as an Agricultural Consultant. Those who eventually obtain Accredited Agricultural Consultant (AAC) certification must successfully complete consulting courses offered by the American Society of Farm Managers and Rural Appraisers, including Ag Consulting Principles, Standards and Ethics, Communications for Agribusiness Professionals, and other specialized courses. In addition, AAC status requires 60 hours of continuing education and completion of the Standards and Ethics course every five years.

Special Requirements

The American Society of Farm Managers and Rural Appraisers offers industry professionals the opportunity to earn the designation of Accredited Agricultural Consultants (AAC). To achieve the status of AAC, the applicant must meet specific education and experience requirements and successfully pass the ASFMRA Accreditation Exam.

Experience, Special Skills, and Personality Traits

Generally speaking, there are different pathways of entry into the consulting field. A number of Agricultural Consultants enter the profession after gaining considerable experience in other areas of the agriculture or agribusiness industries. However, recent college graduates can obtain entry-level positions with an existing firm, receive on-the-job training, and gain additional responsibility with experience. Internships and an agricultural background are extremely helpful for new graduates who wish to enter the agricultural consulting field.

Successful Agricultural Consultants are creative, self-motivated, patient, enthusiastic, tactful, dependable, and detail-oriented. They are able to work independently or with others, and possess initiative, sound judgment, determination, and confidence. In addition, agricultural consulting work requires that one have strong oral communications, mathematical, analytical, computer, communication, customer service, organizational, technical, business, and leadership skills.

Unions and Associations

Agricultural Consultants have a nationwide trade organization, the American Society of Farm Managers and Rural Appraisers. Founded in 1929, the Denver, Colorado–based association offers its members strong support in the political and professional arena. It also provides continuing education and professional designations for members who wish to increase their professionalism. In addition, many Agricultural Consultants belong to professional associations at the state level.

Tips for Entry

1. During high school, take courses in business, accounting, agricultural education, math, and computers.
2. Learn about programs offered by the National FFA (changed in 1988 from Future Farmers of America) Organization that promote skills needed for this specific career by visiting http://www.ffa.org/index.cfm?method=c_job.ShowSearchDetails&careerid=12.
3. Shadow an Agricultural Consultant on the job to find out what the profession is like.
4. In college, complete an agricultural consulting internship in order to increase your prospects for entry-level employment.

Portions of the information contained in this career profile were provided by the American Society of Farm Managers and Rural Appraisers and the National FFA Organization.

COMMERCIAL BEEKEEPER

CAREER PROFILE

Duties: Make management decisions and oversee implementation of tasks necessary to maintain colonies of honey bees for the purposes of producing honey, pollinating crops, and/or producing queens and bulk bees for sale.

Alternate Title(s): Apiculturist; Honey Producer

Salary Range: $10,000 to $100,000

Employment Prospects: Fair

Advancement Prospects: Good

Prerequisites:

Education or Training—A course in honeybee biology and small business management.

Experience—Entry-level positions can be obtained with little or no experience.

Special Skills and Personality Traits—Independent, self-reliant, patient, flexible, adaptable, and not allergic to honey bee stings.

Special Requirements—A commercial driver's license may be required.

CAREER LADDER

```
┌──────────────────────────────────┐
│  Beekeeping Operation Owner       │
└──────────────────────────────────┘

┌──────────────────────────────────┐
│  Beekeeping Operation Part Owner  │
└──────────────────────────────────┘

┌──────────────────────────────────┐
│  Beekeeping Employee              │
└──────────────────────────────────┘
```

Position Description

Commercial Beekeepers raise bees to produce honey and pollinate crops. Beekeeping is a form of animal husbandry. Honeybees are not domesticated, but they can be managed in a manner that meets the requirements of the bees and produces income for the Beekeeper. Beekeepers must be aware of the requirements of the colonies for survival, and they must be able to plan on uses of the bees to produce income adequate to cover the cost of operation, including salaries for the manager and the laborers.

Beekeeping income can be generated by using honeybees for one or more of the following: Colonies with strong populations can be rented to growers for crop pollination; when weather conditions are favorable, blooming plants can provide abundant nectar and the bees produce excess honey that can be harvested and sold; Beekeepers also can rear honeybee queens for sale. This is a specialized undertaking, requiring unique beekeeping equipment and practices that are fairly exacting.

Most Beekeepers work with the Italian honeybee, which is gentle and hardworking. Under good management, honeybees make much more honey than they need for themselves. Each hive contains a queen bee to lay eggs, hundreds of drones for reproduction only and 40,000 to 50,000 worker bees. From 1995 to 2005, commercial honey producers have averaged 75.2 pound honey crops, producing anywhere from 67.8 pounds to 84.1 pounds. Beekeepers gather surplus honey and sell it.

Spring is the time when Commercial Beekeepers set up new hives or take care of old ones. They normally buy a package of bees (two or three pounds of bees and one queen) from a dealer. When the bees settle in, beekeepers screen the entrance and move the colony to an orchard, clover field, or other place where the bees can find nectar.

Old colonies also need care in the spring. Beekeepers make sure the colony has a healthy queen bee and that the bees have enough food stored to last until they start making honey. If the food supply is insufficient, beekeepers provide the bees with high fructose corn syrup or a sugar-and-water syrup.

Commercial beehives commonly consist of three boxes, called supers, that each contain a number of frames. The bottom box, or two, is dedicated to the brood nest, and is home to the queen bee and her offspring, while the upper boxes are called honey supers. Beekeepers regularly inspect hives to make sure they are not crowded, that they are clean and free of disease and parasites, and that the bees are producing a good amount of honey. They fight diseases and parasites using drugs and chemicals recommended by their state agricultural department or extension agents. Beekeepers open the hive and examine each honeycomb. Specifically, they check the brood in the combs. In addition, Beekeepers move hives to different locations for various reasons, including escaping contact with insecticides.

When the honey is ripe, or thick, Beekeepers harvest it. The first harvest may come in late spring or summer. Early in the season, when bees are gathering nectar and making honey, Beekeepers may take off the filled supers and replace them with empty ones. They keep the different flows of honey separate since the spring crop is usually a lighter colored, mild-flavored honey, and the honey harvested in the fall is darker and more robust in flavor.

For retail sales, Beekeepers package honey in jars or small cans. In many states, laws require labels to contain contact information to the retailer, the weight of honey in the container, and the grade of the honey. Description of the kinds of blossoms from which the honey was made, as well as nutritional data, was optional as of 2006. Beekeepers keep records on their bees and colonies. They list the age of the queen, when they added supers, amount of extra food supplied, number of filled combs, kind of honey, and amounts. In the fall Beekeepers prepare their hives for winter.

Commercial beekeeping jobs are found throughout the United States. Beekeepers spend a great deal of time working outdoors year-round. They also work indoors when they keep their business records and clean and repair equipment. In addition to working with supers and frames, Commercial Beekeepers use a variety of specialized equipment to carry out their work, including protective clothing and hive tools, smokers for colony examination, bee brushes, trucks, and forklifts.

Beekeeping is a very labor-intensive occupation. Even with the assistance of mechanical devices, this profession requires workers to be in good physical condition. Beehives are placed on or near the ground, and colony examinations require bending over the boxes for many consecutive hours. When filled with honey, the boxes weigh nearly 80 pounds. After the bees are driven down out of the boxes with repellents or forced air, the boxes are carried by hand to the truck or to the stack waiting to be mechanically lifted onto the truck. Beekeeping is very hard on the back.

Salaries

Beekeepers usually do not have a written contract with their operation for a specific, monthly salary. As revenue comes in, some is used as salary. According to Eric Mussen, cooperative extension apiculturist at the University of California, Davis, salaries for Commercial Beekeepers are highly variable, ranging anywhere from $10,000 to $100,000. Revenue does not accrue on a regular basis. Pollination fees and income from honey sales or from selling bees varies from season to season. Judicious financial planning is required to meet the needs of both the operation and the operators.

Employment Prospects

While employment opportunities in the commercial beekeeping field were somewhat limited in 2006, many Commercial Beekeepers were approaching retirement age and should be amenable to "phased retirement." Both the previous and future owners benefit from such an arrangement.

Advancement Prospects

Many Commercial Beekeepers start their careers by working for someone who owns their own beekeeping operation. In time, they may become a part owner in the operation and eventually assume full ownership. With increased experience, a Beekeeper can increase the size of an operation or diversify into different aspects of the business. Such growth usually requires hiring and supervising more permanent employees.

Education and Training

Commercial Beekeepers learn about their profession through on-the-job experience. Although there is no requirement for any level of education to become a Beekeeper, many do attend college and obtain a four-year degree. Courses in business management are extremely useful. Not only does such training help the Beekeeper to run a business efficiently, it also prepares them to generate detailed, convincing business plans, which are essential to obtain funding from lending institutions.

Special Requirements

Because operating forklifts and trucks is a central part of a beekeeping enterprise, Commercial Beekeepers may be required to hold a commercial driver's license.

Experience, Special Skills, and Personality Traits

Entry-level beekeeping jobs can be obtained with little or no experience, although prior exposure to bees and beekeeping is helpful. Manipulating hives of bees and recognizing colony conditions within the hives are skills that can be learned only through experience. Bee stings are part of the occupation. Beekeepers cannot be allergic to honeybee stings and must be able to tolerate the discomfort of frequent stings.

Many Beekeepers are attracted to the profession because they wish to be self-employed. Beekeeping can be very satisfying or very frustrating. Therefore, a beekeeper must be an optimist. Beekeepers must be highly motivated, patient, detail-oriented, and capable of working independently. They must possess good manual dexterity, sound judgment, and steady nerves. In addition, Commercial Beekeepers have solid decision-making and business skills, and are able to work under pressure.

Unions and Associations

Beekeepers sometimes form county beekeeping clubs. There are three regional societies in the United States: the Eastern Apicultural Society, the Heartland Apicultural Society, and the Western Apicultural Society. Many commercial beekeepers belong to one or both of the national associations: the American Beekeeping Federation or the American Honey Producers' Association.

Tips for Entry

1. In high school, put particular emphasis on English and the sciences, including biology, zoology, chemistry, and math.
2. In college, choose courses that relate to conservation, ecology, biology, and financial management.
3. Attend meetings of beekeeping groups to learn about beekeeping practices and employment opportunities.
4. Shadow a beekeeper to find out what the job is really like.
5. Volunteer at or seek part-time employment with a beekeeping business in order to gain valuable hands-on experience.

Portions of the information contained in this career profile were provided by the National FFA Organization, as well as Eric Mussen, cooperative extension apiculturist at the University of California, Davis.

CROP FARMER

CAREER PROFILE

Duties: Plant, cultivate, harvest, and store grain, fiber, fruits, or vegetable crops for cash or livestock feed; study crops to improve quality and quantity; stay current on the latest equipment, varieties, production, marketing, and nutrient management practices; maintain knowledge of the market and selling/distribution processes; hire, train, supervise, and coordinate activities of other farm workers

Alternate Title(s): Fruit Grower; Rice Farmer; Tobacco Farmer; Vegetable Farmer

Salary Range: Variable

Employment Prospects: Poor

Advancement Prospects: Fair

Prerequisites:

Education or Training—Two-year degree in agriculture

Experience—An entry-level farm worker position can be obtained with little or no experience, but experience is required to manage or own a farm.

Special Skills and Personality Traits—Strong mathematical, organizational, mechanical, scientific, decision-making, business, stress management, communication, research, and computer skills; responsible, logical, persistent, self-motivated, detail-oriented, goal-oriented, physically fit, patient, and orderly; possess initiative, good judgment, determination, confidence, manual dexterity, and the ability to work independently

CAREER LADDER

```
┌─────────────────────────────┐
│   Farm Manager or           │
│   Agricultural Consultant   │
└─────────────────────────────┘

┌─────────────────────────────┐
│   Crop Farmer               │
└─────────────────────────────┘

┌─────────────────────────────┐
│   Intern                    │
└─────────────────────────────┘
```

Position Description

Broadly speaking, farmers raise crops and livestock for human consumption. They are businesspeople who invest in and profit from their activities. Farmers must have a high degree of knowledge and skill in business management, as well as the technical knowledge and skills of agriculture.

The farming profession involves establishing output goals, determining financial constraints, and monitoring production and marketing. Farmers may be involved with large corporate farms or small individual family farms. They may own or lease the land used to produce their products. Farmers operate and maintain daily farming operations, including the care of crops, machinery, finances, and labor. In addition, they also plan for future farm enterprises.

Crop Farmers grow crops for cash or to feed farm-raised livestock. They may raise grain, fiber, fruits, or vegetables. Some Crop Farmers raise one specialty crop (such as pineapple), while others raise diversified crops (one or more fruits or vegetables with different growing cycles).

First and foremost, Crop Farmers must understand how to plant, cultivate, harvest, and store their crops. This involves studying crops to improve the quality and quantity of produce, and staying current on the latest varieties, production, and nutrient management practices. Crop Farmers seek to improve crop yield while controlling pests and weeds.

They combine scientific knowledge and technical skills to grow and develop plants for better human nutrition, and to improve the aesthetic quality of the environment.

In addition to being knowledgeable about crops, Crop Farmers also must be good businesspeople. This requirement calls for them to be knowledgeable of the market and the selling/distribution processes needed to maximize the value of what they grow. Diversified Crop Farmers plan the combination of crops they will raise so that if the price of one crop drops, they will have income from another.

Crop Farmers must consider many factors at once when making decisions, including market and weather conditions, growing cycles, the kinds of seeds and fertilizers that are best for the soil and climate, and operational costs. Other decisions Crop Farmers make range from choosing what types of new technology would be the most suitable or beneficial for their farm to deciding when to replace or buy new equipment such as combines and tractors.

Crop Farmers also must stay current on new varieties of seeds or rootstock, new equipment, and new processing and marketing methods. They also maintain extensive financial records and inventories. Many Crop Farmers arrange for credit from banks in order to purchase farm equipment, machines, and supplies such as seeds, fertilizers, and chemicals. In addition, they are charged with hiring, training, supervising, and coordinating activities of other farm workers.

Generally speaking, the farming profession is both complicated and risky. Farmers constantly face unpredictable threats, such as fluctuating weather and market conditions and insect infestations. In addition, they must contend with complex environmental rules and regulations at the state and federal government levels. Since 2005 a growing emphasis is being placed on more environmentally friendly production practices, including the use of ground covers for soil erosion control and prescription pesticide and nutrient management schemes.

Diversified Crop Farmers may grow a wide variety of different crops for wholesale or retail distribution, including beans, corn, tomatoes, potatoes, and squash. Specialty crops include the likes of rice and tobacco, which can be complicated to grow in their own right. For example, rice farmers must be knowledgeable of soil enrichment, planting, water management, pest control, harvest, straw incorporation, and storage. In addition, there are four classes of rice, including long grain rough rice, medium grain rough rice, short grain rough rice, and mixed rough rice.

In the case of tobacco farming, tobacco varieties undergo rigorous testing before being released for commercial production. This testing includes small plot trials on experiment stations, warehouse evaluations, determination of chemical and physical properties, and finally on-farm testing to evaluate how the potential variety performs in a commercial situation. A variety must meet certain quality standards before being released. When commercial planting begins, each tobacco farmer may have different requirements for the variety or varieties to be grown on his farm. Ease of growing and curing, disease and nematode resistance, and market acceptance are a few examples of the factors they consider when selecting a variety.

The vast majority of farming jobs are located in rural areas, and Crop Farmers spend a great deal of their time outdoors, working in fields or greenhouses. Diversified crop farmers and vegetable farmers work throughout the United States. However, certain types of crops are either limited to or are more common in specific regions. Corn is a typical crop in the Midwest, cotton is found in the Southwest, and wheat fields blanket the West. Tobacco farms are located in the states of Florida, Georgia, Alabama, South Carolina, North Carolina, and Virginia. Rice is grown in the southern United States along coastal waters and in California.

In general, the work of farmers is often strenuous; their work hours are frequently long, and their days off are sometimes infrequent. Of those who work full time, half work 60 or more hours a week. Nevertheless, these disadvantages are often outweighed by the opportunities for living in a more rural area, working outdoors, being self-employed, and making a living by working the land.

Salaries

Income from farming varies considerably due to crop production and prices. According to the 2006–07 edition of the U.S. Department of Labor's *Occupational Outlook Handbook*, the U.S. Department of Agriculture reported that farm operator households earned an average net cash farm business income of $15,603 in 2004. This figure does not include government subsidies or other forms of supplemental income.

Employment Prospects

Through 2014, the U.S. Department of Labor anticipates that many farms will go out of business because of falling prices for agricultural goods. This trend will promote further consolidation and result in a smaller number of large, well-funded farms dominating the industry. Productivity increases also will cause the overall demand for farm laborers to fall, as farms gain the ability to produce more with fewer workers. A number of small farmers have found success by specializing in a specific niche, such as organic farming or selling directly to farmers' markets or cooperatives.

Advancement Prospects

Some Crop Farmers begin their careers at a very young age, working on a family farm. In college, they may work as interns in areas such as production, sales and marketing, and pest management. A number of Crop Farmers go on to become farm managers or agricultural consultants. Others pursue careers in sales, government affairs, or communications.

Education and Training

According to the U.S. Department of Labor, the complex nature of agriculture now requires prospective farmers to receive formal training. At minimum, a two-year degree in agriculture is needed, but many farmers earn four-year bachelor's degrees. Every state university system in the United States has a land grant university with a school of agriculture. Courses of study commonly include agricultural economics, agricultural production, agronomy, animal science, business, crop and fruit science, dairy science, and horticulture.

Experience, Special Skills, and Personality Traits

Farmers must possess strong mathematical, organizational, mechanical, scientific, decision-making, business, stress management, communication, research, and computer skills. They are responsible, logical, persistent, self-motivated, detail-oriented, goal-oriented, physically fit, patient, and orderly. Farmers possess initiative, good judgment, determination, confidence, manual dexterity, and the ability to work independently.

Unions and Associations

About 250,000 farm and ranch families throughout the United States are members of the Washington, D.C.-based National Farmers Union, which was established in 1902. The NFU's mission is "to protect and enhance the economic well-being and quality of life for family farmers and ranchers and their rural communities." While its membership is nationwide, the NFU has organized chapters in 26 states.

Tips for Entry

1. During high school, take courses in agriculture, horticulture, biology, botany, agronomy, earth sciences, accounting, math, business, computers, and mechanics.
2. Learn about programs offered by the National FFA Organization that promote skills needed for farming careers by visiting http://www.ffa.org.
3. Shadow a Crop Farmer on the job to find out what the profession is like.
4. Review college catalog course descriptions in the departments of agriculture, agronomy, or plant and soil science to identify a curriculum that interests you.
5. In college, secure internships that provide valuable experience and increase your qualifications for entry-level employment.

Some of the information contained in this career profile was provided by the National FFA Organization.

CROP SCIENTIST

CAREER PROFILE

Duties: Serve in technical, consulting, and research roles related to a variety of agronomic crops; gather information from satellites and airplanes; identify crop types and crop diseases; measure moisture conditions of both crops and soils; predict crop conditions and yields; engage in computer modeling

Alternate Title(s): Crop Breeder; Crop Chemist; Crop Cytogeneticist; Crop Cytologist; Crop Ecologist; Crop Geneticist; Crop Marketing Specialist; Crop Physiologist; Crop Production Specialist; Crop Protection Specialist; Crop Quality Specialist; Crop Utilization Specialist

Salary Range: $30,660 to $88,840+

Employment Prospects: Fair

Advancement Prospects: Good

Prerequisites:

Education or Training—Bachelor's, master's, or doctorate degree in agronomy, crop science, earth science, environmental science, natural resources, plant biochemistry, plant physiology, plant genetics/breeding, or molecular genetics

Experience—Crop science fieldwork, as well as familiarity with computer modeling, digital mapping, and GIS and GPS systems

Special Skills and Personality Traits—Analytical thinking, writing, communication, problem-solving, and computer skills; logical, self-reliant, independent, adaptable, flexible, detail-oriented, careful, and thorough

Special Requirements—Certified Crop Adviser (CCA), Certified Professional Agronomist (CPAg) (ARCPACS), and Certified Professional Soil Scientist/Classifier (CPSS/CPSC) certifications are voluntary, but may be required by employers.

CAREER LADDER

```
┌─────────────────────────────────────┐
│   Senior Scientist or Consultant     │
└─────────────────────────────────────┘

┌─────────────────────────────────────┐
│            Crop Scientist            │
└─────────────────────────────────────┘

┌─────────────────────────────────────┐
│        Crop Science Technician       │
└─────────────────────────────────────┘
```

Position Description

The well-being of humankind depends on the profitability and sustainability of agriculture. The corn fields that cover the Midwest, the acres of cotton drying under the Southwestern sun, the green pastures of the Northeast, and the wheat fields of the West are not endless and do not just happen. Hard work on the part of the grower and inputs from experts in science and technology are required.

Crop science is the study of growing food, feed, forage, fiber, and pharmaceutical crops. This field involves working with plants and all of the factors that promote their development, such as light, water, temperature, and nutrients, as well as those conditions that inhibit their development including diseases, weeds, and insects. Examples of agronomic crops include corn, cotton, peanuts, rice, soybeans, sunflowers, sugarcane, turfgrass, and wheat.

Crop Scientists identify, interpret, and manage crops for agriculture, urban uses, and rangeland in an environmentally responsible way. They work to provide food that is healthy, safe, and plentiful. Professionals in this field help to protect the environment and use land resources more efficiently and are involved in the discovery of new research to make food and feed more nutritious. Without careful planning, food shortages that commonly exist in many parts of the world will occur in the United States. Therefore, an important challenge for the Crop Scientist is to increase food production in the United States and around the world while using available resources more efficiently.

Crop Scientists work in a wide range of specialty areas, including:

- Environmental quality
- Ecology
- Biotechnology
- Plant physiology
- Turfgrass science
- Pest management
- Genetics
- Plant breeding
- Molecular biology
- Seed science
- Nutrition
- Plant diseases
- Mathematics and modeling
- International development

Crop Scientists are on the cutting edge of technology. Their work involves gathering information from satellites or airplanes to identify crop types and crop diseases and to measure moisture conditions of both crops and soils. This information helps experts to predict crop conditions and yields worldwide and provides valuable input in domestic and foreign policy decisions.

Crop Scientists draw knowledge from a number of disciplines while performing their work. In addition to specific training in crop science, professionals in this field are often knowledgeable in fields such as general biology, chemistry, earth/environmental science, ecology, farm and ranch management, food production, forestry, geography, geology, horticulture, hydrology, limnology, mathematics, physics, plant science, statistics, weed science, and wetland ecology.

Crop science graduates can choose from a range of excellent professional opportunities and challenging careers. Employment opportunities are available as certified crop consultants, agricultural producers, laboratory technicians and managers, laboratory and field researchers, government

and academic research scientists, educators, and extension specialists.

Crop Scientists serve in technical, consulting, and research capacities in many sectors of the economy. In the private sector they are employed by both for-profit and nonprofit organizations, including consulting firms, seed companies, life science companies, fertilizer industries, commercial farms, agriculture cooperatives, colleges and universities, crop management firms, chemical producers, agricultural service firms, food products companies, and commercial research and development laboratories.

Opportunities also exist with a variety of different government agencies. According to the U.S. Department of Labor, in mid-2004 approximately 25 percent of salaried agricultural and food scientists were employed by governments at the local, state, or federal level. The U.S. Department of Agriculture is a leading federal government employer.

While Crop Scientists perform some of their work in laboratory and office settings, they also spend a great deal of time outdoors, working in farm fields or at agricultural research stations. Positions that are physically demanding require scientists to be in good physical condition. In addition to their primary job functions, Crop Scientists may conduct seminars, give public or professional presentations, and write articles for professional journals.

Salaries

While the U.S. Department of Labor does not list specific salary information for Crop Scientists, it does provide data for the related category of soil and plant scientists. According to the 2006–07 edition of the department's *Occupational Outlook Handbook*, in mid-2004 soil and plant scientists' annual salaries ranged from $30,660 to more than $88,840, with a median of $51,200. Data from the National Association of Colleges and Employers put average annual starting salaries for those with bachelor's degrees in plant sciences at $31,649 a year, while those with other types of agricultural science degrees earned $36,189 a year.

Employment Prospects

Through 2014, the U.S. Department of Labor anticipates average job growth for agricultural scientists. Although prior research activities have led to the development of crops with higher yields and a greater ability to withstand disease and insects, growth will be driven by the need to constantly combat pathogens and pests that develop the ability to attack these hardier crop varieties. Growth also will stem from the growing global demand for food and the need to grow crops that use reduced levels of herbicide, pesticide, and fertilizer.

Advancement Prospects

After gaining experience as college interns or technicians, Crop Scientists regularly obtain entry-level positions that involve working under the supervision of experienced crop professionals. Eventually, they may progress on the career ladder and obtain scientific positions with greater responsibility, while some pursue positions with private consulting firms. Crop Scientists who earn advanced degrees may become involved in research and education, or obtain senior-level positions that involve managing other scientists or research programs.

Education and Training

A bachelor of science (B.S.) degree or its equivalent is the minimum educational requirement to work as a Crop Scientist. Numerous positions in teaching, research, or extension require training beyond the B.S. degree. Students eligible for advanced work usually receive financial assistance in the form of scholarships, fellowships, or assistantships. These students specialize in one or more areas of crop science as they work toward a master's or doctorate degree.

Special Requirements

The American Society of Agronomy (ASA) offers the Certified Crop Adviser (CCA) program for Crop Scientists, and the Soil Science Society of America (SSSA) offers the Certified Professional Agronomist (CPAg) (ARCPACS) and Certified Professional Soil Scientist/Classifier (CPSS/CPSC) programs. Although they are voluntary, these certifications may be required for employment by some private firms.

Experience, Special Skills, and Personality Traits

Crop Scientists must be detail-oriented, with the ability to perform tasks in a careful and thorough manner. They also must be logical and analytical thinkers, with excellent problem-solving abilities. Due to the many variables involved in scientific work, the ability to be adaptable and flexible also is critical for professionals in this field. Because projects may take them to remote locations where it is necessary to work in relative isolation, Crop Scientists must be self-reliant and capable of working independently. On the other hand, because they often work on project teams and are required to communicate with others, Crop Scientists must be team players.

Report writing and presentations are important aspects of this profession. Therefore, strong written and oral communication skills are required, along with proficiency in statistics. Basic computer experience is required for word processing and developing presentations. In addition, Crop Scientists may be required to perform modeling using computers, and carry out digital mapping and data integration activities. Therefore, experience with geographic information systems (GIS) and global positioning systems (GPS) may be helpful or required.

Unions and Associations

At the national level, many Crop Scientists are members of the Soil Science Society of America, the Crop Science Society of America, and the American Society of Agronomy. These three autonomous societies share many common interests, as well as the same headquarters in Madison, Wisconsin. Their members "are dedicated to the conservation and wise use of natural resources to produce food, feed, and fiber crops while maintaining and improving the environment."

Tips for Entry

1. In high school, take courses that provide exposure to earth science, geology, biology, mathematics, chemistry, physics, and engineering, and hone your English language skills.
2. Download a free career brochure from the Crop Science Society of America by visiting http://www.crops.org.
3. Review college catalog course descriptions in the departments of agriculture, agronomy, soil science, earth science, environmental science, or natural resources to identify a curriculum that interests you.
4. In college, secure internships that provide valuable field and lab experience and increase your qualifications for entry-level employment.

Some of the information contained in this career profile was provided by the Crop Science Society of America.

DAIRY FARMER

CAREER PROFILE

Duties: Feed and care for dairy animals; maintain clean barns and other farm buildings; oversee breeding and marketing activities; sell milk; sell livestock to other farmers; clean stalls; sterilize, maintain, and repair equipment; oversee the planting, fertilizing, and cultivating of crops such as hay, grain, and corn; keep inventories and financial records; hire, train, supervise, and coordinate activities of other farm workers

Alternate Title(s): Dairy Herdsman

Salary Range: Variable

Employment Prospects: Poor

Advancement Prospects: Fair

Prerequisites:

Education or Training—Two-year degree in agriculture

Experience—An entry-level farm worker position can be obtained with little or no experience, but experience is required to manage or own a dairy farm.

Special Skills and Personality Traits—Strong mathematical, organizational, mechanical, scientific, decision-making, business, stress management, communication, research, and computer skills; responsible, logical, persistent, self-motivated, detail-oriented, goal-oriented, physically fit, patient, and orderly; possess initiative, good judgment, determination, confidence, manual dexterity, and the ability to work with animals

CAREER LADDER

```
┌─────────────────────────────┐
│     Farm Manager or          │
│  Agricultural Consultant     │
└─────────────────────────────┘

┌─────────────────────────────┐
│       Dairy Farmer           │
└─────────────────────────────┘

┌─────────────────────────────┐
│         Intern               │
└─────────────────────────────┘
```

Position Description

Broadly speaking, farmers raise crops and livestock for human consumption. They are businesspeople who invest in and profit from their activities. Farmers must have a high degree of knowledge and skill in business management, as well as the technical knowledge and skills of agriculture.

The farming profession involves establishing output goals, determining financial constraints, and monitoring production and marketing. Farmers may be involved with large corporate farms or small individual family farms. They may own or lease the land used to produce their products. Farmers operate and maintain daily farming operations, including the care of animals, crops, machinery, finances, and labor. In addition, they also plan for future farm enterprises.

Dairy Farmers raise milk-producing cows, sell the milk, and may sell livestock to other farmers. They must feed and care for dairy animals as well as maintain clean barns and other farm buildings. Dairy Farmers also oversee breeding and marketing activities.

Dairy Farmers' work revolves around a twice-daily milking routine (generally around 5:00 A.M. and 5:00 P.M.). Commercial Dairy Farmers use milking parlors and around-the-barn pipelines so that one person can handle several automatic milking units at a time. Another important responsibility of Dairy Farmers is cleaning stalls and sterilizing equipment. Cleanliness is very important because unsanitary conditions foster disease in cows, resulting in contaminated milk. Dairy Farmers schedule breeding, vaccinating, and dehorning of the animals. They also may artificially inseminate the cows. Dairy Farmers must be prepared to handle emergencies such as machinery breakdowns, cattle illnesses, storms, droughts, and labor shortages.

Dairy cows cannot thrive on pasture or forage crops alone. They need grain to supplement their diet. Most Dairy Farmers, except those in the West and the Southwest, also raise hay, grain, and corn to feed their dairy herds. In this role they oversee the planting, fertilizing, and cultivating of any crops such as hay, grain, and corn. Those in northern states also must provide feed during the winter months when the cows remain indoors. Dairy Farmers plow, seed, harvest, and store hay, grains, and ensilage. In some parts of the country, however, Dairy Farmers buy much of the feed they use.

Dairy Farmers also maintain and repair tractors, cultivators, and other equipment. They must be knowledgeable about farm management, disease control, soil preparation/cultivation, and equipment maintenance and repair. In addition to being knowledgeable about animals, Dairy Farmers also must be good businesspeople. This requirement calls for them to be knowledgeable of the market and the selling/distribution processes needed to maximize the value of their milk. Dairy Farmers must be able to wear many hats to be successful. Managing money and a budget well enough to realize a profit from year to year can be a challenge. Starting from scratch is difficult and cost-prohibitive; most farmers in this field either work for someone else or have had the operation in the family for several generations.

Dairy Farmers must consider many factors at once when making decisions, including market and weather conditions, feed prices, and operational costs. Other decisions Dairy Farmers make range from choosing what types of new technology would be the most suitable or beneficial for their farms to deciding when to replace or buy new equipment, such as milking parlors.

Dairy Farmers also must stay current on new varieties of equipment, and new processing and marketing methods. They also maintain extensive financial records and inventories. Many Dairy Farmers arrange for credit from banks in order to purchase farm equipment, machines, and supplies. In addition, they are charged with hiring, training, supervising, and coordinating activities of other farm workers.

The dairy farming field also includes opportunities for dairy herdsmen, who produce cattle for use in the dairy herd. Specifically, herdsmen manage the operation of the dairy herd, define and supervise animal care and husbandry methods to minimize net cost of herd operations, oversee the herd budget, and assist in the preparation of new budgets.

They also advise on capital improvements and renovations needed for the herd, and arrange for acquisition, transport, and disposal of animals to facilitate efficient herd operation. Herdsmen also may coordinate with veterinary services to maximize cow health and performance, and define, calculate, record, and communicate specific performance measures about the herd to show current status and progress toward goals. Their coordination activities include supplying feed and bedding, handling manure, moving cattle, sharing equipment, and maintaining facilities.

Generally speaking, the farming profession is both complicated and risky. Farmers constantly face unpredictable threats, such as fluctuating weather and market conditions and insect infestations. In addition, they must contend with complex environmental rules and regulations at the state and federal government levels. In the 2000s, a growing emphasis is being placed on more environmentally friendly production practices, including the use of ground covers for soil erosion control and prescription pesticide and nutrient management schemes.

The vast majority of dairy farming jobs are located in rural areas, mainly in the states of California, Oregon, Washington, Wisconsin, Michigan, Minnesota, Pennsylvania, and New York. Other than milking, farmers spend a great deal of their time outdoors in all kinds of weather. Dairy farming can be hazardous, because farmers may sustain injuries from machine accidents or develop and suffer from allergies to dust, animal dander, and pollen.

In general, the work of farmers is often strenuous; their work hours are frequently long, and their days off are sometimes infrequent. Of those who work full time, half work 60 or more hours a week. Dairy Farmers who also grow crops may be busier during the planting and harvest periods. However, like livestock farmers, they are busy year-round because they must continually feed, care for, and milk their cows. Dairy Farmers are tied down to their milking schedules—every day at specific times. This aspect of their work makes vacations or time away from the dairy farm difficult. Nevertheless, these disadvantages are often outweighed by the opportunities for living in a more rural area, working outdoors, being self-employed, and making a living working the land.

Salaries

Income from dairy farming varies considerably. Profits can fluctuate greatly from year to year based on several variables, such as market value, weather conditions, and feed prices. According to the 2006–07 edition of the U.S. Department of Labor's *Occupational Outlook Handbook*, the U.S. Department of Agriculture reported that farm operator households earned an average net cash farm business income of $15,603 in 2004. This figure does not include government subsidies or other forms of supplemental income.

Employment Prospects

Through 2014, the U.S. Department of Labor anticipates that many farms will go out of business because of falling prices for agricultural goods. This trend will promote further consolidation and result in a smaller number of large, well-funded farms dominating the industry. Productivity increases also will cause the overall demand for farm laborers to fall, as farms gain the ability to produce more with fewer workers.

Advancement Prospects

Some Dairy Farmers begin their careers at a very young age, working on a family farm. In college, they may work as interns in areas such as production, sales and marketing, and pest management. Some Dairy Farmers go on to become farm managers or agricultural consultants. Others pursue careers in sales, government affairs, or communications.

Education and Training

According to the U.S. Department of Labor, the complex nature of agriculture now requires prospective farmers to receive formal training. At minimum, a two-year degree in agriculture is needed, but many farmers earn four-year bachelor's degrees. Every state university system in the United States has a land grant university with a school of agriculture. Courses of study commonly include agricultural economics, agricultural production, agronomy, animal science, business, crop and fruit science, dairy science, and horticulture.

Experience, Special Skills, and Personality Traits

Farmers must possess strong mathematical, organizational, mechanical, scientific, decision-making, business, stress management, communication, research, and computer skills. They are responsible, logical, persistent, self-motivated, detail-oriented, goal-oriented, physically fit, patient, and orderly. Farmers possess initiative, good judgment, determination, confidence, manual dexterity, and the ability to work with animals.

Unions and Associations

About 250,000 farm and ranch families throughout the United States are members of the Washington, D.C.–based National Farmers Union, which was established in 1902. The NFU's mission is "to protect and enhance the economic well-being and quality of life for family farmers and ranchers and their rural communities." While its membership is nationwide, the NFU has organized chapters in 26 states.

Tips for Entry

1. During high school, take courses in agriculture, horticulture, biology, botany, agronomy, earth sciences, accounting, math, business, computers, and mechanics.
2. Learn about programs offered by the National FFA Organization that promote skills needed for farming careers by visiting http://www.ffa.org.
3. Shadow a Dairy Farmer on the job to find out what the profession is like.
4. Review college catalog course descriptions in the departments of agriculture, agronomy, or plant and soil science to identify a curriculum that interests you.
5. In college, secure internships that provide valuable field and lab experience and increase your qualifications for entry-level employment.

Some of the information contained in this career profile was provided by the National FFA Organization.

FARM MANAGER

CAREER PROFILE

Duties: Assess farm resources; recommend operating procedures; implement management plans; hire, fire, instruct, and supervise workers; plan and execute marketing programs; purchase supplies and equipment; direct maintenance and upkeep of equipment and buildings; optimize land utilization

Alternate Title(s): Agricultural Manager; Ranch Manager

Salary Range: $27,000 to $150,000+

Employment Prospects: Fair

Advancement Prospects: Good

Prerequisites:

Education or Training—A bachelor of science degree in an agriculture-related field is often required.

Experience—Agriculture operations experience is required

Special Skills and Personality Traits—Interpersonal relations, verbal/written communications, negotiating, organization/planning, and budgeting/financial skills; knowledge of horticultural/crop production, soil fertility, drainage/irrigation, commodity marketing, farm equipment/labor issues, business law, and governmental regulations

Special Requirements—A real estate license is required to manage property in most states. Managers must pursue continuing education.

CAREER LADDER

```
┌─────────────────────────────────┐
│  Farm Management Executive or   │
│     Independent Contractor      │
└─────────────────────────────────┘

┌─────────────────────────────────┐
│          Farm Manager           │
└─────────────────────────────────┘

┌─────────────────────────────────┐
│             Farmer              │
└─────────────────────────────────┘
```

Position Description

Professional farm management can prove to be an exciting, educational career opportunity, providing wide exposure to various crops, geographic regions, and business situations. Farm Managers typically develop a very broad and intensive knowledge of the agricultural community.

Professional Farm Managers work for anyone who owns an agricultural property and does not have the time or expertise to operate it. Property owners share in any profits from the land, and the Farm Manager takes care of the work. Farm Managers strive to help landowners achieve the highest possible financial returns from their property while preserving and protecting the land.

Upon being hired, a Farm Manager typically assesses a farm's resources, recommends the best operating procedures, and implements a plan on behalf of the landowner. Generally, the Farm Manager will lease the property to an area farmer and will work with the farmer to determine the best operating procedures. Operating arrangements vary from cash rent leases, net share leases, and participating crop shares (50/50, for example) to custom farming or direct farming.

Farm management is beneficial to all of the parties involved. The landowner knows that the farmer is putting forth every effort to make the property produce to its full potential. The farmer has the opportunity to farm more property. This is especially helpful for young farmers who are trying to get their start but are not able to afford their own property. The landowner, the Farm Manager, and the farmer are all dedicated to preserving the value of the farm property in terms of fertility, soil erosion, condition of improvements, general productivity, and income earning potential.

The Farm Manager combines agricultural and business methods to operate one or more farms. It is common for the manager to be responsible for 20 to 35 or more units at a time. He or she directs the farming activities with the amount of authority designated by the owner to best make the farm productive and profitable. The size and type of farm or farms under management, and the policies of the owner(s), are influencing factors that determine the Farm Manager's duties. Managers may be free to run the farm according to their best judgment, or they may be guided by the owner in varying degrees.

In the case of large farms, managers spend most of their time organizing and administering work. This involves determining labor needs, the use of land, and planting, harvesting, and marketing schedules. Farm Managers also may direct methods in the care and feeding of livestock. They may be involved in the marketing of products, as well as maintaining financial records and performing bookkeeping tasks. In some instances, an accounting firm may be engaged by the owner to handle the finances, in which case the Farm Manager's financial responsibility may be to operate within a prescribed budget.

When several farms are under the manager's supervision, he or she spends time at each farm organizing resources for maximum profit and instructing and supervising workers regarding farm activities. This involves observing procedures, evaluating progress, and deciding on future activities.

In managing one or more farms in which products are to be sold exclusively to processing firms or others, there exists little or no need for the Farm Manager to be directly concerned with marketing problems. In other situations, he or she spends considerable time planning and executing marketing programs.

Farm Managers also are concerned with hiring, firing, and supervising labor; determining agricultural methods to be used; purchasing supplies and equipment; directing maintenance and upkeep of equipment and buildings; and utilizing the land to its best advantage.

Professional Farm Managers work for a variety of different employers, including banks, insurance companies, county tax/assessor offices, and independent fee appraisal offices. Many opportunities also exist with state and federal land management agencies, such as the Bureau of Land Management, Bureau of Indian Affairs, Bureau of Reclamation, Forest Service, and Fish and Wildlife departments.

Private farm management companies range in size from one-person firms owned by Farm Managers to large firms that typically are owned by financial institutions or banks. Both types of firms can be very effective in their chosen territories or crop specialties. Many firms also provide agricultural real estate brokerage and agricultural consulting services.

Farm Managers rely heavily on certain types of equipment during the course of their work, namely financial calculators, computers, and printers. Examples of the computer software they use include productivity suites that contain a word processor, spreadsheet, and database program; business accounting software; and Uniform Agricultural Appraisal Report software (optional, but accepted by some agencies and institutions). In addition to maps, atlases, and reliable transportation, Farm Managers also use standard 35mm or digital cameras.

Professional farm management positions normally require significant amounts of business travel to farm properties. Time is usually divided between an outdoor and office setting. The Farm Manager's hours are regulated according to the demand and need for his or her services. Working days are often longer than eight hours, particularly during busy periods of the year. Positions typically involve considerable walking, and managers may operate farm equipment when their job requires active labor participation.

Salaries

The Farm Manager's salary varies considerably, according to specific responsibilities and the size, type, and number of farms under management. During the mid-2000s, the American Society of Farm Managers and Rural Appraisers indicated that it was common for managers to receive annual salaries ranging from $27,000 for an entry-level position to $150,000 or more for those with a great deal of experience.

Employment Prospects

The number of opportunities in farming is limited because of the decline in the overall industry, especially among small farmers. However, management and technical skills are recognized as essential ingredients for success in modern farming. Competition will be keen and those with specialized training plus some experience or a background in agriculture will have the best chances to enter this occupational field.

Advancement Prospects

After gaining several years of experience, it is possible for Farm Managers to pursue supervisory or management roles in private organizations or government agencies. In addition, some may go into business for themselves as independent contractors or owners of their own farm management firms.

Education and Training

A bachelor of science degree in an agriculture-related area with experience and training in farm operations usually provides the best background for a career in farm management. A college education may include agricultural economics, business, and engineering; agronomy; animal science; poultry husbandry; and other related specialties.

Many Farm Managers have master's degrees in specialty fields.

Special Requirements

Most states require Farm Managers to obtain a real estate license in order to manage property. To stay current, Farm Managers also are required to participate in continuing professional education programs.

Experience, Special Skills, and Personality Traits

The typical Farm Manager has agricultural experience of some kind, having worked or been raised on a farming operation. Farm Managers need strong business skills in the areas of interpersonal relations, verbal/written communications, negotiating, organization/planning, budgeting/financial work, and business law. Managers also must possess agricultural expertise in areas such as horticultural/crop production, soil fertility, drainage/irrigation, commodity marketing, farm equipment, labor issues, and governmental regulations. Farm Managers must be highly motivated self-starters who can manage their assigned accounts with a minimum of direct supervision. Owner/client relations are critical to their success.

Unions and Associations

Professional Farm Managers have a nationwide trade organization, the American Society of Farm Managers and Rural Appraisers. Founded in 1929, the Denver, Colorado-based association offers its members strong support in the political and professional arena. It also provides continuing education and professional designations for members who wish to increase their professionalism.

Tips for Entry

1. During high school, complete a college entrance program with electives in agricultural subjects.
2. Join the National FFA Organization or a 4-H Club to gain training and experience in vocational agriculture.
3. Shadow a Farm Manager on the job to find out what the job is like.

Information contained in this career profile was provided by the American Society of Farm Managers and Rural Appraisers.

FISHER

CAREER PROFILE

Duties: Operate and maintain small boats and large fishing vessels; use fishing rods, traps, nets, and other devices to capture fish in the wild

Alternate Title(s): Fisherman

Salary Range: $322 to $775 per week

Employment Prospects: Poor

Advancement Prospects: Good

Prerequisites:

Education or Training—Fishers mainly learn on the job.

Experience—Not usually required for entry-level positions.

Special Skills and Personality Traits—Fishers possess endurance and manual dexterity; they are physically strong, patient, decisive, attentive, alert, and team-oriented.

Special Requirements—U.S. Coast Guard licenses may be required for certain Fisher professions.

CAREER LADDER

```
┌─────────────────────────────────────┐
│       Fishing Vessel Captain          │
└─────────────────────────────────────┘

┌─────────────────────────────────────┐
│    Boatswain or First/Second Mate     │
└─────────────────────────────────────┘

┌─────────────────────────────────────┐
│            Deck Hand                  │
└─────────────────────────────────────┘
```

Position Description

Humankind relies on fish for a variety of purposes, ranging from food and sport to pharmaceutical production and medical research. To fulfill these needs, fish are obtained via different methods. Working from both small boats and large fishing vessels, professional Fishers use fishing rods, traps, nets, and other devices to capture fish in their natural environments.

Many Fishers are part of sizable commercial fishing operations that involve large vessels. Capable of transporting thousands of pounds of fish at a time, vessels such as these take Fishers far away from shore and into deep waters. According to the U.S. Department of Labor, they are characterized by a formal crew structure that usually includes a captain or skipper, first mate, second mate, boatswain, and specialized deckhands.

On large fishing vessels, the captain is in charge of the planning and administrative aspects of the operation, including determining where and how the fishing will take place, the types of fish desired, selling the fish once the crew returns to shore, obtaining licenses and equipment, dealing with personnel matters, navigating the boat, and paying crew members.

The first and second mates assist the captain, providing backup in the area of ship operations and navigation. With leadership from the captain and assistance from the boatswain—a lead deckhand who functions in a supervisory capacity—mates direct the fishing crew in their efforts to catch, preserve, store, and ultimately unload fish. The mates also play a key role in operating and maintaining the ship, as well as overseeing or making repairs.

Fishers who are regular crew members or deck hands perform virtually every task involved to successfully carry out a commercial fishing operation. Some tasks, such as loading equipment and supplies, are related to getting a vessel ready to sail. While boatswains often operate the actual fishing equipment at sea, deckhands help to secure and store the catch. They also ensure that the vessel's engine and other equipment are in good working order, and that the ship's deck is clean. At shore, deckhands may help to unload fish.

Some Fishers work near land from small boats with a handful of crew members. During the course of their work day, they place different types of nets in lakes and bays, and across inlets and river mouths. They also use scrapes and dredges to collect scallops, oysters, and other shellfish and set traps to capture crabs and lobsters. A handful of commercial Fishers work underwater, using diving equipment to capture abalone, coral, sea urchins, sponges, and shellfish with spears and nets.

Commercial Fishers use a wide range of manual equipment to carry out their work, including rods, reels, lines, tackle, weights, hooks, blades, tongs, shovels, rakes, nets, traps, dredges, slings, markers, cables, and hoists. Fishing operations also involve the use of sensitive and high-tech equipment, including compasses, radar, and Global Positioning Satellite devices, as well as devices for determining depth and finding fish.

The U.S. Department of Labor indicated that approximately 38,000 fishing vessel operators were employed in 2004, half of whom were self-employed. The majority of fishing activities occur in coastal areas—especially Alaska, California, Louisiana, Massachusetts, and Virginia.

Fishing is among the most hazardous occupations, according to the U.S. Department of Labor. Fishers are exposed to all kinds of weather conditions, including fog and ice, which may endanger their lives or cause a fishing operation to be postponed or cancelled. In addition to the weather, Fishers are exposed to a range of sharp and dangerous fishing equipment, as well as potentially hazardous conditions such as slippery decks and collisions with other vessels. Making conditions even more dangerous is that immediate medical care is usually unavailable to injured Fishers.

Fishers often spend extended periods at sea, sometimes for several months at a time. In addition to being away from friends and family, living in a contained, dangerous environment with others can be stressful. Fishing is physically demanding, requiring candidates to be in good physical condition. Individuals who wish to work at sea should be relatively tolerant of motion sickness, and able to work very long hours.

Salaries

According to the U.S. Department of Labor, approximate weekly earnings for Fishers were $322 to $775 per week during the mid-2000s. This amount varies at different times of the year, given the seasonal nature of fishing. With this in mind, Fishers often supplement their earnings by working in other jobs during the slow season. Income for fishing vessel captains, or those with a stake in a commercial fishing operation, varies depending on numerous factors, including operating expenses and the price received for fish.

Employment Prospects

The U.S. Department of Labor anticipates that employment opportunities for Fishers and fishing vessel operators will decline through 2014. The *Occupational Outlook Handbook* explains that a number of factors, including more efficient operations, heightened competition from imports and domestically farmed fish, and the destruction of fish habitats and spawning grounds, are contributing to the decline.

Advancement Prospects

Fishers who make long-term commitments to the profession can rise through the ranks on a large commercial vessel, beginning as deckhands and advancing to boatswain, first mate, or ship engineer. Some start their own fishing enterprises and become captains of their own vessels, while others pursue administrative roles with the government or trade associations.

Education and Training

Beyond a Coast Guard class for those who plan to operate their own vessels, there are no educational requirements to pursue a career as a commercial Fisher. Skills are commonly learned on-the-job and through workshops. However, two-year vocational degrees are available from community colleges in coastal areas. Such programs offer hands-on and academic training related to fishing gear technology, seamanship, and vessel operations.

Special Requirements

The U.S. Coast Guard requires licenses for captains and mates on fishing vessels of 200 gross tons or more and for crew members on some fish-processing vessels.

Experience, Special Skills, and Personality Traits

Fishers can obtain entry-level employment with little or no experience. They must be mechanically inclined, physically strong, patient, decisive, attentive, and alert. Fishers also must possess endurance and manual dexterity and have the capability to work under pressure in dangerous conditions. The ability to function as part of a team is critical for Fishers, because crew members depend on one another in order to carry out a successful operation.

Unions and Associations

Some commercial Fishers belong to regional associations and unions. Such organizations often are focused on a specific type of fishing. Examples include the Deep Sea Fisher's Union of the Pacific; the North Pacific Fishing Vessel Owners' Association; and the Atlantic Offshore Lobstermen's Association.

Tips for Entry

1. In high school, take classes in biology, earth science, chemistry, math, and computers.
2. Gain exposure to the field through summer employment at a marina or marine supply store.
3. View the Marine Technology Society's listing of postsecondary fishing and related marine education programs at http://www.mtsociety.org.

Some of the information contained in this career profile was provided by the National FFA Organization.

FISH FARMER

Duties: Breed, grow, and harvest fish in captivity

Alternate Title(s): Aquaculturalist; Fish Hatchery Technician

Salary Range: $10,000 to $60,000+

Employment Prospects: Poor

Advancement Prospects: Good

Prerequisites:

Education or Training—A two-year aquaculture degree may be required.

Experience—Not usually required for entry-level positions

Special Skills and Personality Traits—Fish Farmers have strong mathematical, analytical, organizational, business, computer, scientific, technical, team, decision-making, and communication skills.

```
┌─────────────────────────────┐
│   Fish Hatchery Manager     │
└─────────────────────────────┘

┌─────────────────────────────┐
│       Fish Farmer           │
└─────────────────────────────┘

┌─────────────────────────────┐
│   Fish Hatchery Intern      │
└─────────────────────────────┘
```

Position Description

Humankind relies on fish for a variety of purposes, ranging from food and sport to pharmaceutical production and medical research. To fulfill these needs, fish are obtained via different methods. Fish Farmers breed, grow, and harvest fish in captivity. They work in fish and shellfish hatcheries and in related operations to produce fish for sale in consumer markets and for stocking lakes, ponds, streams, and oceans. In federal and state hatcheries, Fish Farmers also maintain fish hatcheries for research purposes.

Fish farming, also known as aquaculture, may involve a range of different fish and seafood. According to the National Aquaculture Association, "The US aquaculture industry is comprised of a wide diversity of plant and animal species, including trout, shellfish, salmon, catfish, marine shrimp, baitfish, hybrid striped bass, freshwater shrimp, tilapia, crawfish, alligators, ornamental fish, and many others." Farming methods vary, depending on the kind of fish or seafood involved. Some farms maintain captive brood stock (stock maintained as a source of population replacement or for the establishment of new populations) such as catfish in ponds or tanks. Other farms trap game fish, such as bass, in order to incubate the eggs and rear the fry or small fish in fish hatcheries.

Fish Farmers periodically inspect eggs and, using a syringe, pick out ones that are dead, infertile, or off-color. After the fish hatch, they transfer them to rearing tanks. To feed the fry, or small fish, workers use many techniques ranging from hand feeding to a blower that automatically scatters food over the water. Some marine species require live feeds such as phytoplankton and zoo plankton until they become large enough to subsist on artificial feeds.

Fish Farmers must keep a close watch on the fish to spot disease. They may add medicine to the food or water. In some parts of the United States, Fish Farmers have indoor tanks to keep young fish alive when winter weather prevails. Later, they transfer the maturing fish to outdoor tanks or farm ponds. To transport fish to the market, they use tanker trucks.

A number of Fish Farmers work in management roles. Using their knowledge of fish culture, fish hatchery managers develop and carry out methods for the rearing of fish in hatcheries. Much of their work consists of directing fish farming workers who perform the tasks of raising the fish. Fish hatchery managers often confer with fish pathologists, biologists, and other experts to get facts on the diseases, environmental requirements, and habits of fish. Fish hatchery managers study the life cycles of fish; they keep records on fish size, condition, and production and work to improve the hatching and growth rates and to prevent disease in hatcheries. Fish hatchery managers also prepare reports required by state and federal laws. They complete budget reports and records on income, costs, and expenditures.

Fish Farmers are especially concentrated in Arkansas, Idaho, Louisiana, Maryland, Massachusetts, Mississippi, Montana, northern Maine, and Virginia. Opportunities also exist at points along the Mississippi River. Finally, the Pacific Northwest is a large producer of cultured shellfish and some salmon.

Working conditions for Fish Farmers vary depending upon the facilities in which they work, as well as the specific tasks they perform. Managers or owners work in an office where they prepare reports and keep records. At other times they work outdoors, directing workers around holding pens or incubation installations. Workers may wade in water when releasing fish into lakes or streams. Shellfish farming workers work in shallow water along sea fronts and on boats.

Salaries

According to information posted on the Woods Hole Oceanographic Institution Sea Grant Program's Web site in 2006, those engaged in small fish farming start-ups may earn as little as $10,000 per year in the beginning, while those managing large aquaculture operations may earn $60,000 per year or more. Based on various job postings, salaries in the $25,000 to $30,000 range were common for experienced aquaculturists at cooperative research and extension services in the 2000s.

Employment Prospects

In 2006 the National FFA Organization reported that slight to declining growth was expected for Fish Farmers. Growth in fish imports was one limiting factor for this profession.

Advancement Prospects

Fish Farmers have good opportunities for advancement. After working in entry-level roles, some accept supervisory positions or become fish hatchery managers. In addition, some Fish Farmers go into business for themselves by starting their own fish farms.

Education and Training

According to the National FFA Organization, a two-year aquaculture degree is often required for those who wish to work as Fish Farmers. This is especially true in the case of fish hatchery managers.

Experience, Special Skills, and Personality Traits

Fish Farmers can obtain entry-level employment with little or no experience. However, preference is sometimes given to candidates pursuing an academic degree in aquaculture.

Fish Farmers must have strong mathematical, analytical, organizational, computer, scientific, sales, technical, management, decision-making, and communication skills. In addition to possessing sound judgment, good manual dexterity, determination, and confidence, successful Fish Farmers are creative and detail-oriented. They are knowledgeable of basic business principles and are capable of working independently or as part of a team.

Unions and Associations

Some Fish Farmers are members of the National Aquaculture Association (NAA), a nonprofit, producer-based association based in Charles Town, West Virginia. The NAA serves every area of the U.S. aquaculture community, providing "a unified national voice for aquaculture that ensures its sustainability, protects its profitability, and encourages its development in an environmentally responsible manner."

Tips for Entry

1. In high school, prospective Fish Farmers can prepare by pursuing classes in biology, earth sciences, chemistry, math, and computers.
2. Become a student member of the National Aquaculture Association. Memberships can be obtained by sending an e-mail to naa@frontiernet.net.
3. View the Marine Technology Society's listing of postsecondary fishing and related marine education programs at http://www.mtsociety.org.

Some of the information contained in this career profile was provided by the National FFA Organization.

LIVESTOCK FARMER

CAREER PROFILE

Duties: Breed and raise livestock; maintain knowledge of animal nutrition, reproduction, marketing, and health; select and mate breeding stock; tend to newborn animals; maintain records; inspect and examine livestock; prevent livestock problems; sell livestock at auctions or to individuals; negotiate with buyers; groom and exhibit livestock at shows; grow crops for animal feed

Alternate Title(s): Cattle Rancher; Diversified Livestock Producer; Horse Rancher

Salary Range: Variable

Employment Prospects: Poor

Advancement Prospects: Fair

Prerequisites:

    Education or Training—Two-year degree in agriculture

    Experience—An entry-level farm worker position can be obtained with little or no experience, but experience is required to manage or own a farm or ranch.

    Special Skills and Personality Traits—Strong mathematical, organizational, mechanical, scientific, decision-making, business, stress management, communication, research, and computer skills; responsible, logical, persistent, self-motivated, detail-oriented, goal-oriented, physically fit, patient, and orderly; possess initiative, good judgment, determination, confidence, manual dexterity, and the ability to work with animals

CAREER LADDER

```
┌─────────────────────────────┐
│      Farm Manager or         │
│   Agricultural Consultant    │
└─────────────────────────────┘

┌─────────────────────────────┐
│      Livestock Farmer        │
└─────────────────────────────┘

┌─────────────────────────────┐
│          Intern              │
└─────────────────────────────┘
```

Position Description

Broadly speaking, farmers raise crops and livestock for human consumption. They are businesspeople who invest in and profit from their activities. Farmers must have a high degree of knowledge and skill in business management, as well as the technical knowledge and skills of agriculture.

The farming profession involves establishing output goals, determining financial constraints, and monitoring production and marketing. Farmers may be involved with large corporate farms or small individual family farms. They may own or lease the land used to produce their products. Farmers operate and maintain daily farming operations, including the care of animals, crops, machinery, finances, and labor. In addition, they also plan for future farm enterprises.

Livestock Farmers breed and raise livestock, such as beef cattle, dairy cattle, goats, horses, reindeer, sheep, and swine, for such purposes as the sale of meat, for riding or working stock breeding, for show, or for products such as milk, wool, and hair. They are knowledgeable in areas of animal nutrition, reproduction, marketing, and health.

Livestock Farmers select and mate breeding stock to breed for the qualities of offspring desired. They perform the necessary management practices on newborn animals, and they maintain the records needed for making breeding and selection decisions. They also determine quantity and types of feed needed, and perform the necessary approved practices that promote efficient and rapid growth while maintaining the health of the livestock herds.

Livestock Farmers regularly inspect and examine livestock and make decisions that prevent problems and correct existing problems. They sell the breeding stock at auctions or to individuals, and they negotiate with buyers for sale of animals for meat. They also may groom and exhibit livestock at livestock shows, or they may grow crops to provide some or all of the feed needed for the livestock herds.

In addition to those who raise many different types of animals, some Livestock Farmers specialize in one type of animal. Examples include cattle ranchers and horse ranchers. In the United States, there are basically two types of cattle producers: purebred and commercial. Purebred cattle producers produce breeding stock for area commercial producers. They are concerned with developing and merchandising a product that will improve the quality of offspring produced by commercial breeders. The commercial producer is in business to produce beef for consumption by the world's population. Commercial producers will sell their calves at weaning or shortly thereafter.

There are many different types of horse ranches in the United States. Purebred producers are in the business of producing breeding stock and animals for show. They are concerned with developing and merchandising a product that will improve the quality of others' herds and provide a high-quality show animal. Ranchers also may raise animals for the average horseperson to ride and show for pleasure and fun. They typically sell their horses after weaning, when they have been "green broke" or trained to the specifications of the buyer. Horse ranchers also may board and train horses for other people.

In addition to raising livestock on farms and ranches, this area of the agricultural field also includes employment opportunities in livestock yards. Workers in this setting perform a range of different feed lot activities, such as marking, de-horning, and castrating cattle; herding cattle to and from pens; applying prescribed medication; cleaning pens and shelters; and stacking and loading hay or other bedding.

Livestock yard supervisors inspect cattle, pens, shelters, equipment, and feed supplies. They note tasks to be done and assign them to crews or individual workers. They may perform other duties, such as record keeping and buying and selling of feedlot cattle. In addition, they may be responsible for health and sanitation management.

In addition to being knowledgeable about animals, Livestock Farmers also must be good businesspeople. This requirement calls for them to be knowledgeable of the market and the selling/distribution processes needed to maximize the value of their livestock. Livestock Farmers must be able to wear many hats to be successful. Managing money and a budget well enough to realize a profit from year to year can be a challenge. Starting from scratch is difficult and cost-prohibitive; most farmers or ranchers in this field either work for someone else or have had the operation in the family for several generations.

Livestock Farmers must consider many factors at once when making decisions, including market and weather conditions, feed prices, and operational costs. Other decisions Livestock Farmers make range from choosing what types of new technology would be the most suitable or beneficial for their farm to deciding when to replace or buy new equipment.

Livestock Farmers also must stay current on new varieties of equipment, as well as new processing and marketing methods. They also maintain extensive financial records and inventories. Many Livestock Farmers arrange for credit from banks in order to purchase farm equipment, machines, and supplies. In addition, they also are charged with hiring, training, supervising, and coordinating the activities of other farm and ranch workers.

Generally speaking, the farming profession is both complicated and risky. Farmers constantly face unpredictable threats, such as fluctuating weather and market conditions and insect infestations. In addition, they must contend with complex environmental rules and regulations at the state and federal government levels.

The vast majority of livestock farming jobs are located in rural areas, and farmers spend a great deal of their time outdoors, working in fields or barns. In general, the work of farmers is often strenuous; their work hours are frequently long, and their days off are sometimes infrequent. Of those who work full time, half work 60 or more hours a week.

Unlike crop farmers, who are busiest during the planting and harvest periods, Livestock Farmers are busy year-round, as they must continually feed and care for animals. This aspect of their work makes vacations or time away from the farm or ranch difficult. Nevertheless, these disadvantages are often outweighed by the opportunities for living in a more rural area, working outdoors, being self-employed, and making a living by working the land.

Salaries

Income from livestock farming varies considerably. Profits can fluctuate greatly from year to year based on several variables, such as market value, weather conditions, and feed prices. According to the 2006–07 edition of the U.S. Department of Labor's *Occupational Outlook Handbook*, the U.S. Department of Agriculture reported that farm operator households earned an average net cash farm business income of $15,603 in 2004. This figure does not include government subsidies or other forms of supplemental income.

Employment Prospects

Through 2014, the U.S. Department of Labor anticipates that many farms will go out of business because of falling prices for agricultural goods. This trend will promote further consolidation and result in a smaller number of large, well-funded farms dominating the industry. Productivity increases also will cause the overall demand for farm laborers to fall, as farms gain the ability to produce more with fewer workers.

Advancement Prospects

Some Livestock Farmers may begin their careers at a very young age, working on a family farm. In college, they may work as interns in areas such as production, sales and marketing, and pest management. Some Livestock Farmers may go on to become farm managers or agricultural consultants. Others may pursue careers in sales, government affairs, or communications.

Education and Training

According to the U.S. Department of Labor, the complex nature of agriculture now requires prospective farmers to receive formal training. At minimum, a two-year degree in agriculture is needed, but many farmers earn four-year bachelor's degrees. Every state university system in the United States has a land grant university with a school of agriculture. Courses of study commonly include agricultural economics, agricultural production, agronomy, animal science, business, crop and fruit science, dairy science, and horticulture.

Experience, Special Skills, and Personality Traits

Farmers must possess strong mathematical, organizational, mechanical, scientific, decision-making, business, stress management, communication, research, and computer skills. They are responsible, logical, persistent, self-motivated, detail-oriented, goal-oriented, physically fit, patient, and orderly. Farmers possess initiative, good judgment, determination, confidence, and manual dexterity and are able to work with animals.

Unions and Associations

About 250,000 farm and ranch families throughout the United States are members of the Washington, D.C.–based National Farmers Union, which was established in 1902. The NFU's mission is "to protect and enhance the economic well-being and quality of life for family farmers and ranchers and their rural communities." While its membership is nationwide, the NFU has organized chapters in 26 states.

Tips for Entry

1. During high school, take courses in agriculture, horticulture, biology, botany, agronomy, earth sciences, accounting, math, business, computers, and mechanics.
2. Learn about programs offered by the National FFA Organization that promote skills needed for farming careers by visiting http://www.ffa.org.
3. Shadow a Livestock Farmer on the job to find out what the profession is like.
4. Review college catalog course descriptions in the departments of agriculture, agronomy, or plant and soil science to identify a curriculum that interests you.
5. In college, secure internships that provide valuable field and lab experience and increase your qualifications for entry-level employment.

Some of the information contained in this career profile was provided by the National FFA Organization.

RURAL APPRAISER

CAREER PROFILE

Duties: Estimate the value of improved or unimproved rural real estate; research, verify, and analyze property information; prepare narrative reports for clients

Alternate Title(s): Appraiser; Agricultural Appraiser

Salary Range: $30,000 to $100,000

Employment Prospects: Good

Advancement Prospects: Good

Prerequisites:

Education or Training—A bachelor's degree in agriculture, agricultural economics, real estate, or business is helpful but not required

Experience—Employment at the trainee level does not require experience.

Special Skills and Personality Traits—Data interpretation and communication skills; knowledge of agriculture, land values, and economic conditions; honest, self-confident, accurate, detail oriented

Special Requirements—Many states have licensure and continuing education requirements.

CAREER LADDER

```
┌─────────────────────────────────┐
│   Farm Manager or Consultant     │
└─────────────────────────────────┘

┌─────────────────────────────────┐
│        Rural Appraiser           │
└─────────────────────────────────┘

┌─────────────────────────────────┐
│     Rural Appraiser Trainee      │
└─────────────────────────────────┘
```

Position Description

Professional rural appraisal can prove to be an exciting, educational career opportunity. It has something to offer for a wide variety of people, including those who are just starting their careers, professionals outside of agriculture who wish to expand their expertise, and college-educated individuals who come from a family farming background. Anyone interested in real estate, valuation issues, agricultural issues, or natural resources should consider the agricultural appraisal field.

While some appraisers evaluate several different types of real estate, others specialize in the appraisal of residential, commercial, or industrial types of properties. Rural Appraisers estimate the value of improved or unimproved rural real estate. Appraisals generally are made to establish investment or loan values when property is being bought or sold. However, appraisals also may be needed for determining taxes, fair compensation and condemnation proceedings, rental payments or lease provisions, market value, legal distribution of property among individuals, or determining property assets of individuals, firms, or corporations.

Rural Appraisers research and analyze information on a subject property, including comparable sale information, in order to estimate the property's value. Depending on the individual assignment, the Rural Appraiser is most often responsible for estimating values of and for land and improvements; easements; condemnation; natural resources such as water rights, timber, or minerals; partial interests; and personal property.

Professional Rural Appraisers are needed to satisfy requirements for such things as eminent domain; estate planning, gift valuations, or inheritance issues; litigation involving land valuations, damages, or crop losses; partitions; loan purposes; expert witness services; and assistance to banks and trustees in handling real estate holdings.

Rural Appraisers estimate the value of a specific piece of agricultural property through an inspection procedure and an evaluation of the properties' attributes. They then complete a narrative report for the client that includes, at minimum, the following information:

- Identification of property
- Purposes of appraisal
- Value of definition
- Effective date of appraisal
- Definition of estate under appraisal
- County, regional and neighborhood data
- Description of subject property
- Highest and best use, sales comparison approach, income approach, cost approach
- Correlation and conclusions
- Certificate of appraiser
- Maps, photos, and charts
- General information such as report format, explanations, and data presentation

Importantly, the appraiser's report must be written in such a way that the reader can adequately understanding the conclusion, as well as any limiting conditions or assumptions.

Rural Appraisers also collect information about the type of rent or ownership, along with data regarding a property's condition, maintenance, and cost. This information is then analyzed, along with the cost of real estate taxes, insurance, maintenance, services, and other expenses. After all of the necessary information has been gathered and analyzed, the appraiser then estimates the property value based on the information that has been collected. In legal disputes regarding eminent domain (condemnation) procedures, the appraiser may be asked to serve as an expert witness in court proceedings.

There are many career pathways into the agricultural appraisal field, including but not limited to college graduates with degrees in business, economic, or agricultural fields; those with institutional lending experience; people with agricultural backgrounds; and individuals currently involved in other professional real estate-related fields such as real estate sales, agricultural consulting, and property management. In addition, current real estate appraisers may wish to pursue agricultural appraisal as a specialty.

Professional Rural Appraisers serve a number of different customers, including loan officers, trusts, attorneys, accountants, municipalities, government agencies, and private individuals. Employment opportunities for qualified appraiser candidates exist in established independent appraisal offices, state and federal government agencies, banks, property management offices, insurance companies, and with county and state tax assessor offices.

Most Rural Appraisers are employed by organizations and work a five-day week or longer. Their hours are irregular and may range from less than 25 to more than 50 hours a week. Rural Appraisers spend the majority of their work time in office settings where they complete reports, study data, and maintain records. However, they do travel to prop-

erty sites to make inspections and examinations. Considerable standing and walking is required while measuring and evaluating properties. When appraising rural properties, the appraiser usually does not wear a three-piece suit, but would be more inclined to wear boots, jeans, and a sports shirt. Sometimes, working conditions involve exposure to unusual types of weather conditions.

Salaries

According to the 2006–07 edition of the U.S. Department of Labor's *Occupational Outlook Handbook*, in mid-2004 salaries for real estate appraisers and assessors ranged from $22,300 to more than $81,240. Earnings of real estate appraisers vary considerably, depending on their experience and training and the geographic location in which they work. Generally, appraisers make less money in rural markets.

According to data from the American Society of Farm Managers and Rural Appraisers, annual salaries of trainee Rural Appraisers range from about $30,000 to $40,000. Earnings increase as the individual gains experience and may exceed $100,000 after several years of employment. The same level of compensation applies to independent (self-employed) Rural Appraisers. After experience, they may earn in excess of $100,000 when working for federal and state agencies, as well as insurance companies. Generally speaking, salaries are contingent upon an appraiser's workload.

Employment Prospects

In most areas of the country, the employment outlook for qualified Rural Appraisers is expected to be good in the near future. There is a lesser demand for Rural Appraisers in the eastern states due to the lack of rural property, while demand is stronger in other parts of the country. Employment opportunities will result from the need to replace appraisers who retire or leave the profession. However, competition for available positions is expected to be keen and employment prospects will be best for persons who are well trained and experienced.

Advancement Prospects

After entering the field as a trainee and gaining general experience, some Rural Appraisers specialize in areas such as agribusiness valuation, permanent crops, dry land or irrigated crops, or specialized agricultural structures. The agricultural appraisal profession provides opportunities for advancement and expansion into other real estate related fields such as sales, farm management, and consulting.

Education and Training

A bachelor's degree with a major in agriculture, agricultural economics, and real estate or business is helpful, but not required, for those who wish to become Rural Appraisers. Emphasis of courses in real estate, urban land, economics, business, and journalism is helpful. Many colleges, universities, and junior colleges offer courses in agriculture, real estate and rural appraising.

Special Requirements

Most states require various types of licensing for real estate appraisers, even though most appraisers are required to have a sales or broker's license. Continuing education for appraisers is also now required at the state level and is administrated through the real estate appraisal board.

Experience, Special Skills, and Personality Traits

Entry-level employment at the trainee level can be secured with little or no experience. Individuals wishing to become Rural Appraisers should have an interest in and be capable of acquiring knowledge of land values, economic conditions, and interpreting data. They should have a sound agricultural background and possess honesty, integrity, self-confidence, and tact. Rural Appraisers place an emphasis on accuracy and attention to detail. In addition, they are able to express themselves clearly, both orally and in writing.

Unions and Associations

Professional Rural Appraisers have a nationwide trade organization, the American Society of Farm Managers and Rural Appraisers. Founded in 1929, the Denver, Colorado-based association offers its members strong support in the political and professional arena. It also provides continuing education and professional designations for members who wish to increase their professionalism.

Tips for Entry

1. During high school, complete a college entrance program.
2. Shadow a Rural Appraiser on the job to find out what the profession is like.
3. Join a professional appraisal society and take advantage of the advanced training offered. This will provide an edge in preparing for entry-level employment.

Information contained in this career profile was provided by the American Society of Farm Managers and Rural Appraisers.

FORESTRY

FORESTER

CAREER PROFILE

Duties: Plan and supervise forestry projects; develop short- and long-term forest management plans; negotiate contracts; supervise others; ensure compliance with government regulations; monitor tree growth rates and species prevalence; prepare land for new tree growth; prevent and control forest fires; minimize environmental impact of timber cutting and removal

Alternate Title(s): Area Forester; Chief Unit Forester; Environmental Protection Forester; Fire Prevention Forester; Regional Forester; Resource Forester; Service Forester; Urban Forester

Salary Range: $25,000 to $72,050+

Employment Prospects: Poor

Advancement Prospects: Good

Prerequisites:

    Education or Training—Bachelor's degree in forestry, range management, or related field

    Experience—Seasonal, part-time, or internship positions help entry-level Foresters secure full-time employment.

    Special Skills and Personality Traits—Knowledge of science and the outdoors; systems perspective; proficiency in statistics; familiarity with laws and regulations; active learner; self-reliant; team player; ability to supervise, manage, direct, and motivate others; solid decision-making, written and oral communication, critical thinking, and problem-solving skills

    Special Requirements—Some states require Foresters to meet licensing or registration criteria.

CAREER LADDER

```
┌─────────────────────────────────┐
│   Chief Forester or Consultant   │
└─────────────────────────────────┘

┌─────────────────────────────────┐
│            Forester              │
└─────────────────────────────────┘

┌─────────────────────────────────┐
│      Forestry Technician         │
└─────────────────────────────────┘
```

Position Description

Forestry is the science, art, and practice of creating, managing, using, and conserving forests in a sustainable manner to meet desired goals, needs, and values. In simpler terms, the forestry profession focuses on caring for trees, soils, water, wildlife, and other forest elements, for both current and future generations.

There are a number of specialties within the forestry profession, including forest management, pest management, disease management, fire management, wildlife and fisheries management, wilderness management, watershed management, research and teaching, forest recreation, agro- and urban forestry, policy and economics, communications, technology applications, genetics, and environmental education.

A Forester is a uniquely qualified professional who cares for trees and forests. Foresters go to college to learn the art and practice of forestry; through comprehensive coursework and practical field experience they acquire the knowledge, skills, and abilities to practice their profession.

There are several exciting career paths to pursue within the field of forestry. As forest managers or consultants, Foresters grow trees for forest products like lumber, paper, boxes, or any of the more than 5,000 things that come from the forest. Foresters in this role also are responsible for water quality, wildlife habitats, endangered plants and animals, recreational issues, and ensuring aesthetic beauty.

Some Foresters work in the field of urban forestry. Urban and community forests are made up of trees and associated vegetation within the environs of populated places—from the smallest villages to the largest cities. Urban foresters help communities to conserve forests and "green spaces" as they develop urban areas. Foresters also work as researchers. In such roles they may discover ways to grow trees faster, healthier, or taller. In addition, forestry specialists serve on college and university faculties, and run school forests and nature centers.

In addition to working in the field and the classroom, Foresters also work on forest policy issues in the halls of Congress and with state legislatures. They also can be found at local newspaper offices, helping people to understand the complexities of conserving forested resources.

There are a number of common tasks that Foresters perform. These include planning and supervising forestry projects; developing short- and long-term forest management plans; negotiating contracts for leasing, managing, and harvesting forest land; supervising other workers; making sure that forestry contracts and activities are in compliance with government regulations; monitoring the growth rates and prevalence of different tree species; preparing areas of land for new tree growth through the use of herbicides, controlled burning, and heavy equipment; preventing and controlling forest fires; and making sure timber cutting and removal efforts are carried out optimally, with minimal environmental impact.

In the field, Foresters use a variety of tools to carry out their work. As the U.S. Department of Labor explains in its *Occupational Outlook Handbook*: "Clinometers measure the height of trees, diameter tapes measure the diameter, and increment borers and bark gauges measure the growth of trees so that timber volumes can be computed and growth rates estimated. Remote sensing (aerial photographs and other imagery taken from airplanes and satellites) and geographic information systems (GIS) data often are used for mapping large forest areas and for detecting widespread trends of forest and land use. Once the map is generated, the data are digitized to create a computerized inventory of information required to manage the forest land and its resources. Moreover, hand-held computers, global positioning systems (GPS), and World Wide Web–based applications are used extensively."

Foresters also use fire as a tool for reducing underbrush and preparing planting sites. In addition, they work with and

supervise firefighters and smoke jumpers, who control wildfire that threatens both forests and residential areas.

Like other conservationists, including range managers, Foresters are subject to a variety of working conditions. While some may spend a portion of their time in a laboratory, classroom, or office setting, Foresters spend a considerable amount of time working outdoors in all kinds of weather—including rain, extreme heat, and bitter cold. This profession can be physically demanding; in addition to walking long distances, Foresters must sometimes travel over rough terrain and through dense brush and forests. Therefore, being in good or excellent physical condition may be a job requirement.

Foresters have a variety of employment scenarios from which to choose. America's forests are owned by private individuals (49 percent), the public (42 percent), and private industries (9 percent). Foresters work with and for all of these owners to develop and implement management plans. Owners of tree farms or woodlots frequently hire forestry consultants to manage their land. These consultants, who may work for themselves or for large firms, offer services ranging from estate planning to writing management plans to marketing timber.

A large number of Foresters work in the government sector. Major federal government employers include the U.S. Forest Service (Department of Agriculture), the Bureau of Land Management, the Park Service (Department of the Interior), and branches of the military. Foresters also work for state agencies, usually in departments of natural resources, and at the community level, often as urban Foresters.

Private industry employers include manufacturers of paper and wood products, as well as smaller sawmills. Foresters working with these companies are often focused on growing trees faster and stronger and developing more environmentally friendly methods of harvesting trees and making forest products.

Not-for-profit organizations, ranging from local to national in scope, also employ Foresters. In addition to working in educational roles with colleges and universities, Foresters also serve as consultants for banks and law firms specializing in land investment or estate law.

Salaries

Salaries for Foresters vary, depending on factors such as level of education, years of experience, employer group (government, industry, university, etc.), and geographic region. According to the 2006–07 edition of the Department of Labor's *Occupational Outlook Handbook*, in mid-2004 annual salaries for Foresters ranged from less than $29,770 to more than $72,050, with a median of $48,230. In general, those with a bachelor's degree in forestry or natural resources can expect to make about $25,000 to $35,000 upon graduation, according to the Society of American Foresters. Starting salaries for those with a master's or doctorate degree are $40,000 to $50,000, respectively.

Employment Prospects

The U.S. Department of Labor anticipates slower-than-average job growth for conservation scientists and Foresters through 2014. According to the *Occupational Outlook Handbook*, government cutbacks mean that the best opportunities will exist with consulting firms in the private sector. The publication explains that "demand will be spurred by a continuing emphasis on environmental protection, responsible land management, and water-related issues. Growing interest in developing private lands and forests for recreational purposes will generate additional jobs for foresters and conservation scientists. Fire prevention is another area of growth for these two occupations."

Advancement Prospects

Some Foresters begin their careers as forestry technicians and advance on the career ladder after gaining additional experience and academic training. After securing an entry-level position, Foresters may advance to senior or supervisory roles in the field, while others pursue careers as executives or consultants.

Education and Training

The minimum educational requirement for professional Foresters is a bachelor's degree in forestry, range management, or a related field, while technicians opt for a two-year technical degree. Forestry programs combine technical and scientific courses with training in policy and economics, quantitative methods, and communications. Forestry students learn about forest ecology, inventory, water quality, wildlife habitat, and the identification of tree species. Most forestry courses add advanced computer applications such as geographic information systems and resource assessment programs. Forestry programs also teach students how to integrate biological, social, political, economic, and historical considerations into forest management decisions.

Special Requirements

While some states require Foresters to meet licensing or registration criteria, many states have no such requirements. In states that do, an examination is often required to obtain a license, and candidates must meet certain criteria related to education and forestry experience.

Experience, Special Skills, and Personality Traits

Entry-level Foresters can increase their employment prospects by completing internships or working in seasonal or part-time positions while in college. These are prime opportunities to gain valuable hands-on experience.

A number of skills and personality traits are essential for Foresters. In addition to sound judgment and decision-making abilities, successful Foresters must be active learners with solid knowledge of science and the outdoors. They must have excellent critical thinking and problem-solving skills, as well as the ability to take a systems perspective and determine how the outcome of a process can be affected by changing different variables. In addition, Foresters must be self-reliant and capable of working independently at remote sites, and also on teams that involve communication with others.

Report writing, documentation, and interaction with others are important aspects of this profession. Therefore, strong written and oral communication skills are required, along with proficiency in statistics. In addition to scientific knowledge, Foresters must be familiar with applicable laws and regulations. Finally, because many Foresters oversee staff and volunteers, they must be able to supervise, manage, direct, and motivate others.

Unions and Associations

The Society of American Foresters is the world's largest professional society for Foresters. In addition to natural resource professionals and researchers, this leading scientific and educational organization includes CEOs, administrators, educators, and students among its members.

Tips for Entry

1. In high school, take courses that provide exposure to the sciences, including Earth science, biology, and zoology, as well as courses in mathematics, chemistry, physics, and English.
2. Make sure that your personal goals, talents, and lifestyle requirements dovetail with the requirements to become a Forester.
3. Shadow a Forester on the job to discover what their work is really like.
4. Search the Society of American Foresters' listing of Accredited Professional Forestry Degree Programs at http://www.safnet.org/education/pforschools.cfm.
5. As a high school student and college undergraduate, volunteer for a conservation organization to gain hands-on experience.

Information contained in this career profile was provided by the Society of American Foresters

FORESTRY TECHNICIAN

CAREER PROFILE

Duties: Conserve water, soil, and other natural resources; survey, measure, and map out sections of forest; maintain areas of tree growth; control weed and insect populations; maintain recreation areas, campsites, and other facilities; prevent, detect, and extinguish forest fires; train and educate others; work with data; participate in logging activities

Alternate Title(s): Conservation Technician; Conservationist; Forest Ranger; Forest Technician; Forestry Aide; Natural Resources Technician; Park Ranger; Resource Manager; Resource Technician; Wildlife Technician

Salary Range: $25,338 to $62,291+

Employment Prospects: Poor

Advancement Prospects: Good

Prerequisites:

Education or Training—High school diploma, GED, or associate's degree in forest technology

Experience—Internships or seasonal/part-time positions can increase chances of finding entry-level employment.

Special Skills and Personality Traits—Knowledge of science and the outdoors; systems perspective; proficiency in statistics; awareness of laws and regulations; active learner; self-reliant; team player; ability to supervise and motivate others; solid decision-making, written and oral communication, critical thinking, and problem-solving skills

Special Requirements—Valid driver's license

CAREER LADDER

```
┌─────────────────────────┐
│       Supervisor        │
└─────────────────────────┘

┌─────────────────────────┐
│    Forestry Technician  │
└─────────────────────────┘

┌─────────────────────────┐
│         Intern          │
└─────────────────────────┘
```

Position Description

Forestry is the science, art, and practice of creating, managing, using, and conserving forests in a sustainable manner to meet desired goals, needs, and values. In simpler terms, the forestry profession focuses on caring for trees, soils, water, wildlife, and other forest elements for both current and future generations.

Forestry Technicians play a key role in the fields of conservation and forestry. Working under the direction of foresters, they perform a wide range of tasks to care for the environment. Their responsibilities range from forest protection, monitoring, and management to fish and wildlife management, timber harvesting, and parks management. Some Forestry Technicians are involved in education, training, and research.

While most Forestry Technicians work in traditional settings, such as rural areas and forests, in the 2000s many are specializing in nontraditional areas, such as urban forestry. Urban and community forests are made up of trees and associated vegetation within the environs of populated places, from the smallest villages to the largest cities.

There are a number of common tasks that Forestry Technicians perform. These can be grouped into a number of broad categories. In the area of forest evaluation and maintenance,

Forestry Technicians provide technical assistance to help conserve water, soil, and other natural resources. In addition, they survey, measure, and map out sections of forest in order to identify specific areas that have been cut, burned, or designated for timber sales or experimental purposes.

Forestry Technicians may thin areas of tree growth, prune individual trees, and cut down diseased trees. Working with chemicals, they also treat areas of the forest where weeds and insects have become problematic. Forestry Technicians frequently clear brush and fallen trees from forest areas, campsites, trails, and roadways following bad weather or fires and then plant and cultivate seedlings as part of reforestation efforts. They also may be called upon to maintain recreation areas, campsites, and other facilities. Such tasks can involve cleaning, stacking firewood, making repairs, and installing signs or fences.

In the area of forest protection, Forestry Technicians work alone or with foresters, range managers, and other conservation scientists to manage a variety of different initiatives. These may include coordinating programs for protecting wildlife habitats, detecting forest fires, training fire crews, and educating the public about fire prevention. Forestry Technicians also patrol parks and forests, and enforce regulations related to accident prevention, fire safety, and environmental protection.

Many Forestry Technicians spend a considerable amount of time working with data. In this area, they gather a wide range of forest-related information. Examples include data about the size and condition of land tracts, tree populations and species, the mortality of tree seedlings, insect damage, diseases, and potential hazards. Technicians may use the data they collect to develop plans for thinning forest areas, designating logging areas, or creating new access roads.

Finally, many Forestry Technicians are involved in logging initiatives. In this area they evaluate, grade, and mark trees for cutting, monitor the activities of contractors and loggers who harvest timber from the forest, record the number of logs taken to sawmills, and help to deliver forest products to buyers.

In the field, Forestry Technicians use a variety of tools to carry out their work. These include hand tools such as axes and shovels, fishing nets, special meters that measure soil moisture, and reforestation equipment such as tree planter spades, plug spades, and brush hooks. They also use computer software. In addition to database and inventory management applications, Forestry Technicians use a variety of specialized programs for creating maps and geomechanical design, as well as ones for remote sensing and modeling the behavior of fire. Forestry Technicians may be required to wear uniforms on the job, as well as protective clothing and gear like gloves, hard hats, and safety goggles.

The majority of Forestry Technician jobs are found at private and national parks and forests, as well as lumber-producing forests, located in southeastern and western United States. According to the U.S. Department of Labor, Forestry Technicians held about 33,000 jobs in 2004. Of these, 75 percent worked for the federal government, while state governments employed another 13 percent. Opportunities in the private sector are limited, but may be found with forestry consulting firms; forestry contractors; colleges and universities; pulp, paper, and sawmilling companies; equipment manufacturers and distributors; and trade/professional organizations in the areas of forestry and wood products.

Forestry Technicians often work regular 40-hour weeks. However, employment may be seasonal. In addition, long or unusual hours are required when technicians are called upon to fight forest fires. Like foresters, Forestry Technicians are subject to a variety of working conditions. They spend a considerable amount of time working outdoors in all kinds of weather—including rain, extreme heat, and bitter cold. This profession can be physically demanding; in addition to walking long distances, Forestry Technicians must sometimes travel over rough terrain and through dense brush and forests. Therefore, being in good or excellent physical condition may be a job requirement.

Forestry Technicians face a number of potential occupational hazards including animals that may bite, insects that may sting, burns that can result from working with or trying to extinguish fires, as well as cuts and scrapes resulting from saws and other tools or equipment. Although Forestry Technicians frequently work in remote areas where they are isolated from others, they do interact with foresters, fellow technicians, loggers, graduate foresters from universities, government officials, students, and members of the public.

Salaries

Salaries for Forestry Technicians vary, depending on factors such as level of education, years of experience, employer group (government, industry, university, etc.), and geographic region. According to the 2006–07 edition of the Department of Labor's *Occupational Outlook Handbook*, in mid-2004 forest and conservation technicians earned median hourly wages of $13.14. However, based on data obtained from various job postings, in 2006 annual salaries ranged from $25,338 to $62,291 or more.

Employment Prospects

The U.S. Department of Labor anticipates slower-than-average job growth for Forestry Technicians through 2014. According to the *Occupational Outlook Handbook*, this is because of federal government cutbacks in general, as well as reduced timber management activity on federal land. Although limited opportunities exist within the private sector, some new job growth may occur with local and state governments—namely within specialized areas such as geographic information systems (satellite-based location systems) and urban forestry. A growing emphasis on specific conservation issues, including environmental protection and the preservation of water resources, may also provide employment opportunities.

Advancement Prospects

Some Forestry Technicians gain their first hands-on experience as interns while pursuing a two-year degree. Others begin with no experience and receive all of their training on the job by assisting experienced technicians. Forestry Technicians may advance to supervisory roles after gaining more experience.

Advancement may happen more formally in government positions. In some states forest commissions place Forest Technician positions at different levels. Level I positions commonly require a high school diploma and focus on more routine tasks, including fire suppression and prevention. Level II positions may involve more complex tasks like prescribed burning, wildlife management, and operating heavy equipment, and usually require a two-year degree in forestry or an equivalent amount of experience. Finally, Level III technicians often supervise lower-level technicians. In addition to holding two-year degrees, they receive advanced forest firefighting and law enforcement training and are responsible for enforcing laws and directing firefighting operations. Level III technicians also may assist foresters with a number of tasks, including harvest site inspection, timber marking, and planting.

Education and Training

The minimum education requirement for employment as a Forestry Technician is a GED or high school diploma. However, a two-year associate's degree in forest technology—available from a community college or technical school—is required for many positions. A number of two-year degree programs are accredited by the Society of American Foresters. Degree programs provide a combination of field and lab experience, and focus mainly on the areas of forestry, forest technology, forest resource management, and environmental studies.

Special Requirements

A valid driver's license is required for many Forestry Technician positions.

Experience, Special Skills, and Personality Traits

Entry-level Forestry Technicians can increase their employment prospects by completing internships or working in seasonal or part-time positions while in college. Many forest technology students work in state or federal forests and parks during the summer months to gain valuable hands-on experience. In particular, exposure to fighting wildfires is especially valuable.

A number of skills and personality traits are essential for Forestry Technicians. In addition to sound judgment and decision-making abilities, successful technicians must be active learners with solid knowledge of science and the outdoors. They must have excellent critical thinking and problem-solving skills, as well as the ability to take a systems perspective and determine how the outcome of a process can be affected by changing different variables. Forest Technicians have to be precise in their work, because mistakes can cause significant damage to plant and animal life. In addition, they must be self-reliant and capable of working independently at remote sites, and also on teams that involve communication with others.

Report writing, documentation, and interaction with others are important aspects of this profession. Therefore, strong written and oral communication skills are required, along with proficiency in statistics. Forestry Technicians must be aware of applicable laws and regulations. Finally, technicians who pursue supervisory positions must be able to supervise and motivate others.

Unions and Associations

The Society of American Foresters is the world's largest professional society for foresters and Forestry Technicians. In addition to natural resource professionals and researchers, this leading scientific and educational organization includes CEOs, administrators, educators, and students among its members.

Tips for Entry

1. In high school, take courses that provide exposure to the sciences, including Earth science, biology, environmental science, and zoology, as well as courses in mathematics, computer and information sciences, and physical education.
2. Make sure that your personal goals, talents, and lifestyle requirements dovetail with the requirements to become a Forestry Technician.
3. Shadow a Forestry Technician on the job to discover what their work is really like.
4. Search the Society of American Foresters' listing of Recognized Technical Forestry Education Programs at http://www.safnet.org/education/ftschools.cfm.
5. In high school or college, volunteer for a conservation organization or work on a farm or ranch to gain hands on experience.

Information contained in this career profile was provided by the Society of American Foresters

LOGGER

CAREER PROFILE

Duties: Evaluate logging conditions; inspect suitability of trees for cutting; clear areas of brush and vegetation; cut down trees and remove branches; transport and sort logs; construct and repair logging roads; remove tree stumps; cut and stack firewood; service tools and equipment; operate and maintain manual tools, power tools, and heavy equipment

Alternate Title(s): Lumberjack; Forest Worker; Log Grader; Log Scaler

Salary Range: $12.29 to $14.29 (median hourly)

Employment Prospects: Poor

Advancement Prospects: Fair

Prerequisites:

Education or Training—No degree is required; training is primarily on-the-job

Experience—No experience is needed for entry-level jobs, but skilled logging positions require previous experience

Special Skills and Personality Traits—Solid decision-making, communication, critical thinking, mechanical, and problem-solving skills; sound judgment; physical stamina; manual dexterity; self-reliant; team player

CAREER LADDER

```
┌─────────────────────────────────────┐
│        Logging Contractor            │
└─────────────────────────────────────┘

┌─────────────────────────────────────┐
│ Bucker, Faller, or Equipment Operator │
└─────────────────────────────────────┘

┌─────────────────────────────────────┐
│         Manual Laborer               │
└─────────────────────────────────────┘
```

Position Description

Logging is a centuries-old profession, steeped in the legend of Paul Bunyan and his trusty blue ox, Babe. Also known as lumberjacks, Loggers fulfill a critical and essential need within the wood products industry—cutting down trees so that the industry has the wood it needs to supply lumber and hundreds of other wood-related products. Although advancements in technology have changed some aspects of the logging profession, by the early 21st century many elements of this occupation had remained unchanged for more than a century.

Logging is an extremely dangerous profession. In May of 2005, *U.S. News & World Report* indicated that, based on figures from the U.S. Department of Labor, loggers outpaced other occupations in terms of fatalities. In 2003 fatality rates for loggers totaled 131.6 deaths per 100,000 workers, surpassing those for fishermen (115.0), aircraft pilots (97.4), and police officers (20.9).

Generally speaking, there are a number of common tasks that Loggers perform. These include searching areas of forestland to evaluate logging conditions; inspecting trees to determine their suitability for cutting; marking undesirable trees with ribbons so they are left standing; and using axes, chain saws, and tractors to clear areas of brush and vegetation to create "falling areas" for logging activities.

There are several different types of Loggers, and each is responsible for a different aspect of the timber-cutting process. The different varieties of Loggers commonly form logging crews that consist of four to eight workers. Crews always include a "faller," whose job is to cut down trees. Specifically, fallers determine the best way to direct a falling tree. Once this has been decided, they score cutting lines on the tree with an axe and proceed to cut it down with a chain saw. Special jacks and wedges are used during this process, in order to prevent saws from getting stuck. Finally, when a tree begins to tip the faller must run to safety to avoid injury.

Once a tree has been felled, "buckers" remove branches and tree tops and cut or "buck" logs to a certain length. After "rigging slingers" or "choke setters" attach chains or cables to the logs, equipment operators use tractors, crawlers, and self-propelled forwarders or skidders to move them to a sorting area where they are categorized in various ways. Some logs are reduced to wood chips, while others are placed onto trucks and rail cars using lifting machines called grapple loaders or prepared for removal by helicopter. Loggers known as "chippers," "markers," "log sorters," and "movers" are involved in these final stages of the logging process.

After logs are loaded onto vehicles for removal from the forest, they usually are transported to sawmills or pulp mills. At these locations, equipment operators use forklift-like equipment to remove logs and transport them for inspection. Log graders and scalers evaluate logs for defects, estimate their market value, and enter related data into handheld computers.

In addition to felling trees, other common tasks that loggers perform include the construction and repair of logging roads; removing tree stumps; and cutting and stacking firewood. Many Loggers are required to service the tools and equipment they use, in order to minimize operational costs. Loggers rely on a variety of different manual and power tools to carry out their work. These include axes, mauls, wedges, pole saws, hand saws, chain saws, and various types of heavy equipment such as trucks, tractors, and even helicopters.

Self-employed logging contractors are the leading employer of Loggers. According to the 2006–07 edition of the Department of Labor's *Occupational Outlook Handbook*, approximately 75,000 logging workers were employed in mid-2004, including 43,000 logging equipment operators; 15,000 fallers; and 9,000 log graders and scalers. While the majority of tree fallers work in the field for logging contractors, employment of equipment operators is divided equally between logging operations and sawmills or planing mills. Most log graders and scalers work for sawmills and planing mills.

Loggers spend the majority of their time working outdoors in every kind of weather—including rain, extreme heat, and bitter cold. Despite the increasing use of machinery to perform many logging tasks, this remains a physically demanding profession. In addition to walking long distances over rough terrain and through dense brush and forests, Loggers have to be able to lift heavy loads, stand for long periods of time, bend frequently, and climb trees. While some loggers live in bunkhouses in logging camps, many have to travel long distances between where they live and work.

Occupational hazards await Loggers at every turn. These range from falling branches, slippery terrain, and hearing loss from exposure to noisy equipment to insect bites, snakebites, and exposure to poisonous plants. Research has shown that heat exhaustion and dehydration are major risks for Loggers, because they lose a great deal of body fluid working in high heat and humidity. Loggers have cited a number of reasons for improper hydration, including the inability to carry both equipment and a personal water supply, the potential for water supplies to be contaminated with gas and oil, and social reasons (e.g., the need to keep working instead of taking a break).

Logging can be a seasonal occupation, but this varies depending on the part of the country in which operations are located. Logging goes on year-round in the northeast, while periods of rainy weather during the spring may prevent continuous logging in the south. In addition to the weather, employment also can be affected by conditions within the wood products and construction industries.

Salaries

According to the 2006–07 edition of the Department of Labor's *Occupational Outlook Handbook*, in mid-2004 earnings for Loggers varied. Wages are influenced by factors such as experience, geography, and the size of a logging operation. In mid-2004 log graders and scalers earned the lowest median hourly wage, at $12.29, while equipment operators earned $13.18. Hourly earnings were highest for fallers ($13.23) and other types of logging workers ($14.29).

Employment Prospects

The U.S. Department of Labor anticipates slower-than-average job growth for Loggers through 2014. According to the *Occupational Outlook Handbook*, job opportunities result from turnover within the industry as Loggers retire or pursue other opportunities. Industry consolidation, the mechanization of some logging functions, and competition from sources of cheaper foreign lumber have negatively affected industry employment.

Advancement Prospects

Entry-level Loggers are normally assigned to manual tasks. Those with manual dexterity can advance to become buckers or fallers. Generally speaking, the advancement path often involves moving into roles that require the operation of complicated heavy equipment. Depending on the size and structure of the employer, some Loggers may advance to roles as crew leaders or supervisors. Those with small business skills and the capital to purchase the equipment needed to run a logging operation may go into business for themselves. In such cases, these owner-operators usually work alongside their crews in a supervisory capacity.

Education and Training

A college education is not required to work as a Logger. Most workers in this occupation learn what they need to know from experienced coworkers who teach them while working on the job. However, more formal training opportunities are offered by industry associations at the state and national levels, logging companies, and equipment manufacturers. Involving classroom time, field instruction, or both, this type of education often focuses on safety and the proper operation of equipment. However, training also may focus on matters such business management, the protection of endangered species, or complying with environmental laws and regulations.

Experience, Special Skills, and Personality Traits

Entry-level workers with little or no experience are usually tasked with manual duties. However, Loggers who wish to work as buckers, fallers, or equipment operators must have previous experience because of the specialized skills needed to operate equipment. A number of skills and personality traits are essential for Loggers. In addition to being quick thinkers with sound judgment and decision-making abilities, successful Loggers must have excellent critical thinking and problem-solving skills. In addition, they must possess the physical stamina, manual dexterity, and mechanical skills required for this profession. Loggers must be self-reliant and capable of working independently at remote sites, and also on teams that involve communication with others. Those who wish to work as logging contractors need to have solid business skills.

Unions and Associations

In addition to a number of state and regional associations, more than 50,000 loggers and some 10,000 logging contractors are represented by the American Loggers Council (ALC). Based in Hemphill, Texas, the ALC is a coalition of state and regional associations and councils. The organization seeks to provide professional loggers with a "unified, national voice."

Tips for Entry

1. In high school or college, secure seasonal employment working for a nursery, park service, or county/ state forest.
2. Make sure that your personal goals, talents, and lifestyle requirements dovetail with the requirements to become a Logger.
3. Visit the American Loggers Council online and submit questions regarding Loggers and logging on the association's Ask a Logger page, located at http:// www.americanloggers.org/ask_a_logger.htm.
4. Shadow a Logger on the job and learn what their work is really like.

URBAN FORESTER

CAREER PROFILE

Duties: Plan and supervise forestry projects; develop short- and long-term forest management plans; negotiate contracts; supervise others; ensure compliance with government regulations; monitor tree growth rates and species prevalence; prepare land for new tree growth; prevent and control forest fires; minimize environmental impact of timber cutting and removal

Alternate Title(s): City Forester; Community Forester

Salary Range: $25,000 to $72,050+

Employment Prospects: Fair

Advancement Prospects: Good

Prerequisites:

Education or Training—Bachelor's degree in forestry, urban forestry, arboriculture, range management, or related field

Experience—Seasonal, part-time, or internship positions help entry-level foresters secure full-time employment; three to five years of arboricultural, supervisory, and administrative experience may be required.

Special Skills and Personality Traits—Knowledge of science and the outdoors; systems perspective; proficiency in statistics; familiarity with laws and regulations; active learner; self-reliant; team player; ability to supervise, manage, direct, and motivate others; solid decision-making, written and oral communication, critical thinking, and problem-solving skills

Special Requirements—Some states require foresters to meet licensing or registration criteria; a valid driver's license and pesticide applicator's license are commonly required to work as an Urban Forester; some city governments require Urban Foresters to be Certified Arborists.

CAREER LADDER

```
┌─────────────────────────────────┐
│  Chief Forester or Consultant    │
└─────────────────────────────────┘

┌─────────────────────────────────┐
│         Urban Forester           │
└─────────────────────────────────┘

┌─────────────────────────────────┐
│       Forestry Technician        │
└─────────────────────────────────┘
```

Position Description

Forestry is the science, art, and practice of creating, managing, using, and conserving forests in a sustainable manner to meet desired goals, needs, and values. In simpler terms, the forestry profession focuses on caring for trees, soils, water, wildlife, and other forest elements for both current and future generations.

A forester is a uniquely qualified professional who cares for trees and forests. Foresters go to college to learn the art and practice of forestry; through comprehensive course work and practical field experience they acquire the knowledge, skills, and abilities to practice their profession. Among the many specialties within the forestry profession, urban forestry is an increasingly important one. Urban and community forests are made up of trees and associated vegetation within the environs of populated places—from the smallest villages to the largest cities. Urban Foresters, who normally work for city governments, help communities to conserve forests and "green spaces" or "green infrastructure" as they develop urban areas. Urban forests provide numerous benefits to cities. Beyond their aesthetic appeal, they help to reduce soil erosion, provide residents with shade and shelter from the elements, reduce energy costs, promote relaxation, provide a habitat for local wildlife, and produce oxygen.

One primary responsibility of the Urban Forester is to care for the trees and shrubs that dot the urban landscape. This function is sometimes accomplished by providing technical advice regarding tree care and landscape maintenance to city employees. However, Urban Foresters also work in the field to identify problems with trees involving disease or insects. These include various kinds of beetles, bagworms, webworms, and caterpillars that defoliate trees; leafminers that eat leaves from the inside out; root and shoot feeders such as weevils that destroy plants from underground; and insects such as boxelder bugs that are not harmful, but which may be a nuisance to residents. Urban Foresters implement the best treatment, including the use of pesticides and insecticides.

Developing and implementing urban forest management programs is another key area of responsibility for Urban Foresters. Such plans cover the planting, maintenance, and removal of shrubs and trees in city parks and public areas throughout a city, including rights-of-way. One example is a street tree program that involves maintaining inventory data on trees along streets. Another example might be a "re-leaf" program designed to increase the tree population in a specific area of a city.

In addition to working with other city government departments, Urban Foresters frequently serve as liaisons between a city and outside parties in regard to requests for information, forestry services, and complaints. These outside parties include both private organizations and public agencies with an interest or involvement in the urban green infrastructure, architects, developers, contractors, the news media, and the public at large.

Many Urban Foresters review construction and land use plans in order to ensure that they comply with tree-related city codes and ordinances. They often have a voice in housing and urban development projects, sit on neighborhood or community planning committees, attend town hall meetings, and help residents to obtain community block grants. Many successful Urban Foresters also work hard to meet and maintain relations with opinion leaders and elected officials in urban areas.

In particular, public outreach is one of the most critical aspects of the Urban Forester's profession. They must contend with social and economic issues while carrying out their work. The need for green infrastructure, including healthy tree cover, is equally as important in economically depressed urban areas as it is in wealthier sectors of a city. However, food and housing are often more of a priority for low-income individuals than investing in and maintaining green spaces. Therefore, Urban Foresters are often challenged to find creative, nontraditional ways of helping residents in depressed areas deal with natural resources issues. This often includes helping residents to become "citizen foresters" by helping them to plan and fund neighborhood beautification projects and tree planting initiatives. Such projects help residents to increase the value of their property.

Like all professionals, Urban Foresters perform a variety of administrative tasks and duties. These include maintaining logs and databases, supervising contracts, preparing and maintaining budgets, and writing reports and articles. Additionally, Urban Foresters also write ordinances, policies, and procedures related to tree management and other aspects of urban forestry, and provide education and training to other city employees.

In the field, Urban Foresters use a variety of tools to carry out their work. Beyond cameras, personal computers, and cell phones, these include a number of tools that are occupation-specific. Included are tree injectors for injecting chemicals into tree tissue; measurement devices such as bark gauges, diameter tapes, and clinometers (to measure tree height); and equipment related to the use of geographic information systems (GIS), remote sensing (aerial and satellite photographs), and the Global Positioning Systems (GPS).

While most Urban Foresters spend a portion of their time in an office setting, they also spend time working outdoors in all kinds of weather—including rain, extreme heat, humidity, and bitter cold. This profession can be physically demanding, requiring frequent walking and standing. Although some outdoor work is carried out in parks and on city streets, Urban Foresters sometimes travel to proposed land development sites and construction zones to perform inspections. Such areas may consist of rough terrain. Therefore, being in good or excellent physical condition may be a requirement for this profession.

Salaries

Salaries for Urban Foresters vary, depending on factors such as level of education, years of experience, employer group (government, industry, university, etc.), and geographic region. According to the 2006–2007 edition of the Department of Labor's *Occupational Outlook Handbook*, in mid-2004 annual salaries for Urban Foresters ranged from less than $29,770 to more than $72,050, with a median of $48,230. In general, those with a bachelor's degree in forestry or natural resources can expect to make about $25,000 to $30,000 upon graduation, according to the Society of American Foresters. Starting salaries for those with a master's or doctorate degree are $35,000 to $45,000, respectively.

Employment Prospects

The U.S. Department of Labor anticipates slower-than-average job growth for conservation scientists and foresters through 2014. Because of government cutbacks, the best opportunities will exist with consulting firms in the private sector. However, the never-ending process of land development, as well as the need for responsible land management, should help to maintain demand for Urban Foresters.

Advancement Prospects

Some Urban Foresters begin their careers as forestry technicians and advance on the career ladder after gaining additional experience and academic training. After securing an entry-level position, Urban Foresters may advance to senior or supervisory roles in the field, while others pursue careers as executives or consultants.

Education and Training

The minimum educational requirement for professional foresters is a bachelor's degree in forestry, range management, or a related field. Some Urban Foresters hold specialized undergraduate degrees in urban forestry or arboriculture. Forestry programs combine technical and scientific courses with training in policy and economics, quantitative methods, and communications. Forestry students learn about forest ecology, inventory, water quality, wildlife habitat, and the identification of tree species. Most forestry courses add advanced computer applications such as geographic information systems and resource assessment programs. Forestry programs also teach students how to integrate biological, social, political, economic, and historical considerations into forest management decisions.

Special Requirements

While some states require Urban Foresters to meet licensing or registration criteria, many states have no such requirements. In states that do, an examination is often required to obtain a license, and candidates must meet certain criteria related to education and forestry experience. A valid driver's license and pesticide applicator's license are commonly required to work as an Urban Forester. Some city governments require Urban Foresters to be Certified Arborists, a credential available from the International Society of Arboriculture.

Experience, Special Skills, and Personality Traits

Entry-level Urban Foresters can increase their employment prospects by completing internships or working in seasonal or part-time positions while in college. These are prime opportunities to gain valuable hands-on experience. However, many urban forestry positions require three to five years of experience performing arboricultural work, as well as supervisory or administrative duties.

A number of skills and personality traits are essential for Urban Foresters. In addition to sound judgment and decision-making abilities, successful Urban Foresters must be active learners with solid knowledge of science and the outdoors. They must have excellent critical thinking and problem-solving skills, as well as the ability to take a systems perspective and determine how the outcome of a process can be affected by changing different variables. In addition, Urban Foresters must be effective communicators who are capable of working with groups or committees that include people from different professional and socioeconomic backgrounds.

Report writing, documentation, and interaction with others are important aspects of this profession. Therefore, strong written communication skills are required, along with proficiency in statistics. In addition to scientific knowledge, Urban Foresters must be familiar with applicable laws and regulations. Finally, because many Urban Foresters oversee staff and volunteers, they must be able to supervise, manage, direct, and motivate others.

Unions and Associations

The Society of American Foresters is the world's largest professional society for foresters. In addition to natural resource professionals and researchers, this leading scientific and educational organization includes CEOs, administrators, educators, and students among its members.

Tips for Entry

1. In high school, take courses that provide exposure to the sciences, including Earth science, biology, and zoology, as well as courses in mathematics, chemistry, physics, and English.
2. Make sure that your personal goals, talents, and lifestyle requirements dovetail with the requirements to become an Urban Forester.
3. Shadow an Urban Forester on the job to discover what their work is really like.
4. Search the Society of American Foresters' listing of Accredited Professional Forestry Degree Programs at http://www.safnet.org/education/pforschools.cfm.
5. As a high school student and college undergraduate, volunteer for a conservation organization to gain hands-on experience.

Information contained in this career profile was provided by the Society of American Foresters

LEGAL AND REGULATORY

ENVIRONMENTAL ATTORNEY

CAREER PROFILE

Duties: Prosecuting or representing parties in legal and regulatory matters related to the air, water, and land; performing legal transactions; consulting with scientists and engineers; performing other duties as required by clients or the government

Alternate Title(s): Associate Attorney; Junior Partner; Senior Partner; Staff Attorney; Corporate Counsel; Chief Legal Counsel

Salary Range: $34,000 to $181,000+

Employment Prospects: Good

Advancement Prospects: Good

Prerequisites:

Education or Training—Undergraduate degree, as well as a law (J.D.) degree

Experience—Internship with a private law firm or government agency specializing in environmental law

Special Skills and Personality Traits—Strong work ethic; self-motivation; self-confidence; ability to work in a team environment; excellent communication skills; well-organized; proficient in research, analysis, and writing; attention to detail; ability to think conceptually

Special Requirements—Attorney's license and passage of written bar exam

CAREER LADDER

```
┌─────────────────────────────────┐
│  Senior Partner or Chief Counsel │
│           or Director            │
└─────────────────────────────────┘

┌─────────────────────────────────┐
│ Junior Partner or Associate Attorney │
└─────────────────────────────────┘

┌─────────────────────────────────┐
│             Intern               │
└─────────────────────────────────┘
```

Position Description

Environmental Attorneys deal with regulation and legal matters related to the air, water, and land. Specifically, cases may include a wide range of issues, including natural resources protection, endangered species, public lands use, transportation, forestry, pollution, hazardous materials, toxic waste, public health, and international environmental matters.

The field of environmental law is a substantial category within the larger legal field, and includes many specific sub-specialties. Attorneys often focus on one area of concentration, such as air, water, or land pollution, and may specialize even further within those sub-categories, dealing with particular types of work, such as solid waste.

Environmental Attorneys work in either the private or government sector. While the specialization of law is the same, attorneys in each sector are on opposing sides. For example, attorneys in the private sector normally defend and represent the interests of business entities who face government action over environmental concerns, while attorneys working for a government agency represent the public interest by prosecuting parties that are responsible for pollution. While government attorneys enforce environmental laws and regulations, private sector attorneys ensure that the government has the lawful authority to make requirements of companies, and if so, to make sure those mandates are reasonable.

Major environmental laws at the federal level cover everything from the maintenance and remediation of underground storage tanks to wetlands and surface mining. Examples include:

- Clean Air Act
- Clean Water Act
- Emergency Planning and Community Right to Know Act (EPCRA)
- Hazardous Materials Transportation Authorization Act
- Resource Conservation and Recovery Act (RCRA)
- Safe Drinking Water Act
- Superfund (CERCLA)
- Toxic Substances Control Act (TSCA)

Environmental Attorneys generally begin their careers in the government sector, where opportunities exist within city and state attorneys' offices; air, water, and land bureaus within state environmental protection agencies; and at the federal level with organizations such as the U.S. Environmental Protection Agency. Although their salary and benefits are generally low, government attorneys are able to gain immediate and valuable experience through involvement in cases that, at a private firm, would be relegated to counsel with more experience.

Local, state, and federal agencies often work together, exchanging information and sharing resources while enforcing environmental protection laws. Government agencies prosecute a variety of environmental crimes. They pursue civil and criminal actions to enforce ordinances, statutes, and regulations at the city, state, and federal levels. In addition to complex litigation cases involving environmental remediation, government agencies also are involved with public nuisance abatements and injunctions that involve matters such as lead-based paint. They also work in partnership with public interest or environmental advocacy organizations.

Government attorneys often begin as interns and then obtain employment as new associate attorneys within a state agency's division of legal counsel, which includes a group of attorneys who service the entire environmental agency. These divisions vary in size depending on the state, and often include sub-groups of attorneys who serve particular bureaus, such as land, air, or water. After a period of several years, government attorneys may obtain supervisory positions that, after a period of 15 to 20 years, may lead to a position as the division's director or chief legal counsel.

After "cutting their teeth," many government attorneys cross over to the private sector, armed with knowledge of the inner workings, mindset, and philosophies of government agencies. However, in some instances, conflict of interest laws may prevent government attorneys from immediately working for the private sector for a certain period of time.

In the private sector, Environmental Attorneys mainly work with corporate clients in matters of environmental risk management, compliance, and defense. They deal with environmental issues that arise during the course of business, including mergers, acquisitions, and real estate transactions. In addition to providing advisement, counsel, and strategy development, law firms represent businesses and corporations of all sizes in environmental litigation matters that may involve:

- Brownfield restoration and site remediation
- Indoor air quality
- Land use and natural resources
- Occupational safety and health
- Real estate
- Solid and hazardous waste management
- Toxic tort defense

When companies are required to clean up the environment, private and government attorneys are often at odds over what the company's obligation is. Sometimes, this issue is unclear under environmental laws or regulations. Complicating matters is the fact that environmental cleanups are not always black-and-white matters. For example, in the early days of environmental law, companies were often required to remove all contaminants from the environment. Remediation became more risk-based during the 1990s, and in the 2000s, regulations allow contaminants to be removed to the point where pollution is deemed to be at an "acceptable level," or where it is not an imminent threat to human health or the environment. This is due to a better understanding of natural attenuation, whereby contaminants naturally diffuse over time, as well as factors such as geology, hydrogeology, and the exposure pathways that contaminants follow.

In addition to working for the environmental division of a large law firm, which may place clusters of attorneys in major cities throughout the country, environmental lawyers also might find employment in "boutique" firms that specialize exclusively in environmental law. Another option is for attorneys to go into private practice, either alone or in partnership with other attorneys. A small percentage of environmental attorneys go into private practice and pursue public interest work, marketing themselves to national organizations like the Sierra Club, which often require local representation.

Some private sector attorneys find employment as in-house counsel for large corporations. In particular, chemical companies and waste disposal firms often have large in-house legal departments, sometimes employing as many as 25 to 30 attorneys. Rather than representing their employers exclusively, in-house counsel frequently work in tandem with Environmental Attorneys at private firms who are more intimately familiar with local politics and culture, the personalities of local authorities, and local laws and regulations. While corporate counsel may perform more general environmental law work, they rely on private firms to provide expertise in particular concentrations of environmental law.

On the private side, new attorneys typically work as associates for seven to nine years before becoming junior or non-capital partners. After another six or seven years, promotions may lead to a role as senior or equity partner.

Within corporations, new attorneys typically begin as associates within the division or department of legal counsel. Within five years, in-house attorneys may progress to supervisory positions, overseeing two or three other attorneys. After 20 or 25 years, an in-house attorney may become general counsel for the organization's environmental affairs department.

It is not unusual for Environmental Attorneys, in both the government and private sectors, to work long hours. When they are very busy, some attorneys work 60 hours per week or more.

Salaries

Salaries vary considerably for Environmental Attorneys, depending on skill, experience, location, whether one is employed in the government or private sector, and law firm size. According to estimates from the U.S. Department of Labor's Bureau of Labor Statistics, 352,090 lawyers were employed in the United States in May 2004, earning a mean annual salary of $114,540. In its *2004 Public Sector and Public Interest Attorney Salary Report*, the National Association for Law Placement (NALP) revealed that entry-level attorneys in civil service organizations earned first-year median salaries of $34,000. By comparison, those working for public interest organizations earned $36,656, local prosecuting attorneys earned $40,000, and state prosecuting attorneys earned $40,574. With 11 to 15 years of experience, these salaries increased to $51,927; $64,000; $69,255; and $68,139, respectively. According to the NALP's *2005 Associate Salary Survey*, first-year associates earned $67,500 to $125,000, depending on the size of the law firm, while eighth-year associates earned $109,000 to $181,500.

Employment Prospects

Employment in the legal field is competitive, as law school graduates outnumber available positions. According to the U.S. Department of Labor's Bureau of Labor Statistics, lawyers are expected to experience average employment growth through 2014. The bureau cited environmental law and increasing levels of business activities as two factors driving employment growth. Looking ahead, some observers have noted that because of rising levels of vehicle traffic, increased levels of industrialization in emerging economies such as China, and the issue of global warming, air pollution is an especially promising concentration of environmental law.

Advancement Prospects

There are a number of things that attorneys can do to maximize their chances of succeeding in environmental law. On the government side, winning big cases is especially helpful. Winning cases also is very important at private firms, as well as generating revenue by billing as many hours as possible. In-house attorneys are successful by doing an adequate job of legal administration and, importantly, minimizing the company's outlays in the way of fines and penalties. In-house attorneys and those at private firms often succeed or fail together, because their jobs are closely interconnected.

Education and Training

Those interested in pursuing a career in environmental law must first obtain an undergraduate degree from an accredited college or university. Some attorneys have undergraduate training in agriculture or environmental studies. However, there are many academic pathways to a career in environmental law. Undergraduate backgrounds in biology, chemistry, engineering, mathematics, or physics are beneficial, because Environmental Attorneys must be able to grasp scientific concepts regarding the nature of contaminants, their concentration and molecular makeup, and the rate at which they migrate through air, water, or land. Environmental Attorneys frequently deal with computer and mathematical models that help them to determine how quickly a contaminant will move from one point to another over a period of years and in what concentrations. Although a background in science, engineering, or mathematics is helpful, it is not required for a successful environmental law career, because attorneys rely on environmental consultants and other experts to provide them with current and accurate information.

According to the Law School Admission Council (LSAC), the demonstrated ability to perform well in a rigorous academic setting is important for those who wish to attend law school. An undergraduate education that hones skills in written and oral expression, critical analysis, and logical reasoning also is important.

As undergraduates, students often receive guidance from pre-law advisers. After receiving an undergraduate degree and taking the Law School Admission Test (LSAT), students must gain entrance to a law school accredited by the American Bar Association (ABA). Over the course of three years, ABA-accredited law schools provide all students with training that furthers their creative, analytical, debating, and logical reasoning skills. Students receive sufficient training in American law so that they are prepared to take the bar examination in any state.

Law schools generally follow the "case method" of instruction, according to the LSAC. During their first year, students usually take classes covering legal methods, civil procedure, constitutional law, legal writing and research, contracts, criminal law and criminal procedure, torts, and so on. Students receive specialized training via internships. In addition, some law schools offer programs that blend academic concentrations like business and science with law. Upon graduation from law school, students are awarded a juris doctor (J.D.) degree.

Special Requirements

In order to practice law, attorneys must pass a bar exam and obtain a license in the state, district, or territory where they plan to practice. Each state has a different bar exam, and some attorneys pass the bar in multiple states. Likewise, each individual state sets its own criteria for taking the bar examination or qualifying for bar admission.

Most bar exams last two days, with the first day devoted to the Multistate Bar Examination (MBE), which covers constitutional law, real property, contracts, evidence, torts, and criminal law. According to the American Bar Association (ABA), the second day usually involves "locally crafted essays from a broader range of subject matters." However, more states are using nationally developed exams during the second day. These include the Multistate Performance Test (MPT) and the Multistate Essay Examination (MEE). The ABA further explains that "almost all jurisdictions require that the applicant present an acceptable score on the Multistate Professional Responsibility Examination (MPRE)."

Before granting a law license, bar examiners also evaluate candidates in regard to their character and fitness. This is accomplished by reviewing information about a candidate's background. After receiving a law license, attorneys must pursue continuing education to maintain their licensure.

Experience, Special Skills, and Personality Traits

Successful Environmental Attorneys possess the same traits that lawyers in other legal concentrations have, such as a strong work ethic, self-motivation, self-confidence, and the ability to work in a team environment. In addition to excellent communication skills, they must be well organized and proficient in research, analysis, and writing. Because of the extensive work that must be performed with numbers and scientific concepts, attention to detail is especially important. The ability to think conceptually, or three-dimensionally, also is key, because Environmental Attorneys must be able to conceptualize what they are told by a particular computer model or expert.

Unions and Associations

Environmental Attorneys belong to a number of associations to further their professional development and stay abreast of legal developments and court decisions in their particular field. The American Bar Association (ABA) has a section devoted to environmental law. Additionally, large industrial states such as California, Florida, Illinois, New Jersey, New York, and Texas have state bar associations with substantial environmental law sections. Organizations such as the Environmental Law Institute (ELI) offer seminars, training courses, and research programs in conjunction with organizations like the ABA, the American Law Institute, and the Smithsonian Institution. Attorneys also may belong to specialized trade associations that focus on particular aspects of environmental practice, such as the American Groundwater Association or the Solid Waste Alliance of North America.

Tips for Entry

1. Learn more about legal careers from the National Association for Law Placement, http://www.nalp.org.
2. Find out more about law school and the Law School Admission Test (LSAT) from the Law School Admission Council, http://www.lsac.org.
3. Pursue an undergraduate degree in a field that relates to the environment.
4. As a college undergraduate, work with a pre-law adviser to learn more about and prepare for law school.
5. In law school, gain valuable exposure by pursuing an internship with a private law firm or government agency specializing in environmental law.

ENVIRONMENTAL CAMPAIGN STAFF WORKER

CAREER PROFILE

Duties: Engage in public outreach activities that might include telephone, door-to-door, and street campaigns; participate in the creation of campaign goals and objectives and work toward achieving them; recruit campaign participants and supporters; raise funds in both the public and private sector

Alternate Title(s): Environmental Activist; Environmental Advocate; Environmental Organizer; Forest Campaigner

Salary Range: $20,000 to $50,000

Employment Prospects: Good

Advancement Prospects: Good

Prerequisites:

Education or Training—A minimum of a high school diploma, although many positions require some level of college coursework in public policy, political science, community organizing, communications or similar field

Experience—Fund-raising, canvassing via phone or door-to-door, mobilizing and organizing people; communicating with elected officials

Special Skills and Personality Traits—Passionate about environmental, social, and political change; team-oriented, yet also self-motivated; strong leadership and public speaking skills

Special Requirements—Stamina and flexibility to work varied and long hours, particularly as campaign deadlines draw near

CAREER LADDER

Environmental Campaign Director

Environmental Campaign Assistant Director

Environmental Campaign Staff Worker

Environmental Campaign Volunteer

Position Description

Environmental Campaign Staff Workers are normally part of a team that operates under the guidance of some sort of manager or director. Typically, the director and the staff workers draft some sort of goal related to environmental policy and devise a plan for achieving that goal. While the director or assistant director might oversee the entire campaign and make higher level decisions about the types of activities their staff will undertake throughout the campaign, it is the Environmental Campaign Staff Workers who are on the front lines, talking to citizens about the issues and motivating them to get involved in campaigns—by voting, volunteering, writing a letter, making a donation, etc.—in an effort to effect change. Deeply committed to their cause, which might range from slowing down logging activity in certain forests to increasing the frequency of water quality testing in a specific community, Environmental Campaign Staff Workers attempt to mobilize community members to take action in the hope of impacting environmental legislation not only locally but also at the state or even national level.

Organized efforts to raise awareness and solicit support from community members, a process often referred to as "canvassing," include calling people on the telephone, going door-to-door, or approaching people on the street. Environmental Campaign Staff Workers might also be called upon to foster relationships with relevant agencies, such as environmental or public health organizations, public and private businesses, public officials, civic leaders, and any other organizations or individuals who might offer campaign assistance and support. Other tasks include writing media releases, attending and speaking at news conferences, meeting with editorial boards, and developing various media contacts in an effort to maximize media coverage for the campaign.

Many Environmental Campaign Staff Workers work well over 40 hours per week, particularly as campaign deadlines, such as fund-raising goals, draw near. Hours are oftentimes irregular, and include evening and weekend work, mainly because that is the easiest time to reach community members at their homes and out in public. Given the intensity of the job, as well as the personal passion that fuels the career choice, Environmental Campaign Staff Workers can be vulnerable to burnout, particularly if campaigns prove less than successful or if goals are not achieved.

Salaries

According to Harley Jeben, author of *100 Jobs in Social Change*, pay for campaign workers ranges from roughly $20,000 to $50,000 per year, depending on experience, education, and the type of organization overseeing the campaign. Smaller nonprofit organizations tend to pay less than larger groups with deeper pockets.

Employment Prospects

Jobs for Environmental Campaign Staff Workers are expected to grow, as the trend in the nonprofit sector is to hire professional campaign organizers, fund-raisers, etc. At the same time, however, as with all candidates seeking jobs within the nonprofit sector, it is important to remember that employment largely depends upon funding, which is oftentimes directly tied to the economy. During recessionary times, one way that both individuals and businesses tend to tighten their belts is to reduce charitable donations; consequently, these types of jobs may be vulnerable to economic downturns, as well as increasingly dependent upon the success of fund-raising campaigns.

Advancement Prospects

Many environmental organizations that hire Environmental Campaign Staff Workers also train these individuals in their own advocacy and organization techniques. While many positions do prefer candidates who have some back-ground in advocacy or fund-raising, others tend to look more closely at whether or not a candidate appears to have the personality characteristics of a successful campaigner. Gaining volunteer experience at any sort of environmentally minded nonprofit agency can be helpful, particularly if the work is somehow related to fund-raising or public outreach. Sometimes, successful volunteers are offered part-time or even full-time employment after a certain period of time. After a few successful years as an Environmental Campaign Staff Worker, individuals may be able to advance into assistant director or director positions; however, jobs at this level usually require at least a four-year degree in public policy, political science, communications, environmental advocacy, or a similar field.

Education and Training

While some Environmental Campaign Staff Workers may possess nothing more than a high school diploma and a passion for environmental issues, many have completed some college course work in public policy, political science, environmental science, environmental advocacy, community organization, communications, or a similar field. Many positions require a four-year degree in one of these fields, as well as specific training in advocacy and organization. Many agencies provide this type of training themselves.

EnviroEducation.com lists nearly 800 colleges and universities that offer environmental studies degree programs with a specialization in either environmental advocacy/leadership or environmental justice. Some of these postsecondary institutions offer specific degrees in environmental advocacy, rather than simply a specialization that is part of an environmental studies curriculum. For example, Antioch University New England offers a graduate program called Environmental Advocacy and Organizing.

Experience, Special Skills, and Personality Traits

Environmental Campaign Staff Workers must be passionate about environmental, social, and political change. Because the ability to communicate this passion to others is equally important, well-developed public-speaking and persuasion skills are necessary to inspire and motivate citizens to take action. While most Environmental Campaign Staff Workers will operate within a team setting, they should also possess the self-motivation to complete tasks on their own.

Unions and Associations

Some of the most well-known environmental advocacy groups that regularly engage in highly publicized environmental campaigns include Greenpeace, World Wildlife Federation, the Sierra Club, the Nature Conservancy, Clean Water Action,

Alliance for a Healthy Tomorrow, and the Center for Health, Environment, and Justice.

Tips for Entry

1. In high school, take courses in interpersonal communication, public speaking, sociology, and writing.
2. Gain experience in fund-raising by volunteering at a local nonprofit agency.
3. Research colleges and universities that offer specializations in environmental advocacy/leadership or environmental justice at EnviroEducation.com.
4. Search for environmental advocacy and communications jobs at the Environmental Career Opportunities Web site, http://www.ecojobs.com/jobs.php?sec=1EW.

ENVIRONMENTAL COMPLIANCE SPECIALIST

CAREER PROFILE

Duties: Inspecting waste disposal and treatment operations; investigating violations and complaints related to waste disposal; writing reports; making recommendations for maintaining compliance with local, state, and federal environmental laws; issuing citations

Alternate Title(s): Environmental Compliance Officer; Wastewater Treatment Compliance Specialist; Conservation Compliance Specialist

Salary Range: $40,000 to $70,000

Employment Prospects: Good

Advancement Prospects: Limited

Prerequisites:

Education or Training—Bachelor's degree in environmental science, environmental engineering, chemistry, or similar field

Experience—Knowledge of local, state, and federal environmental laws and regulations; ability to use, calibrate, and repair technical equipment, such as hydraulic pumps

Special Skills and Personality Traits—Communication skills, including verbal and written; attention to detail; ability to work independently; public speaking; problem solving

Special Requirements—A valid driver's license; certifications may vary by specialty

CAREER LADDER

```
┌─────────────────────────────────┐
│  Environmental Services Manager  │
└─────────────────────────────────┘

┌─────────────────────────────────┐
│     Senior Environmental         │
│     Compliance Specialist        │
└─────────────────────────────────┘

┌─────────────────────────────────┐
│ Environmental Compliance Specialist │
└─────────────────────────────────┘

┌─────────────────────────────────┐
│     Environmental Compliance     │
│       Specialist Trainee         │
└─────────────────────────────────┘
```

Position Description

Environmental Compliance Specialists visit a variety of waste disposal and treatment sites and conduct a series of tests to determine whether or not operations are in compliance with environmental regulations. They analyze test results and, if necessary, make recommendations for improving the effectiveness of processes and procedures. In some cases, they may also issue citations for violations. Hired by both governmental agencies and private businesses, Environmental Compliance Specialists may be responsible for assessing a broad range of activities related to waste disposal and treatment:

- Wastewater treatment
- Water pretreatment
- Occupational health and safety compliance
- Solid waste treatment and disposal
- Handling of hazardous substances
- Contamination of water, soil, and air
- Industrial discharge

During a routine visit, the specialist normally examines any waste disposal and treatment plans the site already has in place; reviews permits, certifications, and other records to determine if licensure is adequate; inspects facilities and grounds; and takes samples of waste products, such as wastewater or soil containing industrial runoff. Along with deciding where to take samples and which sampling methods are most effective, Environmental Compliance Specialists must also be well versed in sample preservation method as some samples require transportation to a laboratory. Sampling may also involve operating testing and sampling equipment, which may require calibrations and/or troubleshooting. For example, individuals working in the wastewater treatment sector often make use of hydraulic pumps and measurement apparatuses when sampling and analyzing wastewater, and specialists are expected to have enough familiarity with the equipment to make minor repairs and adjustments to these devices as needed.

Environmental Compliance Specialists responsible for reviewing the occupational safety and health practices of a waste disposal and treatment facility will discuss standard practices with employees and employers, test employee equipment, observe when and how employees make use of safety devices or protective clothing, monitor any activities that may put employees at risk; measure any exposure to toxic materials, and assess employee knowledge of emergency procedures. They may also offer environmental compliance training to groups of employees and employers.

In some cases, Environmental Compliance Specialists may find themselves investigating consumer and employee allegations of illegal activities, such as dumping of pesticides or other hazardous products; faulty labeling; noncompliance with labeling requirements of toxic substances, or tampering with regulatory devices that restrict levels of industrial runoff. Along with investigating the sites and examining the products in question, specialists may also need to question individuals to gather more information about reported violations. In addition, they may find themselves coordinating activities with other regulatory agencies, such as the Environmental Protection Agency or the Occupational Safety and Health Administration.

Jobs for Environmental Compliance Specialists can vary considerably. A city might hire such an individual to monitor one specific program, such as its wastewater pretreatment program, while a zoo might want a specialist to analyze and implement state, federal, or local requirements to maintain an approved program for disposing of animal waste. These individuals might also find themselves researching a variety of hazardous waste programs not only to uncover any potential problems or risks, but also to develop a variety of treatment and disposal options at various costs.

Environmental Compliance Specialists typically work 40 hours per week. They divide their time between fieldwork, which includes visiting sites and transporting samples to laboratories, and the more administrative tasks of their job, such as reviewing laboratory results and writing reports. Work can be physically demanding as it oftentimes requires long periods of standing, as well as walking and even climb-

ing. From time to time, specialists are also exposed to toxic substances and other hazardous environmental conditions.

Salaries

According to the 2006–07 edition of the Department of Labor's *Occupational Outlook Handbook*, the annual median salary for an Environmental Compliance Specialist was $48,530 in 2004. While newcomers to the industry tend to start at roughly $40,000, those with more extensive experience can earn upwards of $70,000. Individuals with graduate degrees tend to earn more than those with undergraduate degrees.

Employment Prospects

Through 2014, job growth for Environmental Compliance Specialists will range from 10 percent to 20 percent, a figure comparable to most other occupations. According to the Department of Labor, increased public awareness of environmental hazards, partly due to threats of bioterrorism following the September 11 terrorist attacks in New York City and Washington, D.C., has helped bolster demand for environmental compliance and offset the impact of cuts in funding for many environmental programs.

Advancement Prospects

Due to the highly technical nature of this work, gaining entry into this field can be difficult for individuals with no experience. Therefore, while in school pursuing the bachelor's degree required by most employers, students are best served by securing an internship of some sort. Most new hires undergo some sort of on-the-job training, and they typically report to either a senior specialist or an environmental director. Larger organizations may offer opportunities for advancement into managerial positions.

Education and Training

Environmental Compliance Specialists are required to hold a bachelor's degree in environmental engineering, environmental science, chemistry, or a related field. Many also pursue graduate degrees. A number of colleges and universities across the country offer accredited programs in these fields.

Special Requirements

Every Environmental Compliance Specialist needs an in-depth understanding of local, state, and national environmental laws, particularly as they pertain to waste disposal and toxic substances. As they often are required to review existing blueprints and other facility plans, candidates must be able both to understand and to interpret these plans. In addition, because they handle questionable materials themselves, it is essential that candidates understand chemical structure and composition, as well as how chemicals react to each other, and be skilled in safe handling and disposal techniques. Because site visits may require a great deal of walking, standing, and/or climbing, physical fitness is also important. Qualified applicants typically possess a valid driver's license, and they may be subject to drug tests, background checks, medical examinations, and a written test.

Some positions require certification, which varies by state. The Association of Boards of Certification compiles a state-based list of contacts for various certification credentials, such as biological industrial wastewater, physical/chemical industrial waste, inspection, solid waste, water treatment, and wastewater collection. Normally, before securing permission to take a certification examination, candidates must meet education and experience requirements.

Experience, Special Skills, and Personality Traits

Environmental Compliance Specialists need the ability to communicate both verbally and in writing, as well as to give public presentations and training seminars when required. In addition, they must possess solid analytic, critical thinking, and problem-solving skills. Because they may face challenging situations from time to time, particularly when investigating things like allegations of corporate violations of environmental laws, Environmental Compliance Specialists rely extensively on interpersonal communication skills.

To use specialized equipment and write detailed technical reports also requires considerable attention to detail.

Unions and Associations

The Association of Boards of Certification offers state-based certification credentials to individuals working in the environmental compliance field. The Water Environment Federation represents water quality professionals in a variety of disciplines. Other associations include the American Water Works Association and the Air and Waste Management Association.

Tips for Entry

1. Visit the Association of Boards of Certification's Web site, http://www.abccert.org/certcontacts.html, to find the contact in your state for certifications such as biological industrial wastewater, physical/chemical industrial waste, inspection, solid waste, water treatment, and wastewater collection.
2. In high school, take courses in chemistry, physics, and mathematics.
3. Visit the Student Center at the American Water Works Association's Web site, http://www.awwa.org/careercenter/studentcenter/, to learn more about careers in the wastewater industry.
4. Search for jobs at the Water Environment Federation's Web site, http://wef.jobcontrolcenter.com/search.cfm.

ENVIRONMENTAL ECONOMIST

CAREER PROFILE	CAREER LADDER

Duties: Analyzing the economic costs and benefits of environmental programs and activities; explaining environmental and economic data; developing economic models for various economic trends; preparing detailed reports and making presentations

Alternate Title(s): Conservation Economist

Salary Range: $50,000 to $80,000+

Employment Prospects: Limited

Advancement Prospects: Limited

Prerequisites:

Education or Training—Bachelor's degree in environmental economics, economics, statistics, environmental science, or similar field

Experience—Understanding of theoretical economic concepts and social science research practices; familiarity with statistics and various economic and mathematical models; knowledge of environmental concepts, programs, activities, and regulations

Special Skills and Personality Traits—Ability to use statistical analysis software, as well as database, spreadsheet, and presentation programs; attention to detail and accuracy; leadership skills; report writing; public speaking

```
┌─────────────────────────────────────┐
│   Senior Environmental Economist      │
└─────────────────────────────────────┘

┌─────────────────────────────────────┐
│      Environmental Economist          │
└─────────────────────────────────────┘

┌─────────────────────────────────────┐
│   Junior Environmental Economist      │
└─────────────────────────────────────┘
```

Position Description

Environmental Economists research and analyze economic and statistical data related to the environment. They offer their professional opinions on various relationships between economics and the environment to public and private companies, governmental agencies, and other organizations. Along with conducting specific cost-benefit analyses for various proposals—such as a piece of conservation legislation that will restrict development in the natural habitats of certain animals—these individuals use various economic models and statistical computations to explain existing economic trends and forecast future activity. For example, they might analyze existing data for current consumption levels of non-renewable resources to predict areas of depletion that might be of concern and also to calculate the economic impact of such a phenomenon.

The data compiled, analyzed, and consolidated into reports by Environmental Economists forms the basis for the advice they give to clients. This advice might take the form of specific recommendations to improve economic weaknesses, as well as plans to bolster economic strength. For example, Environmental Economists might draft policies designed not only to protect the environment, but also to create new jobs or promote responsible consumer spending. In other situations, they might be called upon to develop a set of economic guidelines that will be used by legislators and other government officials for drafting a variety of environmental and economic programs. As economic theories can differ depending upon political orientation, Environmental Economists might need to analyze data from different perspectives and offer clients opposing points of view. They may also be called to give expert testimony in hearings related to the economic impact of environmental legislation.

The work of an experienced Environmental Economist calls for both innovation and leadership skills. Along with developing their own procedures for gathering, analyzing, evaluating, and compiling data, these individuals also conduct original research projects, for which they may have to secure grants and other sources of funding. Based on this analysis and research, they work in conjunction with other professionals to develop programs designed to be both environmentally and economically sustainable. For example, they might work with irrigation auditors and resource conservation specialists to devise a community-based water restriction program that not only conserves water but also reduces costs for the water company, the community, and its residents.

Environmental Economists work an average of 40 hours per week. However, this number may increase when project deadlines loom or when legislation is under debate. Most of their work takes place in an office.

Salaries

Salaries for Environmental Economists range from $50,000 to more than $80,000. The Bureau of Labor Statistics reported the annual median salary for Environmental Economists as $72,370 in 2004. Many individuals in this profession pursue graduate studies, including doctorate degrees; earnings for these individuals are oftentimes markedly higher than for those with undergraduate degrees. Doctorate-level economists may be able to boost their income further with teaching appointments, research grants, consulting work, and other supplementary projects.

Employment Prospects

Job growth for Environmental Economists is expected to be slower than average through 2014, according to the Department of Labor's Bureau of Labor Statistics.

Advancement Prospects

Many individuals enter this field via internships, which are offered by many colleges and universities at both the undergraduate and graduate level. The National Center for Environmental Economics offers a series of summer internships when funding is available. Temporary and summer employment programs are also offered by the Environmental Protection Agency and other governmental bodies.

While advancement prospects are limited, due in part to recent funding cuts in environmental programs, experienced Environmental Economists with advanced degrees do have opportunities to branch out into other areas where their expertise is needed. They are, for example, qualified to teach university-level economics and environmental economics courses. Other academic activities including overseeing research projects and supervising student projects. Environmental Economists can also market themselves as independent consultants.

Education and Training

A bachelor's degree in economics, environmental economics, environmental science, statistics, or a related field is required for an entry-level position as an Environmental Economist. Master's degrees are common for individuals in this field, and many experienced economists further their education with a Ph.D. A number of colleges and universities across the country offer these degrees.

Along with understanding various theoretical economic concepts and economic models, Environmental Economists should possess in-depth knowledge of environmental concepts, programs, activities, and regulations. The research-oriented nature of the work requires familiarity with social science research standards and practices. Also required is the ability to understand, interpret, and use statistics.

Experience, Special Skills, and Personality Traits

Environmental Economists use statistical analysis software—as well as electronic databases, spreadsheets, and presentation programs—on a regular basis; as a result, a high level of proficiency with computers is essential; the mathematical basis of most economic models requires the ability to work with sophisticated numerical equations. For data compilation and the interpretation and evaluation of statistical data, economists need also the ability to think critically, a high level of accuracy, and attention to detail. Also important are program-development, leadership, and written and oral communication skills.

Unions and Associations

The National Center for Environmental Economics represents Environmental Economists throughout the United States, as does the Association of Environmental and Resource Economics. Other organizations that provide resources and career development opportunities to industry professionals include the American Agricultural Economics Association, the International Society for Ecological Economics, and the International Environmetrics Society.

Tips for Entry

1. Visit the National Center for Environmental Economics's Web site, http://www.yosemite1.epa.gov/ee/ epa/eed.nsf/webpages/SummerInternships.html, for information about summer internships for high school and college students.
2. In high school, take courses in mathematics, statistics, and environmental science.
3. Visit the Student Center at the Environmental Protection Agency's Web site, http://www.epa.gov/ohr/ student/studentoffices.htm, to learn about student temporary and summer employment.
4. Search for graduate schools at the Association of Environmental and Resource Economics's Web site, http://www.aere.org.

ENVIRONMENTAL HEALTH OFFICER

CAREER PROFILE

Duties: Inspecting public and private sites—such as apartments, restaurants, schools, hospitals, businesses, manufacturing plants, community swimming pools, and other facilities—for compliance with local, state, and federal environmental health laws

Alternate Title(s): Environmental Health Inspector, Environmental Sanitation Specialist

Salary Range: $35,000 to $90,000

Employment Prospects: Fair

Advancement Prospects: Limited

Prerequisites:

    Education or Training—Bachelor's degree in environmental health, public health, biological sciences, or similar field

    Experience—Knowledge of local, state, and federal laws and regulations regarding environmental health hazards

    Special Skills and Personality Traits—Ability to work independently; attention to detail; interpersonal communication skills; report writing; problem solving

    Special Requirements—Varies by agency; state or national certification is typically required, as is a valid driver's license

CAREER LADDER

```
┌─────────────────────────────────────┐
│      Director of Public Health       │
└─────────────────────────────────────┘

┌─────────────────────────────────────┐
│  Senior Environmental Health Officer │
└─────────────────────────────────────┘

┌─────────────────────────────────────┐
│     Environmental Health Officer     │
└─────────────────────────────────────┘

┌─────────────────────────────────────┐
│        Environmental Health          │
│        Officer-in-Training           │
└─────────────────────────────────────┘
```

Position Description

Typically hired by public health departments, Environmental Health Officers work to ensure compliance with local, state, and federal environmental health laws. They pay scheduled and unscheduled visits to restaurants, schools, hospitals, zoos, hotels, childcare providers, factories, and other public and private facilities. Their primary job at these sites is to conduct a thorough inspection of not only buildings and grounds but also the operations that take place there and pinpoint any environmental health violations. For example, Environmental Health Officers who visit a restaurant not only examine the cleanliness of the kitchen and bathroom, but also they observe how food is stored, how staff prepare and serve food, and how dishes are washed. They may also collect food samples for testing. At a meat manufacturing plant, an Environmental Health Officer not only inspects the quality and freshness of the packaged product, but also monitors the processes leading up to packaging, as well as how the meat is then stored and shipped to grocery stores, restaurants, etc. Similarly, at a public recreational facility, Environmental Health Officers might do things like review how often public pool cleaning and maintenance is scheduled, as well as test current chlorine levels.

Environmental Health Officers also inspect how the activities of certain businesses, such as factories or waste disposal firms, impact air and water quality and pollution. In some cases, they may collect water or soil samples for laboratory analysis and issue an order to reduce pollution levels, if necessary.

After an inspection—whether a routine visit or one undertaken in response to employee or consumer complaints—Environmental Health Officers meet with owners or other responsible parties to discuss their findings. If these findings include violations, Environmental Health Officers then issue citations and schedule a repeat visit where they check to see necessary changes have been implemented. For repeat offenders, Environmental Health Officers can file court complaints, and some are authorized to order business owners to appear in court. In cases where a violation results in a court case, an Environmental Health Officer may also have to appear in court to testify.

A key component of the Environmental Health Officer's job is to maintain detailed records of findings and to write reports, many of which are ultimately made public. In fact, some newspapers regularly publish "report cards" for local restaurants; these are based upon the findings of Environmental Health Officers. Other job duties include giving presentations on environmental health and safety issues; investigating public health outbreaks to determine the cause; and making recommendations for new processes and procedures that promote environmental health.

Large public health departments may hire several Environmental Health Officers, each of whom is assigned to a specific activity, such as water quality, air pollution, or restaurant sanitation. In smaller operations, a single officer may be responsible for all environmental health activities. Normally, Environmental Health Officers work 40 hours a week. They divide their time between writing reports in their office and making field visits, which can be physically demanding if the site requires extensive walking, climbing, or stooping.

Salaries

Beginning Environmental Health Officers make between $35,000 and $50,000 per year. Those who take on managerial duties typically earn between $45,000 and $60,000 annually. A director can garner a salary of up to $80,000. Individuals working for larger public health departments in urban areas tend to garner a higher wage than those in smaller, more rural settings. Advanced degrees also tend to boost earnings.

Employment Prospects

The Bureau of Labor Statistics expects the job outlook for Environmental Health Officers through 2014 to be slower than average for most other occupations. This is due both to recent budget cuts and also to the fact that positions typically become open only when an officer retires or secures a promotion.

Advancement Prospects

Beginning Environmental Health Officers need both a bachelor's degree and state or national certification. Some may gain entry into the field by securing an internship with a local, state, or national public health agency. Sometimes officers may be hired as trainees who work with a senior officer while they gain experience in inspection processes and procedures, as well as increase their knowledge of specific laws and regulations pertinent to their position. Environmental Health Officers who secure a master's degree in public health and a few years of experience are eligible for promotion to a supervisory position that includes overseeing junior officers. Environmental Health Officers with a number of years in the field and considerable managerial experience may pursue a position as a director of public health; these positions may require a doctorate degree.

Education and Training

The minimum educational requirement for an Environmental Health Officer is a bachelor's degree in public health, environmental health, biology, or related field. Environmental Health Officers must be able to prepare accurate and detailed official reports that may be used in court. They also need an in-depth understanding of the environmental rules and regulations of their jurisdiction.

Special Requirements

Certification at either the state or national level is typically required; for entry-level positions, individuals may be given a period of six months or one year to obtain required certification. The National Environmental Health Association offers five types of certification for Environmental Health Officers. Typically, individuals must possess a minimum of a bachelor's degree in environmental or public health to sit for the certification examination. Those with a bachelor's degree in another field need two years of experience before they qualify to take the exam.

As the job requires fieldwork in of all sorts of settings, a certain degree of physical fitness is usually necessary. A valid driver's license is a common requirement because officers must travel from site to site. As with most governmental positions, candidates may also be subject to drug tests, background checks, medical examinations, and a written test.

Experience, Special Skills, and Personality Traits

Environmental Health Officers need the interpersonal skills to handle difficult situations, as they may encounter angry business owners from time to time. Because they quite often spend a considerable amount of time working independently, officers must also be able to manage their own time well and be self-motivated.

Unions and Associations

The National Environmental Health Association and the American Public Health Association represent Environmental Health Officers and related professionals. The Environmental and Occupational Health Sciences Institute provides educational and career information to individuals pursing career advancement in this field.

Tips for Entry

1. Visit the National Environmental Health Association's Web site, http://www.neha.org/credential/index.shtml, to learn about certification as an Environmental Health Officer.

2. Search for jobs at the American Public Health Association's Web site, http://www.apha.org/career/, or at National Environmental Health Association's Web site, http://www.neha.org/CareerOp.html.

3. Research internships offered by your state's Department of Public Health.

4. Begin making professional contacts by joining a public health association in your state. (See http://www.apha.org/state_local/affiliates/ for more information.)

FISH AND WILDLIFE OFFICER

CAREER PROFILE

CAREER PROFILE

Duties: Enforcing state and local hunting and fishing laws; responding to accidents and emergencies; investigating complaints; issuing warnings to lawbreakers and making arrests of repeat offenders; keeping an inventory of animals and fish in designated wildlife areas and collecting water samples; conducting training classes in firearm safety

Alternate Title(s): Conservation Officer; Game Warden

Salary Range: $30,000 to $80,000

Employment Prospects: Fair

Advancement Prospects: Limited

Prerequisites:

  Education or Training—A minimum of an associate's degree, preferably in criminal justice, forestry, or a similar field

  Experience—Law enforcement and work in conservation areas

  Special Skills and Personality Traits—Ability to work independently; familiarity with outdoor settings; problem solving; writing, public speaking, and interpersonal skills

  Special Requirements—U.S. citizenship; 21 years of age; valid driver's license; no previous convictions; drug test

CAREER LADDER

```
┌─────────────────────────────────────┐
│   Chief Fish and Wildlife Officer    │
└─────────────────────────────────────┘

┌─────────────────────────────────────┐
│  Senior Fish and Wildlife Officer    │
└─────────────────────────────────────┘

┌─────────────────────────────────────┐
│      Fish and Wildlife Officer       │
└─────────────────────────────────────┘

┌─────────────────────────────────────┐
│ Fish and Wildlife Officer-in-Training│
└─────────────────────────────────────┘
```

Position Description

As full-time government employees, Fish and Wildlife Officers work at either the state or national level for wildlife and conservation departments within the United States. Uniformed police officers licensed to carry firearms, Fish and Wildlife Officers spend a considerable amount of time patrolling the area to which they are assigned. This may take place on foot, in some sort of truck or jeep, or via boat. While on patrol, duties include issuing hunting and fishing licenses, investigating complaints about illegal hunting and fishing activities, and enforcing state and federal hunting, fishing, and boating laws. While Fish and Wildlife Officers normally issue verbal or written warnings for various violations, particularly to first-time offenders, they also possess the authority to make arrests, depending upon the severity of the violation, as well as the number of previous warnings given. At times, Fish and Wildlife Officers are called upon to write incident reports, as well as to testify in court.

Another key responsibility of Fish and Wildlife Officers is to teach courses on topics such as firearm, boating, and wilderness safety; hunting and fishing rules and regulations; and the importance of wildlife preservation. While these seminars oftentimes take place within the area to which the Fish and Wildlife Officer is assigned, they are sometimes held at a nearby school or community center, to which the officer must travel. Fish and Wildlife Officers may also find themselves fighting forest fires and organizing and leading a search party. When investigating calls about wild animals that have made their way into suburban or urban settings, officers may need to sedate and transport the animals back to their natural habitat. If a visitor to a wildlife area is harmed, officers are expected to administer first aid and CPR and either to transport injured persons to appropriate sources of medical help or to request emergency assistance if necessary.

Some Fish and Wildlife Officers work with environmental and natural resource scientists and biologists to maintain counts of wildlife and fish in certain areas and to record their observations of the wildlife and natural setting. A portion of this work involves not only maintaining accurate and detailed records but also writing lengthy reports.

The majority of Fish and Wildlife Officers are full time and work approximately 40 hours per week; however, these hours fluctuate considerably. For example, hours increase dramatically during the most popular hunting and fishing seasons. Most officers are required to work weekends because these days are more popular for hunting and fishing than weekdays; they also typically begin their shifts very early in the morning, as this can be a peak time of day for such activities. Also, many Fish and Wildlife Officers remain on call while they are off the clock.

Salaries

A beginning Fish and Wildlife Officer makes roughly $30,000 annually. Because they are considered on probation for a specific period of time, such as six months or one year, these individuals usually receive on-the-job training. After completing probation and gaining certification, Fish and Wildlife Officers earn between $40,000 and $60,000 per year. Promotions to senior positions typically result in additional wages as well. Chief Fish and Wildlife Officers, a title reserved for experienced officers with years of management and administrative experience, can garner more than $80,000.

Employment Prospects

Because only a limited number of positions exist for Fish and Wildlife Officers, competition for these jobs is intense. According to the North America Wildlife Enforcement Officers Association, the state and federal governments in the United States and Canada combined employ no more than a total of 12,000 Fish and Wildlife Officers. As job growth for the industry is minimal, positions tend to open only when officers quit, secure a promotion, or retire.

Advancement Prospects

To gain entry into the field before finishing school, many prospective Fish and Wildlife Officers gain experience by securing part-time employment or volunteer positions with the U.S. Fish and Wildlife Service, which operates a temporary employment program for students. Similarly, the Student Conservation Association offers a variety of summer internships for high school and college volunteers interested in eventually working for public parks and forests in the United States.

After they secure their first full-time position, Fish and Wildlife Officers who gain supervisory and administrative experience can pursue managerial promotions, although these positions are even more limited than officer positions. Some officers end up advancing their careers by specializing in an area such as investigations, forensics, or training. The National Conservation Training Center, operated by the U.S. Fish and Wildlife Service, offers six specialized training programs: Aquatic Resources, Education Outreach, Leadership and Employee Development, Environmental Conservation, Technology, and Wildlife.

Education and Training

The majority of Fish and Wildlife Officer positions require at least an associate's degree in criminal justice, forestry, environmental or natural resources, or a similar field. Some states do allow experience to substitute for education; however, given the significant number of candidates who typically apply for each position, those with an associate's or bachelor's degree stand a better chance of landing an interview and securing a job.

Special Requirements

Specific state and federal requirements vary. Most Fish and Wildlife Officers are expected to pass a Civil Service Examination; complete a CPR course, as well as additional medical and safety training depending upon the jurisdiction in which the position is open; complete medical and physical agility tests; undergo drug tests; and possess other qualifications required of all commissioned police officers: U.S. citizenship, 21 years of age, valid U.S. driver's license, and no criminal record. While interviewing, potential Fish and Wildlife Officers may also be subject to a polygraph test, a background check, and psychological review.

Experience, Special Skills, and Personality Traits

Fish and Wildlife Officers are expected to have an understanding of both law enforcement and wildlife conservation. Expected to work independently, officers also need well developed interpersonal and communication skills, as they quite often interact with hunters, fishers, boaters, and others. Good public-speaking skills are also helpful when officers are called upon to teach hunting and boating safety courses. Finally, given the fact that officers spend considerable amounts of time outdoors, they need experience with a variety of outdoor activities, such as using a compass, reading a map, operating a boat, hiking, and interacting with wild animals.

Unions and Associations

Nearly every state operates a fish and wildlife association. The North American Wildlife Enforcement Officers Association serves Fish and Wildlife Officers in both the United States and Canada. The U.S. Fish and Wildlife Service also represents officers working within the States, as does the Federal Wildlife Officers Association.

Tips for Entry

1. Secure a temporary student position with the U.S. Fish and Wildlife Service. Search for openings at their Web site, http://www.fws.gov/jobs/STEP.gov.

2. Apply for a summer internship with the Student Conservation Association, http://www.sca-inc.org.

3. Learn more about your state's fish and wildlife department by finding the link to your state at the U.S. Fish and Wildlife Service's Web site, http://www.fws.gov.

4. Search for jobs at the Federal Wildlife Officers Association, http://www/fwoa.org/careers.html.

IRRIGATION AUDITOR

CAREER PROFILE

Duties: Examining irrigation systems; determining where irrigation operations can be made more efficient both in terms of saving money and reducing impact on the environment; making recommendations for improvements.

Alternate Title(s): Environmental Auditor; Irrigation Specialist

Salary Range: $40,000 to $70,000

Employment Prospects: Good

Advancement Prospects: Limited

Prerequisites:

Education or Training—High school diploma with five years of experience; otherwise a minimum of a two-year technical degree with a focus on environmental engineering or waste management

Experience—Knowledge of irrigation systems and related technology

Special Skills and Personality Traits—Accuracy and attention to detail; ability to work independently; troubleshooting and problem solving; verbal and written communication skills; mathematical skills

Special Requirements—A valid driver's license; certifications may vary by specialty

CAREER LADDER

```
┌─────────────────────────────────┐
│    Senior Irrigation Auditor     │
└─────────────────────────────────┘

┌─────────────────────────────────┐
│      Irrigation Auditor          │
└─────────────────────────────────┘

┌─────────────────────────────────┐
│    Irrigation Auditor Trainee    │
└─────────────────────────────────┘
```

Position Description

Irrigation Auditors examine all kinds of irrigation systems, from those used in small golf course operations to those serving large cities. The job of Irrigation Auditors is oftentimes twofold: they collect and document evidence of whether or not an organization's irrigation system complies with local, state, and federal environmental regulations, and they also evaluate the efficiency of the system in an effort to reduce costs for the organization. For example, they may determine that a system produces too much runoff, which is not only violating local runoff limits, but also impacting the water quality of an area. Fixing this problem may force an organization to incur costs in the form of purchasing new irrigation equipment or modifying standard procedures. However, for a different organization, an Irrigation Auditor may also discover that although runoff levels are in compliance with all regulations, inefficiencies with the runoff processes and procedures are boosting operation and maintenance costs. As a result, they may be able to make recommendations that will actually save money.

Prior to making a site inspection, an Irrigation Auditor normally reviews irrigation blueprints, schedules, and other plans and photos that demonstrate how an irrigation system is currently operating. Activities that take place during an inspection include the following:

• Walking the site
• Observing how the irrigation system works
• Pinpointing areas with visible problems
• Taking soil and water samples to discover hidden problems

- Measuring irrigation levels at different areas within a site
- Calculating real-time evaporation and transpiration levels
- Using historical evaporation and transpiration levels with landscape coefficients to determine water requirements
- Testing irrigation equipment, such as sprinkler heads, water pumps, pipes, and hoses
- Interviewing workers about their practices, interaction with the system, and observations about how the system works
- Recording findings

Once they have finished an inspection and compiled all data, Irrigation Auditors then consolidate their findings into a report, which they typically present to management in a face-to-face meeting, so they can explain their recommendations and answer any questions. Audits are also forwarded to any regulatory bodies deemed necessary.

Irrigation Auditors can specialize in certain industry sectors, such as landscape design. An individual who chooses this specialization will develop very specific goals when working with a client. When first touring a site, the Irrigation Auditor will make special note of problem areas in the landscape, such as drooping plants, waterlogged areas, or dry patches. They will typically test how much water the irrigation system distributes and whether or not this is consistent across the landscape. The information they seek will be quite specific, such as how often and for what duration of time the landscape is irrigated, how the schedule is adjusted when seasons change, when the irrigation system was first put into place, what types of repairs were necessary, and how often they were required.

Irrigation Auditors spend the majority of their time conducting on-site inspections, which require considerable walking, and the remainder of their time in an office working with the information they have gathered. Normally, they work a standard 40-hour workweek.

Salaries

The median annual salary for an Irrigation Auditor was $48,530 in 2004, as reported by the 2006–07 edition of the Department of Labor's *Occupational Outlook Handbook*. Yearly wages range from roughly $40,000 to $70,000, depending on experience and education.

Employment Prospects

Average job growth is expected for Irrigation Auditors through 2014, according to the Department of Labor's Bureau of Labor Statistics. Landscape architecture is considered a key growth sector for this profession.

Advancement Prospects

Irrigation Auditors can gain entry-level experience by securing a summer job with the U.S. Department of Agriculture (USDA) or a seasonal landscaping firm. Another option

is to apply for an internship through the Irrigation Association Education Foundation. Most entry-level Irrigation Auditors also receive on-the-job training. Eventually, after gaining years of experience, candidates may be eligible for a senior position that includes managerial or administrative responsibilities. Some Irrigation Auditors may decide to work independently as consultants.

Education and Training

While postsecondary education is not a requirement for all Irrigation Auditor positions, holding a four-year degree in environmental engineering, landscape architecture, or a similar field can certainly improve a candidate's potential for landing a job. Salaries for degreed individuals also tend to be higher. The Irrigation Association publishes a directory of postsecondary institutions that offer programs in irrigation.

Along with an in-depth understanding of water-related rules, regulations, and restrictions, Irrigation Auditors need to grasp the scientific concepts that determine how weather impacts water sources. As they are required to review existing blueprints and other irrigation plans, the ability to read and interpret these plans is essential.

Special Requirements

Some states require certification. The Irrigation Association offers two credentials: Certified Landscape Irrigation Auditor and the Certified Gold Irrigation Auditor. Examinations are offered at sites throughout the United States.

Physical fitness is also important, as site visits may require a great deal of walking, standing, and/or bending. Because auditors must travel from site to site, qualifications also include possessing a valid driver's license.

Experience, Special Skills, and Personality Traits

Irrigation Auditors need mathematical skills to complete the various calculations necessary for determining water requirements. Being able to use specialized equipment and then consolidate and analyze resulting data is also important. Additional requirements include problem solving, technical report writing, presentation, and verbal communication skills.

Unions and Associations

The Irrigation Association represents irrigation industry professionals of all kinds, as does the American Society of Irrigation Consultants. Other associations include the American Water Works Association and the Water Environment Federation.

Tips for Entry

1. Look for summer and student jobs with the USDA's Agriculture Research Service. Regional contacts

are listed at http://www.ars.usda.gov/Careers/docs. htm?docid=1345.

2. Research scholarships available through the American Water Works Association. More information is available at http://www.awwa.org/careercenter/studentcenter.

3. Apply for summer internships listed on the Irrigation Association Education Foundation's Web site, http://www.irrigation.org.

4. Search for jobs at the Water Environment Federation's Web site, http://wef.jobcontrolcenter.com/search.cfm.

OCCUPATIONAL SAFETY AND HEALTH OFFICER

CAREER PROFILE

Duties: Inspecting work sites, both public and private, for compliance with local, state, and federal occupational safety and health laws; investigating accidents and complaints related to workplace safety; issuing citations for violations; making recommendations for improvements.

Alternate Title(s): Workplace Safety Compliance Officer; Occupational Safety and Health Specialist; Environmental Workplace Safety Technician

Salary Range: $30,000 to $80,000

Employment Prospects: Good

Advancement Prospects: Limited

Prerequisites:

Education or Training—Bachelor's degree in environmental science, industrial hygiene, biology, chemistry, or similar field

Experience—Knowledge of local, state, and federal laws and regulations regarding workplace safety

Special Skills and Personality Traits—Strong observational skills; ability to work both independently and with teams; attention to detail; interpersonal communications skills; report writing; problem solving

Special Requirements—Varies by jurisdiction, although certification is typically required, as is a valid driver's license and U.S. citizenship

CAREER LADDER

```
┌─────────────────────────────────┐
│  Senior Occupational Safety and │
│         Health Officer          │
└─────────────────────────────────┘

┌─────────────────────────────────┐
│ Occupational Safety and Health Officer │
└─────────────────────────────────┘

┌─────────────────────────────────┐
│      Occupational Safety and    │
│   Health Officer-in-Training    │
└─────────────────────────────────┘
```

Position Description

Typically hired by the Occupational Safety and Health Administration (OSHA) to work at either the state or federal level, Occupational Safety and Health Officers work to ensure compliance with local, state, and federal workplace safety and health laws. They follow OSHA guidelines—regulations put in place to protect employees, the environment, and the public—to conduct routine worksite inspections and then write detailed technical reports of their findings. After finishing their inspections, Occupational Safety and Health Officers discuss their findings with employers and employees. Due to the technical nature of their job, officers may

need to offer detailed explanations of regulations, violations, various types of citations, how penalties are assessed, how citations can be appealed, and what changes must be made to ensure compliance with occupational safety and health standards.

To prepare for a workplace visit, Occupational Safety and Health Officers do things like review the emergency action plans of the organization, become familiar with any safety training currently offered at the site, and analyze the frequency and nature of on-the-job injuries. During a site inspection, Occupational Safety and Health Officers conduct a thorough tour of the facilities and grounds, talking with employees about their practices; taking air, water, and soil samples; and pinpointing any potential environmental hazards. They test equipment, monitor employee use of any protective devices or clothing, observe how hazardous substances are both handled and stored, assess the emergency preparedness level of the organization, and measure employee exposure to any types of unsafe or unhealthy conditions ranging from poor lighting and aging equipment to toxic chemicals and dangerous molds. If they find violations, Occupational Safety and Health Officers may issue either a warning or a citation and schedule a follow-up visit to ensure compliance measures have been taken.

While Occupational Safety and Health Officers conducting routine visits examine all safety and health aspects of an operation, when responding to a specific concern, such as a hazardous spill, chemical fire, or a series of on-the-job injuries, their work is much more targeted. They may interview employees to find out what happened, investigate the site of an incident, and recommend measures to reduce future risk. If they are able to determine cause, they may also issue a citation, ask employers to make immediate improvements, or remove employees from an area, if warranted.

The duties of a higher-level Occupational Safety and Health Officer include training less experienced colleagues and leading special investigation or task-based teams. They might also find themselves giving presentations to employers and employees regarding environmentally hazardous work conditions, testifying in cases that have gone to court, and offering professional expertise to attorneys.

Occupational Safety and Health Officers may be hired to work in a specific sector, such as construction, or they may work across a variety of industries. Occupational Safety and Health Officers tend to work 40 hours a week, some of which is spent in an office writing reports and the remainder of which is spent on-site. Work can be physically demanding as it oftentimes requires long periods of standing as well as walking and even climbing. Officers are also exposed to hazardous work conditions and substances, as well as unsafe environmental conditions, from time to time.

Salaries

Entry-level Occupational Safety and Health Officers make roughly $30,000, while those with considerable experience earn nearly $80,000. According to the Bureau of Labor Statistics, the median yearly salary for an Occupational Safety and Health Officer in 2004 was $48,710. Individuals with graduate degrees tend to earn more than those with undergraduate degrees.

Employment Prospects

Job growth for Occupational Safety and Health Officers through 2014, as reported by the Bureau of Labor Statistics, will be comparable to most other occupations. Since the

September 11 terrorist attacks in New York City and Washington, D.C., demand for emergency preparedness in the workplace has risen, a phenomenon which has subsequently increased demand for Occupational Safety and Health Officers. Also influencing employment in this sector is increased public attention on job-related environmental hazards.

Advancement Prospects

Entry-level Occupational Safety and Health Officers typically possess a four-year degree in industrial hygiene, environmental science, or a related field. Sometimes officers may be hired as trainees who work with a senior officer while they gain experience in OSHA inspection processes and procedures as well as increase their knowledge of specific laws and regulations pertinent to their position. Experienced Occupational Safety and Health Officers who secure a graduate degree may be eligible for promotion to supervisory positions, although these tend to be quite limited as turnover typically happens only when an individual retires or receives a promotion. One area for advancement is the private sector, as the number of occupational health and safety consulting businesses has grown in recent years.

Education and Training

The minimum educational requirement for Occupational Safety and Health Officers is a bachelor's degree in industrial hygiene, environmental science, biology, chemistry, or a related field. Many Occupational Safety and Health Officers possess master's degrees. The American Society of Safety Engineers compiles a list of postsecondary institutions that offer degrees for individuals interested in safety-related professions. The American Industrial Hygiene Association offers a similar list of educational options for those who want to pursue a degree in industrial hygiene.

Special Requirements

Certification at either the state or national level is typically required; for entry-level positions, individuals may be given a period of six months or one year to obtain required certification. The American Board of Industrial Hygiene offers two credentials: the Certified Industrial Hygienist or the Certified Associate Industrial Hygienist. The Board of Certified Safety Professionals offers the Certified Safety Credential. Also, the Council on Certification of Health, Environment, and Safety Technologists offers both the Occupational Health and Safety Technologist certification and the Construction Health and Safety Technician certification. Most certification programs have education and experience requirements that must be met prior to gaining approval to sit for an examination.

Occupational Safety and Health Officers must understand highly detailed and technical occupational safety laws and regulations. As they are required to prepare governmental reports regarding their findings, officers must also possess an in-depth understanding of industrial work and potential hazards. Because site visits make up a significant portion of the job, at least an average level of physical fitness is important as well. Other common requirements include U.S. citizenship, a valid driver's license, and the ability to pass drug tests, background checks, medical examinations, and a written test.

Experience, Special Skills, and Personality Traits

Occupational Safety and Health Officers need strong observational skills as well as the ability to work both independently and with teams. Because they may find themselves in emotionally charged situations, particularly when investigating things like industrial accidents, officers also need considerable interpersonal communication and problem-solving skills. Also, tasks like the compilation of highly technical information and the creation of detailed reports require considerable accuracy.

Unions and Associations

The Board of Certified Safety Professionals represents individuals working in safety-related professions. More specialized associations include the American Board of Industrial Hygiene; the Council on Certification of Health, Environmental, and Safety Technologists; the American Society of Safety Engineers; and the American Industrial Hygiene Association.

Tips for Entry

1. Visit the Board of Certified Safety Professionals' Web site, http://www.bcsp.org, to learn about the Certification Safety Professional credential. Other organizations offering certification include the Board of Industrial Hygiene, http://www.abih.org, and the Council on Certification of Health, Environmental, and Safety Technologists, http://www.cchest.org.

2. To learn more about colleges and universities offering specialized degree programs, visit the Web sites of organizations like the American Society of Safety Engineers, http://www.asse.org, or the American Industrial Hygiene Association, http://www.aiha.org.

3. Gain experience as a student through the Student Temporary Employment and Student Career Experience Component programs offered by the Office of Personnel Management. A list of openings for students is available at http://www.usajobs.opm.gov.

4. Search for jobs at the Department of Labor's Web site, http://www.dol.gov/dol/jobs.htm, which posts positions for the Occupational Safety and Health Administration.

PARK MANAGER

CAREER PROFILE

Duties: Managing the operation of one or more federal or state parks; establishing strategic plans and goals; planning, developing, and implementing new park programs; overseeing budgetary and fiscal considerations; ensuring compliance with all municipal, state, and federal regulations; hiring and supervising park rangers and other employees

Alternate Title(s): Park Director; Park Superintendent; District Manager

Salary Range: $75,000 to $100,000+

Employment Prospects: Limited

Advancement Prospects: Limited

Prerequisites:

Education or Training—Minimum of an undergraduate degree in some form of management, preferably parks and recreation management, natural resources management, or similar field; a graduate degree is desirable

Experience—Previous managerial and administrative work; understanding of specific issues related to park operations, including site safety and risk, ecological impact, and grounds maintenance

Special Skills and Personality Traits—Strong leadership skills; ability to multitask and delegate responsibilities; mentoring; interpersonal communication skills; writing, public-speaking, and problem-solving skills

Special Requirements—Familiarity with state and federal laws and regulations regarding public parks

CAREER LADDER

```
┌─────────────────────────────┐
│      District Manager        │
└─────────────────────────────┘

┌─────────────────────────────┐
│       Park Manager           │
└─────────────────────────────┘

┌─────────────────────────────┐
│       Park Ranger            │
└─────────────────────────────┘
```

Position Description

Park Managers are responsible for the operation and administration of an entire park or series of parks within the state and federal park system of the United States. As a result, Park Managers must possess a very broad range of skills that include the oversight of personnel development, park maintenance, park resources, strategic planning, community relations, educational programs, and visitor services. Whether they conduct specific tasks themselves or delegate them to an assistant of some sort, Park Managers are accountable for everything that takes place within their parks.

Park Managers oversee all aspects of personnel development, from employee recruitment and retention to scheduling. They are responsible for the interviewing, hiring, training, and supervising of rangers and all other park employees and volunteers. Typically, they also handle all employee discipline issues and conduct all employee evaluations. It is also the job of the Park Manager to ensure that all human resource laws and regulations are followed.

Along with ensuring the proper maintenance of park grounds, Park Managers are also responsible for both historical and nonhistorical buildings, as well as equipment and vehicles such as trucks, boats, small aircraft, and skis used by employees. Other activities related to park maintenance include managing the construction of new facilities, overseeing recycling processes and procedures, and ensuring compliance with all Occupational Safety and Health Administration (OSHA) regulations.

To manage park resources, Park Managers oversee the design and construction of any new trails, decide how to deal with invasive species of plants and animals that might disrupt the ecosystem of the park, and supervise the processes and procedures related to the inventory of park plants and animals. They may need to draft ecological impact statements, oversee the acquisition of land, work to protect endangered species, predict future trends, foresee future problems, and deal with boundary encroachments.

The administrative tasks of Park Managers are extensive. Along with developing and monitoring the park's budget, Park Managers are also expected to contract all necessary services, such as concession stands; make public presentations; write grants; develop marketing and fund-raising strategies; manage park records; write necessary reports; prepare for audits; and ensure compliance with all rules and regulations.

Park Managers are also responsible for strategic planning. This involves establishing not only a mission, vision, and goals, but also a park identity, which can include anything from landscape design and program offerings to specific park traditions, such as free botanical tours in the spring. Oftentimes, Park Managers will work with their entire staffs to develop specific park philosophies, such as how law enforcement activities will be handled.

Another important component of park management is public relations. Park Managers are responsible for developing and maintaining relationships with various community organizations, as well as with the media. Oftentimes, they solicit volunteer groups to handle certain tasks, such as promoting events. Park Managers also work to develop governmental contacts that might prove useful for promoting pieces of legislation relevant to park funding or operations. To this end, Park Managers are expected to facilitate meetings with congressional representatives, committee chairpersons, and the public, and to advocate for their parks by negotiating with county, state, and federal officials.

As most public parks in the state and federal park system offer educational programs and special events of some sort, program development, promotion, and implementation are important aspects of park management. Other visitor services, such as signs, maps, exhibits, displays, and first aid, are also the responsibility of the Park Manager.

As park use in the United States tends to be quite seasonal, hours for Park Managers can vary quite a bit. They work a minimum of 40 hours per week; however, this number can climb considerably higher during high season, when the need for managerial intervention typically peaks.

Salaries

According to the National Park Service, Park Managers made annual salaries ranging from $75,000 to $100,000 in 2005. Individuals with extensive management experience, even in other fields, tend to earn more than individuals whose management experience is more limited.

Employment Prospects

Due to recent budget cuts in funding for parks and other natural resources, competition is fierce within the U.S. state and federal park system at all grade levels, including management. Given the low rate of job growth for the industry, Park Manager positions tend to open only when existing managers quit, secure a promotion, or retire. District Park Manager positions are even fewer in number.

Advancement Prospects

Park Managers typically advance their careers in two ways. They may work as park rangers for several years, gaining experience while they wait for a management position to become available. Other individuals gain management experience in other industries and then transfer these skills into the field of park management; however, even in these cases, candidates are most successful when they have some sort of experience in the park system.

Prospective Park Managers can gain valuable experience by working as seasonal assistants or in some other entry-level capacity while student. After completing their degrees and finding full-time work, individuals interested in management work can take on additional responsibilities—such as mentoring new employees, writing reports, and preparing budgets—in an effort to build their base of managerial skills. Eventually, experienced Park Managers might be able to advance their careers further by becoming District Park Managers, responsible for a group of parks.

Education and Training

Park Managers who are promoted from park ranger positions usually possess at least an undergraduate degree in environmental or natural resources, parks and recreation management, or a similar field. A significant number of candidates, however, come from different sorts of backgrounds. Individuals who shift into park management from another industry tend to have graduate degrees in business or management, as well as some sort of experience with or knowledge of the state and federal park system.

Special Requirements

Applicants must be U.S. citizens. During the interview process, Park Managers may have to undergo a background check and drug screening, as well as psychological and medical review and a confidential financial disclosure. In addition, most candidates are expected to complete a supervisor/managerial probationary period upon hire.

Experience, Special Skills, and Personality Traits

Park Managers are expected to have substantial and wide ranging managerial skills, as well as an understanding of the natural environment within parks. Also essential are strong leadership skills; the ability to mentor employees and delegate responsibilities; problem-solving capabilities; public relations experience, including the ability to speak and write persuasively; and interpersonal skills. Park Managers must also be able to handle a fast-paced work environment with multiple and varied demands.

Unions and Associations

The National Association of State Park Directors is the professional organization serving the senior administrator of each state's park agency. The Center for Park Management, a branch of the National Parks Conservation Association, represents all park managers working within the U.S. National Park Service. The National Recreation and Parks Association serves all industry professionals, regardless of their level.

Tips for Entry

1. Learn more about national and state parks by visiting the National Park Service Web site, http://www.nps.gov.
2. Gain experience either by volunteering at your local park or by securing a part-time or seasonal position.
3. Apply early for a seasonal job. Visit http://www.nps.gov/personnel to learn more about the early recruitment efforts of the National Park Service. The site accepts online applications.
4. Search for Park Manager position openings at the National Parks Conservation Association Web site, http://www.npca.org.

OTHER

GROUNDS MAINTENANCE WORKER

CAREER PROFILE

Duties: Grade land; build retaining walls; install walkways; lay sod; plant grass seed and other greenery; fertilize, water, and mow lawns; care for plants, shrubs, and trees; maintain and repair outdoor areas; trim and prune trees and shrubs; apply weed treatments, fertilizers, herbicides, fungicides, and pesticides

Alternate Title(s): Groundskeeper, Landscaper, Tree Trimmer, Pesticide Handler

Salary Range: $9.57 to $16.99 (median hourly)

Employment Prospects: Excellent

Advancement Prospects: Good

Prerequisites:

Education or Training—No education is needed for entry-level positions.

Experience—Previous experience is helpful but not required.

Special Skills and Personality Traits—Responsibility; strong work ethic; excellent communication skills; ability to understand and follow oral and written instructions; ability to work cooperatively with others

Special Requirements—State licenses are sometimes required for applying pesticides or working as a landscape contractor. A driver's license and good driving record are required for some positions. Optional certifications are provided by trade associations.

CAREER LADDER

```
┌─────────────────────────────────────┐
│   Landscape Designer or Arborist     │
└─────────────────────────────────────┘

┌─────────────────────────────────────┐
│     Crew Leader or Supervisor        │
└─────────────────────────────────────┘

┌─────────────────────────────────────┐
│    Grounds Maintenance Worker        │
└─────────────────────────────────────┘
```

Position Description

In addition to jobs that involve the preservation of forests, rangelands, wetlands, lakes, and oceans, the conservation and environmental field offers opportunities for individuals who are interested in creating and maintaining natural spaces in and around buildings, homes, and other public areas. Grounds Maintenance Workers are employed in the broad occupational area of grounds maintenance, which encompasses several areas of specialization.

Landscaping and groundskeeping are the two principal specialties for Grounds Maintenance Workers. However, other areas include tree trimming and pruning, as well as pesticide application. While some Grounds Maintenance

Workers concentrate exclusively on one of these areas, many perform work related to them all.

Grounds Maintenance Workers who focus on landscaping frequently create new green space and areas of natural beauty. In addition to grading the earth to make sure that an area is sloped or formed in a certain way, landscapers may build retaining walls, dig holes in the ground for man-made ponds, and install walkways. After "roughing out" the land, landscapers lay sod or plant seed to create grassy areas. This may involve covering the ground with straw or erosion matting to prevent seed from washing away.

Landscapers also transport and plant a variety of greenery including shrubs, bushes, trees, plants, and flowers. Finally, they enhance the beauty and sustainability of green areas with finishing touches that range from fountains and sprinkler systems to lights, decks, and areas of colored mulch or stone. In addition to creating new green areas, landscapers also perform maintenance tasks that include fertilizing, watering, and mowing lawns and caring for plants, shrubs, and trees.

As groundskeepers, Grounds Maintenance Workers perform some of the same tasks that landscapers do, such as mowing, fertilizing, and watering grassy areas; raking leaves; and caring for trees and plants. However, their focus usually is on the upkeep and maintenance of outdoor areas. In addition to caring for green spaces, groundskeepers frequently keep roads, parking lots, and walkways free of ice and snow during the winter. They also install snow fences, remove litter and debris, and make repairs to broken equipment, benches, fences, fountains, swimming pools, picnic shelters, signs, sidewalks, and the like.

Grounds Maintenance Workers who specialize in tree trimming and pruning use their skills to work with trees and shrubs. On the practical side, they may cut away dead or low-hanging branches that are in the way of roads, walkways, or utility lines. However, some tree trimmers have specialized skills for shaping ornamental shrubs and trees.

Some Grounds Maintenance Workers are employed by services that concentrate on applying weed treatments, fertilizers, herbicides, fungicides, and pesticides to lawns and greenery on both commercial and residential properties. This work is more specialized than other types of grounds maintenance, and requires workers to perform inspections, develop pest or lawn management plans, mix chemical applications, and follow specific safety procedures.

Finally, some Grounds Maintenance Workers serve in supervisory capacities, either as independent business owners or as employees of larger enterprises. As such, they must prepare cost estimates and schedule crew assignments. Supervisors also train workers, keep track of employees' time records, and even help workers when deadlines require.

Regardless of their specialty, Grounds Maintenance Workers have a seemingly unlimited number of work settings from which to choose. These include homes; businesses such as offices, shopping malls, amusement parks, hospitals, and hotels; real-estate development and property management firms; lawn and garden equipment stores; private and public gardens, parks, forest preserves, and arboretums; sod farms; schools; government agencies; nurseries; athletic fields; golf courses; cemeteries; and college and university campuses. Some of these work settings require specialized skills or the performance of unique tasks. For example, Grounds Maintenance Workers who work on golf courses (known as greenskeepers) relocate holes on putting greens, and those who work in cemeteries must dig graves.

The U.S. Department of Labor indicated that some 1.5 million people were employed as Grounds Maintenance Workers in 2004. Of these, the majority (nearly 1.2 million) were either groundskeepers or landscapers. Approximately 33 percent worked for firms that served dwellings and buildings, and nearly 25 percent were self-employed.

Grounds Maintenance Workers use a wide range of tools and equipment to carry out their work. They frequently use simple hand tools including axes, rakes, shovels, hedge clippers, handsaws, pruning hooks, sod cutters, and shears. In addition, Grounds Maintenance Workers use motorized equipment such as chain saws, hedge trimmers, lawnmowers, snow throwers, lawn tractors, and backhoes.

For many Grounds Maintenance Workers, especially landscapers, employment is seasonal, with work occurring during the warmer months of the year. Workdays can be especially long, ranging from 12 to 14 hours in some cases. This is due to a variety of factors, including pressure to complete as many projects as possible during the warm season.

Employees in this field are subject to extreme temperatures and weather conditions—namely heat and severe storms. Non-seasonal Grounds Maintenance Workers work in winter weather that includes exposure to cold, snow, and ice. This occupation is physically demanding, with work that is characterized by heavy lifting, frequent bending and standing, and repetitive motion. Occupational hazards include a risk of heat stroke, skin cancer, dehydration, injury from hand and power tools, exposure to harmful pesticides and chemicals, and hearing loss from loud equipment and power tools. However, proper safety precautions can reduce the likelihood of many of these hazards.

Salaries

Salaries for Grounds Maintenance Workers vary, depending on factors such as area of specialization and employer. According to the 2006–07 edition of the Department of Labor's *Occupational Outlook Handbook*, in mid-2004 median hourly earnings for Grounds Maintenance Workers ranged from a low of $9.57 to a high of $16.99. The highest wages were earned by supervisors and managers, as well as tree trimmers and pruners and pesticide handlers. Elementary and secondary schools, as well as local governments, tended to pay higher wages than other employers.

Employment Prospects

The U.S. Department of Labor anticipates faster-than-average job growth for Grounds Maintenance Workers through 2014. According to the *Occupational Outlook Handbook*, a number of factors will drive this growth, namely high turnover due to low wages and the physically demanding nature of the work. Other factors include growth in residential and commercial construction, an increasing number of two-income households, and an aging population.

Advancement Prospects

Beyond entry-level, hands-on work, Grounds Maintenance Workers may advance to roles as crew leaders or supervisors. After working for someone else, some Grounds Maintenance Workers go into business for themselves by opening their own landscape contracting or landscape design firms. With specialized training, tree trimmers and pruners may advance to positions as arborists, who plant and care for trees.

Education and Training

Most jobs in the field of grounds maintenance have no educational requirements. Those that do usually require applicants to hold a high school diploma. In the 2000s, the U.S. Department Labor revealed that the majority of Grounds Maintenance Workers had either a high school education or less. While previous experience is helpful, most entry-level workers acquire the skills needed for this line of work via on-the-job training. Generally speaking, it takes only a short time for new workers to learn how to use equipment properly and safely, and to make repairs when needed.

Special Requirements

In most states, Grounds Maintenance Workers who apply pesticides must hold a license. In addition, landscape contractors are required to hold licenses in some states. Optional certification is provided by trade associations. For example, the Professional Landcare Network (PLANET) offers designations such as Certified Landscape Technician, Certified Landscape Professional, and Certified Turfgrass Profes-

sional. Finally, a driver's license and good driving record is required for positions that involve driving motor vehicles.

Experience, Special Skills, and Personality Traits

Although helpful, previous experience is not needed to work as a Grounds Maintenance Worker. In order to succeed and advance to lead or supervisory roles, employees must be responsible, have a strong work ethic, and possess excellent communication skills. In addition, they must be able to understand and follow both oral and written instructions. Finally, Grounds Maintenance Workers must be able to work cooperatively with others.

Unions and Associations

Some Grounds Maintenance Workers are members of the Professional Landcare Network. Known as PLANET, this international association was formed when the Associated Landscape Contractors of America (ALCA) and the Professional Lawn Care Association of America (PLCAA) combined in 2005. Other associations include the Professional Grounds Management Society, the International Society of Arboriculture, and the Tree Care Industry Association.

Tips for Entry

1. In high school, take courses in science, math, and business, which will help to prepare you for lead or supervisory positions.
2. Prior to entering the workforce, familiarize yourself with the operation of manual and motorized lawn care equipment, such as mowers and trimmers.
3. Pursue work in warmer regions of the country, where non-seasonal positions are more plentiful.

LANDSCAPE ARCHITECT

CAREER PROFILE

Duties: Plan the location and arrangement of buildings, walkways, roads, water features, site furnishings, plants, flowers, and trees; design and plan the restoration of wetlands, stream corridors, mined areas, and forested land; work with architects, city planners, civil engineers, and other professionals; undertake preservation planning projects for national, regional, and local historic sites and areas

Alternate Title(s): Designer, Golf Course Architect, Land Planner, Landscape Designer, Planner, Project Manager

Salary Range: $32,390 to $90,850+

Employment Prospects: Good

Advancement Prospects: Good

Prerequisites:

Education or Training—Bachelor of landscape architecture (B.L.A.), bachelor of science in landscape architecture (B.S.L.A.), master of landscape architecture (M.L.A.), or M.A./M.S. in landscape architecture

Experience—Basic technical skills; understanding of and proficiency in the use of computer-aided design and mapping software programs

Special Skills and Personality Traits—Sensitivity to landscape quality; understanding of the arts; humanistic approach to design; ability to analyze problems in terms of design and physical form; technical competence; management skills; professional ethics

Special Requirements—State licensure and passing of the national Landscape Architect Registration Examination

CAREER LADDER

```
┌─────────────────────────────────┐
│      Associate or Partner        │
└─────────────────────────────────┘

┌─────────────────────────────────┐
│   Licensed Landscape Architect   │
└─────────────────────────────────┘

┌─────────────────────────────────┐
│            Intern                │
└─────────────────────────────────┘
```

Position Description

Combining art and science, landscape architecture is the analysis, planning, design, and management of the natural and built environment. Landscape Architects enhance the quality of life by adding beauty, but they also are problem solvers who analyze the environmental impact of proposed developments, plan for pedestrian and automobile traffic, and determine the best use of each site.

The term *landscape architecture* became common after 1863 when Frederick Law Olmsted and Calvert Vaux designed New York's Central Park. Today, landscape architects deal with the increasingly complex relationships between the built and natural environments. Landscape Architects plan and design traditional places such as parks, residential developments, campuses, gardens, cemeteries, commercial centers, resorts, transportation facilities, corporate and institutional centers, and waterfront developments.

Landscape Architects also design and plan the restoration of natural places disturbed by humans such as wetlands, stream corridors, mined areas, and forested land. Working with architects, city planners, civil engineers, and other professionals, Landscape Architects play an important role in environmental protection by designing and implementing projects that respect the needs both of people and of our environment. In addition, their appreciation for historic landscapes and cultural resources enables landscape architects to undertake preservation planning projects for national, regional, and local historic sites and areas.

By sketching and using computer-aided design tools and computer mapping systems, landscape architects plan the location and arrangement of buildings, walkways, roads, water features, site furnishings, plants, flowers, and trees. Just a few of the things Landscape Architects do include:

- Analyzing the natural elements of a site, such as climate, soil, drainage, vegetation, and where sunlight falls at different times of the day. What plants will grow there? Where will each plant grow best?
- Considering how the site will be used. Will children play there? Will cars drive there and need to park? Will there be stores and shoppers?
- Assessing existing buildings, roads, water features, and utilities. Will new roads need to be built? Will electrical power lines need to be added?
- Evaluating the project's impact on the natural environment and local wildlife. Will the project disrupt the habitat of local wildlife? Will stormwater runoff cause an existing stream to flood?
- Taking into account laws and regulations that may affect the site
- Producing detailed site plans, including sketches, models, photographs, land use studies, written reports, and cost estimates for approval by the client and regulatory agencies
- Developing a plant list and plan of what plants, trees, flowers, and shrubs will go where

More than 70 percent of Landscape Architects spend at least part of their time designing residential projects, such as play areas, gardens, pools, fences, and other amenities. Residential design constitutes 40 percent of the U.S. market for landscape architecture services.

There is a wide range of opportunities for Landscape Architects. They may be employed in a variety of private, public, and academic organizations. In addition, many landscape architects are self-employed, start their own firms, or work on a consultant basis.

Most Landscape Architects work in the private sector for landscape architectural, engineering, architectural, and planning firms. Landscape Architects may also work with other types of private corporations that have physical planning departments—such as college campuses or retail chains—or that offer products and services related to land planning and development.

Public sector employment opportunities are found within federal, state, regional, and municipal agencies involved in land planning, development, and preservation. Federal agencies employing landscape architects include the U.S. Forest Service (employing the greatest number of landscape architects in the United States), National Park Service, Soil Conservation Service, Bureau of Land Management, U.S. Army Corps of Engineers, Department of Transportation, Veteran's Administration, and others. State and local governments offer landscape architects many more opportunities.

Landscape Architects in the academic sector practice, teach, and conduct research in the professional programs offered by colleges and universities across the country. They are on the faculties in departments of architecture, art, planning, and other related fields, and also teach in community colleges and continuing education programs.

Salaries

Salaries for Landscape Architects vary depending on years of experience, geographical location, and type of position. According to the U.S. Department of Labor's 2006–07 *Occupational Outlook Handbook*, in mid-2004 annual salaries for Landscape Architects ranged from less than $32,390 to more than $90,850, with a median of $53,120. According to the American Society of Landscape Architects (ASLA), in 2004 the average salary for entry-level Landscape Architects was $34,700. That year, those with up to five years of experience earned average salaries of $41,803, and practitioners earned $74,644.

Employment Prospects

There are about 30,000 Landscape Architects in the United States and many more are needed. Meeting human needs by making wise use of environmental resources is work that is in demand today and will continue to be needed in the future. While most Landscape Architects work for private firms, nearly 23 percent are self-employed—more than three times the average for all professionals. Therefore, opportunities are excellent for those who have an entrepreneurial spirit.

Advancement Prospects

During the first few years of their careers, beginning Landscape Architects normally work in an intern capacity under the supervision of a licensed Landscape Architect. Work responsibilities and tasks tend to be of a lower order at this time, with little involvement in actual project designs. After five years of experience many Landscape Architects have taken, or are preparing for, the Landscape Architect Registration Exam (LARE), which legally allows them to work on projects from start to finish. After about ten years, Landscape Architects may become associates or partners in a private firm, or start firms of their own.

Education and Training

Professional education in landscape architecture can be obtained at the undergraduate or graduate level. There are two undergraduate professional degrees: a Bachelor of

Landscape Architecture (B.L.A.) and a Bachelor of Science in Landscape Architecture (B.S.L.A.). These usually require four or five years of study in design, construction techniques, art, and history, as well as natural and social sciences.

There are generally three types of graduate degree programs including an M.L.A. for people who have an undergraduate degree in landscape architecture or another field, or an M.A. or M.S. degree for people who want to conduct research in landscape architecture, but don't want to become professional practitioners.

Special Requirements

In 2006, 47 states licensed Landscape Architects. There are two different types of mandated licensing known as "title acts" and "practice acts." In states with "title acts," no one without a license may use the title of Landscape Architect. Under the provisions of "practice acts," no one without a license may perform the work of a Landscape Architect. Each state sets its own requirements for registration, but all require candidates to pass the Landscape Architect Registration Examination (LARE). Many states also require candidates to have completed an approved program of professional education and to practice for a time under the supervision of a licensed Landscape Architect. The Council of Landscape Architectural Registration Boards (CLARB) develops and administers the LARE, and also maintains current information on the various states' licensing requirements.

Experience, Special Skills, and Personality Traits

Experience requirements for entry-level Landscape Architects vary from firm to firm. However, most firms require candidates to possess basic technical skills. In addition, entry-level Landscape Architects must have basic understanding and proficiency in the use of computer-aided design and mapping software programs.

Along with sensitivity to landscape quality, successful Landscape Architects must have an understanding of the arts and a humanistic approach to design. They must be able to analyze problems in terms of design and physical form. Technical competence is needed to translate a design into a completed work. Finally, Landscape Architects must be skilled in all aspects of professional practice including management and professional ethics.

Unions and Associations

The American Society of Landscape Architects (ASLA) is the national professional association for landscape architects, representing more than 15,000 members. ASLA promotes the landscape architecture profession and advances the practice through advocacy, education, communication, and fellowship. The Council of Educators in Landscape Architecture (CELA) represents faculty members and others interested in landscape architectural education.

Tips for Entry

1. While looking for a school, develop a list of questions that will help you make the best decision. A list of questions is available from the ASLA's Web site, http://www.asla.org.
2. Visit at least one landscape architecture program while classes are in session and, if possible, visit at least one or two landscape architecture offices.
3. Visit the ASLA's Web site for a list of books, journals, and magazines about the field of landscape architecture.
4. Join the ASLA as a Student Affiliate member. Membership includes a one-year subscription to *Landscape Architecture* magazine.

Information contained in this career profile used with permission of the American Society of Landscape Architects

NATURE PHOTOGRAPHER

CAREER PROFILE

Duties: Conduct research; propose photo-story ideas to editors; travel to remote locations; arrange photo compositions; transport, set up, and take down equipment; evaluate environmental factors; make technical adjustments to cameras; develop negatives; upload digital images; edit or touch up photos; send negatives or digital images to editors or make prints; write grant applications; write articles

Alternate Title(s): Wildlife Photographer

Salary Range: $15,000 to $54,180+

Employment Prospects: Fair

Advancement Prospects: Limited

Prerequisites:

Education or Training—Degree helpful but not required

Experience—Previous experience not required

Special Skills and Personality Traits—Business and technical skills; good color vision and eyesight; physical dexterity, stamina, and coordination; ability to work independently or collaboratively; artistic, creative, original, curious, efficient, flexible, patient, realistic, independent, and disciplined

CAREER LADDER

```
┌─────────────────────────────────┐
│   Photo Editor or Instructor     │
└─────────────────────────────────┘

┌─────────────────────────────────┐
│       Nature Photographer        │
└─────────────────────────────────┘

┌─────────────────────────────────┐
│ Intern or Photography Assistant  │
└─────────────────────────────────┘
```

Position Description

The field of photography contains a number of specialties, one of which is nature or wildlife photography. Nature Photographers capture images of animals, sea creatures, insects, and other forms of wildlife in their natural habitats. The often breathtaking results of their work can be seen in many places including museum exhibits, books, and articles in magazines such as *National Geographic*. Nature Photographers have documented everything from commercial fishing in the Bering Sea to the impact of oil spills on animal life.

Most Nature Photographers are self-employed. They work as freelancers who propose and/or receive assignments from magazine and book editors. In addition, they also submit their work to stock photography services, which catalog and cross reference images and make them available to editors, companies, and other parties for a fee, via catalogs and online databases. In turn, these services pay a royalty back to the photographer for the use of their work.

While taking great pictures is important, good business skills are critical in order to succeed in this field. As the U.S. Department of Labor explains in the 2006–07 edition of its *Occupational Outlook Handbook*, "Photographers who operate their own business, or freelance, need business skills as well as talent. These individuals must know how to prepare a business plan; submit bids; write contracts; keep financial records; market their work; hire models, if needed; get permission to shoot on locations that normally are not open to the public; obtain releases to use photographs of people; license and price photographs; and secure copyright protection for their work. To protect their rights and their work, self-employed photographers require basic knowledge of licensing and copyright laws, as well as knowledge of contracts and negotiation procedures."

Several key survival strategies are essential for independent photographers. First is the ability to consistently sell enough work to maintain a sustainable income. This requires photographers to keep several projects going simultaneously, due to factors such as assignment cancellations or clients who are late in providing payment.

Another strategy is differentiation, whereby a photographer sets his or her work apart from competing photographers. While emulating the career paths of successful photographers might seem logical, Nature Photographer Niall Benvie discourages this approach. In the article "Photos for Food," which appeared in *Nature Photographers Online Magazine*, Benvie explained: "This is a business where individuality is valued highly. Under no illusion are qualifications or professional distinctions going to cut any ice with editors. While established photographers find it easier to have their work seen, superior pictures from an unknown photographer on the same light table will normally be selected ahead of those from a 'name.'" Benvie also recommends that photographers strive to add value to the photos they take by offering prospective buyers complete packages that offer pictures along with concepts and words.

While some Nature Photographers travel the globe to shoot photographs of wildlife, some focus on specific geographic areas or regions. By developing an intimate familiarity with local landscapes and wildlife, specializing photographers have an edge over visiting photographers who do not possess the same knowledge. In addition, specialists may develop relationships with area officials and authorities that allow them to gain access to areas that would likely be restricted to other photographers, or to access wildlife preserves during off hours. Photographers who specialize in photographing their immediate environment also have the advantage of keeping overhead low—especially if they choose to live in or near the areas they photograph, as opposed to traveling from urban or suburban communities.

In order to prepare for a photo shoot, Nature Photographers often spend a great deal of time doing research before they take any pictures. In addition to developing a list of subjects and developing mental images of shots they would like to take, some photographers may even do rough sketches in a notebook. Following the planning stage, Nature Photographers devote varying amounts of time to their assignments. While photo shoots for a magazine article or print collateral may last only a day or two, a wildlife photography book could require many shots over the course of several years.

Nature Photographers use a range of equipment during the course of their work, including traditional and digital cameras, as well as a variety of lenses, tripods, film, and media cards. With the advent of digital photography, the use of traditional photo processing in dark rooms has given way to computerized photo editing. Because computers also have become important tools for photo storage and distribution, they are as essential as cameras for the serious photographer.

There are a number of common tasks that Nature Photographers perform. These include conducting research; proposing photo story ideas to editors; traveling to remote locations for photo shoots; arranging photo compositions; and transporting, setting up, and taking down equipment. After evaluating such environmental factors as lighting, subject motion, distance, field depth, and film speed/type, Nature Photographers make a variety of technical adjustments to their cameras including shutter speed, aperture, and focus.

After taking pictures, photographers develop negatives or upload digital images from their camera to a computer. They then review large numbers of photographs to find the best images, which may require digital editing or traditional touch-up methods. Finally, Nature Photographers may send negatives or digital images directly to editors, or make prints. Nature Photographers also search for sources of financial support to fund their work, which may involve writing grant applications.

The majority of Nature Photographers are self-employed. However, some work for magazines, publishing companies, newspapers, and government agencies. Nature Photographers work in natural environments that can be dangerous and uncomfortable at times. In their quest for the perfect photo they may encounter rain, snow, wind, rough seas, and extreme heat and cold, as well as a range of potentially dangerous insects and animals. As they wait for animals to cooperate, Nature Photographers may sit or stand for long periods of time, sometimes with no results. Finally, Nature Photographers work long and unusual hours that may require them to be away from home for weeks or months at a time, depending on the nature of their assignments.

Salaries

According to the U.S. Department of Labor's 2006–07 *Occupational Outlook Handbook*, in mid-2004 annual salaries for photographers ranged from less than $15,000 to more than $54,180, with a median of $26,080. In general, freelance photographers tend to earn more than those who earn regular, full-time salaries. However, freelance photographers must make significant investments in equipment.

Employment Prospects

In general, the U.S. Department of Labor projects that overall employment rates for photographers will increase about as fast as the average for all occupations through 2014. However, because photography is a popular career choice and there are more candidates than positions, competition for salaried or hourly positions is extremely high. While the Internet has made it easier for freelance photographers to market their work, affordable digital photography equipment has increased competition.

Advancement Prospects

Many photographers begin their careers by working in assistant roles for experienced photographers. After building their portfolios and forging contacts, some photographers become freelancers, while others pursue careers with newspapers or magazines. These photographers may ultimately become photography editors. Still other photographers become instructors at colleges, universities, and technical schools.

Education and Training

No degree is required to work as a Nature Photographer. However, courses and degree programs are helpful in building a solid base of technical skill and proficiency. These educational offerings are available via community and junior colleges, universities, vocational-technical institutes, and trade/technical schools. Bachelor's degree programs, including ones in photojournalism, may provide valuable business-related courses.

Experience, Special Skills, and Personality Traits

No experience is needed to work as a Nature Photographer. Once they have acquired basic camera skills, photographers begin building their portfolios and submitting work to editors for consideration. This experience is usually gained independently, while working on a freelance basis. There are several key skills that successful Nature Photographers have. These include good business sense and the ability to network with others and promote themselves. Technical skills also are important. In particular, Nature Photographers must have a working knowledge of the equipment they use, including cameras, digital imaging technology, and lighting gear. Good color vision and eyesight are important requirements for this career, along with physical dexterity, stamina, and coordination. While Nature Photographers must be able to work independently in remote locations, they also must be able to work collaboratively with editors and other clients. Successful photographers are artistic, creative, original, curious, efficient, flexible, patient, realistic, independent, and disciplined.

Unions and Associations

In addition to a variety of state and local clubs or associations, many Nature Photographers are members of the Wheat Ridge, Colorado–based North American Nature Photography Association, or the Atlanta, Georgia-based Professional Photographers of America.

Tips for Entry

1. Learn how to use traditional and digital cameras.
2. While in high school, familiarize yourself with the field of nature photography by subscribing to related magazines and newsletters.
3. Seek summer or part-time employment in a photo studio or camera store, or if possible, as an intern or assistant to a Nature Photographer.
4. Develop contacts by joining a local or regional group of nature photography enthusiasts.
5. Assemble a portfolio of your best nature photographs and try to get published as often as possible.

OUTDOOR/ENVIRONMENTAL EDUCATION

ECOLOGICAL RESTORATION INSTRUCTOR

CAREER PROFILE

Duties: Teach theory and practice of ecological restoration, which the Environmental Protection Agency defines as "the process of returning polluted or otherwise disturbed ecosystems to a close approximation of their condition prior to contamination"; lead hands-on activities that include gathering and testing soil and water samples, reintroducing any indigenous plant and animal species that may have become endangered, and maintaining records of activities; training elementary and high school science teachers how to incorporate various ecological restoration activities into their curriculum; preparing educational materials; maintaining equipment and materials; overseeing assistants and volunteers.

Alternate Title(s): Ecological Restoration Trainer; Watershed Restoration Teacher; Watershed Restoration Trainer

Salary Range: $25,000 to $50,000

Employment Prospects: Good

Advancement Prospects: Fair

Prerequisites:

Education or Training—Most positions require a bachelor's degree in environmental science, ecological restoration, conservation science, or similar field

Experience—Working on environmental restoration projects; collecting and analyzing environmental samples; developing educational materials and giving presentations; leading field trips

Special Skills and Personality Traits—Leadership, team building, and public-speaking skills; detail-oriented and organized; knowledge of local flora and fauna, as well as land use practices

Special Requirements—CPR and first aid training may be required; comfortable walking and standing, sometimes for hours at a time; physically fit enough to collect samples and to carry samples and equipment

CAREER LADDER

```
┌─────────────────────────────────┐
│  Ecological Restoration Program  │
│           Coordinator            │
└─────────────────────────────────┘

┌─────────────────────────────────┐
│  Ecological Restoration Instructor │
└─────────────────────────────────┘

┌─────────────────────────────────┐
│  Ecological Restoration Assistant │
└─────────────────────────────────┘

┌─────────────────────────────────┐
│  Ecological Restoration Volunteer │
└─────────────────────────────────┘
```

Position Description

Ecological Restoration Instructors teach both the scientific concepts underpinning ecological restoration and the process of evaluating an ecosystem, planning a restoration, implementing that plan, and evaluating its success. Some instructors focus on a specific type of restoration, such as watershed restoration, while others are broader in focus. Topics typically covered in a restoration curriculum include the following:

- How to preserve existing ecosystems and prevent further degradation
- How to gather historical data on an ecosystem's evolution, including the extent and magnitude of various changes over time, to predict future conditions
- How to evaluate existing resources, including project funding and community support, and locate additional resources, if necessary
- How to develop concrete, measurable, and realistic goals for restoration that can ultimately sustain itself without artificial support such as man-made irrigation or landscape maintenance
- How to restore previous conditions, such as water levels, nutrient levels in soil, and riverbank integrity
- How to make use of bioengineering, a process of combining live and dead plants to create a viable ecosystem designed to minimize the impact of things like erosion and pollutants, as well as provide a habitat for the reintroduction of native species
- How to restore previous processes, such as sediment deposits, water flow fluctuations, and runoff patterns
- How to determine the impact of structural alterations—such as deforestation in a natural park, dredging of a riverbed, and erecting sea walls along a shoreline—and develop plans to restore previous structures or minimize the impact of existing alternations to the extent possible
- How to restore native flora and fauna and eliminate invasive, non-native species
- How to evaluate conditions, processes, and structure to determine if restorative efforts have been successful
- How to develop plans that take into consideration the impact of activities, such as clear cutting and development, planned within adjacent ecosystems
- How to identify the direct and indirect causes of degradation, both natural and man-made, and eliminate them; if elimination is not possible, how to develop strategies to minimize their impact
- How to secure the expertise necessary to oversee a restoration project by consulting experts not only in ecology, but also in geology, engineering, developing, planning, social science, etc.

Ecological Restoration Instructors work with a variety of students, including elementary, middle, and high school students who sometimes participate in an ecological restoration project as part of their science curriculum or as an extracurricular activity. Others train science teachers who want to learn more about ecological restoration and how to incorporate its concepts into their classrooms. Still others train and lead teams of volunteers interested in becoming involved in community-based restoration efforts. Given the variety of students seeking ecological restoration education, it stands to reason that those interested in pursuing this career have a wide range of potential employers. Ecological Restoration

Instructors can work for school districts, alternative school programs, colleges and universities, ecology or science centers, arboretums or botanical gardens, government agencies, public and private businesses, and nonprofit agencies.

No matter where they are employed, these instructors can lead tours of sites at which ecological restoration projects are under way; show slide shows demonstrating what an ecosystem looks like before, during, and after restoration efforts; lead students in sample collecting and analyzing activities; oversee students and volunteers engaged in specific restoration tasks; and speak to community members about restoration projects.

Full-time Ecological Restoration Instructors tend to work a standard, 40-hour week, although some positions might include weekend hours. Some positions may be grant-funded, and thus temporary. If a project is taking place in a particularly remote area, instructors might be required to live on site; these positions typically include free housing and food. Individuals working for a public school system might have summers off; however, many school districts hire Ecological Restoration Instructors for summertime programming, particularly in areas where the weather dictates that restoration efforts be limited to spring, summer, and fall months.

Salaries
Temporary Ecological Restoration Instructors, particularly those working for grant-funded initiatives, are often paid stipends, which can be quite modest. However, full-time Ecological Restoration Instructors earn annual salaries that range from $25,000 to $50,000 per year, depending on education and experience.

Employment Prospects
According to the Environmental Protection Agency, the number of restoration projects is on the rise throughout the United States. As a result, future job prospects for Ecological Restoration Instructors are considered good.

Advancement Prospects
Volunteering for a local ecological restoration project is an excellent mode of entry into the field, particularly as most full-time positions require experience teaching or leading restoration crews. Advancement opportunities beyond a full-time position as Ecological Restoration Instructors are good, given the growing number of restoration projects that will likely require administrators, such as program coordinators and directors.

Education and Training
While temporary positions may not require a bachelor's degree, most expect candidates to have completed some college course work in ecological restoration, environmental science, biology, botany, natural history, or a similar field.

Most also require teaching experience. Full-time Ecological Restoration Instructors typically need an undergraduate degree along with teaching or training experience. Advancement into administrative positions normally requires a graduate degree in some sort of environmental science or in education.

Special Requirements

A certain level of physical fitness is necessary for Ecological Restoration Instructors, as they often spend a considerable amount of time outdoors standing, walking, collecting specimens, and carrying equipment. Due to safety concerns, many employers require CPR certification and first aid training.

Experience, Special Skills, and Personality Traits

Given the fact that they are often overseeing groups of students or volunteers engaged in restoration activities, Ecological Restoration Instructors must possess both leadership and team-building skills, as well as the ability to work with people of all ages. Solid public-speaking skills are also helpful. The ability to identify a wide range of plants and animals is also necessary. Finally, given the data-collection and record-keeping requirements of restoration projects, instructors must also be detail-oriented and organized.

Unions and Associations

The Society for Ecological Restoration International and the Society for Conservation Biology are two professional associations that Ecological Restoration Instructors can join. Another organization that serves this profession is the Watershed Ecology Team of the Office of Wetlands, Oceans, and Watersheds, a branch of the Environmental Protection Agency.

Tips for Entry

1. While an undergraduate, research internships like those listed on the Web site for the North American Association for Environmental Educators(http://www.eelink.net/eejobsdatabase.html) and by the Student Conservation Association (http://www.sca-inc.org).
2. Gain experience by volunteering for a local ecological restoration project.
3. Join organizations like the North American Association for Environmental Educators (http://www.naaee.org), the Society for Ecological Restoration International (http://www.ser.org), and the Society for Conservation Biology (http://www.conbio.org).
4. Search for job openings at the Society for Conservation Biology (http://www.conbio.org/Jobs/search.cfm).

ENVIRONMENTAL EDUCATION PROGRAM DIRECTOR

CAREER PROFILE

Duties: Managing all aspects of an environmental education program, including scheduling, budgeting, and facilities maintenance; overseeing curriculum development; hiring, supervising, and evaluating teachers; assessing program success; developing goals and objectives; collaborating with community agencies and other education programs; developing marketing materials and overseeing all promotional and outreach efforts

Alternate Title(s): Outdoor Education Program Director; Natural History Program Director; Adventure Education Program Director

Salary Range: $30,000 to $60,000

Employment Prospects: Average

Advancement Prospects: Limited

Prerequisites:

Education or Training—A minimum of a bachelor's degree in environmental education or similar field; a master's degree in educational leadership or curriculum development is desirable

Experience—Desire to work with children, teenagers, or other population targeted by program; understanding of administrative issues specific to managing environmental education programs, including both day programs and longer term programs where students live on-site; knowledge of safety concerns related to the various types of outdoor and adventure education courses that are often offered in environmental education programs

Special Skills and Personality Traits—Strong leadership and mentoring skills; ability to delegate responsibilities; problem solving, conflict resolution, and interpersonal communication skills

Special Requirements—Physically fit enough to accompany students and teachers on field trips that might involve hiking, rock climbing, or similarly strenuous activities; state teaching certification may be required

CAREER LADDER

```
┌─────────────────────────────────────┐
│  Environmental Education Program     │
│              Director                │
└─────────────────────────────────────┘

┌─────────────────────────────────────┐
│  Environmental Education Program     │
│         Assistant Director           │
└─────────────────────────────────────┘

┌─────────────────────────────────────┐
│  Environmental Education Teacher     │
└─────────────────────────────────────┘

┌─────────────────────────────────────┐
│     Environmental Education          │
│        Part-time Teacher             │
└─────────────────────────────────────┘
```

Position Description

Environmental Education Program Directors manage all aspects of an environmental education program. Responsibilities range from hiring and mentoring teaching staff, observing classroom and field activities, and disciplining students, to reviewing schedules and budgets, developing various community collaboration and program marketing strategies, and overseeing facility grounds and building maintenance. While directors are expected to possess a broad set of teaching and administrative skills that would allow them to complete specific tasks by themselves, a key component of their job is to delegate appropriate responsibilities to assistant administrators, teachers, and other employees. As with most upper-level management positions, however, Environmental Education Program Directors are ultimately responsible for everything that takes place within their program.

Environmental education programs come in all shapes and sizes. Some are seasonal, lasting only a few hours a day for a week or two in the summertime. For programs like these, students may go home every day, or they may live on-site for the duration of the program. Other seasonal programs might be more intensive, lasting all summer long. Places like science and nature centers and parks also offer a wide variety of year-round programs that students might attend for a single day, perhaps as a school field trip, a week, or even an entire semester. Many of these facilities offer programs that are open to the public and geared toward a wide variety of age groups, including adults and senior citizens.

The types of environmental education courses offered might include adventure and outdoor recreation, nature walks, slide shows, wilderness and survival training, etc. Topics covered range from natural history, ecology, biodiversity, and watershed restoration to animal behavior and habitats, botany, and resource conservation. Environmental education programs might be offered by businesses, by parks and recreation departments of various jurisdictions, by public or private schools, or by nonprofit organizations like the National Wildlife Federation. No matter what the setting or structure of the program, Environmental Education Program Directors are responsible for all aspects of operation.

Specific duties of Environmental Education Program Directors include the following:

- Draft environmental education curriculum and develop activities designed to foster learning and meet educational objectives
- Develop rules designed to ensure the safety of all teachers and students; monitor compliance of rules, and give any necessary feedback, or undertake any necessary disciplinary actions
- Schedule classes and activities, assign teachers, and assess and place students appropriately
- Host orientation sessions in which students and teachers meet one another and discuss classroom conduct, rules, schedules, etc.
- Observe teachers and provide feedback and mentoring on what takes place throughout lessons and activities
- Evaluate effectiveness of educational activities and implement changes to meet student needs and ensure favorable outcomes
- Develop policies and procedures for handling any necessary first aid services, as well as emergencies; conduct

routine drills to prepare teachers and students to respond to emergencies appropriately
- Reach out to community organizations, public schools, and other educational agencies in an effort to establish collaborative relationships
- Create marketing materials and promotional plans designed to boost attendance
- Tour facility and grounds to ensure cleanliness and safety
- Check equipment and supplies to ensure functionality and safety

Depending on the type of program offered, Environmental Education Program Directors may live on-site or off-site. Those who live on-site typically work 10 hour days and are quite often on-call on their days off. Those who run day programs usually work about eight hours a day, with no on-call duties. Full-time directors of seasonal programs may have time off during the off-season, or they engage in tasks like developing new programs, recruiting students and teachers, and forging alliances with other agencies.

Salaries

Salaries for Environmental Education Program Directors range from $30,000 to $60,000, depending on things like the duration and number of courses offered, whether or not the director is expected to live on-site, and the number of students served. Both year-round and seasonal positions tend to be full-time for the duration of the program. Additional perks often include free room and board and standard benefits packages.

Employment Prospects

Full-time, year-round positions for Environmental Education Program Directors are more competitive than part-time or seasonal positions, which are expected to grow from 10% to 20% through 2014, according to the Bureau of Labor Statistics.

Advancement Prospects

Many Environmental Education Program Directors gain initial experience in the field by volunteering at local nature or science centers, parks or forests, or nonprofit agencies. Eventually, volunteers might be permitted to lead certain activities or to assist teachers with various tasks. Many directors work as environmental education instructors prior to pursuing an administrative position; these instructors are typically required to complete some level of college coursework in either education or environmental science or to obtain a bachelor's degree in one of these fields.

Many Environmental Education Program Directors work as assistant directors for a few years to gain the managerial and administrative experience to oversee an entire program. Advancement opportunities beyond the position of Environmental Education Program Director are rather limited. Individuals directing a single, small program might advance their career by seeking employment with a large parks and recreation department, where they might oversee a variety of programs. Others might eventually create their own programs.

Education and Training

Environmental Education Program Directors are expected to possess at least a bachelor's degree in environmental science, education, management, business administration, or a similar field. Many positions at this level also require a master's degree and teaching experience. Five to 10 years' experience managing educational, enrichment, or recreational programs is also often desired.

Special Requirements

Some positions require state teaching certification by the Board of Education. Others might require certification by the National Recreational and Parks Association or other credentials related to outdoor educational activities. Other potential requirements might include background checks and drug and alcohol tests. Candidates are also expected to be familiar with local, state, and federal regulations related to working with youth, particularly if they live on-site.

Experience, Special Skills, and Personality Traits

Environmental Education Program Directors must possess solid interpersonal communication, organizational, team-building, and managerial skills, all of which help them both to mentor teachers and to delegate responsibilities when necessary. Directors are also expected to be creative, motivational, and people-oriented. Additional skills include marketing, grant writing, and fund-raising.

Unions and Associations

The North American Association for Environmental Educators serves environmental education professionals, students, and volunteers in the public school system, in colleges and universities, in government agencies, in the private sector, and in nonprofit agencies. Two organizations specifically targeting outdoor education students and professionals are Outdoor Ed and America Outdoors. Other relevant organizations include the National Recreation and Parks Association, the Active Network, and the American Alliance for Health, Physical Education, Recreation, and Dance.

Tips for Entry

1. Gain experience by volunteering with environmental education programs at a local nature or science center or park.
2. In high school, take courses in business, communication, psychology, and education.
3. Search for environmental education programs at Enviroeducation.com: The Environmental Education Directory, http://www.enviroeducation.com/.
4. Search for job openings at Web sites like America Outdoors, http://www.americaoutdoors.org/job-results.asp; Outdoor Ed: The Professional's Resource, http://www.outdoored.com; and The North American Association for Environmental Educators, http://eelink.net/pages/EE+Jobs+Database.

ENVIRONMENTAL SCIENCE PROFESSOR

CAREER PROFILE

Duties: Teaching a broad range of both undergraduate and graduate environmental science classes covering topics such as climatology, environmental chemistry, physical geography, natural resource management, conservation, population dynamics, and natural history; conducting research in specialized areas of interest, presenting findings at academic conferences, and publishing results in scholarly journals; overseeing research and teaching assistants; and serving on various committees ranging from curriculum development and textbook selection to campus administration

Alternate Title(s): Environmental Science Instructor; Environmental Science Lecturer; Environmental Studies Professor; Environmental Studies Instructor; Environmental Studies Lecturer

Salary Range: $15,000 to $100,000

Employment Prospects: Excellent

Advancement Prospects: Average

Prerequisites:

    Education or Training—Master's degree or Ph.D. in environmental science, biological sciences, or similar field

    Experience—Teaching college-level students complex concepts and theories; conducting research in accordance with university policies and procedures; giving presentations at academic conferences; publishing work in scholarly journals

    Special Skills and Personality Traits—Excellent comprehension and critical thinking skills; ability to understand statistics and use statistical software; public speaking, writing, and research skills

    Special Requirements—Familiarity with stringent academic research protocols and standards

CAREER LADDER

```
┌─────────────────────────────────┐
│       Department Chair          │
└─────────────────────────────────┘

┌─────────────────────────────────┐
│          Professor              │
└─────────────────────────────────┘

┌─────────────────────────────────┐
│ Assistant or Associate Professor│
└─────────────────────────────────┘

┌─────────────────────────────────┐
│      Adjunct (part-time)        │
│    Instructor or Lecturer       │
└─────────────────────────────────┘

┌─────────────────────────────────┐
│  Teaching or Research Assistant │
└─────────────────────────────────┘
```

Position Description

Of the professionals who teach college-level courses related to conservation and the environment, Environmental Science Professors are the least specialized. At the postsecondary level, environmental science departments tend to offer courses that focus specifically on the physical environment, such as environmental chemistry, geology, and natural history, as well as courses such as ecology, population dynamics and resource conservation, which also examine the interaction between human beings and the environment. Some colleges and universities, particularly those with large environmental science departments, might hire specialized professors, such as ecology professors or natural history professors, who focus solely on these more narrow disciplines. However, the institutions that hire Environmental Science Professors typically expect them to teach a broad spectrum of courses.

At the postsecondary level, Environmental Science Professors do much more than teach. In fact, most Environmental Science Professors working at four-year colleges or universities teach only two or three classes a semester. Required to hold a Ph.D., these professionals spend considerable time supervising the teaching assistants who teach introductory level courses, designing and overseeing research projects, writing articles and even books, and presenting papers at academic conferences. Other duties include mentoring Ph.D. candidates as they write their dissertations, serving on campus committees, and developing curricula for new courses.

Environmental Science Professors working at community colleges tend to have a slightly different focus, as they are oftentimes required to teach a minimum of four classes a semester and also to hold a certain number of office hours, during which time they are expected to be available to students; as a result, research and publication requirements are not quite as stringent. Many two-year institutions require only a master's degree, rather than a full Ph.D., even for tenured professors. Also, as two-year institutions do not offer Ph.D. programs, they do not make use of teaching and research assistants; as a result, these Environmental Science Professors may be expected to teach more basic science classes, such as biology or chemistry, and they typically have to grade tests and papers themselves, rather than delegate these tasks to assistants, as university professors are often able to do.

Postsecondary Environmental Science Professors may work in a variety of settings. Along with lecturing in large halls filled with 300 or more undergraduate students, these professors might also find themselves leading small graduate seminars or laboratory sessions, or holding classes in the field. As distance learning continues to grow in popularity, many Environmental Science Professors are also now required to develop and conduct classes via the Internet.

Work on various research projects often requires Environmental Science Professors to collaborate with governmental agencies, businesses, or other academic institutions. For example, if the Environmental Protection Agency decides to fund a water quality assessment project in a certain area, government officials might contact an Environmental Science Professor at a nearby university to help oversee the project, while local businesses might supply necessary equipment, and environmental engineering students at a nearby vocational school might help collect water samples. Many institutions also expect faculty members to conduct original research, which involves developing a research question that has not yet been answered, conducting experiments, collecting data, analyzing data, and drawing conclusions. Typically, these conclusions are then presented at conferences or published in academic journals or books.

Committee work is also expected of Environmental Science Professors. While many committees focus on academic matters—such as curriculum development, textbook selection, and resource procurements for libraries and laboratories—many also focus on more administrative matters, including the selection of new environmental science faculty members, reviewing student applications to the environmental science program, and changes to existing policies and procedures or the creation of new university bylaws.

As with many teaching positions, Environmental Science Professors tend to sign nine- or 10-month contracts and have summers off, during which time they might be expected to pursue research interests or develop new courses. Some postsecondary institutions do require professors to teach during the spring and summer semesters as part of their regular schedule; however, many offer additional pay for these courses as they fall outside of the contracted workload. Environmental Science Professors have flexible schedules with the freedom to select the days of the week and times of day they teach courses, make themselves available to students, conduct research, grade tests and papers, etc. However, due to their various responsibilities, most professors find themselves working between 50 and 60 hours a week. And while semester breaks allow for more vacation time than many other professions, many Environmental Science Professors use at least a portion of their time off to catch up on grading and create schedules and syllabi for the upcoming semester.

Salaries

At the postsecondary level, part-time Environmental Science Professors, also known as adjunct instructors, are usually paid a set amount for each course, earning anywhere from $1,500 to $3,000 per course per semester. These positions usually do not offer benefits, and they are oftentimes filled by professionals in the field who are interested in teaching an evening course or two. According to the American Association of University Professors, the average annual salary for a full-time professor was $68,500 during the 2004–05 school year. Instructors and lecturers with master's degrees averaged between $39,000 and $45,000 per year; assistant professors with Ph.D.'s garnered roughly $55,000; associate professors, $65,000; and full professors, $92,000.

Employment Prospects

The Bureau of Labor Statistics projects considerable growth in employment for postsecondary educators, including Environmental Science Professors, through 2014. However, this projection comes with the caveat that many of the positions available will likely be part-time. In 2004, approximately 30% of all postsecondary faculty were part-time, and this percentage is expected to grow as educational institutions of all types continue to experience cutbacks in government funding.

Advancement Prospects

Environmental Science Professors at postsecondary institutions tend to start out as assistant or associate professors. The best way for Ph.D. candidates to prepare for these positions is to serve as teaching or research assistants while pursuing their degrees. Both two- and four-year institutions also offer part-time positions to instructors, sometimes known as lecturers. While they do not pay very well, these positions are numerous and fairly easy to obtain, and they allow individuals to gain access to an institution and the experience oftentimes required for full-time positions.

The most desirable full-time positions are known as tenure-track, offering a career path designed to ultimately reward successful assistant and associate professors with tenure, a guarantee of full-time employment that cannot be revoked without due process. While the process varies by institution, securing tenure typically involves completing a probationary period, quite often several years long, during which time the candidate's teaching, research, and publication efforts are regularly reviewed. At the end of the probationary period, candidates may have to submit a portfolio of their contributions to the college or university and undergo a committee review. Those determined to be successful receive tenure; those who do not qualify are expected to leave the institution at the end of the semester and seek employment elsewhere. The number of tenure-track positions is expected to decline; as a result, competition for these positions is projected to remain intense through 2014.

Education and Training

The minimum education requirement for an Environmental Science Professor is a master's degree. Many positions require a Ph.D., which typically takes nine or 10 years to complete. Whether in high school or college, students interested in becoming Environmental Science Professors can benefit from taking public-speaking classes, as well as courses in statistics, biology, chemistry, conservation, natural history, and botany. To gain experience in the field, a student might also consider getting an undergraduate degree in environmental science and working as an industry professional for a few years prior to applying to a Ph.D. program. This experience is oftentimes helpful in gaining access to a Ph.D. program and is also considered valuable by colleges and universities seeking Environmental Science Professors.

Special Requirements

While no specific teaching certifications or licensing requirements exist for Environmental Science Professors, familiarity with academic research protocols and standards is required.

Experience, Special Skills, and Personality Traits

Clearly, Environmental Science Professors must possess excellent public-speaking skills. These individuals should also enjoy mentoring graduate students and teaching and research assistants, as they may be assigned to oversee various research projects undertaken by students and to serve on committees reviewing the dissertations published by Ph.D. candidates. As research is a key function of many of these professionals, the ability to compile data in accordance with university standards and to use statistical software to interpret this data is required. Excellent writing skills are also essential.

Unions and Associations

Some universities and colleges belong to unions, which faculty members may or may not opt to join. Unions often charge dues that are deducted from paychecks. The Society for College Science Professors, a division of the National Science Teachers Association, serves postsecondary science teachers of all scientific disciplines, while the Association of Environmental Engineering and Science Professors serves science professors specializing in environmental issues. The National Association of Biology Teachers represents life science teachers at both the secondary and postsecondary levels, while the North American Association for Environmental Educators provides resources and networking opportunities for environmental educators of all kinds, including postsecondary environmental sciences teachers and college students aspiring to become environmental educators of some sort.

Tips for Entry

1. Take classes in public speaking, writing, and statistics.
2. While an undergraduate, research internships like those listed on the Web site for the North American Association for Environmental Educators (http://www.eelink.net/eejobsdatabase.html) and graduate assistant and fellowship opportunities posted at the Association of Environmental Engineering and Science Professors Graduate Jobs page (http://www.aeesp.org/jobs/graduatejobs.php).
3. Join organizations like the North American Association for Environmental Educators (http://www.naaee.org), the Association of Environmental Engineering and Science Professors (http://www.aeesp.org), National Association of Biology Teachers (http://www.nabt.org), and the Society of College Science Teaching (http://www.scst.org).
4. Search for job openings at the *Chronicle of Higher Education,* http://chronicle.com.

ENVIRONMENTAL SCIENCE TEACHER, HIGH SCHOOL

CAREER PROFILE

Duties: Teaching environmental science classes covering topics such as ecology, biodiversity, conservation, population dynamics, geology, climatology, and natural history; developing lesson plans that include hands-on activities for students to complete in the lab and in the field; maintaining classroom safety and addressing issues related to student conduct; creating homework assignments and tests; grading student work and maintaining student records; holding parent-teacher conferences

Alternate Title(s): High School Biology Teacher; High School Life Sciences Teacher; High School Science Teacher

Salary Range: $25,000 to $60,000

Employment Prospects: Excellent

Advancement Prospects: Average

Prerequisites:

Education or Training—Bachelor's degree in environmental science, biological sciences, or similar field; official teaching certification is also required for public school jobs

Experience—Teaching high school students complex concepts and theories related to environmental science; devising assignments that foster critical thinking; planning and implementing hands-on activities designed to appeal to different learning styles; maintaining classroom discipline

Special Skills and Personality Traits—Public speaking; leadership and problem-solving skills; creativity; patience

Special Requirements—Teaching certificate

CAREER LADDER

```
┌─────────────────────────────────┐
│        Department Chair          │
└─────────────────────────────────┘

┌─────────────────────────────────┐
│   High School Environmental      │
│      Science Teacher             │
└─────────────────────────────────┘

┌─────────────────────────────────┐
│        Student Teacher           │
└─────────────────────────────────┘
```

Position Description

At the high school level, Environmental Science Teachers work with students from grades nine through 12, and typically carry a course load of four to five classes a day. As environmental science is often an elective course that is offered only once or twice a day, many schools require environmental science teachers to also teach required science classes, such as biology or chemistry.

In the public school system, classes range in size from 20 to 40 students. Private schools oftentimes offer a lower student-teacher ratio. No matter what the size of the class, teachers are expected to meet individual student needs.

Some students are mainly visual learners who do well when teachers do things like write on the blackboard or use overhead projectors to draw pictures. Auditory learners have the most success with lectures that include verbal descriptions, examples, stories, classroom discussions, etc. Kinesthetic learners tend to learn most by taking part in hands-on activities. To be sure they reach all three types of learners, teachers must develop lessons that have visual, auditory, and kinesthetic components. Teacher are also expected to spend extra time with students who fall behind or have difficulty with certain concepts and to design enrichment activities for more advanced students.

Environmental Science Teachers do more than teach scientific concepts. They also help foster critical thinking about the environment and various conservation issues and help students develop the skills to form their own opinions and to take action based upon those opinions. For example, an Environmental Science Teacher might devise a research project that involves having each student study a piece of environmental legislation and write a letter, perhaps to a local state representative, that demonstrates not only an understanding of the scientific concepts underlying the issue, but also expresses an opinion about the issue and offers a logical, well-supported justification for this opinion.

Teachers at the high school level are also expected to take on extracurricular responsibilities, including coaching and mentoring. For example, Environmental Science Teachers might also help students form and operate an environmental advocacy club, lead various field trips, or advise students who are interested in a career in the sciences.

Teachers sometimes have to deal with serious problems among students, such as fighting and bullying. They also need to be on the lookout for signs of drug and alcohol problems, abuse, and depression. These things affect students' attendance and class work, so teachers can be the first adults to notice when a young person is in trouble.

Whether in the public school system or at a private school, most high school teachers work nine months a year and have the summers off. Due to planning and grading responsibilities, many high school teachers work between 50 and 60 hours a week. And while school breaks allow for more time off around the holidays than many other professions, many Environmental Science Teachers use at least some of this vacation time to grade tests, assignments, and papers, as well as to record those grades, revise old lesson plans, and develop new ones.

Salaries

High school Environmental Science Teachers with a bachelor's degree and a teaching certificate earned roughly $49,000 in 2005, according to the American Federation of Teachers. Beginning teachers tend to start at $30,000 annually, while those with master's degrees and several years

of experience can earn upwards of $50,000. Teachers can also supplement their income with extracurricular activities, such as coaching. Private school teachers typically make substantially less than public school teachers.

Employment Prospects

The Bureau of Labor Statistics projects better-than-average growth in employment for high school teachers, particularly those in math and the sciences, through 2014. This is mainly due to projected retirements.

Advancement Prospects

All certified teachers are required to spend a minimum of one semester as a student teacher, gradually taking on more responsibilities as they work directly with students in the classroom alongside an experienced teacher. Not only does this provide college graduates with experience, but it also affords many of them the foot in the door they need to secure full-time employment.

In the public school system, most teaching positions are tenure-track, meaning they offer a career path designed to ultimately reward successful teachers with tenure, a guarantee of full-time employment that cannot be revoked without just cause and due process, which is typically developed by a teacher's union. While the process varies by institution, securing tenure typically involves completing a probationary period, quite often two or three years long, during which time the candidate's lesson plans and classroom teaching techniques are reviewed at least once a year. At the end of the probationary period, those considered successful are granted tenure; those who do not qualify may be expected to resign at the end of the school year.

Education and Training

The minimum education requirement for a high school Environmental Science Teacher is a bachelor's degree, as well as a teaching certificate, which requires completion of a teacher education program. Most teacher education programs are one year in length and require a combination of course work and student teaching. Whether in high school or college, students interested in becoming Environmental Science Teachers can benefit from taking public-speaking classes, as well as courses in biology, chemistry, geology, conservation, natural history, and botany.

Special Requirements

Public school systems require high school teachers to secure and maintain professional certification to be eligible for full-time employment. Requirements for certification are set by state boards of education, but they typically involve completing a one-year teacher education program that involves course work in things like educational psychology, testing and measurement, and classroom management, as well as completing at least one semester of student teaching. While the National Board for Professional Teaching Standards also certifies teachers on the national level, most states still require state-based certification as a condition of employment.

Experience, Special Skills, and Personality Traits

Along with excellent public-speaking skills, high school Environmental Science Teachers must also enjoy working with teenagers and have the patience, conflict resolution, and problem-solving skills to manage issues such as fights, students who talk out of turn, and other forms of disruptive classroom behavior.

Unions and Associations

Many public schools belong to unions, which teachers may or may not opt to join. Unions often charge dues that are deducted from paychecks. The National Science Teachers Association serves both high school and college science teachers. The National Association of Biology Teachers represents life science teachers at both the secondary and postsecondary levels, while the North American Association for Environmental Educators provides resources and networking opportunities for environmental educators of all kinds, including high school environmental sciences teachers and college students aspiring to become environmental educators of some sort.

Tips for Entry

1. Take classes in public speaking, educational psychology, biology, chemistry, geology, botany, and environmental science.

2. While a high school or college student, research summer internships like those listed on the Web site for the North American Association for Environmental Educators (http://www.eelink.net/eejobsdatabase.html).

3. Join organizations like the North American Association for Environmental Educators; the National Association of Biology Teachers (http://www.nabt.org); and the National Science Teachers Association (http://www.nsta.org/highschool).

4. Many colleges and universities with teacher education programs also hold jobs fairs on campus. Talk to your academic advisor to learn more about the job search services offered by your school. Also, search for job openings at Teachers-Teacher.com (http://www.teachers-teachers.com/teaching-jobs.cfm).

FIELD EDUCATION COORDINATOR

CAREER PROFILE

Duties: Coordinating all aspects of an environmentally based field education program; coordinating the logistics of various field education programs; establishing and fostering collaborative relationships with community agencies, schools, nature centers, etc.; recruiting, hiring, and mentoring teachers and volunteers; participating in the development of goals, objectives, curricula, and activities; evaluating program success; assisting with marketing and fund-raising efforts

Alternate Title(s): Outdoor Education Coordinator; Adventure Education Coordinator

Salary Range: $30,000 to $50,000

Employment Prospects: Good

Advancement Prospects: Average

Prerequisites:

Education or Training—A minimum of a bachelor's degree in environmental education, ecology, biology, teaching, or similar field; a master's degree in educational leadership or administration is desirable

Experience—Understanding of logistical and safety issues specific to coordinating field experiences, which may include day programs as well as more long-term programs where students spend several days at a facility; desire to work with children, teenagers, or other populations targeted by a particular program; skilled in establishing collaborative relationships with various community organizations.

Special Skills and Personality Traits—Self-directed; strong time management, organizational, and problem-solving skills; excellent interpersonal communication skills; ability to communicate effectively verbally and in writing; comfortable working in an outdoor setting

Special Requirements—Physically fit enough to accompany students and teachers on field trips that might involve hiking, rock climbing, or similarly strenuous activities; knowledge of CPR and first aid techniques

CAREER LADDER

Field Education Program Director

Field Education Coordinator

Field Education Assistant Coordinator

Field Education Teacher

Position Description

Field Education Coordinators are responsible for overseeing the field-based experiences of students enrolled in environmental education programs that require some form of fieldwork. Coordinators normally work in conjunction with program directors, executive directors, and other administrative staff members to develop, implement, and evaluate a variety of field experiences for students. Normally, the Field

Education Coordinator heads a team of educational professionals working together to draft field education objectives, curriculum materials, program activities, evaluation tools, etc. Sometimes, coordinators also spend a portion of their time teaching, both in the classroom and in the field.

One of the first steps in creating a viable environmental education field program is to develop relationships with local schools, community agencies, parks, beaches, nature centers, museums, governmental agencies, businesses, and other organizations that might contribute in some way to a field education program. Collaborative alliances are at the core of field programs, as the goal is to provide students with a range of experiences within the community. To this end, Field Education Coordinators must clearly and persuasively communicate their program's objectives to potential collaborators.

Coordinators can engage in a variety of activities designed to solicit community support. These include speaking at community events, such as fund-raisers; arranging private meetings with local business leaders and elected officials; contacting environmental advocacy agencies and other non-profit organizations interested in promoting environmental education; developing relationships with teachers and administrators at local school districts, community colleges and postsecondary vocational institutions, and public and private colleges and universities; and reaching out to administrators at local parks, nature centers, museums, and other entities whose mission it is to offer recreational, enrichment, and environmental education activities to the public.

Once collaborative relationships have been established, Field Education Coordinators are responsible for scheduling various activities, which can range from daytime field trips, after-school activities, and special workshops to week-long camping trips or adventure education-based weekends. Coordinators are also responsible for arranging transportation and ensuring that students and teachers arrive at various sites on time; periodically visiting sites to monitor the behavior of students, teachers, volunteers, and any other individuals involved in the field experience; communicating safety policies and procedures to all involved parties and implementing reviews to ensure compliance; and engaging in any other activities that will help foster mutually supportive relationships with area organizations.

Additional tasks for which Field Education Coordinators may find themselves responsible are listed below:

- Ordering supplies and equipment necessary for various activities; checking for functionality and safety
- Recruiting, interviewing, training, and mentoring teachers and volunteers
- Writing grants and assisting with any other fund-raising or marketing initiatives spearheaded by program managers, executive directors, etc.
- Hosting on-site orientations for students, volunteers, and teachers
- Touring various facilities and grounds to ensure cleanliness and safety

Field Education Coordinators typically work 40 hours a week. Schedules may vary a bit if certain field activities take place in the evening or on weekends. Coordinators may also be expected to attend fund-raisers and other functions that take place in the evening or on weekends. Hours may be divided between the office and field.

Salaries

Depending on their educational background and level of experience, Field Education Coordinators typically earn salaries that range from $30,000 to $50,000. Earnings might also depend upon the size of the agency for which the coordinator works.

Employment Prospects

Given the growing popularity of field education in all disciplines, including environmental education, the job outlook for Field Education Coordinators, particularly those who are also to able teach some courses or lead certain activities, is considered good.

Advancement Prospects

Many Field Education Coordinators have teaching backgrounds. Others might gain experience in field education coordination by volunteering at local nature or science centers, parks or forests, or nonprofit agencies. Particularly well-organized volunteers are often allowed to schedule various activities, make appointments for coordinators, and observe and participate in certain courses and field experiences. Some Field Education Coordinators might have to work as assistants for a few years prior to securing a full-fledged position as a coordinator. Those seeking to advance their careers further can pursue promotions to program director or even executive director. In these cases, a master's degree in educational leadership or administration is quite often required.

Education and Training

Most Field Education Coordinators are expected to have a bachelor's degree in biological sciences, environmental science, education, or a similar field. Other requirements include teaching experience, both in the classroom and outdoors. Some level of public relations training is also desirable.

Special Requirements

While no specific certification requirements exist for Field Education Coordinators, an official elementary or secondary teaching certificate or familiarity with National Science Education Standards for K–12 might set one candidate apart from the others. Some employers may also require CPR and first aid training.

152 CAREER OPPORTUNITIES IN CONSERVATION AND THE ENVIRONMENT

Experience, Special Skills, and Personality Traits

Due to the amount of time they might spend in the field, coordinators must be able to withstand various weather conditions, walk and hike for several hours at a time, lift equipment that might weigh up to 50 pounds, and engage in similarly strenuous tasks. For their work in the community, Field Education Coordinators must also possess excellent interpersonal communication, negotiation, persuasion, relationship-building, and problem-solving skills, as well as creativity in procuring various resources. While in the office, Field Education Coordinators must have the ability to gather and analyze data, draw sound conclusions and make appropriate recommendations, and speak and write in a clear and concise manner.

Unions and Associations

The North American Association for Environmental Educators serves environmental education professionals, students, and volunteers in the public school system, in colleges and universities, in government agencies, in the private sector, and in nonprofit agencies. Two organizations specifically targeting field education students and professionals are Outdoor Ed and America Outdoors. Other relevant organizations include the National Recreation and Parks Association, the Active Network, the American Alliance for Health, Physical Education, Recreation, and Dance, and the National Science Teachers Association.

Tips for Entry

1. In high school, take courses in business, communication, science, marketing, and education.
2. Volunteer with environmental education programs at local nature centers, parks, or similar sites.
3. Search for environmental education programs at Enviroeducation.com: The Environmental Education Directory, http://www.enviroeducation.com/.
4. Search for job openings at Web sites like America Outdoors, http://www.americaoutdoors.org/job-results. asp; Outdoor Ed: The Professional's Resource, http://www.outdoored.com; and the North American Association for Environmental Educators, http://eelink.net/pages/EE+Jobs+Database.

FIELD TEACHER/NATURALIST

CAREER PROFILE

Duties: Deliver formal and informal environmental education presentations, both indoors and outdoors, on topics such as forestry, natural history, biodiversity, and field ecology to a wide variety of audiences; prepare educational materials and equipment; travel to different sites to lead field trips; maintain facilities, grounds, and live collections of animals, when appropriate.

Alternate Title(s): Natural History Teacher; Field Instructor; Park Guide

Salary Range: $20,000 to $40,000

Employment Prospects: Fair

Advancement Prospects: Limited

Prerequisites:

Education or Training—While part-time, seasonal jobs may not require a college degree, most full-time positions, even seasonal ones, require a bachelor's degree in environmental science, ecology, conservation science, biological sciences, or similar field

Experience—Creating educational materials, conducting formal and informal presentations about various environmental topics; leading field trips

Special Skills and Personality Traits—Public speaking; leadership skills; ability to explain and answer questions about a variety of ecosystems

Special Requirements—Ability to lead walking tours, maintain grounds, and handle animals; knowledge of CPR and first aid

CAREER LADDER

```
┌─────────────────────────────────┐
│      Field Teacher/Naturalist    │
└─────────────────────────────────┘

┌─────────────────────────────────┐
│       Part-time or Seasonal      │
│      Field Teacher/Naturalist    │
└─────────────────────────────────┘

┌─────────────────────────────────┐
│    Field Teacher/Naturalist Aide │
└─────────────────────────────────┘
```

Position Description

Field Teachers/Naturalists develop and deliver presentations on the ecological features of parks, forests, beaches, and other natural sites. To learn more about the natural history of an area, Field Teachers/Naturalists conduct research about the cultural, historical, and natural developments that have taken place at various sites over time. They then create educational materials such as brochures, displays, and handouts to use on field trips, nature walks, and other types of tours. Expected to create engaging and innovative activities for their students, Field Teachers/Naturalists might create lesson plans that include interactive water quality testing, live archaeological digs, and similar hands-on experiences. A large component of this job involves answering questions and responding to requests from schools, community members, tourists, and other groups and individuals seeking specific information.

Field Teachers/Naturalists give presentations in a wide variety of settings. Some might be hired by a school district to visit various schools and give presentations on-site or to lead off-site field trips for students. Others might find work at various campgrounds, where they develop and deliver presentations designed to teach children about their natural setting; at resorts, where they might lead tourists on walking trips through various natural habitats; at nature centers or museums, where they might offer regular field-based natural history classes to community residents; and at similar sites offering environmental education to their visitors.

Because Field Teachers/Naturalists often work in conjunction with local school districts or with nonprofit environmental agencies, they may find themselves in charge of training public school teachers or volunteers. Those working at campsites might be expected to teach things like outdoor living skills to residents.

Many state and national parks hire Field Teachers/Naturalists to respond to questions about the ecological history and development of the park, conservation efforts taking place within the park, the habitats of various animals living within the park, etc. Field Teachers/Naturalists working within a park system are also typically expected to design, build, and tear down exhibits; to create brochures and other informational materials for public distribution; and to lead guided tours and hikes, some of which require varying fitness levels.

While Field Teachers/Naturalists working with a park or forest system are not faced with the law enforcement responsibilities of park rangers or wildlife officers, they do share some similar tasks. For example, many Field Teachers/Naturalists are required to maintain a site's natural resources, a task that includes landscaping park grounds, checking the quality of any bodies of water that exist within the site, maintaining trails, monitoring and restoring habitats, and overseeing the removal of garbage. In addition, Field Teachers/Naturalists may find themselves doing things like tracking wildlife behavior and maintaining collections of live animals.

Hours for Field Teachers/Naturalists can vary considerably, due to the seasonal nature of many natural settings open to the public. Weekend positions are plentiful for those seeking part-time work. Many summer positions exist at sites like camps, parks, and beaches; oftentimes these positions require the Field Teacher/Naturalist to live on-site. For on-site positions, free housing and food are often considered part of the compensation package. Those individuals working for a public school system might find themselves with the summer off, although many school districts make use of Field Teachers/Naturalists for enrichment programs offered during the summertime. Most full-time Field Teachers/Naturalists work roughly 40 hours per week, except during peak seasons, when overtime may be required.

Salaries

Part-time Field Teachers/Naturalists make anywhere between $9 and $12 an hour. Daily pay rates range from $50 to $100 and may include free room, board, food, and laundry. Full-time Field Teachers/Naturalists make anywhere from $20,000 to $40,000 per year, depending on experience.

Employment Prospects

Over the past several years, budget cuts in funding for schools, parks, forests, and other natural resources have increased the competitiveness for full-time positions. Given the low rate of job growth for the industry, Field Teacher/Naturalist positions tend to open only when someone retires or resigns.

Advancement Prospects

Many Field Teachers/Naturalists gain experience by volunteering for environmental organizations or securing part-time jobs at parks, forests, camps, and similar sites. As most full-time positions require some experience teaching or working with the target population, volunteer or part-time work is nearly essential for individuals hoping to land a full-time position in this field.

Education and Training

While seasonal and part-time positions do not require a bachelor's degree, many do require some college course work in environmental science, biology, botany, natural history, or a similar field. Some level of teaching experience is also typically required to secure a part-time position. Qualifications for a full-time Field Teacher/Naturalist position normally include an undergraduate degree in environmental science, biology, botany, natural history, or a similar field, as well as teaching or public-speaking experience.

Special Requirements

Because most Field Teachers/Naturalists work outdoors and lead groups on tours that require some level of physical fitness, many employers require CPR certification and first aid training.

Experience, Special Skills, and Personality Traits

Due to their regular contact with the public, Field Teachers/Naturalists need to enjoy working with people of all ages. The ability to lead is also important, as is a tolerance for physically demanding work, which might include walking and lifting, in both indoor and outdoor settings. Field Teachers/Naturalists must also possess the problem-solving skills necessary to anticipate and subvert potential natural hazards.

Unions and Associations

The American Society of Naturalists is the most well known national organization of naturalists. The North American

Association for Environmental Educators serves environmental educators of all kinds, while America Outdoors specifically serves outdoor educators. Field Teachers/Naturalists also have a variety of state associations from which to choose.

Tips for Entry

1. While an undergraduate, research internships like those listed on the Web site for the North American Association for Environmental Educators (http://www.eelink.net/eejobsdatabase.html) and the Student Conservation Association (http://www.sca-inc.org).

2. Gain experience either by volunteering as a tour guide at a local park or nearby forest or by securing a part-time or seasonal position.

3. Join organizations like the North American Association for Environmental Educators (http://www.naaee.org) and the American Society of Naturalists (http://www.amnat.org).

4. Search for job openings at America Outdoors (http://www.americaoutdoors.org/job-results.asp) and at the North American Association for Environmental Educators Jobs Database (http://eelink.net/pages/EE+Jobs+Database).

FORESTRY AND CONSERVATION SCIENCE PROFESSORS

CAREER PROFILE

Duties: Teaching both undergraduate and graduate forestry and conservation science classes covering topics such as conservation policy, forest pathology, forest mapping, natural resource management, and natural history; conducting research in specialized areas of interest, presenting findings at academic conferences, and publishing results in scholarly journals; overseeing research and teaching assistants; serving on various committees ranging from curriculum development and textbook selection to campus administration.

Alternate Title(s): Forestry and Conservation Science Instructor; Forestry and Conservation Science Lecturer

Salary Range: $15,000 to $100,000

Employment Prospects: Excellent

Advancement Prospects: Average

Prerequisites:

Education or Training—Master's degree or Ph.D. in forestry, conservation science, environmental science, biological sciences, or similar field

Experience—Teaching college-level students complex concepts and theories; conducting research in accordance with university policies and procedures; giving presentations at academic conferences; publishing work in scholarly journals

Special Skills and Personality Traits—Public speaking; writing and research skills; excellent comprehension and critical thinking skills; ability to understand statistics and use statistical software

Special Requirements—Familiarity with stringent academic research protocols

CAREER LADDER

```
┌─────────────────────────────────────┐
│          Department Chair            │
└─────────────────────────────────────┘

┌─────────────────────────────────────┐
│             Professor                │
└─────────────────────────────────────┘

┌─────────────────────────────────────┐
│  Assistant or Associate Professor    │
└─────────────────────────────────────┘

┌─────────────────────────────────────┐
│        Adjunct (part-time)           │
│      Instructor or Lecturer          │
└─────────────────────────────────────┘

┌─────────────────────────────────────┐
│    Teaching or Research Assistant    │
└─────────────────────────────────────┘
```

Position Description

Forestry and Conservation Science Professors must be well versed in all aspects of forestry, including forest creation, growth, and conservation; pest, disease, and fire management; wildlife management; watershed management; and forest recreation. Along with teaching students the scientific concepts underlying the lifecycles of trees, soils, water, wildlife, and other forest elements, these professors also cover the legal, ethical, and political issues surrounding forestry and conservation science in their courses.

Along with their teaching duties, Forestry and Conservation Science Professors—particularly those who work at four-year colleges or universities and teach only two or three classes a semester—are also required to publish a certain number of articles per year and to secure funding for research projects. Other responsibilities might include presenting papers at academic conferences, supervising the graduate students who teach introductory level courses and advising these students as they undertake their thesis projects or their dissertations, joining campus committees, and developing new courses.

Community college-based Forestry and Conservation Science Professors are likely to have a more narrow focus, as they typically teach at least four classes per semester and are required by contract to be available to students via a prescribed number of office hours per course. Many community colleges do not require their Forestry and Conservation Science Professors to engage in research and publication efforts, although many professors still do so for the sake of professional development. Many two-year institutions require only a master's degree, rather than a full Ph.D., even for tenured professors. Also, as two-year institutions do not offer Ph.D. programs, they do not make use of teaching and research assistants; as a result, despite their specialization in forestry and conservation science, these teachers might find themselves teaching a broader base of environmental science classes than they would at a four-year college or university.

Forestry and Conservation Science Professors may work in a variety of indoor settings, including large lecture halls, smaller seminar rooms, and laboratories. Given the field-based nature of this discipline, these professors oftentimes work outdoors, leading nature walks on campus and overseeing visits to nearby destinations, such as forests, parks, nature and ecology centers, etc. As distance learning continues to grow in popularity, many Forestry and Conservation Science Professors are also now required to develop and conduct classes via the Internet.

Forestry and Conservation Science Professors also collaborate with governmental agencies, businesses, and/or nonprofit agencies on various research projects. For example, after securing a government-funded grant to study the impact of clear cutting—the process of chopping down all of the trees in a geographic area without concern for their size or longevity—on certain species of plants and animals, a professor might contract with local businesses for necessary soil sampling equipment or contact a nonprofit organization, such as the National Parks Conservation Association, to solicit volunteers to help monitor animal behavior, collect soil samples, record data, etc. Data collection efforts for a research project such as this can last for months or even years. Along with writing a grant proposal, planning and coordinating collaborative efforts, and overseeing data collection, at some point Forestry and Conservation Science Professors must also analyze this data and draw conclusions. Findings are then normally presented at conferences and/or published in academic journals or books.

Committee work is also expected of Forestry and Conservation Science Professors. While many committees focus on academic matters—such as curriculum development, textbook selection, and resource procurements for libraries and laboratories—many also focus on more administrative matters, including the selection of new faculty members, reviewing student applications to the program, and changes to existing policies and procedures or the creation of new university bylaws.

As with many teaching positions, Forestry and Conservation Science Professors tend to sign nine- or 10-month contracts and have summers off, during which time they might be expected to pursue research interests or develop new courses. Some postsecondary institutions do require professors to teach during the spring and summer semesters as part of their regular schedule; however, many offer additional pay for these courses as they fall outside of the contracted workload. Forestry and Conservation Science Professors have flexible schedules with the freedom to select the days of the week and times of day they teach courses, make themselves available to students, conduct research, grade tests and papers, etc. However, due to their various responsibilities, most professors find themselves working between 50 and 60 hours a week. And while semester breaks allow for more vacation time than many other professions, many Forestry and Conservation Science Professors use at least a portion of their time off to catch up on grading and create schedules and syllabi for the upcoming semester.

Salaries

At the postsecondary level, part-time Forestry and Conservation Science Professors, also known as adjunct instructors, are usually paid a set amount for each course, earning anywhere from $1,500 to $3,000 per course per semester. These positions usually do not offer benefits, and they are oftentimes filled by professionals in the field who are interested in teaching an evening course or two. According to the American Association of University Professors, the average annual salary for a full-time professor was $68,500 during the 2004–05 school year. Instructors and lecturers with master's degrees averaged between $39,000 and $45,000 per year; assistant professors with Ph.D.'s garnered roughly $55,000; associate professors, $65,000; and full professors, $92,000.

Employment Prospects

The Bureau of Labor Statistics projects considerable growth in employment for postsecondary educators, including Forestry and Conservation Science Professors, through 2014. However, this projection comes with the caveat that many of the positions available will likely be part-time. In 2004, approximately 30% of all postsecondary faculty were part-time, and this percentage is expected to grow as educational institutions of all types continue to experience cutbacks in government funding.

Advancement Prospects

Forestry and Conservation Science Professors tend to start out as assistant or associate professors. The best way for Ph.D. candidates to prepare for these positions is to serve as teaching or research assistants while pursuing their degree. Both two- and four-year institutions also offer part-time positions to instructors, sometimes known as lecturers. While they do not pay very well, these positions are numerous and fairly easy to obtain, and they allow individuals to gain access to an institution and the experience often required for full-time positions.

The most desirable full-time positions are known as tenure-track, offering a career path designed to ultimately reward successful assistant and associate professors with tenure, a guarantee of full-time employment that cannot be revoked without due process. While the process varies by institution, securing tenure typically involves completing a probationary period, quite often several years long, during which time the candidate's teaching, research, and publication efforts are regularly reviewed. At the end of the probationary period, candidates may have to submit a portfolio of their contributions to the college or university and undergo a committee review. Those determined to be successful receive tenure; those who do not qualify are expected to leave the institution at the end of the semester and seek employment elsewhere. The number of tenure-track positions is expected to decline; as a result, competition for these positions is projected to remain intense through 2014.

Education and Training

The minimum education requirement for a Forestry and Conservation Science Professor is a master's degree. Many positions require a Ph.D., which typically takes nine or 10 years to complete. Whether in high school or college, students interested in becoming Forestry and Conservation Science Professors can benefit from taking public-speaking classes, as well as courses in statistics, biology, chemistry, conservation, natural history, and botany. To gain experience in the field, a student might also consider getting an undergraduate degree in environmental or conservation science and working in the field for a few years prior to applying to a Ph.D. program. This experience is oftentimes not only helpful in gaining access to a Ph.D. program, but also is considered valuable by colleges and universities seeking Forestry and Conservation Science Professors.

Special Requirements

While no specific teaching certifications or licensing requirements exist for Forestry and Conservation Science Professors, familiarity with academic research protocols and standards is required.

Experience, Special Skills, and Personality Traits

Clearly, Forestry and Conservation Science Professors must possess excellent public speaking-skills. These individuals should also enjoy mentoring graduate students and teaching and research assistants, as they may be assigned to oversee various research projects undertaken by students and to serve on committees reviewing the dissertations published by Ph.D. candidates.

As research is a key function of many of these professionals, the ability to compile data in accordance with university standards and to use statistical software to interpret this data is required. Excellent writing skills are also essential.

Unions and Associations

Some universities and colleges belong to unions, which faculty members may or may not opt to join. Unions often charge dues that are deducted from paychecks. The Society for College Science Professors, a division of the National Science Teachers Association, serves postsecondary science teachers of all disciplines. The National Association of Biology Teachers represents life science teachers at both the secondary and postsecondary levels, while the North American Association for Environmental Educators provides resources and networking opportunities for environmental educators of all kinds, including postsecondary forestry and conservation science teachers and college students aspiring to become forestry and conservation educators of some sort.

Tips for Entry

1. Take classes in public speaking, writing, and statistics.
2. While an undergraduate, research internships like those listed on the Web site for the North American Association for Environmental Educators (http://www.eelink.net/eejobsdatabase.html) or those offered by the Student Conservation Association (http://www.sca-inc.org).
3. Join organizations like the North American Association for Environmental Educators (http://www.naaee.org); the National Association of Biology Teachers (http://www.nabt.org); and the Society for College Science Teachers (http://www.scst.org).
4. Search for job openings at the *Chronicle of Higher Education* (http://chronicle.com).

MARINE SCIENCE INSTRUCTOR

CAREER PROFILE

Duties: Give presentations, both in the classrooms and in the field, on topics related to marine ecology; lead snorkeling, kayaking, and similar trips in freshwater and saltwater environments, such as natural springs, coral reefs, and mangroves; prepare educational materials; travel to different sites, operate watercraft; maintain equipment and live marine specimens, when appropriate

Alternate Title(s): Marine Science Teacher; Marine Biology Instructor; Marine Biology Teacher; Marine Science Educator; Marine Biology Educator

Salary Range: $15,000 to $50,000

Employment Prospects: Fair

Advancement Prospects: Limited

Prerequisites:

Education or Training—Although part-time, seasonal jobs do not always require a college degree, most full-time positions, seasonal or year-round, require a bachelor's degree in environmental science, environmental education, marine biology, or similar field

Experience—Developing educational materials, giving formal and information presentations about environmental topics, particularly those related to marine science; leading snorkeling and other water-based trips

Special Skills and Personality Traits—Public-speaking and leadership skills; ability to explain scientific concepts and field questions about marine ecology

Special Requirements—SCUBA and Red Cross life guard certifications or equivalents; licensure as a coast guard captain or similar boating experience; CPR and first aid training

CAREER LADDER

```
┌─────────────────────────────────────┐
│   Marine Science Program Director    │
└─────────────────────────────────────┘

┌─────────────────────────────────────┐
│  Full-time Marine Science Instructor │
└─────────────────────────────────────┘

┌─────────────────────────────────────┐
│  Part-time Marine Science Instructor │
└─────────────────────────────────────┘

┌─────────────────────────────────────┐
│   Marine Science Instructional Aide  │
└─────────────────────────────────────┘
```

Position Description

Marine Science Instructors develop and deliver presentations on the ecological features of oceans, intracoastal and intercoastal waterways, natural springs, and similar ecosystems. Marine Science Instructors typically conduct their own research about the historical and ecological development of a particular area and then create lesson plans that include lectures and discussions, as well as field-based experiences that might include hiking, kayaking, canoeing, snorkeling, scuba diving, and other activities designed to immerse students in various marine environments. Given the focus of the curriculum, specific activities that Marine Science Instructors might arrange for students include interacting with marine mammals by using bioacoustic equipment; touring various aquariums or lighthouses; exploring coral reefs, wetlands, marshes, etc.; profiling beaches; and observing fishing practices aboard a seiner, a ship that drags a large net through the water to capture entire schools of fish.

Marine Science Instructors work in a wide variety of settings. Some nonprofit organizations hire marine science educators to develop and teach programs to targeted populations, such as at-risk youth or children who are out of school for the summer. Public and private school districts might contract a marine science teacher to deliver on-site presentations at various schools prior to leading off-site field experiences for students. Others opportunities include marine science centers that offer hands-on programs designed to educate children and adolescents about local marine science issues, resorts and tour companies that arrange snorkeling or scuba diving trips through various marine ecosystems, coastal park systems that provide regular marine science presentations to community residents, and similar organizations with an interest in providing marine science education.

No matter what the setting, most Marine Science Instructors can expect to be responsible for the same types of tasks, which include the following:

- Drafting marine science curriculum and developing activities designed to foster learning and meet educational objectives
- Training any volunteers, assistants, or teachers who are helping in the classroom or on field-based activities
- Teaching things like camping, fishing, cooking, and other outdoor skills, particularly in settings where participants spend the night
- Preparing equipment, such as scuba or snorkeling gear, and any teaching materials prior to the students' arrival
- Training participants on how to use equipment properly and behave responsibly while interacting with marine life
- Giving safety presentations that cover topics like boating behavior, water safety, radio use, first aid, and emergency procedures
- Becoming familiar with park regulations and holding students accountable for following them
- Answering questions about marine ecology
- Transporting students to and from various sites, or working with a bus driver to schedule transportation
- Maintaining any collections of marine life, both indoors and outdoors

Many state and national parks, particularly those in coastal areas, hire Marine Science Instructors to respond to questions about the ecological history and development of the park and waterways, any environmental issues faced by the area, and the habits of various marine mammals, fish, etc. Marine Science Instructors working within such a park system are also typically responsible for creating various exhibits; developing brochures and other informational materials for public distribution; and leading guided tours, some of which require wading, swimming, etc.

Hours for Marine Science Instructors can vary considerably, due to the seasonal nature of many natural settings open to the public. Those looking for part-time work can often find weekend and seasonal jobs, such as summer positions at camps, coastal parks, and beaches; although these positions often require instructors to live on-site, they do tend to offer free room and board, along with a salary. Those working for a school system tend to have summers off, although many school districts make use of Marine Science Instructors for enrichment programs offered during the summertime. Most full-time Marine Science Instructors work roughly 40 hours per week, except during peak seasons, when overtime may be required.

Salaries

The rate of pay for part-time Marine Science Instructors ranges from $9 to $12 an hour. Those paid per day tend to make $250 to $500 weekly, and they usually have access to free housing and food. Depending on their educational level and experience, full-time Marine Science Instructors earn anywhere from $25,000 to $40,000 annually. Those who direct an entire marine science program can earn up to $50,000 per year.

Employment Prospects

While part-time and seasonal positions are plentiful, recent cuts in funding for educational, environmental, and conservation programs have made full-time Marine Science Instructor positions more difficult to land. Given the relatively low rate of industry job growth, as well as an overall lack of funding for new program development in this field, full-time positions tend to open only when someone retires or resigns.

Advancement Prospects

The majority of full-time positions require at least some teaching experience; consequently, volunteering or working part-time at coastal parks, beaches, or marine-focused camps is the easiest mode of entry for Marine Science Instructors ultimately seeking a full-time position. Several years of teaching experience is typically required for advancement into an administrative position, such as a program director.

Education and Training

While seasonal and part-time positions do not require a bachelor's degree, many do require some college course work in marine science, marine biology, environmental science, or a similar field. Full-time Marine Science Instructor positions normally require both teaching experience and a bachelor's degree in marine science, marine biology, environmental science, or a similar field.

Special Requirements

Marine Science Instructors must be able to swim, tolerate the sun and various weather conditions, operate watercraft, lift equipment, and lead a variety of water-based activities. As a result, they must be physically fit and enjoy working outdoors. Many employers also require CPR certification, first aid training, SCUBA and Red Cross lifeguard certifications or equivalents, and licensure as a coast guard captain.

Experience, Special Skills, and Personality Traits

Due to their regular contact with the public, Marine Science Instructors need to enjoy working with people of all ages. They must also possess the ability to lead groups and manage student behavior in both indoor and outdoor settings. It is also important that Marine Science Instructors have the problem-solving skills necessary to anticipate and subvert potential natural hazards.

Unions and Associations

A variety of national professional associations—including the National Oceanic and Atmospheric Administration, the American Society of Limnology and Oceanography, and the National Marine Educators Association—serve Marine Science Instructors. A variety of regional organizations also exist, particularly in states such as Florida, Georgia, New York, New Jersey, and other states with significant coastal areas.

Tips for Entry

1. While an undergraduate, research marine science educator internships like those listed on the Web site for the Student Conservation Association, http://www.sca-inc.org.
2. Gain experience by either volunteering or working part time at a coastal park, beach, or aquarium.
3. Join organizations like the National Marine Educators Association, http://www.marine-ed.org.
4. Search for job openings at the America Outdoors (http://www.americaoutdoors.org/job-results.asp) and North American Association for Environmental Educators (http://www.eelink.net/eejobsdatabase.html) Web sites.

OUTDOOR EDUCATION INSTRUCTOR

CAREER PROFILE

Duties: Create and implement outdoor activities designed to teach team-building, problem-solving, leadership, and other social skills, as well as raise environmental consciousness and awareness of human impact on the environment; teach specific wilderness survival skills, such as camping, cooking, and map and compass reading; develop an activities-based curriculum that covers topics such as ecology, geology, biology, and natural history

Alternate Title(s): Outdoor Education Leader; Outdoor Environmental Education Instructor; Adventure Education Instructor; Adventure Education Leader

Salary Range: $15,000 to $50,000+

Employment Prospects: Average

Advancement Prospects: Limited

Prerequisites:

Education or Training—A minimum of a high school diploma; many positions require some college course work, or even a bachelor's degree, in environmental science, biology, education, or related field

Experience—Understanding of ecology, natural history, and human impact on the environment; experience teaching, particularly children or young adults, in an outdoor setting

Special Skills and Personality Traits—Ability to plan and organize activities; time management; attention to detail; public speaking; problem solving

Special Requirements—Basic first aid skills and CPR certification

CAREER LADDER

```
┌─────────────────────────────────────┐
│ Outdoor Education Program Developer  │
└─────────────────────────────────────┘

┌─────────────────────────────────────┐
│    Outdoor Education Instructor      │
└─────────────────────────────────────┘

┌─────────────────────────────────────┐
│        Part-Time Outdoor             │
│       Education Instructor           │
└─────────────────────────────────────┘
```

Position Description

Outdoor Education Instructors teach a variety of science- and nature-based skills and concepts, typically to either children or young adults, in an outdoor setting. Often offered in the form of trips or excursions, outdoor education courses can range from a single day of activities designed to expose students to various facets of environmental ethics or forest ecology to weeklong rock climbing, river-rafting, wilderness-backpacking, or kayak-surfing expeditions.

Specific activities might include constructing a shelter from materials found outside, searching for examples of both macro and micro invertebrates, using telescopes to identify various stars and planets, building a tower and using an earthquake seismology simulator to test its stability, and completing an obstacle course that requires a team to help each member scale a rock wall and use a zip line.

No matter the duration of the class or the activities involved, subjects covered can include biology, geology, engineering, resource conservation, ecosystem management, forest ecology, etc. Typically, activities are designed to help students also develop social skills in things like team building, leadership, decision making, problem solving, risk taking, interpersonal communication, and personal responsibility, as well as physical skills such as map reading, navigation, cooking, camping, and other outdoor survival tactics.

Outdoor Education Instructors, particularly those leading overnight excursions, must also monitor weather conditions at planned destinations, assess the physical fitness levels of students, and monitor the progress and ensure the safety of students for the duration of the course. These instructors typically also demonstrate for students how to use necessary equipment and review safety guidelines and any other rules students are expected to follow.

Given the fact that Outdoor Education Instructors typically work with children and young adults, some of whom might be troubled or have a history of prior behavior problems in traditional classroom settings, these professionals are also responsible for holding students accountable for their actions. Along with being able to handle personality conflicts, disruptive behavior, and other discipline issues in the moment they occur, Outdoor Education Instructors oftentimes must anticipate potential problems before they arise and take preventive action, such as creating lists of course expectations or rules on the first day of class and posting these lists in a place students can see, contracting with individual students regarding the type of behavior expected of them, or role playing various scenarios and discussing appropriate student or team behavior.

Outdoor Education Instructors can be either part-time or full-time. Full-time instructors often live on-site and have evening responsibilities such as helping students cook meals, supervising cabins or campgrounds, and leading evening entertainment, which can range from telling ghost stories around a campfire to setting up and operating karaoke equipment. For part-time instructors, hours may be sporadic, depending on the types of courses taught, and work is often seasonal as many outdoor education programs are limited to the summer months in various regions of the country.

Salaries

Outdoor Education Instructors paid by the week tend to earn from $275 to $600 per week, depending upon their qualifications. Those paid by the hour make anywhere from $10 to $15 per hour. If educators are expected to live on-site, free room and board may be included as part of the compensation package. Outdoor Education Instructors who eventually oversee entire programs and take on administrative responsibilities can make upwards of $50,000.

Employment Prospects

Employment for Outdoor Education Instructors is expected to grow roughly 10 to 15 percent annually through 2014. This is considered an average rate of growth compared to other types of careers.

Advancement Prospects

Outdoor Education Instructors can gain experience by volunteering at local parks, nature centers, and other sites that typically offer environmental education of some sort. Finding part-time work also allows an educator access to the field, well as the chance to increase skills and knowledge. Experienced Outdoor Education Instructors interested in advancing into an administrative position are often hired to develop and/or direct an entire outdoor education program.

Education and Training

The minimum education requirement for an Outdoor Education Instructor is a high school diploma. However, many positions require some college-level course work in science, particularly in life sciences or environmental sciences. Community colleges and universities across the country offer a variety of courses in the environmental sciences. Enviroeducation.com, an online directory of environmental education programs, lists 197 different postsecondary schools that offer undergraduate- and graduate-level environmental education programs. Most positions also require that candidates have some previous teaching experience with the target population. As with many careers, the more education and experience a candidate has, the higher the wage he or she will earn.

Whether in high school or college, students interested in becoming Outdoor Education Instructors will benefit from course work in biology, geology, nature studies, conservation, recreation studies, environmental science, public speaking, and education. Business and management courses are helpful for those who plan to move into administration.

Special Requirements

Due to the physical nature of outdoor education experiences, many Outdoor Education Instructors are required to have training in CPR and first aid. While most of these positions do not require official teaching certification, many do require some previous teaching experience. For programs involving mountain or rock climbing, white water rafting, or similar outdoor activities, specialized training is required.

Experience, Special Skills, and Personality Traits

Excellent group leadership, motivational, conflict resolution, and public-speaking skills are required of all Outdoor Education Instructors. As many outdoor education activities require a significant amount of hiking or other potentially strenuous activity, a basic level of physical fitness is also typically necessary.

Unions and Associations

The North American Association for Environmental Educators serves environmental education professionals, students, and volunteers in the public school system, in colleges and universities, in government agencies, in the private sector, and in nonprofit agencies. Two organizations specifically targeting outdoor education students and professionals are Outdoor Ed and America Outdoors.

Tips for Entry

1. While in high school, take courses in environmental science, biology, geology, physical fitness and recreation, public speaking, and education.

2. Search for environmental education programs at Enviroeducation.com: The Environmental Education Directory, http://www.enviroeducation.com/.

3. Apply for outdoor education scholarships like those offered by Outdoor ED, http://www.outdoored.com.

4. Search for job openings at Web sites like America Outdoors, http://www.americaoutdoors.org/job-results.asp; Outdoor Ed: The Professional's Resource, http://www.outdoored.com; and the North American Association for Environmental Educators, http://eelink.net/pages/EE+Jobs+Database.

RECREATION AND FITNESS STUDIES PROFESSOR

CAREER PROFILE

Duties: Teaching college-level courses in fitness, recreation, and leisure, covering topics like exercise physiology, recreational program development, and facilities management; designing and overseeing research projects; attending academic conferences; publishing scholarly articles and books; mentoring research and teaching assistants; and joining a variety of campus committees, including those related to recreation and fitness studies and those dealing with campus administration in general.

Alternate Title(s): Physical Education Professor; Health and Physical Education Professor; Health, Physical Education, and Recreation Professor; Kinesiology Professor; Sports Management Professor

Salary Range: $15,000 to $100,000

Employment Prospects: Good

Advancement Prospects: Average

Prerequisites:

Education or Training—Master's degree or Ph.D. in physical education, health and recreation, kinesiology, or similar field

Experience—Teaching college-level students complex concepts and theories; conducting research in accordance with university policies and procedures; giving presentations at academic conferences; publishing work in scholarly journals

Special Skills and Personality Traits—Strong public-speaking, leadership, and mentoring abilities; proficient in writing and research; excellent comprehension and critical thinking skills; detail-oriented; self-motivated

Special Requirements—Ability to lead students in a wide variety of physical activities; proficiency with statistical software; understanding of research protocols

CAREER LADDER

```
┌─────────────────────────────────┐
│       Department Chair          │
└─────────────────────────────────┘

┌─────────────────────────────────┐
│          Professor              │
└─────────────────────────────────┘

┌─────────────────────────────────┐
│ Assistant or Associate Professor│
└─────────────────────────────────┘

┌─────────────────────────────────┐
│  Adjunct (part-time) Instructor │
│          or Lecturer            │
└─────────────────────────────────┘

┌─────────────────────────────────┐
│  Teaching or Research Assistant │
└─────────────────────────────────┘
```

Position Description

Recreation and Fitness Studies Professors develop and teach courses such as exercise physiology, recreational program development, facilities management, anatomy, therapeutic recreation, and conditioning theory to both undergraduate and graduate students. Teaching college-level courses involves the following basic responsibilities:

- Developing measurable course objectives and monitoring student progress in an effort to ensure those objectives are met
- Creating and implementing activities, which can include lectures, classroom discussions, group work, hands-on activities, homework projects, and tests
- Leading fitness activities in the school's gymnasium or fitness center
- Writing and distributing course syllabi and schedules and distributing these at the beginning of each semester; revising these documents, if necessary, and redistributing updated versions to students and administration
- Grading assignments, tests, and papers
- Recording grades and maintaining student records
- Scheduling office hours each semester for students seeking additional help with their course work or guidance related to career plans

Teaching is only one component of the work performed by a Recreation and Fitness Studies Professor. To stay up-to-date with the latest developments in their field, these professionals also read scholarly journals, attend professional conferences, and meet regularly with their colleagues. In addition, Recreation and Fitness Studies Professors are also expected to write articles for publication, present papers at conferences, and undertake research projects, a lengthy process that involves creating an original research question, conducting experiments, gathering data, analyzing data, and drawing conclusions that are then typically published in academic journals or books. In fact, those working at four-year colleges or universities sometimes teach only two or three classes a semester to ensure that they have time for these activities.

Most four-year institutions require their Recreation and Fitness Studies Professors to possess a Ph.D. and to mentor graduate students, as well as research and teaching assistants, many of whom teach introductory-level courses in place of the professors themselves. Other duties at this level include overseeing Ph.D. candidates as they write their dissertations and developing curricula for new courses.

Community college Recreation and Fitness Studies Professors may face fewer research and publication requirements, as they tend to carry course loads of four to five classes a semester. A master's degree, rather than a full Ph.D., may suffice to secure employment at a two-year institution. Also, because two-year institutions do not offer Ph.D. programs, they typically do not recruit teaching and research assistants; as a result, Recreation and Fitness Studies Professors at this level are not responsible for mentoring these individuals, nor do they have the luxury of delegating tasks, such as grading tests and papers, to them.

Recreation and Fitness Studies Professors may find themselves teaching in diverse settings, such as large lecture halls, smaller classrooms, gymnasiums, laboratories, or even outdoors. The increasingly popularity of distance learning has also prompted many postsecondary institutions to begin offering classes via the Internet. As a result, Recreation and Fitness Studies Professors may find themselves expected to develop and conduct certain classes online.

Recreation and Fitness Studies Professors are also expected to sit on various committees, many of which are devoted to academic issues, including textbook selection, curriculum modifications, and grading policies. Other committees, such as hiring committees, student selection committees, and campus safety committees, are more administrative in nature.

Most contracts for Recreation and Fitness Studies Professors are nine or ten months long. Although professors are not necessarily obligated to teach courses during the summers, many do work during this period by pursuing new research interests or developing new courses. While some colleges and universities require their professors to teach spring and summer courses, many offer additional pay for these courses.

Recreation and Fitness Studies Professors enjoy flexible schedules as they are able to choose which days of the week and times of day they teach classes, when they offer office hours, and when they complete their additional responsibilities, such as research, writing, and grading. To complete their work, most professors find themselves logging between 50 and 60 hours a week. Although the time off between semesters results in more vacation days than offered by many other professions, many Recreation and Fitness Studies Professors use their semester breaks to complete grading, rewrite schedules and syllabi, and develop new courses.

Salaries

Part-time Recreation and Fitness Studies Professors are also known as adjunct instructors. Each semester, these instructors typically sign a contract whereby pay—roughly $1,500 to $3,000 per course—is based on the number of courses taught. These positions usually do not offer any type of benefits, and they are filled either by individuals hoping to gain experience and eventually land a full-time job or by professionals in the field who are interested in making extra money by teaching an evening course or two.

The average annual salary for full-time Recreation and Fitness Studies Professors, according to the American Association of University Professors, was $68,500 during the 2004–05 school year. Average pay for instructors and lecturers with master's degrees ranged from $39,000 and $45,000 per year; assistant professors with Ph.D.'s earned roughly $55,000; associate professors, $65,000; and full professors, $92,000.

Employment Prospects

The National Institute of Health's Office of Science Education projects better-than-average growth in employment for Recreation and Fitness Studies Professors. However, a large portion of these new positions are expected to be part time. Roughly 30 percent of all college-level teachers were part-time in 2004, and this percentage are expected to grow as funding for educational institutions of all kinds continues to decline.

Advancement Prospects

Recreation and Fitness Studies Professors tend to start out at the assistant or associate level. Many Ph.D. candidates gain the teaching experience typically required to qualify for the position by securing a teaching assistantship while in graduate school. Others build their résumés by accepting a part-time teaching position at either a two-year or four-year institution. While these positions are notorious for not paying very well, particularly for the master's degree they typically require, they are fairly easy to obtain.

The most desirable full-time positions are known as tenure-track, offering a career path designed to ultimately reward successful assistant and associate professors with tenure, a guarantee of full-time employment that cannot be revoked without due process. While the process varies by institution, securing tenure typically involves completing a probationary period, quite often several years long, during which time the candidate's teaching, research, and publication efforts are regularly reviewed. At the end of the probationary period, candidates may have to submit a portfolio of their contributions to the college or university and undergo a committee review. Those whose accomplishments are deemed successful receive tenure; those who do not qualify are expected to leave the institution at the end of the semester and seek employment elsewhere. As the number of tenure-track positions is expected to decline through 2014, competition for these slots will likely remain intense.

Education and Training

At minimum, Recreation and Fitness Studies Professors are expected to hold a master's degree in physical education, health and recreation, kinesiology, or a similar field. A full Ph.D., which typically takes nine or 10 years to complete, is required of many positions. Both high school and undergraduate students planning to become Recreation and Fitness Studies Professors can benefit from course work in public speaking, physical fitness, anatomy, business management, and statistics. Those who find the idea of nine or 10 consecutive years of schooling daunting might also consider getting an undergraduate degree in physical education, as well as a teaching certificate, and working as an elemen-

tary or secondary school physical education teacher for a few years prior to applying to a graduate program.

Special Requirements

While no specific teaching certifications or licensing requirements exist for Recreation and Fitness Studies Professors, due to the physical nature of some courses, CPR and first aid training might be expected by certain institutions.

Experience, Special Skills, and Personality Traits

Along with excellent public-speaking and leadership skills, Recreation and Fitness Studies Professors must also possess the desire and ability to mentor graduate students, teaching assistants, and research assistants, as they may be assigned to oversee various student research projects and to serve on committees reviewing the dissertations published by Ph.D. candidates. As research is a key function of many of these professionals, the ability to compile data in accordance with university standards and to use statistical software to interpret this data is also required. Excellent writing skills are also essential.

Unions and Associations

Some universities and colleges belong to unions, which faculty members may or may not opt to join. Unions often charge dues that are deducted from paychecks. The Society for College Science Professors, a division of the National Science Teachers Association, serves postsecondary science teachers of all disciplines. Associations specifically serving Recreation and Fitness Studies Professors include the American Alliance for Health, Physical Education, Recreation, and Dance and the National Association for Sport and Physical Education.

Tips for Entry

1. Take classes in physical education, anatomy, public speaking, writing, and statistics.
2. While a student, join organizations like the National Association for Sport and Physical Education, http://www.aahperd.org/NASPE/.
3. Search for job openings at the Web sites of the *Chronicle of Higher Education* (http://chronicle.com) and American Association for Health, Physical Education, Recreation, and Dance (http://member.aahperd.org/careercenter/).

RECREATION PLANNER

CAREER PROFILE

Duties: Compile information about current and projected recreation trends, preferences, and needs of a community; use this information to develop plans for recreational programming that takes into consideration the social, economic, and environmental impact of these plans; give public presentations that detail development plans; write reports that include how to implement tasks, projected costs, and potential sources of funding.

Alternate Title(s): Sports and Recreation Planner; Recreation Developer; Sports and Recreation Developer

Salary Range: $30,000 to $80,000+

Employment Prospects: Good

Advancement Prospects: Good

Prerequisites:

Education or Training—Bachelor's degree in planning with a master's degree in parks and recreation or similar field, or a bachelor's degree in parks and recreation or similar field with a master's degree in planning

Experience—Understanding of how various recreational opportunities impact a community; knowledge of building and landscape design, particularly as they relate to recreational facilities

Special Skills and Personality Traits—Interpersonal and business communication skills; attention to detail; public speaking; report writing

Special Requirements—Proficiency with database, statistical and computer modeling software; interest in promoting recreational and fitness activities within a community

CAREER LADDER

```
┌─────────────────────────────┐
│      Senior Planner         │
└─────────────────────────────┘

┌─────────────────────────────┐
│         Planner             │
└─────────────────────────────┘

┌─────────────────────────────┐
│      Junior Planner         │
└─────────────────────────────┘
```

Position Description

Recreation Planners work with community groups, governmental agencies, and existing recreational organizations within a community to assess things like existing recreational opportunities for all residents; current and future recreational needs; and projected recreational trends. While gathering data, planners might pinpoint gaps in recreational services and overlapping programs. This data can then be used to determine how well the recreational needs of community residents are being met, how often recreational opportunities are utilized, and whether or not additional programming or enhancements to existing programming might be necessary.

For example, a planner might realize that recreational programs are accessed regularly by senior citizens in certain zip codes and hardly used at all by senior citizens living in other zip codes. Rather than assuming that the programs simply do not appeal to those senior citizens and discontinuing them, a Recreation Planner might conduct further research and uncover transportation issues for residents in certain zip codes; future planning might then include either placing a facility within one of those zip codes or offering a bus or shuttle service to existing facilities. Or a planner might discover that most of an urban community's recreational programming focuses on young adult males from the ages of 16 to 25 and largely ignores young women in this age group. This discovery might prompt a Recreation Planner to begin interviewing this demographic group to ascertain what types of recreational activities hold the most appeal.

If planning efforts include something as extensive as the creation of a new facility, Recreation Planners might then need to consult with construction firms, building engineers, landscape architects, and similar industry professionals. This type of planning also tends to involve meeting with local governmental officials, such as city council members, to resolve issues of concern to residents, as well as working with zoning boards, building inspectors, and similar entities to ensure compliance with building codes and other regulations.

When developing plans for the construction of new recreational facilities or upgrading or remodeling existing facilities, Recreation Planners must also take into consideration things like location, landscape design, environmental impact, and adequacy of resources. Ultimately, planners condense all of this information into a detailed report that outlines specific plans, an implementation schedule for those plans, and all projected costs.

In many cases, Recreation Planners might not be working on facility design as much as on recreational programming. They might be hired by a municipality, park system, public or private business, nonprofit agency, school system, or any other organization to oversee all recreational opportunities. In these cases, Recreation Planners use what they know about their target population to develop specific recreational programs—such as arts and crafts, dance, drama, music, nature studies, outdoor and adventure education, and sports—that take into consideration things like existing facilities and equipment, the number of recreation workers available, and the amount of money budgeted for recreation.

Recreation Planners tend to work a 40-hour workweek. However, they may also find themselves having to schedule evening and weekend meetings, particularly if they are doing things like talking with community groups or attending city council meetings. Hours may also increase when deadlines for reports and presentation are imminent.

Salaries

The Bureau of Labor Statistics reported average annual salaries for Recreation Planners as $53,000 in 2004. Annual salaries range from $30,000 to $80,000, depending on education and experience. Beginning planners tend to earn from $30,000 to $40,000, although those with master's degrees might make a bit more than this. Planners with roughly five

years of experience garner annual salaries of $40,000 to $50,000. Professionals with upwards of 10 years of experience, often titled senior planners, can make earn more than $80,000 per year. Positions with the state and local governments tend to be the most lucrative.

Employment Prospects

The job outlook for Recreation Planners is projected to be on par with most other occupations through 2014, according to the Bureau of Labor Statistics.

Advancement Prospects

Nearly all Recreation Planners must possess a bachelor's degree to secure an entry-level position. Many postsecondary programs offer internships, which may prove invaluable to students, as they provide an opportunity to gain industry experience as well as to meet other professionals and perhaps find a mentor. Most often, new college graduates are hired for entry-level "junior planner" positions, which require candidates to assist experienced planners to gather data, write reports, and prepare presentations. A master's degree is normally required prior to promotion to the next level. A senior planner typically has at least five or 10 years of experience. In larger organizations, senior planners may also be expected to perform administrative and managerial duties.

Special Requirements

Recreation Planners must be able to understand demographic information to draw conclusions about current and future recreational needs, as well as be able to comprehend building and landscape design concepts. Proficiency with statistical, computer drafting, and database software is also necessary.

Education and Training

Most Recreation Planner positions require a bachelor's degree, if not a master's degree. Master's degrees in planning are available at roughly 70 colleges and universities, and 15 of these institutions also offer undergraduate degrees in planning. Some students secure bachelor's degrees in planning and then pursue master's degrees in things like parks and recreation management or sports and recreation administration. Others get undergraduate degrees in parks and recreation or sports and recreation and then pursue a graduate degree in planning.

Roughly 100 colleges and universities offer four-year parks and recreation degrees that are accredited by the National Recreation and Park Association. Students pursuing this course of study have the option of specializing in outdoor recreation, therapeutic recreation, or commercial recreation, as well as either business or camp management for those hoping to secure administrative positions some day. Along with offering classes on topics such as recreation and administration and community organization, these programs also require students to complete some sort of supervised internship.

The American Planning Association's American Institute of Certified Planners offers a certification credential for individuals who pass their examination. To be eligible to sit for the examination, planners need between two and four years of experience, depending on their level of education. The National Recreation and Park Association also offers the Certified Park and Recreational Professional credential for individuals with a bachelor's degree, two years of full-time experience in the field, and successful completion of the Certified Park and Recreation Professional examination.

Experience, Special Skills, and Personality Traits

Recreation Planners must possess solid interpersonal and business communication skills, particularly for interactions with community groups and government agencies. Other skills include public speaking, report writing, and attention to detail.

Unions and Associations

The American Planning Association represents planners throughout the United States. The Association of Collegiate Schools of Planning promotes educational options for planners and offers information on degree programs, scholarships, and awards. Recreation Planners can also join the National Association of Recreation Resource Planners, the National Recreation and Park Association, the American Alliance for Health, Physical Education, Recreation, and Dance, and the American Association for Physical Activity and Recreation.

Tips for Entry

1. In high school, take courses in computers, business public speaking, communications, and recreation and physical fitness.
2. Visit the Association of Collegiate Schools of Planning's Web site, http://www.acsp.org, to research schools that offer degrees in planning.
3. Search for jobs at the American Planning Association's Web site, http://www.planning.org/jobsonline/ads.htm.
4. Review industry Web sites such as Planners Web, http://www.plannersweb.com, and Planners Network, http://www.plannersnetwork.org, to learn more about the industry.

RECREATION WORKER

CAREER PROFILE

Duties: Develop and lead various recreational activities, such as arts and crafts, camping, games, music, sports, theater, and other hobbies; create recreation programs designed to meet the needs of various populations; create schedules; promote activities; recruit participants

Alternate Title(s): Recreation and Fitness Worker; Sports and Recreation Worker; Recreation Leader; Recreation and Fitness Leader; Sports and Recreation Leader;

Salary Range: $13,000 to $35,000

Employment Prospects: Average

Advancement Prospects: Fair

Prerequisites:

Education or Training—A minimum of a high school diploma, although many positions require a college degree in recreation and fitness or similar field

Experience—Depends on focus of organization; oftentimes, experience with the specific type of recreation, such as dance or theater, is desired

Special Skills and Personality Traits—Energetic and enthusiastic; creative; self-motivated; strong leadership, public-speaking, and interpersonal communication skills

Special Requirements—Vary by employer; may need certifications in various activities, CPR training

CAREER LADDER

```
┌─────────────────────────────┐
│    Recreation Director      │
└─────────────────────────────┘

┌─────────────────────────────┐
│     Recreation Leader       │
└─────────────────────────────┘

┌─────────────────────────────┐
│     Recreation Worker       │
└─────────────────────────────┘

┌─────────────────────────────┐
│    Recreation Assistant     │
└─────────────────────────────┘
```

Position Description

Recreation Workers develop, promote, and lead various recreational activities—including arts and crafts, biking, camping, dance, games, music, sports, tai chi, theater, and yoga—in all sorts of settings. Some businesses hire recreation workers to develop enrichment programs for employees. Theme parks and resorts might use Recreation Workers to lead tourists in a variety of activities, such as nature walks, bird watching, or rock climbing. Other organizations that hire Recreation Workers include campgrounds, community centers, jails, nursing homes, parks and forests, playgrounds, religious organizations, and zoos.

Depending on their experience level, responsibilities for a Recreation Worker might vary. Those who are involved in a wide variety of recreation activities for an organization might create daily or weekly schedules to meet the needs of various participants, develop promotional materials and recruit participants for various activities, order necessary equipment, oversee use of facilities and equipment, and actually lead the activities themselves. In other cases, Recreation Workers might be limited to overseeing a single activity, such as leading walks through botanical gardens several times a day. Some Recreation Workers might specialize in a single activity, such as camping or fly fishing, and also recruit activity specialists to offer other classes in art, music, theater or sports like gymnastics, swimming, or tennis. Depending upon the setting in which they work, Recreation Workers often report to a general manager, such as the director of a campground, park, or playground.

The daily activities of a Recreation Worker can vary considerably. On some days, they might spend their time outdoors engaged in physically demanding activities, such as river rafting and rock climbing; on other days, they might find themselves in a classroom leading groups in drawing, guitar playing, painting, or pottery making; and at other times, they may not be engaged in leading activities, but rather recruiting participants for a new activity planned for the following week.

Due to the physical nature of the work, recreation workers do risk suffering injuries, particularly during the more demanding activities. Most full-time Recreation Workers log about 40 hours a week, including evenings and weekends, as these are the times people most often engage in recreational activities. Hours vary for part-time and seasonal jobs. Some jobs, particularly those at sites like campgrounds and large parks, require Recreation Workers to live on-site.

Salaries

According to the Bureau of Labor Statistics, average earnings for full-time Recreation Workers were $20,000 in 2004. Recreation leaders or directors typically earn a much higher salary. While full-time positions tend to include a standard benefits package, the majority of part-time and seasonal positions do not offer benefits.

Employment Prospects

Jobs for Recreation Workers are expected to grow at an average rate through 2014, according to the Bureau of Labor Statistics. However, this growth projection comes with the caveat that many new positions will be either part-time or seasonal and not require a college-level education or experience; as a result, they will not pay a professional wage. Competition for permanent, full-time positions will remain intense, as this type of work, as well as the setting in which it takes place, is considered desirable by many applicants.

Advancement Prospects

The large number of part-time and seasonal positions makes gaining experience fairly easy for Recreation Workers. Volunteer opportunities are also plentiful, particularly at non-profit agencies, nursing homes, jails, and other settings with populations that might prove difficult for some.

Recreation Workers who want to develop new skills are sometimes able to do this while working. For example, Recreation Workers might assist an activity specialist in yoga or karate for several months in an effort to gain enough experience to eventually lead the activity. Experienced Recreation Workers who are interested in pursing administrative work may have the opportunity to advance into recreation leader or recreation director positions at some point; however, these jobs do tend to require a minimum of a four-year degree in recreation and fitness, or some form of business.

Education and Training

While part-time and seasonal positions typically require nothing more than a high school diploma and a desire to work with a certain population, full-time Recreation Workers are usually expected to have completed some college course work. Many positions require either an associate's or a bachelor's degree in recreation and fitness or a similar field. In some cases, a bachelor's degree in a liberal arts field may suffice. Specific experience in the types of activities offered by the organization is also highly desirable.

Roughly 100 colleges and universities offer four-year degrees in parks and recreation that are accredited by the National Recreation and Park Association. Students pursuing this course of study have the option of specializing in outdoor recreation, therapeutic recreation, and commercial recreation, as well as either business or camp management for those hoping to secure administrative positions some day. Along with offering classes on topics such as recreational needs with special populations, community organization, and administration, these programs also require students to complete some sort of supervised internship.

The National Recreation and Park Association also offers three certifications for park and recreation professionals: Associate Park and Recreation Professional, for individuals who do not yet have a four-year degree; Provisional Park and Recreation Professional, for individuals with a bachelor's degree who do not yet have the experience required for full certification; and Certified Park and Recreation Professional, for individuals with a bachelor's degree, two years of full-time experience in the field, and successful completion of the Certified Park and Recreation Professional examination.

Special Requirements

Candidates, particularly those applying for full-time positions, are often expected to undergo drug tests and background checks. Certification in CPR and other specialized training related to various activities might also be required.

Experience, Special Skills, and Personality Traits

Recreation Workers are expected to work well with others, to possess a wide range of solid interpersonal communication skills, and to be comfortable leading various activities. Experience working with the target population, or an interest in working with this population, is also desirable. Recreation Workers are expected to be enthusiastic and energetic, as well as personable, motivational, and sensitive to the needs of participants. As activities might involve a considerable level of physical exertion, candidates must also be quite fit.

Unions and Associations

The National Recreation and Parks Association, the American Alliance for Health, Physical Education, Recreation, and Dance, and the National Association of Recreation Resource Planners are three professional organizations serving Recreation Workers. The American Camp Association represents camp professionals of all types, including Recreation Workers.

Tips for Entry

1. Gain experience with whatever population interests you most by volunteering with an organization such as a playground, campground, or nursing home that serves this population.
2. In high school, take courses in interpersonal communication, public speaking, and physical fitness, and also sign up for any extracurricular programs related to your career interests.
3. Join organizations like the American Association for Physical Activity and Recreation and the National Association for Sport and Recreation Planners to gain access to professional development and additional training opportunities for Recreation Workers.
4. Search for jobs at the Career Center of the National Recreation and Parks Association's Web site, http://nrpa.jobcontrolcenter.com/search/ and at Outdoor ED, http://www.outdoored.com.

SCIENTIFIC

ATMOSPHERIC SCIENTIST

CAREER PROFILE

Duties: Gather, analyze, and interpret data; collect air samples; conduct meteorological research; use computer models and numerical simulations; develop weather forecasts, maps, and reports; apply knowledge of meteorology to environmental problems; broadcast weather information and warnings

Alternate Title(s): Meteorologist

Salary Range: $30,220 to $92,430+

Employment Prospects: Fair

Advancement Prospects: Good

Prerequisites:

Education or Training—Some entry-level positions may be obtained without a college degree, but most positions require a bachelor's, master's, or doctorate degree in atmospheric science, meteorology, or a related field

Experience—Requirements vary; internships usually provide hands-on field experience needed for entry-level employment

Special Skills and Personality Traits—Analytical thinking, writing, oral communication, problem-solving, statistical, and computer skills; logical, self-reliant, independent, adaptable, flexible, detail-oriented, careful, thorough

Special Requirements—Certification from the American Meteorological Society may be required for consulting meteorologists.

CAREER LADDER

Administrator

Supervisor

Staff Meteorologist or Consultant

Intern

Position Description

Atmospheric Scientists study the physical properties and characteristics of the atmosphere—the mass of air that surrounds the Earth. In addition to examining atmospheric processes and motions, scientists in this field study how the atmosphere affects the environment.

Also known as meteorologists, Atmospheric Scientists engage in a wide range of interesting work. While weather forecasting is one of their more recognizable jobs, they have many others. In addition to analyzing present-day weather, Atmospheric Scientists seek to understand past weather and identify and interpret climate trends. As the U.S. Depart-

ment of Labor's *Occupational Outlook Handbook* explains, "Weather information and meteorological research also are applied in air-pollution control, agriculture, forestry, air and sea transportation, defense, and the study of possible trends in the Earth's climate, such as global warming, droughts, or ozone depletion."

In fact, there are several broad areas of specialization within the field of atmospheric science. Applied meteorology includes weather forecasting, consulting, marketing and sales, and atmospheric measurements and instrumentation. In addition to applied meteorology, opportunities also exist in education and research.

Atmospheric Scientists constitute the largest grouping of operational meteorologists. They are responsible for developing weather forecasts. According to the U.S. Department of Labor's *Occupational Outlook Handbook*, operational meteorologists "study information on air pressure, temperature, humidity, and wind velocity; and apply physical and mathematical relationships to make short-range and long-range weather forecasts. Their data come from weather satellites, weather radars, sensors, and weather stations in many parts of the world. Meteorologists use sophisticated computer models of the world's atmosphere to make long-term, short-term, and local-area forecasts. More accurate instruments for measuring and observing weather conditions, as well as high-speed computers to process and analyze weather data, have revolutionized weather forecasting. Using satellite data, climate theory, and sophisticated computer models of the world's atmosphere, meteorologists can more effectively interpret the results of these models to make local-area weather predictions."

While some weather forecasters work in the media sector, producing forecasts for television, newspapers, radio, and the Internet, many more work in non-media roles. Although the forecasts developed by operational meteorologists obviously benefit the general public, they also are of use to industries that rely on accurate weather data for operational, economic, or safety purposes. Examples of such end-users include businesses in the fields of agriculture, air transportation, aviation, fishing, forestry, shipping, and utilities.

Many Atmospheric Scientists work in the consulting field. Consulting work may include virtually any service related to meteorological science. However, according to the American Meteorological Society (AMS), the majority of consulting services offered by Atmospheric Scientists focus on environmental quality (especially the air); forensic meteorology, which involves the weather as it relates to police investigations and legal matters; weather-related decision support for certain industries; and meteorological software and systems development.

Applied atmospheric science positions also exist in marketing and sales, where technical knowledge is needed to effectively sell meteorological products and services to end-users. Scientists in these roles may work for companies that develop atmospheric instruments, which can range from simple rain gauges to Doppler radar systems and weather satellites.

Some Atmospheric Scientists are involved in research initiatives at universities, government agencies, and private firms. Under the larger umbrella of research, scientists may specialize in a number of different areas:

- Environmental meteorologists study a range of environmental issues and problems, from water shortages to air pollution.
- Physical meteorologists concentrate on the physical and chemical properties of the atmosphere. These may include atmospheric energy transfer, cloud formation, and the properties of severe storms.
- Climatologists study variations in the Earth's climate that range from hundreds to millions of years. They obtain, analyze, and draw conclusions from historic weather data from different regions of the world. The results of their work are put to use in agriculture, architecture, and environmental control systems in buildings.
- Synoptic meteorologists are involved in the development of weather forecasting tools. Their work involves the use of computers and complex mathematical models of the atmosphere.

Atmospheric Scientists perform different tasks, depending on the specific positions they hold. However, there are a number of common duties that this type of scientist performs. These include gathering, analyzing, and interpreting data from satellites, weather stations, and weather bureaus; collecting air samples via airplanes and ships; conducting meteorological research; using computer models and numerical simulations; developing weather forecasts, maps, and reports; applying knowledge of meteorology, mathematics, physics, and climate theory to environmental problems; broadcasting weather information and warnings via different forms of media; and using sophisticated equipment to monitor the atmosphere, including Doppler radar.

Because weather conditions affect all areas of the planet, Atmospheric Scientists work everywhere. Employment settings include tiny one-person weather stations in remote locations, large weather offices with multiple employees, television and radio stations, and even airplanes and airports. These settings are found in both rural and urban areas. While some Atmospheric Scientists work relatively normal hours, those who develop forecasts may have erratic schedules that vary with weather conditions. Positions such as these regularly require work during day and nighttime hours, and also on weekends and holidays.

Salaries

According to the 2006–07 edition of the Department of Labor's *Occupational Outlook Handbook*, in mid-2004 annual salaries for Atmospheric Scientists ranged from $34,590 to more than $106,020, with a median of $70,100. In 2005 meteorologists employed by the federal government in nonsupervisory, supervisory, and management jobs earned average annual salaries of $80,499.

Employment Prospects

Average demand for Atmospheric Scientists is expected through 2014, according to the U.S. Department of Labor. Because hiring by the federal government—the largest employer of civilian meteorologists—is projected to be relatively flat, the best job opportunities will exist in the private sector. This is especially the case with consulting firms that provide forecasting to companies in industries with a vested interest in the weather. Of particular interest to such industries are seasonal and long-range forecasts.

Advancement Prospects

Many operational meteorologists begin their careers by securing internships with the federal government. Entry-level positions typically involve collecting, computing, and analyzing routine weather information, as well as basic forecasting. After learning about forecasting procedures and equipment, scientists with the National Weather Service work in staff roles at one of many weather stations. These jobs may lead to supervisory or administrative jobs—especially for those who pursue either a second undergraduate degree or a master's degree. Finally, some meteorologists leave the government sector to work as consultants.

Education and Training

The number of colleges and universities that offer degrees in atmospheric science is relatively small because this field is highly specialized. However, even though many schools do not have formal programs, the appropriate course work is often offered via departments of earth science, geography, geophysics, and physics. Because the National Weather Service and certain private sector employers have specific educational requirements, students are advised to make sure that they attend schools that offer the right courses.

Some entry-level Atmospheric Scientist positions may be obtained without a college degree if a candidate has an appropriate combination of experience and education. However, most positions require a bachelor's degree in atmospheric science, meteorology, or a related field. Undergraduate meteorology programs often include course work in weather systems analysis and prediction, atmospheric dynamics and thermodynamics, physical meteorology, and instrumentation. While a doctorate degree is often required for research positions, it does not have to be in meteorology. Advanced degrees in engineering, physics, and mathematics are appropriate for those who wish to work in research.

Special Requirements

The American Meteorological Society (AMS) offers professional certification for consulting meteorologists who are able to demonstrate their expertise and meet certain criteria in the areas of education, knowledge, experience, and character.

Experience, Special Skills, and Personality Traits

Atmospheric Scientists must be detail-oriented, with the ability to perform tasks in a careful and thorough manner. They also must be logical and analytical thinkers, with excellent problem-solving abilities. Due to the many variables involved in scientific work, as well as the weather, the ability to be adaptable and flexible also is critical for professionals in this field. While they must be able to work independently, Atmospheric Scientists also must be team players because they frequently interact with the public and other professionals regarding research projects and the interpretation of forecasts.

Report writing and presentations are important aspects of this profession. Therefore, strong communication skills are required, along with proficiency in statistics. In particular, Atmospheric Scientists who wish to work in broadcasting roles must have exceptional oral communication skills. They also must be knowledgeable of media production methods and techniques. Entry-level applied meteorologists may be required to have some field experience, as well as working knowledge of electronics, computer equipment, and computer programming methods.

Unions and Associations

Many Atmospheric Scientists belong to the American Meteorological Society (AMS). The AMS's approximately 11,000 members include professionals as well as students and weather enthusiasts. In addition to sponsoring twelve annual conferences, the society publishes nine journals related to atmospheric, oceanic, and hydrologic matters. Some Atmospheric Scientists also belong to the National Weather Association, whose mission is to support and promote excellence in operational meteorology and related activities.

Tips for Entry

1. Familiarize yourself with the field of atmospheric science by exploring the American Meteorological Society's online *Career Guide for the Atmospheric Sciences*, available from http://www.ametsoc.org/atmoscareers/index.html.
2. In high school, take courses in earth science, physics, mathematics, and chemistry.
3. Find information about AMS fellowships and scholarships online at http://www.ametsoc.org/AMS.
4. In college, secure internships and summer positions that provide valuable field experience and increase your qualifications for entry-level employment.

CHEMICAL LABORATORY TECHNICIAN

CAREER PROFILE

Duties: Operate laboratory equipment; set up apparatuses for chemical reactions; conduct experiments; handle materials; prepare compounds; collect samples; conduct analyses; contribute to experiment designs; measure material properties; record and report experimental results; write technical reports; maintain safety and quality standards

Alternate Title(s): Chemical Technician, Formulation Technician, Laboratory Analyst, Laboratory Technician, Laboratory Tester, Research and Development Technician, Research Associate, Research Technician

Salary Range: $27,400 to $49,300+

Employment Prospects: Fair

Advancement Prospects: Good

Prerequisites:

Education or Training—Associate of applied science degree or bachelor's in chemistry

Experience—Technical experience sampling and handling chemical materials, measuring physical properties of materials, performing chemical and instrumental analysis, designing and conducting experiments, and synthesizing compounds

Special Skills and Personality Traits—Manual dexterity; attention to detail; adaptability; personal motivation; customer focus; technical, analytical thinking, problem-solving, communication, organizational, and teamwork skills

CAREER LADDER

```
┌─────────────────────────────────────┐
│            Supervisor                │
└─────────────────────────────────────┘

┌─────────────────────────────────────┐
│   Chemical Laboratory Technician     │
└─────────────────────────────────────┘

┌─────────────────────────────────────┐
│              Intern                  │
└─────────────────────────────────────┘
```

Position Description

Environmental-related career opportunities in the field of science are not limited to high-level scientific positions; a wide range of entry-level jobs also exists at the technician level. Generally speaking, science technicians serve in practical support roles for scientists in a specific discipline or field. Through the application of scientific theories and principles, they help to solve research and development problems. In addition, they make improvements to existing processes and products and also help to develop new ones.

Chemical Laboratory Technicians team with chemists and chemical engineers in the laboratory to study and develop new chemical processes and materials to meet society's changing needs. They are highly skilled scientific professionals with increasing responsibility who play a critical role in all aspects of the chemical process industry.

In 2004, the U.S. Department of Labor reported that about 35 percent of Chemical Laboratory Technicians worked in the chemical manufacturing industry, while 26 percent worked for scientific, technical, or professional services firms. In general, Chemical Laboratory Technicians fall within two broad categories. Process control technicians work in manufacturing or industrial facilities, while research and development technicians work mainly in experimental laboratories.

Chemistry is the science of matter. It involves studying the composition of substances, as well as their properties, processes, and reactions. Because all living things are composed of chemicals, the field of chemistry is very broad in nature; it is not limited to the study of man-made compounds. The field of chemistry includes many subspecialties, including environmental chemistry. Some Chemical Laboratory Technicians work with environmental chemists, who focus on the interaction between chemicals and the environment. They help to determine the impact that chemicals have on land, air, and water, and also how the environment affects different chemicals.

Chemistry began to play a more central role in environmental cleanup initiatives during the late twentieth century. During the early days of environmental law, companies found responsible for pollution were often required to remove all contaminants from the environment. However, science eventually provided a better understanding of natural attenuation, whereby contaminants naturally diffuse over time, as well as the role of geology, hydrogeology, and the exposure pathways that contaminants follow. This allowed remediation, or cleanup efforts, to become more risk-based during the 1990s. By the 2000s, regulations allowed contaminants to be removed to the point where pollution was deemed to be at an "acceptable level," or where it was not an imminent threat to human health or the environment.

Chemical Laboratory Technicians operate laboratory equipment, set up apparatuses for chemical reactions, conduct experiments, handle materials, prepare compounds, collect samples, and conduct analyses that evaluate product quality and consistency. They often contribute to the design of experiments. Much of their work involves measuring properties of materials used and produced in chemical reactions. In addition, they record and report experimental results; write technical reports; and make sure that processes are carried out safely, cost-effectively, and according to the highest professional standards.

According to the Department of Labor's *Occupational Outlook Handbook*, "Many research and development chemical technicians conduct a variety of laboratory procedures, from routine process control to complex research projects. For example, they may collect and analyze samples of air and water to monitor pollution levels, or they may produce compounds through complex organic synthesis. Most process technicians work in manufacturing, testing packaging for design, integrity of materials, and environmental acceptability. Often, process technicians who work in plants also focus on quality assurance, monitoring product quality or production processes and developing new production techniques. A few work in shipping to provide technical support and expertise for these functions."

Most Chemical Laboratory Technicians work normal schedules in clean, well-lit research and development laboratories and/or analytical laboratories. Both types of laboratories contain complex and sophisticated instrumentation that technicians are trained to use and maintain. Research and development laboratories also have experimental work areas, such as benches that may be equipped with cooling water, natural gas, and vacuum pumps.

During the course of their work, Chemical Laboratory Technicians come into contact with chemicals, radioactive isotopes, and toxic materials that may be hazardous. However, proper safety procedures eliminate many of the risks associated with these substances. Most laboratories place an emphasis on safety equipment that may include ventilation hoods, eye wash fountains, showers, specialized storage cabinets, fire equipment, and spill equipment. They also comply with waste management and minimization practices.

Salaries

According to the U.S. Department of Labor's 2006–07 *Occupational Outlook Handbook*, in mid-2004 Chemical Lab Technicians earned median hourly wages of $18.35. Based on data from various job postings, salaries for this profession ranged from $27,400 to $49,300 or more. Generally speaking, the most competitive salaries are offered to those holding bachelor's degrees in chemistry.

Employment Prospects

Because a significant portion of the chemical industry workforce will be retiring in the next decade, the American Chemical Society reports that there is a large and growing demand for Chemical Laboratory Technicians. However, the U.S. Department of Labor projects that Chemical Laboratory Technicians will see overall employment increase at a rate that is slower than the average for all occupations through 2014. This is due to anticipated downsizing in the chemical manufacturing industry, which employs the majority of Chemical Laboratory Technicians. The best opportunities are expected to exist in the areas of medicine and pharmaceutical manufacturing, due to the demand for newer and more effective drugs.

Advancement Prospects

While pursuing two- or four-year degrees to prepare for careers as Chemical Laboratory Technicians, students normally complete internships that allow them to interact with prospective employers and network with other technicians and scientists. These experiences help students to initiate their careers. After gaining valuable hands-on experience, Chemical Laboratory Technicians may advance to supervisory roles or continue their education and pursue careers as chemists.

Education and Training

Today's chemical industry companies demand a solid foundation in applied basic chemistry and math, plus experience using a variety of standard labware and instrumentation. The best preparation is a two-year associate of applied science degree. However, a number of technicians hold bachelor's degrees in chemistry. Employers value their technicians and often provide additional in-house training in specific areas to supplement their formal chemical technology training.

Experience, Special Skills, and Personality Traits

Employers seek Chemical Laboratory Technicians with solid technical skills. These include sampling and handling chemical materials, measuring physical properties of materials, performing chemical and instrumental analysis, designing and conducting experiments, and synthesizing compounds. In addition, Chemical Laboratory Technicians must be able to work with their hands, think analytically, pay attention to details, and solve problems. Employers look for an individual's adaptability; personal motivation; customer focus; and communication, organizational, and teamwork skills.

Unions and Associations

Many Chemical Laboratory Technicians belong to the American Chemical Association, which has a special division devoted to their specific profession. Some also belong to state and regional professional organizations.

Tips for Entry

1. Familiarize yourself with the field of chemistry by exploring the American Chemical Association's page for students and educators at http://www.chemistry.org/portal/a/c/s/1/educatorsandstudents.html.

2. In high school, take courses in chemistry, as well as biology, earth science, physics, and mathematics.

3. Find an American Chemical Society-approved educational program by downloading the *Directory of Chemistry-Based Technology Programs* at http://www.chemistry.org/portal/resources/ACS/ACSContent/education/technicians/contacts/Updated_Directory.pdf.

4. In college, secure internships that provide valuable field and lab experience and increase your qualifications for entry-level employment.

ENVIRONMENTAL CHEMIST

CAREER PROFILE

Duties: Analyze inorganic and organic compounds using spectrophotometry, chromatography, and spectroscopy; prepare test compounds and solutions; change the composition of substances; improve, develop, and customize formulas, methods and processes, products, and equipment; coordinate research projects

Alternate Title(s): Analytical Chemist; Biochemist; Organic Chemist; Physical Chemist

Salary Range: $33,170 to $98,010+

Employment Prospects: Fair

Advancement Prospects: Excellent

Prerequisites:

Education or Training—Bachelor's, master's, or doctorate degree in chemistry; course work in environmental studies

Experience—Familiarity with government regulations and legislation; experience working with computer modeling, simulation, and computerized laboratory equipment

Special Skills and Personality Traits—Logical and analytical thinking, computer, communication, and problem-solving skills; detail-oriented, careful, thorough, self-reliant, patient, adaptable

Special Requirements—Certified Professional Chemist (CPC) or Environmental Analytical Chemist credential may be required

CAREER LADDER

```
┌─────────────────────────────────────┐
│           Senior Chemist             │
└─────────────────────────────────────┘

┌─────────────────────────────────────┐
│      Staff Environmental Chemist     │
└─────────────────────────────────────┘

┌─────────────────────────────────────┐
│   Environmental Chemistry Technician │
└─────────────────────────────────────┘

┌─────────────────────────────────────┐
│               Intern                 │
└─────────────────────────────────────┘
```

Position Description

Chemistry is the science of matter. It involves studying the composition of substances, as well as their properties, processes, and reactions. Because all living things are composed of chemicals, the field of chemistry is very broad in nature; it is not limited to the study of man-made compounds. The field of chemistry includes many subspecialties, including environmental chemistry. Generally speaking, Environmental Chemists focus on the interaction between chemicals and the environment. They are concerned with the impact that chemicals have on land, air, and water, and also how the environment affects different chemicals.

One important aspect of environmental chemistry deals with pollution, or how chemicals end up in the environment.

Pollution results from illegal or improper waste disposal, as well as ineffective treatment methods at industrial sites or water treatment facilities. In this regard, Environmental Chemists play important roles as consultants and scientific experts. They provide professional opinions and scientific data to businesses, attorneys, and also government officials at environmental protection agencies. This information is of critical importance in disputes over pollution, because when companies are required to clean up the environment they are often at odds with government agencies over what the company's obligation is. Oftentimes, issues are unclear even under environmental laws or regulations.

Chemistry began to play a more central role in environmental cleanup initiatives during the late twentieth century.

During the early days of environmental law, companies found responsible for pollution were often required to remove all contaminants from the environment. However, science eventually provided a better understanding of natural attenuation, whereby contaminants naturally diffuse over time, as well as the role of geology, hydrogeology, and the exposure pathways that contaminants follow. This allowed remediation, or cleanup efforts, to become more risk-based during the 1990s. By the 2000s, regulations allowed contaminants to be removed to the point where pollution was deemed to be at an "acceptable level," or where it was not an imminent threat to human health or the environment.

According to the American Chemical Society, "As the technology for measuring leakage from landfills was developed, for example, industry recognized the potential for chemicals to negatively impact the environment—and the attendant social, political, and economic ramifications. As a result of these new data, chemists were able to help design pollution abatement systems that minimize the unwanted elements escaping into the environment. They also applied their knowledge to develop remediation systems to clean up contaminated areas."

Even within the field of environmental chemistry, there are many opportunities for specialization. For example, analytic chemists focus on a substance's structure or composition. They often are the Environmental Chemists who are involved in detecting environmental pollution. Biochemists work in the ever-advancing field of biotechnology, which involves the use of whole or partial living organisms to create or enhance products, or make improvements to existing living organisms. They may be involved in the development of better pesticides, more productive or disease-resistant plants, or microorganisms that remove water pollution. Organic chemists deal with carbon compounds and the development of such things as fertilizers, plastics, and pharmaceuticals. Finally, physical chemists deal with chemicals at the molecular or atomic level.

Environmental Chemists perform different tasks depending on the industry in which they work and the nature of their specific jobs. However, common tasks may involve developing or redeveloping chemical compounds that are more environmentally friendly or compatible, improving the efficiency of industrial processes, or discovering new solutions to waste disposal problems.

The U.S. Department of Labor lists a number of common responsibilities that many chemists share. One is determining the chemical and physical properties, structure, and composition of inorganic and organic compounds. By using analytic techniques such as spectrophotometry, chromatography, and spectroscopy, chemists are able to learn about reactions and relationships between such compounds.

In addition to preparing test compounds and solutions, chemists change the composition of substances through the introduction of energy, light, heat, and other chemicals. They also are involved in the improvement, development, and customization of formulas, methods, processes, products, and equipment. While coordinating research projects, chemists may direct others during test procedures and analyses.

Environmental Chemists draw from a number of other disciplines while performing their work. In addition to specific training in water and soil chemistry, scientists in this field are often knowledgeable in general biology, earth/environmental science, ecology, engineering, genetics, geology, hydrology, mathematics, mineralogy, physics, sedimentology, and statistics.

Most Environmental Chemists work normal hours. They often perform varying degrees of lab, office, and fieldwork. Laboratories range from very small and crude setups to elaborate research complexes with the latest equipment. Work performed in a laboratory may involve developing new products or performing analytical tests, while office work involves preparing written reports, working on research studies, and performing administrative tasks. Fieldwork often involves gathering water and soil samples and interacting with people who use chemicals in different settings. Finally, some Environmental Chemists are involved in education, and spend much of their time in classroom settings.

Salaries

According to the 2006–07 edition of the Department of Labor's *Occupational Outlook Handbook*, in mid-2004 annual salaries for chemists ranged from $33,170 to more than $98,010, with a median of $56,060. According to the American Chemical Society (ACS), in 2004 those with bachelor's degrees earned median salaries of $62,000, while those with master's and doctorate degrees earned $72,300 and $91,600, respectively. Inexperienced chemistry graduates with bachelor's degrees earned mean starting salaries of $33,981 in 2004, while those with master's and doctorate degrees earned $44,796 and $63,547, respectively.

Employment Prospects

The weak economy of the early 2000s had a negative impact on employment for chemists. The ACS reported that 86.7 percent of chemists responding to its 2004 employment survey were employed full-time. This stood in comparison to 91.8 percent in 2001 and was the lowest percentage the society recorded since the early 1970s. Nevertheless, the U.S. Department of Labor anticipates near average job growth for chemists through 2012. According to the *Occupational Outlook Handbook*, chemists in the environmental sector "will be needed to develop and improve the technologies and processes used to produce chemicals for all purposes, and to monitor and measure air and water pollutants to ensure compliance with local, State, and Federal environmental regulations. Environmental research will offer many new opportunities for chemists and materials scientists. To satisfy public concerns and to comply with government regulations, the chemical industry will continue to invest billions of dollars each year in technology that reduces pollution and cleans up existing waste sites. Chemists also are needed to find ways to use less energy and to discover new sources of energy."

Advancement Prospects

Environmental Chemists have excellent advancement opportunities. Many advance into positions as lead or senior scientists, or secure management positions. Those who no longer wish to engage in lab or field work often pursue additional education and put their expertise to use in fields such as business, public policy, or law. They may become environmental attorneys or work for corporations in the areas of regulatory compliance or government affairs.

Education and Training

Like chemists in all specialties, Environmental Chemists must hold a bachelor's degree in chemistry or a related field to obtain an entry-level position. Master's degrees, and in many cases doctorate degrees, are required for many jobs. This is especially true of positions that involve conducting research or teaching at the university level.

Required undergraduate course work usually includes organic, inorganic, analytical, and physical chemistry, as well as other course work in areas such as physics, biology, and mathematics. According to the U.S. Department of Labor, "those interested in the environmental field also should take courses in environmental studies and become familiar with current legislation and regulations. Computer courses are essential, because employers prefer job applicants who are able to apply computer skills to modeling and simulation tasks and operate computerized laboratory equipment."

Special Requirements

Some chemists obtain the Certified Professional Chemist (CPC) credential from the American Institute of Chemists. In addition, the National Registry of Certified Chemists offers certification for different types of chemists, including environmental analytical chemists. These organizations have specific requirements related to education, lab experience, and professional involvement.

Experience, Special Skills, and Personality Traits

Environmental Chemists must be detail-oriented, with the ability to perform tasks in a careful and thorough manner. They also must be logical and analytical thinkers, with excellent problem-solving abilities. Due to the many variables involved in scientific work, the ability to be adaptable and flexible also is critical for professionals in this field. While they must be able to work independently, Environmental Chemists also must be team players because they frequently interact with other professionals—including attorneys, engineers, consultants, and scientists—regarding research projects and the interpretation of test results.

Report writing and presentations are important aspects of this profession. Therefore, strong written and oral communication skills are required, along with proficiency in statistics. Computer experience is required for word processing and developing presentations. In addition, Environmental Chemists perform complex analyses using computers and sophisticated laboratory instruments.

Unions and Associations

Chemists may belong to a number of national organizations, including the American Chemical Association and the American Institute of Chemists, as well as environmental impact organizations such as Environmental Defense. Some also belong to state and regional professional organizations.

Tips for Entry

1. Familiarize yourself with the field of chemistry by exploring the American Chemical Association's page for students and educators at http://www.chemistry.org/portal/a/c/s/1/educatorsandstudents.html.
2. In high school, take courses in chemistry, as well as biology, earth science, physics, and mathematics.
3. Find an American Chemical Society-approved chemistry program by visiting http://www.chemistry.org.
4. In college, secure internships that provide valuable field and lab experience and increase your qualifications for entry-level employment.

ENVIRONMENTAL TECHNICIAN

CAREER PROFILE

Duties: Collect, analyze, label, preserve, store, and dispose of environmental samples, including waste; operate, maintain, decontaminate, and repair equipment; maintain records; prepare reports

Alternate Title(s): Air Sampling and Monitoring Technician; Cartography/Mapping Technician; Decontamination Technician; Environmental Compliance Technician; Industrial Technician; Land Survey Technician; Soil Conservation Technician; Solid Waste Landfill Technician; Wastewater Analyst; Water Supply Technician; Wildlife Technician; Environmental Health Practitioner; Registered Sanitarian; Registered Environmental Health Specialist

Salary Range: $33,218 to $59,197+

Employment Prospects: Good

Advancement Prospects: Good

Prerequisites:

Education or Training—Associate's or bachelor's degree in environmental science, engineering, chemistry, biology, or geology

Experience—Experience using technical software related to environmental modeling and emergency response may be helpful or required, as well as experience operating and maintaining scientific instruments and equipment

Special Skills and Personality Traits—Analytical thinking, problem-solving, communication, computer, technical, and mechanical skills; detail-oriented; careful; thorough; patient; logical; adaptable; and flexible

Special Requirements—State or federal certification may be required to work with hazardous materials, wastewater, and radiation, or to perform a variety of abatement services.

CAREER LADDER

```
┌─────────────────────────────┐
│         Supervisor          │
└─────────────────────────────┘

┌─────────────────────────────┐
│  Environmental Technician   │
└─────────────────────────────┘

┌─────────────────────────────┐
│           Intern            │
└─────────────────────────────┘
```

Position Description

Environmental-related career opportunities in the field of science are not limited to high-level scientific positions; a wide range of jobs also exists at the technician level. Generally speaking, science technicians serve in practical support roles for scientists in a specific discipline or field. Through the application of scientific theories and principles, they help to solve research and development problems. In addition, they make improvements to existing processes and products and also help to develop new ones.

There are some common tasks that most science technicians perform, regardless of the particular niche or sub-specialty in which they work. These tasks include the setup, operation, and maintenance of lab instruments; making observations; monitoring experiments; calculating and recording results; and developing conclusions. In addition, science technicians must maintain careful documentation of the work they do. By the early twenty-first century, technicians in a variety of scientific fields were becoming more involved in research and development activities due to the growing complexity of laboratory procedures and instruments.

In the 2006–07 edition of the *Occupational Outlook Handbook*, the U.S. Department of Labor explained: "In addition to performing routine tasks, many technicians now develop and adapt laboratory procedures to achieve the best results, interpret data, and devise solutions to problems, under the direction of scientists. Moreover, technicians must master the laboratory equipment, so that they can adjust settings when necessary and recognize when equipment is malfunctioning.

"The increasing use of robotics to perform many routine tasks has freed technicians to operate more sophisticated laboratory equipment. Science technicians make extensive use of computers, computer-interfaced equipment, robotics, and high-technology industrial applications, such as biological engineering."

While some technician positions related to conservation and the environment focus mainly on specific scientific areas, such as biology or chemistry, a broad range of job opportunities exist under the banner of Environmental Technician that may involve work in a variety of scientific and other areas. As the Advanced Technology Environmental Education Center (ATEEC) explains, "Environmental technology is a career field that utilizes the principles of science, engineering, communication, and economics to protect and enhance safety, health, and natural resources."

The ATEEC lists eleven major categories or sub-specialties of environmental technology:

• Air
• Field services
• Information management systems
• Laboratory services
• Natural resources management
• Pollution prevention
• Regulatory affairs: government and industry
• Remediation
• Safety and health
• Solid and hazardous waste
• Water and wastewater

Generally speaking, technicians in this broad field apply technical, scientific, and communications skills to carry out tasks in their chosen niche. They collect, analyze, label, pre-serve, store, and dispose of environmental or waste samples; operate, maintain, decontaminate, and repair equipment; maintain records; and prepare reports. Technicians that work for organizations often help to eliminate or reduce the amount of waste and pollution that a facility discharges into the environment. In addition to having a positive impact on the environment, this reduces an organization's liability and the number of compliance requirements it must meet.

In addition to these common tasks that are shared by most Environmental Technicians, technicians also perform tasks that are specific to their niche or subspecialty. For example, technicians in the water and wastewater category work with ground water, surface water, drinking water, and wastewater. They may evaluate stormwater runoff and help facilities to develop plans to prevent stormwater pollution; assess and develop corrective measures related to soil erosion; help to delineate wetland areas; add chemicals to water and wastewater treatment tanks; measure the level and flow of groundwater; and drain/clean wastewater treatment tanks.

Technicians in the remediation field remove dangerous substances from the environment. Specific job responsibilities may include the abatement of lead and asbestos, the removal of underground storage tanks, and responding to chemical spills.

In the areas of safety and health, technicians help organizations to comply with standards related to occupational safety and health set forth by the Occuaptional Safety and Health Administration (OSHA); develop workplace health and safety plans; conduct internal inspections; communicate with government officials, media representatives, and the public; identify contamination; and contain, clean, and dispose of hazardous material following spills.

In the area of regulatory affairs, technicians who work for government agencies review permit requests for accuracy and ensure that organizations and other parties are in compliance with environmental laws and regulations. Those who work for organizations help to ensure compliance with environmental laws and regulations by assisting with policy and procedure development, conducting internal audits, and maintaining records.

Environmental Technicians specializing in information management systems work in the areas of mapping, cartography, geographic information systems, marketing, cost-recovery, and regulatory compliance. They may use computer software to produce maps needed for specific projects.

Technicians in the area of pollution prevention often devote a considerable amount of time to helping their organization comply with environmental rules and regulations. In addition to staying knowledgeable in this area, they apply for environmental permits, maintain related records, collect data that is used for environmental audits by regulatory agencies, and submit a variety of reports as required.

In the natural resources management field, technicians work in areas such as wildlife management, ecology, recreation, fire management, and forestry. Their job responsibilities may include working with wildlife, including rare or endangered species.

In the private sector, Environmental Technicians find employment opportunities with environmental engineering and consulting firms, which are often called upon to perform independent or "third party" services that companies cannot objectively perform on their own. In addition, a wide range of companies employ Environmental Technicians, especially those engaged in chemical production and waste disposal.

At the federal government level, potential employers include the U.S. Environmental Protection Agency, the Bureau of Land Management, the USDA Agricultural Research Service, and the National Oceanic and Atmospheric Administration. At the state government level employment opportunities exist with departments of fish and game; environment, health and natural resources; and agriculture. At the city, county, and township level, employers may include health departments, public works commissions, and stormwater management commissions.

Environmental Technicians have many different types of work environments from which to choose. These range from office and laboratory settings to working in industrial locations, water and waste treatment plants, and outdoor locations that can range from construction sites to wetlands and forests. While some technicians may work exclusively in one type of environment, many divide their time between different settings. Environmental Technicians usually work normal schedules.

Environmental Technicians may be subject to a range of occupational hazards, including chemicals, toxic waste, and potentially dangerous equipment. In the field, technicians may be exposed to extreme weather conditions. Fieldwork also can be physically demanding at times, requiring technicians to stand frequently, bend, and walk long distances. Therefore, good physical condition may be a job requirement.

Salaries

According to the U.S. Department of Labor's 2006–07 *Occupational Outlook Handbook*, in mid-2004 environmental science and protection technicians, including health, earned median hourly earnings of $16.99. Nuclear technicians earned median hourly salaries of $28.46, geological and petroleum technicians earned $19.35, chemical technicians earned $18.35, and biological technicians earned $15.97. In 2005 federal government positions (nonsupervisory, supervisory, and managerial positions) averaged $38,443 for biological science technicians and $50,264 for physical science technicians.

Employment Prospects

In general, the U.S. Department of Labor projects that environmental science and protection technicians will see over-
all employment rates increase about as fast as the average for all occupations through 2014. Candidates who obtain special certifications prior to applying for a position will increase their employment prospects and may secure higher entry-level salaries.

Advancement Prospects

While pursuing two- or four-year degrees to prepare for environmental technology jobs, students normally complete internships that allow them to interact with prospective employers and network with other technicians and scientists. These experiences help students to initiate their careers. After gaining valuable hands-on experience, science technicians may advance to supervisory roles or continue their education and pursue careers as scientists in their chosen field.

Education and Training

While some positions may require an associate's degree in environmental science or an applied area, many Environmental Technician jobs require an undergraduate degree in environmental science. Many candidates hold undergraduate degrees in engineering, chemistry, biology, or geology and complement their education with additional classes in environmental science. In particular, those wishing to work as Environmental Technicians should take classes in ecology, environmental law, mathematics, and occupational safety.

Special Requirements

Depending on their particular area of specialization, Environmental Technicians must often hold special certifications that are required by an employer's insurance company or by state and federal government. Certifications most often are related to working with hazardous materials, such as lead, wastewater, or radiation.

Experience, Special Skills, and Personality Traits

Environmental Technicians must be detail-oriented, with the ability to perform tasks in a careful and thorough manner. They also must be logical and analytical thinkers, with excellent problem-solving abilities. Due to the many variables involved in scientific and technical work, the ability to be patient, adaptable, and flexible also is critical for professionals in this field. Environmental Technicians must be able to closely follow established procedures and protocols.

Environmental Technicians must be self-reliant and capable of working independently at remote sites and also on teams that involve communication with other technicians, scientists, and the public. Because documentation is an important aspect of this profession, basic computer experience is required for word processing. Strong written communication skills also are required, along with proficiency in statistics.

Environmental Technicians must be proficient in using computer software. Beyond common productivity software such as word processing and spreadsheet programs, technicians in this field are required to use technical programs related to environmental modeling and emergency response.

Because operating, maintaining, and repairing sophisticated instruments and equipment is often a primary job responsibility, Environmental Technicians must be mechanically inclined and skilled in the use of technology, including sensors, as well as geographic information systems (GIS) and global positioning satellites (GPS).

Unions and Associations

More than 4,500 environmental health practitioners belong to the Denver, Colorado–based National Environmental Health Association. In addition, scientific technicians may belong to a number of associations in their chosen field. For example, the American Chemical Society maintains a division for chemical technicians.

Tips for Entry

1. In high school, take courses that provide broad exposure to science, including biology, chemistry, earth science, geology, and zoology, as well as courses in mathematics, physics, and English.
2. Learn more about the many different areas of specialization within the environmental technology field and identify areas that interest you.
3. Identify community colleges and technical institutes that offer applied environmental science technology degrees in your areas of interest and request program information.
4. Obtain any special certifications before applying for a position, which will give you an edge over other applicants and possibly result in a higher starting salary.

GEOSCIENTIST

CAREER PROFILE

Duties: Collect, examine, measure, analyze, and classify rock, water, soil, mineral, and fossil samples; analyze and interpret scientific data; plan and conduct field studies; write reports and create charts, graphs, diagrams, and maps

Alternate Title(s): Environmental Consultant; Geochemist; Geologist; Geophysicist; Geotechnical Engineer; Oceanographer; Petroleum Engineer; Surveyor

Salary Range: $37,700 to $130,750+

Employment Prospects: Good

Advancement Prospects: Good

Prerequisites:

Education or Training—Bachelor's, master's, or doctorate degree in geoscience, geology, environmental science, or earth-systems science

Experience—Fieldwork in relevant geoscience specialty, as well as familiarity with computer modeling, digital mapping, data integration, and geographic information systems and global positioning satellites systems

Special Skills and Personality Traits—Analytical thinking, writing, communication, problem-solving, and computer skills; logical, self-reliant, independent, adaptable, flexible, detail-oriented, careful, and thorough

Special Requirements—Geologist in Training (GIT) or Professional Geologist (PG) license may be required

CAREER LADDER

Senior Researcher

Project Leader or Manager

Staff Geoscientist

Lab Technician or Research Assistant

Position Description

The field of geosciences offers a wide range of occupational opportunities for those who are interested in working with the Earth. As the U.S. Department of Labor's *Occupational Outlook Handbook* explains, "geoscientists study the composition, structure, and other physical aspects of the Earth. With the use of sophisticated instruments and by analyzing the composition of the earth and water, geoscientists study the Earth's geologic past and present."

Geoscientists usually work within one of two closely related fields: geology or geophysics. According to the *Occupational Outlook Handbook*, "geologists study the composition, processes, and history of the Earth. They try to find out how rocks were formed and what has happened to

them since their formation. They also study the evolution of life by analyzing plant and animal fossils." There are many different kinds of geologists:

- Economic geologists study mineral deposits and are involved in the search for valuable geologic materials.
- Engineering geologists apply geological principles to environmental and civil engineering projects, including environmental clean-up efforts and the construction of buildings and bridges.
- Glaciologists study the movement and properties of ice sheets and glaciers.
- Hydrogeologists study the quality, distribution, and movement of ground water.

- Marine geologists concentrate on the borders and boundaries that separate oceans and continents, including continental shelves and ocean basins.
- Medical geologists investigate the biological impact that minerals have on humans.
- Mineralogists study the formation, composition, and properties of minerals.
- Paleontologists attempt to understand and reconstruct past environments by studying fossils.
- Petroleum geologists use geological knowledge to find and produce natural gas and petroleum.
- Stratigraphers study the formation of rock layers, along with the fossils and minerals they contain.
- Structural geologists study the Earth's crust and analyze how it has deformed, fractured, and folded.
- Volcanologists attempt to forecast volcanic eruptions by studying volcanoes and volcanic phenomena.

The *Occupational Outlook Handbook* further explains that "geophysicists use the principles of physics, mathematics, and chemistry to study not only the Earth's surface, but also its internal composition; ground and surface waters; atmosphere; oceans; and magnetic, electrical, and gravitational forces." As with geologists, there are a variety of geophysicists:

- Geodesists study various aspects of the Earth, including its gravitational field, polar motion, rotation, shape, and size.
- Geomagnetists measure the Earth's magnetic field and develop theories about the planet's origin based on past measurements.
- Paleomagnetists record continental wandering, the polarity of the Earth's magnetic field, and the expansion of the sea floor through the interpretation of fossil magnetization in sediments and rocks from the planet's oceans and continents.
- Seismologists interpret the Earth's structure by studying the location and characteristics of earthquakes.

Oceanographers are another form of Geoscientist. They study the Earth's coastal waters and oceans, drawing knowledge from the fields of geophysics, geology, chemistry, and biology. More specifically, the *Occupational Outlook Handbook* explains that oceanographers "study the motion and circulation of the ocean waters; the physical and chemical properties of the oceans; and how these properties affect coastal areas, climate, and weather." There are many different types of oceanographers. For example, geophysical and geological oceanographers study the physical properties and topography of the ocean floor; physical oceanographers concentrate on the interplay between the ocean, weather, and climate; and chemical oceanographers study the chemical makeup of the ocean and ocean floor.

Geoscientists perform different job tasks, depending on the positions they hold and their scientific subspecialties. However, common tasks include collecting, examining, measuring, analyzing, and classifying rock, water, soil, mineral, and fossil samples. Geoscientists also are involved in the analysis and interpretation of scientific data obtained from logs, surveys, and photographs. In addition to planning and conducting field studies and performing scientific analyses, Geoscientists write reports and create charts, graphs, diagrams, and maps to share their findings with employers, clients, and the public. They provide valuable advisement regarding the environment as it relates to land use; the construction of buildings, roadways, and dams; waste management and disposal; the probability and mitigation of natural disasters; mineral extraction; and exploration for oil and natural gas.

In addition to a strong understanding of scientific concepts and principles in the areas of geography, chemistry, physics, mathematics, and engineering, Geoscientists must often possess knowledge about public safety, government codes and regulations, and the political climate in which they work. Because Geoscientists use sophisticated instruments and satellites to analyze the environment, they must be skilled in the use of computers and technology.

Geoscientists are sound decision-makers and problem-solvers who are able to think creatively. In addition to engaging in scientific analysis and discovery, they must be able to communicate their findings to others in a clear and concise manner. This may involve conveying highly technical or scientific information to businesspeople, consumers, and others with little or no scientific training, and helping them to understand and apply that information. For this reason, successful Geoscientists have a strong command of the English language, along with strong written and oral communication skills.

Because of the wide variety of subspecialties that exist within the geosciences, Geoscientists have many different types of work environments from which to choose. These range from office and laboratory settings to outdoor environments and classrooms. Fieldwork can involve long travel times to remote or foreign locations, sometimes via all-terrain vehicles or helicopters. Scientists may be required to work unusual hours and under extreme temperatures. Positions that are physically demanding require candidates to be in good physical condition. Many Geoscientists divide their time between fieldwork and an office or lab setting.

Geoscientists find employment opportunities with government agencies, nonprofit environmental organizations, museums, engineering and geological consulting firms, mining and exploration companies, and gas and oil companies. Geoscientists also are employed in the education field at the secondary and college levels.

Salaries

According to the 2006–07 edition of the U.S. Department of Labor's *Occupational Outlook Handbook*, in mid-2004 annual salaries for Geoscientists ranged from $37,700 to more than $130,750, with a median of $68,730. Data from the National Association of Colleges and Employers put average annual starting salaries for those with bachelor's degrees in geology and related sciences at $39,365 in mid-2005. In general, the mineral, mining, and petroleum industries pay higher-than-average salaries for Geoscientists.

Employment Prospects

Overall, slower-than-average job growth is expected for Geoscientists through 2014, according to the U.S. Department of Labor. However, good job opportunities will exist due to a large number of retirements and a short supply of qualified geoscience graduates. Historically, employment stability for Geoscientists in the mineral, mining, and petroleum industries has been volatile. Because these industries are susceptible to energy prices and economic conditions, exploration-related employment tends to be cyclical. Geoscientists with foreign language abilities and a willingness to travel can increase their employment prospects.

Advancement Prospects

Geoscientists commonly secure entry-level positions as technicians or assistants in lab or research settings. Such positions frequently involve increasingly complex field assignments. Typically, Geoscientists progress on the career ladder to become project leaders or managers. Some pursue high-level research positions.

Education and Training

While some entry-level positions may be obtained with an undergraduate degree, most geoscience positions require a master's degree in geoscience, geology, environmental science, or earth-systems science. Those with a master's degree obtain specialized knowledge in a particular area of geoscience. Doctorate degrees are required for those who wish to pursue a teaching career at the university level or an advanced-level research position.

Special Requirements

Individual states often require geologists to hold a Geologist in Training (GIT) or Professional Geologist (PG) license. GIT examinations can often be taken upon college graduation, while the PG exam may be taken after several years of work experience under the supervision of a PG.

Experience, Special Skills, and Personality Traits

Geoscientists must be detail-oriented, with the ability to perform tasks in a careful and thorough manner. They also must be logical and analytical thinkers, with excellent problem-solving abilities. Due to the many variables involved in scientific work, the ability to be adaptable and flexible also is critical for professionals in this field. Because projects may take them to remote locations where it is necessary to work in relative isolation, Geoscientists must be self-reliant and capable of working independently. On the other hand, because they often work on project teams and are required to communicate with others, Geoscientists also must be team players.

Report writing and presentations also are important aspects of this profession. Therefore, strong written and oral communication skills are required, along with proficiency in statistics. Basic computer experience is required for word processing and developing presentations. In addition, geoscientists may be required to perform computer modeling, digital mapping, and data integration activities. Therefore, experience with geographic information systems (GIS) and global positioning satellite (GPS) systems may be helpful or required.

Unions and Associations

Geoscientists often belong to state geological surveys and associations. Leading national organizations include the American Geological Institute (AGI), the Geological Society of America (GSA), and the American Geophysical Union (AGU). Geoscientists also belong to specialized associations such as the Tulsa, Oklahoma–based American Association of Petroleum Geologists.

Tips for Entry

1. In high school, take courses that provide exposure to earth science, geology, biology, mathematics, chemistry, physics, and engineering, and hone your English language skills.
2. Request career information from the American Geological Institute by visiting http://www.agiweb.org. The institute's *Directory of Geoscience Departments* lists approximately 800 degree-granting geoscience programs in North America.
3. Review college catalog course descriptions in the departments of earth-systems science, environmental science, geology, or geosciences to identify a curriculum that interests you.
4. In college, secure internships that provide valuable field and lab experience and increase your qualifications for entry-level employment.

MARINE BIOLOGIST

CAREER PROFILE

Duties: Study and classify aquatic organisms; study biochemical processes in living cells; plan and carry out experimental studies; collect and analyze data and samples; estimate marine life distributions and populations; observe the characteristics and behavior of marine life; document the origin, evolution, and history of species; provide professional opinions regarding environmental impact

Alternate Title(s): Aquatic Biologist; Fisheries Biologist; Marine Ichthyologist; Marine Scientist

Salary Range: $31,258 to $81,200+

Employment Prospects: Limited

Advancement Prospects: Fair

Prerequisites:

  Education or Training—Bachelor's, master's, or doctorate degree in marine biology, aquatic science, or similar field

  Experience—Ability to operate a boat and use SCUBA and snorkeling equipment; fieldwork in marine science; familiarity with research fundamentals, electronics, computer modeling, digital mapping, data integration, and geographic information systems and global positioning satellites systems

  Special Skills and Personality Traits—Logical and analytical thinking, computer, communication, problem-solving, and stress management skills; detail-oriented, careful, thorough, self-reliant, patient, adaptable, flexible

  Special Requirements—Certification to perform scientific diving, licenses for handling hazardous materials, and physical examinations may be required

CAREER LADDER

```
┌─────────────────────────────────┐
│  Senior Scientist or Professor  │
└─────────────────────────────────┘

┌─────────────────────────────────┐
│        Marine Biologist         │
└─────────────────────────────────┘

┌─────────────────────────────────┐
│         Lab Technician          │
└─────────────────────────────────┘

┌─────────────────────────────────┐
│            Intern               │
└─────────────────────────────────┘
```

Position Description

Marine Biologists are aquatic biologists who study saltwater animal and plant species. In addition to studying interactions between species, they also observe the different ways in which plants and animals influence and are influenced by the environment. For example, they may seek to understand how changes in ocean temperature or levels of chemical pollution impact aquatic life. The closely related field of limnology involves the study of organisms that live in fresh water.

Marine Biologists have made a variety of important discoveries and observations about mankind's interaction with aquatic life. These findings have raised awareness about a number of issues and problems, leading to changes that minimize or prevent harm to the environment. Marine Biologists have documented the declining numbers of certain species, charted the migratory patterns of whales, chronicled man's damage to coral reefs, observed tuna fishermen capturing dolphins, counted the decreasing numbers of certain species, and performed valuable work related to the improvement and control of both commercial and sport fishing.

While many believe that Marine Biologists spend the majority of their time working with large sea creatures such as dolphins, sharks, and whales, in reality this is not the case; such work is normally the purview of zoologists. In fact, Marine Biologists spend a great deal of their time studying and classifying smaller organisms, including algae, bacteria, fish larvae, plankton, shrimp, and worms. A great deal of their work involves molecular biology, or the biochemical processes that occur in living cells.

Marine Biologists are involved in a wide range of activities related to marine science. One of their primary job functions is to plan and carry out experimental studies, either in controlled settings or in natural habitats. Marine Biologists frequently collect and analyze data and samples from oceans and tidal pools that may be used to classify different organisms; estimate marine life distributions and populations; learn about the characteristics and behavior of marine life; and document the origin, evolution, and history of particular species. Even in the early 21st century, marine biology remains an exciting field because a great deal of the world's oceans have yet to be explored, and many new organisms are awaiting discovery.

In addition to performing these fundamental scientific tasks, Marine Biologists use what they learn to make important determinations and recommendations as planners or consultants. They provide professional opinions regarding the impact that mankind is having on oceans and coastal zones in regard to matters like industrial activities, tourism, and sewage disposal.

As with other scientific professions, Marine Biologists are required to share their findings through written reports, scientific papers, and professional presentations. They also may conduct training seminars and give public presentations for clubs, schools, special interest groups, and businesses. Those with management or administrative responsibilities may be involved with public relations, fund-raising, and budgeting. Marine Biologists frequently write grant proposals to fund their work because much of their research is dependent on private, state, or federal funds for support. In some cases, proposals are difficult to write and grants have very specific requirements.

Marine Biologists find employment in a variety of settings. Many work within the government sector. In fact, the U.S Department of Labor reveals that local, state, and federal governments employed half of all biological scientists in 2002. Government opportunities exist within a number of agencies including the Environmental Protection Agency, the Fish and Wildlife Service, and the National Oceanic and Atmospheric Administration.

Marine Biologists also work in the private sector for environmental consulting firms, foundations, independent research laboratories, biotechnology firms, and pharmaceutical companies. In addition, some work for aquariums, museums, and zoos. Finally, some Marine Biologists devote their careers to training others at colleges and universities.

Marine Biologists have many different types of work environments from which to choose. These range from office and laboratory settings to research vessels, oceans, tidal pools, aquariums, and classrooms. Most Marine Biologists divide their time between fieldwork and an office or lab. Periodically, their job may require them to be at sea for weeks or months at a time. However, Marine Biologists often spend more time doing lab work and reading journals than working underwater.

For those who are engaged in fieldwork, long travel times to remote or foreign locations are involved. Scientists are frequently required to work unusual hours because they are at the mercy of the marine populations being studied and unpredictable weather conditions. They also may be subject to extreme underwater temperatures and forced to face dangerous conditions above and below the ocean's surface. In addition to the weather, they may find themselves in the presence of dangerous marine life, including fish.

Marine Biologists frequently gather samples from the deck of a ship, but they also spend a lot of time exploring underwater environments. These underwater expeditions require the researchers to operate water vessels and SCUBA dive, which involves special underwater breathing equipment and wetsuits. When working underwater, Marine Biologists use a special device called a slurp gun to capture fish without harming them. In addition, they take great care not to disturb the delicate underwater environment. Fieldwork can be physically demanding, requiring scientists to withstand underwater pressure, stand frequently, bend, and walk long distances. Therefore, good physical condition is a job requirement when working in the field.

Salaries

While the U.S. Department of Labor does not list specific salary information for Marine Biologists, it does provide data for the related fields of zoology and wildlife biology. According to the 2006–07 edition of the department's *Occupational Outlook Handbook*, in 2004 annual salaries for zoologists and wildlife biologists ranged from $31,450 to more than $81,200, with a median of $50,330. Data from the National Association of Colleges and Employers put average annual starting salaries for those with bachelor's degrees in biological and life sciences at $31,258 in 2005.

Employment Prospects

While demand for Marine Biologists is expected to exist through 2014, the U.S. Department of Labor indicates that opportunities will be limited due to the highly specialized nature and small size of this field. According to the 2006–07 *Occupational Outlook Handbook*, the number of applicants generally far outnumbers the few openings that occur each year in the exciting research positions to which many aspire.

Advancement Prospects

Many Marine Biologists begin their careers as entry-level lab technicians or research assistants and progress to more senior roles. After furthering their education, those with master's degrees qualify for basic research positions, serve as staff scientists, or pursue administrative and management roles. After gaining additional work experience and education, some Marine Biologists pursue jobs as senior scientists or senior researchers. Some scientists also choose to teach marine biology at the college or university level.

Education and Training

While some entry-level positions may be obtained with an undergraduate degree, most positions require a master's degree in marine biology or aquatic science. Such degrees are commonly offered at larger colleges and universities. Undergraduate programs provide a solid educational base in the aquatic sciences, with course work that may include oceanography, marine invertebrate biology, and ichthyology. Master's degrees, which offer opportunities to specialize in a certain aspect of marine science, are the bare minimum for research positions. Doctorate degrees are usually required, especially for those wishing to pursue a teaching career at the university level or obtain an independent or advanced-level research position.

Special Requirements

State licensure is normally not required for Marine Biologists. However, those engaging in underwater fieldwork must obtain special certification from the Professional Association of Diving Instructors or a similar organization that provides the training needed for scientific diving. In addition, special licenses may be required to handle hazardous materials. Because of the strenuous nature of positions that require fieldwork, some employers may require candidates to take physical examinations.

Experience, Special Skills, and Personality Traits

In addition to a familiarity with research fundamentals, Marine Biologists usually must have experience operating boats and using SCUBA and snorkeling equipment. They must be detail-oriented, with the ability to perform tasks in a careful and thorough manner. They also must be logical and analytical thinkers, with excellent problem-solving abili-

ties. Due to the many variables involved in scientific work and the length of research projects, the ability to be patient, adaptable, and flexible also is critical for professionals in this field.

Because projects may put Marine Biologists in dangerous situations with underwater creatures and plants, self-control and a calm disposition are important, as well as stress management abilities. Marine Biologists must be self-reliant and capable of working independently at remote sites and also on teams that involve communication with other scientists, the public, and government officials.

Report writing and presentations are important aspects of this profession. Therefore, strong written and oral communication skills are required, along with proficiency in statistics. In addition to scientific knowledge, Marine Biologists in management roles must be familiar with the political process, laws, and regulations, as well as principles of business and management.

Marine Biologists may be required to work with sensors and computer chips, and perform computer modeling, digital mapping, and data integration activities. Therefore, experience with computers, electronics, geographic information systems (GIS), and global positioning satellite (GPS) systems may be helpful or required.

Unions and Associations

Marine Biologists may belong to one or more professional organizations, including advocacy groups like the Ocean Conservancy, as well as scientific associations like the American Society of Limnology and Oceanography and the American Institute of Biological Sciences.

Tips for Entry

1. In high school, take courses that provide exposure to the biological sciences, including biology and zoology, as well as courses in mathematics, chemistry, physics, and English.
2. Make sure that your personal goals, talents, and lifestyle requirements dovetail with the requirements to become a Marine Biologist.
3. Explore the different settings in which Marine Biologists work to identify career paths that interest you the most.
4. If possible, gain hands-on experience by volunteering or working for a local aquarium.
5. As a high school student and college undergraduate, participate in summer internships and research programs to gain research experience and meet other scientists.
6. During your junior and senior years of college, get involved with undergraduate research programs.

MARINE SCIENCE TECHNICIAN

CAREER PROFILE

Duties: Perform traditional field and lab work in applied scientific areas; set up, maintain, and operate a variety of instruments, equipment, and gear; perform maintenance and repair on engines and mechanical devices; help to solve research and development problems

Alternate Title(s): Marine Environmental Specialist; Marine Safety Specialist; Oil and Hazardous Materials Spill Responder; Computer Systems Analyst; Weather Forecaster

Salary Range: $33,217 to $50,264+

Employment Prospects: Good

Advancement Prospects: Good

Prerequisites:

Education or Training—Associate's degree in applied science or marine science or two years of specialized training

Experience—Qualifications vary, but previous shipboard and mechanical experience is helpful for entry-level positions

Special Skills and Personality Traits—Analytical thinking, problem-solving, communication, computer, technical, and mechanical skills; detail-oriented, careful, thorough, patient, logical, adaptable, flexible

CAREER LADDER

```
┌─────────────────────────────┐
│         Supervisor          │
└─────────────────────────────┘

┌─────────────────────────────┐
│  Marine Science Technician  │
└─────────────────────────────┘

┌─────────────────────────────┐
│          Intern             │
└─────────────────────────────┘
```

Position Description

Environmental-related career opportunities in the field of science are not limited to high-level scientific positions; a wide range of entry-level jobs exist at the technician level. Generally speaking, science technicians serve in practical support roles for scientists in a specific discipline or field. Through the application of scientific theories and principles, they help to solve research and development problems. In addition, they make improvements to existing processes and products and help to develop new ones.

Marine Science Technicians are employed in a wide range of different roles. Some Marine Science Technicians perform traditional field and lab work in applied scientific areas such as oceanography, geophysical exploration, and marine biology. In this role, technicians help marine scientists to study the biological and physical characteristics of lakes and oceans. During the course of their work they may play a hand in mapping sections of the ocean floor, studying the ocean's impact on weather and climate patterns, and determining and documenting the effects of pollution. They also may be involved in the search for different forms of marine life, energy sources, and precious minerals. Unlike scientists, Marine Science Technicians play a more hands-on role in the maintenance and operation of scientific instruments and equipment.

Other Marine Science Technicians work in roles that are more environmentally focused. Environmental positions may range from various types of monitoring to working with nuclear power plants, analyzing water and wastewater at treatment facilities, and carrying out environmental cleanup initiatives following disasters such as oil spills. Still other Marine Science Technicians work in the fishing industry, where their work may involve commercial fishing activities, the construction and repair of fishing gear, and the maintenance and repair of small engines. Finally, some technicians work in the area of marine salvage.

Marine Science Technicians also are employed in military roles. According to the U.S. Coast Guard (USCG), technicians "conduct marine-safety activities such as investigating pollution incidents, monitoring pollution cleanups, conducting foreign-vessel boardings to enforce pollution and navigation safety laws, conducting harbor patrols for port safety and security, inspecting waterfront facilities and supervising the loading of explosives on vessels. They may be assigned to the National Strike Force for oil and hazardous-material response."

On-shore, Marine Science Technicians act as the USCG's experts in safety and environmental health matters. They also are assigned to its icebreaking fleet, and due to their advanced training, provide assistance to scientists in the areas of weather forecasting and oceanography.

There are a number of common tasks that most science technicians perform, regardless of the scientific discipline in which they work. These include the setup, operation, and maintenance of lab instruments, making observations, monitoring experiments, calculating and recording results, and developing conclusions. In addition, science technicians must maintain careful documentation of the work they do. By the early twenty-first century, technicians in a variety of scientific fields were becoming more involved in research and development activities due to the growing complexity of laboratory procedures and instruments.

In the 2006–07 edition of the *Occupational Outlook Handbook*, the U.S. Department of Labor explained: "In addition to performing routine tasks, many technicians now develop and adapt laboratory procedures to achieve the best results, interpret data, and devise solutions to problems, under the direction of scientists. Moreover, technicians must master the laboratory equipment, so that they can adjust settings when necessary and recognize when equipment is malfunctioning.

"The increasing use of robotics to perform many routine tasks has freed technicians to operate more sophisticated laboratory equipment. Science technicians make extensive use of computers, computer-interfaced equipment, robotics, and high-technology industrial applications, such as biological engineering."

Specifically, Marine Science Technicians maintain and use sophisticated equipment aboard everything from small boats to large ocean-going vessels. Such equipment includes electronic navigation devices, chemical and physical measuring instruments, data acquisition and reduction systems, and various types of sampling devices. In addition to working with equipment, technicians commonly are involved in the collection of data, as well as the gathering of water and marine life samples for further analysis.

Marine Science Technicians find employment opportunities at colleges, universities, and private sector firms. Specific examples of potential employers include private and university-run marine labs, research stations, education centers, and oceanography institutes; aquariums; fisheries; marinas; underwater testing, research, and evaluation centers; engineering firms; environmental consulting agencies; marine construction firms; dredging and dock companies; wildlife refuges; and large corporations in the food, chemical, automotive, energy, telecommunications, and pharmaceutical industries.

At the federal government level, potential employers include the U.S. Navy; U.S. Coast Guard; National Oceanic and Atmospheric Administration; and the U.S. Army Corps of Engineers. At the state government level, employment opportunities exist with departments of fish and game; environment, health and natural resources; and agriculture. Local government employers may include port authorities, storm-water management commissions, and public works commissions.

Like higher-level marine scientists, Marine Science Technicians have many different types of work environments from which to choose. These range from office and laboratory settings to research vessels, oceans, lakes, tidal pools, fisheries, aquariums, and classrooms. While some Marine Science Technicians may work exclusively in one type of environment, others divide their time between field situations and an office or lab. Periodically, their job may require them to be at sea for weeks or months at a time.

While lab work usually is done during normal working hours, technicians who are engaged in fieldwork may be subject to long travel times to remote or foreign locations. They may be required to work long or unusual hours due to the nature of scientific studies involving marine populations. In addition, technicians may be subject to extreme underwater temperatures and forced to face dangerous conditions above and below the ocean's surface. In addition to the weather, they may find themselves in the presence of dangerous marine life, as well as hazards from chemicals, toxic materials, and equipment.

Although Marine Science Technicians may gather samples from the deck of a ship, they also may explore underwater environments with remote operated vehicles and SCUBA dive, which involves special underwater breathing equipment and wetsuits. Fieldwork can be physically demanding, requiring technicians to withstand underwater pressure, stand frequently, bend, and walk long distances. Therefore, good physical condition may be a job requirement.

Salaries

While the U.S. Department of Labor does not list specific salary information for Marine Science Technicians, it does provide data for related types of science technicians. According to the 2006–07 edition of the department's *Occupational Outlook Handbook*, in 2004 chemical technicians earned a median hourly wage of $18.35, while biological technicians earned $15.97 per hour. For nonsupervisory, supervisory, and managerial positions, the federal government paid average annual salaries of $38,443 for biological science technicians and $50,264 for physical science technicians in 2005.

Employment Prospects

According to the College of the Redwoods, which operates certificate and degree programs in marine science technology, a rapidly growing need for Marine Science Technicians exists. In general, the U.S. Department of Labor projects that science technicians will see overall employment rates increase at a rate that is about as fast as the average for all occupations through 2014. Employment opportunities will be the best for those with degrees from applied science technology programs, and those who have received training to use advanced equipment and instruments.

Advancement Prospects

While pursuing applied science technology certificates or degrees, students normally complete internships that allow them to interact with prospective employers and network with other technicians and scientists. Such internships often students initiate their careers. After gaining valuable hands-on experience, technicians may advance to supervisory roles or continue their education and pursue careers as scientists in their chosen field.

Education and Training

In general, most science technician jobs require an associate's degree in an applied area, or two years of specialized training. However, some technician positions require additional undergraduate course work in mathematics, or a bachelor's degree in biology, chemistry, or a related field. Associate's degrees can be earned from various community colleges or technical institutes. The latter institutions generally provide more hands-on training and less general education and theory than community colleges.

Marine technology programs are commonly offered at institutions in coastal states, with ready access to the ocean. Curricula are designed to provide the practical education and training needed for a career in marine scientific support. Programs normally include classroom instruction combined with training aboard an oceangoing vessel, where students learn to use and repair various types of equipment and instruments.

Some military training programs last approximately seven weeks and cover topics such as port security and anti-terrorism techniques, conducting investigations, monitoring pollution removal, commercial fishing-vessel safety, handling explosives, and weather forecasting.

Experience, Special Skills, and Personality Traits

Marine Science Technicians must be detail-oriented, with the ability to perform tasks in a careful and thorough manner. They also must be logical and analytical thinkers, with excellent problem-solving abilities. Due to the many variables involved in scientific work and the length of research projects, the ability to be patient, adaptable, and flexible also is critical for professionals in this field.

Marine Science Technicians must be self-reliant and capable of working independently at remote sites and also on teams that involve communication with other technicians, scientists, and the public. Because documentation is an important aspect of this profession, basic computer experience is required for word processing. Strong written communication skills also are required, along with proficiency in statistics.

Because operating, maintaining, and repairing sophisticated instruments and equipment is often a primary job responsibility, Marine Science Technicians must be mechanically inclined and skilled in the use of technology, including sensors, as well as geographic information systems (GIS) and global positioning satellite (GPS) systems. An aptitude for physics and mathematics is helpful.

Unions and Associations

Scientific technicians may belong to a number of associations in their chosen field. Some Marine Science Technicians belong to the Marine Technology Society. In addition to publishing a quarterly, peer-reviewed journal, the society hosts a number of conferences and offers four technical divisions and twenty-four technical committees.

Tips for Entry

1. In high school, take courses that provide exposure to the biological sciences, including biology and zoology, as well as courses in mathematics, chemistry, physics, and English.
2. Volunteer at a local aquarium, marina, fishery, or marine lab to gain practical hands-on experience.
3. Identify community colleges and technical institutes that offer applied marine science technology degrees and request information from the schools that interest you.
4. As a high school student, participate in summer marine science internships and research programs to gain experience and meet others in the profession.

OCEANOGRAPHER

CAREER PROFILE

Duties: Conduct field studies; perform scientific analyses; collect, examine, measure, analyze, and classify samples of marine life, rock, water, soil, and fossils; collect, analyze, and interpret scientific data

Alternate Title(s): Geoscientist; Limnologist

Salary Range: $37,700 to $130,750+

Employment Prospects: Good

Advancement Prospects: Good

Prerequisites:

Education or Training—Bachelor's degree in biology, geology, physics, or chemistry; master's or doctorate degree in oceanography

Experience—Shipboard experience, especially in a fieldwork or research setting; familiarity with geographic information systems (GIS) and global positioning satellite (GPS) systems may be helpful or required

Special Skills and Personality Traits—Ability to repair equipment during research expeditions; analytical thinking, decision-making, writing, communication, problem-solving, and computer skills; logical, self-reliant, independent, adaptable, flexible, detail-oriented, careful, thorough

CAREER LADDER

```
┌─────────────────────────────────────┐
│         Senior Researcher            │
└─────────────────────────────────────┘

┌─────────────────────────────────────┐
│      Project Leader or Manager       │
└─────────────────────────────────────┘

┌─────────────────────────────────────┐
│        Staff Oceanographer           │
└─────────────────────────────────────┘

┌─────────────────────────────────────┐
│  Lab Technician or Research Assistant │
└─────────────────────────────────────┘
```

Position Description

Oceanographers are geoscientists who study the Earth's coastal waters and oceans. The U.S. Department of Labor's *Occupational Outlook Handbook* explains that oceanographers "study the motion and circulation of the ocean waters; the physical and chemical properties of the oceans; and how these properties affect coastal areas, climate, and weather."

Oceanographers have made many contributions to the field of science, including the discovery of exotic organisms that live near hydrothermal vents and confirmation that the Earth's surface is divided into large plates that move over time (plate tectonics). In addition, Oceanographers provide insight into the impact that oceans—which store considerable amounts of carbon dioxide and heat—have on the Earth's climate. They are able to help predict changes in sea levels, as well as future temperature changes.

Oceanography is a multidisciplinary field in that it involves the application of virtually all branches of science—including biology, physics, chemistry, and geology—to the ocean. This broad scope is reflected in the different oceanographic subspecialties:

- Geophysical and geological Oceanographers study the structure, physical properties, and topography of the ocean floor. They evaluate how the ocean floor has changed over time by examining layers of sediment.
- Physical Oceanographers concentrate on the interplay between the ocean, weather, and climate. They study the ocean's movement and circulation by studying waves, currents, water temperature, density, and the transmission of sound and light. While some oceanographers may study a particular area, such as coastal or bay areas,

others focus on oceanic conditions on a global or planetary level.

- Chemical Oceanographers and marine geochemists study and analyze the chemical makeup of seawater and the ocean floor. Their work may involve desalinating seawater, mapping current flow through the presence of trace chemicals, discovering ways to extract desirable chemicals from the sea, and understanding the impact that pollution has on the ocean.
- Ocean engineers focus on the development of structures that allow humans to live and work in marine environment. They may be involved with the design and construction of marine equipment, offshore drilling platforms, and port facilities. During the course of their work, they contend with factors such as beach erosion, water pressure, salinity changes, and sedimentation.

Oceanographers perform different job tasks, depending on the positions they hold and their particular subspecialties. However, most conduct field studies and perform scientific analyses. These job functions involve collecting, examining, measuring, analyzing, and classifying samples of marine life, rock, water, soil, and fossils. Oceanographers also collect, analyze, and interpret scientific data. The results of their work are often used to produce scientific manuals, reports, charts, and graphs.

In addition to a strong understanding of scientific concepts and principles in the areas of geography, chemistry, physics, mathematics, and biology, Oceanographers must be skilled in the use of computers and technology because they use sophisticated instruments to analyze the environment. Examples include robots that perform underwater exploration, satellites that provide images of the world's oceans from outer space, underwater cameras, submersible exploration vehicles called bathyscaphes, thermometers, and other highly specialized devices made specifically for oceanography.

Because there are a number of subspecialties within the field of oceanography, Oceanographers have many different types of work environments from which to choose. These range from office and laboratory settings to oceangoing vessels. Many Oceanographers divide their time between the field and an office or lab setting at a shore station or research center, although some work exclusively onshore. Generally speaking, Oceanographers tend to work normal 40-hour weeks in onshore settings, although this varies depending on the position. For example, those in academic roles often work longer hours to accommodate research and teaching responsibilities.

Fieldwork can involve extended periods of time at sea and long travel times to remote or foreign locations. Due to the nature of experiments, scientists may be required to work unusual hours in hazardous or extreme weather conditions. Positions that are physically demanding require candidates to be in good physical condition. Individuals who wish to work at sea should be relatively tolerant of motion sickness.

The majority of Oceanographers work in states with coastal or bay areas, including Virginia, Maryland, Florida, Hawaii, and California. According to an estimate from the University of Delaware, the federal government employs about 40 percent of Oceanographers, while 30 percent work for private industry and another 30 percent work for colleges and universities. At the federal government level, employment opportunities exist with the Fish and Wildlife Service, the Environmental Protection Agency, the U.S. Geological Survey, and the National Oceanic and Atmospheric Administration. In addition, opportunities also exist within some state governments.

Salaries

According to the 2006–07 edition of the U.S. Department of Labor's *Occupational Outlook Handbook*, in 2004 annual salaries for geoscientists (the general category that includes Oceanographers) ranged from $37,700 to more than $130,750, with a median of $68,730. Data from the National Association of Colleges and Employers put average annual starting salaries for those with bachelor's degrees in geology and related sciences at $39,365 in mid-2005. The average federal government salary for Oceanographers in 2005 (including nonsupervisory, supervisory and management positions) was $87,007.

Employment Prospects

Slower than average demand for geoscientists is expected through 2014, according to the U.S. Department of Labor. Although government cutbacks will reduce the number of new jobs available in the geosciences, a large number of projected retirements, as well as a shortage of qualified geoscience graduates, will help to offset this situation and create good employment conditions. The *Occupational Outlook Handbook* further indicates that "a small number of new jobs will result from the need for oceanographers to conduct research for the military or for Federal agencies such as the National Oceanic and Atmospheric Administration (NOAA) on issues related to maintaining healthy and productive oceans."

Advancement Prospects

While most entry-level oceanography positions call for master's or doctorate degrees, those with undergraduate degrees may begin working as technicians and then advance to higher level positions after gaining additional experience and pursuing graduate degrees. Entry-level technicians who have some field experience may be able to obtain positions with more responsibility. As scientists in this field progress on the career ladder, they may become project leaders, managers, administrators, or pursue high-level research positions. Strong competition exists for academic positions.

Education and Training

Individuals wishing to work as Oceanographers must first earn an undergraduate degree in a scientific discipline such as biology, geology, physics, or chemistry. Course work in mathematics also is important. Most formal oceanography programs are available only at the graduate level and offer several areas of specialization. Doctorate degrees are required for those who wish to pursue a teaching career at the university level, or an advanced-level research position.

Experience, Special Skills, and Personality Traits

Shipboard experience is helpful for those who wish to become Oceanographers, because many positions require at least some time at sea. In particular, the ability to repair equipment is a desired trait, as breakdowns sometimes occur during research expeditions, and engineers and repair technicians may not always be available.

Oceanographers must be sound decision-makers and problem-solvers who are able to think critically and creatively. Due to the many variables involved in scientific work, they also must be adaptable and flexible. Oceanographers must be able to work independently or as part of a team. In addition, they must be able to communicate with others clearly and concisely. For this reason, successful Oceanographers must have a strong command of the English language, along with strong written and oral communication skills.

In addition to basic computer knowledge for word processing, modeling, and developing presentations, Oceanographers may be required to perform digital mapping and data integration activities. Therefore, experience with geographic information systems (GIS) and global positioning satellite (GPS) systems may be helpful or required.

Unions and Associations

Many Oceanographers are members of the American Society of Limnology and Oceanography. This professional association meets the specialized development needs of educators and researchers alike through research journals, interdisciplinary meetings, and symposia. In addition, it is involved in matters of public policy and provides public education and outreach activities.

Tips for Entry

1. In high school, take courses that provide exposure to mathematics (through calculus), English, computer science, and as many scientific disciplines as possible.

2. Request educational and career information from the American Geophysical Union, http://www.agu.org, or the American Society of Limnology and Oceanography, http://www.aslo.org.

3. In college, secure internships that provide valuable field and lab experience and increase your qualifications for entry-level employment.

4. Before choosing a graduate oceanography program, explore the different areas of specialization within the field and identify the ones that most interest you.

PLANT SCIENTIST

CAREER PROFILE

Duties: Conduct research studies, experiments, and investigations; identify and classify plant species; analyze and interpret scientific data; provide advice regarding environmental matters

Alternate Title(s): Ecologist, Natural Resources Manager, Horticulturist, Arborist

Salary Range: $30,660 to $88,840+

Employment Prospects: Fair

Advancement Prospects: Good

Prerequisites:

    Education or Training—Bachelor's, master's, or doctorate degree in botany or related field

    Experience—Fieldwork in plant science; familiarity with research fundamentals, electronics, computer modeling, digital mapping, data integration, and geographic information systems and global positioning satellites systems

    Special Skills and Personality Traits—Logical and analytical thinking, computer, communication, and problem-solving skills; detail-oriented, careful, thorough, self-reliant, patient, adaptable, flexible

    Special Requirements—Special licenses are normally not required for most Plant Scientists. Horticulturalists may obtain certification from the American Society for Horticultural Science.

CAREER LADDER

```
┌─────────────────────────────────────────┐
│   Senior Scientist or Senior Researcher   │
└─────────────────────────────────────────┘

┌─────────────────────────────────────────┐
│                 Manager                   │
└─────────────────────────────────────────┘

┌─────────────────────────────────────────┐
│             Staff Scientist               │
└─────────────────────────────────────────┘

┌─────────────────────────────────────────┐
│   Lab Technician or Research Assistant    │
└─────────────────────────────────────────┘
```

Position Description

Plant Scientists work in the broad scientific field of botany, which involves the study of plants and their environment. In addition to furthering general scientific knowledge about plants, their work impacts areas such as conservation, environmental protection, and public health. Plant Scientists also help to identify new and better sources of medicine, food, building materials, and clothing fibers. Agronomy-related work employs thousands of Plant Scientists in the areas of agricultural production and crop research.

The types of plant life studied by scientists in this field include algae, conifers, ferns, flowering plants, fungi, lichens, and mosses. In addition, the plant sciences offer multiple areas of specialization. Examples include plant identification and classification, plant part structure/function, plant disease, plant biochemistry, and the interaction between plants and other organisms and environmental elements. Some scientists even study the geological history of plants.

For those who are interested in plant science, the career possibilities are virtually unlimited. At the most fundamental level Plant Scientists can choose to work with plant life at the microscopic level, focusing on individual cells, while others engage in fieldwork that involves working with entire plants. Some Plant Scientists are involved in work that includes varying degrees of these approaches.

According to the Botanical Society of America (BSA), there are many different areas of specialization within the field of plant science. In addition to ecology, genetics, and molecular biology, there are other areas of specialization:

- Taxonomy is the identification, naming, and classification of plants.
- Plant anatomy encompasses the study of plant structure, even at the microscopic level.
- Cytology concentrates on plant cells, including their history, function, and structure.
- Physiology encompasses the vital plant processes and functions, such as photosynthesis.
- Biophysics involves applying physics to the life processes of plants.
- Biochemistry concentrates on plant processes and products at the chemical level.
- Paleobotany deals with the evolution and biology of fossil plants.
- Morphology deals with plants at the macroscopic level, including the development and evolution of roots, stems, and leaves.

Plant Scientists also may focus on a particular area of applied plant science, such as forestry or natural resources management. The BSA recognizes many different areas of applied science:

- Biotechnology involves inserting desirable genes into plants.
- Breeding involves matching and crossing plants to develop better ones.
- Economic botany focuses on commercial aspects of plants, including plant products.
- Food science and technology focuses on plants that are used as food sources.
- Plant pathology concentrates on plant diseases.
- Agronomy involves working with crops and soils.
- Horticulture involves working with ornamental plants, fruits, and vegetable crops, as well as landscape design.

In addition to specializing in different plant biology disciplines or types of applied plant science, plant scientists also may concentrate on a particular type of organism, including mosses (bryology), lichens (lichenology), fungi (mycology), microorganisms (microbiology), ferns (pteridology), and algae (phycology).

Finally, a large number of Plant Scientists are involved in education. In addition to teaching at the secondary, junior college, or university level, some work in educational roles at universities, arboretums, and botanical gardens, while others develop curricula and instructional materials.

Plant Scientists perform different job tasks, depending on the positions they hold and their scientific subspecialties. However, common tasks include conducting research studies, experiments, and investigations, and identifying and classifying plant species. Plant Scientists also are involved in the analysis and interpretation of scientific data obtained from other sources. Plant Scientists who are involved in research often focus on genetics, as well as the chemical processes that occur within plants. They may concentrate on processes that have taken place over thousands or millions of years or in a fraction of a second. Some Plant Scientists provide advice to lawmakers regarding environmental protection matters.

In addition to planning and conducting field studies and performing scientific analyses, Plant Scientists write reports and create charts, graphs, diagrams, and maps to share their findings with their employers, clients, colleagues, and the public. The results of their work may lead to the development of new drugs; crops and plants with more desirable attributes, including larger size or improved disease resistance; new or improved methods for planting, spraying, cultivating, and harvesting; and better methods for plant processing, storage, and transportation.

In addition to a strong understanding of scientific concepts and principles in the areas of biology, geography, chemistry, physics, and mathematics, Plant Scientists must often possess knowledge about education and training methods, economics, and food production. Because they use sophisticated laboratory instruments and devices to analyze plant samples and the environment, Plant Scientists must be skilled in the use of computers and technology.

Plant Scientists are sound decision makers and problem solvers who are able to think creatively. In addition to engaging in scientific analysis and discovery, they must be able to communicate their findings with others in a clear and concise manner. This may involve conveying highly technical or scientific information to students, businesspeople, consumers, and others with little or no scientific training and helping them to understand and apply that information. For this reason, successful Plant Scientists have a strong command of the English language, along with strong written and oral communication skills.

Employment opportunities for Plant Scientists exist with a wide range of organizations. These include colleges and universities, government agencies dealing with the environment, nonprofit environmental organizations, museums, arboretums, botanical gardens, private consulting and research firms, and companies in the energy, pharmaceutical, agricultural, and food industries.

Because of the wide variety of subspecialties and potential employers that exist within the plant sciences, Plant Scientists have many different types of work environments from which to choose. These range from office, classroom, and laboratory settings to outdoor environments such as farm fields, research plots, forests, tropical areas, arboretums, and botanical gardens. Fieldwork can involve long travel times to remote or foreign locations. Scientists in the field may be required to work unusual hours and under extreme temperatures. Positions that are physically demanding require candidates to be in good physical condition. Many Plant Scientists divide their time between fieldwork and an office or lab setting.

Salaries

According to the 2006–07 edition of the U.S. Department of Labor's *Occupational Outlook Handbook*, in mid-2004 soil and plant scientists earned annual salaries of less than $30,660 to more than $88,840, with a median of $51,200. Data from the National Association of Colleges and Employers put average 2005 starting salaries for those with bachelor's degrees in plant sciences at $31,649, while salaries for those with degrees in agricultural sciences averaged $36,189.

Employment Prospects

According to the U.S. Department of Labor, some 18,000 Plant Scientists were employed in 2002. Through 2012, the department anticipates slower than average job growth for Plant Scientists, with a need for approximately 5,000 additional employees. Slower than average growth also is expected for agricultural and food scientists. This is largely due to slow growth in local, state, and federal government sectors. Existing job growth will be supported by greater overall awareness of environmental issues, the need to determine and monitor the environmental impact of industry, growing pressure on the global food supply and the related need for sustainable agriculture, and the need to discover and develop new or more effective pharmaceuticals.

Advancement Prospects

Entry-level Plant Scientists commonly work as interns, lab technicians, or research assistants. After working for several years as an assistant or associate level scientist, Plant Scientists can obtain senior level positions through promotion. Scientists who earn advanced degrees may become involved in research or education, or obtain positions that involve managing other scientists or research programs.

Education and Training

Those with undergraduate degrees in botany or a related field qualify for jobs as technicians or research assistants at museums, botanical gardens, parks, laboratories, private companies, and government agencies. Most professional positions require a master's degree. A doctorate degree is almost always required for those who wish to pursue a teaching career at the university level or an independent or advanced-level research position. In addition to course work in the sciences, the Botanical Society of America recommends that students round out their education with classes in humanities, social sciences, language, and arts. Foreign language courses are recommended for those who wish to work abroad or in the tropics.

Special Requirements

Special certifications or licenses are normally not required for Plant Scientists, including botanists. However, the American Society for Horticultural Science offers professional certification for horticulturalists who are able to meet certain standards in the areas of education, experience, and ethics. Because of the strenuous nature of positions that require fieldwork, some employers require candidates to take physical examinations.

Experience, Special Skills, and Personality Traits

Plant Scientists are required to be familiar with research fundamentals. They must be detail-oriented, with the ability to perform tasks in a careful and thorough manner. They also must be logical and analytical thinkers, with excellent problem-solving abilities. Due to the many variables involved in scientific work and the length of some research projects, the ability to be patient, adaptable, and flexible also is critical for professionals in this field. Plant Scientists must be self-reliant and capable of working independently at remote sites and also on teams.

Because report writing and presentations are important aspects of this profession, strong written and oral communication skills are required, along with proficiency in statistics. In addition to scientific knowledge, Plant Scientists in management roles must be familiar with the political process, laws, and regulations, as well as principles of business and management.

Basic computer experience is required for word processing and developing presentations. In addition, Plant Scientists may be required to work with advanced laboratory equipment and perform computer modeling, digital mapping, and data integration activities. Therefore, experience with electronics, geographic information systems (GIS), and global positioning systems (GPS) may be helpful or required.

Unions and Associations

Plant Scientists may belong to a number of different nonprofit, scientific, or cause-related professional organizations. These include the Botanical Society of America, the American Society for Horticultural Science, the American Society of Plant Biologists, the Ecological Society of America, the American Society of Plant Taxonomists, and the American Institute of Biological Sciences.

Tips for Entry

1. In high school, take courses that provide exposure to the biological sciences, including biology and zoology, as well as courses in mathematics, chemistry, physics, English, and preferably a foreign language.
2. Make sure that your personal goals, talents, and lifestyle requirements dovetail with the requirements to become a Plant Scientist.

3. Participate in science clubs and science fairs, and pursue internships or summer employment at a camp, plant nursery, landscaping company, floral shop, botanical garden, laboratory, park, or farm.

4. Contact Plant Scientists in different specialties to discuss possible career paths. The Botanical Society of America, http://www.botany.org, maintains a contact list of botanists throughout the United States.

5. If possible, shadow a Plant Scientist on the job to discover what their work is really like.

6. During your junior and senior years of college, get involved with undergraduate research programs.

RANGE MANAGER

CAREER PROFILE

Duties: Protect rangelands from damage; plan and oversee rangeland improvements; restore degraded ecosystems; inventory animals, plants, and soils; develop resource management plans, technical standards, and specifications; develop or improve methods and instruments used for reseeding; maintain vegetation and soil stability; maintain sustainable rangeland yield; help ranchers to optimize livestock production

Alternate Title(s): Consultant; Educator; Land Manager; Ranch Manager; Range Conservationist; Range Ecologist, Range Scientist

Salary Range: $27,950 to $78,470+

Employment Prospects: Poor

Advancement Prospects: Good

Prerequisites:

Education or Training—Bachelor's degree in range management, range science, or related field

Experience—Seasonal, part-time, or internship positions must often precede full-time employment

Special Skills and Personality Traits—Knowledge of science and the outdoors; systems perspective; proficiency in statistics; familiarity with laws and regulations; active learner; self-reliant; team player; ability to supervise, manage, direct, and motivate others; solid decision-making, written and oral communication, critical thinking, and problem-solving skills

Special Requirements—Voluntary certifications are available from the Society for Range Management

CAREER LADDER

```
┌─────────────────────────────────┐
│  Administrator or Consultant     │
└─────────────────────────────────┘

┌─────────────────────────────────┐
│  Range Manager                   │
└─────────────────────────────────┘

┌─────────────────────────────────┐
│  Intern                          │
└─────────────────────────────────┘
```

Position Description

Range Managers are conservation scientists who are responsible for studying, improving, managing, and protecting the Earth's rangelands, which include alpine, deserts, grasslands, marshes, prairies, savanna, and some forests. Range Managers have the sometimes difficult job of keeping rangelands safe, while at the same time maximizing their use for commercial and recreational activities.

According to the U.S. Department of Labor's *Occupational Outlook Handbook*, "rangelands cover hundreds of millions of acres of the United States, mostly in Western States and Alaska. They contain many natural resources, including grass and shrubs for animal grazing, wildlife habitats, water from vast watersheds, recreation facilities, and valuable mineral and energy resources." While some rangelands are privately owned, many exist on public land.

The Society for Range Management explains that rangelands, which constitute more than 40 percent of the Earth's land, "are extremely productive and rich in biodiversity, providing: A source of high quality water, clean air and open spaces; essential wildlife habitat and carbon sequestration; an environment for recreation such as hiking, camping, hunting and fishing; economic means for agriculture, mining and local communities; [and] a setting for social, cultural and aesthetic activities."

Opportunities abound for those interested in the field of range management. In fact, careers are as diverse as the many different types of rangelands. Range Managers may specialize in one of several different scientific areas. These include agriculture, ecosystems, fisheries, hydrology, plant science, soil science, social economics, and wildlife.

During the course of their daily work, Range Managers may interact with a variety of people. In addition to members of the public, government officials, and representatives of special interest groups, they also communicate with other Range Managers, conservation scientists, foresters, and forestry technicians, as well as landowners, farmers, and loggers. However, many Range Managers spend a considerable amount of time working by themselves in isolated areas.

Range Managers are responsible for the maintenance of healthy ecosystems. When engaging in rangeland planning, monitoring, and assessment activities, balancing the elements of climate, plant physiology, and soil productivity are essential. Range Managers also work with the land following activities that disturb the land, such as droughts, gas and oil extraction, and fire. In such situations, they are engaged in the assessment and implementation of rehabilitation and land reclamation techniques.

Range Managers perform a variety of tasks and use a number of different techniques during the course of their work. Common tasks include the restoration of degraded ecosystems; the inventorying of animals, plants, and soils; and the development of resource management plans, technical standards, and specifications.

Range Managers protect rangelands from damage that could result from poisonous plants, rodents, and fire; plan and oversee improvements such as watering reservoirs, corrals, fencing, and structures for controlling soil erosion; develop or improve methods and instruments used for reseeding; determine the best varieties of forage plants for a given rangeland; and maintain sustainable rangeland yield through the use of revegetation, herbicide use, and controlled burning.

As the U.S. Department of Labor explains in its *Occupational Outlook Handbook*, some Range Managers manage ranches. In this line of work, "they may help ranchers attain optimum livestock production by determining the number and kind of animals to graze, the grazing system to use, and the best season for grazing. At the same time, however, range managers maintain soil stability and vegetation for other uses such as wildlife habitats and outdoor recreation."

Like other conservationists, including foresters, Range Managers are subject to a variety of working conditions. While some may spend a portion of their time in an office setting, Range Managers spend a considerable amount of time working outdoors in all kinds of weather—including rain, extreme heat, and bitter cold. This profession can be physically demanding; in addition to walking long distances, Range Managers must sometimes travel over rough terrain and through dense brush and forests. Therefore, being in good or excellent physical condition may be a job requirement.

In the United States, the majority of Range Managers work for the federal government. Three federal departments—the Bureau of Land Management, the Forest Service, and the Natural Resource Conservation Service—are the main employers of Range Managers. However, the Agricultural Research Service, Department of Defense, Environmental Protection Agency, Fish and Wildlife Service, and National Park Service are other federal employers.

At the state, county, and local government levels, opportunities exist with various agencies including cooperative extensions, county planning departments, fish and wildlife departments, natural resource departments, and park districts.

Within the private sector Range Managers work for consulting firms, as well as companies involved in agriculture, land management, mining, and real estate. Some work for nonprofit organizations, including land trusts. Finally, other Range Managers are involved in education and research at colleges and universities.

Salaries

According to the 2006–07 edition of the Department of Labor's *Occupational Outlook Handbook*, in mid-2004 annual salaries for conservation scientists ranged from less than $30,740 to more than $78,470, with a median of $52,480. Data from the National Association of Colleges and Employers put average annual starting salaries for those with bachelor's degrees in conservation and renewable natural resources at $27,950 in 2005. That year, Range Managers employed by the federal government in nonsupervisory, supervisory, and management jobs earned average annual salaries of $58,162. Starting salaries for those with undergraduate degrees tend to be comparable between the federal government and private sector firms, while local and state governments usually pay smaller salaries.

Employment Prospects

The U.S. Department of Labor anticipates slower-than-average job growth for conservation scientists through 2014. According to the *Occupational Outlook Handbook*, because of government cutbacks the best opportunities will exist with consulting firms in the private sector. The publication explains that "demand will be spurred by a continuing emphasis on environmental protection, responsible land management, and water-related issues. Growing interest in developing private lands and forests for recreational purposes will generate additional jobs for foresters and conservation scientists. Fire prevention is another area of growth for these two occupations."

Advancement Prospects

After working in entry-level positions that involve heavy fieldwork, Range Managers often advance to administrative jobs that involve planning, supervising others, and writing reports. Some Range Managers go into business as private consultants or ranchers. Finally, opportunities also exist in the areas of research and education.

Education and Training

A bachelor's degree in range management or range science is usually required to work as a Range Manager. However, some conservation scientists in this field hold degrees in agriculture, biology, ecology, environmental science, natural resource management, or a similar field. Teaching and research positions almost always require a master's or doctorate degree. Courses in rangeland management and rangeland science are available at many colleges and universities. These often are available as part of a broader program in natural resource science or agricultural science. However, there are a few schools that offer formal programs.

Special Requirements

Optional certifications for this profession are available from the Society for Range Management. These include the Certified Professional in Rangeland Management (CPRM) and Certified Range Management Consultant (CRMC). In addition to passing a written exam, candidates must meet specific requirements related to education and work experience.

Experience, Special Skills, and Personality Traits

In general, beginning Range Managers seeking full-time employment must first hold a number of seasonal or part-time positions. Internships and summer work while in college are prime opportunities to gain this experience.

A number of skills and personality traits are essential for Range Managers. In addition to sound judgment and decision-making abilities, successful Range Managers must be active learners with solid knowledge of science and the outdoors. They must have excellent critical thinking and problem-solving skills, as well as the ability to take a systems perspective and determine how the outcome of a process can be affected by changing different variables. In addition, Range Managers must be self-reliant and capable of working independently at remote sites and also on teams that involve communication with others.

Report writing, documentation, and interaction with others are important aspects of this profession. Therefore, strong written and oral communication skills are required, along with proficiency in statistics. In addition to scientific knowledge, Range Managers must be familiar with applicable laws and regulations. Finally, because many Range Managers manage staff and volunteers, they must be able to supervise, manage, direct, and motivate others.

Unions and Associations

Many Range Managers are members of the Society for Range Management (SRM). Based in Lakewood, Colorado, this professional and scientific organization is concerned with studying, conserving, managing and sustaining the varied resources of rangelands.

Tips for Entry

1. In high school, take courses that provide exposure to the sciences, including earth science, biology, and zoology, as well as courses in mathematics, chemistry, physics, and English.
2. Make sure that your personal goals, talents, and lifestyle requirements dovetail with the requirements to become a Range Manager.
3. Shadow a Range Manager on the job to discover what their work is really like.
4. Search the SRM's listing of schools offering degrees in rangeland management and rangeland science, including accredited programs, at http://www.rangelands. org/links_universities.shtml.
5. As a high school student and college undergraduate, volunteer for a conservation organization or work on a farm or ranch to gain hands-on experience.

SOIL SCIENTIST

CAREER PROFILE

Duties: Conduct soil surveys; perform site evaluations for land use and waste disposal applications; monitor construction projects; conduct research; carry out chemical analyses on soil samples; develop corrective action plans

Alternate Title(s): Environmental Consultant; Land Use Manager; Soil Analyst; Soil Chemist; Soil Conservationist; Soil Ecologist; Soil Microbiologist; Soil Physicist; Soil Surveyor

Salary Range: $27,950 to $78,470+

Employment Prospects: Fair

Advancement Prospects: Excellent

Prerequisites:

Education or Training—Bachelor's, master's, or doctorate degree in soil science, earth science, environmental science, or natural resources

Experience—Soil science fieldwork, as well as familiarity with computer modeling, digital mapping, geographic information systems, and global positioning satellites

Special Skills and Personality Traits—Analytical thinking, writing, communication, problem-solving, and computer skills; logical, self-reliant, independent, adaptable, flexible, detail-oriented, careful, thorough

Special Requirements—Certification is voluntary, but may be required by employers

CAREER LADDER

```
┌─────────────────────────────┐
│      Senior Scientist        │
└─────────────────────────────┘

┌─────────────────────────────┐
│   Environmental Consultant   │
└─────────────────────────────┘

┌─────────────────────────────┐
│       Soil Scientist         │
└─────────────────────────────┘

┌─────────────────────────────┐
│    Soil Science Technician   │
└─────────────────────────────┘
```

Position Description

Soil Scientists study the biological, chemical, and physical properties and characteristics of soils and arrange them into standard classifications. As the Soil Science Society of America explains, "soil scientists explore and seek to understand the earth's land and water resources. Students of soil science learn to identify, interpret, and manage soils for agriculture, forestry, rangeland, ecosystems, urban uses, and mining and reclamation in an environmentally responsible way."

Soil Scientists draw knowledge from a number of disciplines while performing their work. In addition to specific training in soil conservation, soil fertility, and soil microbiology, scientists in this field are often knowledgeable in fields such as general biology, chemistry, earth/environmental science, ecology, farm and ranch management, food production, forestry, geography, geology, horticulture, hydrology, limnology, mathematics, physics, plant science, statistics, weed science, and wetland ecology.

The field of soil science is broad and offers a variety of challenging career choices. For example, Soil Scientists may help developers to determine the most effective use of land and natural resources, estimate the cost of conservation practices, plan or evaluate septic and storm-water systems, and enhance land through landscape design. They also may assist in dispute resolution by gathering facts and facilitating mediation sessions involving landowners, government agencies, and other parties.

In the agricultural sector, Soil Scientists work with farmers to plan crop rotations, manage the use of fertilizers and agrichemicals, conserve water, identify the best soil for growing certain plants, and develop sustainable agriculture. Another area in which Soil Scientists work is environmental protection, which may include the coordination of resource protection projects for government agencies. Common environmental issues include sewage and industrial waste management, mine reclamation, and the removal or remediation of contaminated soils.

Soil Scientists also may engage in soil systems research on behalf of universities and other private or public institutions. In some cases, their work may focus exclusively on the lithosphere (soils), including issues like soil fertility, soil heat transfer, soil quality and sustainability, biogeochemical processes, trace element accumulations, and carbon/nitrogen cycling and balances. However, Soil Scientists also perform interrelated research that involves the atmosphere (global climate change, grazing lands, and deforestation/reforestation), the biosphere (crop production, rangeland ecosystems, and forest ecosystems), and the hydrosphere (groundwater contamination, solute movement and fate, and pesticide use).

Depending on their specific positions, Soil Scientists may conduct a range of different job tasks, often in cooperation with other professionals who are not familiar with or knowledgeable of soil systems. These typically include conducting soil surveys (soil description, classification, and mapping), performing site evaluations for land use and waste disposal applications, using engineering manuals and technical guides, monitoring construction projects, carrying out chemical analyses on soil samples, and developing corrective action plans. When carrying out these tasks, Soil Scientists may evaluate soil characteristics such as sustainability, stability, drainage, moisture retention, and chemical concentration.

Soil Scientists serve in technical, consulting, and research capacities in many sectors of the economy. In the private sector they work for companies and consulting firms, as well as for nonprofit organizations and universities. The construction and agricultural sectors are significant employers for scientists in this field. Opportunities also exist with government agencies. Soil Scientists work for various state conservation and land management agencies, as well as the Bureau of Land Management, the USDA Agricultural Research Service, and other federal agencies.

Because Soil Scientists have many career opportunities from which to choose, their work can take them to a variety of different settings. In addition to residential and commercial land developments, work sites may include farms, forests, mines, wetlands, and even archeological sites. Many Soil Scientists divide their time between fieldwork and an office or lab setting. Fieldwork can involve long travel times to remote or foreign locations, and scientists may be required to work unusual hours and under extreme temperatures. Positions that are physically demanding require scientists to be in good physical condition. In addition to their primary job functions, Soil Scientists may conduct seminars, give public or professional presentations, and write articles for professional journals.

Salaries

While the U.S. Department of Labor does not list salary information specifically for Soil Scientists, it does provide data for the related occupation of conservation scientist. According to the 2006–07 edition of the department's *Occupational Outlook Handbook*, in mid-2004 conservation scientists' annual salaries ranged from $30,740 to more than $78,470, with a median of $52,480. Data from the National Association of Colleges and Employers put average annual starting salaries for those with bachelor's degrees in conservation and renewable natural resources at $27,950 in 2005.

Employment Prospects

Through 2014, the U.S. Department of Labor anticipates slower than average job growth for conservation scientists. This is largely due to government budget cutbacks and an increase in government contracts with private consultants. While opportunities still exist in the government sector, the best opportunities for Soil Scientists will likely be with private scientific research and development services, as well as private consulting firms. Factors supporting job growth include a growing number of environmental regulations and laws, including those related to soil erosion and land management, as well as greater overall awareness of environmental issues. In the agricultural sector, the Department of Labor cites a continued need to practice sustainable agriculture. This can be accomplished through the development and implementation of plans that address pest and crop management, soil fertility and erosion, and animal waste in such a way that minimal damage occurs to the natural environment. Such plans often call for a reduction in the amount of chemicals used.

Advancement Prospects

After gaining experience as college interns or soil science technicians, Soil Scientists regularly obtain entry-level positions with county conservation districts. After working under the supervision of experienced professionals, they may progress on the career ladder or move to jobs with state departments of environmental quality or federal agencies. Others pursue positions with private consulting firms, as well as reclamation or mining companies. Scientists who earn advanced degrees may become involved in research or education or obtain senior-level positions that involve managing other scientists or research programs.

Education and Training

Soil Scientists earn degrees in soil science or closely related fields such as earth science, environmental science, or natural resources. Students in undergraduate programs gain a comprehensive understanding of the soil environment and the interrelationships between soil forming factors, soil morphology, soil biology, soil chemistry, and soil physics. General course work is heavily focused in core scientific areas, while more specialized classes cover topics such as food production, soil classification, soil management, and waste management. A master's degree is required for many staff-level jobs. Soil Scientists who pursue a research career or wish to teach at the university level must earn a doctorate degree.

Special Requirements

The Soil Science Society of America (SSSA) offers three certifications for Soil Scientists, which vary according to career path. These include Certified Crop Adviser (CCA), Certified Professional Agronomist (CPAg) (ARCPACS), and Certified Professional Soil Scientist/Classifier (CPSS/CPSC). Although they are voluntary, these certifications may be listed as requirements for employment by private firms.

Experience, Special Skills, and Personality Traits

Soil Scientists must be detail-oriented, with the ability to perform tasks in a careful and thorough manner. They also must be logical and analytical thinkers, with excellent problem-solving abilities. Due to the many variables involved in scientific work, the ability to be adaptable and flexible also is critical for professionals in this field. Because projects may take them to remote locations where it is necessary to work in relative isolation, Soil Scientists must be self-reliant and capable of working independently. On the other hand, because they often work on project teams and are required to communicate with others, Soil Scientists also must be team players.

Report writing and presentations also are important aspects of this profession. Therefore, strong written and oral communication skills are required, along with proficiency in statistics. Basic computer experience is required for word processing and developing presentations. In addition, Soil Scientists may be required to analyze and model soil processes using computers and carry out digital mapping and data integration activities. Therefore, experience with geographic information systems (GIS) and global positioning systems (GPS) may be helpful or required.

Unions and Associations

Soil Scientists commonly belong to one of 48 professional state associations, boards, registries, or societies for Soil Scientists or classifiers. At the national level, associations include the Soil Science Society of America, Crop Science Society of America, American Society of Agronomy, and the Association of Women Soil Scientists.

Tips for Entry

1. In high school, take courses that provide exposure to earth science, geology, biology, mathematics, chemistry, physics, and engineering, and hone your English language skills
2. Download free career brochures from the Soil Science Society of America and the Crop Science Society of America by visiting http://www.soils.org and http://www.crops.org, respectively.
3. Review college catalog course descriptions in the departments of soil science, earth science, environmental science, or natural resources to identify a curriculum that interests you
4. In college, secure internships that provide valuable field and lab experience and increase your qualifications for entry-level employment

VETERINARIAN

CAREER PROFILE

Duties: Diagnose animal health problems; dress wounds; set fractures; perform surgery; help birthing animals; administer medication; vaccinate animals; provide instruction regarding animal breeding, feeding, housing, and behavior; euthanize sick animals

Alternate Title(s): Epidemiologist, Poultry Inspector, Disease Control Worker, Director of Environmental Health, Public Health Department Director

Salary Range: $39,020 to $118,430+

Employment Prospects: Good

Advancement Prospects: Excellent

Prerequisites:

Education or Training—Doctor of veterinary medicine (D.V.M. or V.M.D.) degree

Experience—Previous hands-on experience with animals is helpful

Special Skills and Personality Traits—Appreciation of animals; interest in science; good manual dexterity; good communication, people, business, and time-management skills

Special Requirements—State licensure; pass national board exam and national clinical competency exam

CAREER LADDER

```
┌─────────────────────────────┐
│    Private Practitioner or   │
│   Board-certified Specialist │
└─────────────────────────────┘

┌─────────────────────────────┐
│    Staff Veterinarian or     │
│    Associate Veterinarian    │
└─────────────────────────────┘

┌─────────────────────────────┐
│      Intern or Resident      │
└─────────────────────────────┘
```

Position Description

Veterinarians are medical professionals who care for animals. In addition, through research and other efforts they also help to protect and improve the health of humans. While the majority of Veterinarians work in private practice settings and care mainly for pets or companion animals, others play roles that focus more on the environment.

Even in private practice settings, about 25 percent of Veterinarians work in so-called "mixed" practices that involve caring for both small and large animals, including goats, cows, pigs, llamas, and sheep. A smaller number of Veterinarians focus exclusively on the care of large animals. Working mainly in the field of agriculture, they travel to ranches and farms where they provide urgent and preventive care for individual animals, as well as entire herds.

In addition to agriculture, Veterinarians also work in the area of wildlife preservation. In this niche, they provide care for animals in aquaria, animal parks, and zoos. Rather than working directly for these organizations, Veterinarians commonly provide their services on a contract or fee basis.

Veterinarians also work in the areas of environmental and public health. In the environmental health field, Veterinarians manage or participate in programs that determine how certain contaminants, such as industrial pollutants, pesticides, and other substances, impact both animals and humans.

In the public health arena Veterinarians function as epidemiologists at all levels of government, investigating outbreaks of disease that affect both animals and humans. They have benefited mankind in numerous ways. Examples include producing an anticoagulant that is used to treat heart disease, helping to discover cures for yellow fever and malaria, solving the mystery of botulism, and pioneering advancements in such areas as organ and limb transplantation and joint replacement surgery. Procedures and pharmaceuticals that are intended for eventual use on humans are often tested on animals first, under the care of trained veterinarians.

Veterinarians also work in regulatory capacities. They ensure the safety of the food supply by inspecting livestock and helping to prevent the spread of disease between animals and humans. Some Veterinarians evaluate and inspect poultry and meat processing plants to ensure that government sanitation and quality standards are being met. This type of work may involve evaluating live animals, as well as inspecting animal carcasses.

In the private sector, some Veterinarians find employment in technical, research, sales, marketing, and management roles. A wide range of companies rely on Veterinarians who have specialized expertise in areas such as bacteriology, endocrinology, laboratory animal medicine, nutrition, parasitology, pathology, pharmacology, toxicology, and virology.

Specifically, agricultural companies rely on Veterinarians for their expertise in the areas of disease control and nutrition, which helps poultry and livestock producers to optimize production and quality. Private sector Veterinarians also are employed by firms engaged in biomedical research and the production of pharmaceuticals, chemicals, animal feed, and pet foods.

In addition to technical, business, and direct animal-care roles, Veterinarians also work in the educational sector, where they share their knowledge with others and contribute to new developments in veterinary medicine and public health. According to the American Veterinary Medical Association (AVMA), some 3,800 Veterinarians work in this area. In addition to providing classroom and lab instruction, Veterinarian-educators also conduct research and contribute to scientific journals and other publications.

Veterinarians perform different tasks depending on the kind of work they do. Those who work in clinical settings diagnose health problems, dress wounds, set fractures, perform surgery, help birthing animals, administer medication, and vaccinate animals to prevent conditions such as rabies and distemper. In addition, Veterinarians also provide instruction regarding matters such as animal breeding, feeding, housing, and behavior. Finally, Veterinarians euthanize animals that are too injured or sick to recover.

While caring for animals, Veterinarians use a wide variety of medical equipment, ranging from sophisticated laboratory instruments (such as centrifuges and microscopes) and medical imaging apparatuses (such as X-ray, MRI, CT, and ultrasound machines) to surgical instruments and stethoscopes.

In addition to working in private practice, or for large clinical practices, Veterinarians work for private and government laboratories, and for government agencies at every level. Beyond county and state health departments, Veterinarians find federal employment opportunities with the Agriculture Research Service, the Environmental Protection Agency, the Fish and Wildlife Service, the Food and Drug Administration, the National Institutes of Health, and the National Library of Medicine.

Because part of their job involves providing urgent medical care, Veterinarians in clinical roles often work long or unusual schedules. In addition to keeping regular office hours, they often are on call to respond to emergency situations. However, the growing number of emergency care facilities for animals has helped to alleviate some of the need for private practitioners to be on call. Nevertheless, the majority of Veterinarians put in more than 50 hours per week, according to the AVMA; only 20 percent work 40-hour weeks. Generally speaking, Veterinarians who are just starting their careers tend to work longer hours.

Veterinarians in research or administrative roles tend to work relatively regular schedules in clean, well-lit lab or office environments. In clinic settings, those caring for large animals travel to ranches and farms in remote locations. In such roles they must often provide care in a variety of weather and under unsanitary conditions. Animals that are sick or frightened present a potential occupational risk for Veterinarians, because they may be inclined to scratch, bite, or kick. However, the use of tranquilizers and proper procedures can alleviate much of this risk.

Salaries

According to the 2006–07 edition of the U.S. Department of Labor's *Occupational Outlook Handbook*, in 2004 annual salaries for Veterinarians ranged from $39,020 to more than $118,430, with a median of $66,590. Data from the AVMA put average annual starting salaries for Veterinarians between $38,628 and $50,878 in 2004. Those caring exclusively for horses earned the smallest starting salaries, while those caring mainly for smaller animals earned the highest salaries.

Employment Prospects

The U.S. Department of Labor projects that Veterinarians will see overall employment rates increase at a rate that is about as fast as the average for all occupations through 2014. While growth is expected to be slower than average for Veterinarians who care mainly for large animals, lower earnings in this area, as well as a reluctance to work in isolated or rural areas, may lead to better than average job prospects for Veterinarians who wish to work with farm animals. The Department of Labor explains that the demand for Veterinarians will benefit from ongoing support in areas such as human-health-related biomedical research, public health and food safety, and national disease control programs. However, jobs in these niche areas are limited.

Advancement Prospects

Most Veterinarians begin their careers as employees of established clinical practices, and some go on to establish their own clinics. Outside of traditional, pet-focused clinical practices, Veterinarians have excellent advancement opportunities. According to the AVMA this is especially the case for those who have pursued postgraduate education in a specific area, such as diagnostic pathology, environmental medicine, immunology, laboratory animal medicine, molecular biology, or toxicology. After obtaining entry-level technical, research, teaching, or management positions, Veterinarians often advance on the career ladder to more senior level roles.

Education and Training

Pre-veterinary students must earn an undergraduate degree that includes heavy course work in science and mathematics, as well as additional course work in English, social science, and business. Candidates then apply to one of twenty-eight accredited colleges of veterinary medicine. Admission to veterinary school is highly competitive; approximately 40 percent of applicants are accepted. Depending on the college to which they apply, candidates must earn a satisfactory score on the Veterinary College Admission Test (VCAT), the Medical College Admission Test (MCAT), or the Graduate Record Examination (GRE). After a period of four years, students earn a doctor of veterinary medicine (D.V.M. or V.M.D.) degree.

After leaving veterinary school, some students go on to complete an optional one-year internship in a particular specialty and a two- or four-year residence program that leads to board certification in a specialty such as cardiology, internal medicine, neurology, or oncology.

Special Requirements

With the exception of some who work for state and federal agencies, all Veterinarians must be licensed in the state where they practice. While requirements vary from state to state, all states require that Veterinarians earn a D.V.M. degree or its equivalent and pass a national board exam and a clinical competency exam. Most states also require Veterinarians to pass exams related to state regulations and laws, and some administer clinical competency tests. In addition, most have specific requirements related to continuing education.

Experience, Special Skills, and Personality Traits

Prior to entering veterinary school, candidates should gain hands-on experience working with animals in a formal setting such as a veterinary clinic or research facility. Experience also may be gained by working at an animal shelter, farm, or ranch. In addition to an appreciation of animals and an interest in science, Veterinarians must possess good manual dexterity and have good communication, people, and time-management skills. Solid business skills are required for Veterinarians who wish to successfully own their own clinical practice, as they will need to market their business, maintain financial and billing operations, and manage other employees.

Unions and Associations

Veterinarians are often members of their state veterinary medical association. At the national level, the American Veterinary Medical Association counted approximately 70,000 Veterinarians as members in 2006—representing about 86 percent of all U.S. Veterinarians.

Tips for Entry

1. In middle school and high school, take courses that will prepare you for a career in veterinary science, including biology, chemistry, zoology, and mathematics.
2. In high school or college, volunteer or work for a veterinary office, farm, or animal shelter to gain valuable hands-on experience working with animals.
3. As a college undergraduate, identify prospective veterinary schools and learn about their specific admission requirements.
4. After veterinary school, complete an internship or residency program to increase your chances of earning the best entry-level starting salary or going into private practice.

WETLAND SCIENTIST

CAREER PROFILE

Duties: Assess and evaluate wetland environments; plan, execute, and manage mitigation and restoration projects; delineate wetlands; collect and analyze samples; write technical reports; prepare proposals

Alternate Title(s): Wetland Ecologist, Wetland Specialist, Wetland Project Coordinator, Water Resources Engineer, Stream Restoration Scientist, Field Biologist

Salary Range: $31,366 to $94,460+

Employment Prospects: Excellent

Advancement Prospects: Good

Prerequisites:

Education or Training—Bachelor's, master's, or doctorate degree in environmental science, ecology, environmental studies, biology, chemistry, hydrology, or related field

Experience—Wetland delineation experience; familiarity with government legislation and permit requirements, as well as the characteristics of specific geographic regions

Special Skills and Personality Traits—Teamwork, project-management, writing, communication, organization, analytical, and computer skills; highly motivated, self-starter

Special Requirements—Certification as a wetland professional in training (WPIT) or professional wetland scientist (PWS) may be required

CAREER LADDER

```
┌─────────────────────────────────┐
│     Senior Wetland Scientist     │
└─────────────────────────────────┘

┌─────────────────────────────────┐
│      Staff Wetland Scientist     │
└─────────────────────────────────┘

┌─────────────────────────────────┐
│  Associate or Assistant Scientist │
└─────────────────────────────────┘

┌─────────────────────────────────┐
│             Intern               │
└─────────────────────────────────┘
```

Position Description

Wetland Scientists are ecologists, soil scientists, hydrologists, and related professionals who are engaged in the practice of wetland science. According to the U.S. Environmental Protection Agency, wetlands are "areas where water covers the soil, or is present either at or near the surface of the soil all year or for varying periods of time during the year, including during the growing season." Wetlands can serve as a natural means of removing suspended silt and chemicals from water, and are helpful in minimizing the impact of drought and floods.

With the exception of Antarctica, wetlands are found throughout the world. Generally speaking, wetlands fall into one of two broad categories: inland/nontidal and coastal/tidal.

However, many different types of wetlands exist within these classifications due to regional variations in vegetation, soil, climate, topography, water chemistry, and hydrology. In addition, the plant and animal communities that live within wetlands also vary, depending on the aforementioned factors.

Wetland Scientists are actively involved in assessing and evaluating wetland environments. They determine water quality, as well as the presence and condition of wildlife and wildlife habitats. Wetland Scientists also are involved in the planning, execution, and management of mitigation and restoration projects, which involve efforts to create new wetlands or improve and revitalize existing ones. Some wetland science projects involve delineation, or the demarcation of wetland boundaries.

Wetland Scientists are often responsible for managing complex environmental projects. Junior or entry-level scientists often work under the supervision and guidance of senior scientists and project managers. They may spend a greater portion of their work time in the field than more experienced scientists, who often concentrate on legislative or policy issues. Fieldwork involves working in wetland environments and collecting samples that will be taken back to a laboratory for evaluation and analysis. While the prospect of outdoor work may sound appealing, Wetland Scientists often work in environments that have been damaged by man. Furthermore, work settings are often muddy, requiring scientists to wear rubber pants known as "waders." Although some jobs require comparative amounts of fieldwork and office time, this varies depending on the position.

In addition to project management, Wetland Scientists frequently write technical reports and prepare proposals. They must possess excellent written and oral communication skills, and must be adept at analyzing and interpreting data. Wetland Scientists must have the ability to work independently, as well as collaboratively with co-workers, clients, and third parties. Beyond general knowledge of their chosen scientific field, Wetland Scientists may be required to demonstrate familiarity with the flora and wildlife of specific states, regions, or localities.

Wetland Scientists are employed by nonprofit organizations, such as the National Wildlife Foundation, and at the state government level by departments of natural resources, parks and wildlife departments, water management districts, and environmental protection agencies. At the federal level, opportunities exist with the EPA; Army Corps of Engineers; U.S. Department of Agriculture, Natural Resources Conservation Service; and the U.S. Department of Interior, U.S. Fish and Wildlife Service. Within the private sector, a large number of Wetland Scientists work for engineering and environmental consulting firms, as well as environmental testing firms.

Wetland Scientists who work for local, state, or federal government agencies are involved in the management, restoration, and protection of wetland resources. They may be involved in programs that involve shoreline stabilization or erosion control. In addition, Wetland Scientists work to ensure compliance with government water quality standards. For example, states are required to comply with Section 401 of the federal Clean Water Act in order to ensure that development projects do not adversely impact wetlands. In the government sector, Wetland Scientists also are involved with issuing permits related to projects that impact, create, or destroy wetlands or water bodies.

In the private sector, Wetland Scientists who are employed by consulting firms frequently help clients deal with legislative requirements, including the National Environmental Policy Act of 1969 (NEPA), which requires government agencies, as well as nongovernmental organizations that use federal funds, to assess and consider the impact their actions will have on the environment.

Also common is compliance with Section 404 of the Clean Water Act, which regulates the discharge of dredged and fill material into U.S. waters. When wetlands are converted for farming or forestry, or when they may be impacted by the construction of dams and levees, residential developments, or highways, special permits must be obtained from the Army Corps of Engineers. Wetland Scientists who are employed by consulting firms help clients to obtain these permits, working as part of a team that may include compliance experts and engineers.

Wetland Scientists may work in a wide range of different settings, including wet meadows, wet prairies, marshes, bogs, swamps, playas, basins, areas along the edges of ponds and lakes, floodplains near streams and rivers, and tidal areas. Some of these areas are seasonal wetlands, meaning that they are dry for certain periods of the year.

In addition to performing their core job responsibilities, Wetland Scientists may write articles for professional journals and share their knowledge or expertise by presenting at professional conferences or leading training programs. In fact, some scientists pursue education as a career, devoting their time to training other wetland scientists at the college or university level.

The typical work hours for Wetland Scientists can vary considerably, and are dependent upon a wide range of factors. For example, projects and work time may be dictated by seasonal or tidal conditions in a particular area, as well as the migratory patterns of birds. Therefore, scientists may be busier at certain times of the year. In addition, they may be required to work late at night or early in the morning to observe specific conditions or phenomena.

Salaries

While the U.S. Department of Labor does not list salary information specifically for Wetland Scientists, it does provide data for environmental scientists and hydrologists. According to the 2006–07 edition of the department's *Occupational Outlook Handbook*, in mid-2004 annual salaries for environmental scientists ranged from $31,610 to more than $85,940, with a median of $51,080. Hydrologists' annual salaries ranged from $38,580 to more than $94,460, with a median of $61,510. Generally speaking, scientists in management positions earn more than their nonmanagerial counterparts. Data from the National Association of Colleges and Employers put average annual starting salaries for those with bachelor's degrees in environmental science at $31,366 in mid-2005.

Employment Prospects

As companies are forced to comply with a growing number of environmental regulations and laws, including those related to flood control, soil erosion, and the impact that development projects have on wetlands and other environmentally sensitive areas, industry observers expect growing demand for Wetland Scientists. In addition to greater overall awareness of environmental issues, rising sea levels and deteriorating coastal environments will create average job growth for environmental scientists and faster-than-average growth for hydrologists through 2014, according to the U.S. Department of Labor. Because the prospect of working outdoors is attractive, strong competition exists for entry-level positions.

Advancement Prospects

Students with internship experiences will have better chances of obtaining a junior or entry-level position as a Wetland Scientist. After working for several years as an assistant- or associate-level scientist, Wetland Scientists can obtain senior-level positions through promotion. Some industry observers have indicated that there is an abundance of Wetland Scientists with doctoral degrees. For this reason, there is very strong competition for positions requiring this level of education, such as teaching positions at the university level.

Education and Training

Wetland Scientists must earn an undergraduate degree in environmental science, ecology, environmental studies, biology, chemistry, or a related field. Many go on to earn advanced degrees, but these are not required for all entry-level positions. In college, students may pursue course work in chemistry, coastal resources management, conflict resolution, conservation biology, environmental planning, fisheries management, hydrogeology, limnology, marsh ecology, economics, soil science, stream ecology, water resources law, and wildlife science. In addition, fieldwork and laboratory time are essential components of the educational experience. Students pursuing training in wetlands science will learn to collect and analyze samples.

Special Requirements

The SWS Professional Certification Program Inc. is a nonprofit corporation that was established by the Society of Wetland Scientists to provide professional certification. The program offers the Wetland Professional in Training (WPIT) and Professional Wetland Scientist (PWS) certifications. Although they are not required by government agencies, these certifications are sometimes listed as requirements for employment by private firms.

Experience, Special Skills, and Personality Traits

Successful Wetland Scientists are highly motivated individuals who can work alone or as part of a team. Because the field of wetland science involves extensive project management and analyses, Wetland Scientists must be self-starters with strong organizational skills. Report writing and presentations also are important aspects of this profession. Therefore, strong written and oral communication skills are required, along with proficiency in statistics. In fact, some firms require Wetland Scientists to be proven technical writers.

Basic computer experience is required for word processing and developing presentations. However, Wetland Scientists also may be required to work with geographic information systems (GIS) and global positioning systems (GPS). With the exception of entry-level positions, Wetland Scientists are often expected to have experience with wetland or stream delineation and be familiar with government legislation and permit requirements, as well as the soil characteristics, flora, and wildlife of specific geographic regions.

Unions and Associations

Many Wetland Scientists are members of the Society of Wetland Scientists, a nonprofit organization based in McLean, Virginia, that was established to "promote wetland science and the exchange of information related to wetlands." Founded in 1980, the society claimed some 4,000 members throughout the world in the mid-2000s. In addition to its annual meeting, where scientific and technical information is presented, the society publishes a journal called *Wetlands* and the *SWS Bulletin* and maintains regional chapters that publish newsletters. It also supports student research and wetland science programs.

Tips for Entry

1. As a high school student, take courses that will prepare you for a career in wetland science, including biology, chemistry, earth science, and zoology.
2. Learn more about wetlands by visiting the U.S. Environmental Protection Agency online at http://www.epa.gov and downloading the agency's Wetlands Fact Sheets.
3. In college, seek opportunities to gain valuable field experience, including internships.
4. Learn more about careers in wetland science by visiting the Society of Wetland Scientists online at http://www.sws.org. The society's journal, *Wetlands*, is available online at no cost.

WILDLIFE REHABILITATOR

CAREER PROFILE

Duties: Capture and transport injured wild animals; feed baby birds and mammals; assist with fluid therapy and bandaging; clean cages; maintain databases; supervise paid staff and/or volunteers; provide public presentations; engage in fund-raising

Alternate Title(s): Animal Caretaker; Veterinary Technician; Wildlife Care Worker

Salary Range: $13,000 to $30,000+

Employment Prospects: Good

Advancement Prospects: Poor

Prerequisites:

Education or Training—Internships or volunteer work are needed to enter the field. An undergraduate degree in biology or ecology is recommended, but not required.

Experience—Hands-on animal care experience under the supervision of a licensed Wildlife Rehabilitator

Special Skills and Personality Traits—Concern for wildlife, people, and the environment; commitment to learning; strong communication skills; creative, resourceful, realistic, self-motivated, honest, cooperative, energetic, flexible, confident, responsible, positive, pleasant

Special Requirements—Ability to withstand frequent exposure to stressful and potentially dangerous situations involving animal illness and death; demanding time and financial requirements; liability insurance; complicated paperwork; special state and federal permits

CAREER LADDER

```
┌─────────────────────────────┐
│     Executive Director      │
└─────────────────────────────┘

┌─────────────────────────────┐
│   Coordinator or Supervisor │
└─────────────────────────────┘

┌─────────────────────────────┐
│    Wildlife Rehabilitator   │
└─────────────────────────────┘

┌─────────────────────────────┐
│     Intern or Volunteer     │
└─────────────────────────────┘
```

Position Description

Wildlife Rehabilitators provide professional care to sick, injured, and orphaned wild animals so they can ultimately be returned to their natural habitats. Wildlife rehabilitation is not an attempt to turn wild animals into pets; animals are held in captivity only until they are able to live independently in the wild. Wildlife Rehabilitators come from diverse backgrounds. While some are average citizens with specialized training, others are veterinarians, veterinary technicians, biologists, and educators.

Wildlife rehabilitation is a genuine public service. Because of their training, Wildlife Rehabilitators help concerned people to decide whether an animal truly needs help. They provide instructions for how to reunite wildlife families, keeping the safety of the animals and the rescuers in mind, and suggest humane, long-term solutions when conflicts arise between humans and their wild neighbors.

A great variety of tasks are involved with wildlife rehabilitation. There is no "typical" job description that defines what is expected of a Wildlife Rehabilitator. Generally speaking, the wildlife rehabilitation profession involves three main components: hands-on animal care, education and outreach, and wildlife medicine. Individual Wildlife Rehabilitators may perform varying degrees of work in each of these areas, depending on their position.

Paid wildlife rehabilitator positions can involve some or all of the following: feeding baby birds or mammals, assisting with fluid therapy and bandaging, supervising paid staff and/or volunteers, providing public presentations about animals and the environment, cleaning cages, maintaining databases on animals and/or members, fund-raising, capturing and transporting injured wild animals, and talking to concerned citizens who call with animal- and environmental-related situations.

Wildlife Rehabilitators often work with veterinarians to assess injuries and diagnose a variety of illnesses. They must be able to administer basic first aid and physical therapy. Because wild animals are very different from domestic animals, Wildlife Rehabilitators need extensive knowledge about the species in their care, including natural history, nutritional requirements, behavioral issues, and caging considerations. They also need to understand any dangers the animals may present. While many are generalists, some Wildlife Rehabilitators specialize in caring for specific animals or animal groups.

Fear of humans is a necessary survival trait for wild animals. While carrying out their work, Wildlife Rehabilitators make every effort to minimize human contact and prevent the taming of rehabilitation patients. This often is an elaborate and time-consuming process. Those animals who sustain injuries or illnesses that prevent them from living successfully in the wild are usually euthanized; they have their suffering ended in a humane fashion. Occasionally, animals that recover from their injuries but are not able to survive in the wild are placed in education facilities.

Wildlife rehabilitation is many things, but glamorous is not one of them. Jobs can be both repetitive and challenging. Some people may consider routine animal care boring. Others may get discouraged by callers who do not share their concern and respect for wildlife or who do not believe that their advice is the best for the animal. Wildlife Rehabilitators also deal with the death and suffering that is often encountered when rehabilitating wild animals. However, there also are many rewarding aspects of wildlife rehabilitation: helping animals, relieving suffering, working with others, helping people to regain a connection with nature, and the joy of releasing animals back into the wild.

A great many Wildlife Rehabilitators are independent; they work for themselves out of their homes or smaller facilities. However, others work at large wildlife rehabilitation centers, which are usually large enough to offer a variety of jobs covering the many aspects of wildlife rehabilitation. Positions at these larger facilities may require specific levels of wildlife or supervisory experience.

Wildlife Rehabilitators are often busiest during the warmer periods of the year, when interactions between humans and animals are most frequent. During the winter, it is common for them to catch up on paperwork, record keeping, and similar tasks. Work hours can be long and erratic, depending on the specific rehabilitation needs of animals. For example, baby birds must be fed every 15 to 30 minutes during daylight hours (14 hours a day).

Salaries

U.S. Wildlife Rehabilitators by law cannot charge a fee for animals brought to them, and this makes treating wildlife a nonprofit endeavor. Salaries for Wildlife Rehabilitators who work for nonprofit organizations vary considerably. For example, those providing full-time direct animal care may earn annual wages of approximately $13,000 to $15,000, while those in supervisory, education, or administrative rolls may earn salaries of $25,000 to $30,000 or more. Some internships pay small weekly stipends, plus housing.

Employment Prospects

Wildlife rehabilitation jobs are usually found in areas with high human populations. The larger wildlife rehabilitation centers are typically located near these areas due to the more frequent interactions between humans and wildlife. Employment opportunities exist within both the private and public sectors. Publicly funded jobs exist at various city, county, and state nature and environmental education facilities. Jobs in the private sector are usually with nonprofit foundations and organizations. Continuing residential and commercial development activities, which will increase the number of interactions between humans and animals, will support a growing demand for Wildlife Rehabilitators.

Advancement Prospects

After volunteering or completing a wildlife rehabilitation internship, many Wildlife Rehabilitators work independently in this profession. However, those who seek employment at wildlife rehabilitation centers may advance on a more traditional career ladder, holding supervisory or management positions. Finally, some Wildlife Rehabilitators become executive directors and use their skills in the areas of administration, public relations, and fund-raising.

Education and Training

Wildlife Rehabilitators learn on their own through internships, volunteer work, classes, seminars, conferences, books, journals, and networking with other experienced rehabilitators and professionals in related fields. Individuals must seek out the information needed to round out their own education and training by consulting interested wildlife rehabilitators, biologists, and veterinarians.

Although a college degree is not required to become a licensed Wildlife Rehabilitator, the National Wildlife Rehabilitators Association recommends that most rehabilitators earn a degree in biology or ecology. Curricula should include ornithology, mammalogy, animal behavior, ecology, and related wildlife and environmental subjects. A biology-related degree provides knowledge that is essential for quality hands-on animal care, develops an understanding of wildlife as they relate to humans and the environment, and gives Wildlife Rehabilitators an edge in this increasingly competitive field.

Within biology or animal ecology degree programs, several schools now offer areas of specialization in wildlife, wildlife care, and/or pre-veterinary medicine. Many schools offer classes related to wildlife rehabilitation such as wildlife management, behavior, ecology, field techniques, restraint, raptor physiology, and others. There are more than 60 colleges offering accredited veterinary technology or animal health technology programs in North America, as well as 27 veterinary schools. Many of these schools now offer specific courses or additional study opportunities in wildlife medicine.

Special Requirements

Wildlife Rehabilitators must be prepared to treat distressed wild animals and interact with the people who find them. In addition, they must be prepared to spend less time with their family and friends, experience animal suffering and death, and face the danger associated with handling wild animals.

Wildlife rehabilitation can be expensive. In addition to purchasing books, joining organizations, and attending training sessions, most rehabilitators pay for food, cages, medicines, transportation, liability insurance, and other things out of their own pockets. Most Wildlife Rehabilitators eventually form nonprofit corporations, which makes it easier to collect donations. Because nonprofit status involves complicated paperwork and accounting, the assistance of an attorney or accountant is often needed.

Almost all birds are protected by federal law; state laws protect most other kinds of wildlife. To work with mammals, reptiles, and amphibians, Wildlife Rehabilitators must be issued special permits from their state wildlife agencies. Before receiving their permits, they must meet various requirements such as specialized training, participation in mentorship programs, facility inspections, and written or oral exams. Rehabilitators who wish to care for birds must get permits from the U.S. Fish and Wildlife Service.

Experience, Special Skills, and Personality Traits

Successful Wildlife Rehabilitators are concerned about wildlife, people, and the environment. They are creative, resourceful, and realistic. In addition to possessing an initiative to learn and continue learning, Wildlife Rehabilitators are able to acknowledge their strengths and weaknesses. Employers may look for a person who is self-motivated, honest, well-spoken, a good listener, willing to work, cooperative, energetic, flexible, confident, responsible, positive, and pleasant.

Unions and Associations

Many Wildlife Rehabilitators are members of the National Wildlife Rehabilitators Association (NWRA), which is dedicated to improving and promoting the profession of wildlife rehabilitation and its contributions to preserving natural ecosystems. In addition to publishing a directory of members from around the world, the NWRA strives to provide the most correct and up-to-date information available through association publications. The association also sponsors an annual symposium.

Tips for Entry

1. Visit one or more wildlife rehabilitators or rehabilitation centers. Make an appointment and ask lots of questions.
2. Volunteer a few hours a week to see firsthand what wildlife rehabilitation is all about.
3. Read more about the profession. Several informative books are available from the NWRA by visiting http://www.nwrawildlife.org.
4. Join various organizations and networks for wildlife rehabilitators. A list is available from the NWRA.
5. Contact your state wildlife agency to find the office that governs wildlife rehabilitation activities and ask them to provide information on permit requirements, training, and rehabilitators in your area that you can contact.
6. Training opportunities are available all over the continent, including volunteer positions, paid and unpaid internships, and seasonal positions. The NWRA lists training opportunities on its Web site.

Information contained in this career profile was provided courtesy of the National Wildlife Rehabilitators Association.

WILDLIFE SCIENTIST

CAREER PROFILE

Duties: Plan and carry out experimental animal studies; collect and analyze data; estimate wildlife distributions; make determinations and recommendations about wildlife populations; make recommendations about habitat management to address wildlife concerns

Alternate Title(s): Conservation Resources Management Biologist, Environmental Specialist, Wildlife Biologist, Wildlife Manager, Zoologist

Salary Range: $31,258 to $81,200+

Employment Prospects: Fair

Advancement Prospects: Good

Prerequisites:

Education or Training—Bachelor's, master's, or doctorate degree in wildlife biology, ecology, wildlife management, conservation biology, zoology, or similar field

Experience—Fieldwork in wildlife science; familiarity with research fundamentals, electronics, computer modeling, digital mapping, data integration, and geographic information systems and global positioning satellites systems

Special Skills and Personality Traits—logical and analytical thinking, computer, communication, problem-solving, and stress management skills; detail-oriented, careful, thorough, self-reliant, patient, adaptable, flexible

Special Requirements—Certified Wildlife Biologist certification may be required

CAREER LADDER

```
┌─────────────────────────────────────────┐
│  Senior Scientist or Senior Researcher   │
└─────────────────────────────────────────┘

┌─────────────────────────────────────────┐
│                 Manager                   │
└─────────────────────────────────────────┘

┌─────────────────────────────────────────┐
│             Staff Scientist               │
└─────────────────────────────────────────┘

┌─────────────────────────────────────────┐
│            Research Assistant             │
└─────────────────────────────────────────┘
```

Position Description

Wildlife Scientists study the behavior, origins, life processes, genetics, and diseases of wildlife and animals, according to the U.S. Department of Labor's *Occupational Outlook Handbook*. Generally speaking, scientists who work in this particular field may focus on working with live animals in either natural or controlled environments, or the dissection and study of dead animals. They often are engaged in the monitoring of a particular species or working with a specific natural "zone" or habitat.

Wildlife Scientists commonly fall within one of two classifications: wildlife biologists or zoologists. According to the Wildlife Society, "a professional wildlife biologist is a person with demonstrated expertise in the art and science of applying the principles of ecology to the sound stewardship and management of the wildlife resource and its environment." By comparison, zoologists specialize in a particular grouping of animal life. For example, ichthyologists study fish, mammalogists study mammals, herpetologists study reptiles, and ornithologists study birds.

Wildlife Scientists are involved in a wide range of activities related to wildlife management and research. One of their primary job functions is to plan and carry out experimental animal studies, either in controlled settings or natural habitats. Wildlife Scientists also collect and analyze data that may be used to classify different animal groups; estimate wildlife distributions and populations; understand the characteristics of wildlife; gain insight into animal behavior; and document the origin, evolution, and history of particular species or ecological niches.

In addition to performing these fundamental scientific tasks, Wildlife Scientists use what they learn to make important determinations and recommendations as planners or consultants. They may provide professional opinions regarding the impact that commercial, industrial, or residential developments will have on wildlife and wildlife habitats. They also may assess the impact that man already is having on wildlife populations and suggest changes to protect animals from harm. For declining or rare species, they identify habitat needs and management priorities based upon research.

Wildlife Scientists often are involved in wildlife population planning and the coordination of programs to control disease outbreaks. Scientists who are employed by wildlife parks and zoos may help zoo management to care for and control resident animals, and provide advisement regarding habitat maintenance and overall facilities management. State and federal employees use their population estimates and previous harvest data to set bag limits or harvest quotas during hunting and fishing seasons. This determines how many of a species can be taken in an area during a season or per day.

As with other scientific professions, Wildlife Scientists are required to share their findings through written reports, scientific papers, and professional presentations. They also may conduct training seminars and give public presentations for clubs, schools, special interest groups, park programs, and businesses. Those with management or administrative responsibilities may be involved with public relations, fundraising, and budgeting. Because many scientific jobs depend on private, state, or federal funds to support research programs, Wildlife Scientists frequently write grant proposals to fund their work. In some cases, such proposals are difficult to write and have very specific requirements.

Wildlife Scientists find employment in a variety of settings. Many work within the government sector. In fact, the U.S Department of Labor reveals that local, state, and federal governments employed half of all biological scientists in 2002. At the state level, common employers include resource protection authorities, forest services, and natural resource conservation boards. At the federal level, opportunities exist with the Bureau of Land Management, Environmental Protection Agency, Natural Resources Conservation Service, U.S. Geological Survey, National Park Service, Fish and Wildlife Service, and the Food and Drug Administration.

Wildlife Scientists also work in the private sector for environmental consulting firms, foundations, independent research laboratories, biotechnology firms, pharmaceutical companies, and companies that produce pesticides and agricultural products. They also work for aquariums, theme parks, museums, and zoos. Finally, some Wildlife Scientists devote their careers to training others at secondary schools, technical schools, junior and community colleges, and four-year colleges and universities.

Wildlife Scientists have many different types of work environments from which to choose. These range from office and laboratory settings to outdoor environments and classrooms. Many Wildlife Scientists divide their time between fieldwork and an office or lab, while some may work exclusively in a particular setting. Therefore, working conditions and hours vary depending on the job.

For those who are engaged in fieldwork, long travel times to remote or foreign locations may be involved. Scientists may be required to work unusual hours, because they are at the mercy of the animal populations being studied. They also may be subject to extreme temperatures and forced to live in primitive conditions. Because fieldwork can be physically demanding, requiring scientists to stand frequently, bend, and walk long distances, good physical condition may be a job requirement.

Salaries
According to the 2006–07 edition of the U.S. Department of Labor's *Occupational Outlook Handbook*, in mid-2004 annual salaries for zoologists and wildlife biologists ranged from $31,450 to more than $81,200, with a median of $50,330. Data from the National Association of Colleges and Employers put average annual starting salaries for those with bachelor's degrees in biological and life sciences at $31,258 in mid-2005.

Employment Prospects
Approximately 15,000 zoologists and wildlife biologists were employed in 2002, according to the U.S. Department of Labor. Slower than average job growth is projected through 2012, with a projected need for about 6,000 workers.

Advancement Prospects
Wildlife Scientists often begin their careers as lab technicians, research assistants, high school instructors, or as sales or service representatives. Those with master's degrees qualify for basic research positions, serve as staff scientists, or pursue administrative and management roles. After gaining seven to 10 years of work experience and assuming greater levels of responsibility, Wildlife Scientists with advanced education may pursue jobs as senior scientists or senior researchers. Some scientists also choose to teach wildlife science at the college or university level.

Education and Training
While some entry-level positions may be obtained with an undergraduate degree in wildlife biology, ecology, wildlife

management, conservation biology, zoology, or a similar field, most wildlife science positions require a master's degree. For those without a master's degree, it may be necessary to work several seasonal positions before securing full-time employment. Master's degrees are commonly offered at larger universities and colleges. Students can sometimes enter the field with a degree in botany if they take additional coursework in animal and life sciences. Master's degrees are essential for research positions, and doctorate degrees are required for those who wish to pursue a teaching career at the university level or an independent or advanced-level research position.

Special Requirements

Special state certifications or licenses are normally not required for Wildlife Scientists. However, the Wildlife Society offers professional certification for wildlife biologists who are able to demonstrate their expertise and meet certain standards in the areas of education, experience, and ethics. The society's Certified Wildlife Biologist certification program is available to member scientists, as well as nonmembers and the public. Because of the strenuous nature of positions that require fieldwork, some employers require candidates to take physical examinations.

Experience, Special Skills, and Personality Traits

Wildlife Scientists are required to be familiar with research fundamentals. They must be detail-oriented, with the ability to perform tasks in a careful and thorough manner. They also must be logical and analytical thinkers, with excellent problem-solving abilities. Due to the many variables involved in scientific work and the length of research projects, the ability to be patient, adaptable, and flexible also is critical for professionals in this field. A background in statistics can be particularly useful.

Because projects may put Wildlife Scientists in dangerous situations with wild animals, self-control and a calm disposition are important, as well as stress-management abilities.

Wildlife Scientists must be self-reliant and capable of working independently at remote sites, and also on teams that involve communication with other scientists, the public, and government officials.

Report writing and presentations are important aspects of this profession. Therefore, strong written and oral communication skills are required, along with proficiency in statistics. In addition to scientific knowledge, Wildlife Scientists in management roles must be familiar with the political process, laws, and regulations, as well as principles of business and management.

Basic computer experience is required for word processing and developing presentations. In addition, Wildlife Scientists may be required to work with sensors and computer chips, and perform computer modeling, digital mapping, and data integration activities. Therefore, experience with electronics, geographic information systems (GIS), and global positioning systems (GPS) may be helpful or required.

Unions and Associations

Wildlife Scientists may belong to a number of different nonprofit, scientific, or cause-related professional organizations. These include the Wildlife Society, the Ecological Society of America, and the Nature Conservancy.

Tips for Entry

1. In high school, take courses that provide exposure to the biological sciences, including zoology, as well as courses in mathematics, chemistry, physics, and English.
2. Make sure that your personal goals, talents, and lifestyle requirements dovetail with the requirements to become a Wildlife Scientist.
3. Explore the different settings in which Wildlife Scientists work to identify career paths that interest you the most.
4. Shadow a Wildlife Scientist on the job to discover what their work is really like.
5. As a high school student and college undergraduate, participate in summer internships and research programs to gain research experience and meet other scientists.
6. During your junior and senior years of college, get involved with undergraduate research programs.

APPENDIXES

I. Education and Training Resources

II. Professional Associations

III. Professional Certifications

IV. Government Agencies

V. Internet Resources

VI. National Forests

VII. National Parks

VIII. State Environmental Resources

APPENDIX I
EDUCATION AND TRAINING RESOURCES

This appendix contains helpful listings of education and training programs for some of the jobs and job categories profiled in this book. Listings are organized by state within each job category.

ECOTOURISM

BUSINESS AND MANAGEMENT

CALIFORNIA

New College of California
Green MBA
99 Sixth Street
Santa Rosa, CA 95401
Phone: (707) 523-9034
Fax: (707) 568-0114
http://www.greenmba.com

FLORIDA

Florida Atlantic University
Environmental Management MBA
   Program
P.O. Box 3091
Boca Raton, FL 33431-0991
Phone: (561) 297-0052
Fax: (561) 297-2675
http://www.fau.edu/enviro-mba/

MARYLAND

University of Maryland, University
   College
Environmental Management
3501 University Boulevard
Adelphia, MD 20783
Phone: (301) 985-4617
Fax: (301) 985-7544
http://www.umuc.edu/mkting/env2.html

NEW YORK

Rensselaer Polytechnic Institute
MBA with Environmental Management
   Concentration
RPI—Lally School of Management &
   Technology
110 8th Street—Pittsburgh Building
Troy, NY 12180-3590
Phone: (518) 276-6565

Fax: (518) 276-2665
http://lallyschool.rpi.edu/

OKLAHOMA

Northeastern State University
Environmental Management
600 North Grand
Tahlequah, OK 74464
Phone: (918) 456-5511
http://arapaho.nsuok.edu/%7Eindustry/

PENNSYLVANIA

University of Pennsylvania
The Wharton School, Environmental
   Management Program
1030 Steinberg Hall-Dietrich Hall 3620
   Locust Walk
Philadelphia, PA 19104
Phone: (215) 898-5000
Fax: (215) 898-1883
http://lgst.wharton.upenn.edu/
   Environment/

RHODE ISLAND

Roger Williams University
Environmental Management Certificate
   Program
150 Washington Street
Providence, RI 02903
Phone: (401) 276-4800
Fax: (401) 276-4848
http://www.rwuonline.cc/programs/uvc/
   opencollege/cert.html

TENNESSEE

Vanderbilt University
Center for Environmental Management
   Studies
401 21st Avenue South
Nashville, TN 37203
Phone: (615) 322-8004

Fax: (615) 343-7177
http://www.vanderbilt.edu/vcems

TEXAS

Hardin-Simmons University
Environmental Management Program
2200 Hickory
Box 16210
Abilene, TX 79698-6210
Phone: (888) 478-1222
http://www.hsutx.edu/academics/eman/
   eman1.html

VIRGINIA

George Mason University
Environmental Management Programs
4400 University Drive
Fairfax, VA 22030-4444
Phone: (703) 993-1050
Fax: (703) 993-1066
http://www.gmu.edu/departments/Biology/
   environmental_management.htm

HOSPITALITY MANAGEMENT

VERMONT

Green Mountain College
Hospitality Management Program
One College Circle
Poultney, VT 05764
Phone: (802) 287-8000
http://www.greenmtn.edu

PLANNING

CALIFORNIA

Art Center College of Design
Environmental Design Program
1700 Lida Street
Pasadena, CA 91103

Phone: (626) 396-2373
http://www.artcenter.edu/accd/programs/
    undergraduate/environmental.jsp

San Francisco Institute of Architecture
Ecological Design Programs
P.O. Box 2590
Alameda, CA 94501
Phone: (510) 523-5174
Fax: (510) 529-5175
http://www.sfia.net/EcoDes.asp

Sonoma State University
Department of Environmental Studies
    and Planning
1801 East Cotati Avenue
Rohnert Park, CA 94928
Phone: (707) 664-2306
Fax: (707) 664-4202
http://www.sonoma.edu/ENSP/

GEORGIA

University of Georgia
College of Environment & Design
609 Caldwell Hall
Athens, GA 30602-1845
Phone: (706) 542-1816
Fax: (706) 542-4485
http://www.ced.uga.edu

KANSAS

Kansas State University
Environmental Design Studies Program
Manhattan, KS 66506-5506
Phone: (785) 532-5047
Fax: (785) 532-6722
http://aalto.arch.ksu.edu/

ENVIRONMENTAL ENGINEERING

ALASKA

University of Alaska, Anchorage
Environmental Quality Engineering &
    Science Programs
3211 Providence Drive, ENGR 201
Anchorage, AK 99508
Phone: (907) 786-1900
Fax: (907) 786-1079
http://www.engr.uaa.alaska.edu/soe/
    AcadProgs/EQE/EQEIntro.htm

University of Alaska, Fairbanks
Environmental Engineering &
    Environmental Quality Science

NEW YORK

Cornell University
Department of Design and Environmental
    Analysis
E104 MVR Hall
Ithaca, NY 14853
Phone: (607) 255-1954
Fax: (607) 255-0305
http://www.human.cornell.edu/dea/index.
    cfm

New York University
Wagner Graduate School
Urban Planning Program
Environmental Management Focus
4 Washington Square North
New York, NY 10003-6671
Phone: (212) 998-7400
http://www.nyu.edu/wagner/urban.planning/

NORTH CAROLINA

Appalachian State University
Department of Geography and Planning
Boone, NC 28608
Phone: (828) 262-3000
Fax: (828) 262-3067
http://www.geo.appstate.edu/

North Carolina A & T State University
Department of Natural Resources &
    Environmental Design
Carver Hall
Greensboro, NC 27411
Phone: (336) 334-7543
Fax: (336) 334-7844
http://www.ag.ncat.edu/academics/natres/
    index.html

ENGINEERING

P.O. Box 755900
Fairbanks, AK 99775-5590
Phone: (907) 474-7241
Fax: (907) 474-6087
http://www.uaf.edu/civileng/enveng/
    index.html

ARIZONA

Northern Arizona University
Environmental Engineering Program
P.O. Box 15600
Building #22 Beaver Street
Flagstaff, AZ 86011
Phone: (928) 523-5251
Fax: (928) 523-2300
http://www.cet.nau.edu/Academic/
    EnvEng/esources

OHIO

Kent State University
Environmental Design Program
Kent, OH 44242
Phone: (330) 672-2444
http://www.saed.kent.edu/SAED/

OREGON

University of Oregon
Department of Planning Public
    Policy & Management
119 Hendricks Hall
1209 University of Oregon
Eugene, OR 97403-1209
Phone: (541) 346-3635
Fax: (541) 346-2040
http://utopia.uoregon.edu/

VIRGINIA

**Virginia Polytechnic Institute
    and State University**
Urban Affairs and Planning
201 Architecture Annex
Blacksburg, VA 24060
Phone: (540) 231-5485
Fax: (540) 231-3367
http://www.uap.vt.edu/

WASHINGTON

Washington State University
Environmental Science & Regional
    Planning
P.O. Box 644430
Pullman, WA 99164-4430
Phone: (509) 335-8538
http://www.esrp.wsu.edu

University of Arizona
Mining and Geological Engineering
    Department
1235 East North Campus Drive, Mines 229
P.O. Box 210012
Tucson, AZ 85721
Phone: (520) 621-6063
Fax: (520) 621-8330
http://www.mge.arizona.edu/

CALIFORNIA

California Institute of Technology
Department of Environmental Science
    and Engineering
M/C 150-21
1200 East California Boulevard
Pasadena, CA 91125-7800

Phone: (626) 395-2447
Fax: (626) 585-1917
http://www.ese.caltech.edu

Stanford University
Department of Civil and Environmental
    Engineering
M42 Terman Engineering Center
Stanford, CA 94305-4020
Phone: (650) 723-3074
http://www-ce.stanford.edu/

University of California, Davis
Civil and Environmental Engineering
116 Everson Hall
One Shields Avenue
Davis, CA 95616
Phone: (530) 752-1441
Fax: (530) 752-7872
http://cee.engr.ucdavis.edu/student/
    Prospective/graduate/env.htm

University of California, San Diego
Environmental Engineering Program
9500 Gilman Drive
La Jolla, CA 92093
Phone: (858) 534-0114
http://www.jacobsschool.ucsd.edu/
    students/prospective_undergrads/
    degree_programs/environmental_
    engineering.shtml

COLORADO

Colorado School of Mines
Division of Environmental Science
    and Engineering
1500 Illinois Street
Golden, CO 80401
Phone: (303) 273-3467
http://www.mines.edu/Academic/envsci/

University of Colorado, Boulder
Environmental Engineering Program
428 UCB
Boulder, CO 80309-0428
Phone: (303) 735-0253
http://www.colorado.edu/engineering/
    EnvEng/index.htm

CONNECTICUT

University of New Haven
Department of Civil & Environmental
    Engineering
300 Orange Avenue
West Haven, CT 06516

Phone: (203) 932-7159
Fax: (203) 932-7158
http://www.newhaven.edu/seas/ce/index.
    htm

DISTRICT OF COLUMBIA

Catholic University of America
Environmental Engineering and
    Management
620 Michigan Avenue
Washington, DC 20064-0001
Phone: (202) 319-5163
Fax: (202) 319-6677
http://engineering.cua.edu/civil/
    generalinfo/

FLORIDA

Florida A&M University
Engineering, Technology and Agriculture
Perry-Paige Building
Room 217 South
Tallahassee, FL 32307
Phone: (850) 561-2644
http://www.famu.edu/acad/colleges/cesta/

Florida International University
College of Engineering and Computing
10555 West Flagler Street, EC 2460
Miami, FL 33174
Phone: (305) 348-2522
Fax: (305) 348-6142
http://www.eng.fiu.edu

University of Central Florida
Environmental Engineering Program
P.O. Box 162450
Orlando, FL 32816-2450
Phone: (407) 823-2814
Fax: (407) 823-3315
http://www.cee.ucf.edu/

University of Florida
Department of Environmental
    Engineering Sciences
Academic Office
216 Black Hall, P.O. Box 116450
Gainesville, FL 32611-6450
Phone: (352) 392-0841
Fax: (352) 392-3076
http://www.ees.ufl.edu

GEORGIA

Georgia Institute of Technology
School of Civil and Environmental
    Engineering

790 Atlantic Drive
Atlanta, GA 30332-0355
Phone: (404) 894-2201
Fax: (404) 894-2278
http://www.ce.gatech.edu/

INDIANA

Rose-Hulman Institute of Technology
MS Environmental Engineering
5500 Wabash Avenue
Terre Haute, IN 47803
Phone: (812) 877-1511
http://www.rose-hulman.edu/ce/
    enviro-curriculum.htm

MARYLAND

Johns Hopkins University
Department of Geography and
    Environmental Engineering
313 Ames Hall
3400 North Charles Street
Baltimore, MD 21218-2686
Phone: (410) 516-7092
Fax: (410) 516-8996
http://www.jhu.edu/~dogee/

MASSACHUSETTS

**Massachusetts Institute of Technology
    (MIT)**
Department of Civil and Environmental
    Engineering
77 Massachusetts Avenue
Room 1-290
Cambridge, MA 02139-4307
Phone: (617) 253-7101
http://web.mit.edu/civenv/

Northeastern University
Department of Civil and Environmental
    Engineering
130 Snell Engineering Center
360 Huntington Avenue
Boston, MA 02115
Phone: (617) 373-2445
Fax: (617) 373-4419
http://www.coe.neu.edu/Depts/CIV/
    civil/

University of Massachusetts, Amherst
Department of Civil and Environmental
    Engineering
Box 5-3205 Marston Hall
Amherst, MA 01003
Phone: (413) 545-2508

Fax: (413) 545-2840
http://www.ecs.umass.edu/cee/

University of Massachusetts, Lowell
Energy Engineering Program
One University Avenue
Lowell, MA 01854
Phone: (978) 934-2950
Fax: (978) 934-3048
http://m-5.uml.edu/energy.htm

University of Massachusetts, Lowell
Graduate Program in Environmental
  Studies
Department of Civil & Environmental
  Engineering
108 Falmouth Hall
One University Place
Lowell, MA 01854
Phone: (978) 934-2280
Fax: (978) 934-3052
http://civil.caeds.eng.uml.edu/

MICHIGAN

Michigan State University
Department of Civil and Environmental
  Engineering
3546 Engineering Building
East Lansing, MI 48824-1226
Phone: (517) 355-5107
Fax: (517) 432-1827
http://www.egr.msu.edu/cee/

University of Michigan
Environmental and Water Resources
  Engineering Program
Department of Civil & Environmental
  Engineering
2350 Hayward, 2340 G.G.
  Brown Building
Ann Arbor, MI 48109-2125
Phone: (734) 764-8495
Fax: (734) 764-4292
http://www.engin.umich.edu/dept/cee/
  program/ewre/overview.htm

MISSOURI

Washington University
Environmental Engineering Science
  Program
School of Engineering and Applied
  Science
One Brookings Drive, Campus Box 1180
Saint Louis, MO 63130-9989
Phone: (314) 935-5548
Fax: (314) 935-5464
http://www.env.wustl.edu

NEBRASKA

University of Nebraska, Lincoln
Graduate Program in Environmental
  Engineering
W348 NH
Lincoln, NE 68588-0531
Phone: (402) 472-5020
Fax: (402) 472-8934
http://bse.unl.edu/Grad/EnvEng.htm

NEW MEXICO

**New Mexico Institute of Mining &
  Technology**
Environmental Engineering Department
801 Leroy Place
Socorro, NM 87801
Phone: (505) 835-5467
Fax: (505) 835-5509
http://www.nmt.edu/~enve/

NEW YORK

Cornell University
School of Civil and Environmental
  Engineering
219 Hollister Hall
Ithaca, NY 14853-3501
Phone: (607) 255-7560
http://www.cee.cornell.edu/

Hofstra University
Environmental Engineering Program
104 Weed Hall
Hempstead, NY 11549-1330
Phone: (516) 463-6672
Fax: (516) 463-4939
http://www.hofstra.edu/Academics/
  HCLAS/Engineering/egg_envr_dsc.cfm

Manhattan College
Environmental Engineering Discipline
Manhattan College Parkway
Riverdale, NY 10471
Phone: (718) 862-7205
http://www.manhattan.edu/catalog/
  engineer.html

NORTH CAROLINA

Louisburg College
Environmental Engineering Program
501 North Main Street
Louisburg, NC 27549
Phone: (919) 497-3240
http://www.louisburg.edu/academics/
  premajors/engineering.htm

OHIO

University of Cincinnati
Civil and Environmental Engineering
P.O. Box 210071
Cincinnati, OH 45221-0071
Phone: (513) 556-3648
Fax: (513) 556-2599
http://www.cee.uc.edu/

Youngstown State University
Civil and Environmental Engineering
  Department
3001 Jones Hall
Youngstown, OH 44503-9955
Phone: (330) 742-3027
Fax: (330) 742-1580
http://www.eng.ysu.edu/~jalam/civil/

OKLAHOMA

University of Oklahoma
School of Civil Engineering &
  Environmental Science
Carson Engineering Center
202 West Boyd, Room 334
Norman, OK 73019-0631
Phone: (405) 325-5911
Fax: (405) 325-4217
http://www.cees.ou.edu/

OREGON

Oregon Graduate Institute
Environmental Science & Engineering
  Program
20000 Northwest Walker Road
Beaverton, OR 97006-8921
Phone: (503) 748-1196
Fax: (503) 748-1273
http://www.ese.ogi.edu/

Oregon State University
Civil, Construction and Environmental
  Engineering
202 Apperson Hall
Corvallis, OR 97331-2302
Phone: (514) 737-6149
Fax: (541) 737-3052
http://ccee.oregonstate.edu/

PENNSYLVANIA

Carnegie Mellon University
Department of Civil & Environmental
  Engineering
5000 Forbes Avenue
Pittsburgh, PA 15213-3890
Phone: (412) 268-2940

Fax: (412) 268-7813
http://www.ce.cmu.edu/

Drexel University
Department of Civil, Architectural
    and Environmental Engineering
3141 Chestnut Street
Curtis Hall 251
Philadelphia, PA 19104
Phone: (215) 895-2283
Fax: (215) 895-1363
http://www.cae.drexel.edu/

Gannon University
Department of Environmental Science
    and Engineering
University Square
Erie, PA 16541-0001
Phone: (814) 871-7240
http://www.gannon.edu/resource/dept/
    enviro/

Lafayette College
Department of Environmental and Civil
    Engineering
319 Acopian Engineering Center
Easton, PA 18042
Phone: (610) 330-5437
Fax: (610) 330-5059
http://ww2.lafayette.edu/~ce-enve/home.htm

Lehigh University
Environmental Engineering Program
13 East Packer Avenue
Fritz Engineering Laboratory

Bethlehem, PA 18015
Phone: (610) 758-3566
Fax: (610) 758-6405
http://www.lehigh.edu/~inenviro/inenviro.
    html#faculty

Penn State Harrisburg
Environmental Engineering Program
Science & Technology Building TL177
777 West Harrisburg Pike
Middletown, PA 17057-4898
Phone: (717) 948-6358
Fax: (717) 948-6580
http://www.hbg.psu.edu/envprog/

Villanova University
Department of Civil and Environmental
    Engineering
800 Lancaster Avenue
Villanova, PA 19085-1681
Phone: (610) 519-4960
Fax: (610) 519-6754
http://www.engineering.villanova.edu/
    academics/ce/index.htm

SOUTH DAKOTA

**South Dakota School of Mines and
    Technology**
Civil and Environmental Engineering
    Department
501 East Saint Joseph Street
Rapid City, SD 57701-3995
Phone: (605) 394-2438
Fax: (605) 394-5171

http://www.hpcnet.org/cgi-bin/global/
    a_bus_card.cgi?SiteID=51209

TEXAS

Rice University
Department of Civil & Environmental
    Engineering
MS-318
P.O. Box 1892
Houston, TX 77251
Phone: (713) 348-4949
Fax: (713) 348-5268
http://www.ruf.rice.edu/~ceedept/

University of Texas, Arlington
Environmental Science and Engineering
    Program
Box 19308
Arlington, TX 76019-0498
Phone: (817) 272-2405
Fax: (817) 272-2855
http://www.uta.edu/ese/

WISCONSIN

Marquette University
Department of Civil & Environmental
    Engineering
P.O. Box 1881
Milwaukee, WI 53201
Phone: (800) 222-6544
Fax: (414) 288-7302
http://www.eng.mu.edu/~ceen/

ENVIRONMENTAL TECHNOLOGY

ARIZONA

Arizona State University
Environmental Technology Management
    Program
7001 East Williams Field Road,
    Technology Center
Mesa, AZ 85212
Phone: (480) 727-1499
Fax: (480) 727-1684
http://etmonline.asu.edu/

CALIFORNIA

Hartnell College
Environmental Technology
156 Homestead Avenue
Salinas, CA 93901
Phone: (813) 755-6700

http://www.hartnell.cc.ca.us/academics/
    degrees/env.html

CONNECTICUT

Briarwood College
Environmental Technology Program
2279 Mount Vernon Road
Southington, CT 06489
Phone: (800) 952-2444
Fax: (860) 628-6444
http://www.briarwood.edu/programs/
    catalog/associate/details.asp?ID=18

MINNESOTA

Carleton College
Environmental and Technology Studies
    Program

One North College Street
Northfield, MN 55057
Phone: (800) 447-8688
http://www.carleton.edu/curricular/
    ENTS/

Vermilion Community College
Natural Resource Technology
1900 East Camp Street
Ely, MN 55731
Phone: (800) 657-3608
Fax: (218) 365-7218
http://www.vcc.mnscu.edu

MISSISSIPPI

Jackson State University
School of Science and Technology
P.O. Box 18750

Jackson, MS 39217-1050
Phone: (601) 979-2153
Fax: (601) 979-2058
http://www.jsums.edu/%7Esst/index2.htm

TENNESSEE

Middle Tennessee State University
Department of Environmental Science &
    Technology
P.O. Box 19

Murfreesboro, TN 37132
Phone: (615) 898-2113
http://www.mtsu.edu/%7Eest

UTAH

Utah Valley State College
Environmental Technology Department
800 West University Parkway
Orem, UT 84058-5999
Phone: (801) 863-8679

Fax: (801) 863-7077
http://www.uvsc.edu/envt/

WEST VIRGINIA

Marshall University
Environmental Science and Safety
    Technology Division
Huntington, WV 25755
http://www.marshall.edu/cite/academics/
    DivESandST.htm

FARMING AND FISHING

AGRICULTURE

ALABAMA

Alabama A & M University
School of Agriculture and Environmental
    Science
4900 Meridian Street
Normal, AL 35762
Phone: (256) 372-5783
Fax: (256) 372-5906
http://saes.aamu.edu

ALASKA

University of Alaska, Fairbanks
School of Natural Resources and
    Agricultural Sciences
P.O. Box 757140
Fairbanks, AK 99775
Phone: (907) 474-5550
Fax: (907) 474-6184
http://www.uaf.edu/snras/

ARIZONA

Central Arizona College
Agricultural Science Program
Signal Peak Campus
Paul Pearce Center for Technology Studies
8470 North Overfield Road
Coolidge, AZ 85228
Phone: (520) 426-4326
Fax: (520) 426-4580
http://www.cac.cc.az.us/ag/

ARKANSAS

Arkansas State University
College of Agriculture
P.O. Box 1080
State University, AR 72467
Phone: (870) 972-2085
http://www.agri.astate.edu/

North Arkansas College
Agriculture Program
1515 Pioneer Drive
Harrison, AR 72601
Phone: (870) 391-3343
Fax: (870) 391-3250
http://www.northark.edu/users/
    Agriculture/Index.htm

University of Arkansas, Pine Bluff
School of Agriculture, Fisheries &
    Human Sciences
1200 North University Drive
Mail Slot 4990
Pine Bluff, AR 71601
Phone: (870) 575-8529
http://www.uapb.edu/safhs/

CALIFORNIA

California State University, Chico
College of Agriculture
400 West First Street
Chico, CA 95929-0310
Phone: (530) 898-5844
Fax: (530) 898-5845
http://www.csuchicoag.org/

University of California, Davis
College of Agricultural & Environmental
    Sciences
CA&ES Dean's Office
One Shields Avenue
Davis, CA 95616-8571
Phone: (530) 752-0108
Fax: (530) 752-9049
http://caes.ucdavis.edu/Default.htm

University of California, Riverside
College of Natural and Agricultural
    Sciences
300 College Building North
Riverside, CA 92521-0127
Phone: (909) 787-4799

Fax: (909) 787-4190
http://cnas.ucr.edu/

COLORADO

Fort Lewis College
Agriculture Department
1000 Rim Drive
Durango, CO 81301-3999
Phone: (970) 247-7446
http://www.fortlewis.edu/academics/
    school_arts_sciences/agriculture/
    index.htm

DELAWARE

Delaware State University
Department of Agriculture and Natural
    Resources
1200 North DuPont Highway
Dover, DE 19901
Phone: (302) 857-6290
http://www.dsc.edu/schools/Agriculture/
    deptofagri.html

GEORGIA

Fort Valley State University
College of Agriculture
State University Drive
Fort Valley, GA 31030
Phone: (478) 825-6344
http://souari.forest.net/~fvsu/Colleges/
    COAg_HE_Allied_Programs_index.
    htm

IOWA

Iowa State University
College of Agriculture
Ames, IA 50011-1010
Phone: (515) 294-2518
http://www.ag.iastate.edu/

KANSAS

Fort Hays State University
Agriculture Department
600 Park Street
Hays, KS 67601-4099
Phone: (785) 628-4196
Fax: (785) 628-4183
http://www.fhsu.edu/agriculture/

Kansas State University
College of Agriculture
117 Waters Hall
Manhattan, KS 66506
Phone: (785) 532-6151
Fax: (785) 532-6897
http://www.ag.ksu.edu/

McPherson College
Agriculture Program
1600 East Euclid
P.O. Box 1402
McPherson, KS 67460
Phone: (800) 365-7402
http://www2.mcpherson.edu/academics/
agriculture/index.asp

KENTUCKY

**Berea College, Agriculture and
Natural Resources**
Berea, KY 40404
Phone: (859) 985-3590
http://www.berea.edu/ANR/

LOUISIANA

Louisiana State University
College of Agriculture
Baton Rouge, LA 70803-6200
Phone: (225) 578-2065
Fax: (225) 578-2526
http://www.coa.lsu.edu/

McNeese State University
Agricultural Sciences Department
4205 Ryan Street
Lake Charles, LA 70609
Phone: (337) 475-5000
http://www.mcneese.edu/colleges/sci/
deptag/index.asp

Nicholls State University
Agriculture Program
6 Family and Consumer Sciences
Building
Thibodaux, LA 70310
Phone: (504) 448-4691
Fax: (504) 449-7087
http://www.nicholls.edu/ag/

**Northeast Louisiana University
at Monroe**
Department of Agriculture
CNSB 310
Monroe, LA 71209-0510
Phone: (318) 342-1766
Fax: (318) 342-1779
http://www.ulm.edu/agriculture/
AGRIBUSINESSHOME.html

MISSISSIPPI

Alcorn State University
School of Agriculture, Research,
Extension, and Applied Sciences
1000 ASU Drive 690
Room 517
Alcorn State, MS 39096-7500
Phone: (601) 877-6137
Fax: (601) 877-6219
http://www.alcorn.edu/academic/academ/
ags.htm

MISSOURI

Northwest Missouri State University
Department of Agriculture
800 University Drive
Maryville, MO 64468-6001
Phone: (660) 562-1155
http://www.nwmissouri.edu/academics/ag/

MONTANA

Montana State University
College of Agriculture
P.O. Box 172860
Bozeman, MT 59717
Phone: (406) 994-5744
Fax: (406) 994-6579
http://ag.montana.edu/

NEBRASKA

University of Nebraska, Lincoln
College of Agriculture and Natural
Resources
103 Ag Hall
Lincoln, NE 68583-0702
Phone: (402) 472-2201
http://casnr.unl.edu/index.htm

NEW YORK

Cornell University
College of Agriculture and Life Sciences
177 Roberts Hall
Cornell University
Ithaca, NY 14853

Phone: (607) 255-2036
http://www.cals.cornell.edu/

**State University of New York (SUNY),
Alfred**
Agriculture and Horticulture Programs
10 Upper College Drive
Alfred, NY 14802
Phone: (800) 425-3733
http://www.alfredtech.edu/academics/
ag_programs.html

**State University of New York (SUNY),
Cobleskill**
Agriculture & Natural Resources Division
Curtis Mott 100
Cobleskill, NY 12043
Phone: (518) 255-5323
http://www.cobleskill.edu/Academic/AG/

**State University of New York (SUNY),
Morrisville**
College of Agriculture & Technology
Brooks Hall
Morrisville, NY 13408
Phone: (315) 684-6046
http://www.morrisville.edu/academics/
ag_natural%20resources/

NORTH CAROLINA

North Carolina A & T State University
School of Agriculture & Environmental
Sciences
1601 East Market Street
Greensboro, NC 27411
Phone: (336) 334-7979
http://www.ag.ncat.edu/

North Carolina State University
College of Agriculture & Life Sciences
115 Patterson Hall
Box 7642
Raleigh, NC 27695-7642
Phone: (919) 515-2614
Fax: (919) 515-1965
http://www.cals.ncsu.edu/

NORTH DAKOTA

Dickinson State University
Agricultural and Technical Studies
291 Campus Drive
Dickinson, ND 58601
Phone: (800) 279-4295
http://www.dickinsonstate.com/d_ag_
tech.asp

Williston State College
Agriculture Program
P.O. Box 1326

Williston, ND 58801
Phone: (701) 774-4269
http://www.wsc.nodak.edu/WSCFact
    Sheets_/011703/Agriculture.pdf

OKLAHOMA

Cameron University
Department of Agriculture
2800 West Gore Boulevard
Lawton, OK 73505
Phone: (580) 581-2275
Fax: (580) 581-2880
http://www.cameron.edu/academic/
    science/agriculture/index.html

Langston University
Agriculture Program
Langston, OK 73050
Phone: (405) 466-2231
http://www.lunet.edu/agric.html

**Northwestern Oklahoma State
    University**
Department of Agriculture
709 Oklahoma Boulevard
Alva, OK 73717
Phone: (580) 327-8503
Fax: (580) 327-8502
http://www.nwosu.edu/bea/Agriculture/
    index.html/

OREGON

Eastern Oregon State College
Agriculture Program
One University Boulevard
Zabel Room, No. 204
La Grande, OR 97850-2899
Phone: (541) 962-3612
http://www3.eou.edu/osuag/

SOUTH CAROLINA

Clemson University
College of Agriculture, Forestry and
    Life Sciences
101 Barre Hall
Clemson, SC 29634-0303
Phone: (864) 656-3013
Fax: (864) 656-1286
http://virtual.clemson.edu/groups/CAFLS/

TENNESSEE

Austin Peay State University
Agriculture Department
Sundquist Science Complex, Room D232

P O Box 4607
Clarksville, TN 37044
Phone: (931) 221-7272
Fax: (931) 221-6385http://www.apsu.
    edu/agriculture

Middle Tennessee State University
School of Agribusiness & Agriscience
Murfreesboro, TN 37132
Phone: (615) 898-2440
http://www.mtsu.edu/~deptabas/

University of Tennessee
College of Agricultural Sciences and
    Natural Resources
125 Morgan Hall
Knoxville, TN 37901-4500
Phone: (865) 974-7303
Fax: (865) 974-9329
http://web.utk.edu/~casnr/

TEXAS

Abilene Christian University
Agricultural and Environmental Sciences
    Department
ACU Box 27986
Abilene, TX 79699
Phone: (325) 674-2401
http://www.acu.edu/academics/cas/agenv.
    html

Angelo State University
Department of Agriculture
P.O. Box 10888
San Angelo, TX 76909
Phone: (325) 942-2027
Fax: (325) 942-2183
http://www.angelo.edu/dept/agriculture/

Sul Ross State University
School of Agriculture and Natural
    Resource Sciences
P.O. Box C-114
Alpine, TX 79832
Phone: (432) 837-8201
Fax: (432) 837-8409
http://www.sulross.edu/pages/497.asp

Tarleton State University
Department of Agribusiness, Agronomy,
    Horticulture, and Range Management
Box T-0050
Stephenville, TX 76402
Phone: (254) 968-9359
Fax: (254) 968-9228
http://www.tarleton.edu/~aahrm/

Texas A&M University
College of Agriculture and Life Sciences
109 Kleberg Building

2402 TAMU
College Station, TX 77843-2402
Phone: (979) 845-3712
http://coals.tamu.edu/

Texas Tech University
College Agricultural Sciences and
    Natural Resources
Box 42123
Lubbock, TX 79409
Phone: (806) 742-2808
http://www.depts.ttu.edu/
    agriculturalsciences/

UTAH

Brigham Young University
College of Biology & Agriculture
Provo, UT 84602
Phone: (801) 378-4636
http://bioag.byu.edu/

Southern Utah University
Division of Agriculture
351 West Center Street
Cedar City, UT 84720
Phone: (435) 586-7923
http://www.suu.edu/sast/sci/agriculture/

WASHINGTON

Clark College
Agriculture/Horticulture Department
1800 East McLoughlin Boulevard
Vancouver, WA 98663
http://www.clark.edu/academic_
    programs/technical/agriculture_
    horticulture/index.html

WISCONSIN

University of Wisconsin, Madison
Department of Agronomy
1575 Linden Drive
Madison, WI 53706
Phone: (608) 262-1390
http://agronomy.wisc.edu/

AQUACULTURE

KENTUCKY

Kentucky State University
Division of Mathematics and Sciences
Aquaculture Program
132 Carver Hall
400 East Main Street
Frankfort, KY 40601

Phone: (502) 597-6603
http://www.kysu.edu/artsscience/
    MathSciences/home.html/fbigdeli@
    gwmail.kysu.edu

MICHIGAN

Hillsdale College
Aquatic & Field Biology Program
33 East College
Hillsdale, MI 49242
Phone: (517) 437-7341
Fax: (517) 437-3923
http://www.hillsdale.edu/academics/bio/
    Swinehart/Aquatics/Home.html

Lake Superior State University
Fisheries and Wildlife Management
650 West Easterday Avenue
Sault Ste. Marie, MI 49783
Phone: (888) 800-LSSU
Fax: (906) 635-2111
http://www.lssu.edu/academics/degrees/
    bachelors/fisheries_wildlife_
    management/default.html

Michigan State University
Department of Fisheries and Wildlife
College of Agriculture and Natural
    Resources
13 Natural Resources Building
East Lansing, MI 48824
Phone: (517) 355-4478
Fax: (517) 432-1699
http://www.fw.msu.edu/

NEVADA

University of Nevada, Las Vegas
Water Resources Management Program
4505 Maryland Parkway
Las Vegas, NV 89154-4029
Phone: (702) 895-4006
http://www.unlv.edu/depts/wrm/

University of Nevada, Reno
Hydrologic Sciences Program
LMR 267
Reno, NV 89557-0180
Phone: (775) 784-6469
http://www.hydro.unr.edu/index.lasso

NEW MEXICO

New Mexico State University
Department of Fishery and Wildlife
    Sciences
2980 South Espina, Knox Hall 132
P.O. Box 30003
Campus Box 4901

Las Cruces, NM 88003-8003
Phone: (505) 646-7051
Fax: (505) 646-1281
http://leopold.nmsu.edu/

OHIO

Heidelberg College
Water Resources Program
310 East Market Street
Tiffin, OH 44883-2462
Phone: (419) 448-2226
Fax: (419) 448-2345
http://www.heidelberg.edu/depts/wtr/
    index.html

OKLAHOMA

Northeastern State University
Fisheries & Wildlife Program
Tahlequah, OK 74464
Phone: (918) 456-5511
http://www.nsuok.edu/catalog/scimath/
    fishwild.html

SOUTH CAROLINA

Clemson University
Department of Aquaculture, Fisheries
    and Wildlife
G08 Lehotsky Hall
Clemson, SC 29634-0362
Phone: (864) 656-3117
Fax: (864) 656-5332
http://virtual.clemson.edu/groups/AFW/
    index.htm

VERMONT

University of Vermont
Water Resources Program
George D. Aiken Center
Burlington, VT 05405
Phone: (802) 656-4057
http://www.EnviroEducation.com/s/
    uvm-rsenr/

WYOMING

Eastern Wyoming College
Wildlife & Fisheries Biology and
    Management
3200 West C Street
Torrington, WY 82240
Phone: (307) 532-8293
Fax: (307) 532-8222
http://ewcweb.ewc.cc.wy.us/catalog/
    programs/wildlife.html

PLANT SCIENCE

ARIZONA

Arizona State University East
Plant Biology Program
P.O. Box 4701
Life Science Building, C Wing,
    Room 206
Tempe, AZ 85287-4701
Phone: (480) 727-6277
http://sols.asu.edu/ugrad/conc_plantbio.php

CALIFORNIA

California Polytechnic State University
Crop Science Program
San Luis Obispo, CA 93407
Phone: (805) 756-1237
Fax: (805) 756-6504
http://www.calpoly.edu/~crsc/

California State University, Fresno
Department of Plant Science
2415 East San Ramon
MS AS72
Fresno, CA 93740
Phone: (559) 278-2861
Fax: (559) 278-7413
http://cast.csufresno.edu/PlantSci/

Carnegie Institution of Washington
Department of Plant Biology
260 Panama Street
Stanford, CA 94305
Phone: (650) 325-1521
Fax: (650) 325-6857
http://carnegiedpb.stanford.edu/

Claremont Graduate University
Botany Department
150 East 10th Street
Claremont, CA 91711-6160
Phone: (909) 621-8000
http://www.cgu.edu/bot/

FLORIDA

Florida Southern College
Citrus & Environmental Horticulture
    Department
111 Lake Hollingsworth Drive
Lakeland, FL 33801
Phone: (800) 274-4131
http://www.flsouthern.edu/citrus/index.htm

MICHIGAN

Northwestern Michigan College
Plant Science Program

2200 Dendrinos Drive, Suite 100
Traverse City, MI 49684-8895
Phone: (231) 929-3902
http://www.nmc.edu/~ucenter/plant.htm

MISSOURI

University of Missouri, Columbia
Department of Horticulture
1-87 Agriculture Building
Columbia, MO 65211
Phone: (573) 882-9632
Fax: (573) 882-1369
http://horticulture.missouri.edu/

NEW JERSEY

Rutgers University
Studies in Plant Biology & Pathology
Foran Hall
Cook College, 59 Dudley Road
New Brunswick, NJ 08901
Phone: (732) 932-9711
Fax: (732) 932-9441
http://aesop.rutgers.edu/%7Eplantbiopath/
    academics/academics.htm

NEW MEXICO

New Mexico State University
Agronomy & Horticulture Program
P.O. Box 30003 Box 3Q
Las Cruces, NM 88003-8003
Phone: (505) 646-3406
http://aghort.nmsu.edu/

NEW YORK

**State University of New York (SUNY),
    Cobleskill**
Plant Science Department
Cobleskill, NY 12043
Phone: (518) 255-5279
Fax: (518) 255-5439
http://www.cobleskill.edu/Academic/AG/
    PlantSci/

**State University of New York (SUNY),
    Delhi**
Golf and Plant Science
Farnsworth Hall
Delhi, NY 13753
Phone: (607) 746-4410
http://plantsci.delhi.edu/

**State University of New York (SUNY),
    Farmingdale**
Department of Ornamental Horticulture
Route 110

Farmingdale, NY 11735-1021
Phone: (516) 420-2113
http://www.farmingdale.edu/
    CampusPages/Business/Horticulture/
    pages/home/homepage.html

NORTH DAKOTA

North Dakota State University
Department of Plant Sciences
Morrill 115
Fargo, ND 58105-5655
Phone: (701) 231-7971
Fax: (701) 231-8474
http://www.ag.ndsu.nodak.edu/plantsci/

OKLAHOMA

Oklahoma State University
Plant and Soil Science Department
324 Student Union
Stillwater, OK 74078-1012
Phone: (405) 744-6425
http://pss.okstate.edu

RHODE ISLAND

University of Rhode Island
Plant Sciences and Entomology
Woodward Hall, Alumni Avenue
Kingston, RI 02881
http://www.uri.edu/cels/pls/

VERMONT

University of Vermont
Plant and Soil Science Department
Hills Agricultural Building
105 Carrigan Drive
Burlington, VT 05404-0082
Phone: (802) 656-0467
http://www.uvm.edu/%7Epss/

WISCONSIN

University of Wisconsin, River Falls
Plant & Earth Sciences Department
310 South Third Street
River Falls, WI 54022-5001
Phone: (715) 425-3345
http://www.uwrf.edu/pes/

SOIL SCIENCE

ALABAMA

Alabama A & M University
Department of Plant and Soil Science

P.O. Box 1208
4900 Meridian Street
Normal, AL 35762-1208
Phone: (256) 372-4174
Fax: (256) 372-5429
http://saes.aamu.edu/sps/IndexSPS.
    html

Auburn University
Department of Agronomy & Soils
202 Funchess Hall
Auburn University, AL 36849-5412
Phone: (334) 844-3952
Fax: (334) 844-3945
http://www.ag.auburn.edu/dept/ay/

COLORADO

Colorado State University
Soil and Crop Sciences Department
Fort Collins, CO 80523-1170
Phone: (970) 491-6517
http://www.colostate.edu/Depts/
    SoilCrop/

MICHIGAN

Michigan State University
Department of Crop and
    Soil Sciences
384F Plant and Soil Sciences Building
East Lansing, MI 48824
Phone: (517) 355-0271
Fax: (517) 353-5174
http://www.css.msu.edu/

MISSOURI

University of Missouri, Columbia
Department of Soil and Atmospheric
    Sciences
116 Gentry Hall
Columbia, MO 65211
Phone: (573) 882-6591
Fax: (573) 884-5133
http://web.missouri.edu/~soil

OKLAHOMA

Oklahoma State University
Plant and Soil Science Department
324 Student Union
Stillwater, OK 74078-1012
Phone: (405) 744-6425
http://pss.okstate.edu

OREGON

Oregon State University
Department of Crop and Soil Science
109 Crop Science Building
Corvallis, OR 97331-3002
Phone: (541) 737-2821
Fax: (541) 737-1589
http://cropandsoil.oregonstate.edu/

PENNSYLVANIA

Pennsylvania State University
Environmental Soil Science
116 ASI
State College, PA 16802
Phone: (814) 865-6541
Fax: (814) 863-7043
http://www.psu.edu/registrar/progsumm/

VERMONT

University of Vermont
Plant and Soil Science Department
Hills Agricultural Building
105 Carrigan Drive
Burlington, VT 05404-0082
Phone: (802) 656-0467
http://www.uvm.edu/%7Epss/

FORESTRY

ALABAMA

Auburn University
School of Forestry and Wildlife Sciences
108 M. White Smith Hall
Auburn, AL 36849
Phone: (334) 844-1001
Fax: (334) 844-1084http://www.forestry.
auburn.edu/

ALASKA

University of Alaska, Fairbanks
Forest Sciences Department
P.O. Box 757140
Fairbanks, AK 99775
Phone: (907) 474-5650
http://www.uaf.edu/snras/forest_sciences/

CALIFORNIA

California Polytechnic State University
Masters Forestry Science
Natural Resource Management
    Department
1 Grand Avenue
San Luis Obispo, CA 93407
Phone: (805) 756-2707
Fax: (805) 756-1402
http://www.nrm.calpoly.edu/fs/fs.html

Humboldt State University
College of Natural Resources and
    Sciences
1 Harpst Street
Arcata, CA 95521
Phone: (707) 826-3256
Fax: (707) 826-3562
http://www.humboldt.edu/~cnrs/

Humboldt State University
Forestry & Watershed Management
    Program
1 Harpst Street
Arcata, CA 95521-8299
Phone: (707) 826-3935
http://www.humboldt.edu/~for/index.shtml

University of California, Berkeley
College of Natural Resources
Office of the Dean
101 Giannini Hall #3100
Berkeley, CA 94720-3100
Phone: (510) 642-7171
http://nature.berkeley.edu/

University of California, Davis
Department of Environmental
    Horticulture and Urban Forestry
178 Mark Hall
Davis, CA 95616-8507
Phone: (530) 752-0130
Fax: (530) 752-1819
http://why.ucdavis.edu/academics/majors/
    ehuf.cfm?majors_list=divenvsci_
    majors.inc

COLORADO

Fort Lewis College
Department of Forestry
1000 Rim Drive
Durango, CO 81301-3999
Phone: (970) 247-7446
http://www.fortlewis.edu/academics/
    index.htm

Trinidad State Junior College
Natural Resources Emphasis
600 Prospect
Trinidad, CO 81082
Phone: (800) 621-8752
http://www.tsjc.cccoes.edu/TransferProg/
    Natural_Resources.htm

CONNECTICUT

Yale University
School of Forestry and Environmental
    Studies
205 Prospect Street
New Haven, CT 06511
Phone: (800) 825-0330
Fax: (203) 432-7297
http://www.yale.edu/environment

FLORIDA

University of Florida
School of Forest Resources & Conservation
P.O. Box 110410
Gainesville, FL 32611-0410
Phone: (352) 846-0850
Fax: (352) 392-1707
http://www.sfrc.ufl.edu

University of Florida
School of Natural Resources and
    Environment
P.O. Box 116455
Gainesville, FL 32611-6455
Phone: (352) 846-1634
http://www.snre.ufl.edu

GEORGIA

Georgia Perimeter College
Fire Management Program
3705 Brookside Parkway
Alpharetta, GA 30022
Phone: (770) 551-3010
http://www.dc.peachnet.edu/~acadaff/cat/
    programs/FireManagement.html

University of Georgia
Warnell School of Forest Resources
Athens, GA 30602
Phone: (706) 542-4284
Fax: (706) 542-3293
http://www.uga.edu/~wsfr/

HAWAII

University of Hawaii, Hilo
College of Agriculture, Forestry and
    Natural Resource Management
200 West Kawili Street
Hilo, HI 96720
Phone: (808) 974-7393
Fax: (808) 974-7674
http://www.uhh.hawaii.edu/academics/
    cafnrm/

ILLINOIS

Augustana College
Environmental Management & Forestry
639 38th Street
Rock Island, IL 61201-2296
Phone: (309) 794-7303
http://www.augustana.edu/academ/
environmental/top.htm

College of DuPage
Fire Science Technology Program
425 Fawell Boulevard
Glen Ellyn, IL 60137-6599
Phone: (630) 942-2107
http://www.cod.edu/Academic/AcadProg/
Occ_Voc/Fire_Occ.htm

INDIANA

Ball State University
Department of Natural Resources and
Environmental Management
Muncie, IN 47306
Phone/Fax: (765) 285-2606
http://www.bsu.edu/nrem/

Indiana University, Fort Wayne
Department of Forestry and Natural
Resources
Science Building, Room G56
Fort Wayne, IN 46805-1499
Phone: (260) 481-6316
http://www.ipfw.edu/academics/
programs/f/forestry/

Indiana University Southeast
School of Natural Sciences
4201 Grantline Road
New Albany, IN 47150
Phone: (812) 941-2284
Fax: (812) 941-2637
http://www.ius.edu/NaturalScience/

Purdue University
Department of Forestry & Natural
Resources
Forestry Building
195 Marsteller Street
West Lafayette, IN 47907-2033
Phone: (765) 494-3591
http://www.agriculture.purdue.edu/fnr/

IOWA

Iowa State University
Forestry Department
253 Bessey Hall
Ames, IA 50010-1021
Phone: (515) 294-1458

Fax: (515) 294-2995
http://www.ag.iastate.edu/departments/
forestry

Luther College
Environmental Management and Forest
Resource Management Program
700 College Drive
Decorah, IA 52101
Phone: (319) 387-1557
http://www.luther.edu/~biodept/forprog.
htm

KANSAS

Kansas State University
Natural Resources & Environmental
Science Program
Manhattan, KS 66506
Phone: (785) 532-6727
http://www.ksu.edu/nres/

KENTUCKY

University of Kentucky
Department of Forestry
College of Agriculture
T.P. Cooper Building, Room 105
Lexington, KY 40546-0073
Phone: (859) 257-7611
Fax: (859) 323-1031
http://www.uky.edu/Agriculture/Forestry/
forestry.html

LOUISIANA

Grambling State University
Wildlife Concentration
403 Main Street
Grambling, LA 71245
Phone: (318) 274-2446
http://www.gram.edu/COST/biology.htm

Louisiana Tech University
School of Forestry
P.O. Box 10138
Ruston, LA 71272
Phone: (318) 257-4985
Fax: (318) 257-5061
http://ans.latech.edu/forestry-index.html

MAINE

University of Maine
College of Natural Sciences, Forestry,
and Agriculture
5782 Winslow Hall, Room 106
Orono, ME 04469-5782
Phone: (207) 581-3206

Fax: (207) 581-3207
http://www.nsfa.umaine.edu/

MARYLAND

**University of Maryland, University
College**
Fire Science Program
3501 University Boulevard East
Adelphi, MD 20783
Phone: (800) 888-UMUC
http://www.umuc.edu/prog/ugp/majors/
fscn.shtml

MASSACHUSETTS

Greenfield Community College
Environmental Studies/Natural Resources
Program
One College Drive
Greenfield, MA 01301-9739
Phone: (413) 775-1455
Fax: (413) 773-5129

Harvard University
Environment and Natural Resources
Program
John F. Kennedy School of Government
79 JFK Street
Cambridge, MA 02138
Phone: (617) 495-1351
Fax: (617) 495-1635
http://bcsia.ksg.harvard.edu/?program=EN

University of Massachusetts, Amherst
College of Natural Resources and
the Environment
Martha Baker, Assistant Dean
111 Stockbridge Hall
Amherst, MA 01003-9285
Phone: (413) 545-1969
Fax: (413) 545-1977
http://www.umass.edu/nre/

MICHIGAN

Michigan State University
Department of Forestry
126 Natural Resources Building
East Lansing, MI 48824
Phone: (517) 355-0092
Fax: (517) 432-1143
http://okemos.for.msu.edu/

Michigan State University
Watershed Management
115 Manly Miles Building
East Lansing, MI 48823-5243
Phone: (517) 353-9785

Fax: (517) 353-1812
http://online-contened.msu.edu/program.
    asp?program=12

Michigan Technological University
School of Forestry and Wood Products
1400 Townsend Drive
Houghton, MI 49931-1295
Phone: (906) 487-2454
Fax: (906) 487-2915
http://forest.mtu.edu/

University of Michigan
School of Natural Resources and
    Environment
Dana Building
430 East University Avenue
Ann Arbor, MI 48109-1115
Phone: (734) 764-6453
Fax: (734) 936-2195
http://www.snre.umich.edu/

MINNESOTA

University of Minnesota
College of Natural Resources
2003 Upper Buford Circle
St. Paul, MN 55108
Phone: (612) 624-1234
Fax: (612) 624-8701
http://www.umn.edu

MISSISSIPPI

Mississippi State University
College of Forest Resources
P.O. Box 9680
Mississippi State, MS 39762-9690
Phone: (662) 325-2952
Fax: (662) 325-8726
http://www.cfr.msstate.edu

MISSOURI

University of Missouri, Columbia
Department of Forestry
203 Anheuser-Busch Natural Resources
    Building
Columbia, MO 65211-7270
Phone: (573) 882-7242
Fax: (573) 882-1977
http://www.snr.missouri.edu/forestry/

MONTANA

University of Montana
College of Forestry and Conservation
Missoula, MT 59812
Phone: (406) 243-5521
Fax: (406) 243-4845
http://www.forestry.umt.edu/

NEW HAMPSHIRE

University of New Hampshire
Department of Natural Resources
215 James Hall
56 College Road
Durham, NH 03824-3589
Phone: (603) 862-1020
Fax: (603) 862-3617
http://www.unh.edu/natural-resources/
    index.html

NEW YORK

**State University of New York (SUNY),
Canton**
Forestry Technology Program
Cornell Drive
Canton, NY 13617
Phone: (800) 388-7123
http://www.canton.edu/can/can_start.
    taf?page=study_program_forest

**State University of New York (SUNY),
Syracuse**
College of Environmental Science and
    Forestry
1 Forestry Drive
Syracuse, NY 13210-2778
Phone: (315) 470-6500
http://www.esf.edu/

NORTH CAROLINA

Haywood Community College
Natural Resource Division
185 Freedlander Drive
Clyde, NC 28721
Phone: (828) 627-4560
Fax: (828) 627-4690
http://potemkin.haywood.cc.nc.us/
    academic/Courses-of-Instruction.htm

Lenoir-Rhyne College
Pre-Forestry, Pre-Environmental
    Management, Environmental Studies
7th Avenue & Eighth Street NE
Hickory, NC 28601
Phone: (828) 328-7270
http://www.lrc.edu/bio/Overview.htm

NORTH DAKOTA

North Dakota State University
Natural Resource Management
Hultz Hall, Room 163
Fargo, ND 58105
Phone: (701) 231-8180
Fax: (701) 231-7590
http://www.ndsu.edu/ndsu/academic/
    factsheets/eng_arch/natresman.shtml

OHIO

Hocking College
School of Natural Resources
3301 Hocking Parkway
Nelsonville, OH 45764-9704
Phone: (740) 753-3591
Fax: (740) 753-1452
http://www.hocking.edu/natural_
    resources/

Ohio State University
School of Natural Resources
2021 Coffey Road
210 Kottman Hall
Columbus, OH 43210-1085
Phone: (614) 292-2265
http://snr.osu.edu

OKLAHOMA

Oklahoma State University
Forestry Department
324 Student Union
Stillwater, OK 74078-1012
Phone: (405) 744-5438
http://www.okstate.edu/OSU_Ag/asnr/fore/

OREGON

Oregon State University
College of Forestry
140 Peavy Hall
Corvallis, OR 97331-5710
Phone: (541) 737-2004
Fax: (541) 737-8508
http://www.cof.orst.edu

PENNSYLVANIA

Lebanon Valley College
Forestry and Environmental Studies
    Program
101 North College Avenue
Annville, PA 17003
Phone: (717) 867-6181
http://www.lvc.edu/forestry/

Pennsylvania College of Technology
Natural Resources Management
One College Avenue
Williamsport, PA 17701
Phone: (800) 367-9222
Fax: (570) 547-6352
http://www.pct.edu/schools/nrm/

Pennsylvania State University
School of Forest Resources
113 Ferguson Building
University Park, PA 16802

Phone: (814) 865-7541
Fax: (814) 865-3725
http://www.sfr.cas.psu.edu/

TENNESSEE

University of the South
Forestry & Geology Program
735 University Avenue
Sewanee, TN 37383
Phone: (931) 598-3219
http://www.sewanee.edu/Forestry_
    Geology/ForestryGeology.html

TEXAS

Stephen F. Austin State University
Arthur Temple College of Forestry
P.O. Box 6109 SFA
Nacogdoches, TX 75962-6109
Phone: (936) 468-3301
Fax: (936) 468-2489
http://www.sfasu.edu/forestry/

UTAH

Utah State University
College of Natural Resources
5200 Old Main Hill
Logan, UT 84322
Phone: (435) 797-2445
http://www.cnr.usu.edu/front.asp

VERMONT

University of Vermont
The Rubenstein School of Environment
    and Natural Resources
81 Carrigan Drive

Burlington, VT 05405
Phone: (802) 656-4380
Fax: (802) 656-8683
http://www.uvm.edu/~envnr/

VIRGINIA

**Virginia Polytechnic Institute and State
    University**
Department of Forestry
313 Cheatham Hall-0324
Blacksburg, VA 24061
Phone: (540) 231-5483
Fax: (540) 231-3698
http://www.fw.vt.edu/forestry/

WASHINGTON

Central Washington University
Graduate Program in Resource
    Management
400 East Eighth Avenue
Ellensburg, WA 98926-7420
Phone: (509) 963-2795
Fax: (509) 963-1047
http://www.cwu.edu/~geograph/rem.html

University of Washington
College of Forest Resources
Box 352100
Seattle, WA 98195-2100
Phone: (206) 543-7081
Fax: (206) 685-0790
http://www.cfr.washington.edu

Washington State University
Environmental and Natural Resource
    Sciences
370 Lightly Student Services Building

P.O. Box 641067
Pullman, WA 99164-1067
Phone: (888) GOTO-WSU
http://www.it.wsu.edu/AIS/ADM/cgi-bin/
    ug_majors.cgi?acad_area=ENATR

WEST VIRGINIA

West Virginia University
Davis College of Agriculture, Forestry
    & Consumer Sciences
1170 Agricultural Sciences Building
P.O. Box 6108
Morgantown, WV 26506-6108
Phone: (304) 293-2395
Fax: (304) 293-3740
http://www.caf.wvu.edu/

WISCONSIN

University of Wisconsin, Madison
Department of Forest Ecology and
    Management
1630 Linden Drive
Madison, WI 53706
Phone: (608) 262-9975
Fax: (608) 262-9922
http://forest.wisc.edu

WYOMING

Casper College
Fire Science Technology
125 College Drive
Casper, WY 82601
Phone: (800) 442-2963
http://www.caspercollege.edu/trades/fire/

LEGAL & REGULATORY

ADVOCACY

HAWAII

Hawaii Tokai International College
Peace Studies Program
2241 Kapiolani Boulevard
Honolulu, HI 96826
Phone: (808) 983-4100
Fax: (808) 983-4107
http://www.tokai.edu/

KANSAS

McPherson College
Environmental Stewardship Program
1600 East Euclid

P.O. Box 1402
McPherson, KS 67460
Phone: (800) 365-7402
http://www2.mcpherson.edu/academics/
    environmental/

NEW YORK

Friends World Program
Environmental Issues
Long Island University
239 Montauk Highway
Southampton, NY 11968-4198
Phone: (631) 287-8474
Fax: (631) 287-8463
http://www.southampton.liu.edu/fw/lac/
    environment/

PENNSYLVANIA

Arcadia University
International Peace and Conflict
    Resolution Program
450 South Easton Road
Glenside, PA 19038
Phone: (215) 572-4094
Fax: (215) 572-2126
http://www.arcadia.edu/enviro.asp

VERMONT

School for International Training
Masters Programs in Intercultural
    Service, Leadership & Management
Kipling Road

P.O. Box 676
Brattleboro, VT 05302-0676
Phone: (800) 336-1616
Fax: (802) 258-3500
http://www.sit.edu/graduate/pim/index.html

ENVIRONMENTAL HEALTH AND SAFETY

ALABAMA

University of Alabama, Birmingham
Department of Environmental Health
    Sciences
1665 University Boulevard
Birmingham, AL 35294
Phone: (205) 934-8488
http://www.soph.uab.edu/ehshome.
    asp?ID=53

CALIFORNIA

California State University, Northridge
Department of Environmental and
    Occupational Health
18111 Nordhoff Street
Northridge, CA 91330-8412
Phone: (818) 677-7476
Fax: (818) 677-7411
http://www.csun.edu/~vchsc00b/EOH/
    EOH.htm

COLORADO

Colorado State University
Environmental and Radiological Health
    Sciences
121A Environmental Health Building
Ft. Collins, CO 80523-1005
Phone: (970) 491-0294
Fax: (970) 491-2194
http://www.cvmbs.colostate.edu/erhs/

GEORGIA

Emory University
Department of Environmental and
    Occupational Health
1518 Clifton Road
Atlanta, GA 30322
Phone: (404) 727-3697
Fax: (404) 727-8744
http://www.sph.emory.edu/hpeoh.html

IOWA

Iowa Wesleyan College
Environmental Health Program
601 North Main Street
Mount Pleasant, IA 52641

Phone: (800) 582-2382
http://www.iwc.edu/pro_stu/majors/
    health.htm

University of Iowa
Department of Occupational and
    Environmental Health
100 Oakdale Campus, 106 IREH
Iowa City, IA 52242
Phone: (319) 335-4558
http://www.public-health.uiowa.edu/oeh/

KENTUCKY

Eastern Kentucky University
Department of Environmental Health
    Science
Dizney 220
Richmond, KY 40475-3135
Phone: (606) 622-1939
http://www.environmentalhealth.eku.edu/

University of Kentucky
Graduate Center for Toxicology
306 Health Science Research Building
Lexington, KY 40536-3760
Phone: (859) 257-3760
Fax: (859) 323-1059
http://www.mc.uky.edu/toxicology/

MARYLAND

University of Maryland, Baltimore
Graduate Program in Toxicology
500 West Baltimore Street
Baltimore, MD 21201
Phone: (410) 706-8196
http://medschool.umaryland.edu/
    departments/epidemiology/grad_tox.
    html

MASSACHUSETTS

Anna Maria College
MS in Occupational and Environmental
    Health and Safety
50 Sunset Lane
Paxton, MA 01612
Phone: (508) 849-3382
http://www.annamaria.edu/ce/public.
    htm#msoeh

Massachusetts Institute of Technology (MIT)
Center for Environmental Health Sciences
77 Massachusetts Avenue
Building 56-235
Cambridge, MA 02139
Phone: (617) 253-6220

Fax: (617) 452-2066
http://web.mit.edu/cehs/

MICHIGAN

Madonna University
Occupational Safety, Health & Fire
    Science Program
36600 Schoolcraft Road
Livonia, MI 48150-1173
Phone: (734) 432-5516
Fax: (734) 432-5393
http://www.madonna.edu/pages/
    occupationalsafety.cfm

MISSOURI

Missouri Southern State University
Department of Biology & Environmental
    Health
3950 East Newman Road
Joplin, MO 64801-1595
Phone: (800) 606-MSSC
Fax: (417) 659-4429
http://www.mssu.edu/biology/home.htm

MISSISSIPPI

Mississippi Valley State University
Department of Natural Sciences and
    Environmental Health
14000 Highway 82 West
Box 7254
Itta Bena, MS 38941
Phone: (662) 254-3377
Fax: (662) 254-3347
http://www.mvsu.edu/Academics/art_
    and_science/nseh.html

MONTANA

Fort Peck Community College
Hazardous Materials/Waste Technology
P.O. Box 398
Poplar, MT 59255
Phone: (406) 768-6300
Fax: (406) 768-6301
http://www.fpcc.edu/

NEW JERSEY

New Jersey Institute of Technology
Hazardous Substance Management
    Research Program
University Heights
Newark, NJ 07102-9895
Phone: (973) 596-3233
Fax: (973) 642-7170
http://www.hsmrc.org/

NEW YORK

Mercy College
Environmental Health & Safety
  Management
555 Broadway
Dobbs Ferry, NY 10522
Phone: (914) 674-7496
http://www.mercynet.edu/acadivisions/
  socbehavsci/EnvHealth.cfm

Rochester Institute of Technology
Environmental, Health & Safety
  Management
78 Lomb Memorial Drive
Rochester, NY 14623
Phone: (585) 475-2183
http://www.rit.edu/~704

NORTH CAROLINA

East Carolina University
Department of Environmental Health
  Sciences and Safety
Belk AH 310
Greenville, NC 27858-4353
Phone: (252) 328-4434
Fax: (252) 328-0380
http://www.ecu.edu/hhp/ehst/

OHIO

Bowling Green State University
Environmental Health
Bowling Green, OH 43403
Phone: (419) 372-6062
http://www.bgsu.edu/departments/envh/

University of Cincinnati
Department of Environmental Health
College of Medicine
P.O. Box 670056
Cincinnati, OH 45267-0056
Phone: (513) 558-5439
Fax: (513) 558-4397
http://www.med.uc.edu/envhealth/

OKLAHOMA

**Oklahoma State University,
  Oklahoma City**
Occupational & Environmental Safety
900 North Portland
Oklahoma City, OK 73107
Phone: (405) 945-3236
http://www.osuokc.onenet.net/111A.
  html

PENNSYLVANIA

Point Park University
Environmental Health Science
  & Protection Program
201 Wood Street
Pittsburgh, PA 15222
Phone: (412) 391-4100
Fax: (412) 392-3962
http://www.pointpark.edu/default.
  aspx?id=117

VIRGINIA

Old Dominion University
Environmental Health Program
Room 228 Spong Hall
Norfolk, VA 23529
Phone: (757) 683-6010
http://www.odu.edu/hs/cohs/envh/index.
  html

SOUTH CAROLINA

Clemson University
Environmental Toxicology Program
509 Westinghouse Road
P.O. Box 709
Pendleton, SC 29670-0709
Phone: (864) 646-2961
Fax: (864) 646-2277
http://www.clemson.edu/entox/

TENNESSEE

East Tennessee State University
Department of Environmental Health
  Sciences
P.O. Box 70720
Johnson City, TN 37614
Phone: (423) 439-5243
http://www.etsu.edu/cpah/environ/index.
  htm

TEXAS

Texas State Technical College, Waco
Environmental Health & Safety
  Technology
3801 Campus Drive
Waco, TX 76705
Phone: (800) 792-8784
http://db.tstc.edu/projects/
  batcave/cat2003/cattechnacd.
  cfm?techcode=EHS

ENVIRONMENTAL
POLICY

ARIZONA

Northern Arizona University
Environmental Politics and Policy
South San Francisco Street
Flagstaff, AZ 86011
Phone: (520) 523-6544
http://jan.ucc.nau.edu/~dss4/EnviroHome.
  htm

CALIFORNIA

**California State University,
  Monterey Bay**
Division of Science and Environmental
  Policy
100 Campus Center
Seaside, CA 93955-8001
Phone: (831) 582-4120
Fax: (831) 582-4122
http://essp.csumb.edu

University of California, Davis
Department of Environmental Science
  and Policy
One Shields Avenue
Davis, CA 95616
Phone: (530) 752-3026
Fax: (530) 752-3350
http://www.des.ucdavis.edu/

CONNECTICUT

University of Connecticut
Environmental Economics and Policy
  Program
1376 Storrs Road
Storrs, CT 06269-4021
Phone: (860) 486-2836
Fax: (860) 486-1932
http://www.are.uconn.edu/EnvPolPr.html

FLORIDA

University of Miami
Center for Ecosystem Science & Policy
P.O. Box 248087
Coral Gables, FL 33124-8087
Phone: (305) 284-2986
http://www.cesp.miami.edu/

University of South Florida
Department of Environmental Science
  and Policy
4202 East Fowler Avenue, SCA 238
Tampa, FL 33620

Phone: (813) 974-0443
Fax: (813) 974-2184
http://www.cas.usf.edu/esp/

IOWA

Drake University
Environmental Science & Policy
    Program
2507 University Avenue
Des Moines, IA 50311
Phone: (515) 271-4801
http://www.drake.edu/artsci/ENV/

KANSAS

Bethel College, Kansas
Global Peace and Justice Program
300 East 27th Street
North Newton, KS 67117
Phone: (316) 283-2500
Fax: (316) 284-5286
http://www.bethelks.edu/academics/
    globaljustice/

MAINE

University of Southern Maine
Environmental Science and Policy
    Program
P.O. Box 9300
Portland, ME 04104-9300
Phone: (207) 780-4141
http://www.usm.maine.edu/~esd/spalsh.
    htm

MARYLAND

Hood College
Environmental Science and Policy
    Program
401 Rosemont Avenue
Frederick, MD 21701-8575
Phone: (301) 663-3131
http://www.hood.edu/academic/programs/
    programs.cfm?pid=_environmental_
    science.htm

Johns Hopkins University
Environmental Sciences and Policy
    Program
Wyman Park Building, Suite G1
3400 North Charles Street
Baltimore, MD 21218
Phone: (410) 516-6057
Fax: (410) 516-6017
http://advanced.jhu.edu/environmental_
    sciences/

University of Maryland, College Park
Environmental Policy Program
School of Public Affairs
Van Munching Hall
College Park, MD 20742-1821
Phone: (301) 405-6330
http://www.puaf.umd.edu/degree_
    programs/Environmental.html

MASSACHUSETTS

Clark University
Environmental Science & Policy
950 Main Street
Worcester, MA 01610
Phone: (508) 793-7711
http://www.clarku.edu/departments/idce/
    environmentalscience/ba/

**Massachusetts Institute of Technology
(MIT)**
Environmental Policy Group
Room 9-312
77 Massachusetts Avenue
Cambridge, MA 02139
Phone: (617) 253-1509
Fax: (617) 253-7402
http://web.mit.edu/dusp/EPG/

Smith College
Environmental Science and Policy
    Program
Bass Hall 107
Northampton, MA 01063
Phone: (413) 585-3951
Fax: (413) 585-3786
http://www.science.smith.edu/
    departments/esp/

MICHIGAN

Michigan Technological University
Graduate Program in Environmental Policy
1400 Townsend Drive
Houghton, MI 49931
Phone: (906) 487-2113
http://www.social.mtu.edu/EP/

University of Michigan
Public Policy Program
School of Natural Resources and
    Environment
1024 Dana Building
Ann Arbor, MI 48109-1115
Phone: (734) 764-6435
Fax: (734) 963-6453
http://www.spp.umich.edu/academics/
    dual-nre.htm

NEW JERSEY

New Jersey Institute of Technology
Graduate Program in Environmental
    Policy Studies
University Heights
Washington Avenue
Newark, NJ 7102
Phone: (800) 925-NJIT
Fax: (973) 596-3461
http://www.njit.edu/Directory/Academic/
    HUM/EPS/

NEW YORK

Bard College
Center for Environmental Policy
P.O. Box 5000
Annandale-on-Hudson, Dutchess, NY
    12504-5000
Phone: (845) 758-7073
Fax: (845) 758-7636

Columbia University
MPA in Environmental Science and Policy
School of International and Public Affairs
1314 International Affairs Building
420 West 118th Street
New York, NY 10027
Phone: (212) 854-3142
http://www.columbia.edu/cu/
    mpaenvironment/

Hartwick College
Environmental Science and Policy
    Program
239 Miller Science Building
Oneonta, NY 13820
Phone: (607) 431-4734
Fax: (607) 431-4374
http://www.hartwick.edu/envirsci/

New York University
Public and Nonprofit Management and
    Policy Program
4 Washington Square North
New York, NY 10003-6671
Phone: (212) 998-7414
Fax: (212) 995-4164
http://www.nyu.edu/wagner/info/pnp.
    html

Syracuse University
Center for Environmental Policy and
    Administration
400 Eggers Hall
Syracuse, NY 13244-1020
Phone: (315) 443-1890
Fax: (315) 443-1075
http://www.maxwell.syr.edu/cepa/
    cepaindx.htm

Union College
Environmental Science and Policy Study
   Abroad Program
807 Union Street
Schenectady, NY 12308-3107
Phone: (518) 388-6123
http://idol.union.edu/~env/ES_abroad

MASSACHUSETTS

Harvard University
Environmental Science and Public Policy
Center for the Environment
42 Church Street
Cambridge, MA 02138
Phone: (617) 496-6995
Fax: (617) 384-8006
http://environment.harvard.edu/espp/

OHIO

Cleveland State University
Center for Environmental Science,
   Technology and Policy
2121 Euclid Avenue, MC-219
Cleveland, OH 44115
Phone: (216) 687-4860
Fax: (216) 687-5393
http://www.csuohio.edu/cestp/

OKLAHOMA

University of Tulsa
Environmental Policy
600 South College
Tulsa, OK 74104
Phone: (918) 631-2952
http://www.cas.utulsa.edu/envpolicy/

PENNSYLVANIA

Carnegie Mellon University
Heinz School of Public Policy and
   Management
Hamburg Hall 1108
5000 Forbes Avenue
Pittsburgh, PA 15213-3890
Phone: (800) 877-3498
Fax: (412) 268-7036
http://www.heinz.cmu.edu

VIRGINIA

College of William and Mary
Thomas Jefferson Program in Public Policy
P.O. Box 8795
Williamsburg, VA 23187
Phone: (757) 221-2368
Fax: (757) 221-2390
http://www.wm.edu/tjppp/

George Mason University
Department of Environmental Science
   and Policy
4400 University Drive
MS 2D2
Fairfax, VA 22030-4444
Phone: (703) 993-3187
http://www.gmu.edu/phdespp.html

**Virginia Polytechnic Institute and State
University**
Environmental Policy & Planning
201 Architecture Annex
Blacksburg, VA 24060
Phone: (540) 231-5485
Fax: (540) 231-3367
http://www.uap.vt.edu/academics/epp/

LAW

CALIFORNIA

Golden Gate University
School of Law
Environmental Law
536 Mission Street
San Francisco, CA 94105-2968
Phone: (415) 369-5356
Fax: (415) 543-6680
http://www.ggu.edu/schools/law/
   graduates/environment/index.html

University of California, Berkeley
School of Law
Environmental Law Program
Boalt Hall School of Law
Berkeley, CA 94720-7200
Phone: (510) 642-2029
Fax: (510) 643-2673
http://www.law.berkeley.edu/cenpro/
   programs/envirolaw.html

COLORADO

University of Denver
Environmental and Natural Resources Law
College of Law
1900 Olive Street
Denver, CO 80208
Phone: (303) 871-6262
Fax: (303) 871-6711
http://www.law.du.edu/naturalresources/

CONNECTICUT

Stanford Law School
Environmental and Natural Resources
   Law and Policy Program
559 Nathan Abbott Way
Stanford, CA 94305-8610
Phone: (650) 723-4057
http://www.law.stanford.edu/
   naturalresources/

Yale University
Yale Center for Environmental Law
   and Policy
205 Prospect Street
New Haven, CT 06511
Phone: (203) 432-3123
Fax: (203) 432-3817
http://www.yale.edu/envirocenter/

DISTRICT OF COLUMBIA

Georgetown University Law Center
Environmental Law Projects
600 New Jersey Avenue, NW
Washington, DC 20001
Phone: (202) 662-9000
http://www.law.georgetown.edu/clinics/
   ipr/environmental.html

ILLINOIS

Chicago-Kent College of Law
Program in Environmental and Energy
   Law
565 West Adams Avenue
Chicago, IL 60661-3691
Phone: (312) 906-5000
Fax: (312) 906-5280
http://www.kentlaw.edu/academics/jdcert/
   env_pgm.html

LOUISIANA

Tulane University
Tulane Law School
Environmental Law Program
Weinmann Hall
6329 Freret Street
New Orleans, LA 70118-6231
Phone: (504) 865-5939

MARYLAND

University of Maryland, Baltimore
Environmental Law Program
500 West Baltimore Street
Baltimore, MD 21201
Phone: (410) 706-8157
Fax: (410) 706-0407
http://www.law.umaryland.edu/
   environment/

NEW YORK

New York University
School of Law
Center on Environmental & Land Use Law
Vanderbilt Hall, 40 Washington Square
   South
New York, NY 10012-1099

Phone: (212) 998-6223
http://www.nyu.edu/pages/elc/

Pace University School of Law
Environmental Law Program
78 North Broadway
White Plains, NY 10603
Phone: (914) 422-4122
Fax: (914) 422-4261
http://law.pace.edu/environment/index.html

OHIO

University of Toledo
Certificate in Environmental Law
School of Law
Toledo, OH 43606-3390
Phone: (419) 530-4131

http://www.utlaw.edu/registrar/environ%
20law%20certification.htm

OREGON

University of Oregon
Environmental and Natural Resources
    Law Program
School of Law
1515 Agate Street
Eugene, OR 97403
Phone: (541) 346-3852
http://enr.uoregon.edu/

PENNSYLVANIA

University of Pittsburgh
Certificate Program in Environmental
    Law, Science and Policy

School of Law
3900 Forbes Avenue
Room 200C
Pittsburgh, PA 15260
Phone: (412) 648-1408
Fax: (412) 624-4843
http://www.law.pitt.edu/academics/
    programs/env.php

VERMONT

Vermont Law School
Environmental Law Center
Chelsea Street
South Royalton, VT 05068-0096
Phone: (800) 227-1395
Fax: (802) 763-2940
http://www.vermontlaw.edu

OTHER

LANDSCAPE ARCHITECTURE

CALIFORNIA

University of California, Berkeley
Landscape Architecture and
    Environmental Planning
230 Wurster Hall, MC #1820
Berkeley, CA 94720-1820
Phone: (510) 642-5577
Fax: (510) 642-7560

University of Southern California
Landscape Architecture Program
School of Architecture
Watt Hall, Suite 204
Los Angeles, CA 90089-0291
Phone: (213) 740-2723

Fax: (213) 740-8884
http://www.usc.edu/dept/architecture/

IOWA

Iowa State University
Department of Landscape Architecture
146 College of Design
Ames, IA 50011
Phone: (515) 294-5676
Fax: (515) 294-2348
http://www.public.iastate.edu/~land_arch/

TEXAS

Texas A&M University
Department of Landscape Architecture
    and Urban Planning
3137 TAMU

College Station, TX 77843-3137
Phone: (979) 845-1046
http://archweb.tamu.edu/laup/
    dept0918/dept_pg.asp?pass_button_
    name='H%20O%20M%20E'&dp_
    id=167

WASHINGTON

Washington State University, Spokane
Landscape Architecture Program
601 West First Avenue
Spokane, WA 99201-3899
Phone: (509) 358-7500
http://www.spokane.wsu.edu/academic/
    design/landscape_architecture_grad.asp

OUTDOOR/ENVIRONMENTAL EDUCATION

CAMP COUNSELORS

The American Camp Association publishes
information about a career as a camp
counselor in its counseling section at http://
www.acacamps.org/staff/counselors.php.

CAMP DIRECTORS

The American Camp Association offers
a class entitled Basic Camp Director
Course, which is designed for site
managers, experienced program directors,
or camp directors with fewer than six
years of experience. They also offer a

New Camp Director Orientation program.
For more information, visit http://www.
acacamps.org/education/pdcourse.php.

COMMUNITY-FOCUSED ENVIRONMENTAL EDUCATION

NEW HAMPSHIRE

Colby-Sawyer College
Institute for Community and Environment
541 Main Street
New London, NH 03257

Phone: (603) 526-3793
Fax: (603) 526-3429
http://www.colby-sawyer.edu/academic/
    ces/

NEW YORK

City University of New York (CUNY)
Clark University
Department of International
    Development, Community and
    Environment
950 Main Street
Worcester, MA 01610-1477

Phone: (508) 793-7201
Fax: (508) 793-8820
http://www.clarku.edu/departments/idce/
index.shtml

WASHINGTON

Antioch University Seattle
Master of Arts in Environment &
Community
2326 Sixth Avenue
Seattle, WA 98121
Phone: (206) 268-4710
Fax: (206) 441-3307
http://www.antiochsea.edu/ec/index.html

University of Washington
IslandWood Graduate Residency
in Education, Environment and
Community
4450 Blakely Avenue Northeast
Bainbridge Island, WA 98110
Phone: (206) 855-4300
Fax: (206) 855-4301

ENVIRONMENTAL COMMUNICATION

COLORADO

University of Colorado, Boulder
Center for Environmental Journalism
School of Journalism and Mass
Communication
Campus Box 287
Boulder, CO 80309-0287
Phone: (303) 492-5008
http://cires.colorado.edu/env_prog/cej.html

ILLINOIS

**University of Illinois at
Urbana-Champaign**
Agricultural and Environmental
Communications & Education
274 Bevier, 905 South Goodwin, MC-180
Urbana, IL 61801
Phone: (217) 333-3790
Fax: (217) 244-7877
http://www.aces.uiuc.edu/~hcd/
undergrad/AECE-catalog-97.html

LOUISIANA

Loyola University, New Orleans
Center for Environmental
Communications
6363 St. Charles Avenue
New Orleans, LA 70118-6195

Phone: (504) 865-3797
Fax: (504) 865-3799
http://www.loyno.edu/lucec/

MICHIGAN

Michigan State University
Knight Center for Environmental
Journalism
382 Communication Arts Building
East Lansing, MI 48824-1212
Phone: (517) 432-1415
Fax: (517) 355-7710
http://environmental.jrn.msu.edu/

MISSOURI

University of Missouri, Columbia
Environmental Reporting Program
120 Neff Hall
Columbia, MO 65211
Phone: (573) 882-4714
http://www.journalism.missouri.edu/grad/
environ.htm

ENVIRONMENTAL EDUCATION

The Association of Environmental Engineering and Science Professors posts
graduate assistant and fellowship opportunities at http://www.aeesp.org/jobs/
graduatejobs.php.

ARIZONA

Northern Arizona University
Center for Environmental Sciences and
Education
Box 5694
Flagstaff, AZ 86011
Phone: (928) 523-9333
http://www.nau.edu/~envsci/

Northern Arizona University
Environmental Education Outreach
Program
P.O. Box 15004
Flagstaff, AZ 86011
Phone: (520) 523-1275
Fax: (520) 523-1266
http://www4.nau.edu/eeop/

CALIFORNIA

**California State University,
San Bernardino**
M.A. in Environmental Education
5500 University Parkway
San Bernardino, CA 92407-2397
Phone: (909) 880-5640
http://nest.csusb.edu/masters_deg.html

CONNECTICUT

Southern Connecticut State University
Science Education & Environmental
Science
501 Crescent Street
New Haven, CT 06515
Phone: (203) 392-6600
http://www.southernct.edu/grad/
programs/EVE-SCE/

FLORIDA

Florida Atlantic University
Pine Jog Environmental Education Program
College of Education
6301 Summit Boulevard
West Palm Beach, FL 33415
Phone: (561) 686-6600
Fax: (561) 687-4968
http://www.pinejog.org/home.htm

MINNESOTA

University of Minnesota, Duluth
Center for Environmental Education
Sports and Health Center 107
1216 Ordean Court
Duluth, MN 55812-3032
Phone: (218) 726-8677
Fax: (218) 726-6243
http://www.d.umn.edu/ceed/

NEW YORK

City College of New York
Program in Environmental Education
160 Convent Avenue
New York, NY 10031-9198
Phone: (212) 650-6977
Fax: (212) 650-6417
http://www.ccny.cuny.edu/

OHIO

University of Findlay
Master of Arts in Education, Emphasis on
Environmental Safety and Health
1000 North Main Street
Findlay, OH 45840
Phone: (800) 521-1292
Fax: (419) 434-5303
http://www.ufctp.org/NCEEMPD/
Masters_Ed.htm | piper@findlay.edu

OREGON

Southern Oregon University
Environmental Education Graduate
Program

Department of Biology
1250 Siskiyou Boulevard
Ashland, OR 97520
Phone: (541) 552-6876
http://www.sou.edu/biology/enved/
   mainpage.htm

VIRGINIA

West Virginia University
Agricultural and Environmental
   Education
P.O. Box 6108
Morgantown, WV 26506
Phone: (304) 293-4832
http://www.caf.wvu.edu/RESM/aee/
   aeehtml.htm

WISCONSIN

University of Wisconsin, Stevens Point
Environmental Education Online
   Program
College of Natural Resources
Stevens Point, WI 54481
Phone: (715) 346-3854
Fax: (715) 346-4385
http://www.uwsp.edu/natres/rwilke/eetap/

University of Wisconsin, Stevens Point
Wisconsin Center for Environmental
   Education
110 College of Natural Resources
Stevens Point, WI 54481
Phone: (715) 346-4973
Fax: (715) 346-3025
http://www.uwsp.edu/cnr/wcee/

WYOMING

Casper College
Environmental Training and Resource
   Center
125 College Drive
Casper, WY 82601
Phone: (800) 442-2963
Fax: (307) 268-2224
http://www.caspercollege.edu/trades/
   environ/resource.asp

ENVIRONMENTAL LITERACY

INDIANA

Saint Mary-of-the-Woods College
Graduate Program in Earth Literacy
Saint Mary-of-the-Woods, IN 47876

Phone: (812) 535-5160
http://www.smwc.edu/prospective/
   graduate/earth/

ENVIRONMENTAL PSYCHOLOGY

CALIFORNIA

California State University, Sonoma
EcoPsychology Program
1801 East Cotati Avenue
Rohnert Park, CA 94928-3609
Phone: (715) 346-2441
http://isis.csuhayward.edu/ALSS/ECO/
   program.htm

NEW YORK

City University of New York (CUNY)
Environmental Psychology
365 Fifth Avenue
New York, NY 10016-4309
Phone: (212) 817-8751
http://web.gc.cuny.edu/psychology/
   environmental/

VIRGINIA

University of Virginia
Environmental Thought and Practice
P.O. Box 400160
Charlottesville, VA 22904
Phone: (434) 982-3200
Fax: (434) 924-3587
http://tree.evsc.virginia.edu/
   ETP%20page2.htm

FIELD EDUCATION

ALABAMA

Huntingdon College
Field Biology Program
1500 East Fairview Avenue
Montgomery, AL 36106-2148
Phone: (334) 833-4222
http://fs.huntingdon.edu/biology/
   fieldmajorblurb.html

IDAHO

Lewis-Clark State College
Environmental Field Biology Program
500 Eighth Avenue
Lewistown, ID 83501
Phone: (208) 792-2295
http://www.lcsc.edu/science/Programs/
   BiologyField.html

Lewis-Clark State College
Environmental Field Geology Program
500 Eighth Avenue
Lewistown, ID 83509
Phone: (208) 792-2283
Fax: (208) 799-2064
http://www.lcsc.edu/science/Programs/
   Geology.html

INDIANA

Hanover College
Environmental Sciences and Field
   Biology Program
P.O. Box 108
Hanover, IN 47243
Phone: (812) 866-7000
http://www.hanover.edu/biology/biology.
   html

WISCONSIN

Edgewood College
Field Science Teaching Program
1000 Edgewood College Drive
Madison, WI 53711
Phone: (608) 663-2294
Fax: (608) 663-3291
http://www.edgewood.edu/academics/
   undergrad/nat_sci/majors/BFS_
   teaching_le.htm

MARINE SCIENCE

CALIFORNIA

University of San Diego
Marine and Environmental Studies
5998 Alcala Park
San Diego, 92110-2492
Phone: (619) 260-4795
http://www.sandiego.edu/mars_envi/

DELAWARE

University of Delaware
Graduate College of Marine Studies
111 Robinson Hall
Newark, DE 19716-3501
Phone: (302) 831-2841
Fax: (302) 831-4389
http://www.ocean.udel.edu/

FLORIDA

Barry University
Marine Biology Program
School of Natural and Health Sciences

11300 NE Second Avenue
Miami Shores, FL 33161-6695
Phone: (305) 899-3100
http://www.barry.edu/marineBiology/

Florida Institute of Technology
Department of Marine and Environmental
   Systems
150 University Boulevard
Melbourne, FL 32901-6975
Phone: (321) 674-8096
Fax: (321) 674-7212
http://www.fit.edu/AcadRes/dmes/

Florida Keys Community College
Marine Environment Technology
   Program
5901 College Road
Key West, FL 33040
Phone: (305) 296-9081
http://www.firn.edu/fkcc/marine.htm

Jacksonville University
Marine Science Program
2800 University Boulevard North
Jacksonville, FL 32211
Phone: (904) 745-7000
http://www.ju.edu/academics/undergrad_
   marineScience.asp

University of Miami
Rosenstiel School of Marine Science
4600 Rickenbacker Causeway
Miami, FL 33149
Phone: (305) 361-4155
Fax: (305) 361-4771
http://www.rsmas.miami.edu/

GEORGIA

Savannah State University
Marine Science Program
P.O. Box 20468
Savannah, GA 31404
Phone: (912) 356-2809
http://www.savstate.edu/scitech/
   MarineSci/mbi.htm

HAWAII

University of Hawaii, Hilo
Marine Science Department
200 West Kawili Street
Hilo, HI 96720-4091
Phone: (808) 974-7554
Fax: (808) 974-7693
http://www.uhh.hawaii.edu/academics/
   cas/natsci/marinesci.php

University of Hawaii, Manoa
School of Ocean & Earth Science &
   Technology
1680 East-West Road, POST 802
Honolulu, HI 96822
Phone: (808) 956-6182
Fax: (808) 956-9152
http://www.soest.hawaii.edu/

MASSACHUSETTS

Five College
Coastal and Marine Science Program
Smith College
Northampton, MA 01063
Phone: (413) 585-3799
http://www.science.smith.edu/
   departments/MARINE/

University of Massachusetts, Boston
Environmental, Coastal and Ocean
   Sciences
100 Morrissey Boulevard
Boston, MA 02125-3393
Phone: (617) 287-7440
Fax: (617) 287-7474
http://www.es.umb.edu/

MISSISSIPPI

University of Southern Mississippi
College of Marine Sciences
703 East Beach Drive
P.O. Box 7000
Ocean Springs, MS 39566-7000
Phone: (228) 872-4200
Fax: (228) 872-4204
http://www.cms.usm.edu/

NEW YORK

State University of New York (SUNY),
   Stony Brook
Marine Science Research Center
343A Harriman Hall
Stony Brook, NY 11794-2250
Phone: (631) 632-8765
Fax: (631) 632-7809
http://www.msrc.sunysb.edu/pages/
   education.html

NORTH CAROLINA

University of North Carolina,
   Wilmington
Marine Science Program
Wilmington, NC 28403-5606
Phone: (910) 962-3459

Fax: (910) 962-3013
http://www.uncwil.edu/mms/

RHODE ISLAND

Robert Williams University
Marine Biology Summer Program
One Old Ferry Road
Bristol, RI 02809-2921
Phone: (401) 254-3108
http://department.rwu.edu/~biology/
   camp.html

VIRGINIA

Hampton University
Marine and Environmental Science
   Program
Hampton, VA 23668
Phone: (757) 727-5783
http://www.hamptonu.edu/science/marine/

NATURALIST

NORTH CAROLINA

Lees McRae College
Naturalist Concentration Program
P.O. Box 128
Banner Elk, NC 28604-0128
Phone: (828) 898-5241

OUTDOOR EDUCATION

ALASKA

Sheldon Jackson College
Outdoor Leadership Program
801 Lincoln Street
Sitka, AK 99835
Phone: (800) 478-4556
http://www.sheldonjackson.edu/519.cfm

University of Alaska, Southeast
Outdoor Leadership Program
11120 Glacier Highway
Juneau, AK 99801
Phone: (907) 465-6362
http://www.uas.alaska.edu/academics/
   ods/index.html | outdoor.leadership@
   uas.alaska.edu

COLORADO

Colorado Mountain College
Outdoor Studies and Environmental Studies
901 South Highway 24
Leadville, CO 80461

Phone: (719) 486-2015
http://www.coloradomtn.edu/programs/
outdoor.html

ILLINOIS

Northern Illinois University
Department of Teaching and Learning
Outdoor/Environmental Education
DeKalb, IL 60115
Phone: (815) 753-9069
Fax: (815) 753-8594
http://www.cedu.niu.edu/tedu/outdoored/
faq.html

NEW HAMPSHIRE

University of New Hampshire
Outdoor Education Program
124 Main Street
Durham, NH 03824
Phone: (603) 862-2070
Fax: (603) 862-0154
http://www.unh.edu/outdoor-education/

RECREATION

The following colleges and universities offer four-year parks and recreation degrees that are accredited by the National Recreation and Park Association. Students pursuing this accredited course of study have the option of specializing in outdoor recreation, therapeutic recreation, or commercial recreation, as well as either business or camp management. Along with offering classes on topics such as recreation and administration and community organization, these programs also require students to complete some sort of supervised internship.

ARKANSAS

Arkansas Tech University
Department of Parks, Recreation &
    Hospitality Administration
Williamson Hall 106
Russellville, AR 72801
Phone: (501) 968-0378
Fax: (501) 968-0600
http://syssci.atu.edu/dept.htm

University of Arkansas
Recreation Program, Department Health
    Sciences, Kinesiology, Recreation, &
    Dance
HPER 306-R
Fayetteville, AR 72701
Phone: (501) 575-2854

Fax: (501) 575-6401
http://www.uark.edu/depts/coehp/HKRD.
htm

ARIZONA

Arizona State University—Main Campus
School of Community Resources and
    Development
411 North Central Avenue, Suite 550
Phoenix, AZ 85004-0690
Phone: (602) 496-0550
Fax: (602) 496-0953
http://scrd.asu.edu

Arizona State University West
Department of Recreation & Tourism
    Management
4701 West Thunderbird
Glendale, AZ 85306-4908
Phone: (602) 543-6617
Fax: (602) 543-6612
http://www.west.asu.edu/chs/RTM/index.
htm

Northern Arizona University
Parks and Recreation Management Program
Box 15016
Flagstaff, AZ 86011-5016
Phone: (928) 523-6655
Fax: (928) 523-2275
http://www.prm.nau.edu/

CALIFORNIA

California Polytechnic State University,
    San Luis Obispo
Recreation Administration Program,
    Natural Resources Management
    Department
San Luis Obispo, CA 93407
Phone: (805) 756-2050
Fax: (805) 756-1402
http://www.nrm.calpoly.edu/

California State University, Chico
Department of Recreation and Parks
    Management
Room 101 Tehama Hall
Chico, CA 95929-0560
Phone: (530) 898-6408
Fax: (530) 898-6557
http://132.241.182.52/RECR/index.html

California State University, Fresno
Recreation Administration & Leisure
    Studies
5310 North Campus Drive, PH 103
Fresno, CA 93740-0103
Phone: (209) 278-2838

Fax: (209) 278-5267
http://www.csufresno.edu/recadmin/

California State University,
    Long Beach
Department of Recreation and Leisure
    Studies
1250 Bellflower Boulevard
Long Beach, CA 90840-4903
Phone: (562) 985-4071
Fax: (562) 985-8154
http://www.csulb.edu/~rls

California State University, Sacramento
Department of Recreation & Leisure
    Studies
6000 J Street
Sacramento, CA 95819-6110
Phone: (916) 278-6752
Fax: (916) 278-5053
http://www.hhs.csus.edu/rls

San Diego State University
Department of Recreation
5900 Campanile Drive
San Diego, CA 92182-0368
Phone: (619) 594-511
Fax: (619) 594-6974
http://psfa.sdsu.edu/rec

San Francisco State University
Department of Recreation and Leisure
    Studies
1600 Holloway Avenue
San Francisco, CA 94132
Phone: (415) 338-1531
Fax: (415) 338-0543
http://www.sfsu.edu/~recdept

San Jose State University
Department of Recreation and Leisure
    Studies
One Washington Square
San Jose, CA 95192-0060
Phone: (408) 924-3000
Fax: (408) 924-2990
http://www2.sjsu.edu/recreation/

COLORADO

Metropolitan State College of Denver
Department of Human Performance,
    Sport & Leisure
1006 Eleventh Street, Campus Box 25
Denver, CO 80217-3362
Phone: (303) 556-3145
Fax: (303) 556-8301
http://www.mscd.edu/academic/scops/
leisure/

DISTRICT OF COLUMBIA

Gallaudet University
Recreation & Leisure Studies, PER
    Department
800 Florida Avenue, NE
Washington, DC 20002
Phone: (202) 651-5591
Fax: (202) 651-5861
http://depts.gallaudet.edu/PE/

FLORIDA

Florida International University
Park & Recreation Management
    Curriculum, HPER
GPA 242, Ziff Education Building
    Room 215A
Miami, FL 33199
Phone: (305) 348-3520
Fax: (305) 348-3571
http://www.fiu.edu/~hper

Florida State University
Recreation and Leisure Studies Program
215 Stone Building
Tallahassee, FL 32306-4458
Phone: (850) 644-5412
Fax: (850) 644-4335
http://www.fsu.edu/~leisure/

University of Florida
Department of Tourism, Recreation and
    Sport Management
Room 300 Florida Gym /
    P.O. Box 118208
Gainesville, FL 32611-8208
Phone: (352) 392-4042
Fax: (352) 392-7588
http://www.hhp.ufl.edu/rpt

GEORGIA

Georgia Southern University
Department of Recreation and Sport
    Management
Hollis Building, Landrum Box 8077
Statesboro, GA 30460-8077
Phone: (912) 681-5462
Fax: (912) 681-0386
http://www2.gasou.edu/RASM/RASM.
    HTM

University of Georgia
Department of Recreation and Leisure
    Studies, School of Health & Human
    Performance
300 River Road
Athens, GA 30602-6555
Phone: (706) 542-5064
Fax: (706) 542-7917
http://www.coe.uga.edu/recleisure/

IDAHO

**University of Idaho, College of
    Education**
Recreation Program Unit, Division of
    HPERD
Dr. Calvin W. Lathen, Division Director
    and Coordinator of Recreation
Physical Education Building #101
Moscow, ID 83843-2401
Phone: (208) 885-6582
Fax: (208) 885-5929
http://www.uidaho.edu/ed/hperd/

ILLINOIS

Aurora University
Recreation Administration Department
347 South Gladstone Avenue
Aurora, IL 60506
Phone: (630) 844-5404
Fax: (630) 844-5532
http://www.aurora.edu/recadmin

Chicago State University
Recreation Program
9501 South King Drive/ JDC 219
Chicago, IL 60628-1598
Phone: (773) 995-2294

Eastern Illinois University
Department of Recreation Administration
Room 1110, McAfee Gym, 610 Lincoln
    Avenue
Charleston, IL 61920
Phone: (217) 581-3018
Fax: (217) 581-7804
http://www.eiu.edu/~leisrstd/

Illinois State University
Recreation and Park Administration
    Program Department of HPER
McCormick Hall Room 101/CB 5121
Normal, IL 61790-5121
Phone: (309) 438-5608
Fax: (309) 438-5561
http://www.kinrec.ilstu.edu

Southern Illinois University
Department of Health Education and
    Recreation
Pulliam Hall 307, Mail Code 4632
Carbondale, IL 62901
Phone: (618) 453-4331
Fax: (618) 453-1829
http://www.siu.edu/departments/coe/
    hedrec/Programs/REC-BS.html

University of St. Francis
Recreation Administration Department
500 Wilcox Street

Joliet, IL 60435
Phone: (815) 740-3691
Fax: (815) 740-4285
http://www.stfrancis.edu/rec/index.htm

Western Illinois University
Department of Recreation, Park,
    & Tourism Administation
400 Currens Hall
Macomb, IL 61455
Phone: (309) 298-1967
Fax: (309) 298-2967
http://www.wiu.edu/users/mirpta

INDIANA

Indiana State University
Department of Recreation & Sport
    Management
Arena B-64
Terre Haute, IN 47809
Phone: (812) 237-2183
Fax: (812) 237-4338
http://web.indstate.edu/rcsm/

Indiana University
Department of Recreation, Park,
    and Tourism Studies
HPER Building
Bloomington, IN 47405
Phone: (812) 855-4711
Fax: (812) 855-3998
http://www.indiana.edu/~recpark

IOWA

University of Iowa
Department of Sport, Health, Leisure
    and Physical Studies
E102A Field House
Iowa City, IA 52242-1111
Phone: (319) 335-9335
Fax: (319) 335-6669
http://www.uiowa.edu/~leisure/

University of Northern Iowa
Leisure, Youth and Human Services
    Division, HPELS
Wellness Recreation Center, Room 203
School of HPELS
Cedar Falls, IA 50614-0161
Phone: (319) 273-2654
Fax: (319) 273-5958
http://www.uni.edu/coe/hpels/ls/ie.html

KANSAS

Kansas State University
Recreation Resources Division

Department of Horticulture, Forestry
& Recreation Resources
2021 Throckmorton Plant Sciences
Center
Manhattan, KS 66506-4002
Phone: (785) 532-6170
Fax: (785) 532-6949
http://www.oznet.ksu.edu/dp_hfrr/

Pittsburg State University
Department of Health, Physical Education
and Recreation
1701 South Broadway
Pittsburg, KS 66762-7557
Phone: (620) 235-4665
Fax: (620) 235-4520
http://www.pittstate.edu/hper/

KENTUCKY

Eastern Kentucky University
Department of Recreation & Park
Administration
Begley Building Room 402
Richmond, KY 40475
Phone: (606) 622-1833
Fax: (606) 622-2971
http://www.recreation.eku.edu

Western Kentucky University
Recreation and Park Administration
Curriculum, Department PER
Diddle Arena
Bowling Green, KY 42101
Phone: (270) 745-3591
Fax: (270) 745-3592
http://edtech.cebs.wku.edu/~perec/
recreation.html

LOUISIANA

Grambling State University
Recreation Careers Program, Department
of HPELS
P.O. Box 4244
Grambling, LA 71245
Phone: (318) 274-2294
Fax: (318) 274-6053
http://www.gram.edu/COE/college_of_
education.htm

MAINE

University of Maine, Machias
Program in Recreation Management
Division of Professional Studies
9 O'Brien Avenue
Machias, ME 04654

Phone: (207) 255-1227
Fax: (207) 255-4864
http://www.umm.maine.edu/programs/
recmgmt/

MARYLAND

Frostburg State University
Recreation Program, HPER
Cordts Physical Education Center
101 Braddock Road
Frostburg, MD 21532-1099
Phone: (301) 687-4474
Fax: (301) 687-7959
http://www.frostburg.edu/dept/phec/
phecmain.htm

MASSACHUSETTS

Springfield College
Department of Sport Management
& Recreation
263 Alden Street
Springfield, MA 01109-3797
Phone: (413) 748-3693
Fax: (413) 748-3685
http://www.spfldcol.edu

MICHIGAN

Central Michigan University
Department of Recreation, Parks &
Leisure Services
Finch 103
Mt. Pleasant, MI 48859
Phone: (517) 774-3858
Fax: (517) 774-2161
http://rpl.cmich.edu/

Ferris State University
Recreation Leadership & Management
Program
Department of Leisure Studies &
Wellness
102 Student Recreation Center
401 South Street
Big Rapids, MI 49307-2744
Phone: (231) 591-2681
Fax: (231) 591-3887
http://www.ferris.edu/colleges/educatio/lsw/

Michigan State University
Department of Park, Recreation &
Tourism
Room 131 Natural Resources
East Lansing, MI 48824-1222
Phone: (517) 353-5190
Fax: (517) 432-3597
http://www.msu.edu/user/prtr/

MINNESOTA

Minnesota State University, Mankato
Department of Recreation, Parks and
Leisure Services
213 Highland North
Mankato, MN 56002-8400
Phone: (507) 389-2127
Fax: (507) 389-2985
http://www.mankato.msus.edu/dept/RPLS/

University of Minnesota
Division of Recreation, Park, & Leisure
Studies
224 Cooke Hall
1900 University Avenue SE
Minneapolis, MN 55455
Phone: (612) 625-5300
Fax: (612) 626-7700
http://www.kls.coled.umn.edu

MISSISSIPPI

University of Mississippi
Department of Exercise Science
& Leisure Management
215 Turner Center
University, MS 38677
Phone: (601) 232-5521
Fax: (601) 232-5525
http://www.olemiss.edu/depts/eslm/
rm.htm

University of Southern Mississippi
Recreation Program, School of Human
Performance & Recreation
Box 5142
Hattiesburg, MS 39406-5142
Phone: (601) 266-5386
Fax: (601) 266-4445
http://www-dept.usm.edu/~hpr/

MISSOURI

Missouri State University
Recreation & Leisure Studies
Health, Physical Education, and
Recreation Department
901 South National Avenue
Springfield, MO 65804-0089
Phone: (417) 836-5411
Fax: (417) 836-4200
http://www.missouristate.edu/HPER/

Southeast Missouri State University
Recreation Program, Department of
Health and Leisure
One University Plaza, PE 311
Cape Girardeau, MO 63701

Phone: (573) 651-2470
Fax: (573) 651-5150
http://www5.semo.edu/health

University of Missouri
Department of Parks, Recreation and
  Tourism
105 Anheuser-Busch Natural Resources
  Building
Columbia, MO 65211-7230
Phone: (573) 882-7088
Fax: (573) 882-9526
http://www.snr.missouri.edu/prt/index.html

MONTANA

University of Montana
Recreation Management Program
School of Forestry
Missoula, MT 59812
Phone: (406) 243-5521
Fax: (406) 243-6656
http://www.forestry.umt.edu/degrees/
  undergraduate/rrmgmt/

NEW HAMPSHIRE

University of New Hampshire
Department of Recreation Management
  and Policy
108 Hewitt Hall
Durham, NH 03824
Phone: (603) 862-3401
Fax: (603) 862-2722
http://www.unh.edu/rmp/index.html

NEW YORK

Ithaca College
Department of Therapeutic Recreation
  & Leisure Services
36 Hill Center
Ithaca, NY 14850
Phone: (607) 274-3335
Fax: (607) 274-1943
http://www.ithaca.edu/hshp/trls/rectxt.htm

**State University of New York—
  Brockport**
Recreation and Leisure Studies Department
350 New Campus Drive
Brockport, NY 14420-2976
Phone: (585) 395-5338
Fax: (585) 395-5246
http://www.brockport.cdu/lcisurc/

**State University of New York—
  Cortland**
Department of Recreation & Leisure
  Studies

P.O. Box 2000
Cortland, NY 13045
Phone: (607) 753-4941
Fax: (607) 753-5982
http://www.cortland.edu/rec/

NORTH CAROLINA

Appalachian State University
Leisure Studies Program, Department
  HLES
206 Varsity Gym
Boone, NC 28608
Phone: (828) 262-3140
Fax: (828) 262-3138
http://www.appstate.edu/www_docs/
  depart/hles/

East Carolina University
Recreation and Leisure Studies Department
School of Health & Human Performance
174 Minges Coliseum
Greenville, NC 27858-4353
Phone: (252) 328-4640
Fax: (252) 328-4642
http://www.ecu.edu/rcls/

North Carolina Central University
Parks & Recreation Management
  Department PER
P.O. Box 19542
Durham, NC 27707
Phone: (919) 560-6186
Fax: (919) 560-5473
http://www.nccu.edu/artsci/pe/pe.htm

North Carolina State University
Department of Parks, Recreation and
  Tourism Management
4008 Biltmore Hall
Raleigh, NC 27695-8004
Phone: (919) 515-3276
Fax: (919) 515-3687
http://www.cfr.ncsu.edu/prtm/

**University of North Carolina—
  Chapel Hill**
Department of Exercise and Sport Science
Recreation and Leisure Specialization
CB #8700
Chapel Hill, NC 27599-8700
Phone: (919) 962-0534
Fax: (919) 962-6325
http://www.unc.edu/depts/exercise/
  recandleisure.htm

**University of North Carolina—
  Greensboro**
Department of Recreation, Parks, and
  Tourism
420 HHP Building
P.O. Box 26169

Greensboro, NC 27402-6169
Phone: (336) 334-5327
Fax: (336) 334-3238
http://www.uncg.edu/rpt/

**University of North Carolina—
  Wilmington**
Parks and Recreation Management,
  Department of HPER
601 South College Road
Wilmington, NC 28403-3297
Phone: (910) 962-3251
Fax: (910) 962-7073
http://www.uncwil.edu/hper/

Winston-Salem State University
Therapeutic Recreation Program
Department of Physical Education
Winston-Salem, NC 27110
Phone: (336) 750-2580
Fax: (336) 750-2591
http://www.wssu.edu/education/
  Departments/PhyEduDepartment/
  phyeddept.htm

OHIO

Bowling Green State University
Sport Management, Recreation
  & Tourism Division
School of Health, Physical Education,
  and Recreation
203 Eppler North
Bowling Green, OH 43403-0248
Phone: (419) 372-6908
Fax: (419) 372-2877
http://www.bgsu.edu/departments/hmsls/
  smrt/rtd/rtd.html

Kent State University
Leisure Studies Program
School of Exercise, Leisure & Sport
P.O. Box 5190
Kent, OH 44242
Phone: (330) 672-2015
Fax: (330) 672-4106
http://www.kent.edu/sels

Ohio University
Recreation Studies Program
School of Recreation & Sports Science
RTEC 318-C
Athens, OH 45701
Phone: (740) 593-4648
Fax: (740) 593-0284
http://www.ohiou.edu/rsps/recstudies/
  index.htm

University of Toledo
Division of Recreation and Leisure Studies
2801 West Bancroft Street

252 Health Education Center
Toledo, OH 43606
Phone: (419) 530-2757
Fax: (419) 530-4759
http://www.hhs.utoledo.edu/dphrsl/

OKLAHOMA

Oklahoma State University
Program in Leisure Studies, School of
    AHEP
103 Colvin Center
Stillwater, OK 74078
Phone: (405) 744-5503
Fax: (405) 744-6507
http://www.okstate.edu/education/sahep/
    leisure/index.html

PENNSYLVANIA

East Stroudsburg University
Department of Recreation & Leisure
    Services Management
Box 138
East Stroudsburg, PA 18301
Phone: (570) 422-3305
Fax: (570) 422-3777
http://www.esu.edu/recr/index.html

Slippery Rock University
Department of Parks & Recreation/
    Environmental Education
101 Eisenberg
Slippery Rock, PA 16057
Phone: (724) 738-2068
Fax: (724) 738-2938
http://academics.sru.edu/pree/

Temple University
Sport & Recreation Management
1700 North Broad Street, Suite 412
Philadelphia, PA 19122
Phone: (215) 204-8701
Fax: (215) 204-8705
http://www.temple.edu/sthm/

York College
Recreation & Leisure Administration
    Program
Country Club Road
York, PA 17405-7199
Phone: (717) 815-6415
Fax: (717) 849-1619
http://www.ycp.edu/besc/besc_rec_
    leisure.html

SOUTH CAROLINA

Clemson University
Department of Parks, Recreation
    & Tourism Management
276 Lehotsky Hall

Clemson, SC 29634-0735
Phone: (864) 656-3400
Fax: (864) 656-2226
http://www.hehd.clemson.edu/PRTM/
    index.htm

TENNESSEE

Middle Tennessee State University
Program in Recreation
Department of Health, Physical
    Education, and Recreation
201 Memorial Gym
P.O. Box 96
Murfreesboro, TN 37132
Phone: (615) 898-2147
Fax: (615) 898-5020
http://www.mtsu.edu/~hperspot/leisure/
    leisure.html

University of Tennessee—Knoxville
Recreation & Tourism Management
    Department
1914 Andy Holt Avenue
Knoxville, TN 37996-2710
Phone: (423) 974-6045
Fax: (423) 974-6439
http://trcs.he.utk.edu/rec/recmain.html

TEXAS

Southwest Texas State University
Recreation Administration Division,
    Department HPER
Jowers Center, 601 University Drive
San Marcos, TX 78666
Phone: (512) 245-2561
Fax: (512) 245-8678
http://www.schooledu.swt.edu/acaddpt/
    hperweb/index.html

Texas A&M University
Department of Recreation, Park
    & Tourism Sciences
107 Frances Hall
College Station, TX 77843-2261
Phone: (409) 845-5411
Fax: (409) 845-0446
http://wwwrpts.tamu.edu/RPTS/index.
    html

University of North Texas
Recreation & Leisure Studies
Department of Kinesiology, Health,
    Physical Education, and Recreation
UNT Box 311337, PEB 209
Denton, TX 76203-1337
Phone: (940) 565-2651
Fax: (940) 565-4904
http://www.coe.unt.edu/khpr/

UTAH

Brigham Young University
Department of Recreation Management
    & Youth Leadership
273 Richards Building
Provo, UT 84602-2031
Phone: (801) 378-4369
Fax: (801) 378-7461
http://www.byu.edu/rmyl

University of Utah
Department of Parks, Recreation and
    Tourism
250 South 1850 East, HPER N-226
Salt Lake City, UT 84112-0920
Phone: (801) 581-8542
Fax: (801) 581-4930
http://www.health.utah.edu/prt/

Utah State University
Parks & Recreation Program
Department of Health, Physical
    Education, and Recreation
UMC 7000 / Old Main Hall
Logan, UT 84322-7000
Phone: (435) 797-1497
Fax: (435) 797-3759
http://www.coe.usu.edu/hper/

VERMONT

Green Mountain College
Department of Recreation and Leisure
    Studies
160 Moses Hall
Poultney, VT 05764
Phone: (802) 287-8330
Fax: (802) 287-8099
http://www.greenmtn.edu/catalog

Lyndon State College
Recreation Resource & Ski Resort
    Management
Lyndonville, VT 05851
Phone: (802) 626-6475
Fax: (802) 626-9770
http://www.lsc.vsc.edu/

VIRGINIA

Ferrum College
Recreation and Leisure Program
P.O. Box 1000
Ferrum, VA 24088
Phone: (540) 365-4387
Fax: (540) 365-4260
http://www.ferrum.edu/frm_acad.htm

George Mason University
Parks, Recreation and Leisure Studies
    Program

School of Recreation, Health and Tourism
10900 University Boulevard
MSN 4E5
Manassas, VA 20110
Phone: (703) 993-2085
Fax: (703) 993-2025
http://rht.gmu.edu/

Longwood University
Therapeutic Recreation Program
Department of Health, Recreation, and
  Kinesiology
201 High Street
Farmville, VA 23909
Phone: (434) 395-2545
Fax: (804) 395-2380
http://www.longwood.edu/hrk/index.htm

Old Dominion University
Norfolk, VA 23529-0196
Phone: (757) 683-4703
Fax: (757) 683-4270
http://web.odu.edu/webroot/orgs/Educ/
  PE/rec_leisure.nsf

Radford University
Department of Recreation, Parks and
  Tourism
Box 6963
Radford, VA 24142
Phone: (540) 831-7720
Fax: (540) 831-6487
http://www.radford.edu/~recparks/

Virginia Commonwealth University
Recreation, Parks & Tourism, Division
  of HPER
317 West Franklin Street, Box 2015
Richmond, VA 23284-2015
Phone: (804) 828-1130
Fax: (804) 828-1946
http://www.soe.vcu.edu/hper/index.htm

Virginia Wesleyan College
Recreation and Leisure Studies Program
Wesleyan Drive

Norfolk, VA 23502
Phone: (757) 455-3305
Fax: (757) 455-5739
http://www.vwc.edu/academic_life/
  divisions/rec/rec.htm

WASHINGTON

Eastern Washington University
Program in Recreation and Leisure
  Services
Department of Physical Education,
  Health, and Recreation
526 Fifth Street, HPERA Complex,
  MS-66
Cheney, WA 99004
Phone: (509) 359-2341
Fax: (509) 359-4833
http://www.aa.ewu.edu/pehr/

Western Washington University
Recreation Program
Physical Education, Health, and
  Recreation Department
Old Carver #6
Bellingham, WA 98225-9067
Phone: (360) 650-3782
Fax: (360) 650-7447
http://www.ac.wwu.edu/~pehr/

WEST VIRGINIA

Marshall University
Park Resources & Leisure Services,
  HPER Department
400 Hal Greer Boulevard
Huntington, WV 25755-2450
Phone: (304) 696-2922
Fax: (304) 696-2928
http://www.marshall.edu/coe/ESSR/
  INDEX.HTML

West Virginia State University
Recreation Program
Department of Health, Physical
  Education, Recreation & Sport

Fleming Hall, Room 126
Institute, WV 25112-1000
Phone: (304) 766-3232
Fax: (304) 766-3365
http://www.wvsc.edu/hhp

West Virginia University
Recreation and Parks Management
  Program
325B Percival Hall
Morgantown, WV 26506-6125
Phone: (304) 293-2941
Fax: (304) 293-2441
http://www.caf.wvu.edu/for/pandr/
  rptmpage.htm

WISCONSIN

Aurora University
School of Experiential Leadership and
  Recreation Administration
George Williams College
350 Constance Boulevard
P.O. Box 210
Williams Bay, WI 53191
Phone: (262) 245-8572
Fax: (262) 245-8595
http://www.aurora.edu/recadmin

University of Wisconsin—LaCrosse
Department of Recreation Management
  & Therapeutic Recreation
128 Wittich Hall
LaCrosse, WI 54601
Phone: (608) 785-8207
Fax: (608) 785-8206
http://perth.uwlax.edu/RMTR/

RECREATIONAL THERAPY

The American Therapeutic Recreation
Association offers a searchable database
of colleges and universities offering programs in therapeutic recreation at http://
www.atra-tr.org/curriculumguide.htm

SCIENTIFIC

BIODIVERSITY

MICHIGAN

Albion College
Biology Department
Biodiversity Program
611 East Porter Street
Albion, MI 49224
Phone: (517) 629-0291

Fax: (517) 629-0888
http://www.albion.edu/biology/

TENNESSEE

Lee University
Environmental Science and Biodiversity
  Concentration
1120 North Ocoee Street
Cleveland, TN 37320-3450

Phone: (423) 614-8000
http://artsandsciences.leeuniversity.edu/
  nsm/info/programs.asp

BIOLOGICAL SCIENCES

ALABAMA

Alabama State University
Biological Sciences Department

206 H. Council Trenhom Hall
915 South Jackson Street
Montgomery, AL 36101-0271
Phone: (334) 229-4467
Fax: (334) 229-1007
http://www.alasu.edu/asu/ASUWEB.aspx?
    ContentID=153&SubUnitID=33

Athens State University
Biology Department
300 North Beaty Street
Athens, AL 35611
Phone: (256) 233-8255
http://www.athens.edu/sos/bi/

Auburn University, Montgomery
Biology Department
P.O. Box 244023
Montgomery, AL 36124-4023
Phone: (334) 244-3000
http://www.aum.edu/Academics/
    Schools/Sciences/Departments_and_
    Undergraduate_Programs/Biology_
    CLS/index.cfm?id=3596

Judson College
Biology Department
Marion, AL 36756
Phone: (334) 683-5179
http://home.judson.edu/academic/
    divisions/science/biology/biodept.
    html

Spring Hill College
Biology Department
4000 Dauphin Street
Mobile, AL 36608
Phone: (334) 380-3030
http://www.shc.edu/academics/undergrad/
    sciences/

University of South Alabama
Biology Department
Mobile, AL 36688-0002
Phone: (215) 460-6331
http://www.southalabama.edu/biology/

ALASKA

University of Alaska, Anchorage
Department of Biological Sciences
3211 Providence Drive
Engineering Building, Room. 333
Anchorage, AK 99508
Phone: (907) 786-4780
http://www.uaa.alaska.edu/biology/

University of Alaska, Southeast
Biology & Marine Biology

11120 Glacier Highway
Juneau, AK 99801
Phone: (907) 465-6510
http://www.uas.alaska.edu/academics/bio/
    index.html

ARKANSAS

Arkansas State University
Department of Biological Sciences
P.O. Box 599
State University, AR 72467
Phone: (870) 972-3082
Fax: (870) 972-2577
http://biology.astate.edu/

Harding University
Department of Biology
Searcy, AR 72149
Phone: (501) 279-4706
http://www.harding.edu/biology/

Henderson State University
Biology Department
1100 Henderson Street
Box 7520
Arkadelphia, AR 71999-0001
Phone: (870) 230-5314
Fax: (870) 230-5144
http://www.hsu.edu/dept/bio/

Hendrix College
Biology Department
1600 Washington Avenue
Conway, AR 72032
Phone: (501) 450-4532
Fax: (501) 450-4547
http://www.hendrix.edu/homes/fac/
    sutherlandM/default.htm

ARIZONA

Arizona State University
Department of Applied Biological
    Sciences
7001 East Williams Field Road
Mesa, AZ 85212
Phone: (480) 727-1444
Fax: (480) 727-1011
http://www.east.asu.edu/ecollege/
    appliedbiologicalsciences/

Grand Canyon University
Biology Department
3300 West Camelback Road,
    P.O. Box 11097
Phoenix, AZ 85017
Phone: (602) 589-2714
http://www.grand-canyon.edu/cos/
    biology/index.html

John Brown University
Biology Program
2000 West University Street
Siloam Springs, AZ 72761
Phone: (479) 524-9500
http://www.jbu.edu/academics/science/
    biology/index.asp

CALIFORNIA

California Institute of Technology
Biology Division
1200 East California Boulevard
Pasadena, CA 91125
Phone: (626) 395-4951
Fax: (626) 449-0756
http://www.biology.caltech.edu/

California Lutheran University
Biology Program
60 West Olsen Road
Thousand Oaks, CA 91360
Phone: (805) 493-3341
http://lupine.clunet.edu/Academic_
    Programs/Departments/Biology/CLU.
    html

California State University, Bakersfield
Department of Biology
9001 Stockdale Highway
Bakersfield, CA 93311-1099
Phone: (661) 664-3089
Fax: (661) 665-6956
http://www.csubak.edu/Biology/

California State University, Chico
Department of Biological Sciences
Holt 281A
Chico, CA 95929-0310
Phone: (530) 898-5356
http://www.csuchico.edu/biol/biology.
    html

**California State University, Dominguez
Hills**
Biology Department
1000 East Victoria Street
Carson, CA 90747
Phone: (310) 243-3381
http://www.csudh.edu/biology/

California State University, Los Angeles
Department of Biology
BS143
5151 State University Drive
Los Angeles, CA 90032
Phone: (323) 343-2050
Fax: (323) 343-6451
http://www.calstatela.edu/academic/biol/

California State University, Northridge
Biology Department
18111 Nordhoff Street
Northridge, CA 91330-8285
Phone: (818) 677-3356
Fax: (818) 677-2034
http://www.csun.edu/~hfbio002/home.htm

California State University,
San Bernardino
Biology Department
5500 University Parkway
San Bernardino, CA 92407
Phone: (909) 880-5305
Fax: (909) 880-7038
http://biology.csusb.edu/

California State University,
San Marcos
Biology Department
333 South Twin Oaks Valley Road
San Marcos, CA 92096
Phone: (760) 750-4103
http://www.csusm.edu/Biology/

Diablo Valley College
Biological and Health Sciences
    Department
321 Golf Club Road
Pleasant Hill, CA 94523
Phone: (925) 685-2799
http://www.dvc.edu/dpts/bio_and_health_
    sciences.htm

Harvey Mudd College
Biology Department
1250 North Dartmouth Avenue
Claremont, CA 91711
Phone: (909) 621-8561
Fax: (909) 607-7172
http://www.bio.hmc.edu/

La Sierra University
Biology Program
4700 Pierce Street
Riverside, CA 92515
Phone: (909) 785-2105
Fax: (909) 785-2111
http://www.lasierra.edu/departments/
    biology/

Loyola Marymount University
Biology Program
7900 Loyola Boulevard
Los Angeles, CA 90045-8220
Phone: (310) 338-7776
Fax: (310) 338-4479
http://www.eng.lmu.edu/~bio_web/
    LMU_BIO.html

Santa Clara University
Biology Department
500 El Camino Real
Santa Clara, CA 95053-0268
Phone: (408) 554-4496
Fax: (408) 554-2710
http://www.scu.edu/biology/

Stanford University
Center for Conservation Biology
Dept. of Biological Sciences
Stanford, CA 94305-5020
Phone: (650) 723-5924
Fax: (650) 723-5920
http://www.stanford.edu/group/CCB/
    index.htm

University of Southern California
Department of Biological Sciences
Allan Hancock Foundation Building—
    Room 107F
Los Angeles, CA 90089-0371
Phone: (213) 740-2777
http://www.usc.edu/dept/LAS/biosci/

COLORADO

Colorado Christian University
Biology Program
180 South Garrison Street
Lakewood, CO 80226
Phone: (303) 202-0100
Fax: (303) 274-7560
http://www.ccu.edu/undergrad/majors/
    biology.htm

Colorado College
Biology Department
14 East Cache La Poudre Street
Colorado Springs, CO 80903-3298
Phone: (719) 389-6395
http://www.coloradocollege.edu/Dept/
    BY/

Mesa State College
Department of Biology
Box 2647
Grand Junction, CO 81502
Phone: (970) 248-1020
http://mesastate.edu/biology/

CONNECTICUT

Central Connecticut State University
Department of Biological Sciences
Room 332 Copernicus Hall
New Britain, CT 06050
Phone: (860) 832-2645

Fax: (860) 832-2594
http://www.artsci.ccsu.edu/Departments/
    Biology.html

Fairfield University
Biology Department
1073 North Benson Road
Fairfield, CT 06824
Phone: (203) 254-4000
http://www.faculty.fairfield.edu/mhill/
    biology/bio_dept/home.html

DELAWARE

Delaware State University
Department of Biology
1200 North DuPont Highway
Dover, DE 19901
Phone: (302) 857-6510
Fax: (302) 857-6563
http://www.dsc.edu/schools/arts_sciences/
    bio/index.html

DISTRICT OF COLUMBIA

Catholic University of America
Biology Department
620 Michigan Avenue, NE
Washington, DC 20064
Phone: (202) 319-5267
Fax: (202) 319-5721
http://biology.cua.edu/

Howard University
Environmental & Systematic Biology
    Program
2400 Sixth Street, NW
Washington, DC 20059
Phone: (202) 806-6933
http://www.biology.howard.edu/ees.html

FLORIDA

Rollins College
Biology Department
Bush Science Center
1000 Holt Avenue
Winter Park, FL 32789-4499
Phone: (407) 646-2494
Fax: (407) 646-5272
http://www.rollins.edu/biology/

GEORGIA

Agnes Scott College
Biology Program
141 East College Avenue
Decatur, GA 30030

Phone: (404) 471-6000
http://www.agnesscott.edu/academics/
p_departments.asp?id=7

Armstrong Atlantic State University
Biology Department
11935 Abercorn Street
Savannah, GA 31419-1997
Phone: (912) 927-5279
Fax: (912) 921-5688
http://www.biology.armstrong.edu/aasu2.
html

Georgia College & State University
Biological and Environmental Sciences
Department
Campus Box 97
Milledgeville, GA 31061-0490
Phone: (912) 445-5004
http://www.gcsu.edu/acad_affairs/coll_
artsci/bioenv_sci/

Georgia State University
Biology Department
MSC 8L0389
33 Gilmer Street SE Unit 8
Atlanta, GA 30303-3088
Phone: (404) 651-2259
Fax: (404) 651-2509
http://biology.gsu.edu/

LaGrange College
Biology Program
601 Broad Street
LaGrange, GA 30240
Phone: (706) 880-8065
Fax: (706) 880-8158
http://www.lagrange.edu/primary.
cfm?linkid=618

**North Georgia College & State
University**
Department of Biology
105 Sunset Drive
Dahlonega, GA 30597
Phone: (706) 864-1953
Fax: (706) 867-2703
http://www.ngcsu.edu/Academic/
Sciences/Biology/biohome.HTM

Spelman College
Biology Department
Box #1183
350 Spelman Lane SW
Atlanta, GA 30314-4399
Phone: (404) 681-3643
Fax: (404) 223-7662
http://www.spelman.edu/~biology/
Biology.html

State University of West Georgia
Department of Biology
Carrollton, GA 30118
Phone: (770) 836-6547
Fax: (770) 836-6633
http://www.westga.edu/~biology/

HAWAII

**Brigham Young University, Hawaii
Campus**
Department of Biology
55-220 Kulanui Street, Box 1967
Laie, HI 96762
Phone: (808) 293-3800
http://w3.byuh.edu/academics/sciences/

Chaminade University
Biology Program
3140 Waialae Avenue
Honolulu, HI 96816-1578
Phone: (800) 735-3733
Fax: (808) 739-8329
http://www.chaminade.edu/catalog/pdf/
Biology.pdf

ILLINOIS

Augustana College
Biology Department
639 38th Street
Rock Island, IL 61201
Phone: (309) 794-3440
http://www.augustana.edu/academics/
biology/

Benedictine University
Biology Department
Birck Hall 348
5700 College Road
Lisle, IL 60532
Phone: (630) 829-6565
Fax: (630) 829-6547
http://www.ben.edu/programs/arts_
sciences/biology.asp

DePaul University
Biology Department
McGowan Science Center
2325 North Clifton Avenue
Chicago, IL 60614
Phone: (773) 325-7595
Fax: (773) 325-7596
http://condor.depaul.edu/~biology/

Elmhurst College
Department of Biology
Campus Box 55
190 Prospect Avenue

Elmhurst, IL 60126-3296
Phone: (630) 617-3588
Fax: (630) 617-6474
http://www.elmhurst.edu/~bio/

MacMurray College
Biology Program
447 East College Avenue
Jacksonville, IL 62650
Phone: (217) 479-7000
http://www.mac.edu/academics/biology.
html

McKendree College
Department of Biology
701 College Road
Lebanon, IL 62254
Phone: (618) 537-6930
http://www.mckendree.edu/McK
Catalogue_03_04/Courses_of_Study/
Biology.htm

North Central College
Biology Department
P.O. Box 3063
Naperville, IL 60148
Phone: (630) 637-5181
http://www.noctrl.edu/academics/
departments/biology/department_site/
biohome.htm

North Park University
Department of Biology
3225 West Foster Avenue
Chicago, IL 60625-4895
Phone: (773) 244-5655
Fax: (773) 244-4952
http://www.northpark.edu/acad/biology/

Rockford College
Biology Department
5050 East State Street
Rockford, IL 61108-2393
Phone: (800) 892-2984
http://www.rockford.edu/departs/f3bio.html

Roosevelt University
Biology Department
430 South Michigan Avenue
Chicago, IL 60605
Phone: (312) 341-3678
http://www.roosevelt.edu/cas/ssm/
biology.htm

INDIANA

Anderson University
Biology Department
1100 East Fifth Street

Anderson, IN 46012
Phone: (800) 428-6414
Fax: (764) 641-3845
http://www.anderson.edu/academics/biol

Butler University
Department of Biological Sciences
4600 Sunset Avenue
Indianapolis, IN 46208
Phone: (317) 940-9411
Fax: (317) 940-9519
http://www.butler.edu/biology/

Indiana Wesleyan University
Biology Program
4201 South Washington Street
Marion, IN 46953-4999
Phone: (765) 674-6901
http://www.indwes.edu/academics/
    Divisions/NaturalSciences/biology/

Marian College
Biological Science Program
3200 Cold Spring Road
Indianapolis, IN 46222-1997
Phone: (800) 772-7264
http://www.marian.edu/Academics_
    AreasOfStudy.asp?Action=VIEW&ID
    =41&Dept=8

University of Saint Francis
Department of Biology
2701 Spring Street
Fort Wayne, IN 46808
Phone: (800) 729-4732
http://www.sf.edu/biology2/

Wabash College
Department of Biology
P.O. Box 352
Crawfordsville, IN 47933
Phone: (765) 361-6237
Fax: (765) 361-6149
http://www.wabash.edu/depart/biology/

IOWA

Briar Cliff University
Biology Department
269 Heelan Hall
3303 Rebecca Street
Sioux City, IA 51104
Phone: (712) 279-5467
http://www.briarcliff.edu/biology/

Buena Vista University
Biology Program
610 West Fourth Street
Storm Lake, IA 50588

Phone: (800) 383-2821
Fax: (712) 749-2037
http://www.bvu.edu/~science/biology/

Coe College
Biology Department
1220 First Avenue, NE
Cedar Rapids, IA 52402
Phone: (319) 399-8000
http://www.coe.edu/Academics/
    BIOLOGY/Faculty.htm

Grand View College
Biology Department
1200 Grandview Avenue
Des Moines, IA 50316-1599
Phone: (800) 444-6083
http://www.gvc.edu/academics/biology/

Grinnell College
Biology Department
1116 Eighth Avenue
Grinnell, IA 50112-1690
Phone: (641) 269-3172
Fax: (641) 269-4984
http://www.grinnell.edu/academic/biology/

Iowa Wesleyan College
Biology Program
601 North Main Street
Mount Pleasant, IA 52641
Phone: (800) 582-2382
http://www.iwc.edu/pro_stu/majors/
    biology.htm

Loras College
Department of Biology
1450 Alta Vista
Dubuque, IA 52001
Phone: (563) 588-7767
http://depts.loras.edu/bio/

Luther College
Environmental Biology and Conservation
    Program
700 College Drive
Decorah, IA 52101
Phone: (319) 387-1557
http://www.luther.edu/~biodept/envprog.
    htm

KANSAS

Benedictine College
Biology Department
1020 North Second Street
Atchinson, KS 66002
Phone: (913) 367-5340
http://campus.benedictine.edu/biology/
    biology.html

Fort Hays State University
Biological Science Department
Albertson Hall 302
600 Park Street
Hays, KS 67601-4099
Phone: (785) 628-4214
Fax: (785) 628-4153
http://www.fhsu.edu/biology/

Mid-America Nazarene University
Biology Department
2030 East College Way
Olathe, KS 66062-1899
Phone: (800) 800-8887
http://www.mnu.edu/science/biol/

University of Saint Mary
Biology Program
4100 South Fourth Street
Leavenworth, KS 66048
Phone: (913) 682-5151
http://www.stmary.edu/extranet/biology/

KENTUCKY

Asbury College
Biology Department
One Macklem Drive
Wilmore, KY 40390
Phone: (859) 858-3511 ext. 2233
http://www.asbury.edu/academics/
    biology/

Bellarmine College
Biology Department
2001 Newburg Road
Louisville, KY 40205
Phone: (800) 274-4723
http://www.bellarmine.edu/cas/
    departments/biology/

LOUISIANA

Louisiana College
Biology Program
1140 College Drive, Box 552
Pineville, LA 71360
Phone: (318) 487-7611
http://www.lacollege.edu/science/
    biology_dept.html

Nicholls State University
Biological Science Program
114 Gouaux Hall
Thibodaux, LA 70310
Phone: (985) 448-4700
http://www.nicholls.edu/biol/default.htm

Northwestern State University
Department of Biological Sciences

Roy Hall
Natchitoches, LA 71497
Phone: (318) 357-5131
Fax: (318) 357-5599
http://scitech.nsula.edu/biology/

MARYLAND

Columbia Union College
Biology Department
7600 Flower Avenue
Takoma Park, MD 20912
Phone: (301) 891-4000
Fax: (301) 270-1618
http://www.cuc.edu/academic/
    departments/biology/index.html

Frostburg State University
Biology Department
201 Compton Science Center
101 Braddock Road
Frostburg, MD 21532-1099
Phone: (301) 687-4166
Fax: (301) 687-3034
http://www.frostburg.edu/dept/biol/
    biolmain.htm

Hood College
Environmental Biology Program
401 Rosemont Avenue
Frederick, MD 21701-8575
Phone: (301) 696-3660
http://www.hood.edu/academic/biology/
    env.html

Loyola College
Department of Biology
4501 North Charles Avenue
Baltimore, MD 21210
Phone: (410) 617-2642
Fax: (410) 617-5682
http://www.loyola.edu/biology/

McDaniel College
Biology Program
Eaton Hall
Westminster, MD 21157-4390
Phone: (410) 857-2400
Fax: (410) 386-4613
http://www.mcdaniel.edu/academics/
    biology/biology.shtml

MASSACHUSETTS

Boston College
Biology Department
140 Commonwealth Avenue
Chestnut Hill, MA 02467
Phone: (617) 552-3540
Fax: (617) 552-2011
http://www.bc.edu/schools/cas/biology

Boston University
Biology Department
5 Cummington Street
Boston, MA 02215
Phone: (617) 353-2432
Fax: (617) 353-6340
http://www.bu.edu/biology

MICHIGAN

Andrews University
Biology Department
Price Hall, Room 216
Berrien Springs, MI 49104-0410
Phone: (269) 471-3243
Fax: (616) 471-6911
http://www.andrews.edu/academic/cas/
    biology.php3

Calvin College
Biology Department
3201 Burton Street SE
Grand Rapids, MI 49546
Phone: (616) 957-6000
Fax: (616) 957-8551
http://www.calvin.edu/academic/biology/

Eastern Michigan University
Biology Department
316 Mark Jefferson
Ypsilanti, MI 48197
Phone: (734) 487-4242
Fax: (734) 487-9235
http://www.emich.edu/public/biology/
    bioweb.htm

Ferris State University
Department of Biological Sciences
ASC 2004
820 Campus Drive
Big Rapids, MI 49307
Phone: (231) 591-2550
Fax: (231) 591-2540
http://www.ferris.edu/HTMLS/colleges/
    artsands/biology/biology.htm

Hope College
Biology Department
35 East 12th Street
Holland, MI 49422-9000
Phone: (616) 395-7720
Fax: (616) 395-7125
http://www.hope.edu/academic/biology/

Madonna University
Biology Program
36600 Schoolcraft Road
Livonia, MI 48150
Phone: (800) 852-4951

http://madonna2.siteobjects.com/pages/
    biology.cfm

MINNESOTA

Augsburg College
Biology Department
Science Hall 219, Campus Box 117
Minneapolis, MN 55454
Phone: (612) 330-1074
http://www.augsburg.edu/biology/

College of Saint Catherine
Biology Department
601 25th Avenue South
Minneapolis, MN 55454
Phone: (651) 690-6631
http://minerva.stkate.edu/offices/
    academic/biology.nsf

College of Saint Scholastica
Biology Department
1200 Kenwood Avenue
Duluth, MN 55811
Phone: (218) 723-6719
Fax: (218) 723-6472
http://saints.css.edu/bio/biohome.htm

Northwestern College
Biology Major
3003 Snelling Avenue North
Saint Paul, MN 55113-1598
Phone: (651) 631-5100
http://www.nwc.edu/academic/science/
    bio.htm

St. Cloud State University
Biological Sciences Department
720 Fourth Avenue South
St. Cloud, MN 56301-4498
Phone: (320) 255-2039
Fax: (320) 308-4166
http://bulletin.stcloudstate.edu/
    departments/biol.asp

MISSISSIPPI

Belhaven College
Biology Department
1500 Peachtree Street
Jackson, MS 39202
Phone: (601) 968-5964
http://www.belhaven.edu/Academics/
    Divisions/Science/Biology/biology.
    htm

Delta State University
Biological Sciences Department
Cleveland, MS 38733

Phone: (662) 846-4797
http://www.deltastate.edu/academics/
    artsci/bio/index.html

University of Mississippi
Department of Biology
University, MS 38677
Phone: (662) 915-7203
Fax: (662) 915-5144
http://www.olemiss.edu/depts/biology/

University of Southern Mississippi
Department of Biological Sciences
Box 5018
Hattiesburg, MS 39406-5018
Phone: (601) 266-4748
Fax: (601) 266-5797
http://www.usm.edu/biology/

MISSOURI

Avila University
Biology Department
11901 Wornall Road
Kansas City, MO 64145-1698
Phone: (816) 501-3654
http://www.avila.edu/departments/
    biology/Bioweb/about_the_biology_
    Departmenthtm

Northwest Missouri State University
Department of Biological Science
800 University Drive
Maryville, MO 64468-6001
Phone: (660) 562-1388
http://www.nwmissouri.edu/academics/
    biology.htm

Rockhurst University
Biology Department
1100 Rockhurst Road
Kansas City, MO 64110
Phone: (816) 501-4237
http://www.rockhurst.edu/academic/
    biology/index.html

Southwest Baptist University
Biology Department
1600 University Avenue
Bolivar, MO 65613
Phone: (417) 328-1659
http://falcon.sbuniv.edu/cosm/BIO/

Southwest Missouri State University
Biology Department
901 South National Avenue
Springfield, MO 65804
Phone: (417) 836-5126
Fax: (417) 836-4204
http://biology.smsu.edu/Default.htm

University of Missouri, St. Louis
Department of Biology
R223 Research Building
8001 Natural Bridge Road
St. Louis, MO 63121-4499
Phone: (314) 516-6200
Fax: (314) 516-6233
http://www.umsl.edu/%7Ebiology/

MONTANA

University of Great Falls
Biology Program
1301 20th Street South
Great Falls, MT 59405-4996
Phone: (800) 856-9544
http://www.ugf.edu/index.html

NEBRASKA

Bellevue University
Biology Program
1000 Galvin Road South
Bellevue, NE 68005
Phone: (800) 756-7920
http://www.bellevue.edu/degrees/biology.
    asp

Chadron State College
Department of Biology
1000 Main Street
Chadron, NE 69337
Phone: (308) 432-6422
http://www.csc.edu/mathsci/Biology/
    default.htm

College of Saint Mary
Biology Program
1901 South 72nd Street
Omaha, NE 68124
Phone: (402) 399-2608
http://www.csm.edu/biodes.html

Hastings College
Biology Department
800 Turner Avenue
Hastings, NE 68901-7696
Phone: (402) 461-7383
Fax: (402) 461-7463
http://www.hastings.edu/academic/
    biology/index.html

Midland Lutheran College
Biology Program
900 North Clarkson
Fremont, NE 68025
Phone: (402) 941-6305
http://www.mlc.edu/academics/majors/
    default.asp?major=3

University of Nebraska, Lincoln
School of Biological Sciences
348 Manter Hall
P.O. Box 880118
Lincoln, NE 68588-0118
Phone: (402) 472-6676
http://ascweb.unl.edu/academics/depts/
    biosci.html

University of Nebraska, Omaha
Biology Department
Allwine Hall 114
60th and Dodge Streets
Omaha, NE 68182-0040
Phone: (402) 554-2641
Fax: (402) 554-3532
http://www.unomaha.edu/

NEVADA

Community College of Southern Nevada
Department of Biological Sciences
3200 East Cheyenne Avenue
North Las Vegas, NV 89030-4296
Phone: (702) 651-4009
Fax: (702) 651-4056
http://www.ccsn.nevada.edu/science/Lsci.
    html

University of Nevada, Las Vegas
Department of Biological Sciences
Las Vegas, NV 89154-4004
Phone: (702) 895-3390
Fax: (702) 895-3956
http://www.unlv.edu/Colleges/Sciences/
    Biology/

NEW JERSEY

Bloomfield College
Biology Department
Science Building
Liberty Street
Bloomfield, NJ 07003
Phone: (973) 748-9000
Fax: (973) 743-3998
http://www.bloomfield.edu/academic/
    programs/biology.htm

Fairleigh Dickinson University
Biology Department
1000 River Road
Teaneck, NJ 7666
Phone: (973) 443-8746
http://alpha.fdu.edu/becton/BioAHS/
    biology.html

Georgian Court College
Biology Program
900 Lakewood Avenue

Lakewood, NJ 08701
Phone: (732) 364-2200
http://www.georgian.edu/biology/

Kean College of New Jersey
Biology Program
1000 Morris Ave
Union, NJ 07083
Phone: (908) 527-2012
http://www.kean.edu/~biology/biowebhp.
    html

Seton Hall University
Biology Department
400 South Orange Avenue
South Orange, NJ 07079
Phone: (973) 761-9044
Fax: (973) 275-2489
http://artsci.shu.edu/biology/

NEW MEXICO

Eastern New Mexico University
Department of Biology
ENMU Station 33
1500 South Avenue K
Portales, NM 88130
Phone: (505) 562-2174
Fax: (505) 562-2192
http://www.enmu.edu/academics/
    undergrad/colleges/las/biology/index.
    shtml

NEW YORK

Fordham University
Biological Science Department
441 East Fordham Road
Bronx, NY 10458
Phone: (718) 817-3642
Fax: (718) 817-3828
http://www.fordham.edu/biology/

Hartwick College
Biology Department
Miller Science Building
Oneonta, NY 13820
Phone: (607) 431-4748
http://www.hartwick.edu/biology/

Hobart and William Smith Colleges
Department of Biology
Geneva, NY 14456
Phone: (315) 781-3000
http://academic.hws.edu/bio/

Hofstra University
Biology Department
130 Gittleson Hall

Hempstead, NY 11549
Phone: (516) 463-5516
http://www.hofstra.edu/Academics/
    HCLAS/Biology/index_Biology.cfme
    Sciences

Houghton College
Major in Biology with Environmental
    Emphasis
1 Willard Avenue
Houghton, NY 14744
Phone: (800) 777-2556
http://www.houghton.edu/academics/
    programs/biology.htm#Environmental

Iona College
Department of Biology
715 North Avenue
New Rochelle, NY 10801
Phone: (914) 633-2253
http://www.iona.edu/academic/arts_sci/
    departments/biology/

Ithaca College
Biology Department
161 CNS
Ithaca, NY 14850-7278
Phone: (607) 274-3161
Fax: (607) 274-1131
http://www.ithaca.edu/hs/biology/

Keuka College
Biology Program
Keuka Park, NY 14478
Phone: (315) 536-5268
http://www.keuka.edu/academic/science/
    biology.html

Marymount College Tarrytown
Department of Biology
100 Marymount Avenue
Tarrytown, NY 10591-3796
Phone: (800) 724-4312
http://www.marymt.edu/academics/
    biology/

St. Bonaventure University
Biology Department
106 DeLaRoche Hall
St. Bonaventure, NY 14778
Phone: (716) 375-2129
Fax: (716) 375-7618
http://www.sbu.edu/academics_bio_bio.
    html

**State University of New York (SUNY),
    Albany**
Department of Biological Sciences
1400 Washington Avenue

Albany, NY 12222
Phone: (518) 442-4300
Fax: (518) 442-4767
http://www.albany.edu/biology/

NORTH CAROLINA

Appalachian State University
Department of Biology
P.O. Box 32027
572 Rivers Street
Boone, NC 28608-2027
Phone: (828) 262-3025
Fax: (828) 262-2127
http://www.biology.appstate.edu/

Bennett College
Biology Department
900 East Washington Street
Greensboro, NC 27401
Phone: (336) 273-4431
http://www.bennett.edu/biology/

Campbell University
Department of Biological Sciences
P.O. Box 488, Baldwin Hall
Buies Creek, NC 27506
Phone: (910) 893-1733
Fax: (910) 893-1887
http://camel.campbell.edu/

Catawba College
Biology Department
2300 West Innes Street
Salisbury, NC 28144
Phone: (704) 637-4402
http://www.catawba.edu/dept/biology/

Mars Hill College
Biology & Health Sciences Department
Mars Hill, NC 28754
Phone: (828) 689-1307
http://www.mhc.edu/biology/

Meredith College
Department of Biology
3800 Hillsborough Street
Raleigh, NC 27607
Phone: (919) 760-8566
http://www.meredith.edu/biology/

St. Andrews Presbyterian College
Biology Department
1700 Dogwood Mile
Laurinburg, NC 28352
Phone: (910) 277-5555
http://www.sapc.edu/academics/bio/
    academ3.htm

University of North Carolina, Greensboro

Department of Biology
312 Eberhart Building
P.O. Box 26170
Greensboro, NC 27402
Phone: (336) 334-5391
Fax: (336) 334-5839
http://www.uncg.edu/bio/

NORTH DAKOTA

Bismarck State College
Biology Program
1500 Edwards Avenue
P.O. Box 5587
Bismarck, ND 58506
Phone: (701) 224-5411
http://www.bsc.nodak.edu/faculty/biology/

Jamestown College
Biology Department
6000 College Lane
Jamestown, ND 58405
Phone: (800) 336-2554
Fax: (701) 253-4318
http://www.jc.edu/Depts/Biology/

Mayville State University
Biology Program
330 Third Street NE
Mayville, ND 58257
Phone: (701) 786-4804
Fax: (701) 788-4748
http://www.mayvillestate.edu/layout_table.cfm?channel=72&program=1

University of North Dakota
Department of Biology
P.O. Box 8038
Grand Forks, ND 58202
Phone: (701) 777-2621
Fax: (701) 777-4397
http://www.und.edu/dept/biology/undergrad/bio_undergrad.html

OHIO

Ashland University
Department of Biology/Toxicology
Kettering Science Center
Ashland, OH 44805
Phone: (419) 289-4142
http://www3.ashland.edu/academics/arts_sci/biology/biology.html

Baldwin-Wallace College
Department of Biology and Geology
275 Eastland Road
Berea, OH 44017

Phone: (440) 826-2325
http://www.bw.edu/~wwwbio

Bluffton College
Biology Program
280 West College Avenue, Suite 1
Bluffton, OH 45817
Phone: (800) 488-3257
http://www.bluffton.edu/sci/biology/

Capital University
Biological Sciences Department
2199 East Main Street
Columbus, OH 43209
Phone: (614) 236-6222
Fax: (614) 236-6518
http://www.capital.edu/acad/as/bio/biology.html

Case Western Reserve University
Biology Program
10900 Euclid Avenue
Cleveland, OH 44106-7080
Phone: (216) 368-3557
Fax: (216) 368-4672
http://www.cwru.edu/artsci/biol/biol.html

Heidelberg College
Department of Biology
310 East Market Street
Tiffin, OH 44883-2462
Phone: (419) 448-2224
Fax: (419) 448-2124
http://www.heidelberg.edu/depts/bio/

John Carroll University
Biology Department
Environmental Studies Concentration
20700 North Park Boulevard
University Heights, OH 44118
Phone: (216) 397-4251
http://www.jcu.edu/envstudies/

Kent State University
Biological Sciences Program
Kent, OH 44242
Phone: (330) 672-3613
Fax: (330) 672-3713
http://dept.kent.edu/biology/

University of Cincinnati
Department of Biological Sciences
614 Rieveschl Hall
Cincinnati, OH 45221-0006
Phone: (513) 556-9700
Fax: (513) 556-5299
http://www.biology.uc.edu/

Ursuline College
Biology Department

2550 Lander Road
Pepper Pike, OH 44124-4398
Phone: (888) URSULINE
http://www.ursuline.edu/acadaff/biology.htm

OKLAHOMA

Cameron University
Department of Biological Sciences
2800 West Gore Boulevard
Lawton, OK 73505
Phone: (580) 581-2373
Fax: (580) 591-8003
http://www.cameron.edu/academic/science/biology/index.html

Langston University
Biological Studies Program
Langston, OK 73050
Phone: (405) 466-2965
http://www.lunet.edu/biology.html

Southwestern Oklahoma State University
Department of Biological Sciences
100 Campus Drive
Weatherford, OK 73096-3098
Phone: (580) 774-3293
Fax: (580) 774-7140
http://www.swosu.edu/depts/biology/

University of Science & Arts of Oklahoma
Biology Program
17th and Grand Avenue
1727 West Alabama
Chickasha, OK 73018-5322
Phone: (800) 933-8726
http://www.usao.edu/Catalog2002/Biology/index2.html

OREGON

Eastern Oregon State College
Biology Program
One University Boulevard
La Grande, OR 97850
Phone: (541) 962-3511
http://www2.eou.edu/~jrinehar/biodept.htm

Southern Oregon University
Biology Department
1250 Siskiyou Boulevard
Ashland, OR 97520
Phone: (541) 552-6341
http://www.sosc.edu/biology/

PENNSYLVANIA

Alvernia College
Biology Program
400 Saint Bernardine Street
Reading, PA 19607
Phone: (610) 796-8200
http://www.alvernia.edu/academics/
    biology/

Carlow College
Biology Program
3333 Fifth Avenue
Pittsburgh, PA 15213
Phone: (800) 333-2275
http://www.carlow.edu/academic/
    sciences/biology.html

Clarion University
Biology Department
230 Peirce Hall
Clarion, PA 16214
Phone: (814) 393-2273
http://www.artsci.clarion.edu/biology/

Edinboro University of Pennsylvania
Department of Biology & Health Services
Cooper Hall 150
Edinboro, PA 16444
Phone: (814) 732-2500
http://www.edinboro.edu/cwis/biology/
    biohome.html

Elizabethtown College
Biology Department
One Alpha Drive
Elizabethtown, PA 17022-2298
Phone: (717) 361-1389
Fax: (717) 361-1243
http://www.etown.edu/biology/

Grove City College
Biology Department
100 Campus Drive
Grove City, PA 16127
Phone: (724) 458-2000
http://science.gcc.edu/biol/

Holy Family University
Biology Program
Grant and Frankford Avenues
Philadelphia, PA 19114-2094
Phone: (215) 637-7700
http://www.hfc.edu/sas/undergprog3.
    shtml#bio

King's College
Department of Biology
133 North River Street
Wilkes Barre, PA 18711
Phone: (570) 208-5900
http://www.kings.edu/biology/

LaSalle University
Biology Department
1900 West Olney Avenue
Philadelphia, PA 19141
Phone: (215) 951-1250
Fax: (215) 951-1772
http://www.lasalle.edu/academ/biology/

Lock Haven University
Biology, Environmental Biology and
    Natural Science Programs
North Fairview Street
Lock Haven, PA 17745
Phone: (570) 893-2058
http://www.lhup.edu/biology

Lycoming College
Biology Department
700 College Place
Williamsport, PA 17701
Phone: (570) 321-4185
http://www.lycoming.edu/biology/

Mansfield University of Pennsylvania
Department of Biology
Grant Science Center
Mansfield, PA 16933
Phone: (570) 662-4531
Fax: (570) 662-4107
http://www.mnsfld.edu/depts/biology/

Messiah College
Department of Biological Sciences
One College Avenue
Grantham, PA 17027
Phone: (717) 766-2511
http://www.messiah.edu/departments/
    bioscience/

Rosemont College
Biology Program
1400 Montgomery Avenue
Rosemont, PA 19010
Phone: (610) 527-0200
http://www.rosemont.edu/root/womens_
    college/academics/biology.html

RHODE ISLAND

Rhode Island College
Biology Department
600 Mount Pleasant Avenue
Providence, RI 02908
Phone: (401) 456-8010
Fax: (401) 456-9620
http://www.ric.edu/biology/

SOUTH CAROLINA

Coastal Carolina University
Biology Department
P.O. Box 261954
Conway, SC 29528-6054
Phone: (843) 349-2238
Fax: (843) 349-2201
http://www.coastal.edu/biology/

Erskine College
Environmental Biology Program
P.O. Box 608
Due West, SC 29639
Phone: (864) 379-2131
http://www.erskine.edu/academics/
    biology.department.html

SOUTH DAKOTA

Black Hills State University
Biology Department
1200 University Street
Jonas 208
Spearfish, SD 57799-9502
Phone: (605) 642-6212
http://math.bhsu.edu/~bsmith/biology/

University of Sioux Falls
Biology Department
1101 West 22nd Street
Sioux Falls, SD 57105
Phone: (800) 888-1047
http://www.usiouxfalls.edu/academic/
    biology/index.html

University of South Dakota
Biology Program
191 Churchill-Haines
Vermillion, SD 57069
Phone: (605) 677-5211
Fax: (605) 677-6527
http://www.usd.edu/biol/

TENNESSEE

Austin Peay State University
Biology Department
P.O. Box 4718
Clarksville, TN 37044
Phone: (931) 221-6323
Fax: (931) 221-6323
http://www.apsu.edu/biol_page/

Belmont University
Biology Department
Hitch Science Building Room 304
1900 Belmont Boulevard

Nashville, TN 37212
Phone: (615) 460-6431
http://www.belmont.edu/biology/

Carson-Newman College
Biology Department
1646 Russell Avenue
P.O. Box 557
Jefferson City, TN 37760
Phone: (865) 471-2000
Fax: (865) 471-3578
http://www.cn.edu/CN.htm

King College
Biology Program
1350 King College Road
Bristol, TN 37620
Phone: (423) 968-1187
Fax: (423) 968-4456
http://www.king.edu/Academics/SOAS/
    Biology/

Lambuth University
Biology Program
705 Lambuth Boulevard
Jackson, TN 38301
Phone: (731) 425-3279
http://www.lambuth.edu/academics/
    mathandsciences/biology/index.html

Lipscomb University
Biology Program
3901 Granny White Pike
Nashville, TN 37204-3951
Phone: (615) 269-1000
http://biology.lipscomb.edu/

TEXAS

Amarillo College
Department of Biology
P.O. Box 447
Amarillo, TX 79179
Phone: (806) 371-5081
Fax: (806) 371-5979
http://sites.actx.edu/~biology/

Angelo State University
Biology Department
Oceanography Program
ASU Station, #10890
San Angelo, TX 76909-0890
Phone: (325) 942-2189
Fax: (325) 942-2184
http://www.angelo.edu/dept/biology/

Austin College
Biology Department
900 North Grand Avenue, Box 61611

Sherman, TX 75090-4400
Phone: (903) 813-2204
http://www.austincollege.edu/Category.
    asp?669

Howard Pane University
Biological Science Department
1000 Fisk Avenue
Brownwood, TX 76801
Phone: (325) 649-8020
http://www.hputx.edu/Academic/Biology.
    HTM

Le Tourneau University
Biology Program
2100 South Mobberly
Longview, TX 75607-7001
Phone: (903) 233-3283
http://www.letu.edu/opencms/opencms/
    future-students/ft-undergrad/
    academics/biology/

Schreiner College
Biology Program
2100 Memorial Boulevard
Kerrville, TX 78028
Phone: (830) 896-5411
http://www.schreiner.edu/academics/
    biology.html

Southern Methodist University
Biological Science Department
P.O. Box 750376
Dallas, TX 75205-0376
Phone: (214) 768-2730
Fax: (214) 768-3955
http://www.smu.edu/biology/

Southwestern Adventist University
Biology Department
100 West Hillcrest Drive
Keene, TX 76059
Phone: (817) 645-3921
Fax: (817) 556-4737
http://biology.swau.edu/biology.html

Southwest Texas State University
Biology Department
601 University Drive
San Marcos, TX 78666
Phone: (512) 245-2111
http://www.bio.swt.edu/

Texas State University, San Marco
Department of Biology
601 University Drive
San Marcos, TX 78666
Phone: (512) 245-2111
http://www.bio.txstate.edu/
    bioprogramsTS.nclk

University of Houston
Department of Biology and
    Biochemistry
4800 Calhoun Road
Houston, TX 77204
Phone: (713) 743-2255
http://www.bchs.uh.edu/

University of North Texas
Department of Biological Sciences
P.O. Box 305220
Denton, TX 76203
Phone: (940) 565-3593
Fax: (940) 565-3821
http://www.biol.unt.edu/NewWeb/index.
    html

UTAH

Southern Utah University
Biology Department
351 West Center Street
Cedar City, UT 84720
Phone: (435) 586-7944
http://www.suu.edu/sci/biology/

Utah Valley State College
Department of Biology
800 West University Parkway
Orem, UT 84058
Phone: (801) 863-8511
Fax: (801) 863-8064
http://www.uvsc.edu/biol/

VERMONT

Castleton State College
Biology Program
86 Seminary Street
Castleton, VT 05735
Phone: (802) 468-1112
Fax: (802) 468-1170
http://www.csc.vsc.edu/NASWebpage/
    page3.html

VIRGINIA

Averett College
Biology Program
420 West Main Street
Danville, VA 24541
Phone: (804) 791-5766
Fax: (804) 791-4392
http://dev.averett.edu/html/biology.html

Bridgewater College
Biology Department
402 East College Street

Bridgewater, VA 22812
Phone: (540) 828-8000
Fax: (540) 828-5479
http://www.bridgewater.edu/departments/
  biology/biology.html

College of William and Mary
Biology Department
P.O. Box 8795
Williamsburg, VA 23187-8795
Phone: (757) 221-2207
Fax: (757) 221-6483
http://www.wm.edu/biology_new/

George Mason University
Biology Department
4400 University Drive, MSN 3E1
Fairfax, VA 22030
Phone: (703) 993-1050
Fax: (703) 993-1046
http://www.gmu.edu/departments/Biology/

Hollins University
Biology Program
P.O. Box 9707
Roanoke, VA 24020
Phone: (540) 362-6457
http://www.hollins.edu/undergrad/
  biology/biology.htm

Longwood University
Biology Program
201 High Street
Farmville, VA 23909
Phone: (804) 395-2587
http://www.longwood.edu/sciences/
  biology.htm

Mary Baldwin College
Department of Biology
Staunton, VA 24401
Phone: (800) 468-2262
http://www.mbc.edu/academic/
  departments/biol.asp

Norfolk State University
Biology Department
700 Park Avenue
Norfolk, VA 23504
Phone: (757) 823-8512
http://www.nsu.edu/schools/sciencetech/
  biology/

WASHINGTON

Central Washington University
Biological Sciences Department
400 East University Way
Ellensburg, WA 98926-7537
Phone: (509) 963-2731
http://www.cwu.edu/~biology/

Eastern Washington University
Biology Department
Mail Stop 72, 526 Fifth Street
Cheney, WA 99004-2431
Phone: (509) 359-2339
Fax: (509) 359-6867
http://www.csmt.ewu.edu/csmt/biol/
  bioldept.HTM

Gonzaga University
Biology Department
AD Box 5, 502 East Boone Avenue
Spokane, WA 99258-0008
Phone: (509) 323-6624
Fax: (509) 323-5804
http://www.gonzaga.edu/Academics/
  Colleges+and+Schools/College+of+
  Arts+and+Sciences/Biology/default.
  htm

Seattle Pacific University
Department of Biology
3307 Third Avenue West
Seattle, WA 98119-1997
Phone: (206) 281-2140
http://www.spu.edu/depts/biology/

ECOLOGY

CALIFORNIA

**California State University,
  Long Beach**
Ecology & Environmental Biology
  Degree
1250 Bellflower Boulevard
Long Beach, CA 90840
Phone: (562) 985-8133
http://www.csulb.edu/depts/biology/
  pages/ecology.shtml

Saddleback College
Environmental Studies and Ecological
  Restoration
28000 Marguerite Parkway
Mission Viejo, CA 92692
Phone: (949) 582-4500
http://www.saddleback.edu/AP/atas/
  Environmental_Studies_and_
  Ecological_Restoration.asp

University of California, Irvine
Department of Ecology and Evolutionary
  Biology
321 Steinhaus Hall
Irvine, CA 92697
Phone: (949) 824-6006
Fax: (949) 824-2181
http://ecoevo.bio.uci.edu/

COLORADO

Colorado State University
Graduate Degree Program in Ecology
A118, Natural and Environmental
  Sciences Building
Fort Collins, CO 80523-1499
Phone: (970) 491-4373
Fax: (970) 491-2796
http://www.colostate.edu/Depts/GDPE/
  Homepage.html

Naropa University
Ecology Program
2130 Arapahoe Avenue
Boulder, CO 80302
Phone: (800) 772-6951
Fax: (303) 444-0410
http://www.naropa.edu

FLORIDA

Barry University
Ecological Studies Program
School of Natural and Health Sciences
11300 NE Second Avenue
Miami Shores, FL 33161-6695
Phone: (305) 899-3100
http://www.barry.edu/ecologicalStudies/

GEORGIA

University of Georgia
Department of Ecological and
  Environmental Anthropology
250A Baldwin Hall, Jackson Street
Athens, GA 30602-1619
Phone: (706) 542-3922
Fax: (706) 542-3998
http://anthro.dac.uga.edu/

HAWAII

Akamai University
Center for Ecological and Environmental
  Studies
P.O. Box 1557
Hilo, HI 96721
Phone: (877) 934-8793
Fax: (808) 934-8793
http://www.akamaiuniversity.us/
  EcologicalandEnvironmentalStudies.
  html

University of Hawaii, Manoa
Ecological Anthropology Program
2424 Maile Way Social Sciences
  Building 346
Honolulu, HI 96822-2223

Phone: (808) 956-8507
http://www2.soc.hawaii.edu/css/anth/
subfields/ecopage.html

KANSAS

University of Kansas
Department of Ecology & Evolutionary
    Biology
1200 Sunnyside Avenue, Room 2041
    Haworth
Lawrence, KS 66045-7534
Phone: (785) 864-5887
Fax: (785) 864-5860
http://www.ku.edu/~eeb/

MARYLAND

University of Maryland, College Park
Certificate in Ecological Economics
3139 Van Munching Hall
College Park, MD 20742
Phone: (301) 405-6075
Fax: (301) 403-4675
http://www.puaf.umd.edu/degree_
    programs/ecolecon.htm

MASSACHUSETTS

Boston University
Study Abroad Program in Tropical
    Ecology in Ecuador
232 Bay State Road
Boston, MA 02215
Phone: (617) 353-9888
http://www.bu.edu/abroad/programs/
    ecuador/tep/

MICHIGAN

University of Michigan
Landscape Ecology
School of Natural Resources and
    Environment
Dana Building, 430 East University
Ann Arbor, MI 48109-1115
Phone: (734) 615-6431
Fax: (734) 615-7100
http://www.snre.umich.edu/ecomgt/
    landscape.htm

MONTANA

Montana State University
Department of Ecology
P.O. Box 172190
Bozeman, MT 59717-2190
Phone: (406) 994-5724
http://www.montana.edu/ecology/

PENNSYLVANIA

Mercyhurst College
Human Ecology Department
501 East 38th Street
Erie, PA 16546
Phone: (814) 824-2462
http://www.mercyhurst.edu/Academics/
    human_ecology.htm

TEXAS

Rice University
Department of Ecology and Evolutionary
    Biology
MS 170
6100 South Main
Houston, TX 77005
Phone: (713) 348-4919
Fax: (713) 348-5232
http://dacnet.rice.edu/~eeb/

VIRGINIA

Marymount University
Ecology Program
2807 North Glebe Road
Arlington, VA 22207
Phone: (703) 522-5600
http://www.marymount.edu/academic/
    artandsci/biology/esconc.htm

WASHINGTON

Seattle University
Ecological Studies Program
900 Broadway
Seattle, WA 98122-4460
Phone: (206) 296-5470
http://www.seattleu.edu/artsci/eco/

ENERGY AND OTHER PHYSICAL SCIENCES

INDIANA

Ball State University
Applied Solar Energy Program
Department of Physics & Astronomy
Muncie, IN 47306
Phone: (317) 285-6268
http://www.bsu.edu/physics/

MASSACHUSETTS

Boston University
Center for Energy and Environmental
    Studies
675 Commonwealth Avenue

Room 141
Boston, MA 02215
Phone: (617) 353-3083
Fax: (617) 353-5986
http://www.bu.edu/cees/

NEW YORK

New York Institute of Technology
Energy Management Program
HSH 116
Old Westbury, NY 11568
Phone: (516) 686-7578
http://iris.nyit.edu/set/set1/html/index.
    html

NEW MEXICO

San Juan College
Renewable Energy Program
4601 College Boulevard
Farmington, NM 87402
Phone: (505) 326-3311
http://www.sanjuancollege.edu/
    academics/technology/RENG/

SOUTH DAKOTA

Black Hills State University
Environmental Physical Science Major
1200 University Street
Spearfish, SD 57779
Phone: (605) 642-6506
http://www-msc.bhsu.edu/eps/eps.html

ENVIRONMENTAL CHEMISTRY

ALABAMA

Spring Hill College
Environmental Chemistry Program
4000 Dauphin Street
Mobile, AL 36608
Phone: (334) 380-3030
http://www.shc.edu/academics/undergrad/
    sciences/

ALASKA

University of Alaska, Fairbanks
Environmental Chemistry Program
P.O. Box 756160
Fairbanks, AK 99775-6160
Phone: (907) 474-5510
Fax: (907) 474-5640
http://www.uaf.edu/chem/echem/index.
    htm

DISTRICT OF COLUMBIA

Catholic University of America
Environmental Chemistry
201 Maloney Hall
Washington, DC 20064
Phone: (202) 319-5397
http://arts-sciences.cua.edu/chem/
environmental.html

MICHIGAN

Kettering University
Environmental Chemistry Program
1700 West Third Avenue
Flint, MI 48504
Phone: (810) 762-7912
Fax: (810) 762-9796
http://www.kettering.edu/acad/scimath/
envchem/

Lake Superior State University
Department of Chemistry and
    Environmental Science
650 West Easterday Avenue
Sault Ste. Marie, MI 49783
Phone: (906) 635-2267
http://natsci.lssu.edu/chemistry/index.
php

PENNSYLVANIA

La Roche College
Environmental Chemistry Program
9000 Babcock Boulevard
Pittsburgh, PA 15237
Phone: (412) 536-1272
http://www.laroche.edu/schools/
arts-sciences/DisciplineDetail.
asp?DisciplineID=23

ENVIRONMENTAL RESEARCH

Columbia University
Center for Environmental Research
    and Conservation
1200 Amsterdam Avenue
New York, NY 10027-5557
Phone: (212) 854-9987
Fax: (212) 854-8188
http://cerc.columbia.edu/

Columbia University
Earth Institute
2960 Broadway
New York, NY 10027-6902
Phone: (212) 854-1754
http://www.earthinstitute.columbia.edu/

GENERAL ENVIRONMENTAL SCIENCE/ENVIRONMENTAL STUDIES PROGRAMS

ALABAMA

Birmingham-Southern College
Environmental Studies Program
Hess Center for Leadership and Service
Box 549065
900 Arkadelphia Road
Birmingham, AL 35254
Phone: (205) 226-4679
http://www.bsc.edu/academics/
cooperative/env_studies/index.htm

Jacksonville State University
Environmental Science Program
Biology Department
Martin Hall
700 Pelham Road
Jacksonville, AL 36265
Phone: (256) 782-5642
Fax: (256) 782-5587
http://www.jsu.edu/depart/biology/

University of West Alabama
Department of Biological and
    Environmental Sciences
Livingston, AL 35470
Phone: (205) 652-3400
http://nsm.uwa.edu/bio/

ARKANSAS

Arkansas State University
Environmental Sciences Program
P.O. Box 847
Jonesboro, AR 72467
Phone: (870) 972-2007
Fax: (870) 972-2008
http://evs.astate.edu/

John Brown University
Environmental Science Program
2000 West University Street
Siloam Springs, AR 72761
Phone: (479) 524-9500
http://www.jbu.edu/academics/science/
gensci/bsenvironment.asp

Lyon College
Environmental Studies
P.O. Box 2317
2300 Highland Road
Batesville, AR 72503
Phone: (800) 423-2542
http://www.lyon.edu/webdata/Groups/
Science/envstud/envstud.html

University of Central Arkansas
Environmental Science
201 Donaghey Avenue
Conway, AR 72035
Phone: (501) 450-5933
http://www.uca.edu/divisions/academic/
environment/

ALASKA

Sheldon Jackson College
Environmental Science Program
801 Lincoln Street
Sitka, AK 99835
Phone: (800) 478-4556
http://www.sheldonjackson.edu/503.cfm

University of Alaska, Southeast
Environmental Science Program
11120 Glacier Highway
Andersen Building, Room 219
Juneau, AK 99801
Phone: (907) 465-8449
Fax: (907) 465-6406
http://www.uas.alaska.edu/envs/

CALIFORNIA

California Lutheran University
Environmental Studies Minor
60 West Olsen Road
Thousand Oaks, CA 91360-2787
Phone: (805) 493-3264
http://lupine.clunet.edu/Academic_
Programs/Departments/Enviromental_
Studies/CLU.html

California State University, Fullerton
Masters of Environmental Studies
Humanities H-420A
Fullerton, CA 92834-6850
Phone: (714) 278-4373
http://hss.fullerton.edu/envstud/

**California State University,
    Sacramento**
Environmental Studies Program
6000 J Street
Sacramento, CA 95819-6001
Phone: (916) 278-6620
Fax: (916) 278-7582
http://www.csus.edu/envs/

California State University, Stanislaus
Environmental & Resource Studies Minor
801 West Monte Vista Avenue
Turlock, CA 95382
Phone: (209) 667-3127
http://www.csustan.edu/EN_Res_Stud/
lead.html

De Anza College
Environmental Studies
21250 Stevens Creek Boulevard
Cupertino, CA 95014
Phone: (408) 864-8655
Fax: (408) 864-5630
http://environmentalstudies.deanza.edu/

Dominican University of California
Environmental Studies Program
50 Acacia Avenue
San Rafael, CA 94901
Phone: (415) 457-4440
http://www.dominican.edu/Academics/
    Department_Natural_Sciences_
    Mathematics.cfm

Harvey Mudd College
Center for Environmental Studies
1250 North Dartmouth Avenue
Claremont, CA 91711
Phone: (909) 621-8561
Fax: (909) 607-7172
http://www.environcenter.hmc.edu/

Merritt College
Environmental Program
12500 Campus Drive
Oakland, CA 94619
Phone: (510) 434-3840
http://merritt.edu/~envst/

San Francisco State University
Department of Environmental Studies
1600 Holloway Ave
San Francisco, CA 94132
Phone: (415) 338-1149
http://bss.sfsu.edu/envstudies/

San Jose State University
Environmental Studies
One Washington Square 118
San Jose, CA 95192-0115
Phone: (408) 924-5450
http://www.sjsu.edu/depts/EnvStudies

University of California, Los Angeles
Institute of Environment
610 Charles E. Young Drive East
1365 Hershey Hall
Los Angeles, CA 90095-1496
Phone: (310) 825-5008
Fax: (310) 825-9663
http://www.ioe.ucla.edu/IoE.html

University of California, Santa Cruz
Environmental Studies Department
405 Interdisciplinary Sciences Building
115 High Street
Santa Cruz, CA 95064

Phone: (831) 459-2634
Fax: (831) 459-4015
http://zzyx.ucsc.edu/ES/es.html

University of Redlands
Center for Environmental Studies
1200 East Colton Avenue
Redlands, CA 92373
Phone: (909) 335-4013
http://newton.uor.edu/
    Departments&Programs/
    EnvironmentalDept/environmental.
    html

University of San Francisco
Environmental Science
2130 Fulton Street
San Francisco, CA 94117-1080
Phone: (415) 422-6373
Fax: (415) 422-2346
http://artsci.usfca.edu/contact/contact.html

University of Southern California
Wrigley Institute for Environmental
    Studies
P.O. Box 5069
Avalon, CA 90704
Phone: (213) 740-6780
Fax: (213) 740-6720
http://wrigley.usc.edu

COLORADO

University of Colorado, Denver
Environmental Sciences Program
P.O. Box 173364
Denver, CO 80217-3364
Phone: (303) 556-4520
Fax: (303) 556-4292
http://www.cudenver.edu//envsci/

University of Denver
Environmental Science
Boettcher Center West
2050 East Iliff Avenue
Denver, CO 80208
Phone: (303) 871-2513
Fax: (303) 871-2201
http://www.du.edu/envir/

CONNECTICUT

Connecticut College
Environmental Studies Program
270 Mohegan Avenue
New London, CT 06320
Phone: (860) 439-2160
Fax: (860) 439-2519
http://www.conncoll.edu/academics/
    departments/envstudies/index.html

Sacred Heart University
Environmental Science Program
5151 Park Avenue
Fairfield, CT 06432
Phone: (203) 371-7999
http://www.sacredheart.edu/academics/
    cas/programs/environmental/

Trinity College
Environmental Science Program
300 Summit Street
Hartford, CT 06106
Phone: (860) 297-2514
http://www.trincoll.edu/pub/academics/
    departments/envsci.html

University of New Haven
Environmental Science Program
300 Orange Ave
West Haven, CT 06516
Phone: (800) DIAL-UNH
http://www.newhaven.edu/UNH/GISWeb/
    qrwweb/graduate.htm

DELAWARE

Wesley College
Environmental Studies Program
120 North State Street
Dover, DE 19901
Phone: (302) 736-2300
http://www.wesley.edu/academics/
    natscience_math/environmental_
    studies.html

DISTRICT OF COLUMBIA

Georgetown University
Center for the Environment
305 O Intercultural Center
Washington, DC 20057
Phone: (202) 687-8399
Fax: (202) 687-5116
http://www.georgetown.edu/centers/
    environment/

**University of the District of Columbia,
    Van Ness Campus**
Department of Biological and
    Environmental Science
4200 Connecticut Avenue, NW
Building 41
Washington, DC 20008
Phone: (202) 274-5194
http://www.udc.edu/cas/dptbes.htm

FLORIDA

Barry University
Environmental Science Program

School of Natural and Health Sciences
11300 NE Second Avenue
Miami Shores, FL 33161-6695
Phone: (305) 899-3100
http://www.barry.edu/snhs/BSprograms/
    EnviromentalScience/default.htm

Eckerd College
Environmental Studies Program
4200 54th Avenue South
St. Petersburg, FL 33711
Phone: (813) 864-7880
http://www.eckerd.edu/academics/other/
    esn/PAGE1~1.HTM

Florida A&M University
Environmental Science Institute
1520 South Bronough Street
Science Research Center
Tallahassee, FL 32307
Phone: (850) 599-3550
Fax: (850) 599-8183
http://www.famu.edu/acad/colleges/esi/

Florida Atlantic University
Charles E. Schmidt College of Sciences
Environmental Sciences Department
777 Glades Road, Room 302
Boca Raton, FL 33483
Phone: (561) 297-2625
Fax: (561) 297-2067
http://www.science.fau.edu/

Florida Gulf Coast University
Environmental Studies Program
10501 FGCU Boulevard South
Fort Myers, FL 33965-6565
Phone: (239) 590-7169
http://www.fgcu.edu/cas/envstu/index.html

Florida Southern College
Environmental Studies Concentration
111 Lake Hollingsworth Drive
Lakeland, FL 33801
Phone: (863) 680-4111
http://www.flsouthern.edu/biology/

Florida State University
Environmental Studies Program
Department of Geography
Room 323, Bellamy Building
Tallahassee, FL 32306-2190
Phone: (850) 644-1706
Fax: (850) 644-5913
http://www.fsu.edu/~geog/ugenv.html

Jacksonville University
Environmental Studies Program
2800 University Boulevard North
Jacksonville, FL 32211

Phone: (904) 745-7000
http://www.ju.edu/academics/undergrad_
    environmentalStudies.asp

GEORGIA

Agnes Scott College
Environmental Studies Program
141 East College Avenue
Decatur, GA 30030
Phone: (404) 471-6000
http://www.agnesscott.edu/academics/
    p_environmental_studies.asp

Berry College
Environmental Sciences Program
2277 Martha Berry Highway
P.O. Box 0430
Mount Berry, GA 30149-0430
Phone: (706) 238-1756
http://www2.berry.edu/academics/
    science/evs/

Mercer University
Environmental Science Program
1400 Coleman Avenue
Macon, GA 31207-0001
Phone: (800) MERCER-U
http://www2.mercer.edu/Admissions/
    AcademicPrograms/environmental.
    htm

Savannah State University
Environmental Science Program
Savannah, GA 31404
Phone: (912) 356-2186
http://www.savstate.edu/scitech/scmath/
    html/Enironmental.htm

HAWAII

American University of Hawaii
Natural and Environmental Science
1063 Lower Main Street
Wailuku, HI 96793
Phone: (808) 534-0816
Fax: (808) 534-0917
http://www.auh.edu/environment.htm

Chaminade University of Honolulu
Department of Environmental Studies
3140 Waialae Avenue
Honolulu, HI 96816-1578
Phone: (808) 735-4834

Hawaii Pacific University
Environmental Science Program
1164 Bishop Street
Honolulu, HI 96813
Phone: (808) 236-5846

http://web2.hpu.edu/index.
    cfm?section=undergrad9

Hawaii Pacific University
Environmental Studies Program
1164 Bishop Street
Honolulu, HI 96813
Phone: (808) 236-5846
http://web2.hpu.edu/index.
    cfm?section=undergrad10

University of Hawaii, Manoa
Environmental Studies
Krauss Annex 19
2500 Dole Road
Honolulu, HI 96822
Phone: (808) 956-7361
Fax: (808) 956-3980
http://www.hawaii.edu/envctr/

University of the Nations, Kona
College of Science and Technology
Environmental Studies Program
75-5851 Kuakini Highway
Kailua-Kona, HI 96740-2199
Phone: (800) 383-4572
Fax: (808) 329-2387
http://www.uofnkona.edu/sat/index.html

IDAHO

Albertson College of Idaho
Environmental Studies Program
2112 Cleveland Boulevard
Caldwell, ID 83605
Phone: (208) 459-5894
Fax: (208) 459-5175
http://www.albertson.edu/environment/

ILLINOIS

Augustana College
Environmental Studies Program
639 38th Street
Rock Island, IL 61201-2296
Phone: (309) 794-7303
http://www.augustana.edu/academics/
    environmental/

Bradley University
Environmental Science Program
1501 West Bradley Avenue
Peoria, IL 61625
Phone: (309) 676-7611
http://www.bradley.edu/academics/las/
    bio/envsci.html

DePaul University
Environmental Science Program
1 East Jackson

121 McGowan Science Center
Chicago, IL 60604
Phone: (773) 325-7422
http://www.depaul.edu/~envirsci/

DePaul University, Barat Campus
Environmental Studies Concentration
700 East Westleigh Road
Lake Forest, IL 60045
Phone: (847) 574-6240
http://barat.depaul.edu/acad_under/
    science_env_studies.asp

Dominican University
Environmental Science and
    Environmental Studies
7900 West Division Street
River Forest, IL 60305
Phone: (708) 524-6800
Fax: (708) 524-5990
http://www.dom.edu/rosary/majors/
    environment.html

Eureka College
Environmental Sciences Major
300 East College Avenue
Eureka, IL 61530-1500
Phone: (309) 467-3721
http://www.eureka.edu/academics/
    programs/envsci.asp

Knox College
Environmental Studies Program
2 East South Street
Galesburg, IL 61401-4999
Phone: (309) 341-7000
http://www.knox.edu/
    environmentalstudies.xml

Lake Forest College
Environmental Studies Program
555 North Sheridan Road
Lake Forest, IL 60045
Phone: (847) 735-5121
http://www.lfc.edu/academics/
    newcatalog/index.php?DeptID=ENVR
    &page=intro

Loyola University, Chicago
Environmental Science/Studies Program
6430 North Kenmore Avenue
Chicago, IL 60626
Phone: (773) 508-2950
Fax: (773) 508-3646
http://www.luc.edu/depts/envsci/index.html

North Park University
Au Sable Institute of Environmental
    Studies
3225 West Foster Avenue

Chicago, IL 60625
Phone: (773) 244-5660
http://campus.northpark.edu/biology/
    programs.html

Northwestern University
Environmental Science Program
1922 Sheridan Road
Evanston, IL 60208-4030
Phone: (847) 491-7560
Fax: (847) 467-7251
http://www.earth.northwestern.edu/ESP/

Roosevelt University
Environmental Programs
1400 North Roosevelt Boulevard
Schaumburg, IL 60173
Phone: (847) 619-8600
http://www.roosevelt.edu/cas/sps/envpro/
    programs.htm

**Southern Illinois University at
    Edwardsville**
Environmental Sciences Program
Box 1099
Edwardsville, IL 62026
Phone: (618) 650-3311
Fax: (618) 650-3174
http://www.siue.edu/ENVS/

University of Chicago
Environmental Studies Program
920 East 58th Street
Chicago, IL 60637
Phone: (733) 834-6021
http://environment.uchicago.edu/studies/

University of Illinois at Springfield
Department of Environmental Studies
UIS PAC 322, P.O. Box 19243
Springfield, IL 62794-9243
Phone: (217) 206-6720
http://www.uis.edu/environmentalstudies/

INDIANA

Earlham College
Environmental Programs
801 National Road West
Richmond, IN 47374-4095
Phone: (765) 983-1620
http://www.earlham.edu/curriculumguide/
    environmental/

Goshen College
Environmental Studies Program
1700 South Main Street
Goshen, IN 46526
Phone: (260) 799-5869
http://www.goshen.edu/envstudies/

Manchester College
Environmental Studies Program
604 East College Avenue
North Manchester, IN 46962
Phone: (219) 982-5310
http://www.manchester.edu/
    Academic/Programs/departments/
    EnvironStudies/

Marian College
Environmental Studies Program
3200 Cold Spring Road
Indianapolis, IN 46222-1997
Phone: (800) 772-7264
http://sonak.marian.edu/academ/
    departments/biology/ENV%20home/
    environmental_studies_homepage.
    htm

IOWA

Central College
Environmental Studies Program
812 University
Pella, IA 50219
Phone: (515) 628-9000

Cornell College
Environmental Studies Program
600 First Street West
Mount Vernon, IA 52314
Phone: (319) 895-4000
http://www.cornellcollege.edu/
    environmental_studies/

Dordt College
Environmental Studies Program
498 Fourth Avenue NE
Sioux Center, IA 51250
Phone: (712) 722-6327
http://www.dordt.edu/academics/
    programs/environmental_studies/

Franciscan University
Environmental Studies Program
400 North Bluff Boulevard
Clinton, IA 52732
Phone: (800) 242-4153
Fax: (563) 242-4023
http://www.tfu.edu/uploads/
    Environmental%20Studies.pdf

Northwestern College, Iowa
Environmental Science Major
101 Seventh Street SW
Orange City, IA 51041
Phone: (712) 737-7008
http://www.nwciowa.edu/dept/env/envsci.
    htm

University of Iowa
Environmental Sciences Program
121 Trowbridge Hall
Iowa City, IA 52242
Phone: (319) 335-1818
Fax: (319) 335-1821
http://www.uiowa.edu/~envsci/

KANSAS

University of Kansas
Environmental Studies Department
517 West 14th Street
Building 138
Lawrence, KS 66044
Phone: (785) 842-2059
Fax: (785) 842-4041
http://www.ku.edu/~kuesp/

KENTUCKY

Centre College
Environmental Studies
600 West Walnut Street
Danville, KY 40422
Phone: (859) 238-5321
http://web.centre.edu/estudies/

Eastern Kentucky University
Environmental Studies Program
Moore 235
521 Lancaster Avenue
Richmond, KY 40475
Phone: (859) 622-1531
Fax: (859) 622-1399
http://www.biology.eku.edu/Enviro.
htm

Georgetown College
Environmental Science Program
400 East College Street
Georgetown, KY 40324
Phone: (502) 863-8088
http://spider.georgetowncollege.edu/
biology/environ/envdescr.htm

Kentucky Wesleyan College
Environmental Science Program
3000 Frederica Street
Owensboro, KY 42301
Phone: (270) 852-3161
http://www.kwc.edu/academic/biology/
kwcensc.htm

Midway College
Environmental Science Program
512 East Stephens Street
Midway, KY 40347
Phone: (800) 755-0031

http://www.midway.edu/degreeprograms/
environmentalscience.html

Northern Kentucky University
Environmental Science Program
Highland Heights, KY 41099
Phone: (859) 572-1409
http://www.nku.edu/~envsci/

LOUISIANA

Centenary College of Louisiana
Environmental Studies
2911 Centenary Boulevard
Shreveport, LA 71104
Phone: (800) 234-4448
http://www.centenary.edu/majors/escience/

Louisiana Tech University
Environmental Science Program
P.O. Box 3178
Ruston, LA 71272
Phone: (318) 257-4573
Fax: (318) 257-4574
http://www.ans.latech.edu/envirsci-index.
html

Loyola University, New Orleans
Environmental Studies Program
6363 St. Charles Avenue, Box 79
New Orleans, LA 70118
Phone: (504) 865-2128
Fax: (504) 865-3883
http://www.loyno.edu/%7Eenvir/

McNeese State University
Department of Biological and
Environmental Sciences
P.O. Box 92000
Lake Charles, LA 70609-2000
Phone: (337) 475-5674
Fax: (337) 475-5677
http://www.faculty.mcneese.edu/
mwygoda/newdept/

MAINE

Bowdoin College
Environmental Studies Program
Adams Hall
Brunswick, ME 04011
Phone: (207) 798-7157
Fax: (207) 725-3689
http://academic.bowdoin.edu/
environmental_studies/

Colby College
Environmental Studies Department
4881 Mayflower Hill Drive
Waterville, ME 04901-8857

Phone: (207) 872-3143
http://www.colby.edu/environ/

University of Maine, Farmington
Environmental Science Program
Natural Science Department
173 High Street
Farmington, ME 04938
Phone: (207) 778-8151
http://departments.umf.maine.edu/
~sciences/enshomp.htm

MARYLAND

Towson University
Environmental Science and Studies
Program
Smith Hall, Room 348
8000 York Road
Towson, MD 21252-0001
Phone: (410) 704-4920
Fax: (410) 704-2604
http://www.towson.edu/ess

MASSACHUSETTS

College of the Holy Cross
Environmental Studies Program
1 College Street
Worcester, MA 01610
Phone: (508) 793-2497
http://www.holycross.edu/departments/
CISS/website/environmental_studies/

Eastern Nazarene College
Environmental Science Program
23 East Elm Avenue
Quincy, MA 02170
http://www.enc.edu/org/science/
EnvMenu.html

Lesley College
Environmental Studies Program
29 Everett Street
Cambridge, MA 02138
Phone: (617) 349-8966
http://www.lesley.edu/ungrad/
environment.html

Merrimack College
Environmental Science Program
315 Turnpike Street
North Andover, MA 1845
Phone: (978) 837-5000
http://www.merrimack.edu/bin/
mcdepartment.cgi?department=Enviro
nmental_Science

Springfield College
Environmental Sciences Program

263 Alden Street
Springfield, MA 01109-3797
Phone: (413) 748-3337

Williams College
The Center for Environmental Studies
P.O. Box 632
Williamstown, MA 01267
Phone: (413) 597-2346
Fax: (413) 597-3489
http://www.williams.edu/CES/welcome.
htm

MICHIGAN

Adrian College
Environmental Studies/Science
    Department
110 South Madison
Adrian, MI 49221
Phone: (800) 877-2246
http://www.adrian.edu/academics/ESS.
php

Alma College
Program of Environmental Studies
614 West Superior Street
Alma, MI 48801
Phone: (989) 463-7191
http://www.alma.edu/academics/
    environstudies/index.htm

Aquinas College
Environmental Science Program
1607 Robinson Road SE
Grand Rapids, MI 49506
Phone: (616) 632-2188
http://www.aquinas.edu/departments/
    environment/

Central Michigan University
Environmental Studies Program
Mount Pleasant, MI 48859
Phone: (989) 774-4000
http://www.cst.cmich.edu/units/env/

Kalamazoo College
Environmental Studies Concentration
1200 Academy Street
Kalamazoo, MI 49006-3295
Phone: (269) 337-7028
http://www.kzoo.edu/regist/depts/envs/

Northwestern Michigan College
Department of Environmental Science
1701 East Front
Traverse City, MI 49686
Phone: (800) 748-0566
http://www.nmc.edu/science-math/
    EnvironmentalScience/envhome.htm

MINNESOTA

Bemidji State University
Center for Environmental Earth and
    Space Studies
Box 27
1500 Birchmont Drive NE
Bemidji, MN 56601-2699
Phone: (218) 755-2910
Fax: (218) 755-4048
http://www.bemidjistate.edu/ceess/

**College of Saint Benedict and Saint
    John's University**
Environmental Studies Program
37 South College Avenue
St. Joseph, MN 56374
Phone: (320) 363-5308
Fax: (320) 363-5010
http://www.csbsju.edu/admission/
    academics/areasofstudy/majors_
    minors/Environmental_studies/
    environmental_studies.htm

Concordia College, Moorhead
Environmental Studies Program
901 Eighth Street South
Moorhead, MN 56562
Phone: (218) 299-4000
http://www.cord.edu/dept/env_studies/

Gustavus Adolphus College
Environmental Studies Program
800 West College Avenue
St. Peter, MN 56802
Phone: (507) 933-8000
http://www.gustavus.edu/oncampus/
    academics/general_catalog/current/
    index.cfm?pr=env

Hamline University
Environmental Studies Program
1536 Hewitt Avenue
St. Paul, MN 55104
Phone: (651) 523-2290
Fax: (651) 523-2620
http://www.hamline.edu/depts/envstud/

MISSOURI

Central Methodist College
Environmental Science Program
411 Central Methodist Square
Fayette, MO 65248
Phone: (660) 248-6371
Fax: (660) 248-1634
http://www.cmc.edu/envsci/

Drury College
Environmental Studies Program

900 North Benton Avenue
Springfield, MO 65802
Phone: (417) 873-7238
http://www.drury.edu/academics/
    undergrad/envstudies/env.cfm

Maryville University of Saint Louis
Environmental Program
13550 Conway Road
Saint Louis, MO 63141
Phone: (800) 627-9855
http://www.maryville.edu/academics/
    sbcontent/lp/environmental/

MONTANA

Carroll College
Environmental Studies Department
1601 North Benton Avenue
Helena, MT 59625
Phone: (406) 447-5476
http://www.carroll.edu/academics/
    environmental/index.php

Montana State University, Billings
Environmental Studies Program
130 Apsaruke Hall
1500 University Drive
Billings, MT 59101-0298
Phone: (800) 565-6782
http://www.msubillings.edu/catalogs/
    generalcatalog/Output/chapt24B2.html

University of Montana
Environmental Studies Program
Missoula, MT 59812
Phone: (406) 243-6273
http://www.umt.edu/evst/

University of Montana, Western
Environmental Sciences Department
710 South Atlantic Street
Dillon, MT 59725
Phone: (406) 683-7615
Fax: (406) 683-7493
http://www.wmc.edu/Academics/
    departments/EnviroSci/

NEBRASKA

Bellevue University
Environmental Science Program
1000 Galvin Road South
Bellevue, NE 68005
Phone: (800) 756-7920
http://www.bellevue.edu/Programs/
    Degrees/environsci.html

Creighton University
Program in Environmental Science

2500 California Plaza
Omaha, NE 68178
Phone: (402) 280-3190
Fax: (402) 280-1731
http://puffin.creighton.edu/evs/

Midland Lutheran College
Environmental Science Program
900 North Clarkson Street
Fremont, NE 68025
Phone: (402) 721-5487
http://www.mlc.edu/academics/majors.
    asp?major=envscience

NEVADA

Nevada State College
Environmental Sciences Program
1125 Nevada State Drive
Henderson, NV 89015
Phone: (702) 992-2000
http://www.nsc.nevada.edu/academics/
    programs/envsci/ | admissions@nsc.
    nevada.edu

University of Nevada, Reno
Environmental Sciences & Health
    Graduate Program
MS/199
Reno, NV 89557-0187
Phone: (775) 784-6400
Fax: (775) 784-1142
http://www.unr.edu/idgrad/esh/

NEW HAMPSHIRE

Dartmouth College
Environmental Studies Program
6182 Steele Hall Room 113
Hanover, NH 03755
Phone: (603) 646-2838
Fax: (603) 646-1682
http://www.dartmouth.edu/~envs/

Franklin Pierce College
Environmental Science Program
20 College Road
Rindge, NH 03461-0060
Phone: (800) 437-0048
http://www.fpc.edu/pages/Academics/
    nscience/envsci/index.htm

Keene State College
Environmental Studies Program
115 Winchester Street 205
Keene, NH 03435
Phone: (603) 358-2571
http://www.keene.edu/programs/enst/

Southern New Hampshire University
Environmental Studies Program
2500 North River Road
Manchester, NH 03106
Phone: (603) 645-9692
http://www.snhu.edu/Southern_
    New_Hampshire_University/
    Academics/General_Info/MINORS/
    Environmental_Studies.html

NEW JERSEY

Drew University
Environmental Studies Minor
Madison, NJ 07940
Phone: (973) 408-3550
http://depts.drew.edu/envstudies/

Essex County College
Environmental Science Program
303 University Avenue
Newark, NJ 07102
Phone: (973) 877-3430
http://www.essex.edu

Princeton University
Princeton Environment Institute
Environmental Studies Program
127 Guyot Hall
Princeton, NJ 08544
Phone: (609) 258-4998
Fax: (609) 258-1716
http://web.princeton.edu/sites/pei/
    undergradprogram.htm

Rutgers University
Environmental Sciences
14 College Farm Road
New Brunswick, NJ 08901-8851
Phone: (732) 932-9185
http://www.envsci.rutgers.edu/

NEW YORK

Adelphi University
Environmental Studies Department
South Avenue
Garden City, NY 11530
Phone: (516) 877-4170
Fax: (516) 877-4209
http://academics.adelphi.edu/artsci/env/

Alfred University
Environmental Studies Program
Saxon Drive
Alfred, NY 14802-1205
Phone: (607) 871-2634
Fax: (607) 871-2697
http://ens.alfred.edu/

Barnard College
Department of Environmental Science
404 Altschul Hall, 3009 Broadway
New York, NY 10027
Phone: (212) 854-5618
Fax: (212) 854-5760
http://www.barnard.edu/envsci/

Canisius College
Environmental Science Program
2001 Main Street
Buffalo, NY 14208-1098
Phone: (716) 888-2567
http://www.canisius.edu/envsci/

Colgate University
Environmental Studies Program
Olin Hall, 13 Oak Drive
Hamilton, NY 13346
Phone: (315) 228-7347
Fax: (315) 228-7997
http://departments.colgate.edu/envir_
    stud/

College of New Rochelle
Environmental Studies Program
29 Castle Place
New Rochelle, NY 10805
Phone: (800) 933-5923
Fax: (914) 654-5464
http://www.cnr.edu/academics/SAS/
    envstudies.html

Columbia University
Department of Earth and Environmental
    Sciences
106 Geoscience
Lamont-Doherty Earth Observatory
61 Route 9W
Palisades, NY 10964
Phone: (212) 854-5029
Fax: (212) 854-7975
http://eesc.columbia.edu

Concordia College, Bronxville
Environmental Science Program
171 White Plains Road
Bronxville, NY 10708
Phone: (714) 337-9300
http://www.concordia.onlinecommunity.
    com/env.pdf

Daemen College
Environmental Studies Program
4380 Main Street
Amherst, NY 14226
Phone: (716) 839-8541
http://www.daemen.edu/academics/
    natural_science/environ-studies.html

Elmira College
Environmental Studies Program
One Park Place
Elmira, NY 14901
Phone: (607) 735-1800
http://www.elmira.edu/academics/am_
  environmental.shtml

Hamilton College
Environmental Studies Program
198 College Hill Road
Clinton, NY 13323
Phone: (315) 859-4698
Fax: (315) 859-4807
http://www.hamilton.edu/academics/
  enviro/default.html

Hobart and William Smith Colleges
Environmental Studies Program
Box 4178, Lansing Hall 206
Geneva, NY 14456
Phone: (315) 781-3918
Fax: (315) 781-3860
http://academic.hws.edu/envstud/

Ithaca College
Environmental Studies Program
315 Muller Center
953 Danby Road
Ithaca, NY 14850
Phone: (607) 274-1347
Fax: (607) 274-3474
http://www.ithaca.edu/esp/

Manhattanville College
Environmental Studies Minor
2900 Purchase Street
Purchase, NY 10577
Phone: (800) 328-4553
http://www.mville.edu/biology/
  envirominor.html

Marist College
Department of Environmental Science
3399 North Road
Poughkeepsie, NY 12601-1387
Phone: (845) 575-3000
http://www.marist.edu/science/
  environmental/

Niagara University
Environmental Studies Program
Timon Hall, Room 11
Niagara, NY 14109
Phone: (716) 286 8092
http://www.niagara.edu/environmental/

Pace University, Pleasantville
Environmental Studies Program
41 Park Row, Third Floor

New York, NY 10038
Phone: (212) 346-1460
Fax: (212) 346-1113
http://appserv.pace.edu/execute/page.
  cfm?doc_id=3921

Paul Smith's College
Environmental Science
Route 86 & 30
P.O. Box 265
Paul Smiths, NY 12970-0265
Phone: (800) 421-2605
Fax: (518) 327-6016
http://www.paulsmiths.edu

**State University of New York (SUNY),
  Binghamton**
Environmental Studies Program
Science 1, Room 161
Binghamton, NY 13902
Phone: (607) 777-2389
http://environ.binghamton.edu/

**State University of New York (SUNY),
  Cortland**
Environmental Science Program
P.O. Box 2000
Cortland, NY 13045
Phone: (607) 753-2815
Fax: (607) 753-2927
http://www.cortland.edu/geology/

**State University of New York (SUNY),
  Fredonia**
Environmental Sciences Program
107A Jewett Hall
Fredonia, NY 14063
Phone: (716) 673-3819
http://www.fredonia.edu/department/
  biology/EnvSci/Web/Title.htm

**State University of New York (SUNY),
  Oneonta**
Environmental Sciences Program
Milne Library 320
Oneonta, NY 13820
Phone: (607) 436-3150
http://www.oneonta.edu/academics/
  envsci/

**State University of New York (SUNY),
  Plattsburgh**
Center for Earth & Environmental
  Science
101 Broad Street
Plattsburgh, NY 12901
Phone: (518) 564-2028
Fax: (518) 564-5267
http://www.plattsburgh.edu/cees/

**State University of New York (SUNY),
  Purchase**
Environmental Science Program
735 Anderson Hill Road
Purchase, NY 10577-1400
Phone: (914) 251-6630
http://www.ns.purchase.edu/envsci/
  default.htm

**State University of New York (SUNY),
  Stony Brook**
Environmental Studies
105 Endeavour Hall
Stony Brook, NY 11794-2250
Phone: (631) 632-8681
http://naples.cc.sunysb.edu/CAS/
  ubdepts0305.nsf/pages/ens

Union College
Environmental Studies Program
807 Union Street
Schenectady, NY 12308
Phone: (518) 388-6000
http://www.union.edu/Academics/
  Departments/deptView.
  php?code=EN&year=2003

Vassar College
Environmental Studies
Box 731
124 Raymond Avenue
Poughkeepsie, NY 12604-0731
Phone: (845) 437-5430
http://environmentalstudies.vassar.edu/

NORTH CAROLINA

Catawba College
Environmental Science & Studies
  Program
2300 West Innes Street
Salisbury, NC 28144
Phone: (704) 637-4402
http://www.catawba.edu/environ/

Elon University
Environmental Studies Program
2625 Campus Box
Elon, NC 27244-2010
Phone: (800) 336-8448
http://www.elon.edu/academics/environ/

Guilford College
Environmental Studies Program
5800 West Friendly Avenue
Greensboro, NC 27410
Phone: (336) 316-2000
http://www.guilford.edu/original/
  academic/envst/

Louisburg College
Environmental Studies Program
501 North Main Street
Louisburg, NC 27549
Phone: (919) 497-3219
Fax: (919) 496-1788
http://www.louisburg.edu/academics/
    sciences.htm

North Carolina Central University
Department of Environmental Science
Room 125 William Jones Building
Durham, NC 27707
Phone: (919) 560-5296
Fax: (919) 560-7990
http://www.nccu.edu/artsci/envirsci/

North Carolina Wesleyan College
Environmental Science Program
3400 North Wesleyan Boulevard
Rocky Mount, NC 27804
Phone: (252) 985-5100
http://www.ncwc.edu/Academics/
    MathScience/environmental.htm

Shaw University
Environmental Science Department
118 East South Street
Raleigh, NC 27601
Phone: (919) 546-8200
Fax: (919) 546-8301
http://www.shawuniversity.edu/ap_cas_
    dept_natural_sciences_mathematics.
    htm#env

**University of North Carolina,
    Wilmington**
Environmental Studies Program
601 South College Road
Wilmington, NC 28403-3297
Phone: (910) 962-7675
Fax: (910) 962-7634
http://www.uncwil.edu/evs/

Warren Wilson College
Department of Environmental Studies
P.O. Box 9000
Asheville, NC 28815
Phone: (828) 298-3325
http://www.warren-wilson.edu/~ens/
    WebPages/bioens/ENS.html

OHIO

Cleveland State University
Department of Biological, Geological
    and Environmental Sciences
2121 Euclid Avenue
Cleveland, OH 44115-2214

Phone: (216) 687-2440
Fax: (216) 687-6972
http://bgesweb.artscipub.csuohio.edu/

Defiance College
Environmental Science Program
701 North Clinton Street
Defiance, OH 43512
Phone: (800) 520-4632
http://www.defiance.edu/pages/
    environmental_science.html

Denison University
Environmental Studies Program
100 South Road
Granville, OH 43023
Phone: (740) 587-5707
http://www.denison.edu/enviro/

Hiram College
Environmental Studies Program
P.O. Box 67
Hiram, OH 44234
Phone: (330) 569-3211
http://www.hiram.edu/academics/majors/
    environmental_studies/index.asp

Lake Erie College
Environmental Science Program
391 West Washington Street
Painesville, OH 44077
Phone: (216) 639-4708
Fax: (216) 352-3533
http://www.lec.edu/academics/academ1.
    html

Marietta College
Environmental Science Program
215 Fifth Street
Marietta, OH 45750
Phone: (740) 376-4643
http://www.marietta.edu/%7Eenvr/

Miami University
Environmental Science Program
Oxford, OH 45056
Phone: (513) 529-1338
http://www.miami.muohio.edu/
    academics/majorsminors/majors/
    environmentalstudies.cfm

Ohio State University
Environmental Science Graduate Program
365 Kottman Hall
2021 Coffey Road
Columbus, OH 43210
Phone: (614) 292-9762
Fax: (614) 292-7432
http://www.osu.edu/units/esgp/
    homebase1.html

Wright State University
Environmental Sciences Ph.D. Program
021 Fawcett Hall
3640 Colonel Glenn Highway
Dayton, OH 45435-0001
Phone: (937) 775-3273
Fax: (937) 775-3068
http://www.wright.edu/academics/envsci/

Youngstown State University
Environmental Studies Program
One University Plaza
Youngstown, OH 44555
Phone: (330) 941-2933
Fax: (330) 941-1754
http://www.cc.ysu.edu/~amjacobs/index3.
    htm

OKLAHOMA

Oklahoma State University
Environmental Sciences Graduate Program
003 Life Sciences East
Stillwater, OK 74078-3011
Phone: (405) 744-9229
Fax: (405) 744-7673
http://environ.okstate.edu/es

OREGON

Lewis & Clark College
Environmental Studies Program
0615 SW Palatine Hill Road
Portland, OR 97219
Phone: (503) 768-7699
http://www.lclark.edu/~esm/

Linfield College
Environmental Studies Program
900 SE Baker Street
McMinnville, OR 97218
Phone: (503) 883-2504
http://www.linfield.edu/env/

Marylhurst University
Environmental Science Program
17600 Pacific Highway
P.O. Box 261
Marylhurst, OR 97036

Oregon Institute of Technology
Environmental Sciences Program
3201 Campus Drive
Klamath Falls, OR 97601-8801
Phone: (541) 885-1150
http://www.oit.edu/index.html?method=aes

Portland State University
Environmental Sciences and Resources
P.O. Box 751
Portland, OR 97207-0751

Phone: (503) 725-4980
http://www.esr.pdx.edu/

Southern Oregon University
Environmental Studies Program
1250 Siskiyou Boulevard
Ashland, OR 97520
Phone: (541) 552-6496
Fax: (541) 552-6415
http://www.sou.edu/envirostudies/index.
  htm

University of Oregon
Environmental Studies Program
5223 University of Oregon
Eugene, OR 97403-5223
Phone: (541) 346-5000
Fax: (541) 346-5954
http://www.uoregon.edu/~ecostudy/

PENNSYLVANIA

Albright College
Environmental Studies
13th and Bern Streets
P.O. Box 15234
Reading, PA 19612
Phone: (610) 921-2381
http://www.albright.edu/catalog/
  environmental_studies.htm

Allegheny College
Environmental Science Department
520 North Main Street
Meadville, PA 16335
Phone: (814) 332-2870
http://www.allegheny.edu/academics/
  envsci/

Bucknell University
Environmental Studies Program
103 Coleman Hall
Lewisburg, PA 17837
Phone: (570) 577-1421
http://www.departments.bucknell.edu/
  environ_studies/

California University of Pennsylvania
Biological and Environmental Sciences
250 University Avenue
California, PA 15419-1394
Phone: (724) 938-4200
http://www.cup.edu/ugcatalog/Programs/
  BioandEnviro/index.htm

Cedar Crest College
Environmental Science Program
100 College Drive
Allentown, PA 18104
Phone: (610) 606-4666, ext. 3515

http://www2.cedarcrest.edu/academic/
  bio/bbenson/envsci.html

Chatham College
Rachel Carson Institute
Environmental Programs
Buhl 234a
Woodland Road
Pittsburgh, PA 15232
Phone: (412) 365-1883
Fax: (412) 365-1505
http://www.chatham.edu/rci/env_curric.
  html

Delaware Valley College
Agronomy and Environmental Science
  Department
700 East Butler Avenue
Doylestown, PA 18901-2697
Phone: (800) 2-DelVal
http://campus.devalcol.edu/linded/

Dickinson College
Environmental Studies Department
Post Office Box 1773
Carlisle, PA 17013
Phone: (717) 243-5121
http://www.dickinson.edu/departments/
  envst/

Duquesne University
Bayer School of Natural & Environmental
  Sciences
100 Mellon Hall
Pittsburgh, PA 15282
Phone: (412) 396-4900
Fax: (412) 396-4881
http://www.science.duq.edu/

Eastern College
Environmental Sciences Program
1300 Eagle Road
St. Davids Road, PA 19087
Phone: (610) 341-5800
http://www.eastern.edu/academic/trad_
  undg/sas/depts/environmental/index.
  html

Gettysburg College
Environmental Studies Department
300 North Washington Street
Gettysburg, PA 17325
Phone: (717) 337-6077
Fax: (717) 337-8550
http://www.gettysburg.edu/academics/env/

Juniata College
Environmental Science & Studies
  Program
1700 Moore Street

Huntingdon, PA 16652
Phone: (814) 641-3000
http://departments.juniata.edu/
  environmental/

Kutztown University of Pennsylvania
Environmental Science Program
Kutztown, PA 19530
Phone: (610) 683-4312
http://www.kutztown.edu/acad/EnvSci/

Lafayette College
Environmental Science Program
Easton, PA 18042
Phone: (610) 330-5196
Fax: (610) 330-5717
http://ww2.lafayette.edu/~envscimp/
  envscimp.html

Lincoln University
Environmental Science Program
1570 Baltimore Pike
Wright Hall, MSC 35, P.O. Box 179
Lincoln University, PA 19352
Phone: (610) 932-8300
Fax: (610) 932-1054
http://www.lincoln.edu/environsci/index.
  htm

Marywood College
Environmental Science Program
2300 Adams Avenue
Scranton, PA 18509
Phone: (570) 348-6211
http://www.marywood.edu/departments/
  Science/Academic_Information/
  Environmental_Science/
  environmental_science.html

Millersville University of Pennsylvania
Environmental Institute
P.O. Box 1002
Millersville, PA 17551
Phone: (717) 871-5425
http://marauder.millersville.edu/
  ~muenviro/

Pennsylvania State University, Altoona
Environmental Studies Program
108 Science Building
3000 Ivyside Park
Altoona, PA 16601-3760
Phone: (814) 949-3760
http://www.aa.psu.edu/envstu/ba.htm

Swarthmore College
Environmental Studies
500 College Avenue
Swarthmore, PA 19081

Phone: (610) 328-8000
http://www.swarthmore.edu/NatSci/es/

Temple University
Environmental Studies Program
330 Gladfelter Hall
Philadelphia, PA 19122-6089
Phone: (215) 204-5918
Fax: (215) 204-7833
http://www.temple.edu/env-stud/

University of Pennsylvania
Master of Environmental Studies
College of General Studies
3440 Market Street, Suite 100
Philadelphia, PA 19104
Phone: (215) 898-6517
Fax: (215) 573-2053

University of Pittsburgh at Bradford
Environmental Studies
300 Campus Drive
Bradford, PA 16701
Phone: (814) 362-0242
http://www.pitt.edu/~robar/

University of Scranton
Environmental Science Program
Scranton, PA 18510
Phone: (570) 941-6286
http://academic.scranton.edu/department/
    envscience/

Ursinus College
Environmental Studies
P.O. Box 1000
601 Main Street
Collegeville, PA 19426-1000
Phone: (610) 409-3000
http://www.ursinus.edu/content.asp?page=
    AcademicPrograms/environStudies.htm

Wilson College
Department of Environmental Studies
1015 Philadelphia Avenue
Chambersburg, PA 17201
Phone: (717) 264-4141
http://www.wilson.edu/Faculty/enviro/
    windex.htm

RHODE ISLAND

Brown University
Center for Environmental Studies
Box 1943
Providence, RI 02912
Phone: (401) 863-3449
Fax: (401) 863-3503
http://envstudies.brown.edu/Dept/

SOUTH CAROLINA

Benedict College
Biology, Chemistry and Environmental
    Health Sciences Department
1600 Harden Street
Columbia, SC 29204
Phone: (803) 253-5000
http://www.benedict.edu/divisions/acadaf/
    sch-science/bio_chem/bc-bio_phys.
    html

Clemson University
School of the Environment
340 Brackett Hall, Box 340976
Clemson, SC 29634-0976
Phone: (864) 656-5567
http://www.ces.clemson.edu/ees/
    schofenviron.html

College of Charleston
Master of Environmental Studies
66 George Street
Charleston, SC 29424
Phone: (843) 953-2000
Fax: (843) 953-2001
http://www.cofc.edu/~environ/

Francis Marion University
Environmental Science Option
Department of Biology
P.O. Box 100547
Florence, SC 29501-0547
Phone: (843) 661-1231
Fax: (843) 661-4660
http://swampfox.fmarion.edu/web/biol/
    envirsci.html

Furman University
Department of Earth and Environmental
    Sciences
3300 Poinsett Highway
Greenville, SC 29613
Phone: (864) 294-2052
Fax: (864) 294-3585
http://alpha.furman.edu/academics/dept/
    ees/newhome/

Lander University
Environmental Science Program
Greenwood, SC 29649
Phone: (864) 388-8132
http://www.lander.edu/science/info_envs.
    html

Newberry College
Environmental Science Program
2100 College Street
Newberry, SC 29108

Phone: (803) 276-5010
http://www.newberry.edu/academics/
    majors/biochemvet.htm

Northern State University
Environmental Science Program
1200 South Jay Street
Aberdeen, SD 57401
Phone: (605) 626-2456
Fax: (605) 626-3365
http://www.northern.edu/cas/biology/
    ProgramsMenu.htm#Environmental%
    20Science

University of South Carolina
School of the Environment
702G Byrnes Building
Columbia, SC 29208
Phone: (803) 777-9153
Fax: (803) 777-5715
http://www.environ.sc.edu/

TENNESSEE

University of Tennessee, Chattanooga
MS in Environmental Science
615 McCallie Ave
Chattanooga, TN 37403-2598
Phone: (423) 425-4666
http://www.utc.edu/gradstudies/environ.
    html

TEXAS

Austin College
Center for Environmental Studies
900 North Grand Avenue
Sherman, TX 75090-4400
Phone: (903) 813-2284
Fax: (903) 813-2420
http://www.austincollege.edu/Category.
    asp?1450

Baylor University
Environmental Studies
One Bear Place, No. 97266
Waco, TX 76798-7266
Phone: (254) 710-3405
Fax: (254) 710-3409
http://www.baylor.edu/Envir_Studies

Lamar University
Environmental Science Program
4400 Martin Luther King Boulevard
P.O. Box 10037
Beaumont, TX 77710
Phone: (409) 880-8255
http://dept.lamar.edu/artssciences/
    biology/bs_in_environmental_science.
    html

McMurry University
Department of Environmental Science
McMurry Station Box 158
Abilene, TX 79697
Phone: (915) 793-3881
http://www.mcm.edu/~martinr/envirsc/
envrsci.htm

Midwestern State University
Environmental Science Program
3410 Taft Boulevard
Wichita Falls, TX 76308
Phone: (940) 397-4000
http://www.mwsu.edu/htmldocs/
departments/enviro_science/
EnviroScience.htm

Southwestern University
Environmental Studies Program
340 Fondren-Jones Science Hall
Georgetown, TX 78626
Phone: (512) 863-1721
Fax: (512) 863-5788
http://www.southwestern.edu/academic/
environmental-studies/

Stephen F. Austin State University
Division of Environmental Science
P.O. Box 6132
Nacogdoches, TX 75962-6132
Phone: (936) 468-6900
Fax: (936) 468-6915
http://www.fp.sfasu.edu/environmental/

Texas A&M University, Corpus Christi
Environmental Science Program
6300 Ocean Drive, NRC 2700
Corpus Christi, TX 78412
Phone: (361) 825-2436
http://www.sci.tamucc.edu/pals/esci/esci.html

Texas Lutheran University
Environmental Studies Programs
1000 West Court Street Admissions Office
Seguin, TX 78155
Phone: (800) 771-8521
http://www.tlu.edu/academics/special/
environmental_studies/

University of North Texas
Environmental Science Program
Institute of Applied Sciences
P.O. Box 310559
Denton, TX 76203-0059
Phone: (940) 565-2694
http://www.ias.unt.edu/

University of Texas, Austin
Environmental Science Institute
Flawn Academic Center, Room 1
Austin, TX 78712
Phone: (512) 471-5847
http://www.utexas.edu/student/connexus

UTAH

University of Utah
Environmental Studies Program
260 South Central Campus Drive, Room 252
Salt Lake City, UT 84112
Phone: (801) 585-3536
http://www.envst.utah.edu/

VERMONT

Castleton State College
Environmental Science Program
Castleton, VT 05735
Phone: (802) 468-1238
Fax: (802) 468-1170
http://www.csc.vsc.edu/NASWebpage/
page4.html

Goddard College
Environmental Studies Concentration
123 Pitkin Road
Plainfield, VT 05667
Phone: (802) 454-8311
http://www.goddard.edu/academic/
Envirostudies.html

Lyndon State College
Environmental Science Program
1001 College Road, P.O. Box 919
Lyndonville, VT 05851-0919
Phone: (802) 626-6500
http://www.lsc.vsc.edu/intranet/
academics/acaddept/nat/envsci.htmy

Marlboro College
Environmental Studies
P.O. Box A, 2582 South Road
Marlboro, VT 05344-0300
Phone: (802) 257-4333
Fax: (802) 257-4154
http://www.marlboro.edu/about/
academics.html

Middlebury College
Environmental Studies Program
Middlebury, VT 05753
Phone: (802) 443-5710
http://www.middlebury.edu/~es/

Norwich University
Environmental Science Program
158 Harmon Drive
Northfield, VT 05663
Phone: (800) 468-6679
http://www.norwich.edu/mathsci/
environmental/

Southern Vermont College
Environmental Studies
982 Mansion Drive
Bennington, VT 05201-6002
Phone: (802) 447-6365
http://www.svc.edu/academics/divisions/
environmental.html

VIRGINIA

Averett College
Environmental Science Program
420 West Main Street
Danville, VA 24541
Phone: (804) 791-5766
Fax: (804) 791-4392
http://dev.averett.edu/html/environmental_
science.html

Bluefield College
Environmental Science Program
3000 College Drive
Bluefield, VA 24605
Phone: (800) 872-0175
http://www.bluefield.edu/index.
php?template=view_academic_
programs&category=Environmental+
Science

Christopher Newport University
Department of Biology, Chemistry and
Environmental Science
1 University Place
Newport News, VA 23606-2998
Phone: (757) 594-7544
Fax: (757) 594-7333
http://www.cnu.edu/bces/

Emory & Henry College
Environmental Studies Program
P.O. Box 947
Emory, VA 24327-0947
Phone: (276) 944-6203

Lynchburg College
Environmental Science Program
1501 Lakeside Drive
Lynchburg, VA 24501
Phone: (804) 544-8370
http://www.lynchburg.edu/academic/envsci/

Mary Washington College
Department of Environmental Science
and Geology

1301 College Avenue
Fredericksburg, VA 22401
Phone: (540) 654-1427
http://www.mwc.edu/eesg/

Shenandoah University
Environmental Studies
1460 University Drive
Winchester, VA 22601
Phone: (540) 665-4587
http://www.su.edu/Faculty/Wbousque/
    ESPages/ESIndex.html

Sweet Briar College
Environmental Programs
Sweet Briar, VA 24595
Phone: (800) 381-6142
Fax: (434) 381-6152
http://environsci.sbc.edu/

University of Richmond
Environmental Studies Program
Gottwald Science Center
Richmond, VA 23173
Phone: (804) 289-8242
Fax: (804) 287-1897
http://environmental.richmond.edu/

University of Virginia
Department of Environmental Sciences
P.O. Box 400160
Charlottesville, VA 22904
Phone: (434) 982-3200
Fax: (434) 924-3587
http://www.evsc.virginia.edu/index.shtml

Washington and Lee University
Environmental Studies Program
Lexington, VA 24450
Phone: (540) 458-8036
http://environmentalstudies.wlu.edu/

WASHINGTON

Clark College
Environmental Science Program
APH 203C, 992-2202
1800 East McLoughlin Boulevard
Vancouver, WA 98663
Phone: (360) 992-2202
http://www.clark.edu/academic_
    programs/transfer/science/
    environmental_science/

Evergreen State College
Master of Environmental Studies
Olympia, WA 98505
Phone: (360) 866-6000
http://www.evergreen.edu/mes/

Northwest College
Environmental Science Program
5520 108th Avenue NE
Kirkland, WA 98033
Phone: (425) 822-8266
http://www.nwcollege.edu/catalog/
    programs/envscimaj.html

Tacoma Community College
Environmental Science Program
6501 South 19th Street
Tacoma, WA 98466
Phone: (253) 566-5348
Fax: (253) 566-5202
http://www.tacoma.ctc.edu/inst_dept/
    science/environmentalscience.asp?Pro
    gram=3&DisplayOrder=1

University of Puget Sound
Environmental Studies Department
1500 North Warner Street
Tacoma, WA 98416
Phone: (253) 879-2819
http://www.ups.edu/environ_studies/
    home.shtml

WEST VIRGINIA

Alderson-Broaddus College
Environmental Science Program
College Hill Road
Philippi, WV 26416
Phone: (304) 457-1700
Fax: (304) 457-6239
http://www.ab.edu/academics/
    environmental_science.html

Davis & Elkins College
Department of Biology and
    Environmental Science
100 Campus Drive
Elkins, WV 26241
Phone: (304) 637-1204
http://www.dne.edu/academ/dept/bes/
    beshpg.htm

WISCONSIN

Alverno College
Environmental Science Program
P.O. Box 343922
Milwaukee, WI 53234-3922
Phone: (800) 933-401
http://www.alverno.edu/academics/
    environment_science.html

Carthage College
Environmental Science Program
2001 Alford Park Drive
Kenosha, WI 53140-1994

Phone: (262) 551-5846
Fax: (262) 551-6208
http://ulysses.carthage.edu/Departments/
    environment/Default.htm

GEOSCIENCE

ALABAMA

Jacksonville State University
Department of Physical and Earth
    Sciences
206 Martin Hall
Jacksonville, AL 36265
Phone: (256) 782-5232
Fax: (256) 782-5336
http://www.jsu.edu/depart/geography/
    geoginto.html

ARIZONA

Arizona State University
Department of Geological Sciences
Box 871404
Tempe, AZ 85287-1404
Phone: (480) 965-5081
Fax: (480) 965-8102
http://www.geology.asu.edu/

ARKANSAS

University of Arkansas
Department of Earth Science
2801 South University Avenue
Little Rock, AR 72204-1099
Phone: (501) 569-3546
Fax: (501) 569-3271
http://www.ualr.edu/~ersc/

CALIFORNIA

American River College
Earth Sciences Department
4700 College Oak Drive
Sacramento, CA 95841
Phone: (916) 484-8638
Fax: (916) 484-8725
http://www.arc.losrios.edu/~earthsci

California Polytechnic State University
Earth & Soil Sciences Department
One Grand Avenue
San Luis Obispo, CA 93407
Phone: (805) 756-2261
Fax: (805) 756-5412
http://www.earth.soils.calpoly.edu

**California State University,
    Dominguez Hills**
Earth Sciences Department

1000 East Victoria Street
Carson, CA 90747
Phone: (310) 243-3376
Fax: (310) 516-4268
http://earth.csudh.edu/

California State University, East Bay
Department of Geography &
   Environmental Studies
25800 Carlos Bee Boulevard
Hayward, CA 94542-3000
Phone: (510) 885-3471
http://isis.csueastbay.edu/dbsw/
   geography/Home_Page.php

California State University, Fresno
Department of Earth and Environmental
   Sciences
2345 East San Ramon Avenue
M/S MH24
Fresno, CA 93740
Phone: (559) 278-3086
Fax: (559) 278-5980
http://www.csufresno.edu/geology/

California State University, Fullerton
Department of Geological Sciences
800 North State College Boulevard
P.O. Box 6850
Fullerton, CA 92834-6850
Phone: (714) 278-3882
Fax: (714) 278-7266
http://geology.fullerton.edu

Mendocino College
Geology Department
P.O. Box 3000
Ukiah, CA 95482
Phone: (707) 468-3128
Fax: (707) 468-3120

University of California, Riverside
Geology Department
P.O. Box 3000
Ukiah, CA 95482
Phone: (707) 468-3128
Fax: (707) 468-3120
http://earthscience.ucr.edu

COLORADO

Colorado School of Mines
Environmental Geochemistry Graduate
   Program
1500 Illinois Street
Guggenheim Hall, Room 314
Golden, CO 80401-1887
Phone: (800) 446-9488
Fax: (303) 273-3247
http://www.mines.edu/Admiss/grad/
   professional_masters.htm

CONNECTICUT

Eastern Connecticut State University
Environmental Earth Science Department
83 Windham Street
Willimantic, CT 06226
Phone: (860) 465-4317
http://www.ecsu.ctstateu.edu/depts/
   eearthsci/index.htm

University of Connecticut
Center for Integrative Geosciences
345 Mansfield Road
U-2045
Storrs, CT 06269-2045
Phone: (860) 486-4435
Fax: (860) 486-1383
http://www.geosciences.uconn.edu

FLORIDA

Department of Geological Sciences
1301 Memorial Drive
43 Cox Science Building
Coral Gables, FL 33124
Phone: (305) 284-4253
Fax: (305) 284-4258
E-mail: geology@umiami.ir.miami.edu

University of Miami
Division of Marine Geology &
   Geophysics
RSMAS
4600 Rickenbacker Causeway
Miami, FL 33149-1098
Phone: (305) 421-4663
Fax: (305) 421-4632
http://rsmas.miami.edu/divs/mgg/

GEORGIA

Fort Valley State University
Cooperative Developmental Energy
   Program
Box 5800 FVSU
1005 State University Drive
Fort Valley, GA 31030
Phone: (912) 825-6454
Fax: (912) 825-6618
http://www.fac.fvsu.edu/as/cd/index.
   htm

Georgia Tech
Earth and Atmospheric Sciences
311 Ferst Drive
Atlanta, GA 30332-0340
Phone: (404) 894-3893
Fax: (404) 894-5638
http://www.eas.gatech.edu/

IDAHO

University of Idaho
Department of Geological Sciences
Seventh & Line Street
Moscow, ID 83844-3022
Phone: (208) 885-6192
Fax: (208) 885-5724
http://geoscience.uidaho.com

ILLINOIS

Augustana College
Department of Geology
639 38th Street
Rock Island, IL 61201
Phone: (309) 794-7318
Fax: (309) 794-7564
E-mail: glwolf@augustana.edu
http://augustana.edu/academ/geology/
   index.htm

City Colleges of Chicago
Earth & Atmospheric Technology
   Program
226 West Jackson Boulevard
Chicago, IL 60606
Phone: (312) 553-3310
Fax: (312) 553-2814
http://www.ccc.edu/district/academics/
   occupational/sro/eatp/index.shtml

Northeastern Illinois University
Department of Geography &
   Environmental Studies
5500 North St. Louis Avenue
Chicago, IL 60625
Phone: (773) 442-5640
Fax: (773) 442-5650
http://www.neiu.edu/~deptges/

Northeastern Illinois University
Earth Science Program
5500 North St. Louis Avenue
Chicago, IL 60625-4699
Phone: (773) 442-6051
http://www.neiu.edu/~deptesci/welcome.
   htm

Wheaton College
Department of Geology & Environmental
   Science
501 East College Avenue
Wheaton, IL 60187
Phone: (630) 752-5063
Fax: (630) 752-5996

INDIANA

Indiana University
Department of Geological Sciences

1001 East 10th Street
Bloomington, IN 47405
Phone: (812) 855-5582
Fax: (812) 855-7899
http://www.indiana.edu/~geosci/

Purdue University
Department of Earth & Atmospheric
 Sciences
550 Stadium Mall Drive
West Lafayette, IN 47907-2051
Phone: (765) 494-3258
Fax: (765) 496-1210
http://www.purdue.edu/eas

IOWA

University of Iowa
Department of Geoscience
121 Trowbridge Hall
Iowa City, IA 52242
Phone: (319) 335-1818
Fax: (319) 335-1821
http://www.uiowa.edu/~geology/

KENTUCKY

Eastern Kentucky University
Department of Earth Sciences
521 Lancaster Avenue
Roark 103
Richmond, KY 40475-3102
Phone: (859) 622-1273
Fax: (859) 622-1451
http://www.earthscience.eku.edu

University of Kentucky
Department of Earth and Environmental
 Sciences
101 Slone Building
Lexington, KY 40506-0053
Phone: (859) 257-3758
Fax: (859) 323-1938
http://www.uky.edu/ArtsSciences/Geology

LOUISIANA

Louisiana State University
Department of Geology & Geophysics
E235 Howe-Russell Geoscience Complex
Baton Rouge, LA 70803-4101
Phone: (225) 578-3353
Fax: (225) 578-2302
http://www.geol.lsu.edu

MARYLAND

Johns Hopkins University
Department of Earth and Planetary Sciences
Olin Building

34th and North Charles Streets
Baltimore, MD 21218
Phone: (410) 516-7135
Fax: (410) 516-7933
http://www.jhu.edu/~eps/home/index.html

MASSACHUSETTS

Amherst College
Geology Department
Amherst, MA 01002-5000
Phone: (413) 542-2233
Fax: (413) 542-2713
http://www.amherst.edu/~geology

Harvard University
Department of Earth and Planetary
 Sciences
20 Oxford Street
Cambridge, MA 02138
Phone: (617) 495-2351
Fax: (617) 495-8839
http://www-eps.harvard.edu/

**Massachusetts Institute of Technology
(MIT)**
Department of Earth, Atmospheric
 & Planetary Sciences
77 Massachusetts Avenue
Cambridge, MA 02139
Phone: (617) 253-0149
http://www-eaps.mit.edu/

MICHIGAN

Adrian College
Earth Science Department
110 South Madison Street
Adrian, MI 49221
Phone: (517) 264-3944
http://www.adrian.edu/academics/ERTH.
 php

Albion College
Geology Department
611 East Porter Street
Albion, MI 49224
Phone: (517) 629-1000
http://www.albion.edu/geology/

Calvin College
Department of Geology, Geography,
 & Environmental Studies
3201 Burton SE
Grand Rapids, MI 49546
Phone: (616) 957-7033
Fax: (616) 957-6501
http://www.calvin.edu/academic/
 geology/

Central Michigan University
Department of Geology
314 Brooks Hall
Mount Pleasant, MI 48859
Phone: (989) 774-3179
Fax: (989) 774-2142
http://www.cst.cmich.edu/units/gel/

Grand Valley State University
Department of Geology
1 Campus Drive
125 Padnos Hall
Allendale, MI 49401
Phone: (616) 895-3728
Fax: (616) 895-3740
http://www.gvsu.edu/

Hope College
Geological and Environmental Science
 Program
35 East 12th Street
Holland, MI 49422-9000
Phone: (616) 395-7133
Fax: (616) 395-7118
http://www.hope.edu/academic/
 geology/

Michigan Technological University
Department of Geological & Mining
 Engineering & Sciences
1400 Townsend Drive
Houghton, MI 49931-1295
Phone: (906) 487-2531
Fax: (906) 487-3371
http://www.geo.mtu.edu

MINNESOTA

University of Minnesota, Duluth
Department of Geological Sciences
229 Heller Hall
1114 Kirby Drive
Duluth, MN 55812
Phone: (218) 726-8385
Fax: (218) 726-8275
http://www.d.umn.edu/geology

University of Minnesota, Twin Cities
Department of Geology & Geophysics
108 Pillsbury Hall
310 Pillsbury Drive SE
Minneapolis, MN 55455-0219
Phone: (612) 624-1333
Fax: (612) 625-3819
http://www.geo.umn.edu

MISSISSIPPI

Mississippi State University
Department of Geosciences

P.O. Box 5448
108 Hilbun Hall
East Lee Boulevard
Mississippi State, MS 39762
Phone: (662) 325-3915
Fax: (662) 325-9423
http://www.msstate.edu/dept/geosciences/
4site/home.htm

MISSOURI

University of Misouri, Kansas City
Department of Geosciences
5100 Rockhill Road
Room 420, Robert H. Flarsheim Hall
Kansas City, MO 64110-2499
Phone: (816) 235-1334
Fax: (816) 235-5535
http://cas.umkc.edu/geo/

MONTANA

Montana State University
Department of Earth Sciences
P.O. Box 173480, Traphagen #200
Bozeman, MT 59717-3480
Phone: (406) 994-3331
Fax: (406) 994-6923
http://www.montana.edu/

Montana Tech
University of Montana
Department of Geological Engineering
Montana School of Mines &
    Engineering
1300 West Park Street
Butte, MT 59701
Phone: (406) 496-4262
Fax: (406) 496-4260
http://www.mtech.edu/geo_eng

Montana Tech
University of Montana
Geophysical Engineering Program
1300 West Park Street
Butte, MT 59701
Phone: (406) 496-4401
Fax: (406) 496-4704
http://www.mtech.edu/geophysics

NEW JERSEY

**Rutgers, the State University of
    New Jersey**
Department of Geological Sciences
Wright Lab
610 Taylor Road
Piscataway, NJ 08854-8066
Phone: (732) 445-2044

Fax: (732) 445-3374
http://geology.rutgers.edu/

NEW MEXICO

**New Mexico Institute of Mining
    & Technology**
Earth and Environmental Science
    Department
801 Leroy Place
Socorro, NM 87801
Phone: (800) 428-TECH
http://www.ees.nmt.edu/

NEW YORK

Binghamton University
Department of Geological Sciences
    and Environmental Studies
P.O. Box 6000
Binghamton, NY 13902-6000
Phone: (607) 777-2264
Fax: (607) 777-2288
http://www.geol.binghamton.edu/

Columbia University
Department of Earth & Environmental
    Sciences
P.O. Box 1000
Route 9W
Palisades, NY 10964
Phone: (845) 365-8550
Fax: (845) 365-8163
http://eesc.columbia.edu

Cornell University
Institute for the Study of the Continents
3122 Snee Hall
Ithaca, NY 14853-1504
Phone: (607) 255-3474
Fax: (607) 254-4780
http://www.eas.cornell.edu/

**Long Island University,
    C.W. Post Campus**
Department of Earth and Environmental
    Science
720 Northern Boulevard
Brookville, NY 11548
Phone: (516) 299-2318
http://www.cwpost.liunet.edu/cwis/cwp/
    clas/earthsci/ees.htm

Queens College
School of Earth and Environmental
    Sciences
Science Building D-216
65-30 Kissena Boulevard
Flushing, NY 11367-1597
Phone: (718) 997-3300

Fax: (718) 997-3299
http://qcpages.qc.edu/EES/

SUNY, Buffalo
Department of Geology
876 Natural Sciences Complex
Buffalo, NY 14260
Phone: (716) 645-6800, ext. 6100
Fax: (716) 645-3999
http://www.geology.buffalo.edu

SUNY, Cortland
Geology Department
341 Bowers Hall
P.O. Box 2000
Cortland, NY 13045
Phone: (607) 753-2815
Fax: (607) 753-2927
http://www.cortland.edu/geology/

SUNY, Stony Brook
Department of Geosciences
Nicolls Road
Stony Brook, NY 11794-2100
Phone: (631) 632-8200
Fax: (631) 632-8240
http://www.geosciences.stonybrook.
    edu

NORTH CAROLINA

Appalachian State University
Department of Geology
195 Rankin Science
Boone, NC 28608
Phone: (828) 262-3049
Fax: (828) 262-6503
http://www.geology.appstate.edu/

East Carolina University
Department of Geology
101 Graham Building
Greenville, NC 27858-4353
Phone: (252) 328-6360
Fax: (252) 328-4391
http://www.geology.ecu.edu

OHIO

Case Western Reserve University
Department of Geological Sciences
10900 Euclid Avenue
A.W. Smith #112
Cleveland, OH 44106-7216
Phone: (216) 368-3690
Fax: (216) 368-3691
http://www.cwru.edu/cwru/dept/artsci/
    geol/geol.html

Miami University
Department of Geology
114 Shideler Hall
Oxford, OH 45056
Phone: (513) 529-3216
Fax: (513) 529-1542
http://www.muohio.edu/geology

University of Akron
Department of Geology
252 Buchtel Commons
Akron, OH 44325-4101
Phone: (330) 972-7630
Fax: (330) 972-7611
http://www.uakron.edu/geology/

Youngstown State University
Department of Geological &
   Environmental Sciences
One University Plaza
Youngstown, OH 44555
Phone: (330) 941-3612
Fax: (330) 941-1754
http://www.as.ysu.edu/geology/

OKLAHOMA

University of Tulsa
Department of Geosciences
600 South College Avenue
Tulsa, OK 74104-3189
Phone: (918) 631-2517
Fax: (918) 631-2091
http://www.geo.utulsa.edu

OREGON

Willamette University
Environment and Earth Science
   Department
900 State Street
Salem, OR 97301
Phone: (503) 370-6587
http://www.willamette.edu/cla/ees/

PENNSYLVANIA

Clarion University
Anthropology, Earth Science and
   Geography Department
335 Peirce Hall
Clarion, PA 16214
Phone: (814) 393-2317
Fax: (814) 393-2004
http://www.clarion.edu/departments/ages/

Franklin and Marshall College
Department of Earth and the
   Environment
P.O. Box 3003
Lancaster, PA 17604-3003

Phone: (717) 291-4118
Fax: (717) 291-4186
http://www.fandm.edu/Departments/
   EnvironmentalStudies/esp.html

LaSalle University
Geology, Environmental Science and
   Physics
1900 West Olney Avenue
Philadelphia, PA 19141-1199
Phone: (215) 951-1268
http://www.lasalle.edu/academ/geo_env/
   index.htm

Lehigh University
Department of Earth & Environmental
   Sciences
31 Williams Drive
Bethlehem, PA 18015
Phone: (610) 758-3660
Fax: (610) 758-3677
http://www.ees.lehigh.edu/

University of Pennsylvania
Master of Science in Applied
   Geosciences
College of General Studies
3440 Market Street, Suite 100
Philadelphia, PA 19104
Phone: (215) 898-6517
Fax: (215) 573-2053

University of Pittsburgh
Department of Geology and Planetary
   Science
200 SRCC
Pittsburgh, PA 15260
Phone: (412) 624-6615
http://collinsm.fdl.pitt.edu/es/index.html

SOUTH CAROLINA

University of South Carolina
Department of Geological Sciences
701 Sumter Street
Columbia, SC 29208
Phone: (803) 777-4535
Fax: (803) 777-6610
http://www.geol.sc.edu/

UTAH

College of Eastern Utah
Life Sciences Department
451 East 400 North
Price, UT 84501
Phone: (435) 637-2120
http://www.ceu.edu/Departmentpages/
   LifeSciences/

VERMONT

Castleton State College
Geology Program
86 Seminary Street
Castleton, VT 05735
Phone: (802) 468-6080
Fax: (802) 468-1170
http://www.castleton.edu/geology/

VIRGINIA

James Madison University
Geology & Environmental Science
   Department
MSC 7703
Harrisonburg, VA 22807
Phone: (540) 568-6130
Fax: (540) 568-8058
http://www.jmu.edu/geology/

WEST VIRGINIA

Concord College
Environmental Geosciences Program
CB-19
Athens, WV 24712-1000
Phone: (304) 384-5238
http://faculty.concord.edu/allenj/geosci.html

WISCONSIN

University of Wisconsin, Madison
Department of Geology & Geophysics
1215 West Dayton Street
Madison, WI 53706
Phone: (608) 262-8960
Fax: (608) 262-0693
http://www.geology.wisc.edu

NATURAL SCIENCES

ALABAMA

Stillman College
Department of Natural Sciences
P.O. Box 1430
Tuscaloosa, AL 35403
Phone: (800) 841-5722
http://www.stillman.edu/stillman/dept_
   natursci/natursci.html

ARIZONA

Arizona State University West
Department of Integrated Natural
   Sciences
4701 West Thunderbird Road
Glendale, AZ 85030

Phone: (602) 543-6050
http://www.west.asu.edu/dins/

ARKANSAS

Arkansas Tech University
School of Physical and Life Sciences
McEver Hall 45
Russellville, AR 72801
Phone: (501) 964-0814
http://pls.atu.edu

CALIFORNIA

California State University, San Bernardino
College of Natural Sciences
5500 University Parkway
San Bernardino, CA 92407
Phone: (909) 880-5300
Fax: (909) 880-7005
http://nsci.csusb.edu/

ILLINOIS

University of St. Francis
Department of Natural Sciences
500 Wilcox Street
Joliet, IL 60435
Phone: (800) 735-7500
http://www.stfrancis.edu/ns/homepage.htm

INDIANA

Bethel College, Indiana
Natural Science Division
1001 West McKinley Avenue
Mishawaka, IN 46545
Phone: (219) 257-3532
http://www.bethelcollege.edu/acadb/undgps/naturalsci/default.php

Franklin College
Natural Sciences Program
501 East Monroe Street
Franklin, IN 46131
Phone: (800) 852-0232
http://www.franklincoll.edu/bioweb/biology.stm

KANSAS

Bethany College
Natural Sciences Division
421 North First Street
Lindsborg, KS 67456-1897
Phone: (785) 227-3311
Fax: (785) 227-2004

http://www.bethanylb.edu/academics/areas_of%20study/natural_sciences/sciences_index.htm

Bethel College, Kansas
Natural Sciences Department
North Newton, KS 67117
Phone: (316) 284-5215
http://www.bethelks.edu/natsci/main.html

Friends University
Division of Natural Science
2100 West University
Wichita, KS 67213
Phone: (800) 794-6945
http://www.friends.edu/Academics/science/default.asp

KENTUCKY

Spalding University
School of Natural Science
851 South Fourth Street
Louisville, KY 40203-2188
Phone: (502) 585-9911
Fax: (502) 585-7158
http://www.spalding.edu/frame.asp?pg=db2.asp?id=785

MARYLAND

Bowie State University
Natural Sciences Department
George M. Crawford Science Hall
14000 Jericho Park Road
Bowie, MD 20715
Phone: (301) 860-3330
http://www.bowiestate.edu/academics/natsci/revision/

Coppin State College
Department of Natural Sciences
2500 West North Avenue
Baltimore, MD 21216-3698
Phone: (410) 591-3000
http://www.coppin.edu/natsci/

University of Maryland, Eastern Shore
Department of Natural Sciences
Princess Anne, MD 21853
Phone: (410) 651-6013
Fax: (410) 651-7739
http://www.umes.edu/sciences

MASSACHUSETTS

Assumption College
Division of Natural Sciences
P.O. Box 15005

Worcester, MA 01615-0005
Phone: (508) 767-7295
http://www.assumption.edu/HTML/Academic/NatSci/

Atlantic Union College
Natural Sciences
338 Main Street
P.O. Box 1000
South Lancaster, MA 01561-1000
Phone: (800) 282-2030
http://www.atlanticuc.edu/acad.biology.php

Hampshire College
School of Natural Science
Cole Science Center
Amherst, MA 01002
Phone: (413) 559-5373
http://www.hampshire.edu/cms/index.php?id=145

Lesley College
Natural Science Program
29 Everett Street
Cambridge, MA 02138-2790
Phone: (617) 349-8966
http://www.lesley.edu/ungrad/natural.html

MICHIGAN

Lake Superior State University
School of Natural Sciences
650 West Easterday Avenue
Sault Sainte Marie, MI 49783
Phone: (906) 635-2231
http://www.lssu.edu/academics/science/schools/natural-sciences/

MISSISSIPPI

Tougaloo College
Natural Sciences Division
500 West County Line Road
Tougaloo, MS 39174
Phone: (601) 977-7782
http://www.tougaloo.edu/matriarch/OnePiecePage.asp?PageID=166&PageName=DivNatSciIntro

MONTANA

Carroll College
Natural Sciences Department
1601 North Benton Avenue
Helena, MT 59625
Phone: (800) 992-3648
http://www.carroll.edu/academics/naturalsci/index.html

NEW JERSEY

Caldwell College
Department of Natural & Physical
  Sciences
9 Ryerson Avenue
Caldwell, NJ 07006
Phone: (973) 618-3000
http://www.caldwell.edu/academics/
  science.html#bimaj

Felician College
Department of Natural Sciences
262 South Main St
Lodi, NJ 07644
Phone: (201) 559-6059
Fax: (201) 559-6188
http://www.felician.edu/departments/
  nat_sci/

Kean University
College of Natural, Applied and Health
  Sciences
1000 Morris Avenue
Union, NJ 07083
Phone: (908) 737-KEAN
Fax: (908) 737-5326
http://www.kean.edu/cnahs.html

NEW YORK

Colgate University
Division of Natural Sciences and
  Mathematics
B1 McGregory Hall
13 Oak Drive
Hamilton, NY 13346
Phone: (315) 228-7226
Fax: (315) 228-6020
http://departments.colgate.edu/
  naturalsciences/

**State University of New York (SUNY),
  Purchase**
Natural Science Department
735 Anderson Hill Road
Purchase, NY 10577-1400
Phone: (914) 251-6630
Fax: (914) 251-6635
http://www.ns.purchase.edu/

NORTH CAROLINA

Fayetteville State University
Department of Natural Sciences
1200 Murchison Road
Fayetteville, NC 28301
Phone: (910) 672-1691
http://www.uncfsu.edu/natsci/index.htm

Gardner-Webb University
Department of Natural Sciences
P.O. Box 976
Boiling Springs, NC 28017
Phone: (704) 406-2361
http://www.naturalsci.gardner-webb.edu/
  index.htm

NORTH DAKOTA

Dickinson State University
Natural Sciences Department
Campus Drive
Dickinson, ND 58601
Phone: (800) 279-4295
http://www2.dsu.nodak.edu/users/
  nascienc/natsc_html/index.html

OREGON

Lewis & Clark College
Environmental and Natural Resource
  Law
10015 SW Terwilliger Boulevard
Portland, OR 97219-7799
Phone: (503) 768-6600
Fax: (503) 768-6671
http://www.lclark.edu/~lawac/LC/jd_
  environmental.htm

PENNSYLVANIA

DeSales University
Department of Natural Sciences
2755 Station Avenue
Center Valley, PA 18034
Phone: (610) 282-1100
http://www.desales.edu/

SOUTH CAROLINA

Claflin University
Division of Natural Sciences and
  Mathematics
400 Magnolia Street
Orangeburg, SC 29115
Phone: (803) 535-5433
http://www.claflin.edu/academics/
  biology.asp

Limestone College
Natural Science Division
1115 College Drive
Gaffney, SC 29340
Phone: (800) 795-7151
http://www.limestone.edu/sfs/acad/
  natural/index.htm

TENNESSEE

Lincoln Memorial University
Mathematics and Natural Sciences
Cumberland Gap Parkway
Harrogate, TN 37752
Phone: (800) 325-0900, ext. 6463
http://www.lmunet.edu/Academics/
  undergrad/math_natscience/index.htm

TEXAS

Lubbock Christian University
Natural Sciences Department
5601 19th Street
Lubbock, TX 79407
Phone: (806) 796-8800
http://www.lcu.edu/natsci.asp

Rice University
Wiess School of Natural Sciences
MS-102
P.O. Box 1892
Houston, TX 77251-1892
Phone: (713) 348-3350
Fax: (713) 348-6149
http://dacnet.rice.edu/~nsci/

VIRGINIA

Virginia Union University
Natural Science Department
1500 North Lombardy Street
Richmond, VA 23220
Phone: (804) 257-5600
http://www.vuu.edu

SUSTAINABLE DEVELOPMENT

ARIZONA

University of Arizona
School of Renewable Natural Resources
Room 325 D, Biological Sciences East
Tucson, AZ 85721
Phone: (520) 621-7260
Fax: (520) 621-8801
http://www.ag.arizona.edu/srnr/

DISTRICT OF COLUMBIA

George Washington University
Center on Sustainability and Regional
  Growth
2000 H Street, NW
Washington, DC 20052
Phone: (202) 994-9709

Fax: (202) 994-5614
http://www.law.gwu.edu/csrg/

KENTUCKY

Berea College
Sustainability and Environmental Studies
305 Goldthwait Agricultural Building
CPO 1921
Berea, KY 40404
Phone: (859) 985-3593
http://www.berea.edu/sens/

MASSACHUSETTS

Hampshire College
Environmental Studies and Sustainability
   Program
893 West Street
Amherst, MA 01002
Phone: (413) 559-5667
http://essp.hampshire.edu/

TEXAS

Texas State University
International Institute for Sustainable
   Water Resources
601 University Drive
San Marcos, TX 78666-4618
Phone: (512) 245-8043
Fax: (512) 245-8346
http://www.swt.edu/iiswr/iiswr_
   collaborators.htmlx

WISCONSIN

College of Menominee Nation
Sustainable Development Institute
P.O. Box 1179
Keshena, WI 54135
Phone: (715) 799-5600
Fax: (715) 799-1336
http://www.menominee.edu/sdi/home1.
   htm

WILDLIFE REHABILITATION

NORTH CAROLINA

Lees McRae College
Wildlife Rehabilitation/Pre-Veterinary
   Science Program
P.O. Box 128
Banner Elk, NC 28604-0128
Phone: (828) 898-5241

APPENDIX II
PROFESSIONAL ASSOCIATIONS

This appendix contains listings for the professional associations listed throughout this book. In addition to serving as a voice for the professions they represent, most of these organizations offer helpful career resources, including job listings, certification information, and links to education and training resources. These listings were current at the time of publication. If a particular link or phone number no longer works, try locating the association or Web site by using a search engine.

ECOTOURISM

American Hotel and Lodging Association
1201 New York Avenue, NW, #600
Washington, DC 20005-3931
Phone: (202) 289-3100
Fax: (202) 289-3199
http://www.ahla.com

American Planning Association
1776 Massachusetts Avenue, NW
Washington, DC 20036-1904
Phone: (202) 872-0611
Fax: (202) 872-0643
http://www.planning.org

American Society of Travel Agents
1101 King Street, Suite 200
Alexandria, VA 22314
Phone: (703) 739-2782
Fax: (703) 684-8319

America Outdoors
P.O. Box 10847
Knoxville, TN 37939
Phone: (865) 558-3595
Fax: (865) 558-3598
http://www.americaoutdoors.org/

International Ecotourism Club
http://ecoclub.com

International Ecotourism Society
1333 H Street, NW
Suite 300, East Tower
Washington, DC 20005
Phone: (202) 347-9203
Fax: (202) 789-7279
http://www.ecotourism.org

National Association of Commissioned Travel Agents
1101 King Street, Suite 200
Alexandria, Virginia 22314
Phone: (703) 739-6826

Fax: (703) 739-6861
http://www.nacta.com

National Tour Association
546 East Main Street
Lexington, KY 40508
Phone: (859) 226-4444
Fax: (859) 226-4414
http://www.ntaonline.com/

Society for Accessible Travel and Hospitality
347 Fifth Ave, Suite 610
New York, NY 10016
Phone: (212) 447-7284
Fax: (212) 725-8253
http://www.sath.org

Travel Industry Association of America
1100 New York Avenue, NW, Suite 450
Washington, DC 20005-3934
Phone: (202) 408-8422
Fax: (202) 408-1255
http://www.tia.org

World Federation of Tourist Guides Association
1555 rue Peel Bureau 600
Montreal, Quebec
Canada H3A 3L8
Phone: (514) 992-0632
Fax: (514) 844-6859
http://www.wftga.org

ENGINEERING

American Academy of Environmental Engineers
130 Holiday Court, Suite 100
Annapolis, MD 21401
Phone: (410) 266-3311
Fax: (410) 266-7653
http://www.aaee.net

American Association for Geodetic Surveying
6 Montgomery Village Avenue, Suite #403
Gaithersburg, MD 20879
Phone: (240) 632-9716
Fax: (240) 632-1321
http://www.aagsmo.org

American Congress on Surveying and Mapping
6 Montgomery Village Avenue,
Suite #403
Gaithersburg, MD 20879
Phone: (240) 632-9716
Fax: (240) 632-1321
http://www.acsm.net

American Planning Association
122 South Michigan Avenue, Suite 1600
Chicago, IL 60603
Phone: (312) 431-9100
Fax: (312) 431-9985
http://www.planning.org

The American Society for Photogrammetry & Remote Sensing
5410 Grosvenor Lane, Suite 210
Bethesda, Maryland 20814-2160
Phone: (301) 493-0290
http://www.asprs.org/society/index.html

The Cartography and Geographic Information Society
6 Montgomery Village Avenue, Suite #403
Gaithersburg, MD 20879
Phone: (240) 632-9716
Fax: (240) 632-1321
http://www.cartogis.org

The Geographic and Land Information Society
6 Montgomery Village Avenue,
Suite #403
Gaithersburg, MD 20879

Phone: (240) 632-9716
Fax: (240) 632-1321
http://www.glismo.org

**National Society of Professional
Surveyors Inc.**
6 Montgomery Village Avenue,
Suite #403
Gaithersburg, MD 20879
Phone: (240) 632-9716
Fax: (240) 632-1321
http://www.nspsmo.org

**The Society for Mining, Metallurgy,
and Exploration Inc.**
8307 Shaffer Parkway
Littleton, CO 80127-4102
Phone: (303) 973-9550 or
(800) 763-3132
Fax: (303) 973-3845
http://www.smenet.org

FARMING & FISHING

American Beekeeping Federation
P.O. Box 1337
Jesup, GA 31598-1038
Phone: (912) 427-4233
Fax: (912) 427-8447
http://abfnet.org

**American Honey Producers'
Association**
11226 Deschutes Road
Palo Cedro, CA 96073
Phone: (530) 549-3500
Fax: (530) 549-5250

**American Society of Farm Managers
and Rural Appraisers**
950 South Cherry Street, Suite 508
Denver, CO 80246-2664
Phone: (303) 758-3513
Fax: (303) 758-0190
http://www.agri-associations.org

**The Eastern Apicultural Society of
North America Inc.**
http://www.easternapiculture.org/
contacts/

Heartland Apicultural Society
100 Fair Oaks, Suite 252
Frankfort, KY 40601
Phone: (502) 564-3956
Fax: (502) 564-7852
http://www.heartlandbees.com

Marine Technology Society
5565 Sterrett Place, Suite 108
Columbia, MD 21044
http://www.mtsociety.org
Phone: (410) 884-5330
Fax: (410) 884-9060

National Aquaculture Association
111 West Washington Street, Suite 1
Charles Town, WV 25414
Phone: (304) 728-2167
Fax: (304) 728-2196
http://www.nationalaquaculture.org

National Farmers Union
400 North Capitol Street, NW,
Suite 790
Washington, DC 20001
Phone: (202) 554-1600
Fax: (202) 554-1654
http://www.nfu.org

The National FFA Organization
P.O. Box 68960
6060 FFA Drive
Indianapolis, IN 46268-0960
Phone: (317) 802-6060
Fax: (317) 802-6061
http://www.ffa.org

Western Apicultural Society
11260 Simpson Road
Monmouth, OR 97361
Phone: (503) 383-2328

FORESTRY

**International Association of Fire
Fighters**
1750 New York Avenue, NW
Washington, DC 20006-5395
Phone: (202) 737-8484
Fax: (202) 737-8418
http://www.iaff.org

Society of American Foresters
5400 Grosvenor Lane
Bethesda, MD 20814-2198
Phone: (301) 897-8720
Fax: (301) 897-3690
http://www.safnet.org

LEGAL & REGULATORY

**Air and Waste Management
Association**
One Gateway Center, Third Floor

420 Fort Duquesne Boulevard
Pittsburgh, PA 15222-1435
Phone: (412) 232-3444
Fax: (412) 232-3450
http://www.awma.org/

**American Agricultural Economics
Association**
415 South Duff Avenue, Suite C
Ames, IA 50010-6600
Phone: (515) 233-3202
Fax: (515) 233-3101
http://www.aaea.org/

American Bar Association
321 North Clark Street
Chicago, IL 60610
Phone: (312) 988-5000 or
(800) 285-2221
Fax: (312) 988-5522
http://www.abanet.org

**American Industrial Hygiene
Association**
2700 Prosperity Avenue, Suite 250
Fairfax, VA 22031
Phone: (703) 849-8888
Fax: (703) 207-3561
http://www.aiha.org

American Public Health Association
800 1 Street, NW
Washington, DC 20001
Phone: (202) 777-APHA
Fax: (202) 777-2534
http://www.apha.org

**American Society of Irrigation
Consultants**
125 Paradise Lane
Rochester, MA 02770
Phone: (508) 763-8140
Fax: (508) 763-8102
http://www.asic.org/

American Society of Safety Engineers
1800 East Oakton Street
Des Plaines, IL 60018
Phone: (847) 699-2929
Fax: (847) 768-3434
http://www.asse.org

American Water Works Association
6666 West Quincy Avenue
Denver, CO 80235
Phone: (303) 794-7711
Fax: (303) 347-0804
http://www.awwa.org

Association of Environmental and Resource Economics
1616 P Street, NW, Box Number 6
Washington, DC 20036
Phone: (202) 328-5125
Fax: (202) 939-3460
http://www.aere.org

Environmental Law Institute
2000 L Street, NW, Suite 620
Washington, DC 20036
Phone: (202) 939-3800
Fax: (202) 939-3868
http://www.eli.org

Federal Wildlife Officers Association
P.O. Box 646□
Harrisburg, PA 17108
http://www.fwoa.org/

International Society for Ecological Economics
P.O. Box 44194
West Allis, WI 53214
Phone: (414) 453-0030
Fax: (877) 230-5110
http://www.ecoeco.org/

Irrigation Association
6540 Arlington Boulevard
Falls Church, VA 22042-6638
Phone: (703) 536-7080
Fax: (703) 536-7019
http://www.irrigation.org

National Association of State Park Directors
8829 Woodyhill Road
Raleigh, NC 27613
Phone: (919) 676-8365
Fax: (919) 676-8365
http://www.naspd.org/

National Environmental Health Association
720 South Colorado Boulevard,
Suite 1000-N
Denver, CO 80246-1926
Phone: (303) 756-9090
Fax: (303) 691-9490
http://www.neha.org

National Environmental, Safety and Health Training Association
5320 North 16th Street, Suite 114
Phoenix, AZ 85016-3241
Phone: (602) 956-6099
Fax: (602) 956-6399
http://www.neshta.org

National Parks Conservation Association□
1300 19th Street, NW, Suite 300
Washington, DC 20036
Phone: (800) 628-7275
Fax: (202) 659-0650
http://www.npca.org

National Recreation and Park Association
22377 Belmont Ridge Road
Ashburn, VA 20148-4150
Phone: (703) 858-0784
Fax: (703) 858-0794
http://www.nrpa.org

National Society for Park Resources
22377 Belmont Ridge Road
Ashburn, VA 20148-4150
Phone: (703) 858-0784
Fax: (703) 858-0794
http://www.nrpa.org

North American Wildlife Enforcement Officers Association
P.O. Box 22
Hollidaysburg, PA 16648
Phone: (250) 567-3106
Fax: (206) 201-6953
http://www.naweoa.org

Park Law Enforcement Association
22377 Belmont Ridge Road
Ashburn, VA 20148-4150
Phone: (703) 858-0784
Fax: (703) 858-0794
http://www.parkranger.com

Water Environment Federation
601 Wythe Street
Alexandria, VA 22314-1994
Phone: (800) 666-0206
Fax: (703) 684-2492
http://www.wef.com

OTHER

American Society of Landscape Architects
636 Eye Street, NW
Washington, DC 20001-3736
Phone: (202) 898-2444
Fax: (202) 898-1185
http://www.asla.org

North American Nature Photography Association
10200 West 44th Avenue, Suite 304
Wheat Ridge, CO 80033-2840

Phone: (303) 422-8527
Fax: (303) 422-8894
http://www.nanpa.org

Professional Grounds Management Society
720 Light Street
Baltimore, MD 21230
Phone: (800) 609-7467
Fax: (410) 752-8295
http://www.pgms.org

The Professional Landcare Network (PLANET)
950 Herndon Parkway, Suite 450
Herndon, VA 20170
Phone: (703) 736-9666 or (800) 395-2522
Fax: (703) 736-9668
http://www.landcarenetwork.org

Professional Photographers of America Inc.
229 Peachtree Street NE, Suite 2200
Atlanta, GA 30303
Phone: (404) 522-8600 or
    (800) 786-6277
Fax: (404) 614-6400
http://www.ppa.com

OUTDOOR/ENVIRONMENTAL EDUCATION

American Association for Health, Physical Education, Recreation, and Dance
1900 Association Drive
Reston, VA 20191-1598
Phone: (703) 476-3400
http://www.aahperd.org

American Camping Association
5000 State Road 67 North
Martinsville, IN 46151-7902
Phone: (765) 342-8456
Fax: (765) 342-2065
http://www.ACAcamps.org

American Society of Naturalists
http://www.amnat.org

American Therapeutic Recreation Association
1414 Prince Street, Suite 204
Alexandria, VA 22314
Phone: (703) 683-9420
Fax: (703) 683-9431
http://www.atra-tr.org

Association of Environmental Engineering and Science Professors
2303 Naples Court
Champaign, IL 61822
Phone: (217) 398-6969
Fax: (217) 355-9232
http://www.aeesp.org

International Association of Culinary Professionals
304 West Liberty Street, Suite 201
Louisville, KY 40202
Phone: (502) 581-9786
Fax: (502) 589-3602
http://www.iacp.com/

National Association for Humane and Environmental Education
67 Norwich Essex Turnpike
East Haddam, CT 06423-1736
Phone: (860) 434-8666
Fax: (860) 434-9579
http://www.nahee.org

National Association for Sport and Physical Education
1900 Association Drive
Reston, VA 20191-1598
Phone: (703) 476-3400
http://www.aahperd.org/NASPE/

National Association of Biology Teachers
NABT, 12030 Sunrise Valley Drive, Suite 110
Reston, VA 20191
Phone: (703) 264-9696
Fax: (703) 264-7778
http://www.nabt.org

National Association of Recreation Resource Planners
2001 Jefferson Davis Highway, Suite 1004
Arlington, VA 22202-3617
Phone: (703) 416-0060
Fax: (703) 416-0014
http://www.narrp.org

National Environmental Education and Training Foundation
1707 H Street, NW, Suite 900
Washington, DC 20006-3915
Phone: (202) 833-2933
Fax: (202) 261-6464
http://www.neetf.org

National Marine Educators Association
P.O. Box 1470
Ocean Springs, MS 39566-1470
http://www.marine-ed.org

National Science Teachers Association
1840 Wilson Boulevard
Arlington, VA 22201
Phone: (703) 243-7100
http://www.nsta.org/

National Therapeutic Recreation Society
22377 Belmont Ridge Road
Ashburn, VA 20148
Phone: (703) 858-0784
Fax: (703) 858-0794
http://www.nrpa.com

North American Association for Environmental Educators
2000 P Street, NW, Suite 540
Washington, DC 20036
Phone: (202) 419-0412
Fax: (202) 419-0415

Society of College Science Teaching
1840 Wilson Boulevard
Arlington, VA 22201
Phone: (703) 243-7100
http://www.nsta.org/college

Society for Conservation Biology
4245 North Fairfax Drive, Suite 400
Arlington, VA, 22203-1651
Phone: (703) 276-2384
Fax: (703) 995-4633
http://www.conbio.org

Society for Ecological Restoration International
285 West 18th Street, Suite 1
Tucson, AZ 85701
Phone: (520) 622-5485
Fax: (520) 622-5491
http://www.ser.org

Wilderness Education Association
900 East Seventh Street
Bloomington, IN 47405
Phone: (812) 855-4095
Fax: (812) 855-8697
http://www.wea.org

SCIENTIFIC

American Association of Petroleum Geologists
1444 South Boulder
P.O. Box 979
Tulsa, OK 74101-0979
Phone: (918) 584-2555 or
(800) 364-2274

Fax: (918) 560-2694
http://www.aapg.org

American Chemical Society
Education and International Activities Division
1155 16th Street, NW
Washington, DC 20036
Phone: (202) 872-4600 or (800) 227-5558
Fax: (202) 872-4615
http://www.chemistry.org

American Geological Institute
4220 King Street
Alexandria, VA 22302-1502
Phone: (703) 379-2480
Fax: (703) 379-7563
http://www.agiweb.org

American Geophysical Union
2000 Florida Avenue, NW
Washington, DC 20009-1277
Phone: (202) 462-6900 or (800) 966-2481
Fax: (202) 328-0566
http://www.agu.org

The American Institute of Biological Sciences
1444 I Street, NW, Suite 200
Washington, DC 20005
Phone: (202) 628-1500
Fax: (202) 628-1509
http://www.aibs.org

American Institute of Chemists
315 Chestnut Street
Philadelphia, PA 19106-2702
Phone: (215) 873-8224
Fax: (215) 925-1954
http://www.theaic.org

American Meteorological Society
45 Beacon Street
Boston, MA 02108-3693
Phone: (617) 227-2425
Fax: (617) 742-8718
http://www.ametsoc.org

American Phytopathological Society
3340 Pilot Knob Road
St. Paul, MN 55121
Phone: (612) 454-7250
Fax: (612) 454-0766
http://www.apsnet.org

American Society for Horticultural Science
600 Cameron Street
Alexandria, VA 22314-2562

Phone: (703) 836-4606
Fax: (703) 836-2024
http://www.ashs.org

American Society of Agronomy
677 South Segoe Road
Madison, WI 53711
Phone: (608) 273-8080
Fax: (608) 273-2021
http://www.agronomy.org

American Society of Limnology and
Oceanography
5400 Bosque Boulevard, Suite 680
Waco, TX 76710
Phone: (800) 929-ASLO or
(254) 399-9635
Fax: (254) 776-3767
http://www.aslo.org

American Society of Plant Biologists
15501 Monona Drive
Rockville, MD 20855-2768
Phone: (301) 251-0560
Fax: (301) 279-2996
http://www.aspb.org

American Society of Plant
Taxonomists
University of Wyoming
Department of Botany 3165
1000 East University Avenue
Laramie, WY 82071
Phone: (307) 766-2556
Fax: (307) 766-2851
http://www.aspt.net

American Veterinary Medical
Association
1931 North Meacham Road,
Suite 100
Schaumburg, IL 60173
Phone: (847) 925-8070
Fax: (847) 925-1329
http://www.avma.org

Association of State Wetland
Managers Inc.
2 Basin Road
Windham, ME 04062
Phone: (207) 892-3399
Fax: (207) 892-3089
http://www.aswm.org

Association of Women Soil Scientists
http://awss.org

Botanical Society of America
4475 Castleman Avenue
P.O. Box 299
St. Louis, MO 63166
Phone: (314) 577-9566
Fax: (314) 577-9515
http://www.botany.org

Crop Science Society of America
677 South Segoe Road
Madison, WI 53711
Phone: (608) 273-8080
Fax: (608) 273-2021
http://www.crops.org

The Ecological Society of America
1707 H Street, NW, Suite 400
Washington, DC 20006
Phone: (202) 833-8773
Fax: (202) 833-8775
http://www.esa.org

Environmental Defense
257 Park Avenue South
New York, NY 10010
Phone: (212) 505-2100
Fax: (212) 505-2375
http://www.environmentaldefense.org

The Geological Society of America
P.O. Box 9140
Boulder, CO 80301-9140
Phone: (303) 447-2020
Fax: (303) 357-1070
http://www.geosociety.org

International Society of
Arboriculture
1400 West Anthony Drive
Champaign, IL 61821
P.O. Box 3129
Champaign, IL 61826-3129
Phone: (217) 355-9411 or
(888) 472-8733
Fax: (217) 355-9516
http://www.isa-arbor.com

National Weather Association
228 West Millbrook Road
Raleigh, NC 27609-4304
Phone/Fax: (919) 845-1546
http://www.nwas.org

National Wildlife Rehabilitators
Association
2625 Clearwater Road, Suite 110
St. Cloud, MN 56301
Phone: (320) 230-9920

Fax: (320) 230-3077
http://www.nwrawildlife.org

The Nature Conservancy
4245 North Fairfax Drive, Suite 100
Arlington, VA 22203-1606
Phone: (703) 841-5300 or
(800) 628-6860
http://www.nature.org

The Ocean Conservancy
2029 K Street
Washington, DC 20006
Phone: (202) 429-5609 or
(800) 519-1541
http://www.oceanconservancy.org

Organization of Wildlife Planners
http://www.owpweb.org

Professional Association of Diving
Instructors
30151 Tomas Street
Rancho Santa Margarita, CA 92688-2125
Phone: (949) 858-7234 or
(800) 729-7234
Fax: (949) 858-7264
http://www.padi.com

Society for Integrative and
Comparative Biology
1313 Dolley Madison Boulevard,
Suite 402
McLean, VA 22101
Phone: (703) 790-1745 or
(800) 955-1236
Fax: (703) 790-2672
http://www.sicb.org

Society for Range Management
445 Union Boulevard, Suite 230
Lakewood, CO 80228
Phone: (303) 986-3309
Fax: (303) 986-3892
www.rangelands.org

Society of Wetland Scientists
1313 Dolley Madison Boulevard,
Suite 402
McLean, VA 22101
Phone: (703) 790-1745
Fax: (703) 790-2672
http://www.sws.org

Soil Science Society of America
677 South Segoe Road
Madison, WI 53711
Phone: (608) 273-8080

Fax: (608) 273-2021
http://www.soils.org

Tree Care Industry Association
3 Perimeter Road, Unit 1
Manchester, NH 03103
Phone: (603) 314-5380 or (800) 733-2622
Fax: (603) 314-5386
http://www.treecareindustry.org

United States Consortium of Soil
    Science Associations
611 Jeffrey Drive
Lincoln, NE 68505
Phone: (402) 483-0604
http://soilsassociation.org/misc/contacts.htm

The Wildlife Society
5410 Grosvenor Lane, Suite 200

Bethesda, MD 20814-2144
Phone: (301) 897-9770
Fax: (301) 530-2471
http://www.wildlife.org

APPENDIX III
PROFESSIONAL CERTIFICATIONS

This appendix includes mandatory and optional certifications related to some of the careers profiled in this book. In addition to the certifications listed below, some professions that involve working with conservation programs and environmental matters require specific permits or licenses issued by governments at the local, state, or federal level. While these are too numerous to list here, more information can be found by contacting working professionals in your state, as well as chapters of professional associations related to a specific career. These listings were current at the time of publication. If a particular link no longer works, try locating the association or Web site by using a search engine.

ECOTOURISM

Sustainable Tourism
The Ecotourism Society, in conjunction with George Washington University, offers distance learning certification in Sustainable Tourism. For more information, visit http://www.ecotourism.org.

Tour Guides
The National Tour Association offers a Certified Tour Professional distance-learning program. For more information, visit www.ntaonline.com.

Travel Agents
The Travel Institute offers three credentials: Certified Travel Associate (CTA), Certified Travel Counselor (CTC), and Certified Travel Industry Executive (CTIE) For more information, visit http://www.thetravelinstitute.com.

Resort Planning
The American Planning Association's American Institute of Certified Planners offers a certification credential for individuals who pass their examination. To be eligible to sit for the examination, planners need between two and four years of experience, depending on their level of education. For more information, visit http://www.planning.org/aicp/index.htm.

ENGINEERING

Geospatial Engineering
The American Society for Photogrammetry & Remote Sensing offers a number of certifications for geospatial engineering professionals, including Certified Photogrammetrist; Certified Mapping Scientist—Remote Sensing; Certified Mapping Scientist—GIS/LIS; Certified Photogrammetric Technologist; Certified Remote Sensing Technologist; and Certified GIS/LIS Technologist. Information is available at http://www.asprs.org/membership/certification.

Surveying
The National Council of Examiners for Engineering and Surveying offers the professional surveyor (P.S.) certification. Information is available from http://www.ncees.org/licensure/licensure_for_land_surveyors.

Surveying and Mapping Technology
The National Society of Professional Surveyors offers the Certified Survey Technician (CST) designation. Details are available at http://www.nspsmo.org/cst/get_certified.shtml.

FARMING & FISHING

Agricultural Consulting
The American Society of Farm Managers and Rural Appraisers offers the Accredited Agricultural Consultant (AAC) designation. Details are available at http://www.asfmra.org/fcourses.htm.

Commercial Fishing
The U.S. Coast Guard Marine Inspection Office, as well as various state Marine Safety Offices, provide licenses for fishing vessel captains and mates, as well as merchant mariner documentation. Details are available from the National Maritime Center's Licensing and Evaluation Branch at http://www.uscg.mil/hq/g-m/nmc/web/contact.htm.

Crop Science
Crop Scientists have three relevant professional certifications from which to choose:
- The American Society of Agronomy (ASA) offers the Certified Crop Adviser (CCA) program. Complete details are available at http://www.agronomy.org/certs_exams.html.
- The Soil Science Society of America (SSSA) offers the designations of Certified Professional Agronomist (CPAg) (ARCPACS) and Certified Professional Soil Scientist/Classifier (CPSS/CPSC). Information is available at http://www.soils.org/certs_exams.html.

Farm Management
The American Society of Farm Managers and Rural Appraisers offers the Accredited Farm Manager (AFM) designation. Details are available at http://www.asfmra.org/fcourses.htm.

Rural Appraisal
The American Society of Farm Managers and Rural Appraisers offers the Accredited Rural Appraiser (ARA) designation. Details are available at http://www.asfmra.org/fcourses.htm.

FORESTRY

General Forestry
The Society of American Foresters offers the Certified Forester credential. Complete details are available at http://www.safnet.org/certifiedforester/becoming/index.cfm.

Urban Forestry
The International Society of Arboriculture offers the Certified Arborists credential. Information is available at http://www.isa-arbor.com/certification/certification.aspx.

LEGAL AND REGULATORY

Environmental Health
The National Environmental Health Association offers five types of certification for Environmental Health Officers. Typically, individuals must possess a minimum of a bachelor's degree in environmental or public health to sit for the certification examination. Those with a bachelor's degree in another field need two years of experience before they qualify to take the exam. For more information, visit http://www.neha.org/credential/index.shtml.

Industrial Hygiene
The American Board of Industrial Hygiene offers two credentials: the Certified Industrial Hygienist or the Certified Associate Industrial Hygienist. For more information, visit http://www.abih.org/certified/index.html.

Irrigation Auditing
The Irrigation Association offers two credentials: Certified Landscape Irrigation Auditor and the Certified Golf Irrigation Auditor. Examinations are offered at sites throughout the United States. For more information, visit http://www.irrigation.org/certification.

Occupational Safety
The following organizations offer certifications for occupational safety professionals:
- The Board of Certified Safety Professionals offers the Certified Safety Credential. For more information, visit http://www.bcsp.org.
- The Council on Certification of Health, Environment, and Safety Technologists offers both the Occupational Health and Safety Technologist certification and the Construction Health and Safety Technician certification. For more information, visit http://www.cchest.org.

Waste Management
The Association of Boards of Certification compiles a state-based list of contacts for various environmental compliance certification credentials, such as biological industrial wastewater, physical/chemical industrial waste, inspection, solid waste, water treatment, and wastewater collection. Normally, before securing permission to take a certification examination, candidates must meet education and experience requirements. For more information, visit http://www.abccert.org/certcontacts.html.

OTHER

Grounds Maintenance
The Professional Landcare Network (PLANET) offers designations such as Certified Landscape Technician, Certified Landscape Professional, and Certified Turfgrass Professional. Information is available at http://www.landcarenetwork.org/cms/certification/categories.html.

OUTDOOR/ ENVIRONMENTAL EDUCATION

Camp Cooks
The American Culinary Federation offers the Master Chef certification. For more information, visit http://www.acfchefs.org.

Camp Directors
The National Recreation and Parks Association offers three levels of certification for industry professionals: Associate Park and Recreational Professional, Provisional Park and Recreational Professional, and Certified Park and Recreational Professional. For more information, visit http://www.nrpa.org.

Parks and Recreation
The National Recreation and Park Association also offers the Certified Park and Recreation Professional credential for individuals with a bachelor's degree, two years of full-time experience in the field, and successful completion of the Certified Park and Recreation Professional examination. For more information, visit http://www.nrpa.org/content/default.aspx?documentId=26.

Recreational Therapy
The National Council for Therapeutic Recreation Certification offers National Certification as a Certified Therapeutic Recreation Specialist. To qualify to sit for the certification exam, candidates must hold a bachelor's degree from an accredited college or university with a major in therapeutic recreation or a major in recreation or leisure with a focus in therapeutic recreation. While a student, candidates must have completed a 12-week internship, offering a minimum of 480 hours of therapeutic recreation services under the supervision of a certified Recreational Therapist. For more information, visit http://www.nctrc.org.

SCIENTIFIC

Atmospheric Science
The American Meteorological Society offers the Certified Broadcast Meteorologist Program, the Certified Consulting Meteorologist Program, and the AMS Seal of Approval for on-air meteorologists. Information is available at http://www.ametsoc.org/amscert/index.html.

Environmental Chemistry
Some chemists obtain status as a Certified Professional Chemist (CPC) from the American Institute of Chemists. Information is available at http://www.theaic.org.

In addition, the National Registry of Certified Chemists offers certification for different types of chemists, including environmental analytical chemists. Details are available at http://www.nrcc6.org.

Geoscience

Individual states often require geologists to hold professional licenses as either a Geologist in Training (GIT) or a Professional Geologist (PG). GIT examinations can often be taken upon college graduation, while the PG exam may be taken after several years of work experience under the supervision of a PG.

Horticulture

The American Society for Horticultural Science offers the ASHS Certified Professional Horticulturist Program. More information is available at http://www.ashs.org/careers/cph_certification.html.

Range Management

The Society for Range Management offers the Certified Professional in Rangeland Management (CPRM) and Certified Range Management Consultant (CRMC) designations. Details are available from http://www.rangelands.org/education_cprm.shtml.

Soil Science

The Soil Science Society of America (SSSA) offers the designations of Certified Professional Agronomist (CPAg) (ARCPACS) and Certified Professional Soil Scientist/Classifier (CPSS/CPSC). Information is available at http://www.soils.org/certs_exams.html.

Wetland Science

Complete details about the Society of Wetland Scientists Professional Certification Program can be found at http://www.wetlandcert.org.

Wildlife Biology

Designation as a Certified Wildlife Biologist may be obtained from the Wildlife Society. More information is available at http://www.wildlife.org/certification/index.cfm.

APPENDIX IV
GOVERNMENT AGENCIES

This appendix includes a listing of federal government agencies that play a role in, or offer resources related to, conservation and environmental issues.

National Oceanic & Atmospheric Administration
U.S. Department of Commerce
14th Street & Constitution Avenue, NW, Room 6217
Washington, DC 20230
Phone: (202) 482-6090
Fax: (202) 482-3154
http://www.noaa.gov

National Science Foundation
4201 Wilson Boulevard
Arlington, Virginia 22230
Phone: (703) 292-5111 or (800) 877-8339
http://www.nsf.gov

U.S. Army Corps of Engineers
441 G Street
Washington, DC 20314-1000
Phone: (202) 761-0010
Fax: (202) 761-1803
http://www.usace.army.mil

U.S. Bureau of Land Management
Office of Public Affairs
1849 C Street, Room 406-LS
Washington, DC 20240
Phone: (202) 452-5125
Fax: (202) 452-5124
http://www.blm.gov

U.S. Department of Agriculture
Natural Resources Conservation Service
14th and Independence Avenue, SW, Room 5105-A
Washington, DC 20250
Phone: (202) 720-7246
Fax: (202) 720-7690
http://www.nrcs.usda.gov

U.S. Department of the Interior
1849 C Street, NW
Washington, DC 20240
Phone: (202) 208-3100
http://www.doi.gov

U.S. Department of the Interior
Bureau of Reclamation
1849 C Street, NW
Washington, DC 20240-0001
Phone: (202) 513-0501
Fax: (202) 513-0315
http://www.usbr.gov

U.S. Department of the Interior
Minerals Management Service
1849 C Street, NW
Washington, DC 20240
Phone: (202) 208-3985
http://www.mms.gov

U.S. Department of the Interior
National Park Service
1849 C Street, NW
Washington, DC 20240
Phone: (202) 208-6843
http://www.nps.gov

U.S. Department of Transportation
400 Seventh Street, SW
Washington, DC 20590
Phone: (202) 366-4000
http://www.dot.gov

U.S. Department of Veterans Affairs
810 Vermont Avenue, NW
Washington, DC 20420
Phone: (202) 273-5400
http://www.va.gov

U.S. Environmental Protection Agency
Ariel Rios Building
1200 Pennsylvania Avenue, NW
Washington, DC 20460
Phone: (202) 272-0167
http://www.epa.gov

U.S. Environmental Protection Agency
Wetlands Helpline
c/o EPA Water Resource Center
Mail Code RC-4100T
1200 Pennsylvania Avenue, NW
Washington, DC 20460
http://www.epa.gov/owow/wetlands/wetline.html

U.S. Fish and Wildlife Service
1849 C Street, NW
Washington, DC 20240
Phone: 800-344-WILD
http://www.fws.gov

USDA Forest Service
1400 Independence Avenue, SW
Washington, DC 20250-0003
Phone: (202) 205-8333
http://www.fs.fed.us

U.S. Geological Survey
USGS National Center
12201 Sunrise Valley Drive
Reston, VA 20192
Phone: (703) 648-4000 or (888) 275-8747
http://www.usgs.gov

APPENDIX V
INTERNET RESOURCES

This appendix provides a listing of Web sites that may provide you with useful information regarding careers in the conservation and environmental field. Additional resources may be found by exploring the Web sites of the many organizations listed in the Professional Associations appendix. These listings were current at the time of publication. If a particular link no longer works, try locating the Web site or organization by using a search engine.

GENERAL

CareerPlanner.com
http://www.careerplanner.com

Conservation International
http://www.conservation.org

Environmental Career Center, LLC.
http://www.environmentalcareer.com

Environmental Career Opportunities
http://www.ecojobs.com/index.php

The Environmental Careers Organization
http://www.eco.org

The Environment Directory
http://www.webdirectory.com

Environmental Expert
http://www.environmental-expert.com

EnviroLink Network
http://www.envirolink.org/about.html

The Global Directory for Environmental Technology
http://www.eco-web.com

Occupational Outlook Handbook
U.S. Bureau of Labor Statistics
http://www.bls.gov/oco/home.htm

O*NET, the Occupational Information Network
http://online.onetcenter.org/

ECOTOURISM

American Planning Association Online Career Center
http://www.planning.org/jobsonline/ads.htm

American Society of Travel Agents Job Board
http://www.astanet.com

ECOCLUB's Ecotourism Job Center
http://www.ecoclub.com/job

Hospitality Online Career Network
http://hotel-online.hospitalitycareernetwork.com/

Student Conservation Association Career Center
http://www.thesca.org/conservation_careers

Travel Industry Association of America Career Center
http://www.tia.org/express/job_intro.html

Travel Industry Association of America Job Bank
http://www.tia.org/express/job_intro.html

ENGINEERING

ASABE Career Center
American Society of Agricultural and Biological Engineers
http://www.asabe.org/membership/career.html

Environmental Technology Links
Advanced Technology Environmental Education Center
http://www.ateec.org/links/links.cfm

Junior Engineering Technical Society (JETS)
http://www.jets.org/

National Society of Professional Surveyors Career Site
http://www.surveyingcareer.com

Society for Mining, Metallurgy, and Exploration
http://www.smenet.org/education/Students/index.cfm.

Ubiquity GIS Jobs Page
http://www.ag.ohio-state.edu/~envjobs/env9.htm

FARMING & FISHING

Agweb.com, The Homepage of Agriculture
http://www.agweb.com

Career Placement Center
Agronomic Science Foundation
American Society of Agronomy
Crop Science Society of America
Soil Science Society of America
http://www.careerplacement.org

National FFA Organization
http://www.ffa.org

FORESTRY

American Loggers Council
http://www.americanloggers.org/ask_a_logger.htm

National Fire Academy
U.S. Fire Administration
http://www.usfa.fema.gov/training/nfa/

Society of American Foresters Career Center
http://www.safnet.org/careercenter/index.cfm

TreeLink
http://www.treelink.org

LEGAL AND REGULATORY

American Public Health Association Career Center
http://www.apha.org/career/

Law School Admission Council
http://www.lsac.org

National Association for Law Placement
http://www.nalp.org

National Environmental Health Association Career Center
http://www.neha.org/CareerOp.html

Federal Wildlife Officers Association Career Center
http://www/fwoa.org/careers.html

USDA's Agricultural Research Service Career Center
http://www.ars.usda.gov/Careers/docs.htm?docid=1345

U.S. Fish & Wildlife Service Career Center
http://www.fws.gov/jobs/STEP.gov

U.S. National Park Service Career Information Center
http://www.nps.gov/personnel

Water Environment Federation Career Center
http://wef.jobcontrolcenter.com/search.cfm

OUTDOOR/ ENVIRONMENTAL EDUCATION

American Association for Health, Physical Education, Recreation, and Dance Career Center
http://member.aahperd.org/careercenter/

America Outdoors Job Listings
http://www.americaoutdoors.org/job-results.asp

Association of Environmental Engineering and Science Professors Jobs Board
http://www.aeesp.org/jobs/jobs.php

Chronicle of Higher Education Jobs Database
http://chronicle.com/jobs/100/

National Parks Conservation Association Job Opportunities Page
http://www.npca.org/jobs/

National Science Teachers Association Career Center
http://careers.nsta.org/

North American Association for Environmental Education Jobs Database
http://eelink.net/pages/EE+Jobs+Database

Outdoor Ed: The Professional's Resource
http://www.outdoored.com/Jobs

Society for Conservation Biology Job Database
http://www.conbio.org/Jobs/search.cfm

Teachers-Teacher.com Job Site
http://www.teachers-teachers.com/teaching-jobs.cfm.

SCIENTIFIC

Advanced Technology Environmental Education Center
http://www.ateec.org

American Chemical Association
http://www.chemistry.org/portal/a/c/s/1/educatorsandstudents.html

American Institute of Biological Sciences
http://www.aibs.org/careers/index.html

American Meteorological Society Career Guide
http://www.ametsoc.org/atmoscareers/index.html

American Phytopathological Society Career and Placement Center
http://www.apsnet.org/careers/top.asp

American Society for Horticultural Science
http://www.ashs.org/careers/index.html

Botanical Society of America
http://www.botany.org/bsa/careers

ChemicalIndustry.com: The Worldwide Search Engine of the Chemical Industry
http://chemindustry.com

MarineBio
http://www.marinebio.com/MarineBio/Careers

National Sea Grant Library
http://www.nsgd.gso.uri.edu

National Wildlife Rehabilitators Association
http://www.nwrawildlife.org

Science Careers Web
http://www.sciencecareersweb.net

Sea Grant's Marinecareers.net
http://www.marinecareers.net/index.htm

Scripps Institution of Oceanography Library
http://scilib.ucsd.edu/sio/guide/career.html

APPENDIX VI
NATIONAL FORESTS

A variety of career opportunities related to conservation and the environment are available in the many national forests and grasslands managed by the Forest Service—an agency of the U.S. Department of Agriculture. Spanning 193 million acres, these public land areas are organized into nine regions* throughout the United States. This appendix lists contact information for the national Forest Service office and each regional office, along with links to corresponding online directories with extensive department phone numbers. In addition, national forests are listed by state, along with individual Web sites when available.

*Regions are numbered 1-6 and 8-10; there is no Region 7

National Headquarters
Forest Service
U.S. Department of Agriculture
Sidney R. Yates Federal Building
201 14th Street, SW
Washington, DC 20250
Phone: (202) 205-8333
http://www.fs.fed.us/intro/directory/wo.htm

Region 1—Northern Region
Federal Building
P.O. Box 7669
Missoula, MT 59807
Phone: (406) 329-3511
Fax: (406) 329-3347
http://www.fs.fed.us/intro/directory/
    Region_1_master.pdf
States: Montana, northern Idaho, North Dakota, northwestern South Dakota

Region 2—Rocky Mountain Region
740 Simms Street
Golden, CO 80401
Phone: (303) 275-5350
http://www.fs.fed.us/intro/directory/rg-2.htm
States: Colorado, Kansas, Nebraska, South Dakota, eastern Wyoming

Region 3—Southwestern Region
333 Broadway, SE
Albuquerque, NM 87102
Phone: (505) 842-3292
Fax: (505) 842-3800
http://www.fs.fed.us/intro/directory/rg-3.htm
States: Arizona, New Mexico

Region 4—Intermountain Region
Federal Building 324

25th Street
Ogden, UT 84401
Phone: (801) 625-5779
Fax: (801) 625-5127
http://www.fs.fed.us/intro/directory/rg-4.htm
States: southern Idaho, Nevada, Utah, western Wyoming

Region 5—Pacific Southwest Region
1323 Club Drive
Vallejo, CA 94592
Phone: (707) 562-USFS
http://www.fs.fed.us/intro/directory/rg-5.htm
States: California, Hawaii, Guam, Trust Territories of the Pacific Islands

Region 6—Pacific Northwest Region
333 SW First Avenue
Portland, Oregon 97204-3440
Phone: (503) 808-2468
http://www.fs.fed.us/intro/directory/rg-6.htm
States: Washington, Oregon

Region 8—Southern Region
1720 Peachtree Road NW
Atlanta, GA 30309
Phone: (404) 347-7226
http://www.fs.fed.us/intro/directory/rg-8.htm
States: Alabama, Arkansas, Florida, Georgia, Kentucky, Louisiana, Mississippi, North Carolina, Oklahoma, Puerto Rico, South Carolina, Tennessee, Texas, Virgin Islands, Virginia

Region 9—Eastern Region
626 East Wisconsin Avenue

Milwaukee, WI 53202
Phone: (414) 297-3600
http://www.fs.fed.us/intro/directory/rg-9.htm
States: Illinois, Indiana, Iowa, Maine, Maryland, Massachusetts, Michigan, Minnesota, Missouri, New Hampshire, New Jersey, New York, Ohio, Pennsylvania, Rhode Island, Vermont, West Virginia, Wisconsin

Region 10—Alaska Region
Federal Office Building
709 West Ninth Street
P.O. Box 21628
Juneau, AK 99802-1628
Phone: (907) 586-8803
http://www.fs.fed.us/intro/directory/rg-10.htm

STATES

ALABAMA

Conecuh, Talladega, Tuskegee, and William B. Bankhead National Forests
http://www.southernregion.fs.fed.us/alabama

ALASKA

Chugach National Forest

Tongass National Forest

ARIZONA

Apache-Sitgreaves National Forest

Coconino National Forest

Coronado National Forest

Kaibab National Forest

Prescott National Forest

Tonto National Forest

ARKANSAS

Ouachita National Forest

Ozark-St. Francis National Forest

CALIFORNIA

Angeles National Forest
http://www.fs.fed.us/r5/angeles/

Cleveland National Forest
http://www.fs.fed.us/r5/cleveland/

Eldorado National Forest
http://www.fs.fed.us/r5/eldorado/

Inyo National Forest
http://www.fs.fed.us/r5/inyo/

Klamath National Forest
http://www.fs.fed.us/r5/klamath/

Lake Tahoe Basin Management Area
http://www.fs.fed.us/r5/ltbmu/

Lassen National Forest
http://www.fs.fed.us/r5/lassen

Los Padres National Forest
http://www.fs.fed.us/r5/lospadres/

Mendocino National Forest
http://www.fs.fed.us/r5/mendocino/

Modoc National Forest
http://www.fs.fed.us/r5/modoc/

Plumas National Forest
http://www.fs.fed.us/r5/plumas/

San Bernardino National Forest
http://www.fs.fed.us/r5/sanbernardino

Sequoia National Forest
http://www.fs.fed.us/r5/sequoia/

Shasta-Trinity National Forest
http://www.fs.fed.us/r5/shastatrinity/

Sierra National Forest
http://www.fs.fed.us/r5/sierra/

Six Rivers National Forest
http://www.fs.fed.us/r5/sixrivers/

Stanislaus National Forest
http://www.fs.fed.us/r5/stanislaus/

Tahoe National Forest
http://www.fs.fed.us/r5/tahoe/

COLORADO

Arapaho National Forest

Comanche National Grassland

Grand Mesa National Forest

Gunnison National Forest

Pawnee National Grassland

Pike National Forest

Rio Grande National Forest

Roosevelt National Forest

Routt National Forest

San Isabel National Forest

San Juan National Forest

Uncompahgre National Forest

White River National Forest

FLORIDA

Apalachicola, Ocala, and Osceola
National Forests
http://www.southernregion.fs.fed.us/
florida/

GEORGIA

Oconee National Forest

Chattahoochee National Forest

IDAHO

Boise National Forest

Caribou National Forest

Challis National Forest

Clearwater National Forest
Curlew National Grassland

Idaho Panhandle National Forests:
Coeur d'Alene, Kaniksu, and
St. Joe National Forests

Nez Perce National Forest

Payette National Forest
http://www.fs.fed.us/r4/payette/

Salmon National Forest

Sawtooth National Forest
http://www.fs.fed.us/r4/sawtooth/

Targhee National Forest
http://www.fs.fed.us/r4/caribou/

ILLINOIS

Midewin National Tallgrass Prairie

Shawnee National Forest

INDIANA

Hoosier National Forest

KANSAS

Cimarron National Grassland

KENTUCKY

Daniel Boone National Forest
http://www.southernregion.fs.fed.us/
boone/
Land Between the Lakes National
Recreation Area
http://www2.lbl.org/lbl/

LOUISIANA

http://www.southernregion.fs.fed.us/
Kisatchie National Forest

MAINE

White Mountain National Forest
http://www.fs.fed.us/r9/white/

MICHIGAN

Hiawatha National Forest

Huron-Manistee National Forest

Ottawa National Forest

MINNESOTA

Chippewa National Forest

Superior National Forest

MISSISSIPPI

Bienville, Delta, Desoto, Holly Springs,
and Homochitto National Forests
http://www.southernregion.fs.fed.us/
mississippi/

Tombigbee National Forest
http://www.southernregion.fs.fed.us/
mississippi/

MISSOURI

Mark Twain National Forest

MONTANA

Beaverhead National Forest

Bitterroot National Forest

Custer National Forest

Deerlodge National Forest

Flathead National Forest

Gallatin National Forest

Helena National Forest

Kootenai National Forest

Lewis and Clark National Forest

Lolo National Forest

NEBRASKA

Nebraska National Forests and
Grasslands

Oglala National Grassland

Samuel R. McKelvie National Forest

NEVADA

Humboldt National Forest

Toiyabe National Forest

NEW HAMPSHIRE

White Mountain National Forest

NEW MEXICO

Carson National Forest

Cibola National Forest

Gila National Forest

Kiowa National Grassland

Lincoln National Forest
http://www.fs.fed.us/r3/lincoln

Rita Blanca National Grassland

Santa Fe National Forest

NEW YORK

Finger Lakes National Forest

NORTH CAROLINA

Croatan, Nantahala, Pisgah, and
Uwharrie National Forests
http://www.cs.unca.edu/nfsnc/

NORTH DAKOTA

Dakota Prairie Grasslands
http://www.fs.fed.us/r1/dakotaprairie/

OHIO

Wayne National Forest

OKLAHOMA

Black Kettle & McClellan Creek
National Grasslands

Ouachita National Forest

OREGON

Crooked River National Grassland

Deschutes National Forest

Fremont National Forest

Malheur National Forest

Mount Hood National Forest

Ochoco National Forest

Rogue River National Forest

Siskiyou National Forest

Siuslaw National Forest

Umatilla National Forest

Umpqua National Forest

Wallowa-Whitman National Forest

Willamette National Forest

Winema National Forest

PENNSYLVANIA

Allegheny National Forest

PUERTO RICO

Caribbean National Forest
http://www.southernregion.fs.fed.us/
caribbean/

SOUTH CAROLINA

Francis Marion-Sumter National Forests

SOUTH DAKOTA

Black Hills National Forest

Buffalo Gap National Grassland

Dakota Prairie Grasslands
http://www.fs.fed.us/r1/dakotaprairie/
Fort Pierre National Grassland

TENNESSEE

Cherokee National Forest
http://www.southernregion.fs.fed.us/
cherokee/

Land Between the Lakes National
Recreation Area
http://www.lbl.org/

TEXAS

Angelina, Davy Crockett, Sabine, Sam
Houston, Caddo/LBJ National
Forests and Grasslands in Texas
http://www.southernregion.fs.fed.us/texas/

UTAH

Ashley National Forest

Dixie National Forest

Fishlake National Forest

Manti-LaSal National Forest

Uinta National Forest

Wasatch-Cache National Forest

VERMONT

Green Mountain National Forest

VIRGINIA

George Washington National Forest
http://www.southernregion.fs.fed.us/gwj/

Jefferson National Forest
http://www.southernregion.fs.fed.us/gwj/

WASHINGTON

Colville National Forest

Gifford Pinchot National Forest

Mount Baker-Snoqualmie National
Forests

Okanogan National Forest

Olympic National Forest

Wenatchee National Forest

WEST VIRGINIA

Monongahela National Forest

WISCONSIN

Chequamegon National Forest

Nicolet National Forest

WYOMING

Bighorn National Forest

Bridger-Teton National Forest

Medicine Bow National Forest

Shoshone National Forest
Thunder Basin National Grassland

APPENDIX VII
NATIONAL PARKS

Numerous career opportunities exist with the National Park Service, a bureau within the U.S. Department of the Interior. In addition to its administrative headquarters, the Park Service is organized into seven regional offices that are responsible for approximately 400 natural, cultural, and recreational sites throughout the United States. This appendix lists contact information for the national headquarters and regional offices, as well as Web pages for each individual state. In addition to searching by state, a complete index of national parks is available at http://www.nps.gov/aboutus/parksindex.htm.

National Park Service Headquarters
1849 C Street, NW
Washington, DC 20240
Phone: (202) 208-6843

Northeast Region
U.S. Custom House
200 Chestnut Street, Fifth Floor
Philadelphia, PA 19106
Phone: (215) 597-7013

National Capital Region
1100 Ohio Drive, SW
Washington, DC 20242
Phone: (202) 619-7000

Midwest Region
601 Riverfront Drive
Omaha, NE 68102-4226
Phone: (402) 661-1524

Intermountain Region
12795 Alameda Parkway
Denver, CO 80225
Phone: (303) 969-2500

Southeast Region
100 Alabama Street SW,
    1924 Building
Atlanta, GA 30303
Phone: (404) 562-3100

Pacific West Region
One Jackson Center
1111 Jackson Street, Suite 700
Oakland, CA 94607
Phone: (510) 817-1304

Alaska Area Region
240 West Fifth Avenue, Suite 114
Anchorage, AK 99501
Phone: (907) 644-3510

STATES

Alabama
http://www.nps.gov/state/AL/

Alaska
http://www.nps.gov/state/AK/

American Samoa
http://www.nps.gov/state/AS/

Arizona
http://www.nps.gov/state/AZ/

Arkansas
http://www.nps.gov/state/AR/

California
http://www.nps.gov/state/CA/

Colorado
http://www.nps.gov/colm/

Connecticut
http://www.nps.gov/state/CT/

Delaware
http://www.nps.gov/state/DE/

District of Columbia
http://www.nps.gov/state/DC/

Florida
http://www.nps.gov/state/FL/

Georgia
http://www.nps.gov/state/GA/

Guam
http://www.nps.gov/state/GU/

Hawaii
http://www.nps.gov/state/HI/

Idaho
http://www.nps.gov/state/ID/

Illinois
http://www.nps.gov/state/IL/

Indiana
http://www.nps.gov/state/IN/

Iowa
http://www.nps.gov/state/IA/

Kansas
http://www.nps.gov/state/KS/

Kentucky
http://www.nps.gov/state/KY/

Louisiana
http://www.nps.gov/state/LA/

Maine
http://www.nps.gov/state/LA/

Maryland
http://www.nps.gov/state/MD/

Massachusetts
http://www.nps.gov/state/MA/

Michigan
http://www.nps.gov/state/MI/

Minnesota
http://www.nps.gov/state/MN/

Mississippi
http://www.nps.gov/state/MS/

Missouri
http://www.nps.gov/state/MO/

Montana
http://www.nps.gov/state/MT/

Nebraska
http://www.nps.gov/state/NE/

Nevada
http://www.nps.gov/state/NV/

New Hampshire
http://www.nps.gov/state/NH/

New Jersey
http://www.nps.gov/state/NJ/

New Mexico
http://www.nps.gov/state/NM/

New York
http://www.nps.gov/state/NY/

North Carolina
http://www.nps.gov/state/NC/

North Dakota
http://www.nps.gov/state/ND/

Northern Mariana Islands
http://www.nps.gov/state/MP/

Ohio
http://www.nps.gov/state/OH/

Oklahoma
http://www.nps.gov/state/OK/

Oregon
http://www.nps.gov/state/OR/

Pennsylvania
http://www.nps.gov/state/PA/

Puerto Rico
http://www.nps.gov/state/PR/

Rhode Island
http://www.nps.gov/state/RI/

South Carolina
http://www.nps.gov/state/SC/

South Dakota
http://www.nps.gov/state/SD/

Tennessee
http://www.nps.gov/state/TN/

Texas
http://www.nps.gov/state/TX/

Utah
http://www.nps.gov/state/UT/

Vermont
http://www.nps.gov/state/VT/

Virginia
http://www.nps.gov/state/VA/

Virgin Islands
http://www.nps.gov/state/VI/

Washington
http://www.nps.gov/state/WA/

West Virginia
http://www.nps.gov/state/WV/

Wisconsin
http://www.nps.gov/state/WI/

Wyoming
http://www.nps.gov/state/WY/

APPENDIX VIII
STATE ENVIRONMENTAL RESOURCES

At the state level, government agencies offer a wide range of career opportunities, as well as information about state laws and regulations. This appendix contains a geographic listing of these agencies. Please note that while specific agency names and responsibilities vary from state to state, these entities all perform similar functions.

ALABAMA

Alabama Department of Conservation and Natural Resources
64 North Union Street, Suite 468
Montgomery, AL 36130
Phone: (334) 242-3486
http://www.dcnr.state.al.us

ALASKA

Alaska Department of Natural Resources
550 West Seventh Avenue, Suite 1260
Anchorage, AK 99501-3557
Phone: (907) 269-8400
Fax: (907) 269-8901
http://www.dnr.state.ak.us

ARIZONA

Arizona Game & Fish Department
2221 West Greenway Road
Phoenix, AZ 85023-4399
Phone: (602) 942-3000
http://www.gf.state.az.us

ARKANSAS

Arkansas Game and Fish Commission
2 Natural Resources Drive
Little Rock, AK 72205
Phone: (501) 223-6300
http://www.agfc.state.ar.us

CALIFORNIA

California Department of Fish and Game
1416 Ninth Street, Room 117
Sacramento, CA 95814
Phone: (916) 445-0411
http://www.dfg.ca.gov

COLORADO

Colorado Division of Wildlife
6060 Broadway
Denver, CO 80216
Phone: (303) 297-1192
http://wildlife.state.co.us

CONNECTICUT

Connecticut Department of Environmental Protection
79 Elm Street
Hartford, CT 06106-5127
Phone: (860) 424-3000
http://www.dep.state.ct.us

DELAWARE

Delaware Department of Natural Resources & Environmental Control
89 Kings Highway
Dover, DE 19901
Phone: (302) 739-9902
http://www.dnrec.state.de.us

FLORIDA

Florida Fish and Wildlife Conservation Commission
Farris Bryant Building
620 South Meridian Street
Tallahassee, FL 32399-1600
Phone: (850) 488-4676
http://floridaconservation org

GEORGIA

Georgia Department of Natural Resources
2 Martin Luther King, Jr. Drive SE, Suite 1262, East Tower
Atlanta, GA 30334
Phone: (404) 656-3500
http://www.gadnr.org

HAWAII

Hawaii Department of Land and Natural Resources
Kalanimoku Building
1151 Punchbowl Street
Honolulu, HI 96813
Phone: (808) 587-0405
Fax: (808) 587-0390
http://www.hawaii.gov/dlnr

IDAHO

Idaho Fish and Game
P.O. Box 25
Boise, ID 83707
Phone: (208) 334-3700
Fax: (208) 334-2148
http://www2.state.id.us/fishgame

ILLINOIS

Illinois Department of Natural Resources
One Natural Resource Way
Springfield, IL 62702
Phone: (217) 782-6302
http://www.dnr.state.il.us

INDIANA

Indiana Department of Natural Resources
402 West Washington Street, Room W160
Indianapolis, IN 46204
Phone: (317) 232-4200
Fax: (317) 233-8654
http://www.state.in.us/dnr

IOWA

Iowa Department of Natural Resources
502 East Ninth Street
Des Moines, IA 50319-0034

Phone: (515) 281-5918
http://www.iowadnr.com

KANSAS

**Kansas Department of Wildlife &
    Parks**
1020 South Kansas, Room 200
Topeka, KS 66612-1327
Phone: (785) 296-2281
http://www.kdwp.state.ks.us

KENTUCKY

**Kentucky Department of Fish and
    Wildlife Resources**
1 Sportsman's Lane
Frankfort, KY 40601
Phone: (800) 858-1549
http://www.kdfwr.state.ky.us

LOUISIANA

**Louisiana Department of Wildlife and
    Fisheries**
2000 Quail Drive
Baton Rouge, LA 70808
Phone: (225) 765-2800
http://www.wlf.state.la.us

MAINE

**Maine Department of Inland Fisheries
    and Wildlife**
284 State Street
41 State House Station
Augusta, ME 04333-0041
Phone: (207) 287-8000
http://www.state.me.us/ifw

MARYLAND

**Maryland Department of Natural
    Resources**
580 Taylor Avenue
Annapolis, MD 21401
Phone: (410) 260-8367
http://www.dnr.state.md.us

MASSACHUSETTS

**Massachusetts Department of Fish and
    Game**
251 Causeway Street, Suite 400
Boston, MA 02114-2104
Phone: (617) 626-1500
http://www.state.ma.us/dfwele

MICHIGAN

**Michigan Department of Natural
    Resources**
Mason Building, Sixth Floor
Lansing, MI 48909
Phone: (517) 373-2329
http://www.michigan.gov/dnr

MINNESOTA

**Minnesota Department of Natural
    Resources**
500 Lafayette Road
St. Paul, MN 55155-4040
Phone: (888) 646-6367
http://www.dnr.state.mn.us

MISSISSIPPI

**Mississippi Department of Wildlife,
    Fisheries and Parks**
1504 Eastover Drive
Jackson, MS 39211-6374
Phone: (601) 432-2400
http://www.mdwfp.com

MISSOURI

Missouri Department of Conservation
2901 West Truman Boulevard
Jefferson City, MO 65109
Phone: (573) 751-4115
Fax: (573) 751-4467
http://www.mdc.mo.gov

MONTANA

Montana Fish, Wildlife & Parks
1420 East Sixth Avenue
Helena, MT 59620-0701
Phone: (406) 444-2535
Fax: (406) 444-4952
http://fwp.state.mt.us

NEBRASKA

Nebraska Game and Parks Commission
2200 North 33rd Street
Lincoln, NE 68503
Phone: (402) 471-0641
http://www.ngpc.state.ne.us

NEVADA

**Nevada Department of Conservation
    & Natural Resources**
901 South Stewart Street, Suite 5001
Carson City, NV 89701

Phone: (775) 684-2700
Fax: (775) 684-2715
http://www.state.nv.us/cnr/nvwildlife

NEW HAMPSHIRE

**New Hampshire Fish and Game
    Department**
11 Hazen Drive
Concord, NH 03301
Phone: (603) 271-3511
Fax: (603) 271-1438
http://www.wildlife.state.nh.us

NEW JERSEY

**New Jersey Division of Fish and
    Wildlife**
P.O. Box 400
Trenton, NJ 08625-0400
Phone: (609) 292-2965
http://www.state.nj.us/dep/fgw

NEW MEXICO

**New Mexico Department of Game
    and Fish**
One Wildlife Way
Santa Fe, NM 87507
Phone: (505) 476-8000
http://www.wildlife.state.nm.us

NEW YORK

**New York State Division of Fish,
    Wildlife and Marine Resources**
625 Broadway
Albany, NY 12233-4750
Phone: (518) 402-8924
Fax: (518) 402-9027
http://www.dec.state.ny.us/website/
    dfwmr/index.html

NORTH CAROLINA

**North Carolina Wildlife Resources
    Commission**
NCSU Centennial Campus
1751 Varsity Drive
Raleigh, NC 27606
Phone: (919) 707-0010
http://www.wildlife.state.nc.us

NORTH DAKOTA

**North Dakota Game and Fish
    Department**
100 North Bismarck Expressway
Bismarck, ND 58501-5095

Phone: (701) 328-6300
Fax: (701) 328-6352
http://gf.nd.gov/

OHIO

Ohio Department of Natural Resources
2045 Morse Road
Columbus, OH 43229
Phone: (614) 265-6875
http://www.dnr.state.oh.us

OKLAHOMA

Oklahoma Department of Wildlife
Conservation
1801 North Lincoln
Oklahoma City, OK 73152
Phone: (405) 521-3851
http://www.wildlifedepartment.com

OREGON

Oregon Department of Fish and
Wildlife
3406 Cherry Avenue NE
Salem, OR 97303
Phone: (503) 947-6000
http://www.dfw.state.or.us

RHODE ISLAND

Rhode Island Department of
Environmental Management
235 Promenade Street
Providence, RI 02908-5767
Phone: (401) 222-6800
http://www.dem.ri.gov

SOUTH CAROLINA

South Carolina Department of Natural
Resources
P.O. Box 167
Columbia, SC 29202
Phone: (803) 734-9100
http://www.dnr.state.sc.us

SOUTH DAKOTA

South Dakota Department of Game,
Fish, and Parks
523 East Capitol Avenue
Pierre, SD 57501
Phone: (605) 773-3485
http://www.state.sd.us/gfp

TENNESSEE

Tennessee Wildlife Resources Agency
P.O. Box 40747
Nashville, TN 37204
Phone: (615) 781-6500
http://www.state.tn.us/twra

TEXAS

Texas Parks and Wildlife
4200 Smith School Road
Austin, TX 78744
Phone: (800) 792-1112
http://www.tpwd.state.tx.us

UTAH

Utah Department of Natural Resources
1594 West North Temple
Salt Lake City, UT 84114-5610
Phone: (801) 538-7200
http://www.nr.utah.gov

VERMONT

Vermont Agency of Natural Resources
103 South Main Street, Center Building
Waterbury, VT 05671-0301
Phone: (802) 241-3600
Fax: (802) 244-1102
http://www.anr.state.vt.us

VIRGINIA

Virginia Department of Game
& Inland Fisheries
4010 West Broad Street
Richmond, VA 23230

Phone: (804) 367-1000
Fax: (804) 367-9147
http://www.dgif.state.va.us

WASHINGTON

Washington Department of Fish
and Wildlife
Natural Resources Building
1111 Washington Street, SE
Olympia, WA 98501
Phone: (360) 902-2200
Fax: (360) 902-2156
http://wdfw.wa.gov

WEST VIRGINIA

West Virginia Division of Natural
Resources
State Capitol
Building 3, Room 669
Charleston, WV 25305
Phone: (304) 558-2754
http://www.wvdnr.gov

WISCONSIN

Wisconsin Department of Natural
Resources
101 South Webster Street
Madison, WI 53707-7921
Phone: (608) 266-2621
Fax: (608) 261-4380
http://www.dnr.state.wi.us

WYOMING

Wyoming Game and Fish
5400 Bishop Boulevard
Cheyenne, WY 82006
Phone: (307) 777-4600
http://gf.state.wy.us

GLOSSARY

abatement   The elimination or reduction of air, water, land, or noise pollution

alpine   Usually in cold environments, high altitude mountainous areas above the timberline

animal husbandry   The practice of caring for breeding animals, including livestock

atmosphere   An envelope of gas that surrounds the planet Earth

attenuation   The process whereby environmental contaminants naturally diffuse over time

audit   A formal examination and verification process, usually performed by an independent party

azimuth   When using a compass, the angle of horizontal deviation from North, where North is 0°, East is 90°, South is 180°, and West is 270°

bacteriology   The study of bacteria

bioengineering   A process of combining live and dead plants or other organic matter to create a viable ecosystem

biomass   The total weight of all living organisms in a certain area, ecosystem, or biological community. This term sometimes refers to plant material that can be used for fuel

brownfield   Former industrial land that has been idled, underused, or abandoned due to perceived or actual environmental contamination

canvassing   An organized effort to contact individuals in a target group, normally in a specific geographic area

clear cutting   The act of cutting of all trees in a geographic area without considering their size or longevity

Doppler radar   A form of radar, used for weather forecasting, that uses the Doppler effect to determine the speed and direction of atmospheric motion

ecological restoration   The process of restoring polluted or otherwise compromised ecosystems to as close to their prior condition as possible

ecology   The study of the relationship between living organisms and their environment

ecosystem   A functional ecological system or unit composed of all the living organisms in a particular area, as well as all nonliving chemical and physical factors

endocrinology   The study of the function and pathology of the body's hormone-secreting endocrine glands, including the pituitary and thyroid glands

enzyme   A protein that functions as a catalyst by triggering and speeding up the rate at which chemical reactions occur

geographic information system (GIS)   A computerized system that is used to collect, store, manipulate, analyze, and display spatial data in a geographic format

Global Positioning System (GPS)   A system of government-owned, earth-orbiting satellites and ground-based receivers that is used to obtain position coordinates

land reclamation   The process of either restoring damaged land to its natural state, or changing the characteristics of natural land, including wetlands, so it is suitable for human use

limnology   The study of inland waters, including lakes, rivers, and ponds

machine vision   Guidance systems composed of video cameras, digital cameras, computers, and other devices that allow robots to acquire and analyze images, often in the context of factory automation and quality control

mass spectrometer   An instrument that uses a magnetic field to distinguish and separate chemical species according to their isotopic masses

mitigation   Efforts taken to minimize or avoid environmental pollution or a natural disaster

modeling   The use of computers, physical representations, or mathematical equations to predict a real-world outcome or event

multispectral   A remote sensing device's ability to detect electromagnetic energy in two or more wavelength or spectral bands, such as infrared and visible

ordinance   A regulation, law, or legislative enactment of a city or other local government body

organism   Any living form of plant, animal, or bacterial life

parasitology   A branch of biology involving the scientific study of parasites and their hosts

pathology   The scientific study of diseases

pharmacology   The scientific study of drugs, including their origins, use, and effects

radioactive isotope   An unstable isotope of a particular element that produces ionizing radiation

reforestation   The natural or artificial process of reestablishing a forest that has been destroyed or harvested

remediation   The removal of harmful contaminants from the environments

remote sensing   Obtaining geospatial information remotely, by measuring variations in how visible light, as well as near-infrared, mid-infrared, thermal, and microwave energy interact with objects

savanna   A tropical or subtropical region consisting of grasslands with scattered, drought-resistant shrubs and trees

seining   The process of catching entire schools of fish with seine nets

statute   A formal written law, passed by a legislative body, that declares or prohibits something

tidal pool   A pool of water that remains on a reef or shore after a tide recedes

topography   The natural and human-made physical features of a particular area, including highways, bridges, forests, rivers, and changes in elevation

tort   An injury or wrong committed against another person or piece of property, resulting in civil liability

toxicology   The study of poisonous substances and their effects on living organisms

virology   The scientific study of viruses and viral diseases

watershed   An area of land that drains into a body of water, such as a stream, river, lake or reservoir

BIBLIOGRAPHY

A. PERIODICALS

Following is a listing of professional trade magazines and journals related to many of the careers profiled in this book. Many of these periodicals offer online editions that may include expanded or exclusive content. While some of these publications may be highly technical, they are useful tools for understanding the issues faced by those working in different professions. These listings were current at the time of publication. If a particular link no longer works, try locating the association or Web site by using a search engine.

GENERAL

Audubon
National Audubon Society, Inc.
http://magazine.audubon.org/index.html

The Ecologist
http://www.theecologist.org/

Environmental Protection
http://www.eponline.com/

E/The Environmental Magazine
http://www.emagazine.com

Frontiers in Ecology and Environment
Ecological Society of America
1707 H Street NW, Suite 400
Washington, DC 20006
Phone: (202) 833-8773
Fax: (202) 833-8775
http://www.frontiersinecology.org/subscriptionInformation.php

Land and Water, Inc.
320 A. Street
Fort Dodge, IA 50501
Phone: (515) 576-3191
http://www.landandwater.com/

National Geographic
http://www.nationalgeographic.com/

Nature
https://secure.nature.com/subscribe/nature

Science News
http://www.sciencenews.org/

ECOTOURISM

EcoCurrents
1333 H Street, NW
Suite 300, East Tower
Washington, DC 20005
Phone: (202) 347-9203
Fax: (202) 789-7279
http://www.ecotourism.org

The International Ecotourism Digital Traveler
1333 H Street, NW
Suite 300, East Tower
Washington, DC 20005
Phone: (202) 347-9203
Fax: (202) 789-7279
http://www.ecotourism.org

The International Ecotourism Digital Traveler—Asia Pacific
1333 H Street, NW
Suite 300, East Tower
Washington, DC 20005
Phone: (202) 347-9203
Fax: (202) 789-7279
http://www.ecotourism.org

International Ecotourism Monthly
http://ecoclub.com

Journal of Ecotourism
http://www.multilingual-matters.net/jet/default.htm

Journal of Sustainable Tourism
http://www.multilingual-matters.net/jost/default.htm

Planning Magazine
American Planning Association
97774 Eagle Way
Chicago, IL 60678-9770
Phone: (312) 431-9100
Fax: (312) 786-6735
subscriptions@planning.org
http://www.planning.org/

RECOMMEND
http://www.recommend.com

ENGINEERING

Environmental Engineer Magazine
The Official Magazine of the American Academy of
    Environmental Engineers
130 Holiday Court, Suite 100
Annapolis, MD 21401
Phone: (410) 266-3311
Fax: (410) 266-7653
http://www.aaee.net/Website/Magazine.htm

Planning Magazine
American Planning Association
97774 Eagle Way
Chicago, IL 60678-9770
Phone: (312) 431-9100
Fax: (312) 786-6735
subscriptions@planning.org
http://www.planning.org/

Pollution Engineering
http://www.pollutioneng.com/

Surveying and Land Information Science Journal
National Society of Professional Surveyors—NSPS
6 Montgomery Village Avenue, Suite #403
Gaithersburg, MD 20879
Phone: (240) 632-9716
Fax: (240) 632-1321
http://www.nspsmo.org/journals/journals.shtml

FARMING AND FISHING

AgDay
http://www.agweb.com/agday.asp

Beef Today
http://www.agweb.com/beeftoday.asp

The Business Farmer
22 West 17th Street
Scottsbluff, NE 69361
Phone: (308) 635-3110
Fax: (308) 635-7435
http://www.thebusinessfarmer.com/subscription_info.php

Dairy Today
http://www.agweb.com/dairytoday.asp

Farm Journal
http://www.agweb.com/farmjournal.asp

*Journal of the American Society of Farm Managers and Rural
    Appraisers*
http://www.asfmra.org/fjournals.htm

Progressive Farmer Magazine
P.O. Box 62376
Tampa, FL 33662-3768
Phone: (800) 292-2340
http://www.progressivefarmer.com/farmer/service/#subs

Successful Farming
1716 Locust Street
Des Moines, Iowa 50309-3023
http://www.agriculture.com/sfsubscribe/

U.S. Farm Report
http://www.agweb.com/usfr.asp

FORESTRY

American Forests Magazine
734 15th Street NW, Suite 800
Washington, DC 20005
Phone: (202) 737-1944
Fax: (202) 737-2457
http://americanforests.org/productsandpubs/magazine/

Forest Products Journal
Forest Products Society
2801 Marshall Court
Madison, WI 53705-2295
Phone: (608) 231-1361
Fax: (608) 231-2152
http://www.forestprod.org/fpjsubs.html

The Forestry Source
Society of American Foresters
5400 Grosvenor Lane
Bethesda, MD 20814-2198
Phone: (301) 897-8720 or (866) 897-8720
Fax: (301) 897-3690
http://www.safnet.org/periodicals/forestrysource.cfm

Journal of Forestry
Society of American Foresters
5400 Grosvenor Lane
Bethesda, MD 20814-2198
Phone: (301) 897-8720 or (866) 897-8720
Fax: (301) 897-3690
http://www.safnet.org/periodicals/journal.cfm

Logging and Sawmilling Journal
http://www.forestnet.com/

LEGAL & REGULATORY

ABA Journal
321 North Clark Street, 15th Floor
Chicago, IL 60610
Phone: (312) 988-6018 or (800) 285-2221
Fax: (312) 988-6014
http://www.abanet.org/journal/redesign/home.html

Air Pollution Consultant
Aspen Publishers Environmental Services
Phone: (800) 638-8437
http://www.aspenpublishers.com/environment.asp

American Journal of Public Health
800 1 Street, NW
Washington, DC 20001

Phone: (202) 777-APHA
Fax: (202) 777-2534
http://www.apha.org/journal

Business & Environment
Aspen Publishers Environmental Services
Phone: (800) 638-8437
http://www.aspenpublishers.com/environment.asp

Ecological Economics
P.O. Box 44194
West Allis, WI 53214
Phone: (414) 453-0030
Fax: (877) 230-5110
http://www.ecoeco.org/

Environmental Forum
2000 L Street, NW, Suite 620
Washington, DC 20036
Phone: (202) 939-3800
Fax: (202) 939-3868
http://www.eli.org

Environmental Law Reporter
2000 L Street, NW, Suite 620
Washington, DC 20036
Phone: (202) 939-3800
Fax: (202) 939-3868
http://www.eli.org

Global Environmental Change Report
Aspen Publishers Environmental Services
Phone: (800) 638-8437
http://www.aspenpublishers.com/environment.asp

Hazardous Waste Consultant
Aspen Publishers Environmental Services
Phone: (800) 638-8437
http://www.aspenpublishers.com/environment.asp

Indoor Environmental Quality
Aspen Publishers Environmental Services
Phone: (800) 638-8437
http://www.aspenpublishers.com/environment.asp

Journal of Environmental Economics and Management
1616 P Street NW, Box Number 6
Washington, DC 20036
Phone: (202) 328-5125
Fax: (202) 939-3460
http://www.aere.org/journal/index.html

Journal of Environmental Health
720 South Colorado Boulevard., Suite 1000-N
Denver, CO 80246-1926
Phone: (303) 756-9090
Fax: (303) 691-9490
http://www.neha.org

Journal of Occupational and Industrial Hygiene
2700 Prosperity Avenue, Suite 250
Fairfax, VA 22031
Phone: (703) 849-8888

Fax: (703) 207-3561
http://www.aiha.org/Content/AccessInfo/joeh/joeh.htm

National Wetlands
2000 L Street, NW, Suite 620
Washington, DC 20036
Phone: (202) 939-3800
Fax: (202) 939-3868
http://www.eli.org

The Nation's Health
800 1 Street, NW
Washington, DC 20001
Phone: (202) 777-APHA
Fax: (202) 777-2534
http://www.apha.org/journal

OSHA Compliance Guide
Aspen Publishers Environmental Services
Phone: (800) 638-8437
http://www.aspenpublishers.com/environment.asp

Planning and Environmental Law
97774 Eagle Way
Chicago, IL 60678-9770
Phone: (312) 431-9100
Fax: (312) 786-6735
subscriptions@planning.org
http://www.planning.org

Professional Safety
1800 East Oakton Street
Des Plaines, IL 60018
Phone: (847) 699-2929
Fax: (847) 768-3434
http://www.asse.org

OTHER

Landscape Architecture
American Society of Landscape Architects
636 Eye Street, NW
Washington, DC 20001-3736
Phone: (202) 898-2444
Fax: (202) 898-1185
http://www.asla.org/lamag/subscribe.html

Nature Photographer Magazine
P.O. Box 220
Lubec, ME 04652
Phone: (207) 733-4201
http://www.naturephotographermag.com/

TurfGrass Trends
http://www.turfgrasstrends.com/turfgrasstrends/

OUTDOOR/ENVIRONMENTAL EDUCATION

American Biology Teacher
12030 Sunrise Valley Drive, #110
Reston, VA 20191-3409
http://www.nabt.org

American Naturalist
http://www.journals.uchicago.edu/AN/

Camping Magazine
5000 State Road 67 North
Martinsville, IN 46151-7902
Phone: (765) 342-8456
Fax: (765) 342-2065
http://www.ACAcamps.org

Current: The Journal of Marine Education
http://www.marine-ed.org/Current.pdf

International Research in Geographic and Environmental Education
http://www.multilingual-matters.net/irgee/default.htm

Journal of Environmental Education
1319 18th Street, NW
Washington, DC 20036-1802
http://www.heldref.org/jenve.php

National Parks
1300 19th Street, NW, Suite 300
Washington, DC 20036
Phone: (800) 628-7275
Fax: (202) 659-0650
http://www.npca.org

Parks and Recreation
22377 Belmont Ridge Road
Ashburn, VA 20148-4150
Phone: (703) 858-0784
Fax: (703) 858-0794
http://www.nrpa.org

SCIENTIFIC

Chemical and Engineering News
http://pubs.acs.org

The Chemist
American Institute of Chemists Inc.
315 Chestnut Street

Philadelphia, PA 19106-2702
Phone: (215) 873-8224
http://www.theaic.org/DesktopDefault.aspx?tabid=49

Genetic Engineering News
http://www.genengnews.com/subscribe.aspx

Geotimes
The American Geological Institute
4220 King Street
Alexandria, VA 22302
Phone: (703) 379-2480
Fax: (703) 379-7563
http://www.geotimes.org

Journal of the Atmospheric Sciences
American Meteorological Society
45 Beacon Street
Boston, MA 02108-3693
Phone: (617) 227-2425
Fax: (617) 742-8718
http://www.ametsoc.org/pubs/journals/waf/index.html

Marine Biology
International Journal on Life in Oceans and Coastal Waters
Springer Science+Business Media
http://www.springer.com

The Plant Cell
http://www.aspb.org/publications

Weather and Forecasting
American Meteorological Society
45 Beacon Street
Boston, MA 02108-3693
Phone: (617) 227-2425
Fax: (617) 742-8718
http://www.ametsoc.org/pubs/journals/waf/index.html

Wetlands
The Journal of the Society of Wetland Scientists
http://www.sws.org/wetlands/#subscribe

B. BOOKS

Following is a list of books related to many careers in conservation and the environment. For additional recommendations, contact your local reference librarian, a professional or trade association that represents the career you are interested in, or someone who is already employed in the field.

GENERAL

Bureau of Labor Statistics, U.S. Department of Labor. *Occupational Outlook Handbook*. 2006–07 edition. Washington, D.C.: U.S. Department of Labor, 2006.
DeGalan, Julie. *Great Jobs for Environmental Studies Majors*. Chicago: VGM Career Books, 2002.
Doyle, Kevin, Sam Heizmann, and Tanya Stubbs. *Environmental Careers in the 21st Century*. Environmental Careers Organization. Washington, D.C.: Island Press, 1999.
The ECO Guide to Careers that Make a Difference. Washington, D.C.: Island Press, 2004.

Fanning, Odom. *Opportunities in Environmental Careers.* Chicago: VGM Career Books, 2002.

Fasulo, Michael, and Jane Kinney. *Careers for Environmental Types & Others Who Respect the Earth.* Chicago: VGM Career Books, 2002.

Fasulo, Michael, and Paul Walker. *Careers in the Environment.* Lincolnwood, Ill.: VGM Career Horizons, 2000.

Miller, Louise. *Careers for Animal Lovers and Other Zoological Types.* 3rd edition. New York: McGraw-Hill, 2007.

Ryder, Tim, and Deborah Penrith. *Working With the Environment.* Oxford: Vacation Work, 2004.

ECOTOURISM

Fennell, David. *Ecotourism.* 2nd edition. New York: Routledge, 2003.

Herremans, Irene M., ed. *Cases in Sustainable Tourism: An Experiential Approach to Making Decisions (Hospitality, Travel and Tourism).* Binghamton, N.Y.: Haworth Hospitality Press, 2006.

Sustainable Development of Ecotourism: A Compilation of Good Practices. Madrid: World Tourism Organization, 2002.

Weaver, David. *Ecotourism.* Hoboken, N.J.: Wiley, 2002.

ENGINEERING

Basta, Nicholas. *Opportunities in Engineering Careers.* Chicago: VGM Career Books, 2002.

Clarke, Keith C. *Getting Started with Geographic Information Systems.* Upper Saddle River, N.J.: Pearson Education, 2003.

Environmental Engineering 2004 Selection Guide. American Academy of Environmental Engineers, Inc., 2004.

Garner, Geraldine O. *Careers in Engineering.* Chicago: VGM Career Books, 2003.

———. *Great Jobs for Engineering Majors.* Chicago: VGM Career Books, 2002.

Kemper, John D., and Billy R. Sanders. *Engineers and Their Profession.* Oxford University Press, Inc., 2001.

Oakes, William C., et al. *Engineering Your Future.* Wildwood, Mo.: Great Lakes Press, Inc., 2006.

FARMING AND FISHING

Anderson, Dale, and Richard Lidz, eds. *Agribusiness, Environment, and Natural Resources,* 4th edition. Mission Hills, Calif.: Glencoe/Macmillan, 1990.

Blacka, Aaron, et al. *Agri-tourism.* Blacksburg, Va.: Virginia Cooperation Extension, 2001.

Collins, Donald N. *Opportunities in Farming and Agriculture Careers.* Lincolnwood, Ill.: VGM Career Horizons, 1996.

Gurney, Gene, and Clare Gurney. *Agriculture Careers.* New York: F. Watts, 1978.

Hrubovcak, James, et al. *Green Technologies for a More Sustainable Agriculture.* Washington, D.C.: U.S. Department of Agriculture, 1999.

Macher, Ron, and Howard W. Kerr Jr. *Making Your Small Farm Profitable.* North Adams, Mass.: Storey Books, 1999.

Smith, Marcella. *Careers in Agribusiness and Industry.* Danville, Ill.: Interstate Publishers, 1991.

Stranger, Marty. *Family Farming: A New Economic Vision.* Lincoln, Nebr.: University of Nebraska Press: San Francisco, Calif.: Institute for Food and Development Policy, 1998.

Whatmore, Sarah. *Farming Women: Gender, Work, and Family Enterprise.* Houndmills, Basingstoke, Hampshire: Macmillan Academic and Professional, 1991.

FORESTRY

Burton, L. DeVere. *Introduction to Forestry Science.* Albany, N.Y.: Delmar Publishers, 1998.

Goldberg, Jan. *Opportunities in Horticulture Careers.* Lincolnwood, Ill.: VGM Career Horizons, 1995.

Robinson, Gordon. *The Forest and the Trees: A Guide to Excellent Forestry.* Washington, D.C.: Island Press, 1988.

Sharpe, Grant, et al. *Introduction to Forest and Renewable Resources.* 7th edition. New York: McGraw-Hill, 2002.

Willie, Chris. *Opportunities in Forestry.* Chicago: VGM Career Books, 2004.

LEGAL AND REGULATORY

Environmental Law Institute. *Environmental Law Desk Book.* 7th edition. Washington, D.C.: Environmental Law Institute, 2002.

Ferrey, Steven. *Environmental Law: Examples and Explanations.* 3rd edition. New York: Aspen Publishers, 2004.

Findley, Roger W., and Daniel A. Farber. *Environmental Law in a Nutshell.* 6th edition. Los Angeles: Loyola School of Law, 2004.

Krages, Bert P. *Total Environmental Compliance: A Practical Guide for Environmental Professionals.* New York: CRC, 2000.

Moffitt, Mary Anne. *Campaign Strategies and Message Design: A Practitioner's Guide from Start to Finish.* West Port, Conn.: Praeger Press, 1999.

Yanuchi, Jeff, Lori Yanuchi, and James R. Morris. *Ranger Trails: Jobs of Adventure in America's Parks.* Healy, Alaska: Ridge Rock Press, 2005.

OUTDOOR/ENVIRONMENTAL EDUCATION

Elder, James L. *A Field Guide to Environmental Literacy: Making Strategic Investments in Environmental Education.* Manchester, Mass.: Environmental Education Coalition, 2003.

Landes, Michael. *The Back Door Guide to Short-Term Job Adventures: Internships, Summer Jobs, Seasonal Work, Volunteer Vacations, and Transitions Abroad.* 4th edition. San Francisco: Ten Speed Press, 2005.

Miller, Louise. *Careers for Nature Lovers & Other Outdoor Types.* Chicago: VGM Career Books, 2001.

Shenk, Ellen. *Outdoor Careers.* Mechanicsburg, Pa.: Stackpole Books, 2000.

Wilke, Richard J., ed. *Environmental Education: A Practical Guide for K-12 Environmental Education.* Thousand Oaks, Calif.: Corwin Press, Inc., 1997.

SCIENTIFIC

Astor, Bart. *What Can You Do with a Major in Biology.* Hoboken, N.J.: Wiley Publishing, 2005.

Belikoff, Kathleen. *Opportunities in Biological Science Careers.* Chicago: VGM Career Books, 2004.

Brind Morrow, Susan. *Wolves and Honey: A Hidden History of the Natural World.* Boston: Houghton Mifflin, 2004.

Brown, Sheldon. *Opportunities in Biotechnology Careers.* Rev. ed. New York: McGraw-Hill, 2007.

Camenson, Blythe. *Great Jobs for Biology Majors.* Chicago: VGM Career Books, 2004.

Camenson, Blythe. *Opportunities in Zoo Careers.* Lincolnwood, Ill.: VGM Career Horizons, 1998.

Echaore-McDavid, Susan. *Career Opportunities in Science.* New York: Checkmark Books, Facts On File, 2003.

Ferguson Publishing Editors. *Careers in Focus: Biology.* 2nd edition. New York: Ferguson, Facts On File, 2006.

Ferguson Publishing Editors. *Careers in Focus: Environment.* 3rd edition. New York: Ferguson, Facts On File, 2004.

Joosten, Sally, and Adele Moore. *Principles of Wildlife Rehabilitation: The Essential Guide for Novice and Experienced Rehabilitators.* 2nd edition. St. Cloud, Minn.: National Wildlife Rehabilitators Association, 2002.

Lee, Mary, and Richard Lee. *Opportunities in Animal & Pet Care Careers.* Chicago: VGM Career Books, 2001.

Maynard, Thane. *Working with Wildlife: A Guide to Careers in the Animal World.* New York: Franklin Watts, 1999.

Samansky, Terry S. *Starting your Career as a Marine Mammal Trainer.* Napa, Calif.: Dolphin Trainer, 2002.

Shenk, Ellen. *Careers with Animals: Exploring Occupations Involving Dogs, Horses, Cats, Birds, Wildlife, and Exotics.* Mechanicsburg, Pa.: Stackpole Books, 2005.

Swope, Robert. *Opportunities in Veterinary Medicine.* Chicago: VGM Career Books, 2001.

INDEX

Page numbers in **boldface** indicate main articles.

A

AAC. *See* Accredited Agricultural Consultant
AAEE. *See* American Academy of Environmental Engineers
ABA. *See* American Bar Association
ABC News xiv
ABET. *See* Accreditation Board for Engineering and Technology, Inc.
Accreditation Board for Engineering and Technology, Inc. (ABET) 45, 51
Accredited Agricultural Consultant (AAC) 55, 56
ACS. *See* American Chemical Association
ACSM. *See* American Congress on Surveying and Mapping
Active Network 10, 143, 152
Advanced Technology Environmental Education Center (ATEEC) 186
advancement prospects, in general ix
agent. *See* travel agent
AGI. *See* American Geological Institute
agricultural consultant **54–56**
agricultural engineer. *See* biological and agricultural engineer
AGU. *See* American Geophysical Union
Air and Waste Management Association 107
ALC. *See* American Loggers Council
ALCA. *See* Associated Landscape Contractors of America
Alliance for a Healthy Tomorrow 104
American Academy of Environmental Engineers (AAEE) xiv, 37, 39
American Agricultural Economics Association 109
American Alliance for Health, Physical Education, Recreation, and Dance
  camp director 10
  environmental education program director 143
  field education coordinator 152
  recreation and fitness studies professor 167
  recreation planner 170
  recreation worker 172
American Association for Geodetic Surveying 48, 51
American Association for Physical Activity and Recreation 170
American Association of Petroleum Geologists 191
American Association of University Professors 145, 157, 166
American Bar Association (ABA) 100
American Beekeeping Federation 59
American Board of Industrial Hygiene 121, 122
American Camp Association 7, 10, 173
American Chemical Association (ACS) 181, 183, 184, 188
American Congress on Surveying and Mapping (ACSM) 48, 51
American Culinary Federation 4
American Geological Institute (AGI) 191
American Geophysical Union (AGU) 191
American Groundwater Association 101
American Honey Producers' Association 59
American Hotel and Lodging Association 13
American Industrial Hygiene Association 122
American Institute of Biological Sciences 194, 203
American Institute of Certified Planners 15, 36, 170
American Institute of Chemists 184
American Law Institute 101
American Loggers Council (ALC) 92
American Meteorological Society (AMS) 177, 178
American Mountain Guide Association 27–28
American Planning Association 15, 16, 35, 36, 170
American Public Health Association 112
American Society for Horticultural Science 203
American Society for Photogrammetry & Remote Sensing (ASPRS) 42
American Society of Agricultural and Biological Engineers (ASABE) 32, 33
American Society of Agronomy (ASA) 65, 210
American Society of Farm Managers and Rural Appraisers (ASFMRA)
  Accreditation Exam 56
  agricultural consultant 55, 56
  farm manager 70, 71
  rural appraiser 80, 81
American Society of Irrigation Consultants 118
American Society of Landscape Architects (ASLA) 132
American Society of Limnology and Oceanography 161, 194, 200
American Society of Naturalists 154
American Society of Plant Biologists 203
American Society of Plant Taxonomists 203
American Society of Safety Engineers 121, 122
American Society of Travel Agents (ASTA) 25
American Veterinary Medical Association (AVMA) 212, 213
American Water Works Association 107, 118
America Outdoors: An Association of Outfitters and Guides
  environmental education program director 143
  field education coordinator 152
  outdoor education instructor 164
  river guide 18
  wilderness guide 27, 28
AMS. *See* American Meteorological Society
Antioch University New England 103
appraiser. *See* rural appraiser
aquacultural engineering (biological and agricultural engineering) 31
architect. *See* landscape architect
Arizona State University 34
ASA. *See* American Society of Agronomy
ASABE. *See* American Society of Agricultural and Biological Engineers

ASFMRA. *See* American Society of Farm Managers and Rural Appraisers
ASLA. *See* American Society of Landscape Architects 132, 133
ASPRS. *See* American Society for Photogrammetry & Remote Sensing
Associated Landscape Contractors of America (ALCA) 130
Associate Park and Recreation Professional 10, 172
Association of Boards of Certification 107
Association of Collegiate Schools of Planning 16, 170
Association of Environmental and Resource Economics 109
Association of Environmental Engineering and Science Professors 146
Association of Management Consulting Firms 55
Association of Women Soil Scientists 210
associations
    ecotourism 284
    engineering 284–285
    farming and fishing 285
    forestry 285
    in general ix, x
    legal and regulatory 285–286
    outdoor/environmental education 286–287
    scientific 287–289
ASTA. *See* American Society of Travel Agents
ATEEC. *See* Advanced Technology Environmental Education Center
Atlanta Journal-Constitution, The xiv
Atlantic Offshore Lobstermen's Association 73
atmospheric scientist **176–178**
attorney. *See* environmental attorney
auditor. *See* irrigation auditor
AVMA. *See* American Veterinary Medical Association

B

bachelor of landscape architecture (B.L.A.) 132–133
bachelor of science in landscape architecture (B.S.L.A.) 133
BAE. *See* biological and agricultural engineer
beekeeper. *See* commercial beekeeper
Benvie, Niall 135
Berger, Eric xiv
biochemistry 202
biological and agricultural engineer (BAE) **30–33**

biological engineering 31
biologist. *See* marine biologist; wildlife scientist
biophysics 202
B.L.A. *See* bachelor of landscape architecture
BLM. *See* U.S. Bureau of Land Management
Board of Certified Safety Professionals 121, 122
Botanical Society of America (BSA) 201, 202, 203
Boy Scouts of America 9
Branson, Richard xiv
Bremmer, Brian xiv
BSA. *See* Botanical Society of America
B.S.L.A. *See* bachelor of science in landscape architecture
bucker, 91. *See also* logger
Bureau of Labor Statistics ix
Bureau of Land Management. *See* U.S. Bureau of Land Management
Bush, George W. xiv
BusinessWeek Online xiv

C

campaign staff worker. *See* environmental campaign staff worker
camp cook **2–4**
camp counselor **5–7**
camp director **8–10**
canvassing 103
career ladder, in general ix
career profile, in general ix
Careers in Focus: Environment 38
cartography 41, 50
Cartography and Geographic Information Society 48, 51
case method of instruction 100
cattle rancher 77. *See also* livestock farmer
CCA. *See* Certified Crop Adviser
CELA. *See* Council of Educators in Landscape Architecture
Center for Health, Environment, and Justice 104
Center for Park Management 125
Central Park (New York) 131
CERCLA. *See* Comprehensive Environmental Response, Compensation and Liability Act
certificates
    ecotourism 290
    engineering 290
    farming and fishing 290
    forestry 291
    in general x
    legal and regulatory 291

    outdoor/environmental education 291
    scientific 291–292
Certified Arborist 95
Certified Associate Industrial Hygienist 121
Certified Crop Adviser (CCA) 65, 210
Certified Gold Irrigation Auditor 118
Certified Industrial Hygienist 121
Certified Landscape Irrigation Auditor 118
Certified Landscape Professional 130
Certified Landscape Technician 130
Certified Park and Recreational Professional 10, 170, 172
Certified Professional Agronomist (CPAg) (ARCPACS) 65, 210
Certified Professional Chemist (CPC) 184
Certified Professional in Rangeland Management (CPRM) 207
Certified Professional Soil Scientist/ Classifier (CPSS/CPSC) 65, 210
Certified Range Management Consultant (CRMC) 207
Certified Rooms Division Specialist 13
Certified Safety Credential 121
Certified Survey Technician (CST) 48
Certified Tour Professional 21
Certified Travel Counselor 25
Certified Turfgrass Professional 130
Certified Wildlife Biologist 222
chemical laboratory technician **179–181**
chemical oceanographer 199. *See also* oceanographer
chemist. *See* environmental chemist
Chief Fish and Wildlife Officer 115
China xiv
chipper 91. *See also* logger
choke setter 91. *See also* logger
citizen foresters 94
Civil Service Examination 115
CLARB. *See* Council of Landscape Architectural Registration Boards
Clean Air Act xiii, 38, 99
Clean Water Act xiii, 38, 99, 215
Clean Water Action 103
climatologist 177. *See also* atmospheric scientist
commercial beekeeper **57–59**
community planner **34–36**
compliance specialist. *See* environmental compliance specialist
Comprehensive Environmental Response, Compensation and Liability Act (CERCLA) xiv, 38, 99
conservation science professor. *See* forestry and conservation science professor

Construction Health and Safety Technician certification 121
consultant. *See* agricultural consultant
cook. *See* camp cook
coordinator. *See* field education coordinator
Council of Educators in Landscape Architecture (CELA) 133
Council of Landscape Architectural Registration Boards (CLARB) 133
Council on Certification of Health, Environment, and Safety Technologists 121, 122
counselor. *See* camp counselor
CPAg ARCPACS. *See* Certified Professional Agronomist
CPC. *See* Certified Professional Chemist
CPRM. *See* Certified Professional in Rangeland Management
CPSS/CPSC. *See* Certified Professional Soil Scientist/Classifier
CRMC. *See* Certified Range Management Consultant
crop farmer **60–62**
Crop Science Society of America 65, 210
crop scientist **63–65**
Cruise Lines International Association 25
CST. *See* Certified Survey Technician
cytology 202

D
dairy farmer **66–68**
Deep Sea Fishermen's Union of the Pacific 73
director. *See* camp director; environmental education program director
District Park Manager 124
doctor of veterinary medicine (D.V.M./V.M.D.) 213
Doppler radar 177
D.V.M. *See* doctor of veterinary medicine

E
Eastern Apicultural Society 59
ecological restoration instructor **138–140**
Ecological Society of America 203, 222
economic geologist 189. *See also* geoscientist
economist. *See* environmental economist
ecotourism
    camp cook **2–4**
    camp counselor **5–7**
    camp director **8–10**
    education and training resources 224–225
    Internet resources 294

professional associations 284
professional certifications 290
resort operator **11–13**
resort planner **14–16**
river guide **17–19**
tour guide **20–22**
travel agent **23–25**
wilderness guide **26–28**
Ecotourism Society 13, 15, 19
education and training. *See also* outdoor/environmental education
    in general ix
    resources x, 224–283
education coordinator. *See* field education coordinator
ELI. *See* Environmental Law Institute
Emergency Planning and Community Right to Know Act (EPCRA) xiv, 38, 99
employment
    industry outlook xiii–xiv
    prospects, in general ix
energy (biological and agricultural engineering) 31
engineer. *See* biological and agricultural engineer; environmental engineer; geospatial engineer; mining and geological engineer
engineering
    biological and agricultural engineer **30–33**
    community planner **34–36**
    education and training resources 225–228
    environmental engineer **37–39**
    geospatial engineer **40–42**
    Internet resources 294
    mining and geological engineer **43–45**
    professional associations 284–285
    professional certifications 290
    surveying and mapping technician **46–48**
    surveyor **49–51**
engineering geologist 189. *See also* geoscientist
EnviroEducation.com 103
Environmental and Occupational Health Sciences Institute 112–113
environmental attorney **98–101**
environmental campaign staff worker **102–104**
environmental chemist **182–184**
environmental compliance specialist **105–107**
environmental economist **108–110**
environmental education program director **141–143**
environmental engineer **37–39**

environmental health officer **111–113**
Environmental Law Institute (ELI) 101
environmental meteorologist 177. *See also* atmospheric scientist
environmental resources
    by state 301–303
    in general x
environmental science professor **144–146**
environmental science teacher, high school **147–149**
environmental technician **185–188**
environmental technology, education and training resources 228–229
EPA. *See* U.S. Environmental Protection Agency
EPCRA. *See* Emergency Planning and Community Right to Know Act
ergonomics, safety and health (biological and agricultural engineering) 32
Evangelical Climate Initiative xiv
experience, skills, and personality, in general ix

F
faller 90–91. *See also* logger
farmer. *See* crop farmer; dairy farmer; fish farmer; livestock farmer
farming and fishing
    agricultural consultant **54–56**
    commercial beekeeper **57–59**
    crop farmer **60–62**
    crop scientist **63–65**
    dairy farmer **66–68**
    education and training resources 229–234
    farm manager **69–71**
    fisher **72–73**
    fish farmer **74–75**
    Internet resources 294
    livestock farmer **76–78**
    professional associations 285
    professional certifications 290
    rural appraiser **79–81**
farm manager **69–71**
Federal Wildlife Officers Association 116
field education coordinator **150–152**
field teacher/naturalist **153–155**
fish and wildlife officer **114–116**
fisher **72–73**
fish farmer **74–75**
fishing. *See* farming and fishing
fitness studies professor. *See* recreation and fitness studies professor
food and bioprocess engineering (biological and agricultural engineering) 31
forest engineering (biological and agricultural engineering) 31

forester **84–86**. *See also* urban forester
forestry
    education and training resources
       234–237
    forester **84–86**
    forestry technician **87–89**
    Internet resources 294
    logger **90–92**
    professional associations 285
    professional certifications 291
    urban forester **93–95**
forestry and conservation science
    professor **156–158**
forestry technician **87–89**

G

geodesist 190. *See also* geoscientist
geodesy 41
geodetic surveyor 50
Geographic and Land Information
    Society 48, 51
geographic information specialist 50
geographic information systems (GIS)
    xiii
geological engineer. *See* mining and
    geological engineer
geological oceanographer 198. *See also*
    oceanographer
Geological Society of America (GSA)
    191
Geologist in Training (GIT) 191
geomagnetist 190. *See also* geoscientist
geophysical oceanographer 198. *See also*
    oceanographer
geophysical prospecting surveyor 50
geophysicist 190. *See also* geoscientist
geoscientist **189–191**
geospatial engineer **40–42**
geospatial technology xiii
Girl Scouts of America 9
GIS. *See* geographic information systems
GIT. *See* Geologist in Training
glaciologist 189. *See also* geoscientist
Global Positioning System (GPS) xiii
global warming xiv
government agencies x, 293
GPS. *See* Global Positioning System
Graduate Record Examination (GRE)
    213
GRE. *See* Graduate Record Examination
Greenpeace 103
greenskeeper. *See* grounds maintenance
    worker
grounds maintenance worker **128–130**
GSA. *See* Geological Society of
    America
guide. *See* river guide; tour guide;
    wilderness guide

H

Hazardous Materials Transportation
    Authorization Act xiv, 38, 99
health (biological and agricultural
    engineering) 32
health officer. *See* environmental health
    officer; occupational safety and health
    officer
Heartland Apicultural Society 59
herdsman 67. *See also* dairy farmer
horse rancher 77. *See also* livestock
farmer
Hospitality Sales and Marketing
    Association 13
Houston Chronicle xiv
hydrogeologist 189. *See also* geoscientist
hydrographic surveyor 50

I

ICTA. *See* Institute of Certified Travel
    Agents
Industrial Revolution xiv
industry outlook xiii–xiv
information and electrical technologies
    (biological and agricultural
    engineering) 31
Institute of Certified Travel Agents
    (ICTA) 25
instructor. *See* ecological restoration
    instructor; marine science instructor;
    outdoor education instructor
International Airlines Travel Agency
    Network 25
International Association of Culinary
    Professionals 4
International Council on Hotel,
    Restaurant, and Institutional Education
    4, 13
International Ecotourism Club
    resort operator 13
    resort planner 16
    river guide 18, 19
    tour guide 21, 22
    travel agent 25
    wilderness guide 27, 28
International Ecotourism Society
    resort operator 13
    resort planner 16
    river guide 19
    tour guide 21, 22
    travel agent 25
    wilderness guide 28
International Environmetrics Society
    109
International Society for Ecological
    Economics 109
International Society of Arboriculture 95,
    130

Internet resources
    ecotourism 294
    engineering 294
    farming and fishing 294
    forestry 294
    in general x, 294
    legal and regulatory 295
    outdoor/environmental education
       295
    scientific 291–295
Irrigation Association
    Education Foundation 118
irrigation auditor **117–119**

J

Jeben, Harley 103
job growth xiii
job profiles, in general ix–x
Journal of Geospatial Engineering 40

L

laboratory technician. *See* chemical
    laboratory technician
landscape architect **131–133**
Landscape Architect Registration Exam
    (LARE) 132, 133
landscape architecture 118
LARE. *See* Landscape Architect
    Registration Exam
Law School Admission Council (LSAC)
    100
Law School Admission Test (LSAT)
    100
legal and regulatory
    education and training resources
       237–242
    environmental attorney **98–101**
    environmental campaign staff worker
       102–104
    environmental compliance specialist
       105–107
    environmental economist **108–110**
    environmental health officer **111–**
       113
    fish and wildlife officer **114–116**
    Internet resources 295
    irrigation auditor **117–119**
    occupational safety and health officer
       120–122
    park manager **123–125**
    professional associations 285–286
    professional certifications 291
Li, Zhilin 40
Lincoln, Abraham 49
livestock farmer **76–78**
Lodging Management Program 13
logger **90–92**

LSAC. *See* Law School Admission Council
LSAT. *See* Law School Admission Test

M

maintenance worker. *See* grounds maintenance worker
manager. *See* farm manager; park manager; range manager
mapping scientist 50
mapping technician. *See* surveying and mapping technician
marine biologist **192–194**
marine geologist 190. *See also* geoscientist
marine science instructor **159–161**
marine science technician **195–197**
marine surveyor 50
Marine Technology Society 197
marker 91. *See also* logger
Master Chef certification 4
MBE. *See* Multistate Bar Examination
MCAT. *See* Medical College Admission Test
Medical College Admission Test (MCAT) 213
medical geologist 190. *See also* geoscientist
MEE. *See* Multistate Essay Examination
meteorologist 176. *See also* atmospheric scientist
Mineralogical Record 44
mineralogist 190. *See also* geoscientist
mining and geological engineer **43–45**
morphology 202
mover, 91. *See also* logger
MPRE. *See* Multistate Professional Responsibility Examination
MPT. *See* Multistate Performance Test
Multistate Bar Examination (MBE) 101
Multistate Essay Examination (MEE) 101
Multistate Performance Test (MPT) 101
Multistate Professional Responsibility Examination (MPRE) 101
Mussen, Eric 58, 59

N

NAA. *See* National Aquaculture Association
NALP. *See* National Association for Law Placement
NASA. *See* National Aeronautics and Space Administration
National Aeronautics and Space Administration (NASA) 32, 41
National Aquaculture Association (NAA) 74, 75

National Association for Law Placement (NALP) 100
National Association for Sport and Physical Education 167
National Association of Biology Teachers 146, 149, 158
National Association of Colleges and Employers
    biological and agricultural engineer 32
    crop scientist 64
    environmental engineer 38
    geoscientist 190
    mining and geological engineer 44
    range manager 206
    soil scientist 209
    wetland scientist 215
    wildlife scientist 221
National Association of Commissioned Travel Agents 25
National Association of Recreation Resource Planners 170, 172
National Association of State Park Directors 125
National Board for Professional Teaching Standards 149
National Center for Environmental Economics 109
National Child Registry 10
National Conservation Training Center 115
National Council of Examiners for Engineering and Surveying 51
National Environmental Health Association 112, 188
National Environmental Policy Act (NEPA) 215
National FAA Organization
    commercial beekeeper 59
    crop farmer 62
    dairy farmer 68
    fisher 73
    fish farmer 75
    livestock farmer 78
National Farmers Union (NFU) 62, 68, 78
National Federation of Tourist Guide Associations 21, 22, 28
National Forests
    by state 296–298
    in general x
National Geodetic Survey 47, 50
National Geographic 134
National Imagery and Mapping Agency (NIMA) 41
National Institutes of Health 212
    Office of Science Education 166
National Library of Science 212
National Marine Educators Association 161

National Oceanic and Atmospheric Administration (NOAA)
    environmental technician 187
    geospatial engineer 41
    marine biologist 193
    marine science instructor 161
    marine science technician 196
    oceanographer 199
National Parks
    by state 299–300
    in general x
National Parks Conservation Association 125, 157
National Recreation and Parks Association
    camp counselor 7
    camp director 10
    environmental education program director 143
    field education coordinator 152
    park manager 125
    recreation planner 169, 170
    recreation worker 172
National Registry of Certified Chemists 184
National Restaurant Association 4
National Science Teachers Association 146, 149, 152, 158, 167
National Society of Professional Surveyors 48, 51
National Strike Force 196
National Tour Association 19, 21, 22, 28
National Weather Service 178
National Wildlife Foundation 215
National Wildlife Rehabilitation Association (NWRA) 219
naturalist. *See* field teacher/naturalist
natural resources (biological and agricultural engineering) 31
Nature Conservancy 103, 222
nature photographer **134–136**
Nature Photographers Online Magazine 135
NEPA. *See* National Environmental Policy Act
NFU. *See* National Farmers Union
NOAA. *See* National Oceanic and Atmospheric Administration
North American Association for Environmental Educators
    environmental education program director 143
    environmental science professor 146
    environmental science teacher, high school 149
    field education coordinator 152
    field teacher/naturalist 154–155
    forestry and conservation science professor 158
    outdoor education instructor 163

North American Nature Photography Association 136
North American Wildlife Enforcement Officers Association 115
North Pacific Fishing Vessel Owners' Association 73
nursery and greenhouse engineering (biological and agricultural engineering) 31–32
NWRA. *See* National Wildlife Rehabilitation Association

O

Occupational Health and Safety Technologist certification 121
occupational safety and health officer **120–122**
Ocean Conservancy 194
ocean engineer 199. *See also* oceanographer
oceanographer 190, **198–200**. *See also* geoscientist
Olmsted, Frederick Law 131
100 Jobs in Social Change 103
operator. *See* resort operator
OSHA. *See* U.S. Occupational Safety and Health Administration
Outdoor Ed: The Professional's Resource 18, 27, 143, 152, 164
outdoor education instructor **162–164**
outdoor/environmental education
    ecological restoration instructor **138–140**
    education and training resources 242–251
    environmental education program director **141–143**
    environmental science professor **144–146**
    environmental science teacher, high school **147–149**
    field education coordinator **150–152**
    field teacher/naturalist **153–155**
    forestry and conservation science professor **156–158**
    Internet resources 295
    marine science instructor **159–161**
    outdoor education instructor **162–164**
    professional associations 286–287
    professional certifications 291
    recreation and fitness studies professor **165–167**
    recreation planner **168–170**
    recreation worker **171–173**

P

paleobotany 202
paleomagnetist 190. *See also* geoscientist

paleontologist 190. *See also* geoscientist
park manager **123–125**
personality, in general. *See* experience, skills, and personality traits, in general
petroleum geologist 190. *See also* geoscientist
PG. *See* Professional Geologist
photogrammetry 41, 50
photographer. *See* nature photographer
"Photos for Food" 135
physical meteorologist 177. *See also* atmospheric scientist
physical oceanographer 198–199. *See also* oceanographer
physiology 202
PLANET. *See* Professional Landcare Network
planner. *See* community planner; recreation planner; resort planner
plant anatomy 202
plant scientist **201–204**
PLCAA. *See* Professional Lawn Care Association of America
Point of Beginning 49
position description, in general ix
power systems and machinery design (biological and agricultural engineering) 31
practice acts 133
predictions. *See* trends and predictions
Professional Association of Diving Instructors 194
professional associations. *See* associations
professional certificates. *See* certificates
Professional Engineer (certified) 45
Professional Geologist (PG) 191
Professional Grounds Management Society 130
Professional Landcare Network (PLANET) 130
Professional Lawn Care Association of America (PLCAA) 130
Professional Photographers of America 136
Professional Wetland Scientist (PWS) 216
professor. *See* environmental science professor; forestry and conservation science professor; recreation and fitness studies professor
program director. *See* environmental education program director
Provisional Park and Recreational Professional 10, 172
PWS. *See* Professional Wetland Scientist

R

range manager **205–207**
RCRA. *See* Resource Conservation and Response Act

recreation and fitness studies professor **165–167**
recreation planner **168–170**
recreation worker **171–173**
regulations xiii–xiv
regulatory. *See* legal and regulatory
rehabilitator. *See* wildlife rehabilitator
releaf program 94
remote sensing 41
requirements, in general ix
resort operator **11–13**
resort planner **14–16**
Resource Conservation and Response Act (RCRA) xiv, 38, 99
resources. *See also* Internet resources
    education and training x
    in general ix
rigging slinger, 91. *See also* logger
river guide **17–19**
rural appraiser **79–81**

S

Safe Drinking Water Act xiv, 38, 99
safety and health (biological and agricultural engineering) 32
safety and health officer. *See* occupational safety and health officer
St. Clair County Community College ix
salaries, in general ix
satellite remote sensing imagery xiii
science professor. *See* environmental science professor; forestry and conservation science professor
science teacher, high school. *See* environmental science teacher, high school
scientific
    atmospheric scientist **176–178**
    chemical laboratory technician **179–181**
    education and training resources 251–237
    environmental chemist **182–184**
    environmental technician **185–188**
    geoscientist **189–191**
    Internet resources 295
    marine biologist **192–194**
    marine science technician **195–197**
    oceanographer **198–200**
    plant scientist **201–204**
    professional associations 287–289
    professional certifications 291–292
    range manager **205–207**
    soil scientist **208–210**
    veterinarian **211–213**
    wetland scientist **214–216**
    wildlife rehabilitator **217–219**
    wildlife scientist **220–222**

scientist. *See* atmospheric scientist; crop scientist; geoscientist; plant scientist; soil scientist; wetland scientist; wildlife scientist

seismologist 190. *See also* geoscientist

"Shape the Future: Careers in Imaging and Geospatial Information Science and Technology" 42

Sheldon, David W. ix

Sierra Club 99, 103

skills, in general. *See* experience, skills, and personality, in general

SME. *See* Society for Mining, Metallurgy and Exploration

Smithsonian Institution 101

Society for Accessible Travel and Hospitality 25

Society for College Science Professors 146, 158, 167

Society for Conservation Biology 140

Society for Ecological Restoration International 140

Society for Mining, Metallurgy and Exploration (SME) 43, 45

Society for Range Management (SRM) 205, 207

Society of American Foresters 86, 89, 95

Society of Wetland Scientists (SWS) 216
 Bulletin 216
  Professional Certification Program 216

Soil Science Society of America (SSSA) 65, 208, 210

soil scientist **208–210**

Solid Waste Alliance of North America 101

sorter 91. *See also* logger

special requirements, in general ix

SRM. *See* Society for Range Management

SSSA. *See* Soil Science Society of America

Stanford University poll xiv

state
 education and training resources 224–283
 environmental resources, in general x, 301–303
  National Forests 296–298
  National Parks 299–300

stratigrapher 190. *See also* geoscientist

street tree program 94

structural geologist 190. *See also* geoscientist

structures and environment (biological and agricultural engineering) 31

Student Conservation Association 115

Superfund. *See* Comprehensive Environmental Response, Compensation and Liability Act

supers (bee boxes) 58

surveying and mapping technician 41, **46–48**, 50

surveyor **49–51**

Sustainable Tourism certification 19, 21, 25, 28

SWS. *See* Society of Wetland Scientists

synoptic meteorologist 177. *See also* atmospheric scientist

T

taxonomy 202

teacher. *See* environmental science teacher, high school; field teacher/naturalist

teaching certification 143

technician. *See* chemical laboratory technician; environmental technician; forestry technician; marine science technician; surveying and mapping technician

Time xiv

Time/ABC News/Stanford University poll xiv

tips for entry, in general ix

title acts 133

tour guide **20–22**

Toxic Substances Control Act (TSCA) xiv, 38, 99

training
 in general. *See* education and training, in general
 resources by state 224–283

travel agent **23–25**

Travel Industry Association of America 25

Tree Care Industry Association 130

trends and predictions xiii–xiv

TSCA. *See* Toxic Substances Control Act

2004 Public Sector and Public Interest Attorney Salary Report 100

2005 Associate Salary Survey 100

U

Uniform Agricultural Appraisal Report software 70

unions and associations, in general ix

United States Armed Forces 3, 196

University of California 58, 59

urban forester **93–95**. *See also* forester

U.S. Army Corps of Engineers 47, 50, 132, 196, 215

U.S. Bureau of Indian Affairs 70

U.S. Bureau of Land Management (BLM)
 environmental technician 187
 farm manager 70
 forester 85
 geospatial engineer 41
 landscape architect 132

 range manager 206
 soil scientist 209
 surveying and mapping technician 47
 surveyor 50
 wildlife scientist 221

U.S. Bureau of Reclamation 70

USCG. *See* U.S. Coast Guard

U.S. Coast Guard (USCG) 73, 196

USDA. *See* U.S. Department of Agriculture

U.S. Department of Agriculture (USDA) 32, 61, 85, 118
 Agricultural Research Service 187, 206, 209, 212
 Natural Resource Conservation Service 206, 215, 221

U.S. Department of Defense 206

U.S. Department of Energy 32

U.S. Department of the Interior 85, 215

U.S. Department of Transportation 132

U.S. Environmental Protection Agency (EPA)
 biological and agricultural engineer 32
 ecological restoration instructor 139
 environmental attorney 99
 environmental compliance specialist 106
 environmental economist 108
 environmental rules and regulations xiv
 environmental science professor 145
 environmental technician 187
 geospatial engineer 41
 marine biologist 193
 oceanographer 199
 Office of Wetlands, Oceans, and Watersheds, Watershed Ecology Team 140
 range manager 206
 veterinarian 212
 wetland scientist 214, 215
 wildlife scientist 221

U.S. Fish and Wildlife Service
 farm manager 70
 fish and wildlife officer 115
 marine biologist 193
 oceanographer 199
 range manager 206
 veterinarian 212
 wetland scientist 215
 wildlife rehabilitator 219
 wildlife scientist 221

U.S. Food and Drug Administration 212, 221

U.S. Forest Service 41, 70, 85, 206

U.S. Geological Survey (USGS) 41, 47, 50, 199, 221

USGS. *See* U.S. Geological Survey
U.S. Mayors Climate Protection
    Agreement xiv
U.S. National Parks Service 125, 132,
    206, 221
U.S. Navy 196
U.S. News and World Report xiii
U.S. Occupational Safety and Health
    Administration (OSHA) 12, 106, 120,
    124, 186
U.S. Park Service 85
U.S. Soil Conservation Service 132
U.S. Veterans Administration 132

V

Vass, Emily E. 49
Vaux, Calvert 131
VCAT. *See* Veterinary College Admission
    Test

veterinarian **211–213**
Veterinary College Admission Test
    (VCAT) 213
Virgin train and airline xiv
V.M.D. *See* D.V.M.; doctor of veterinary
    medicine
volcanologist 190. *See also* geoscientist

W

waders 215
Washington, George 49
Water Environment Federation 107, 118
Western Apicultural Society 59
Wetland Professional in Training (WPIT)
    216
wetland scientist **214–216**
Wetlands journal 216
wilderness guide **26–28**
Wilderness Medical Associates 19, 28

wildlife officer. *See* fish and wildlife
    officer
wildlife rehabilitator **217–219**
wildlife scientist **220–222**
Wildlife Society 220, 222
Woods Hole Oceanographic Institution
    Sea Grant Program 75
World Bank xiv
World Federation of Tourist Guides
    Association 22, 28
World Wildlife Federation 103
WPIT. *See* Wetland Professional in
    Training

Z

zoologist. *See* wildlife scientist